Field Instruction

Field Instruction
Techniques for Supervisors

SUANNA J. WILSON

THE FREE PRESS
A Division of Macmillan Publishing Co., Inc.
NEW YORK

Collier Macmillan Publishers
LONDON

The Free Press
A Division of Macmillan Publishing Co., Inc.
866 Third Avenue, New York, N.Y. 10022

Collier Macmillan Canada, Ltd.

Library of Congress Catalog Card Number: 81–66435

Printed in the United States of America

printing number

1 2 3 4 5 6 7 8 9 10

Library of Congress Cataloging in Publication Data

Wilson, Suanna J.
  Field instruction.

  Bibliography: p.
  Includes index.
  1. Social work education.   2. Social service—Field
work.   3. Social workers—In-service training.   I. Title.
HV11.W593   361.3′07′15   81-66435
ISBN 0-02-934740-8 (Macmillan)   AACR2

This book is dedicated to past, present, and future field instructors everywhere, who put in long hours, often on their own time, in order to contribute to the education of tomorrow's social work professionals. Without their willingness to perform this role and without their competence, dedication, and input into social work education, all of us school-employed, classroom and administrative academicians might as well close up shop and go home.

Contents

Conclusion   223

Appendixes   225

Preface

Most literature concerning social work education is written for academicians by full-time social work educators. The individual who is employed by an agency and who happens to train students as part of a much larger job responsibility is often ignored. This book is written especially for the agency-based field instructor. It is practical, aware of the school's needs, but biased toward the field instructor, and it is virtually self-instructional, so that a practitioner to whom a student is assigned for the first time can learn how to fulfill that role even in the absence of formal training.

The opening chapters describe characteristics of social work education and the accreditation process. Early chapters also discuss criteria for selecting field placements and individual instructors, the use of the preplacement interview, and common needs and anxieties of both students and those who supervise them. Responsibilities and roles of both school and agency are discussed, along with practical guidelines for orienting the new student to the field and making beginning assignments. The field instructor then faces the greatest challenge of all: monitoring and assessing the student's performance and readiness to enter professional social work practice. Several chapters present special techniques for reviewing student work on an ongoing basis. The use of an educational contract is recommended, and concrete guidelines are provided for preparing written performance evaluations and for sharing evaluatory feedback with students. Special chapters discuss unsatisfactory performance and address the question: "Would your written evaluation hold up if challenged?" Frequent causes of unsatisfactory performance are discussed, as are various approaches for responding to it. A final chapter presents legal concepts of field instruction, emphasizing the need for school–agency contracts for the protection of all concerned. A massive appendix provides a variety of "What would you do if . . ." situations typical of those encountered by field

instructors. Special exercises help the supervisor gain increased self-awareness of supervisory style and skill. A number of "case examples" are also provided for use by trainers teaching courses on field instruction, providing material for group analysis and discussion. Several teaching aides are included to help field instructors carry out some of the suggested guidelines.

Every potential and current agency-based field instructor needs to read this book. Field instructors play a key role in social work education, strongly influencing each school's decision regarding whether or not a given student should graduate, and yet most field instructors are entirely *too passive* in fulfilling their role. Those who train students in the field have a great deal to offer to schools of social work, but all too often they are poorly prepared for their educational role, uninformed regarding the social work educational process, and hesitant to give feedback or suggestions to classroom educators. It is a basic tenet of this book that field instructors need to be actively involved in standard setting ("What should a person with a BSW or MSW degree know or be able to do?"), curriculum planning, and evaluating the effectiveness of their local social work educational program. An uninformed field instructor cannot understand what his role involves, cannot determine if he is receiving the kind of training and support from the school that is necessary for effective field instruction, and is ill-equipped to communicate to faculty colleagues the needs of agencies and employers who hire newly graduating students. Thus, this book may generate some controversy as practitioners who read it begin to raise questions that were not voiced before; to request training, information, and other resources from schools; and actively seek ways to increase their input into what is happening in the classroom as well as in field.

The reader will note that some chapters seem to speak to

school faculty, one or two to agency administrators, and the majority to the field instructor. All three parties must be involved in effective field instruction; the three roles overlap in many instances and differ markedly in others. It is beneficial for field instructors to be aware of some of the responsibilities and issues faced by schools in the administration of an effective field instruction program, and vice versa. Likewise, a few chapters have short sections that seem to speak directly to the student who is really the consumer of the field instruction process. I have assumed that the reader will want to know something about the roles of all parties involved so that he can determine where he fits into the total picture.

This book has been designed so that it can be used as a primary text in training courses for both new and experienced field instructors, regardless of whether the courses are offered by a school or by agency personnel. It is also sufficiently self-explanatory to enable isolated practitioners in remote settings to give themselves a ''training course'' through their individual reading of the material.

Deans, chairpersons, and faculty with responsibility for administering field instruction programs will find this book useful in program planning and implementation. While the book assumes that most readers will be field instructors, several chapters speak directly to school faculty and administrators by providing guidelines for developing field instruction settings, selecting field instructors, providing orientation for students, developing appropriate legal documents and insurance coverage, training field instructors, and so forth. The ideas presented in Appendix G could be very useful in planning the content of a field instruction manual. The guidelines in this book do not necessarily reflect the views and standards currently held by the Council on Social Work Education (CSWE) in reference to field instruction; however, in most instances the recommendations made in this book are more stringent than those required by the Council.

The beginning chapters are a review of basic concepts concerning social work education. Some readers of the manuscript who were already familiar with the social work literature responded with such comments as, ''Why so much detail on this material—isn't it obvious?'' Unfortunately, I have encountered many field instructors who simply have had no opportunity to learn about some of the basics that are taken for granted by social work educators and are unaware that they lack this knowledge or embarrassed to reveal their ignorance. There are marked differences between the world of the social work educator and that of the average field instructor. Those already familiar with this material can concentrate on the more advanced chapters.

Every social work student should read this material before entering field placement or concurrently with placement as part of integrative seminars. Students often have a great deal of anxiety about field instruction, including how supervision and evaluation are handled, expectations, common experiences shared by most students in field, and so forth. It is recognized that an informed student can be a threat to field instructor and school alike as he or she challenges tradition and expresses a desire for change. However, it is my hope that all concerned with social work education will make this book readily available to students.

Agency administrators often express a desire to have students, yet many have little understanding of just what kind of commitment such an undertaking requires. Awareness of some of the issues and principles suggested in this text can help them arrive at a more informed decision regarding participation in student education, help them provide effective leadership to agency staff who serve as field instructors, and facilitate maximum effectiveness in the agency's ongoing relationships with local social work educational programs.

This is not a book of techniques for supervising agency staff. However, many of the concepts pertaining to the supervisory process, performance evaluation, and so forth are applicable with paid staff and could prove helpful in orienting and training new supervisors. The primary focus of student supervision is education; the management aspect of supervision is important but secondary. Supervision of paid employees reverses this emphasis: Management of workload (quality and quantity) is the primary objective; education and growth are vital but usually secondary, and very often are achieved through mechanisms outside of the supervisor–supervisee relationship (such as in-service training). If this book is used by persons not involved with student training, this important difference in supervisory emphasis will need to be kept in mind.

The text is concerned with BSW and MSW social work education; no attempt has been made to discuss doctoral-level training. Furthermore, there is a greater emphasis on practice with individuals and families throughout the text than on practice with groups, communities, and organizations. However, case examples, illustrations, and discussions of concepts do make reference to macro practice and are presented in such a way that they can be applied to all areas of practice.

Awkward English and sentence structure often results from attempts to avoid sexist pronouns. I have tried to write this book so that it is easy to read and is written in the everyday language of those who will read it. Thus, the pronoun ''he'' is used throughout the text to designate both male and female persons.

Appreciation

This book is the result of discussions with and input from innumerable students, field instructors, and faculty extending over a decade. While it is impossible to recognize each person individually, those with whom I have worked should consider themselves especially thanked for their direct or indirect contributions to my approach to field instruction and the ideas contained in this book.

Several students and field instructors have given permission for actual samples of their work to be included. Their material helps make the concepts "real," and special thanks are extended to Ellen Calhoun, Ruth Canipe, Sandra Goldstein, Eleanor Grossman, Jennifer Howells, Jean McAmis, Karen Schmidt, Estrella P. Valdes, and John Walker for their contributions.

Thanks are also extended to Mary Alice O'Laughlin, Director of Field Instruction at Loyola University of Chicago, for her review and comments on several key chapters and for arranging permission for inclusion of Loyola's contract with agencies. I am also indebted to Arthur J. Cox of East Tennessee State University for his review and frank critique of several chapters pertaining to social work education, and also to Bob Lewis, Director of Field Instruction at ETSU, for permission to use ETSU's performance evaluation form.

The staff members at Jackson Memorial Hospital Medical Social Services must be mentioned for their contribution of ideas and for their cooperation and competence in enabling me to implement many of the ideas contained in this text over a five-year period. In addition, several who served as field instructors reviewed various drafts of the manuscript and contributed helpful suggestions. Jill Lenney and Phil Plummer deserve special mention for their critique of early drafts of several chapters and for their patience and competence in helping to bring alive the concepts and approaches described here. Diana P. Doyle, Director of the Department, merits special appreciation for her bravery and support in permitting me to develop new and sometimes controversial approaches to field instruction in her department. Several graduate students in placement from Barry College School of Social Work during 1977–1978 also reviewed a number of chapters and contributed reactions and suggestions from the student perspective; their time and efforts are appreciated.

A special salute must be given to Dean Jack Riley and Ruth Stanley, formerly Director of Field Instruction at Barry College School of Social Work; to Yvonne Bacarrisse, Chairperson, and Rosa Jones, Director of Field Instruction, of Florida International University School of Health and Social Services; and to Fred Seaman, Director of Field Instruction at Florida State University, for their encouragement, tolerance, patience, and meaningful interaction mixed with challenges and support as I strove to implement the ideas contained in this text in working with students from their respective schools from 1973 to 1979. Their willingness to let me experiment with "radical" ideas, their frankness in confronting me with opposing ideas, and their flexibility and responsiveness have helped make this entire approach to field instruction, and subsequently this text, a reality.

I must also thank Bob Harrington, Editorial Supervisor at The Free Press, for his competent assistance in editorial matters, including the technical aspects of a rather challenging collection of charts, forms, and illustrations.

Finally, I want to recognize Gladys Topkis, former Senior Editor at The Free Press, whose dedication, skill, knowledge of the social work profession, and commitment to this project helped make it a reality. Her input and support have been invaluable since work began on the text in 1978.

Field Instruction

Introduction

Some Biases and Some Trends in Social Work Education

Every author has some biases, and I am no exception. My years of experience as an agency-employed field instructor have left me with some very strong convictions and concerns about what is happening in social work education today. Not everyone will agree with them. When I finally left practice to join a school of social work in 1979, I thought that some of my biases, acquired while I was a field instructor, would probably change once I got inside the system. However, while I am now more understanding of the school's perceptions and positions, my previous views have actually been reinforced. I share them with you at the outset because these biases prompted me to develop definite approaches to field instruction and to write this book.

My first bias is an obvious one: The ideas in this book *do* work. They have been implemented successfully in a number of field instruction settings by myself and others, both with and without the initial support of all school faculty. Students thrive on a structured approach to field training that involves them as active participants rather than as passive recipients of an unknown process. Students who make it through field placements where high standards are maintained are sought after highly by employers in the local community who know that "any student who came out of that setting is well trained." Both the benefits and the stresses associated with implementing the ideas presented in this text should be evident. The reader must bear in mind that many of the concepts, while workable in some settings, are actually ideals. It is highly unlikely that any school or field instruction agency can implement all the standards presented here. However, I believe in ideals. Without them we have nothing to strive toward and nothing to challenge us to grow and change. Thus, even if a small program with only one field instructor and one student can partially implement just a few of the suggested approaches, the ideals will have value. Change does not come easily to many settings, and

thus even the smallest change can reflect a monumental achievement. Other highly developed programs employing large professional staffs supervising many students may be able to take the ideas presented here and adapt them, build on them, and achieve things heretofore thought impossible. Thus, schools and agencies that are not doing everything exactly as described in this book need not consider themselves failures. Many excellent field placement experiences existed before publication of my thoughts on the subject and will continue to exist either because of or in spite of this book. I recognize that my approach to field instruction is not necessarily the best or the only approach to student training.

There is an unfortunate tendency at times for the Council on Social Work Education (CSWE),* the local school, field placement settings, and employers who hire new graduates to go about their respective business rather independently. There are exceptions, of course, but by and large social work schools and the CSWE, which determine the focus and content of social work programs, often fail to ask a very basic question: "What kind of training, knowledge and skills do the agencies that *hire* social work graduates say the students must have in order to be useful to them and to their clients?" Failure to address this issue and to obtain input from community practitioners forces many employers to set up elaborate training programs, suffer high turnover, and even consciously avoid the graduates of certain schools when filling social work vacancies.

At the time this Introduction is being written, the trend is to prepare BSWs for "beginning professional practice." They will be the ones who actually *do* social work, while MSWs specialize in various practice areas, supervise, train, administer, conduct research, or teach in schools of social

*The accrediting body for schools of social work offering BSW and MSW degrees.

1

work. Thus, the BSW curriculum, according to the CSWE, must be *generic* or *generalist* in its approach. The student is exposed to a wide variety of problem-solving approaches but does not receive in-depth training in any one method. He is a jack of all trades and specialist in none. Schools that offer a specialized concentration at the undergraduate level are viewed with strong disfavor by CSWE. The nagging questions remain: Is this what employers want and need? Is this what is needed to serve consumers in the kinds of jobs that most BSWs will take upon graduation?

The terms "casework," "group work," and "community organization" are now passé at the undergraduate level. Schools seeking accreditation from CSWE avoid using these terms in their course descriptions, written program objectives, and informal discussions, because they imply specialization rather than generalization. Instead, "systems theory" is in, and students are taught "problem solving," "methods," "Practice I and II," and how to "work with individuals and families, groups, organizations, and communities."

Unfortunately, as the French adage has it; *Plus ca change, plus c'est la même chose*—the more things change, the more they remain the same. Many systems theory texts expound at length on the subject with such strange-sounding words as "entitivity" and "throughput," yet all describe basically the same concept that has been taught in social work for years. That is, all individuals interact with, affect, and are affected by significant others in their environment, and social workers must have skills for helping the individual cope with and adjust to the environment as well as for intervening with the environment if that is where the problem lies ("environmental manipulation"). Systems theory has become the glue that bonds the curriculum together in many undergraduate programs as students study problem-solving methods, human behavior, and so forth with attention to systems permeating all course content, including field instruction. While written materials published by CSWE make no reference to systems theory, schools that adopt the systems theory approach receive more favorable feedback from CSWE than do those declining to implement the approach. Is this a passing fad? How long before systems theory becomes obsolete? How much opportunity did practitioners, field instructors, and others have for input as the Council and local schools embraced this approach?

In contrast, there is a very important trend that does promise to be permanent, and that is social work education's focus on the needs of minorities throughout the curriculum. CSWE requires that schools pay special attention to work with blacks, women, the aged, and local minority groups. This content is woven through the curriculum, and virtually no social work student graduates without exposure to a diversity of cultural, ethnic, sexual, and age groups.

A person who works on an assembly line must produce an established minimum number of parts, assemblies, or whatever or else face dismissal; some workers exceed the minimum standards and some cannot achieve them. We are practicing a profession called "social work," which deals with taking apart and putting together *people*—a highly fragile and perishable commodity. Yet, we have no established minimal standards for certifying who shall and shall not receive a degree that entitles him or her to practice social work at either a BSW or an MSW level. We expose students to various kinds of knowledge; we state that students must achieve "effectiveness" at what they do and must "perform satisfactorily," but exactly how much knowledge is enough? What *degree of skill* must be obtained before the student graduates? Some schools have attempted to deal with this issue; however, most faculty, field instructors, and students remain unclear about exactly what must minimally be achieved (other than a certain grade point average) to graduate. As a result, social work degrees often have little meaning. Even though in curriculum content and training approach two schools may appear very similar, they may differ radically in the degree of skill that must be demonstrated by the student to earn a specific grade in each course. Thus, two identical degrees from two different schools may mean two entirely different things in terms of competency and readiness to practice social work. Likewise, two degrees *from the same school* may also represent two entirely different levels of skill, depending on which instructors the student had in the classroom, which field placement was used, the nature of the standards imposed there, and so forth. Thus, when employers hire a BSW or an MSW, they are often hiring an unknown quantity. Field instructors and full-time educators must work together to develop standards and reverse this state of affairs.

The primary reason for this situation is that students are being rewarded for growth rather than for mastery of knowledge or skills. Let us imagine a continuum from 1 to 10, with 1 representing virtually no knowledge or skills and 10 a very superior level of functioning. Where exactly is the cutoff point? In other words, can we say that "In order for the student to graduate, he must have achieved a skill level of ____ or greater"? Let's arbitrarily assume that the minimum level is 5. Many students enter both BSW and MSW programs functioning at level 1—they have limited life or work experience, no prior exposure to social work, and much to learn. Let's say that John enters at that level and works very hard. He attends class regularly, is conscientious, cooperative, mature, gets B's and C's, and is now ready to graduate because he has been in the MSW program for two years and has taken and passed all the required courses. But what if his skill level is only a 3? He worked hard, made progress, and completed the supposed requirements. Do we reward him with a social work degree because he tried hard, or do we reward him with the degree only when he achieves the minimum skills required, regardless of how long it takes or the amount of effort expended? Would a social work employer rather hire a graduate who got his degree on the basis of growth or one whose degree is based on achievement of an established skill level? Which worker would be preferred by a consumer group or an individual client? I believe that the answer to this problem is obvious, though its implications are difficult and challenging, and everyone involved with social work education must address this issue if we are to have maximum credibility and effectiveness as a profession.

Furthermore, many students are graduating without the skills that their degree says they have. I have encountered second-year MSW students taking a clinical concentration who could not name common defense mechanisms, who have never worked with the same individual for more than three weeks, and yet considered themselves highly skilled at long-term treatment. One individual with seven years' pre-master's experience entered an accelerated MSW program to concentrate in staff development. Two months prior to graduation with her MSW degree, the student traveled some distance to observe me doing staff development in my agency. She watched as I taught basic interviewing skills to a group of nurses and emerged from the session white as a sheet, blurting out, "I don't see how you do that—I just can't. I don't even know what the interviewing terms were that you used—I never learned them—how can I possibly teach them?" It also turned out that she was just completing a six-month block field placement in staff development, yet had never seen staff development done, nor had she ever trained anyone. What happens when these students take jobs after graduation, thinking they have the skills their degree says they have? I have had the unfortunate experience of having to fire some of them when they simply could not meet the needs of the agency. What can be done to prevent such highly traumatic outcomes?

One factor in this situation is that many social work students are unsure what they should be getting out of their training. Furthermore, they have little idea what expectations employers will have when they take their first jobs. Thus, they are unable to evaluate or determine whether or not they are getting the skills they need to function as social workers. As a result, many students move through their social work educational experience, including field placement, in a rather passive manner—accepting whatever takes place as "the way it's supposed to be." An informed, maturely assertive student can often do much to ensure that he gets the education he entered school to obtain.

Unfortunately, there is one very serious obstacle that often blocks progress in upgrading the quality of social work education: the quality of the faculty members. There are many bright, dedicated, enthusiastic, creative faculty members who are liked and respected by their students and from whom much can be learned. Some are tenured and some are not. Unfortunately, for every one of these individuals, there seem to be at least two "deadwood" faculty who are resting on their tenure. Such individuals hold tenured positions, making it virtually impossible to fire them, and progressive program chairpersons and deans often find

themselves unable to hire more effective faculty until vacancies occur as a result of retirement. Deadwood faculty rarely engage in research activities, rarely contribute to new knowledge, and may rely on lecture notes that are literally yellowed with age or base class lectures on sentences taken verbatim from the textbook, having been away from social work practice for so long that they are unable to add anything to what is said in the text. These faculty often hold a very limited view of what is happening in social work as a profession and have little knowledge of current skills, expectations, trends, and practice demands. Until change occurs in the promotion and tenure system used in most colleges and universities, this problem will persist.

In addition, many, but not all, schools hire individuals as faculty who have gone from BSW to MSW to PhD or DSW degree with little or no work experience. Some obtain their terminal degree in their mid-twenties and have never laid eyes on a "client" or consumer group except in connection with their training. It is my bias that such persons cannot effectively teach most social work courses, because social work is a *practice* profession. Mere intellectual mastery of knowledge or skills is not adequate; one must also go out and apply the skills. How can those who have never really practiced social work effectively teach others to do so?*

A disturbing number of students in our colleges and universities today are barely literate. I have attempted to teach juniors and seniors in college whose written communication skills are at a grammar school level. I have read papers by graduate students that contained incomplete sentences, obvious misspellings, plagiarism, improperly prepared footnotes and bibliography, and often so awkward a grammatical structure that I could not figure out what the student was saying. I have seen such papers graded "A," accompanied by the notation "well done." Likewise, I have encountered PhDs and DSWs who cannot express themselves using proper sentence structure and whose work must be totally rewritten by someone else in order to render it publishable. Why is this happening? Why do we close our eyes to the problem and allow such students to move on through the system and obtain advanced degrees without correcting these deficiencies? Not only are we doing a vast disservice to the student, but the consumers those students will serve and the social work profession as a whole suffer from our failure to impose adequate literacy standards.

Finally, our general expectations of student performance are often too low. Social work students can often accomplish much more than we realize, yet many settle for the "least I can get by with to get the grade I need" because they know that few faculty or field instructors will encourage them to achieve more. As a result, many of the

---

*It is recognized that some courses, such as research, statistics, and the like, could be taught with a more intellectual approach. However, even instructors of these disciplines would be handicapped in helping students apply the concepts to practice if they have never done so themselves.

brightest, most gifted, most talented students are either not realizing their potential or are being lost to the profession as they switch to psychology and related disciplines. We insist that we are not a ''mediocre'' profession, yet the messages our students receive almost daily convey an attitude of low expectations, nonexistent or unspecified standards, and inadequate intellectual and practice stimulation and challenge. Of course, there are many exceptions, but the picture just described should be the exception rather than the rule. Field instructors are in an excellent position to advocate and implement higher standards.

My comments here are sharply critical and distressing. It was out of my concern over these problem areas that I developed the approaches to field instruction described in this book. Let's all join together—CSWE, classroom faculty and school administrators, field instructors, students, social work employers, and consumers of social work services—to work toward making social work education a meaningful, relevant, high-quality process that will ensure delivery of top-quality professional services to all those who use social work services.

1 The Structure of Social Work Education and Field Instruction

Field instructors have long been an integral part of the social work educational system. Until recently, however, the tendency has been for school-employed faculty to make program planning decisions and for agency-based field instructors to be passive recipients of ideas developed by the school. Fortunately, this trend is changing.

If field instructors are to have increasing input into training programs, clearly they must have some understanding of the general nature and structure of social work education. This chapter presents information that should fill in knowledge gaps and enable field instructors to put their own experiences into a broader perspective. It also suggests some ways in which field instructors may learn more about their own school's program and express their ideas for changes.

Field Instruction as Part of the Total Curriculum

Undergraduate Programs

A college or university with no formal social work program may offer several social work courses under the umbrella of the sociology or other related department. If enough courses are offered to constitute a major in social work, the graduate receives a BS or BA degree in sociology or whatever; he can say that he majored in social welfare or took social work courses, but he cannot get a BSW degree. Such programs vary tremendously in quality and may or may not offer field placement to their students. If the school should decide that it wants to grant the BSW degree, the social work courses and faculty must become a separate entity. The school can then start working toward accreditation by the Council on Social Work Education.

Undergraduate students in accredited BSW programs must first complete two years of basic college courses. Generally they are required to take courses in sociology, economics, psychology, and related areas to provide them with a broad liberal arts base prior to entering the social work program in their junior year. Many schools also specify certain grade point averages as a prerequisite for formal admission as a social work major.

Accredited undergraduate BSW programs are required to offer a core group of courses as follows:

1. *Preparation for Social Work* (Foundation courses). Courses in this group include introduction to social work, self-awareness courses or labs, field observation experiences where students visit various agencies or observe others doing social work, and perhaps a course on interviewing.

2. *Human Behavior and the Social Environment (HBSE)*. These courses, often given over several terms, focus on human growth and development and on relationships between persons/groups/communities and their environment. Such courses provide a social work orientation to the understanding of human behavior, generally with special emphasis on the characteristics and needs of blacks, women, the aged, and other minority groups.

3. *Practice Courses*. In most schools, several courses are offered to introduce students to a variety of interventive methods for use with individuals, families, groups, and communities. These are the "how-to" courses, focusing on problem-solving approaches. A few schools (largely unaccredited programs) still adhere to the traditional "methods" division, with separate courses in casework, groupwork, and community organization. Many programs emphasize the social worker's role as advocate, broker, and change

agent as well as counselor. Students taking practice courses are sometimes required to spend several hours per week in direct client–agency contact of some kind as part of their course work. This is not a field placement, though it is usually supervised closely by the classroom instructor and perhaps also by someone in the agency or the community. The special experience helps both faculty and students determine if continuing in the social work program is best for all concerned and also helps students to begin planning for their formal field placement experience.

4. *Social Welfare Policy.* Students need to learn something about social work as an institution and the historical background of social work programs and policies. One or more courses usually provide this information as well as exploring political aspects of social work, the impact of broad social trends and conditions, and proposals for bringing about institutional and policy change.

5. *Research.* Research is now required in accredited undergraduate programs. Students may actually complete small research projects in connection with classroom assignments and also learn how to interpret data presented in professional journals and reports. Many schools train students to apply basic research principles in examining their individual caseloads and agency systems as well as in evaluating the effectiveness of social work practice. A companion course in statistics is often offered or required as a prerequisite to the research course.

6. *Special Seminars and Electives.* In order to complete a specified number of hours in social work, students are generally required to take some elective courses. A wide variety of topics may be offered, depending on the specialized needs of the local geographical area and the expertise and interests of the faculty. Subjects might include legal aspects of social work, aging, poverty, medical social work, child welfare services, supervision, mental health, substance abuse, rural social work, crisis intervention, and human sexuality.

7. *Field Instruction.* Accredited undergraduate programs must provide a minimum of three hundred clock hours of supervised field instruction. This usually begins in the student's senior year or toward the end of the junior year. While most undergraduate students complete their entire placement in the same agency setting, some programs expose students to several different placements. Students may complete a "block" field placement, where three hundred or more hours of field work are spent in a single quarter or semester; other programs spread field placement out over a longer period of time, perhaps at the rate of sixteen to twenty-four hours per week, while students continue to take some classroom courses. Most schools require students to attend periodic field integration seminars throughout field placement so that field experiences can be discussed. Case presentations may take place, along with discussions about how to integrate material learned in the classroom with what is happening in field. The field instruction portion of the curriculum is designed to help students apply and integrate theoretical concepts learned in the classroom. It is the time when everything comes together.

Undergraduate programs use a wide variety of placements. The local Human Services Department often serves as a placement, especially in the services areas of the program. Traditional family services agencies, public schools, medical and psychiatric settings, and substance abuse programs also make effective placement settings. Nontraditional settings may also be used: community action programs, shelters for battered women, community planning boards, and so forth. Administrative and program-planning experiences can be obtained in both traditional and nontraditional settings.

Supervision is provided by a faculty member assigned to the agency to supervise a unit of students, or by an agency-based field instructor. A faculty member from the school serves as a faculty liaison person, making several visits to the field placement site each term. Field instructors having their MSW degree and several years of post-master's experience are preferred; however, in reality some highly experienced BSW graduates and others without advanced professional training often serve as student supervisors, and many do so quite effectively. If the placement does not provide professional social work supervision, the school usually assigns a faculty member to work very closely with both the student and the agency, providing some direct supervision and meeting frequently with all concerned to ensure proper professional direction of the student's learning experience.

MSW Programs

The accredited MSW program is headed by a dean who usually has a doctorate in social work or a closely related field. He or she administratively oversees the various social work programs offered by the school, which may include an undergraduate program, an MSW program, a doctoral program, or perhaps even separate branches or extension programs located some distance from the dean's office. Heads of BSW programs, who are generally referred to as "chairpersons" or "directors," may have only the MSW degree. However, as baccalaureate education in social work is attaining greater professional status, a DSW is increasingly required.

Graduate programs usually offer two broad areas of concentration: micro (casework, direct service, small systems, clinical) and macro (administration, indirect services, large systems). The macro group includes social work administration, community organization, research, policy and planning, supervision, and staff development or teaching. Students elect one of these areas as their specialty. Both micro and macro students take basic courses in clinical skills, policy, research, human behavior, and the like during their first year of graduate school; the student specializing in micro skills will take more advanced clinical practice courses in the second year. In reality, there is often some duplication between the generic courses offered in the first year of some MSW programs and those offered in the senior year of many progressive BSW programs. Most graduate programs no longer require a formal thesis, but many do require students to complete a major research project in connection with research courses.

All graduate students complete at least one intensive field placement; most are expected to undertake two different placements: one in a traditional direct-services setting working with individuals and famililes, and the second in the student's specialized area of study, such as administration or staff development.

MSW programs usually require the agency-based field instructor to have an MSW plus at least two years of post-master's experience. However, these requirements are not ironclad. Students concentrating in indirect services (macro) may receive supervision from an administrator or community organizer who has little or no social work training or direct experience with "clients." A few schools are so desperate for field placements that brand-new MSW graduates supervise first-year clinical graduate students. At the other extreme, several programs require field instructors to have the MSW plus four or more years of post-MSW experience.

Faculty members in both BSW and MSW programs are sometimes assigned to agencies as full-time field instructors, supervising a unit of six to eight students. They may teach one or more courses on campus as well. Because schools can maintain tight control over the quality and consistency of field instruction experiences by using their own faculties, some schools place all first-year students in units and assign them to individual agency-based field instructors only in their second year.

A substantial problem faced by graduate programs is accommodating to the widely differing backgrounds of their students. A given program may have beginning MSW students who have never worked and others with years of post-BA or BSW experience. Some may be graduates of accredited BSW programs while others know little or nothing about social work. It is not usually practical to develop separate educational tracks for each kind of student. The most common approach to this problem is the abbreviated or accelerated master's program, which enables students to receive the BSW plus the MSW in a total of five years rather than the traditional six. In schools that offer such a program,

BSW students undergo a special senior year experience that is virtually identical to the first year of the regular two-year MSW training. Upon completion of their senior year, they then enter the equivalent of the second year of a traditional MSW program and receive their advanced degrees one year later. Some schools shorten the MSW program for selected students by giving credit for life experiences or by permitting a person with a BSW from another school to enroll in a shortened MSW program. Abbreviated yet complete schedules may permit advanced students to enroll in September and graduate with an MSW twelve months later. Some even fit in field placements for both the first and the second year by doing an initial placement (equivalent to the first-year placement) during the summer, then moving into an intensive second-year schedule. There are many other variations on this theme.

This abbreviated approach to MSW education has its pros and cons. Such programs permit students to move through their educational experience very rapidly. However, the very young graduate may find that his personal maturity and life experience do not equip him for responsible MSW practice. In schools that permit the five-year student to elect a concentration in administration, supervision, community organization, or staff development, this problem becomes more acute, for a twenty-one- or twenty-two-year-old with no significant work experience can theoretically graduate with an MSW degree that certifies his readiness for employment as an agency administrator, supervisor, or coordinator of community programs and services! He is theoretically equipped to hold an MSW clinical position, yet he has only the equivalent of a BSW education in micro practice (the senior year course work and field placement), because the last year was spent concentrating on macro services. Thus, the five-year macro-systems graduate may find himself in a no man's land of unemployment, for most agencies are aware that such a person lacks the training needed to function in their setting. If agencies cannot use these graduates, then the five-year programs are not meeting the manpower needs of the social work community.

It is the author's strong contention that students who select the macro systems concentration must:

1. have at least three years of full-time paid social work experience prior to entering graduate school
2. take the full two years to obtain the MSW degree
3. have demonstrated leadership ability and/or a personality and manner of relating to people that clearly indicate potential
4. receive MSW supervision in all field placements, though non-MSWs may have some major input in the second year

Top-quality schools generally do adhere to these criteria in admitting students into administrative training. However, many other schools hire as faculty individuals who have gone straight from BSW to MSW to DSW without ever having had significant paid social work experience. As long as this trend continues, the quality of graduates from such programs will fail to meet the needs of many social service agencies and consumer groups. Field instructors could have a significant impact by refusing to accept in field placement any administration/supervision/community organization/ staff development students who do not meet the four criteria listed above.

DSW Programs

Doctoral programs in social work usually require two years of residence at the university devoted to coursework plus a dissertation, which normally requires a third year. There is a heavy emphasis on research and scholarship; a wide range of advanced specialities is available: clinical training, administration, research, preparation for college teaching, and the like. Most DSW programs do not include formal field experiences. DSW programs are not subject to review by the Council on Social Work Education.

Quarter Versus Semester Programs

Schools usually follow either a quarter or a semester system. The quarter program offers four full terms per calendar year. By going the year round, a student could conceivably obtain a BSW degree in three instead of four years. Field placements are very short in duration, as most quarters are only ten to twelve weeks in length. Classes may meet for four or five hours once weekly instead of the traditional two or three times a week for one or two hours. The total number of credits necessary to graduate under the quarter system is generally 192 hours. A typical semester program, in contrast, has two semesters: September (or late August) to December and January to May or June. An abbreviated summer session may also be offered. Usually 120 to 130 hours of course credits are required for graduation. In both quarter and semester programs, there are usually long breaks at Christmas, a week or more at Easter, and shorter breaks between quarters. This affects field placement scheduling. If a student is in the field from September to May under a concurrent semester plan, a three- or four-week recess over Christmas and New Year's can disrupt scheduling continuity and service to clients. Those in the administrative track may miss important activities. Many field instructors report that both they and their students regress during these absences, and it may take several weeks after the vacation before they get reinvolved with the field instruction process and build back up to their prior level of learning and involvement.

Block Versus Concurrent Field Placements

As has been mentioned, in both graduate and undergraduate field instruction, either block or concurrent placement may be used. In block placements the student takes no formal courses and reports to the agency for a full thirty-five- or forty-hour week while in placement. Some students take special field integration seminars concurrent with the block placement, which may slightly decrease their actual hours in the field.

In the concurrent plan, students take three or four courses plus field placement simultaneously. Classes are usually scheduled for six to eight hours on each of two days while the student attends field placement for two or three full days a week.

The block plan seems to be preferred by many field instructors and students who have experienced both kinds of schedule. Block placements permit students to do field placements in settings at some distance from their schools. They are therefore mandatory for schools in rural areas where there are insufficient professional programs locally to provide quality field instruction experiences for all students. This arrangement can work well for the student who likes to travel and is free to do so, or who has family he can stay with in a distant city. It does pose some problems for the school in monitoring the student's experience. Faculty visits to a distant field instruction site are expensive and therefore infrequent. Bringing field instructors to the school or getting them together in groups for any kind of training is very costly and impractical. Field instructors may feel a need for closer, more frequent communication with the school. However, block placements do permit students to become totally immersed in their field placement experience. They can attend all staff meetings and special activities and carry out reading and special assignments in connection with field without feeling the additional pressure of classroom assignments. They can become involved in both short-term and long-term activities, knowing that they will be present every day and not miss any unexpected developments. Learning takes place rapidly and intensively as there are no outside educational experiences to intervene or compete for the student's attention.

On the other hand, in the absence of classroom presentation of theory and reading concurrent with field, the student in block placement could have considerable difficulty connecting theory and practice. There may be a gap of several months between the classroom theory the student learned the previous semester or quarter and the time when he is in a position to apply his new knowledge, during which much can be forgotten.

Concurrent placement also has strong advantages and disadvantages. Students are exposed to classroom theory every week and have the opportunity to implement and try out almost immediately the concepts learned. They can bring experiences from the field into the classroom for discussion, as they happen. Because all settings used for concurrent placements must be within commuting distance of the school, not only students but field instructors as well can be assembled on campus (or at other mutually convenient locations) for training and special sessions. Students are not isolated from one another, as occurs with many block placements, but see each other regularly in the classroom and can informally share and compare their experiences in different settings. The school is in an ideal position to offer special field instruction seminars or courses for its students. School library resources are readily available, and faculty advisers or field instruction faculty can visit agencies personally and closely monitor field placement experiences and the selection of agencies and supervisory personnel.

Concurrent placements usually go on longer than block placements. If a student is placed in a setting where long-term counseling is done on a traditional once-a-week basis, he may be able to follow the same individual or family for nine months of concurrent placement, as against only three or four months in block. The longer placement gives the field instructor greater opportunity to get to know the student and the student more time to assimilate field learning. In contrast, if block placements are short-lived (as under a ten-week quarter system), many field instructors find it difficult to prepare midterm and even final performance evaluations; they feel they hardly know the student. In addition, learning must take place very rapidly. There is virtually no time for gradual internalization of concepts.

It is the field instructor who usually experiences the primary disadvantages of the concurrent approach to field instruction. If a student is in the agency on Tuesday and Friday, someone, often the supervisor, must cover his caseload if anything happens on Monday, Wednesday, or Thursday. This can confuse the client, who must relate to two social workers, and can be frustrating to the student; for example, if he returns to the agency on Friday to discover that his client attempted suicide on Wednesday, the field instructor may have become so involved that it is necessary for him to keep the case. In medical and other acute care, crisis, or inpatient settings, the student's client may be discharged unexpectedly while he is absent from field. The student's periodic absences may place an unfair burden on the supervisor or line staff who are asked to handle his cases. Furthermore, special staff meetings, administrative conferences, interdisciplinary meetings, or community activities may take place on days when the student must be at school; he may find himself faced with the choice of missing class to attend something in the agency or missing events at the agency in favor of school. When classroom homework assignments become heavy as midterm or final exam time arrives, students often feel the pressure keenly and slack off noticeably in their involvement in field. Thus,

class and field periodically compete for the student's time and energies.

The pros and cons of block versus concurrent placement could be argued indefinitely. If an agency has a choice and is able to take students from several schools, it may decide that one plan or the other works better for its particular setting and agree to take only students enrolled in that type of program.

Part-Time Programs

Some schools offer part-time programs where fully employed individuals can work toward their degrees by attending classes at night. There is often a requirement that part of the education be on a full-time basis, especially toward the end. Special arrangements are sometimes worked out so that students employed in an agency can remain at full pay and do at least part of their field placement there; subsequent placements must usually be done elsewhere. This arrangement is fraught with hazards for the student, who may be used as a workhorse by his agency, with no real change in assignment or supervisory approach. Another variation permits students to take field placement alone for one term, then only one or two courses per term, enabling them to obtain their degree in three to four years.

The Social Work Education Accreditation Process

CSWE is the accrediting body for schools of social work. It establishes and publishes certain basic criteria that all MSW and BSW programs must meet in order to get its stamp of approval.* The purpose of accreditation is

> ... to help schools of social work achieve maximum educational effectiveness and to identify schools whose competence in the particular educational programs they offer warrants public and professional confidence. Corollary to these basic aims, accreditation of programs of professional education for social work should also serve (1) to help schools achieve high standards rather than standardized educational programs; (2) to encourage well-advised and planned innovation and experimentation in social work education; (3) to foster continuing self-analysis and self-improvement of schools so as to encourage imaginative educational development; (4) to relate professional education for social work to social work practice.†

Thus, the accreditation process assures some consistency regarding faculty qualifications, broad educational objec-

---

*Manual of Accrediting Standards for Graduate Professional Schools of Social Work (with Supplement for Undergraduate Programs) (New York: CSWE, April 1971). Copies can be ordered from CSWE at 111 Eighth Avenue, New York, N.Y. 10011. The standards are currently undergoing some revisions.
†Ibid., Section 1110, p. 4.

tives, and program planning for the BSW and MSW degrees. See Appendix H for more details. It usually takes a school at least three years to gain accredited status. Persons who graduate in the meantime may be granted status retroactively as degree-holders from an accredited program. Only graduates from an accredited undergraduate program may receive a BSW (Bachelor of Social Work) degree. MSW programs simply do not exist unless they are accredited or actively working toward accreditation. Doctoral programs in social work are not subject to a formal CSWE accrediting process.

Accreditation can be granted for up to seven years, with reaccreditation reviews conducted periodically throughout the life of the program. Faculty, particularly those with administrative responsibility, conduct a "self-study" and submit its results to CSWE prior to the site visit of the accreditation team. The self-study is a comprehensive report answering many questions to describe how the program is meeting CSWE standards in specific areas. The school and CSWE together select accreditation team members from a list of trained site visitors. At the time this is being written, serious consideration is being given to appointing at least one field instructor as a member of these teams to provide for input from practitioners as well as full-time social work educators.

The team usually spends two days at the school, going through its records and meeting with faculty, field instructors, students, university administrators, and community groups to determine whether the school is in fact providing what its self-study report claims. The present standards do not permit the site visitors to observe in the classroom. Some schools announce the date and place of the site team's session with field instructors and invite all who wish to attend. Others hand-pick those who are permitted to meet with the team, and the majority of field instructors may not even realize that an accreditation review is taking place.

In its meeting with field instructors, the team usually wants to know what the instructors perceive as the main strengths and problems in the program. They examine communication between school and field; how the classroom curriculum is perceived in preparing students for field and professional practice; and the effectiveness of faculty liaison persons in keeping in touch with both field instructors and students. The discussion is usually informal, but obviously this is not the time for an individual field instructor to grind his personal axe regarding a minute problem or a personality conflict with a faculty member. However, persistent concerns should be brought to the team's attention. Gaps in the educational program and unmet needs for either students or field instructors should be noted as well as inconsistencies between what the school says it is providing and what field instructors perceive as reality. Strong points and positive experiences should be related as well. There is often an opportunity to make recom-

mendations for overcoming problem areas or improving the program in general.

At the conclusion of the site team's visit, a general meeting is held with all faculty, at which the team presents a summary of its findings. This is followed by a formal written report presenting the team's findings and recommendations regarding areas that need improvement. Even the strongest of programs is usually challenged to strengthen some areas. The school then has an opportunity to respond in writing to any concerns raised in the report, and these replies are taken into consideration along with the report when the formal board at CSWE convenes to render its decision regarding the school's accreditation status. This official decision is not usually forthcoming until several months after the site team's visit. Unfortunately, few schools routinely share the details of CSWE reports and recommendations with field instructors, though many undoubtedly would make the report available upon request.

CSWE recommendations are taken very seriously by the school. Many schools undergo significant program or curriculum changes in anticipation of a site visit, and others implement additional changes following receipt of the team's recommendations. For example, a report that the faculty does not contain appropriate representation of minority groups will affect hiring practices. Changes in curriculum or field placement arrangements may be puzzling to field instructors if they do not understand why the changes are needed or lack knowledge of the revised goals the school is striving to meet.

CSWE does provide a mechanism for individual field instructors, groups of field instructors, or members of a local professional group to submit formal complaints or concerns regarding a specific school of social work.* If this is done prior to an accreditation or reaccreditation site visit, the impact can be quite significant. Students also can make use of this provision. Naturally, schools hope few persons will feel a need to apply this mechanism, and those who do must be extremely careful to do so responsibly and as objectively as possible. Neither CSWE nor the local school would appreciate complaints that merely vent emotional frustrations or are designed to retaliate against or harass the school. Likewise, schools must refrain from applying pressure on field instructors or students to communicate or not communicate certain kinds of thoughts to CSWE. It would appear logical that direct communication with CSWE could be used to convey positives as well as negatives.

Roles of the School, the Field Instructor, and Others

Many parties have a role in the field instruction process. Normally the roles are complementary. Difficulties can

---

*See ibid., "Procedures for Receiving and Disposing of Complaints About Accredited Schools," Sections 7C00–7C54, pp. 49–51.

arise when one party feels a need to fill a role it considers essential but views as not being done by the appropriate party, and thus assumes responsibility for doing something that ordinarily someone else should handle. For example, schools traditionally provide training for field instructors. In the absence of such training, some agencies develop their own courses for field instructors. For maximum effectiveness, field instruction must be a *joint* venture among all concerned, and this necessitates considerable ongoing communication among all parties involved.

The chart on pages 12–15 summarizes the key roles of the agency, the individual field instructor within the agency, the overall school program, the director of field instruction within the school, the individual faculty adviser assigned by the school to work with the agency, and the student, as they all work together to bring into being a field placement program and experience for the individual student. These roles are explicated in much greater detail throughout the remainder of this book.

Roles of Key Persons in the Field Instruction Process

Agency	Agency-Based Field Instructor	School*
1. Submits to school a description of what it has to offer students: types of learning experiences available. States the types of students it expects to fit in best with its program and any necessary special requirements.	1. Expresses a desire to be a field instructor and meets all minimum requirements set by the school and/or the agency.	1. Admits students to social work program and rules on readiness for entering field placement.
2. Someone in agency determines who will and will not supervise students in the coming year and gains administrative support for the student program.	2. Takes seminars or training courses offered by school and/or own agency in preparation for field instructor's duties.	2. Develops, in cooperation with the director of field instruction, formal agency-school-student contracts regarding field instruction.
3. Administration develops and/or signs formal written contract providing legal protection in agency's supervision of students.	3. Attends school seminars offered for all field instructors to advise them of current developments in school's program.	3. Develops field instruction manual and offers field instruction training courses or seminars for new, potential, or past field instructors.
4. Tells school exactly how many students, at what level of training and in what areas of specialty, the agency can take in the coming year.	4. Conducts preplacement interview with student.	4. Advises each field placement agency who the faculty adviser will be for each student in placement.
5. When contacted by the school with names of specific potential students, conducts preplacement interview.	5. Advises school whether or not individual field instructor and/or agency will take the student in question.	5. School (often the faculty adviser) prepares formal references for graduating students, abstracted from all classroom and field experience evaluatory material.
	6. Develops educational plan with student; provides day-to-day supervision; evaluates student performance in field.	6. Offers agency personnel opportunity to participate on school committes re field and classroom curriculum. Agency administrators solicited for participation on community advisory committees.
	7. Recommends (or assigns) field placement grade or rating.	
6. Accepts or rejects each student interviewed.		
	8. Keeps faculty adviser informed of students' progress and notifies school of any problems with the student.	7. Takes into consideration suggestions and recommendations for change coming from agencies, incorporates them into school program, and makes necessary changes when appropriate.
7. Completes placement arrangements. If agency is large, designates a senior field instructor or someone to coordinate and oversee the student program ("agency-based liaison person").	9. Participates in conferences with the faculty adviser, school field instruction staff and/or student on a routine basis or whenever problems arise and joint conferences are indicated.	8. Makes certain that field instruction program meets all accreditation requirements; involves field in-
8. Maintains close communication with school		

*Some of these functions may be performed by field instruction faculty.

Director of Field Instruction or Field Instruction Staff	Faculty Liaison Person	Student
1. Contacts existing and potential field placement settings to find out how many students each agency can take during the coming year.	1. Is assigned by school to students/agencies. (In some schools, faculty adviser takes some of the functions listed for field instruction staff).	1. Expresses preference for general type of field placement desired.
2. Reviews files regarding experiences offered in the setting; reviews student's files and feedback from classroom instructors and begins process of matching student to agency.	2. Meets with student periodically to review progress and plan curriculum. Is available to student as needed for questions or problems with course work and field.	2. Participates in interview with field instruction staff for preliminary screening or matching with agency. 3. Attends preplacement interview.
3. May conduct personal interview with student regarding his educational needs and goals in field placement. Informs students of the kinds of experience available in various types of field placement settings as well as with individual field instructors in specific settings.	3. Should visit field placement several times during student's field placement, regardless of whether or not there are problems, to discuss and review student progress in field.	4. Attends school orientation or ongoing seminars designed to prepare student for maximum learning in field. 5. Participates fully in the field placement experience.
4. May interview new field instructors; have them complete resume or application to make certain they meet school's criteria for being a field instructor.	4. Keeps the field instructor informed of happenings in the school that might affect the field placement program. Helps the field instructor work with the student to integrate class and field learning.	6. Communicates with faculty adviser as necessary or when problems arise. 7. Completes evaluation of field placement experience.
5. Calls agency to advise of specific, potential students for placement. Shares basic information from student's application, references, first year experience, and so on.	5. If communication breakdown occurs between student and field instructor, or other problems develop, becomes involved. May talk with student individually and/or meet with field instructor privately or in joint conference with the student.	
6. When advised that agency will accept the student, sends confirmation of the placement. May also send written identifying data regarding the student. Field instructor's name put on mailing list for future correspondence regarding field placement.	6. Informs the Director of Field Instruction of the experiences taking place in the agency. May make recommendations regarding whether a given agency or field instructor should continue to be used by the school.	
7. Supplies field instruction manual to field in-	7. Reviews grade recom-	

(*Continued*)

Roles of Key Persons in the Field Instruction Process (*cont.*)

Agency	Agency-Based Field Instructor	School
throughout placement regarding each student. 9. Offers feedback and suggestion for general improvement of the field instruction program, including suggestions regarding classroom curriculum if necessary.	10. Provides feedback to the field instruction faculty of the school regarding recommendations for improving the overall field instruction program, classroom preparation for field, and related issues that go beyond the needs of a particular student (agency-based liaison person may do this collectively for several field instructors in a large setting). 11. May participate on school committees with faculty and/or students to develop or examine policy for admissions, curriculum planning, field instruction, and related areas.	structors in this process and informs them of the results of accreditation reviews.

Director of Field Instruction or Field Instruction Staff	Faculty Liaison Person	Student

structor; explains educational objectives of field placement and any special requirements or goals.

8. May become involved in conferences with field instructor, faculty adviser, and/or student in complex problem situations.

9. Develops/recommends field instruction policies, with input from the school and possibly also committees on which students and field instructors participate.

10. Reviews student evaluation of field placement experiences and takes them into consideration when planning future placements in each setting.

11. Gives feedback to individual field instructors and agencies concerning student evaluations of their experiences with them, and offers constructive recommendations for improving the quality of the placement; gives positive feedback where warranted.

mended by field instructor and assigns field placement grade.

2 Selection of Agencies and Field Instructors

The selection of appropriate field instructors and agency settings is crucial to the success of any field instruction program. Unfortunately, factors other than who is the best-qualified instructor and which settings can offer the most effective experience often influence the selection.

Agency administrators frequently determine who on their staff will supervise students and how many, leaving the individual practitioner little choice in the matter. On the other hand, in many settings staff who volunteer to be field instructors automatically receive the assignment as long as they meet the minimum educational and/or experience requirements set by the school. An individual who has supervised students for years is automatically assigned more students on the assumption that years of experience are synonymous with good field instruction. A few staff members view volunteering for field instruction as an apple-polishing technique, a way to please the administration and, they hope, gain promotion. If this is the primary motivation for taking on a student, the quality of the field instruction experience often suffers.

Politics can enter into a school's selection of both agencies and individual field instructors. A large agency network or administrative structure may refuse to take any students unless it is free to place them where it wishes, even in those departments known to provide experiences of questionable value. Thus, the school may be forced to accept one or two marginal field instructors in exchange for good placements for a number of students. The sheer size of many social work educational programs forces schools to unearth every conceivable field placement setting and accept some that are poor, for the alternative would be to reduce enrollment and lose funding and faculty positions. If several schools are competing for placements in the same community, outstanding and reasonably effective settings soon become overloaded; schools must then turn to more experimental, high-

risk, or "unknown" agencies and field instructors. As schools become more specialized in their educational programs, it becomes increasingly difficult to find qualified field instructors with the necessary expertise. Schools in locations where few good placements exist may be obliged to accept a mediocre placement or none at all.

Selecting Field Placement Agencies

Almost any setting where social work is practiced or can have a meaningful role can be used as a field placement. Obviously the experiences provided must be compatible with the theory taught in the classroom and enhance the overall educational objectives set up by the school. There must be physical space for the student. A key administrator or supervisor must have a commitment to social work education and some understanding of what social work education is all about. The agency (or department within a large setting) must recognize that student training takes time and must be willing to make certain adjustments to meet the needs of students and schools. There must be individuals within the agency who are willing and able to serve as field instructors and who meet established minimum requirements for affiliation with the school.

Beyond these basics, the nature and quality of a student's field placement experience depend a great deal on the individual field instructor—his competence, his attitude, his approach to student supervision, and the kinds of experience he can provide the student. However, there are a few conditions that indicate that an entire department or agency should not take social work students, regardless of the capability of individual staff within the setting. Unfortunately, schools may not find out about the existence of such factors quickly enough to avoid the setting. To prevent this, an in-depth conversation with an appropriate administrator or even with students previously placed in the setting will usually reveal the presence of complicating elements. There is nothing to prevent an entire agency, unit, or department from eliminating itself if it knows that certain problems are present and then communicating this decision to the school early in its placement process.

A given agency* may be suffering from a morale problem resulting in an abnormally high rate of staff turnover. The cause may be poor working conditions, ineffective supervision or administrative leadership, excessive work loads, or inappropriate use of professional staff. Regardless of the specific cause, the working environment is often tense, anxiety-ridden, and sometimes overtly negative and hostile. An overactive grapevine often initiates new employees and students into all the negatives of the setting and is constantly fueled with gossip regarding the agency, perhaps even attacking the competence and personal character of specific employees, particularly authority figures. There may be passive-aggressive if not open resistance to and resentment toward supervisory and administrative personnel, accompanied by lack of respect for their position, policies, and instructions. Unhappy employees may freely ventilate to all who will listen their dissatisfactions and reasons for leaving the agency.

Some unusually mature learners can weather such an environment and experience growth from the experience, *if* they have an unusually strong and positive field instructor. However, most students simply cannot handle the special anxieties and insecurities created by an overtly problematic work environment in addition to the normal anxiety that goes with being a student. The immature student can easily be persuaded to choose sides and may expend so much energy fighting other people's battles that little significant substantive learning occurs. The anxiety level often rises so high that the student becomes immobilized and learning is virtually impossible.

When schools become aware of such situations, the student is usually moved quickly to another setting. The student's experience would certainly be much less traumatic if problematic settings could be identified in advance of field placement assignments. Agency administrators, supervisors, and field instructors, as well as schools and students, must all assist in identifying situational or chronic problems that indicate a setting should not accept students.

The absence of a key supervisor or administrator in an agency may create chaos for the line staff and prevent otherwise effective field instructors from giving their best to a student. A massive agencywide reorganization can also create turmoil as staff are shuffled to new assignments with accompanying job insecurities, fights for promotion, and disruption of the normal chain of command and communi-

cation channels. Field instructors may find themselves having to serve emotionally disturbed clients or a community population with which they are totally unfamiliar. They may have to learn radically different job skills. Some staff may even resign in the process. If an agency knows it is going to face such an upheaval during the coming school year, this should be communicated to the school as soon as possible, along with a decision not to take students for a while. If certain field instructors are assigned to areas that are not affected by the reorganization and have fairly stable job classifications, perhaps they could still take students. However, large internal changes within an organization commonly force schools to change student field placements in midstream. Some of these changes take place unexpectedly after students are already in the agency. However, why assign students to settings where tumultuous and problematic experiences are predictable?

If an agency has experienced a prolonged period of severe staff shortages, students should be placed elsewhere. Most programs suffer occasional vacancies that create coverage problems until a replacement is hired. However, a prolonged freeze on hiring that prohibits the filling of vacant positions or hefty cutbacks in funds resulting in layoffs put intense pressure on those staff who remain to cover the work load. They may also feel justifiably insecure regarding their own jobs. Students placed in such an environment often suffer from insufficient time with their field instructor, and the temptation to use the extra hands to help carry the work load is greater than most agencies can resist. Students in such placements become unofficial employees with none of the benefits in pay, seniority, or status. Nor do they get the special rights that go along with being a student and for which they are paying—freedom to make mistakes, continuous direction and evaluative feedback, discussions regarding educational goals and special instructional techniques, time for reading during field placement hours and for reflection to integrate material learned, time for gab sessions regarding social work values and philosophy, direct observation of their work by a supervisor, very small work loads, permitting time for all these things to take place, and so on. The student is cheated, yet may feel pleased to be "helping out" and excited about having exposure to so many different experiences. He may receive highly positive feedback because everyone is so glad to have him there to help out. However, no one looks too closely at the quality of his work, because the student's presence is needed so desperately. The naive student usually does not even realize that he is missing a major part of the educational experience to which he is entitled. The school may not become aware of the deficiencies until the student is well into the field placement or not even until after graduation, when the former student talks with others or compares a subsequent experience with what he should have gotten in the questionable field placement. Clearly, such settings should be avoided.

---

*The term "agency" as used here could include a department, unit, or small program within a larger bureaucracy or network of agencies. Some aspects could also apply to the office of one or more professionals who are engaged in private practice.

A field placement facility should believe in hiring those workers it has trained as students whenever possible. Thus, BSW students should not be placed in settings that employ only MSWs. The goal of social work education should be to prepare the new graduate to function at his degree level. If an agency has no commitment to hiring BSWs and little concept of their role in social work practice, how can it meaningfully participate in educating such students? The absence of BSW staff leaves the BSW student with no role model. If an agency does not have a use for BSWs in its program, does it really believe in the value, importance, and role of these persons in social work practice?

A school may need to say no to an agency that consistently refuses to release its staff to attend training courses, seminars, and other special activities provided by the school for field instructors. Such a setting seems to be saying that it wants the benefits of having students but not the extra responsibilities. If the school requires training as a prerequisite for field instructors, such agencies will be eliminated. If exceptions are permitted, untrained field instructors may be providing experiences for students that are not consistent with the school's expectations and the approaches used in other field settings. An individual field instructor who is highly motivated might get around his agency's resistance by using annual leave or personal leave time to attend school sessions. But this should not be necessary in an agency committed to student education. On the other hand, the demands of staff work loads will occasionally prevent most field instructors from attending sessions, and this reality must be recognized and accepted by all concerned.

Agencies sometimes undermine effective field instruction assignments through a game called "the surrogate field instructor." School and agency may contract for supervision of Suzy Smith to be provided by Jack Jones, an experienced field instructor who meets all requirements. In reality, Jack Jones may be quite busy—perhaps acting as consultant to a branch of the agency in another city or taking on some extra duties. So Frank Brown, a bright young man with a master's degree in history and one year's experience in the same position that MSWs occupy in the agency, actually works with the student. Mr. Brown holds supervisory conferences with the student, gives daily guidance and feedback, makes work assignments, and evaluates the student's performance. However, Jack Jones signs the performance evaluation and all official papers. Everything appears in perfect order to the unsuspecting school. The student often sees nothing wrong with the arrangement and just assumes "that's the way it's supposed to be." He may not even know the educational background and experience (or the lack thereof) of his field instructor(s). Only when the student tells someone else that he never sees Jack Jones and a question is raised regarding his supervision is the problem identified.* Students should find out exactly who will be

supervising them on a daily basis, inquire about the professional background and experience of that person and immediately report to the school any differences between the formal assignment and the actual practice.

Finally, all settings used as training sites for students must be in compliance with all pertinent federal, state, and local laws and policies concerning nondiscrimination. Clauses to this effect should be incorporated into formal written contracts between school and agency. Students observing or experiencing genuine discrimination or racist practices in their field placement settings should report their concerns immediately to the school.

Prerequisites for Being a Field Instructor

Most schools of social work require an MSW degree and two or more years of post-master's experience (and/or ACSW certification) before one can become a field instructor. However, there are many exceptions to this policy, some acceptable and others unjustifiable.

Undergraduate programs frequently permit BSWs or even persons without social work degrees to supervise students in field if the supervisors have many years of experience. Graduate students may supervise undergraduates as part of their field placement experience; someone with fewer than the required years of experience may act as a supervisor with a senior field instructor closely overseeing the process and co-signing evaluatory materials. Recent MSW graduates may be foisted into a field-instruction role by their agency or even by a school. Administrators having no social work training whatsoever often act as primary field instructors for macro system students.

Unfortunately, even if an individual meets the minimum education and experience requirements set by a school, we cannot assume that he or she will be an effective field instructor. The following additional prerequisites must be considered:

First, the agency-based practitioner must want to supervise a student. Most agencies do not reduce a staff member's work load when a student is assigned to him. Yet field instructors report consistently that this responsibility consumes anywhere from two to eight or more hours a week in direct student contact time and behind-the-scenes preparation of assignments and review of student work. Thus, the agency's pressure to take a student may be resented, and the astute student almost always detects this attitude. If a staff member must choose between keeping his own work up to date and working with a student, the student may be left to founder from ineffective or insufficient supervisory guidance.

The potential field instructor must have participated in some kind of training in the responsibilities and benefits of

---

*There are situations where schools and agencies agree to an arrangement whereby a normally unqualified field instructor takes a student, but

under close direction and supervision from an experienced field instructor or faculty liaison person. Such situations, when carefully planned and monitored, can work to the student's benefit and permit placement in settings that would otherwise be unavailable to him.

field instruction before he can meaningfully determine whether or not he feels capable of assuming this role and in fact wants to do so.

Once an individual expresses willingness to be a field instructor, he should be required to participate in a course on techniques of field instruction. He will also need to attend ongoing seminars, workshops, or other special activities offered by the school for field instructors. Thus, the individual's employer must be willing to allow time off from work to attend such activities. Many field instructors literally cut their supervisory teeth on students, frequently as a first step toward supervising staff in their agency. Yet these same neophytes are often tossed into a role that demands a very specialized kind of approach, with virtually no guidance on how to function. It is not surprising that a significant number of new field instructors find the process frustrating and anxiety-producing and end up with a genuine reluctance to accept future students.

A field instructor must have basically positive feelings toward students and toward social work education as a process. He may be sharply critical of some aspects of social work education, but must believe that it is a meaningful endeavor and be willing to become a part of it. The field instructor may disagree strongly with the philosophy and approach of a local school of social work, yet he must be able to refrain from joining with the student against the school. He must feel sufficiently positive toward the school's program that he can honestly join with the school in educating the student.

The field instructor must be performing at a satisfactory or better level in his own job and must have basically positive feelings toward his agency and his work environment. He may be very critical of supervisory individuals or of certain procedures and policies; however, he must not be so negative that he unloads his feelings on the student. There must be a sense of loyalty to the agency or department and a willingness to help the student also develop an identity with the program.

A field instructor must be willing and reasonably prepared to deal with difficult as well as outstanding students. Most schools try to assign "easy" students to new field instructors. However, there is no guarantee that an emotionally disturbed, hostile, slow-learning, or other "problem" student won't be assigned instead. Even schools and field instructors who conduct preplacement interviews are not always able to identify these individuals in advance. Thus, the potential field instructor must have a realistic awareness that student supervision can be frustrating, anxiety-producing, stressful, and time-consuming, as well as rewarding, energizing, educational, and self-fulfilling. The beginning field instructor may lack the specific skills necessary for dealing with problem situations, but he must at least have an intellectual commitment to the idea that he could work with a problem student if necessary.

There must be a strong desire to learn and grow both personally and professionally. Students constantly challenge the "old way of doing things" and often will not accept a field instructor's suggested approach or technique without knowing why. The field instructor may find himself frequently questioning and reexamining his own values and techniques and may be reading frantically at home at night to keep one step ahead of his student. If a supervisor provides an effective experience for his student, often he will learn nearly as much as his supervisee in the process. Some of this will be content knowledge regarding social work skills and philosophy, but much will come from self-examination of his instructional style, his supervisory approach, his handling of day-to-day situations with the student, and his commitment to standards in social work education and practice. The insecure or overconfident field instructor may resist this process, resulting in rigidity, failure to meet the individual learning needs of the student, and provision of a rather poor role model for learning.

A field instructor must be physically present on the job during the same hours that the student is in placement. Minor variations cause little difficulty. But how can a student have a meaningful learning experience if he is at the agency from 8 A.M. to 4:30 P.M. and his field instructor doesn't come to work until 3:30 or is gone for large blocks of time? Perhaps the field instructor reports to work only one or two hours per week for supervisory conferences. Most students are unable to confront a field instructor directly with their feeling that he is not spending sufficient time with them. Many postpone reporting the problem, hoping that matters will eventually improve. By the time they do, most of the semester or quarter may have elapsed, leaving the student with gaps in his overall learning experience that must be filled in subsequent field placements, if at all. Thus, there must be a clear understanding among the agency, the school, and the individual field instructor regarding work and field placement hours *before* a commitment is made to take a student.

An agency-based field instructor must have sufficient time to devote to his student to provide a meaningful learning experience. He should expect to spend a minimum of two hours a week in formal conference time, especially during the first few weeks of placement. Several hours more may be necessary for informal on-the-spot contacts. The field instructor will also have to spend time planning assignments, reviewing recording and other work produced by the student, finding appropriate reading material, and perhaps seeking consultation from his own supervisor or from other field instructors regarding his approach with the student. There must be some discussion between the field instructor and his immediate supervisor regarding these extra demands on his time to see if any adjustment in work load is possible. If not, and the staff member still wants to take a student (and most will), he often ends up putting in extra hours or taking work home in order to fulfill his role effectively.

Who Should Not Supervise Students

Certain circumstances are incompatible with good field instruction. These factors must be evaluated before an individual becomes a field instructor. The agency is usually in a better position than the school to know about the existence of these contraindications to field instruction. Thus, the school must clearly state that it will not place students with individuals when these factors are present and then must depend on the agency to take them into consideration when recommending potential field instructors.

Staff members whose own job performance is marginal or unsatisfactory should not be supervising students. Obviously, if an individual is having difficulty meeting performance expectations in the agency, he is going to have difficulty teaching appropriate standards and skills to his student. Furthermore, there may be displacement of negative feelings toward his own superiors or toward the agency onto the student. Most students can sense the tensions when a field instructor is not relating well with his own superiors and will feel insecure and anxious; some immature students may get caught up in the situation out of their own needs. Furthermore, if the field instructor's own performance is inadequate, he will provide a poor role model for his trainee. An individual who knows he is seriously weak in a given area may resist evaluating his student's performance in that area or set too lenient standards for the student to avoid having to deal with his own inadequacies. Others may overcompensate and set impossibly high standards. Finally, if the field instructor's poor performance continues, he may receive disciplinary action and even be suspended or dismissed. Should this occur while a student is under his supervision, the results can be traumatic for the student.

A special problem arises when a staff member with satisfactory performance becomes a field instructor and his performance declines to unsatisfactory while the student is in field. If this is a situational, transitory occurrence and someone is watching out for the student's reactions and special needs in the situation, chances are that the effect on him will be minimal. Indeed, if the field instructor responds positively and nondefensively to critical feedback from his own supervisor, the student probably will not even sense that there is a problem. However, if the decline in performance is prolonged, dramatic, obvious to others, or very serious in nature, the student will need to be reassigned to a new supervisor. For example, in one instance an ordinarily competent field instructor suffered an emotional breakdown while acting as field instructor. Rather bizarre behavior and difficulty functioning were obvious. Some discussion took place with the field instructor regarding what the student would be told as the reason for the transfer. The student was subsequently assigned to a senior field instructor in the same agency, and it was later learned that she was much more aware of what had been happening than had been realized.

She made the transition with comparatively little difficulty. In another situation, the decline in a field instructor's performance was not obvious to the student, but it was felt that the nature of the problem was such that it would be difficult for him to work effectively with the student while striving to improve his own performance. In this kind of situation it is very important to handle the process of transfer to a new field instructor in such a way that the student can maintain his respect for and positive feelings toward his original field instructor. The emphasis must be on the positives and on the "circumstances beyond the field instructor's control" or whatever necessitated the transfer.

Obviously, the school should be advised when such a situation occurs. However, it is the agency, rather than the school, that is able to identify when there is a decline in job performance. Concern for confidentiality and respect for the employee involved may make the agency reluctant to discuss the specifics of the problem with the school. Thus, the agency may make the decision to transfer the student without full discussion with the school. Once the decision is under serious consideration, the school should be contacted. Ideally the student should be kept in the same setting and his learning experience disrupted as little as possible. Only the agency knows whether it has other staff who would be both willing and able to take on a student under these circumstances. It must be an experienced field instructor with whom the agency can share the reason for the transfer. If transfer within the same agency is not possible, the school must be asked for assistance in finding another setting. Some details regarding the problem and the effect on the student will need to be disclosed to enable the school to find a setting and a field instructor there who can handle the situation effectively. Educational objectives, progress, problems, and work in process from the partially completed field placement experience must be shared so the new agency can provide some continuity of experience and expectations.

The situation described above is extremely rare; however, when it does occur, more often than not no action is taken regarding the student. No one likes to face an experienced staff member with "we will be taking your student away from you," and inaction is certainly the least painful course for the agency. That these kinds of problems can arise is a strong argument in favor of the agencies' designation of a senior supervisor or staff member to coordinate the student program, to oversee the selection of field instructors (especially on those factors that only the agency is apt to know about) and the matching of students with individual supervisors, and to act as troubleshooter, consultant, and liaison with the school regarding any special problem situations.

If a field instructor feels there is a possibility that he may resign from the agency, undergo a major change of assignment or experience an extensive absence from the job, he should not take a student.

A staff member with a history of excessive absenteeism

should not become a field instructor until the problem has been resolved.

Persons who do not really want a student should not be coerced into becoming field instructors by an agency or a school. This coercion is often very subtle, as agencies may consciously or unconsciously reward staff who are field instructors with more positive performance evaluations or greater promotional opportunities. Staff are quick to figure out what gets rewarded, and some who are not interested in social work education and do not want to be bothered with a student will suddenly apply to become field instructors.

The potential field instructor's supervisor in the agency should participate in evaluating the individual's readiness for student supervision. If there is some question as to the staff member's fitness for the role because of one or more of the problems listed above or for other reasons, he should not assume this responsibility. A fairly recent graduate may simply need a little more time to develop his own professional skills. Perhaps he hasn't fully internalized his own role within the agency and thus might have some difficulty teaching it to a student. Such individuals should participate in required training courses or seminars on techniques of field instruction in anticipation of the day they will be taking students.

Staff members who are new to the agency or to their particular job assignments should not take students until they have been there long enough to be quite familiar with the client group served, the community resources, the organizational system, and the peculiarities and policies within that system. Staff who have been absent for extended leaves (for example, maternity leave) should not be greeted by a student upon their return unless they have kept in touch with the agency and are returning to their exact same job assignment. Most settings assume that it takes a new employee six months to a year to become really comfortable and productive in his position. Likewise, the line staff member who is promoted to supervisor or who transfers to a different job within the organization may require time before he is able to supervise a student effectively in his new role. If the brand new supervisor has experience in supervising casework students, he could probably take them again fairly quickly after his promotion. However, if he does not carry a caseload, he will be faced with special problems in finding appropriate case assignments, providing day-to-day supervision, and covering activity on cases in the student's absence. A supervisor training a macro system student studying supervision or administration, must have been in his supervisory position for a number of months before he can do so effectively.

The individual with a history of difficulty relating to colleagues, authority figures and others should not supervise students. An agency supervisor whose unit suffers from constant morale problems may not be a good candidate for field instructor. The agency would need to examine the cause of the chronic morale problem: Is it the mix of the individuals in the unit; the nature of the work performed and pressures and demands over which the supervisor has little control; or something about the supervisor's approach that is problematic?

No student should be assigned to a staff member who is experiencing an unusually heavy work load. Most social workers feel their work loads are excessive and complain of high caseloads. However, if for some reason the pressures are unusually high, the individual will find it very difficult to be an effective field instructor. Yet he may eagerly volunteer. This situation can then lead to one of the most common and serious abuses to student education: using the student as a workhorse—a helping hand for the agency—in disregard of his status as a learner. The amount of time required to supervise a student properly exceeds the benefit of his productivity throughout much of field placement. Thus, the seriously overworked staff member will not have sufficient time to devote to student supervision and in all likelihood will be forced to treat him as a staff member and put him to work—without benefit of instructional feedback and other time-consuming but essential educational experiences.

Brand new field instructors must have someone who can provide consultation and guidance as they work with a student for the first time. They will need to use someone as a sounding board—"Are my expectations too high? Are my comments about the student's process recording appropriate? My student seems awfully anxious. Is that normal? I'm thinking of assigning this particular case. Do you think it's a good one for this first assignment?" and so on. The school simply cannot be on the scene and available every time a new field instructor needs help. The individual who has never supervised students has nothing with which to compare his current experience. He does not know if what he is seeing or evaluating is "normal" or unusual. The only way he can validate his observations is through reading and/or discussions with more experienced field instructors. Thus, his own supervisor or an agency-designated overseer of the student program should offer this guidance.

When a staff member feels he does not have enough time to take a student or simply wants a period of respite from taking students, his feelings should be respected. This individual is trying to convey that he doesn't think he can offer a good experience for a student right now. Of course, his feelings should be explored to be certain it is not a form of insecurity that should be worked through. However, all field instructors need occasional rests from student supervision and no one should take students twelve months of the year. Most school schedules permit a three-month or one-quarter rest. An experienced field instructor may occasionally want an entire year off to work on personal or professional self-development or to develop some special program or emphasis in his area of assignment. The temptation to talk such individuals into taking students is great—they often are proven, effective field instructors—but the cost is high as their creativity becomes stifled, they feel trapped, job satisfaction decreases, and eventually their effectiveness as a student supervisor is affected.

Most schools provide a mechanism for students to evaluate field placements and individual field instructors. If such feedback indicates that more than one student has expressed dissatisfaction with a given field instructor, both school and agency must seriously consider retiring him from his role if the difficulties cannot be overcome. If a student reports an especially bad experience, similar action may need to be taken. Certain staff members may be well known in the community and may have become very involved with the school on committees and in field instruction training sessions, but that does not necessarily mean that they are effective as field instructors. If both school and agency have blinders on, continually extolling the excellence of a particular field instructor, the student who is experiencing real difficulties with that instructor is trapped. He usually stops expressing his concerns because he finds that no one will listen. Furthermore, he is often considered to be in the wrong and is labeled a troublemaker. Poor field instruction can continue for years in these circumstances once students stop expressing their honest opinions to the school. However, they often express their feelings to other field instructors in the community and to their fellow students. A situation then develops where the problematic field instructor develops a communitywide reputation for providing poor supervision, and it may seem that everyone except the school and the individual involved is aware of the situation. Personality clashes may occur, and individual student needs may cause some students to be threatened by or critical of effective field instructors, but the average adult learner is generally a reliable judge of a given field instructor's basic effectiveness. Student comments therefore cannot be ignored by either the school or the agency.

Who Chooses the Field Instructor?

It should be obvious by now that neither the school nor the agency alone should select agency-based field instructors. The school must determine its criteria for these individuals, express them in writing, and communicate requirements to field placement settings. However, only the agency is in a position to evaluate some of the more subjective factors, and it thus controls the decision as to who becomes a field instructor by the degree to which it implements the criteria set forth.

The school first determines how many placements it needs in each type of setting (mental health, welfare, the aged). It reviews the backgrounds of students entering field placement and determines which kind of setting each learner should have. Students entering field placement express preferences, which are taken into consideration in matching students with placements. A school representative then contacts a key person in the agency or organization to discuss the number of students the school would like to place there and the number the setting feels it can take. If the agency has applied the guidelines suggested here, it may have determined how many students it can take and who will be field instructors prior to its contact with the school. The sooner this information can be conveyed to the school, the more effective the school can be in matching student needs and desires with a particular setting and its staff. Faculty who arrange field placements need to know such things as: "I have four placements in XYZ agency. One is with Mrs. Smith, who can take first-year graduate students only; the second is with Mr. Jones, who is well known to us and can take difficult students if necessary; the third is Laura Adams, whom we don't know at all as this is her first student," and so on. Or else: "One placement is with cancer patients and their families; the second with the aged ill; the third with children on dialysis," and so on.

The agency may feel that certain individuals can be field instructors if given the right kind of student. For example, a field instructor with just two years of post-MSW experience may be able to take a student if the school sends a young, inexperienced learner as opposed to an older person with several years of social work experience who has gone back to school. Such requirements should be shared with the school.

Thus, the agency does the initial screening of field instructors. Some schools of social work are now also becoming involved in the selection process. Most require submission of a résumé for each field instructor, and some conduct personal interviews to explore the person's grasp of the student supervisory role, to communicate school expectations and benefits and to confirm that the individual is a suitable candidate. Because many of the factors that should eliminate a person from supervising students will not be known by the school, the agency plays a key role in determining that these characteristics are not present before it refers individuals to the school for its screening process.

A school of social work should accept into its program only as many students as it can place in quality field settings. A full implementation of the guidelines presented here would require some schools to cut back severely on the number of new admissions. The alternative is to continue using marginal field placements that fail to provide beginning professional experiences that enable the student to function effectively as an employee after graduation. A poor-quality social work educational experience is *not* better than none at all, and consumers of social work services pay the price.

3 Needs and Anxieties of Students and Field Instructors

The Student

All students experience some degree of anxiety during the early weeks of field placement. Some exhibit behavior that clearly reveals their feelings: forgetfulness, lack of concentration, getting sick the day the first client is to be interviewed, overingratiating mannerisms, and the like. Others are quite skilled at concealing or denying any fears or anxieties: "Oh, I'm doing just fine. I was worried at first, but this field placement experience isn't nearly as bad as I had thought." It may take such a student months before he is finally able to mention casually that he was scared to death for the first three weeks of placement. There is a tendency for field instructors to assume that the older, supposedly more mature student experiences less anxiety than one with less life experience. In fact, quite the opposite is often the case. If someone has been working at a responsible job for a number of years, it is quite an adjustment to return to a dependent, low-status student role, and sometimes sharply reduced financial circumstances. A forty-five-year-old housewife who hasn't worked outside the home in twenty years also has an enormous adjustment to make when she returns to school. Additional life experience gives such students an advantage in access to techniques for concealing their anxiety, but the anxiety is present nonetheless.

The effective field instructor simply assumes that most students will have anxieties and accommodates them. What kinds of anxieties do students experience? The following paragraphs give some ideas. Notice that these behaviors and feelings are not peculiar to immature, maladjusted, or problematic students. These are *typical* needs experienced by most students, even though they are rarely verbalized directly.

Personal Insecurities

A student wants to put his best foot forward at all times—to appear competent and composed even when he isn't. Thus, he may be afraid to reveal ignorance to his supervisor by asking questions. Likewise, he may fear honest performance evaluation feedback. It may be the first time he has been in a situation where his work is being examined closely, and there can be intense anxiety over how the critical feedback will be given.

The trainee often has certain expectations of himself yet does not know exactly what the school and his field instructor expect of him: "Will I be able to meet my own expectations as well as those of others?" He may also wonder if the expectations of the field instructor, the classroom faculty, and the school as a whole will be consistent. He may worry about work assignments: Will there be too much to do or not enough? The mature student knows he has invested considerable money and energy and often drastically altered his life-style in order to go to school. He may wonder whether he will really learn anything in placement: "Will the experience be worthwhile, and what can I do if it isn't?" The student quickly learns that field instruction involves a certain amount of personal risk and self-exposure. But, "How much of myself—my needs, anxieties, values, inadequacies—will I have to expose? How much risk is involved? How much do I *dare* expose?"

The student may feel insecure about whether his classroom experience has prepared him to actually "do" social work in the field and whether he will be able to apply what he's learned in class. He may feel quite guilty if he has taken shortcuts in classes, only to discover that he is handicapped in field because of his failure to learn what was taught in the classroom. He may be extremely preoccupied with grades: Knowing he must pass field or risk not earning his degree, he may struggle desperately to do whatever he perceives his field instructor wants in order to earn a satisfactory or better grade. This anxiety may actually inhibit the student's full participation in learning experiences.

An overriding anxiety faced by many inexperienced students is that they may not know what social work is all about. They may be asking, "Am I really cut out for social work? Suppose I try it and don't like it? Suppose I can't hack it?" Such students may resist verbalizing their anxiety for fear of making their fears come true. They may even become defensive if a supervisor tries to help them examine whether social work is indeed the best profession for them. On a more specific level is concern over the individual field placement. "Am I in the right placement? Is it a good one? What if I don't like it?"

The new student frequently feels lost at the beginning of placement. He doesn't know where the bathroom is, where to eat lunch, or how to find a certain office. He is totally in the dark as to what his role is or should be. Everyone else seems to have found his niche. "Do I introduce myself as a social worker? What if people find out I'm only a student?" The student knows he is low man on the organizational totem pole and may experience real feelings of powerlessness, especially if he was employed in a supervisory or administrative capacity before entering school.

There is also a fear of failure and rejection. The student may be wondering if criticism of any kind from a field instructor or other agency staff means that he is a total failure. There may also be anxiety over having to compete with other students placed in the same agency. "Will I do as well as they do? Can I keep up with them?" Or there may be a resolve that "I must be number one."

The more sophisticated student (especially in a second field placement) may fear being used as a workhorse instead of being treated as a student, especially if he is capable and somewhat productive. The bright student may express hope for an easy experience but inwardly fear that he will not be challenged sufficiently. At the same time, the thought of being challenged in accordance with his abilities may be very anxiety-provoking, because the student will be forced to confront his weaknesses as well as his strengths.

All of us need to feel some sense of control over our environment. Yet the beginnings of most field placements provide scant opportunity for this. The student needs to feel that he is contributing something as well as just taking from placement, yet the early needs of placement provide little opportunity for giving. The adult learner thrust into placement needs to be seen as an individual human being, not as "just" a student, yet he and agency staff are strangers to one another, and he is often just "one of the new crop of students" until familiarity produces individualization.

Concerns Regarding the Field Instructor

Most field instructors would be startled to learn just how scared of them many students are when they enter placement. "Who, *me?* I'm just me. I don't bite, I wouldn't hurt anyone. How can my student be scared of me? He certainly doesn't act scared." Yet students repeatedly express, sometimes weeks and months later, their real fear of their field instructor, because he is viewed as the supreme authority figure. It is he who will determine whether the student passes or fails, whether he gets his degree or not, and whether he is permitted to pursue social work. The student knows this and may react with fear and extreme respect for the field instructor. He may have great difficulty seeing him as a human being as well as an authority figure, teacher, and professional. Some students never achieve this awareness and relaxed comfort in relating to their supervisors.

Discomfort with authority figures is clearly associated with anxiety over the evaluation process. The student does not want to do anything that might bring negative feedback or decrease his evaluation rating. Thus, he may fear retaliation from the supervisor if he communicates honestly, reveals his less-than-perfect self, or—horrors!—disagrees with his supervisor on an issue or points out a simple error. Afraid to express his own opinions, he may sit in silence, appearing to agree with the supervisor rather than risk criticism by expressing his individuality. Students hesitate to confront supervisors with unmet needs. Such fear inhibits student growth and in most instances is unwarranted: Most field instructors will not downgrade a student simply for disagreeing with them. But that fact does not allay the student's fears, especially when the student grapevine carries tales of students who "got flunked out for just looking at their field instructor the wrong way."

Students hope for a good experience with the field instructor. "Will he be likable, friendly, and competent?" The more experienced student may wonder, "Will my supervisor know more than I do, and will I be able to respect him and learn from him? Will he become threatened if he discovers I have specialized knowledge in some areas that exceeds his own competency? Will I like him, and will he like me? What will the supervisor be like—as a professional, a person with a personality, and an authority figure?" The student may have talked to other students who have had placement in that agency or been supervised by his field instructor. Their experiences can heighten or alleviate his own anxieties. He may be wondering anxiously, "What if communication breaks down with my field instructor. What do I do then?" The supervisee wonders if the field instructor will be available when needed or will leave him to founder and embarrass himself when he tries to function as a social worker. He also hopes the field instructor will be able to meet his individual needs as an adult learner with a particular personality. There may be anxiety over the proper role of the field instructor: "How friendly should I be with him? Should I have lunch and coffee breaks with him?" On the other hand, he usually wants to maintain a professional distance and hopes he won't be "caseworked" by the supervisor. If he has talked with other students who feel they have experienced this, or if he is having some upheaval in his personal life concurrent with field placement, he may be afraid that the supervisor will try to probe inappropriately into his personal affairs.

The young, relatively inexperienced student often views his field instructor as *the* role model. He has none other to compare him with. Thus the supervisor's every word and movement are taken as perfection personified—the way it should be—and is copied blindly. A patterning process may occur similar to that experienced by chickens hatched and raised by a human being. Because they've known nothing else, they soon follow the person around as if he were literally a mother hen. Students must be gradually weaned from their field instructor, exposed to various viewpoints and approaches, and encouraged to flex their own professional muscles and assert themselves as individuals.

Client Concerns

The first contact with a "live client" should take place within a few days after the beginning of placement; the longer it is postponed, the higher the anxiety level becomes. It is not unusual for students to procrastinate, become suddenly ill, or find something else to do instead when the dreaded hour arrives. However, with support, virtually everyone survives the first interview intact and experiences enormous relief that it wasn't as bad as had been imagined. Once this hurdle has been cleared, the student begins to build a sense of confidence and security from seeing his own accomplishments, and anxieties decrease markedly.

Many students worry that they might do harm to clients through inexperience. A frank discussion regarding the kinds of behaviors that are damaging to clients versus those that are relatively harmless, including the information that most clients are actually quite tough, is helpful.

If the client is physically ill, the student may be afraid of contracting his disease yet often cannot verbalize the fear directly. Field instructors in hospitals and other settings serving physically ill consumers can alleviate this anxiety by explaining prior to the first client contact that fear of contagion is normal and providing reassurance and instructions regarding any necessary special precautions. Students are sometimes afraid of psychiatric clients or persons exhibiting bizarre behavior. A drooling, mumbling, cross-eyed, mentally retarded adult can be an unnerving sight for the uninitiated student, as can an infant hooked up to artifi-

cial life-support equipment. When students come into direct contact with death, disability, retardation, and other such phenomena for the first time in a professional capacity, there is often much soul-searching and outright fear that "one day I could be like that." Students may suffer the famous third-year medical student's disease, where they begin to identify symptoms in themselves that tell them for certain that they have the same ailments as their clients. Students should be warned in advance that such experiences are normal and can be brought to the field instructor for discussion.

Each of us has unique aspects of our own personal background that make us especially capable of handling certain kinds of problems and especially fearful or uneasy in dealing with others. A student with a parent who is dying of cancer may not mention this to his field instructor and may be placed in a medical setting. When he encounters a sixty-year-old man with terminal cancer, the student's anxiety level can become immobilizing. The inexperienced student may naively believe that because he has lived with a schizophrenic or alcoholic mother, for example, he can handle such problems in others with no difficulty. The more experienced student often, but not always, can identify presenting problems or diagnoses that make him uncomfortable but may experience anxiety over what to do if he is assigned one of these cases; he may worry that his field instructor will think him incompetent if he isn't sufficiently tough and professional to stick with it and work it through. Some frank remarks from the field instructor at the beginning of placement recognizing that these situations could occur, indicating how students typically respond and pointing out what to bring to the field instructor's attention, can be most helpful. Advising the student that not being able to deal with some situations does not mean one is incompetent can help a great deal in relieving anxiety.

Anxieties Regarding the Agency or the System

Students usually wonder if the system and its staff will accept them. A trainee can also become anxious as he tries to analyze the underground politics of the work environment: "Who is it safe to talk to around here? What kind of behavior is accepted or criticized in this setting?" The student may hear gossip through the agency grapevine that can increase his anxiety or perhaps reassure him that some of his fears are not apt to materialize.

The inexperienced student often harbors unrealistic expectations of professional social workers and members of other disciplines. Years of watching "medical programs" on TV may have given him a deeply ingrained impression that all doctors are warm, giving, caring, perfect human beings 100 percent of the time. Such professionals never get angry at their clients, never have insecurities in their own lives, and always interact with everyone with patience and total involvement. Many a student has suffered a rude awakening and considerable anxiety upon encountering a medical student, physician, resident psychiatrist, or social work staff member who reveals his less-than-perfect nature. The student's professional idealism is shattered, and he may even question what he is doing in social work. He may experience some anger before he is able to accept the reality that people come in all shapes and sizes, possess all kinds of personalities and life-styles, and show all degrees of competence and incompetence. It usually takes even longer for the student to accept and use consciously the human side of himself in his own professional practice.

Techniques for Alleviating Student Anxiety

A few basic approaches with the student just beginning a field placement experience have proved helpful in decreasing student anxiety.

The student's innate fear of or excessive respect for the field instructor because of his or her authority position takes time to overcome, and some never succeed. However, many other anxieties regarding the supervisor can be alleviated (but not completely erased) through frank discussion. Experienced field instructors have probably acquired some awareness of their own instructional style, their expectations, what they are like to work for, things they have little tolerance for, what are the positives about their approach to supervision, and so on. This awareness comes through feedback from supervisees as well as school and agency colleagues and from self-assessment.* Why not share it with the student at the very beginning of placement? ''Look, this is what I'm like to work with. This is what you can and cannot expect from me: . . . I want you to be honest with me about . . .'' and so on. The student should be encouraged to share his expectations of the field instructor as well.

The field instructor must be very supportive. Many students require a great deal of hand-holding, spoon-feeding and individual attention during the first few days of placement. Avoid pointing out all the student's faults and areas where growth is needed. Instead, spot the positives and give concrete, specific assignments enabling the trainee to achieve measurable and fairly prompt success. For example, let a student help a client apply for financial assistance or food stamps; have him assist an elderly person with grocery shopping or locate a hospital bed for someone to use at home. Vague, complex assignments where the rewards of effective service delivery are subtle or slow in coming increase anxiety at the beginning of placement. Educational

experiences and instructional feedback must be designed to increase student self-esteem and self-confidence. Of course, feedback must be realistic—students should not receive praise when it is unwarranted. But if assignments are kept simple until the student's capacities are explored more fully, he won't be tested to the limits of his ability right away and can experience some success.

A student needs to know that his field instructor is aware of his anxieties and that they are normal. It is not necessary to run through the entire list presented in this chapter. Simply show a little empathy and understanding that he probably is anxious about a number of things.

Treat the student as an adult learner. Let him know that he is expected to ask questions and that a sign of growth will be increasing ability to form his own opinions. Similarly, recognize with him that he may need to copy the field instructor blindly at first and express hope that he will soon begin to take bits and pieces from others' styles and put them together with his personality and skills to develop his own professional approach. Let him know that this process does not happen overnight.

Much initial student anxiety occurs because expectations are unclear. The development of a formal educational contract alleviates much of this anxiety (see Chapter 6). The student's expectations of the field placement experience and the supervisor, as well as the field instructor's expectations of the student, must be continually reviewed, revised, and shared throughout the placement experience. The field instructor who feels comfortable in sharing a description of his own personal supervisory style will go a long way in helping his student reduce unknowns regarding expectations in the supervisor–student relationship.

Explain the performance evaluation process exactly and show the student copies of the form or outline that will be completed at various points during the placement. Do not assume that most students are familiar with this material. Explain that the written evaluation will contain nothing that the student will not already know: Performance evaluation is an ongoing process throughout placement through frequent verbal feedback. Clearly list and illustrate some of the things that can cause a student to fail field (see pp. 198–203) and what a student must accomplish to earn satisfactory or outstanding ratings in his particular setting (e.g., see pp. 61–66). This discussion is less threatening if presented to a group of students rather than individually. It could also be included in a seminar on ''Being Consumers of Supervision.''

Tell the student that one way he can have some sense of control over his learning experience is through sharing his expectations with the supervisor and giving honest feedback when he feels his needs are not being met. Recognize that he probably will not feel free to do this at first, but express hope that it will come eventually when he feels more comfortable in placement. Allow the student to make as many concrete choices as possible regarding his beginning place-

---

*See Appendix A on increasing one's self-awareness as a field instructor.

ment experience, and structure learning exercises so that he can experience some control over them.

Directly express your feelings that clients are "pretty tough and aren't easily damaged by students." All students make mistakes and sometimes aren't as effective as they might be, but they need to know that the field instructor is aware of this and considers it normal. Explain the use of direct observational methods of assessing student interactions with clients, which enable the field instructor to keep informed of what the student is doing and move in with guidance before irreversible problems develop for the student.

Let the student observe an interview or follow the field instructor around for a few days until he gets a feel for the role of the social worker. Bear in mind that the very inexperienced student will not know enough to appreciate fully or to critique what he is observing; observation soon becomes meaningless unless it is mixed with direct contacts and activity.

Field-instructor feedback should be frequent—almost daily—in the beginning of placement. Long periods of time between completion of an assignment and receipt of supervisory feedback increase anxiety and fears of failing to meet expectations.

Finally, learning should be partialized—broken down into small, manageable parts. The assignment may be to arrange a discharge plan for John Jones, who has been hospitalized. This involves a number of activities. The student can be directed first to interview the patient, then to talk with the doctor regarding physical diagnoses and prognosis and consult with the nurse regarding limitations in activities of daily living. Structure is essential—the student cannot be left on his own for several days to complete a rather vague or highly complex assignment. The student's work schedule should allow him to use field placement time for reading, self-reflection, ventilation of his anxieties, and informal discussions with other students and staff.

Not all students will experience all the anxieties mentioned here. A few exceptionally secure and competent students with considerable life or work experience may have already worked through many of these fears and anxieties. However, they may still feel some discomfort simply because the placement experience offers new people and new expectations to relate to. The mature student often becomes an unofficial leader to whom other students turn as they ventilate their anxieites and seek peer confirmation of feelings. The student who has worked his anxiety through often plays a very significant behind-the-scenes role in offering support, guidance, and interpretation to his peers.

The Field Instructor

Field instructors are human beings first and social work supervisors second. Their individual personalities, needs,

and supervisory styles will surface from time to time and may result in a less-than-perfect approach to the student. Few trainees fully appreciate the private agonies and soul-searching that the conscientious field instructor undergoes both prior to supervising a student (especially the very first one) and during the relationship. Rarely does (or should) a field instructor express his own inner needs, anxieties, and insecurities directly to his student, though he might share them quite openly with the school, with other supervisors, or in training sessions with his peers. If the learner is studying supervision and administration, the secure supervisor will often discuss and share some of his inner feelings with his student, who may be experiencing the same feelings himself as he prepares for supervisory responsibilities.

Even the most experienced field instructor undergoes some self-examination and anxiety when faced with a problematic situation. As with student fears and anxieties, the ones presented here for field instructors are quite common and normal. In fact, there is cause for concern when a supervisor is so self-confident that he fails to experience these feelings from time to time. Sometimes the anxieties seem overwhelming, especially for the brand new field instructor. However, most deal with them effectively through ventilation and consultation with peers, and with support from their own supervisors. Learning that the student does not bite and really isn't as difficult to supervise as he had imagined also helps the supervisor to relax. In a few rare instances, the worst fears and anxieties are confirmed: The student is a problem from the first day of placement, and the supervisor may lack the experience necessary to deal with him effectively and comfortably. However, strong guidance and support from an experienced supervisor as well as from the school can often get him through the situation and result in a meaningful learning experience for the field instructor and an appropriate outcome for the student.

Personal Insecurities

Perhaps the most basic anxiety, especially for the new field instructor, is simply: "Do I have something to offer? Should I really be doing this? Do I know what I'm doing?" Along with these questions comes an internalized recognition that the supervisor is responsible for molding another person's personal and professional growth, and the weight of this responsibility is felt heavily. Field instructors who have never supervised a student before may be keenly aware of their own inadequacies and of the fact that field instruction places heavy emphasis on the instructional component in supervision. While he may feel that he has good practice skills, he may wonder if he can conceptualize them so as to teach them to others. If he is aware of practice areas in which he does not specialize that are not his strongest points, he may wonder how he is going to teach what he himself doesn't know how to do well. These anxieties cause many a conscientious field instructor to head for the nearest library in a desperate attempt to review basic concepts. Texts by Perlman, Compton and Galloway, Kadushin, Pincus and Minahan, and others are devoured eagerly in a frantic effort to keep one step ahead of the student and to make certain that what the supervisor is teaching is not in conflict with what the student is learning in the classroom. The supervisor who responds to his anxieties in this manner and takes the time to do this extra reading (often at home) usually experiences substantial and lasting professional growth.

As the field instructor thinks about the responsibilities involved in student supervision, he may ask himself: "What's in it for me? Why am I doing this?"—followed by: "I should be getting paid for this!" Most schools offer field instructors free use of the library and certain other college facilities, a title that proclaims them (unpaid) faculty members, and perhaps a discount at the university bookstore. The instructor attends special seminars and workshops conducted by the school and often has the opportunity to participate in school planning committees and to lecture or observe in the classroom. In some schools the field instructor is entitled to a given number of tuition-free credit hours in courses of his choosing. Agency-employed field instructors do not get paid for their role; indeed, most agencies do not even reduce their normal work loads to compensate for the extra work involved in student supervision. Thus, the school's benefits alone might not seem enough to entice the average practitioner to become a field instructor. Obviously, field instructors do receive other intangibles and meaningful rewards that often satisfy their question, "What's in it for me?"

Perhaps the biggest reward is seeing the student grow as a professional diamond-in-the-rough is shaped into an approximate facsimile of a functional social worker. In a few instances students do not grow as expected and problems exist. However, if the field instructor is able to take decisive action and is supported by the school, he may derive a feeling of satisfaction from helping a student overcome seemingly insurmountable problems or choose a more appropriate career.

The field instructor himself often experiences significant personal or professional growth through working with students, and many practitioners assume this role primarily because it helps them keep abreast of the latest trends in social work practice. They may also enjoy the challenge of helping to train a practitioner and perhaps a leader of tomorrow. Many field instructors rate their effectiveness low if they do not learn nearly as much as the student during the field instruction process.

Most students will not tell their field instructor directly, "I think you're great. You're doing a great job." If this does happen, it is usually toward the end of placement rather than at the beginning, when the anxious or insecure supervisor could really use the positive feedback. If such compliments come too early in the placement, they must be evaluated carefully. How can the student feel you are doing a good job when he hardly knows you? Perhaps he is so new you haven't yet zeroed in on areas where he needs to improve. Will he still feel the same way after he's received critical as well as positive feedback? The student's own anxiety and extreme desire to please may be causing premature, overingratiating behavior. If it continues to the point that it becomes obviously inappropriate, the pattern should be called to the student's attention and discussed fully. At any rate, most field instructors do not get direct feedback regarding their effectiveness; instead, the feedback comes through more subtle channels. Obviously, student growth indicates supervisory effectiveness in many instances. Students may compare you favorably with other supervisors. Remarks such as, "Boy, I'm glad I don't have so-and-so for a field instructor" or "I was shocked to learn that in ZYA agency they do [or don't do] such-and-such" are actually indirect compliments. Both agencies and individual field instructors within them eventually develop specific reputations among students. It is most rewarding to have students seek out your agency or perhaps you personally because of a positive reputation. Schools may give feedback supporting a supervisor's competence and effectiveness with students, and an effective setting may be told quite directly that "yours is one of the best placements we have."

There are other benefits as well. Students who are placed with an agency may wish to work there after graduation, giving the agency a pool of specially trained candidates to choose from. In addition, if an entire agency or department has an outstanding reputation for the quality of its field instruction program, it will attract post-degree applicants who seek employment there because of the agency's reputation in the community and their desire to be a part of it.

Becoming a field instructor carries a certain status in many agencies, especially those with a reputation for having a good program and high standards in the selection of field instructors. The experience may help prepare a practitioner for assuming supervisory responsibilities later on and give him an advantage over other candidates for promotion who have never supervised anyone. Thus, there may be some tangible long-term rewards.

Anxieties Regarding the Student

Anxieties about students are legion. Perhaps most basic is a fear of failing to meet the student's needs and expectations. There can be very specific anxieties regarding effectiveness as a field instructor: "Will I be able to keep my student sufficiently busy? Will I have enough time for him? Will having a student keep me from getting my other work done? Can I communicate my expectations effectively? How deeply should I dig into my student's personal life and value system? How much should I shelter my student from the realities of social work practice in my agency? Will I be able to be objective with my supervisee? Can I find the right assignments to give him in the beginning? How will I know if my expectations are too high or too low? Will I be able to cope with all my student's needs and anxieties? What if my student asks me questions I can't answer?'' And so on.

Field instructors may feel threatened by certain kinds of students and can become quite anxious, imagining the worst possible outcome. They may fear that the student will know more than they do in some areas. With today's specialized approach to social work education and the increasing number of students with extensive life and work experience, some supervisees actually do know more or are more skilled than their field instructors in certain areas. However, no student knows more than the supervisor in all areas of practice, and the supervisor certainly knows more than his student about the specifics of his own agency and its client group. Furthermore, a teacher does not necessarily need to know more than his student to be effective. His primary role is to facilitate learning, which can come directly from the field instructor or from a host of other sources and experiences. A frank, ''That's not one of my areas of specialty [e.g. research], but if you'd like to pursue it further, I'll see if I can find someone you can work with on that project''— usually earns the student's respect. There may also be anxieties associated with supervising a student who is older or has more work or life experience than the supervisor: ''Will he respect me in spite of my youth? Will he really feel someone as young as I can have something to offer him?'' Many field instructors experience genuine relief when they discover an area in which their student's knowledge or skill is less than perfect: ''Aha, there *is* something I can help him with after all! I *am* needed!''

Field instructors also hope their students will like them. It is difficult for two people to work together when they do not like each other. The student must respect the supervisor if real learning is to occur. If a personal liking for him also exists, this is an added plus. If a supervisor's own need to be liked by his supervisees is too strong, he will have great difficulty giving honest evaluatory feedback or taking any action that he feels might cause his student to dislike him. This can seriously hamper the student's learning experience. Field instructors want to have a good reputation among other students placed in the same agency and with the school and may be quite curious about what their students are saying about them to others. The instructor may worry that his reputation will be tarnished if he has to make evaluatory decisions that are unpopular or disciplinary in nature. Similarly, he hopes his student will do well so he can be proud of him and won't be ashamed to say, ''That's *my* student.''

The conscientious field instructor may worry about his ability to handle student mistakes that could be embarrassing for both student and supervisor. If the student does poorly, the field instructor may fear that others will think it is because he isn't a good supervisor and didn't do a good job. He hopes that all his students will be mature, bright, motivated, eager, responsive, self-directed learners rather than persons with special needs or problems that might test the limits of supervisory skill. On the other hand, the field instructor is often keenly aware of his own limitations and may wonder if areas where he is not strongly competent will be obvious to the student.

''Will the student trust me and communicate openly and honestly? Will he see me as effective in my role?'' Many of the field instructor's past experiences with students and other supervisees and his own relationship with authority figures, both as a student and as an employee, will surface and be reviewed consciously as he performs his field instruction role.

A delicate problem may worry the field instructor. As in a good marriage, it is not beneficial for student and field instructor to be together constantly. Both need periodic breaks from one another. ''How can I tell my student to get lost for a while when I need a break from him?'' may be of concern.

Field instructors can have nearly as many anxieties over the evaluation process as students do (see Chapters 11 and 12). Most new supervisors imagine the worst: ''Suppose I get a student I have to fail or counsel out of social work? What if I get a student who doesn't do well?'' And then: ''If my student does poorly, how will I know if it's the student's fault or because I'm not doing a good job as a field instructor?'' This last question keeps experienced supervisors awake at night when serious problems are encountered. Thus, the supervisory role leads to much self-examination and produces new areas of self-awareness as field instructors agonize over these various concerns. The student may feel that field instruction is 100 percent assessment of the student's performance. However, the wise field instructor knows that it is also a process whereby his own competence and effectiveness are tested. If a supervisor feels that he is not meeting his supervisee's needs, there can be real guilt: ''Maybe the student would be better off if he had someone else as a supervisor.'' Finally, there may be concern over the student's written evaluation of his field placement experience, which is submitted to the school. Many supervisors take this process very seriously and react quite strongly (though usually silently) to critical comments from students who rate them less than positively in their evaluative feedback.

Concerns Regarding the School or Agency

All field instructors hope that the school and its faculty will support them in any recommendations or actions they take. If a school fails to support a field instructor, the community grapevine usually informs student supervisors, resulting in increased anxiety: ''Could the same thing happen to me?'' The field instructor also needs to feel that his own supervisor and other agency staff will support his assessments and actions regarding his student. A department or agency that has clearly defined its approach to field instruction and that provides training for new supervisors and opportunities for all student supervisors to meet periodically to share concerns and hammer out expectations and philosophies usually offers strong, unified support to individual staff who must deal with problematic situations. The support from intra-agency colleagues can give the field instructor the self-confidence and strength needed to take decisive action. The isolated field instructor functioning in a setting that does not offer this kind of support is usually at a distinct disadvantage if faced with having to counsel a student out of placement or assign him a failing grade. He may simply lack the guts to do it, even though professionally he may realize it's what needs to be done.

New field instructors can experience acute anxiety if tossed into the field instruction role without advance training and specific guidance from the school. The role requires new skills for many agency-based practitioners, and they may rightly feel: ''I'm being thrown to the wolves and being given no tools or weapons for dealing with the situation.'' Of course, some staff take on students without fully realizing what they are getting into. Those who are aware of some of the issues discussed throughout this book usually feel a need for specialized training and preparation. How can a school of social work expect quality education if agency staff used as field instructors receive little or no help to carry out their role effectively? If agency-based personnel would refuse to take students unless they first received appropriate training for their new role, this could have a significant impact on the quality of social work education. Likewise, schools could refuse to accept anyone as a field instructor who has not undergone specialized training.

Finally, the field instructor wants his students to have a good experience. He knows he will do his best to be an effective role model and a good teacher/supervisor. But what about others whom the field instructor cannot control? ''Will other staff be good role models for my student, or will they corrupt him?'' A little overprotection may occur. Actually, the student will eventually encounter staff and members of other disciplines who are less than perfect examples of their profession; he can be helped to accept this reality and can learn skills for dealing with his feelings and the other persons involved as part of his educational experience.

The foregoing discussion may give the false impression that all field instructors and students are a seething pool of insecurities and incapacitating anxieties. Such is not the case. The fact that supervisors consciously think about these issues results eventually in a definite stand or approach that comes across as decisive and educational for the student, who is usually unaware of the private problem-solving process that goes on behind the outcome he experiences. Likewise, the field instructor may see little of the student's hidden fears and anxieties. What is important is that both realize that such feelings are a normal, natural part of the field instruction process and that they will surface periodically and can be discussed openly and channeled in a constructive manner.

4 The Preplacement Interview

An effective field placement program strives to match the students' personalities, educational requirements and learning styles with field instruction settings and individual supervisors who can provide what is needed. This is not an easy task. Schools must review résumés, autobiographies, references, and related materials in an effort to get to know incoming students. The field instruction faculty usually interviews each student to learn something about his background and goals. Information from classroom instructors and previous field instructors, if any, is assembled. The school then makes a determination of the type of setting best suited to the student's educational plan. Sometimes students cannot be assigned to the ideal or preferred placement because of geographical restrictions or a scarcity of placements available in the desired setting. Once the school matches a student to a prospective placement setting, the setting is asked whether it will accept the student. Ideally the agency will insist on a preplacement interview at this point to enable both the prospective student intern and the agency to decide whether they can meet each other's needs and work together effectively. If all parties agree to the arrangement, the placement is confirmed.

A number of preliminary stages lead up to the actual preplacement interview.

Data Sharing: From Agency to School

Faculty involved in arranging field placements need to know what kinds of experiences various social work settings can provide for students. Likewise, students need to know what kinds of opportunities exist so that they can express their preferences. Faculty advisers obviously have lists of all the various placement settings used by the school, but they need to know considerably more than the name of the agency and its specialty. For example, some agencies may have found that certain types of students do not do very well in their setting. Some students may have expected a dynamic groupwork experience whereas the setting offers a traditional casework experience with a Freudian orientation. If the school and its students have certain basic information available on each placement setting, many potential mismatches can be avoided in the early stages of the placement process.

Agencies may wish to prepare a summary statement describing their expectations and the experiences available to students placed in their particular setting. Such statements should contain the following kinds of information:*

1. The types of client groups served, including age ranges, key ethnic or cultural groups, socio-economic status, common problem areas, and other descriptive data. Any unusual or unique characteristics should be mentioned, e.g., "We serve hard-core drug addicts who have dropped out of traditional drug treatment programs"; "Most of our clients are from an upper socio-economic group"; or "Our clients are predominantly middle-aged men." This kind of description is important even for students who will be studying administrative or community-focused skills.

2. The organization and internal structure of the agency. What is the purpose of the agency? Who administers or funds its programs? How do consumers get into its service delivery system? What kind of workers and approximately how large a staff does the setting employ? If the program consists of many subunits, the particular units to which students are assigned should be described as well as the overall program.

*See Appendix F-1 for a sample description of a field placement setting.

3. The primary role and typical daily activities of a social worker in the agency and the kinds of learning experiences generally available to students. Mention any unusual experiences that might be available (such as the opportunity to spend twenty-four hours as an inpatient to get an inside look at the system) and any that are absent or insignificant (e.g. community organization or casework), so that students do not come with unrealistic expectations.

4. Preferred characteristics of students placed in the setting. Agencies often develop strong expectations for students in general as they accumulate experiences. A setting may refuse to accept certain types of students or may insist on specific kinds of attributes or background experiences. For example, does the setting accept both first- and second-year graduate students? Both graduate and undergraduate? Block placement and concurrent? Part-time and other special students? Both casework and administration students? Will it accept students who have completed a partial placement elsewhere and are seeking a midstream transfer to another setting because of various difficulties? And so on. These should be stated briefly and discussed in more detail during the preplacement interview.

5. The method and style of supervision provided in the setting. Obviously, this will go along with basic requirements set by the school; however, if a setting has a particular approach to field instruction, this should be described. For example, the agency may develop formal, written educational contracts with all students, even though this approach is not required by the school.

Data Sharing: From School to Agency

The faculty member responsible for student placement usually shares some information with field placement settings in the preliminary contact so that the agencies can decide whether they want to consider the student and can identify areas needing further exploration during the preplacement interview. Some schools volunteer a great deal of information regarding each student; others are not so generous. Field instructors may need to ask for desired details and should feel free to refuse to consider students unless certain kinds of information are provided.

Schools gather information about student readiness for field placement through a variety of sources. Most students submit a detailed biographical statement and several personal references as part of the admission process. Transcripts of grades from an undergraduate or associate degree program may be available. Classroom faculty also submit comments regarding student performance. Copies of evaluations from prior field placements are often available (though the final evaluation from a prior placement may not be available at the time a second field placement is being con-

sidered). Students may be asked to complete a form indicating their field placement preferences and providing some basic information about themselves for consideration in arranging placement. This often includes very practical items such as the availability of a car or what part of town the student lives in. Field instruction faculty often conduct individual or group interviews to explore students' educational needs and desires in placement. Thus, a significant amount of information may be available to a prospective field instructor through the school.

The following information usually proves helpful as an agency considers whether to conduct a preplacement interview with a given student:

1. *Basic identifying information*. Name, age, level of training (first year, second year, etc.), major area of concentration (C.O., casework, administration).

2. *A list of the courses the student has taken and his grades*. This information, of course, indicates how well the student has done with academic concepts and learning but does not necessarily indicate that he would do as well (or poorly) in a field placement program.

3. *For graduate students, the undergraduate major and grade point average*. Is the student a person with a BA in elementary education whose first real exposure to professional social work will occur in the field placement? Or is he someone with a BSW who has already worked for years as a social worker or supervisor?

4. *Previous work and volunteer experience*. Some students come to school with no prior work experience of any kind. They have never worked regular hours, may not know how to use an office phone with multiple lines, have never received formal supervision or evaluation from anyone other than classroom instructors, and have no idea what an office atmosphere is like. The needs of such a student and the demands he places upon the field instructor will be quite different from those of a student with years of post-BSW social work experience under ACSW supervision. Volunteer experiences can be important indicators of student abilities and needs, particularly of older women who are returning to school later in life. Have they been active in the community? Have they had experience in helping others? Have they assumed leadership roles in school, scouting, religious, or political activities?

The kind of previous work experience can also be significant. For example, if a student has four years in public welfare experience, is placement in a public welfare setting appropriate or would it be better for him to experience other areas of social work practice instead?

5. *Previous field placements*. Where was the student previously placed? Who were his field instructors? What kinds

of experiences did he have there and what kind of supervision did he receive? Were there any unusual problems (e.g. change of agency or field instructor midway through the placement, unusual absences, problematic or marginal performance, or irregularities in supervision)? What skills does the school feel the student has acquired? What is he like to supervise? How does he learn best? What kinds of things does the student need to focus on in his subsequent placement? These and related questions help the prospective agency determine the student's current level of functioning, his individual educational needs, and the desired approach of the new field instructor. They also help the agency to determine whether a brand new field instructor could work effectively with the student or whether his needs and background are such that he should be assigned to an experienced supervisor.

Prior work and field placement experiences often differentiate students more meaningfully than educational level. For example, a nineteen-year-old entering a first field placement in the beginning of his senior year in a BSW program may have needs that are very similar to those of a twenty-two-year-old with a BA in English entering his first year of MSW training.

6. *Special strengths, limitations, or potential problem areas.* Many schools are quite frank in sharing students' past and potential problem areas with the field placement setting; others downplay these factors in an effort to encourage the setting to take the student. Some will acknowledge that special problems exist and explore the possibility of a special placement for a difficult or unusually gifted student.

7. *The general nature of the student's life experiences.* Has he led a very sheltered life, or suffered the loss of both parents early in life, functioning as head of household and rearing younger siblings? Does the student appear to be rather naive and uninformed as to some of life's problems and responsibilities, or does he appear to have "been around"?

8. *The student's preference for placement.* Was this agency or its client group the student's first choice, or is he being asked to consider it because nothing else is available or because the school feels it's what he needs?

9. *Has the student interviewed with other prospective field placement settings and been rejected?* This information should not necessarily affect a setting's decision as to whether or not to interview a student. However, it is well known that some students are very hard to place because their manner of dress, attitude, affect, demands, skills, or other characteristics come across so negatively in preplacement interviews that agencies turn them down repeatedly. Most such students are eventually placed, often in settings known for their low expectations and superficial supervi-

sion. On the other hand, a few are assigned to top-quality placements so that they can be evaluated carefully and screened out if necessary.

Acceptance into a field placement setting is a requirement for continuation in a social work program. Students can be admitted into classroom studies, but with the understanding that if they cannot be placed in a field placement setting, they will be dropped from the program. If a student must undergo four or five preplacement interviews before a setting reluctantly accepts him, this communicates a rather powerful evaluation of the student's readiness and suitability for social work practice.

10. *Special recommendations.* The school's knowledge of the student often results in specific recommendations as to the type of supervision and learning experiences he needs in field placement. Perhaps the student dealt with a rather limited client population in the first placement and needs exposure to a wider variety of socio-economic and ethnic groups. Perhaps the first placement concentrated on intake and short-term counseling, and the student now needs to work with some long-term cases, and so on. The school may feel that a highly experienced field instructor should work with the student or that a specific individual's supervisory style is best suited to the student's needs.

With all this information in hand, the agency can decide if it wishes to conduct a preplacement interview. A general rule of thumb should be, "If in doubt, interview." The school's interpretation of certain data and the agency's may differ. The agency may have a fairly positive feeling toward the student after meeting him and may decide to take him on in spite of some known difficulties. On the other hand, it is possible for the agency field instructor to react with enthusiasm to a student prior to the personal contact and then discover after an interview: "I couldn't stand to work with that student!" A medical setting may be so excited about getting a graduate student with "four years of medical social work experience" that it overlooks the fact that the student received no supervision during that time, did little but paperwork, and does not have skills equivalent to those of BA-level social workers employed in the setting. Many students entering graduate programs with impressive-looking credentials do not have strong skills in the areas that many social work educators and field instructors consider important. Thus, an "experienced" student, or one with an advanced degree in a related profession, may present a greater challenge than the individual with limited work experience. In short, *avoid making assumptions!*

Setting Up the Preplacement Interview

Preplacement interviews should be required by every field placement setting. If students are being accepted from a school located some distance from the agency, a long-distance phone call can substitute for the face-to-face interview, but there must be some kind of personal contact between agency and student before any commitments are made so that:

1. The agency can decide if it can meet the student's supervisory and educational needs and whether it wants to accept him
2. The individual field instructor can decide, on a "gut-level," if he and the student will be compatible working together
3. The student can decide if the agency can give him what he wants and needs and whether he would feel comfortable working with the person who interviews him

If an agency has a staff member in charge of all student placements, he may do a rough screening before the preplacement interview with the prospective field instructor to describe the various learning experiences available with all field instructors on staff and help the student choose potential areas of assignment that interest him. From his knowledge of the personality and teaching/supervisory style of each field instructor on staff, he determines which seem best suited to the student's needs and then arranges a preplacement interview between the student and the individual who might actually be his field instructor. Either party can say no following the second interview; if both accept the arrangement, placement is confirmed.

Many students are ill prepared for preplacement interviews. They are anxious, nervous, downright frightened, and often very passive. Unless they have given thought to their educational and supervisory needs, most of them rely on the field instructor to initiate questions. Many sit in silence as the field instructor describes his program in depth. He is obliged to accept (or reject) the applicant without having gotten to know him. There is so much emphasis on the agency's accepting the student that few students realize that a preplacement interview works two ways: They should be evaluating the potential placement as carefully as the interviewer is assessing them. The student must be free to say no to settings that are unappealing or that he suspects will provide poor supervision or limited training. He must be free to reject a field instructor whose approach to student supervision seems superficial, rigid, or inappropriate to the student's own learning style and educational needs. Thus, the student should be asking questions in the interview and participating actively.

Each student should undergo special preparation for preplacement interviews through a seminar or lecture and an individual assessment of his own needs. The "Self-Assessment Questionnaire" (Appendix F-3) is a useful tool for stimulating students' awareness of their supervisory and instructional needs. Students can complete it during field instruction seminars conducted by the school prior to the

preplacement interview, refer to it throughout placement to help in determining their educational objectives, and complete a second form at the end of placement when contemplating a subsequent placement or post-graduation employment. The student who has undergone this preparatory thinking process will come to the interview with appropriate questions and usually will not be content to be a passive participant. If he has completed the questionnaire, he should not be asked or required to share it during the preplacement interview, although most students will volunteer bits and pieces at appropriate points in the interview.

The average preplacement interview lasts approximately one hour and covers a wide range of topics, depending on the agency, the field instructor, and the student involved. The following list suggests areas for discussion, in the approximate order in which these items are typically raised. Not every interview will cover all these items; some will emphasize certain areas more than others. No attempt should be made to follow this list rigidly, insisting that every question be raised and answered. Preplacement interviews should be as relaxed, spontaneous, and informal as possible, with free-flowing conversation that does not appear to assault the student with a list of prepared questions.

Interview Content

1. *Purpose of the preplacement interview.* The field instructor discusses the mutual objectives of student and agency and the fact that either can say no to the placement. The student should be aware of material shared between the agency and the school. The field instructor may need to encourage the student to play an active part during the interview.

2. *"So you want to come here for field placement."* The field instructor elicits the student's feelings about the setting, why he wants to come there for placement, what he hopes to get out of the experience, and whether he knows anything about the agency or its consumers. Does he seem to have an idea of what it would be like to do a placement in this setting? What does he think social workers do in this agency?

3. *Past work experiences.* What kind of work or volunteer experience has the student had? What skills has he acquired, and what experience has he had with supervision? These factors will affect his attitude, performance, and learning in the new setting. Was his former supervisor a social worker? What kind of supervision did he receive? Did he find it adequate? Was it a positive or negative experience for him? What kinds of cases did he carry? What was he expected to do in a typical work day? What kinds of problems did he handle and what techniques did he use? It is not sufficient for him to say he "worked with alcoholics"; was his pri-

mary function the completion of paperwork for admission into a halfway house and for receipt of financial assistance, or did he do intensive counseling with clients and their families? Has he ever had leadership or supervisory responsibilities? What kinds of nonsocial work experience has he had—anything that would require skills in relating to people? And so on.

4. *Past field placement experience*. This area must be explored in some depth. The potential field instructor has already gotten some indication of the scope of the student's experiences and performance from the school prior to the preplacement interview. However, the student may perceive the experience differently from the school, and his perspective is important. Furthermore, the interviewer needs to know what kinds of experiences the student had and what kind of supervision he received so that he can build on these areas and fill in gaps during the forthcoming placement. It is not usually appropriate to say, ''The school says this about you. What do you think?'' The instructor should merely explore the student's experiences and feelings and, except for unusual situations, make comparisons with what he already knows in private.

Many students, when asked about their prior field placement, will say they had a ''good experience.'' Further exploration of just what the student thought was a good experience may identify a rather inadequate one by the field instructor's standards, leaving the student with educational gaps that he may not even be aware of. On the other hand, the instructor may concur with the student that his previous experience was excellent. Thus, pertinent questions must be asked to get a clearer picture of the student's actual experiences. How many clients did he see? What was the longest period of time he followed the same person? How often did he meet with his field instructor? Did he do any work with groups and communities as well as with individuals and families? What techniques did the supervisor use to evaluate his work—process recordings, tapes, direct observation? Did he do any recording in connection with field placement? If so, what kinds of things did he record? Did he do any reading? Did he cover techniques as well as psychodynamics of human behavior in his discussions with his supervisor? What did he actually do with his clients? Can he describe one of his more challenging assignments? What did he like most and least about his prior placement? Does this give him any ideas as to what he would like in this placement? Such questions often provide much more revealing details than the simple statement ''I carried a lot of cases''; or ''I got good supervision''; or ''I didn't get enough time with my field instructor.''

5. *Career goals*. What does the student hope to gain from his social work education? What does he see himself doing professionally three years or ten years from now? Why does he want to go into social work?

These first five items are relatively nonthreatening. Asking the student to talk about himself, describing his goals and past experiences, encourages him to relax and begin to establish some rapport. As the student talks, the field instructor may explore some areas in more detail and begin relating them to the potential field placement experience. It is important that the field instructor's detailed description of the agency come a little later in the interview. Otherwise, there will be a tendency for all subsequent discussion to center on the specific field placement setting, making it more difficult to explore the student's experiences, goals, and needs apart from the potential setting. Furthermore, discussion of these items usually initiates some thought on the student's part regarding his own needs and an examination of his past experiences in light of the potential field placement. By the time the specific field placement is described, the student will often have some definite ideas regarding his needs.

6. *Strengths and areas where growth is needed*. The student should be asked to describe his strengths—areas where he feels he has learned a lot or mastered certain skills. He might also list personal work habits or characteristics that he feels are assets. Again, if the student says his diagnostic skills are ''good,'' he should be asked to illustrate what he means: Why does he feel they are ''good''? Can he describe a case situation or discuss human defense mechanisms or other aspects of diagnosis? What does he feel he needs to learn more about? Is he aware of any limitations or weaknesses? (Phrases such as ''areas where growth is needed'' or ''where you could learn more'' are much less threatening than ''weaknesses,'' ''negatives,'' or ''liabilities.'') If he cannot think of any, the instructor should observe that everyone has *some* areas in which he could learn more. Does he feel he is fully ready for BSW (or MSW) practice right now? Why?

Discussion of strengths and weaknesses provides some insight into the student's level of self-awareness (or his willingness to risk in the preplacement interview). If he has had extensive work and/or prior placement experiences, one would expect some degree of self-awareness gained through supervisory feedback and experience. Its absence could tell the field instructor something significant about the student. On the other hand, a younger student with limited prior experience would not be expected to be very self-aware. He may never have had to think about this question in such a formal manner before.

7. *Description of the field placement setting*. The interviewer should include the types of clients served (age, sex, presenting problems, socio-economic status, educational level, cultural, ethnic or language factors, and so on), learning opportunities available, the role of the social worker, and special requirements (e.g. dress, work hours, workload). If the field instructor is aware that the agency has a

certain reputation in the community pertaining to field instruction, this should be shared. If all students are required to lead a group, make home visits, or engage in other special activities, this should be indicated. The goal should be to paint a picture in words so that the student can visualize what he would be getting into if he accepted placement in the setting. It is far better for the student to eliminate himself at this stage of the game than to accept a placement and then discover that it doesn't provide him with the kind of experiences he wanted. I once interviewed a student who exhibited great eagerness to do placement in my agency. Midway through the interview, I described our setting as one in which students have to work hard because of our high expectations. As we talked on for a few minutes, I noticed the student studying my desk rather closely. As usual, it was piled high with assorted papers, threatening to cascade off onto the floor in apparent disarray. The student suddenly blurted out, "You know, I'm sitting here looking at your desk and all the work piled up on it and thinking that if I have to work that hard in this placement, I'm not sure I want to come here." I quickly reassured him that the condition of my desk was not necessarily reflective of how hard *he* would have to work, but stated realistically, "This is not an easy placement. You will have to work hard to make it here. If you are seeking an easier experience, you should look elsewhere." The interview ended a few minutes later as the student decided this wasn't the right placement for him—a decision that undoubtedly avoided frustration for both of us.

8. *Description of the style of supervision provided and the agency's approach to field instruction.* How does the setting approach the performance evaluation process? What methods are used most commonly to assess student performance and provide learning experiences—process recordings, taping, one-way mirror observation, and so forth? How much time can the field instructor give the student each week? What would he find it like to be your supervisee? What can he expect from the supervisor—and vice versa?*

9. *What the student feels he wants or needs from the field placement experience and his field instructor.* Some of this may already have come out by the time this point is reached in the interview.

10. *The student's personal situation.* Is he working full or part time in addition to field placement? Will this present any problem for him in field? Has the student had life experiences that would make him especially committed to the kind of clients the agency serves or cause him to overidentify or have some difficulty? If a student has had no significant work experience or previous field placements, it can be

*See Appendix A for some self-instructional exercises designed to increase field instructor self-awareness in these areas.

important to determine whether he has had any contact with social workers through family, friends, or professional acquaintances. Has he ever interacted with physicians or psychiatrists socially or professionally, or are his views formed by the mass media?

The Decision

Most preplacement interviews conclude with student and field instructor rather obviously choosing to work together. If this occurs, plans should be made for the student's first day of placement—where and when he should report to the agency. The field instructor may want to suggest reading that the student can do to acquaint himself with the nature of the clients served and the functioning of the agency prior to his arrival.

In some instances, the decision that "this is not the placement for me" may have been communicated by the student, thus terminating the interview. If the instructor feels certain that a student is not suited to his setting but the student's interest remains high, the negative decision may or may not be communicated during the interview. If the field instructor is ambivalent, he can conclude the interview by stating a need to "think about it" and promising to get back to the student with a decision in a few days. In reality, it is often easier for the field instructor to relay his decision to the school and let the faculty member there advise the student of the decision. In many instances, the decision not to accept a given placement or student is made rather obviously and/or jointly during the course of the preplacement interview. Thus, the interview ends with both parties knowing that there is no match.

The field instructor evaluates many factors as he decides whether or not to take a student. What kind of learner is he? Does his learning style fit my teaching style? Do I have anything meaningful to teach him? Do I like him, or am I so turned off by him that I couldn't work with him effectively? Does he seem bright, motivated, and sincerely interested in the placement and in learning? Was he passive, too aggressive, negativistic, overanxious, or contradictory during the interview? Was it hard to get to know the student because of his tendency to give the field instructor what he wanted to hear? Does he seem at ease with people? Can he be warm and empathetic? How much self-awareness does he have regarding his strengths, limitations, and educational needs? Do his perceptions of himself and his experiences seem accurate? Are there potential problem areas? Does the field instructor have a vague feeling that something isn't quite right, without being able to pinpoint it?

One important area that must be evaluated is the kind and degree of skill the student has in relation to the skill he must achieve by the end of the placement. Is he already functioning at a rather high level, or are there serious gaps present because of deficits in the first field placement or limitations on the student's part? If so, will the student be able to acquire the knowledge or skills he should have received from the prior placement *plus* those normally acquired in the second placement—all in one placement? Would he be willing to put in extra hours and do special reading if necessary? Are the gaps so large that no matter how intensively the field instructor worked with him in placement and no matter how hard he worked, he could not be brought up to the required minimum level by the end of placement? If the field instructor is pessimistic, the student probably should not be accepted. If the gaps are real but the student is sincerely willing and apparently able to do extra work *and* he and the field instructor agree to this as a condition of placement, he should probably be accepted.

If a decision is made not to accept a student, the next question is, "Who will tell the student?" If the field instructor has a strong negative personal reaction to the student, it could be most difficult for him to convey the negative decision to the student in an objective, constructive manner. For example, if the field instructor reacts to a student's ethnic background, extreme obesity, physical handicap, or a personality that reminds him of someone he can't stand, the school, rather than the field instructor, should discuss the rejection decision with the student. Ideally, field instructors should not reject students for these reasons; however, in reality these factors and the interviewer's reactions to them can and do sometimes affect preplacement decisions.

Perhaps the most difficult situation arises when a student sincerely wants to come to a particular placement, feels he would do well there, and yet the field instructor has serious reservations and really does not want to accept the student. Inexperienced field instructors should not attempt to communicate a rejection decision to the student. They should share their feelings with the school and let the faculty handle the matter with the student. However, experienced field instructors who have conducted numerous preplacement interviews usually know themselves, their agency, and students as a group rather well. They often can express quite clearly and constructively their reasons for suggesting that the student not attempt placement in their setting in spite of the student's desire to do so. They usually know from experience the kinds of learning attitudes, behaviors, abilities and limitations that characterize students who do well in the setting and those who have serious difficulties. The field instructor may not reveal all of his doubts and observations regarding the interviewee, but he is often able to find a way to share some of them and point out that perhaps the student could do well in a different kind of setting. Thus, experienced field supervisors often can use the context of the interview to share their conclusions regarding nonacceptance of the student.

If a student has had a first field placement and is applying for a subsequent placement, the interview may reveal large gaps in knowledge or skill areas that the field instructor feels he cannot help the student overcome in time for graduation. He might share this observation with the student, pointing out some of the reality demands of social work practice and the apparent gaps between his existing level of preparation and what he must achieve prior to graduation. He might review some of the traits employers look for when interviewing new graduates and some of their expectations once the individual has been hired. Such an explanation will be anxiety-producing for the student and perhaps for the school as well. The school may feel that it provided a good first placement for the student: "And who are you to come along and tell the student you won't take him in your placement because he is poorly prepared?" The school may discourage him from doing extra work or taking special field placements because to permit this would mean acknowledging that he would otherwise graduate with less-than-acceptable skills. The school may feel that it, rather than the field instructor, should set these standards and impose them upon the student. Thus, field instructors who implement the approach discussed above should be aware that the school may have its own viewpoint.

The student may have thought he had a good first field placement, and now a strange practitioner is telling him he didn't learn all he needed to, for which he is being rejected for field placement. However, many students respond to such an honest though hurtful approach maturely, with a determination to fill in those gaps by volunteering to take extra field placements and do other special tasks to prepare them better for professional practice. Rejection on this ground makes some students more aware of what they should be getting in their educational program. As a result they learn much more than they would have if permitted to move through a second field placement with no acknowledgment of the gaps carried over from the first placement. It should be noted that not all of these gaps are the fault of the school or the prior field placement setting; perhaps the student did not work very hard in placement or had personal factors blocking or hindering his learning. It has been my experience that very few students become hostile to the school upon being confronted constructively with the existence of these gaps.

However, the field instructor's communication can have a significant impact on the student's career, and this must be recognized. For example, I have interviewed a number of graduate students who wished to work under my direction to study supervision in an advanced placement. On several occasions, exploration of the student's prior work and field placement activities has revealed limited experience. I ask the student how he can supervise others when he has never been supervised, even in a non–social work job. Will employees listen to and respect what he has to say? Will they feel he understands and can meet their needs? Many students have not previously thought about the reality demands of employment as a supervisor. A number of these students have gone back to their schools and requested reassignment to a casework concentration, realizing that they are not ready to study supervision until they have acquired additional practice and life experience.

When a field instructor makes a decision following a preplacement interview, it is very important that feedback be given to the school as well as to the student. The school needs to know how the student presented himself and came across during the interview. If the school's perception of what took place in the student's initial field placement is different from what the student has reported, this information can be used to evaluate more carefully the kind of placement he now needs. If the student's personal appearance is grossly inappropriate, the school can do some friendly counseling to help him present himself in a more effective light in his next preplacement interview and while in field. Such sharing also increases the school's knowledge of the student. If a student seems to lack a basic ability to relate comfortably to people, feedback from the interviewer may help the school to suggest to the student that he switch to a different profession. Thus, the purpose of the preplacement interview is not only to determine if the student will come to the setting but also to provide a learning experience through receipt of feedback during or after the interview. A rejection by a potential placement can provide an invaluable learning experience if handled properly.

Field instructors may be very tempted to take students who have had ineffective first field placements. There may be genuine empathy for the student who has had an incomplete learning experience through no apparent fault of his own. The field instructor may see the student's deficit as a challenge: *"I can do better than that!"* The student may be very flattering in the interview, reminding the instructor of his excellent reputation and stating his feeling that he can get the "right kind" of training in the agency. The school may even recognize the gaps from the first field placement and encourage the instructor to take the student because "you can provide just what he needs." Again, the gaps between the student's existing skills or knowledge and what he needs to be able to do at the completion of the field placement must be assessed. If it doesn't appear that he can achieve the amount of growth needed in the time allotted, the student should not be accepted. Otherwise, he will finish with significant gaps still present, or the supervisor will have to lower expectations and standards to make it possible for him to pass field instruction. Would you then want to hire this student after he graduates? If you were the client, would you want to be served by him? His degree will appear just as valid as anyone else's, but *you* will know that he never achieved the level of skill his degree says he should have.

It should be quite obvious by now that the preplacement interview actually begins the educational diagnosis part of field instruction. The field instructor begins to form ideas regarding the student's educational needs and learning style. Tentative educational objectives that will later become part of an educational contract* are often identified and agreed upon. Thus, field placement starts not with the first official day of placement but with the preplacement interview itself.

Preplacement Interviews with Macro System Students

Students studying supervision, administration, staff development, research, community organization and related topics should also participate in a preplacement interview. The content of discussion is much the same as that described on the previous pages. However, macro-system students undergo quite different experiences from their casework counterparts, and agencies must therefore look for different qualities before accepting them into placement.

Is this student an emotionally mature individual who can handle responsibly some of the issues and situations he will encounter as an administration student? Will staff feel comfortable having him sit in on confidential and delicate board meetings, administrative planning sessions, and related activities? If he is going to supervise or train staff or other students, does he know enough about social work and have sufficient skills to earn their respect and teach them something? After all, the focus of his training will be not to learn the direct practice skills but to study methods of conveying knowledge to others. Does he have some of the personal qualities necessary for being a good leader? Have his past experiences with authority figures helped or hindered his readiness to become an authority figure himself? Does he have a realistic idea of the kinds of demands and expectations placed upon macro system social workers, and is the level of anxiety he shows about being able to meet these demands appropriate? Or is he overconfident and lacking in self-awareness and/or professional awareness?

The way the student relates to the field instructor in the preplacement interview may be a valid indicator of how he will interact with authority figures and staff in the agency. Was he more at ease in the interview than the average casework student? Did he make the interviewer feel comfortable or uneasy? If he is studying staff development, does he have better-than-average verbal skills? Does he have any experience working with groups, or will it be necessary to teach him the basics of group work as well as the specialized application of group work techniques to in-service training, work with community groups, leading administrative meetings, and the like? Can the interviewer envision this student directing a social work program, acting as a consultant, employed as an educator in a junior college, having charge of staff development for a large agency, or holding similar positions upon graduation? After all, when he finishes field placement in just a few months, his degree will say that he is

*See Chapter 6.

qualified for these kinds of positions. Does the field instructor feel he can teach the student what he needs to know before he graduates? A ''no'' answer to only one or two of these questions would indicate that the student should seriously consider switching to a casework concentration and gaining some postdegree practice experience before taking on macro system responsibilities. The field instructor is the ''gatekeeper of the profession.'' What will he decide?

5 Orienting Students to Field Placement

A Student's Tale*

MONDAY. Hi. My name is Polly Student. My faculty advisor said we have to keep a daily log of our experiences in field placement, so that's what I'm doing.

I had an awful time finding this place. I circled round the block at least a dozen times, in rush hour traffic, before I found the side road that leads to the agency—the miserable street sign was missing. Well, I broke my neck to get here and came in 45 minutes late. I was sure my supervisor would be really mad. But guess what—when I walked in and introduced myself nobody seemed to know who I was and didn't seem to care whether I arrived late or not. My field instructor was out sick today and I sat in the hallway for over an hour until they figured out what to do with me. I guess I should have offered to go home, but somehow that didn't seem the right thing to do. Finally a supervisor (she never did introduce herself) came out and stuck me in an isolated corner and gave me three foot-thick procedure manuals to read.

I read until my eyes got blurry and my bladder was about to burst. I didn't have the slightest idea where the bathroom was and there was nobody around to ask. Things got pretty desperate before I got up nerve to find one of the secretaries and ask her about it. She hollered the instructions for getting there clear across the room and I was so embarrassed I felt like crawling under the desk.

I returned to my desk and read some more. I didn't know when I was supposed to eat and I didn't want to break any rules or anything. About 2pm the supervisor came in and asked how I was doing (boy, would I have liked to tell her a thing or two!) She seemed surprised I hadn't eaten yet and showed me where the snack machines were. When I got back the secretaries were having some kind of loud discussion—I could hear them clear into my cubbyhold. They were really laying it on a Mrs. Smith—something about not doing her reports right. Boy, I hope I don't have to do any reports—I couldn't take that kind of criticism—especially behind my back like that.

I must confess that I fell asleep twice in the afternoon—the stuff is so <u>boring</u>. I sure was glad when my watch said 5pm and I could leave. I hope today isn't an indication of what the rest of this field placement is going to be like. Everybody said it's supposed to be the most interesting part of social work school. Also, I'm not sure I'm wanted here.

TUESDAY. Well, I don't know what to say about today. My field instructor showed up, full of apologies about being absent yesterday. She didn't seem quite ready for me first thing in

*A fictional account based on actual experiences reported by students.

the morning—something about some emergency on her cases. So, I was told to find something to read in the library and to review the procedure manuals some more. The library is an interesting historical collection of outdated stuff nobody reads anymore. I couldn't find any modern textbooks in it—I wonder if staff here really use it?

I finally had my first supervisory conference at 11am. Mrs. Brown talked about her experiences with students and how she really wasn't expecting a student this year but at the last minute her supervisor decided she should have one, so she apologized for not being better prepared for me. She asked me about my family life and what courses I was taking at school and all that. She said I'd be observing and reading for several days. They're in the middle of some internal reorganization and it won't be possible for me to have cases for 2 or 3 weeks. Brother! That's for the birds! But I suppose if that's the way it's done, I'll just have to live with it—she's supposed to be a good field instructor.

This time I had lunch alone in a nearby restaurant. YUK. Think I'll bring my own lunch from now on. In the afternoon I went with Mrs. Brown to a peer review committee meeting. I never did figure out what they were talking about and Mrs. Brown had another meeting right afterwards so I didn't get to ask her about it. I didn't know what to do for the rest of the afternoon, so I worked on an assignment for class that I'd brought with me just in case today was like yesterday. As I was getting ready to leave, Mrs. Brown dropped in to tell me I might go to some other meetings later this week. Monday at 11 is going to be our regular conference time. She said she has only an hour or so a week to spend with her students 'cause she's so busy. Gosh, I've already used up my hour for this week and it's four more days till my next conference. I wonder if other students are doing the same thing? Maybe the school wants us to start in real slow in our first placement. I guess I'll just have to be patient and hope things get better....

The Need for Orientation

Unfortunately, it is not unusual for students to experience the kinds of frustration reported in the illustration above. Yet a student's first few days in field can set the tone for many weeks to come and affect his response to subsequent experiences and assignments. The need for a formal, structured, and well-planned orientation of some kind is obvious when one reviews the list of needs and anxieties that the students have in connection with their internship (see Chapter 3).

The individual who has never experienced a social work field placement usually has a very limited and distorted concept of what the process involves. When students are dumped into a setting with little or no orientation, they must expend a considerable amount of time and energy trying to orient themselves. This leaves them with reduced resources to apply to content learning. A formal orientation from both the school and the agency will reduce (but not eliminate) this energy expenditure as well as student anxiety.

Many students are so anxious at the beginning of placement that they retain very little of the material presented in orientation programs. However, this should not discourage schools and agencies from providing basic orientation experiences. If written materials are distributed during orientation, the student can always review them again for guidance as situations arise in placement weeks or months later.

Social work students are adult learners. They invest a great deal in their education, yet many naively move through the experience without assessing whether it is in fact providing the skills and knowledge they will need to function effectively as social work practitioners after graduation. Many simply do not know what they should be getting in field placement or in the classroom and thus have no yardstick against which to assess their current experience. Thus they fail to take action to improve their experience before an entire placement has elapsed. One of the best methods of preparing students to be active participants in the field instruction process is to provide a meaningful orientation experience.

A school of social work is in a unique position to present an overall view of social work education, its expectations of students, and its concept of and role in the field instruction process. It can prepare students in general for field placement in just about any setting. However, each setting is different. Only the agency knows the peculiar requirements, policies, working conditions, client needs, and internal organization of its service delivery system. Thus, both the school and each individual agency must prepare students for the commencement of field placement.

Scheduling and Format for the Orientation

Schools use various formats for orienting their students to the educational program in general and to field placement. There is usually a formal "orientation day" when general introductory information is presented. Content pertaining to field instruction may be included as part of this larger program. Usually all incoming students participate in one group, but some schools differentiate between new students and those who are entering a second field placement. There may be an initial seminar regarding field instruction followed by periodic seminars throughout the school term to discuss field placement. Some schools present their ideas orally; others distribute written materials to which the student can refer throughout the year. Some programs deliberately withhold certain content during orientation for fear of overwhelming the student in the beginning, bearing in mind his low retention rate. This approach is justifiable only if regularly scheduled followup seminars take place after the initial orientation to provide the missing content. Students should be advised of the schedule for these sessions, as well as the rationale for delaying delivery of certain information.

Agencies with two or more student trainees can cover much orientation material through group sessions conducted by a senior field instructor or various staff. In settings with only one student, obviously all such orientation must be done individually. Not only is this time-consuming for the individual field instructor, but some of the material to be presented by its nature is best covered with a group of orientees. For example, a session on being consumers of supervision is much less threatening if it is received as part of a group rather than individually from a field instructor. Several related departments within a large agency or perhaps several nearby hospitals or mental health clinics could combine their students for selected portions of orientation if common client needs and didactic information must be covered.

Each agency should develop its own written materials for distribution during orientation. These reduce the time that must be spent in oral presentations but should never completely replace them. If reading assignments are given, there should be opportunity for discussion and questions regarding the material.* Some settings develop a student handbook that covers nitty-gritty information. Such materials can save many field instruction hours of having to answer basic questions such as ''Where is the restroom?'' and ''How do I use the telephone?''

Agency orientation could be covered in an intensive series of presentations lasting several days. However, this is overwhelming for most students. Preferably the orientation should be spaced throughout placement. The amount of time the student should spend in orientation is directly related to the number of hours he is at the agency each week.

If the student is present sixteen hours weekly for a ten-week field placement and spends one day a week for a month in orientation, the time available for involvement with actual assignments will be sharply curtailed. Orientation sessions need to be spaced out so that they do not consume more than two or three hours a week, with the possible exception of the first week.

A problem faced by agencies is the fact that students who are from different schools or at different levels of training may not all start placement at the same time. The student in his very first placement may spend several weeks in the classroom before starting field. More advanced students often start placement at the beginning of the term. Thus, an agency may find itself with two students who start placement on September 6 and one who doesn't arrive until September 29. This can cause a very inefficient agency orientation process. There are, however, several possible solutions.

The easiest way to resolve this problem is to provide basic orientation for the early arrivals and hold off on more detailed material until all students have arrived. This requires some duplication of orientation efforts, however, as latecomers must get the same information the other students have already received. Mature students who are already on the scene may be used to assist in orienting those arriving later. However, since they themselves are also very new, agency staff as well will need to participate in the orientation.

A field placement schedule for individual students can sometimes be adjusted. The student who starts at the end of the month might be able to come to the agency for orientation sessions prior to the official starting date of his placement. Such a plan must meet with the school's approval (that is, the student should not be forced to choose between attending classes or seminars at school and attending an agency orientation session). A surprising number of motivated students will eagerly accept this plan and often request reading materials and anything else the field instructor can provide to give them an early start. If necessary, time off can be given later on in the field placement experience to compensate for any initial extra hours. If an agency feels strongly about the need for latecomers to report for early orientation sessions, it might make this a requirement for acceptance of all such students for placement. This policy would then be communicated to the school and discussed thoroughly in the preplacement interview.

Another approach would be to determine if local schools of social work would be willing to agree to a common starting date for field placement in order to facilitate the orientation process for the agency. This has actually been done in some communities with several social work schools. Field instructors and agencies would need to present an organized, unified proposal to the schools that such a plan be implemented and be willing to work with them to arrive at a mutually acceptable arrangement.

*See Suanna Jean Wilson, *Confidentiality in Social Work: Issues and Principles* (New York: The Free Press, 1978), and idem, *Recording: Guidelines for Social Workers* (New York: The Free Press, 1980), for two examples of written materials developed for use in student orientation following several years of repeating the same presentation four times yearly. The response to these materials was so positive and the demand so great that they were eventually rewritten for publication.

Students who are scheduled to arrive ahead of others might be asked to delay the start of their placements. This can be effective with students who are at the agency for only a few days and hours per week. They will miss some field placement hours, and a plan must be made for making up any significant amount of time. The school would need to approve the plan, and the student's classroom schedule and personal commitments must permit this arrangement. Such students may make up the hours missed by putting in a little extra time each week, coming in on a weekend (if supervision is available), attending an agency-related meeting at night to get a special learning experience that would not be available during normal placement hours, or reporting to field during long school breaks. For example, some settings may require students to have client contact during the month-long Christmas recess.

Some orientation sessions might lend themselves to audio- or videotaping. Late students could undergo a self-instructional experience, with periodic sessions scheduled to discuss the material. An added advantage is that the students can go back and review the material whenever they wish.

Content of Orientation Sessions

Once some thought has been given to the mechanical means of providing training, content can be developed, priorities set, and a specific schedule developed. The following suggestions for orientation content are based on the expressed needs of students, field instructors, and schools over several years and have been taught to field instructors in a wide variety of settings and geographical locations. The ideas presented are listed in outline form for use as a checklist if desired. As school and agency programs differ widely, not everything listed will be appropriate to all settings.

There are certain concepts that need to be covered by school faculty before students enter field. This is often done during a special orientation to field placement seminar or in initial field integration seminars. Additional orientation content is often woven into field integration seminars throughout the term. Each school has its own expectations for students in field and generally conveys them to students during orientation programs. In addition, school faculty are well equipped to provide a broad overview of what field placement is all about and how it fits into the overall social work curriculum. Agencies, on the other hand, generally provide a more specialized orientation to their particular settings and their consumer populations. Thus, there will be some differences in both focus and content between orientation provided by the school and that provided by the agency, though there will be some overlapping, especially if either the school or the agency fails to provide a complete orientation, making it necessary for the other party to fill in basic gaps.

The School's Orientation

1. The purpose and place of field placement in social work education
2. Explanation of how agencies and field instructors are selected and how students are matched with specific settings
3. What field placement is like; what generally happens in placement and how students fit into the agency structure
4. The minimum experiences all students should receive in field. This should be provided in writing as well as orally, and there may be a need to distinguish between clinical and administration or other macro system experiences. Specific standards should be communicated regarding
   A. The frequency of formal supervisory conferences
   B. The minimum time the average student spends with a field instructor, especially in the beginning of placement
   C. The kinds of things most agencies should offer in their own orientation for students
   D. How long the average student should expect to wait before getting his first assignment to work with an individual, group, or organization
   E. The average caseload or work assignment that students carry (recognizing that there will be wide variations)
   F. Requirements regarding the type of written recording that students are required to do in field
   G. The fact that the field instructor should be at the agency roughly the same hours that the student is in placement
   H. Other specific experiences that the school wants all students to receive regardless of the type of placement to which they are assigned
5. What a student can do if he is not getting the kinds of experiences described during orientation, including the avenues of communication and chain of command open to the student and the school's role when problems are brought to its attention
6. The roles of the overall school of social work, the dean and the director of field instruction (or other field instruction staff); the student's faculty adviser or field liaison person; classroom faculty, the agency administrator, the individual field instructor and the student in the placement experience (These should be both described and illustrated with examples; e.g., see the chart on pp. 12–15).
7. The importance and continuing problem of integrating classroom theory with what the student is doing in field (Specific suggestions that the student can use to facilitate this process should be offered, such as encouraging reading during placement.)

8. Common needs and anxieties of both students in placement and field instructors

9. Basic expectations of the school, the agency, and field instructors, which might include appropriate dress, professional office behavior, attendance, do's and don'ts of getting along with people in the agency, recognition of the fact that school and field instructors may differ in standards and expectations, and hints for handling this when it occurs

10. The minimal knowledge and skills the school expects its students to achieve and demonstrate before a degree will be awarded and how the field placement experience can help students move toward achieving the required level of competence

11. A description of the kinds of skills employers will expect new graduates to bring to their first job. This discussion can help students examine their present level of preparation against reality demands of social work employment and can result in strong motivation to learn as much as possible so as to become ready for beginning social work practice rather than just to earn a certain grade

12. What it means to be an adult learner, and the student's responsibility to evaluate the field experience critically and participate in structuring it so that he can achieve the best possible learning experience

13. A description of the educational contract (or any other specialized learning tools that the school requires or recommends) and how it should be used in field placement (see Chapter 6)

14. Special requirements. For example, some schools are requiring students to read the National Association of Social Workers (NASW) Code of Ethics and sign a statement agreeing to abide by the Code during field placement. Others require each student join NASW and obtain student malpractice insurance to provide coverage during field placement

15. The concept of the student learner as a "consumer of supervision" in field placement. This discussion should take place in small groups and is most effective during the first or second week of placement. The common expectations that field instructors have of their students and the kinds of things students should expect of their field instructor (a new concept for some students) can be discussed. Describe the use of the supervisory conference and the student's responsibility to let it be known if the field instructor is not meeting his needs. Actually list and give examples of the kinds of things that can cause students to fail in field placement. Most will be enormously relieved to find that it is not easy to fail; only serious problems, not minor ones, would bring about a failing grade. Describe the counseling process that preceeds assignment of an unsatisfactory grade. List the kinds of behaviors, attitudes, work habits, and skills that are necessary for a student to earn an outstanding evaluation in most settings. Finally, give suggestions on what the student can do if communication breaks down with his field instructor

16. A frank discussion of the performance evaluation and grading process, introduced early in the orientation program and discussed in greater detail later during the first month of placement, covering the following areas:

    A. The fact that performance evaluation is an ongoing process, starting with the first day of field placement (If sharing is continual and frank, the final written evaluation should hold no surprises for the student.)

    B. The fact that the student also does an evaluation of his field placement experience and the importance of communicating his evaluatory feedback throughout the field experience

    C. How the school uses the performance evaluation materials received from the field (Explain how it becomes part of the student's reference material and the student's right of access to his records.)*

    D. An explanation of the process by which field placement grades are assigned and the roles of the faculty adviser and field instructor in this process

    E. The various actions a student can take if he does not agree with his evaluation (These might include discussion with the field instructor or agency supervisor, a formal written rebuttal, consultation with faculty adviser and school officials, or initiation of a grievance or other appeal mechanism.)

    F. The repercussions of a failing grade in field placement and its effect on the student's ability to continue in the social work program

    G. Pitfalls associated with receipt of performance evaluations (For example, some students are crushed if they receive "only" satisfactory; students may react strongly to a reading of another's evaluation; and so on.)

    H. Discussion of the performance rating form or outline that field instructors use to evaluate students and of the form that the student will use to evaluate his experience at the end of placement

17. Information on the existence of the school's field instruction manual, what it contains, and where copies can be obtained or borrowed (This manual

---

*This is provided for under the Family Educational Rights and Privacy Act of 1974 (the "Buckley Amendment"), which amends Public Law 93-568, effective November 19, 1974. See also Department of HEW, Office of the Secretary, "Privacy Rights of Parents and Students," Part II, "Final Rule on Education Records," *Federal Register* (June 17, 1976), pp. 24662-24675.

would be ideal required reading for the first month of placement. If a separate student handbook for field instruction exists, copies should be distributed.)

18. Relevant insurance coverage available to students, which might include malpractice coverage; health and accident benefits covering injuries in the field; and car insurance requirements for students who use their private vehicles in connection with field placement

19. Important "don'ts" or "things that should not happen in field"; for example:

    A. Students should not be required to transport clients in their own cars. If they do so, the student must receive the same mileage reimbursement paid to staff members who use their cars on the job. If no reimbursement is possible, the student should be advised of this before he accepts the placement, and his use of his car should occur voluntarily*

    B. Students should never be expected physically to restrain psychotic individuals,† or provide physical care to clients, such as bathing someone or changing bedding or bandages

20. A brief comparison between the field placement experience and the realities of employment as a social worker. Students need to know that there will be differences in the quantity and type of supervision they will receive as social work employees (e.g., more management than educationally oriented). There will also be differences in the way in which cases are assigned and the total number of clients in a typical agency caseload. Students need to begin learning techniques for handling large quantities of work and for setting priorities while still in field, even though they will be working with a much smaller caseload than would an employee in the same agency. Employees also function as part of a system that impacts on them and their clients and can hinder or facilitate services to clients. Students can be helped to apply knowledge learned in the classroom to study the effect of their settings on social work activities and also examine their role as potential change agents

21. A session on techniques of job hunting. This should take place several months before graduation and should cover where to find job openings, how to prepare a résumé and secure job interviews, and what to expect and ask about in employment interviews. Many students benefit from practical hints on how to conduct themselves during an interview, proper dress, salary expectations, and the like‡

22. Assignment of readings pertaining to the field instruction experience, such as this book

Checklist of School's Written Handouts

Student anxiety is usually high during formal orientation sessions, and retention of information presented orally may be low. Therefore, it is suggested that written handouts be used to give students something to refer back to as they progress through their placement experience. Some handouts will repeat material presented orally; others will give information that is best illustrated in written form.

1. A list of minimum experiences all students should have in field placement

2. Performance expectations for students at the end of each period of field placement (These should be expressed in behavioral terms, indicating the level of competence that should be attained as well as the content area to which the student will be exposed.)

3. Forms used by field instructors and students to evaluate performance and the field placement experience

4. A checklist of "don'ts" or "things that should not happen in field"

5. List of assigned readings and suggested completion dates

6. School calendar, with special notations regarding field placements

7. Recording outlines, confidentiality guidelines, and similar materials

The Agency's Orientation

The content of the agency's orientation will be determined to some degree by the nature of the school's orientation program. Agencies must therefore be familiar with the orientation programs provided by their students' schools. If key elements appear to be missing, the placement setting may want to incorporate appropriate content into its own program. If the school's orientation appears adequate and effective, the agency can avoid duplication of content and focus instead on orientation to specifics associated with the particular agency involved. A large agency with considera-

---

*This problem can be more serious than some schools realize. For example, a student on an extremely limited budget was completing a field placement. During an end-of-quarter seminar she complained of being asked to deliver papers between the main agency and its outlying office, more than 50 miles away. It had never occurred to her that this might be an inappropriate use of her time, and she had not thought to inquire whether the agency could reimburse her for the cost of this travel.

†One undergraduate student hesitantly asked, during a field instruction seminar held halfway through placement, whether his agency should be asking him to sit on violent patients to restrain them. He was afraid he might be injured and wondered if the school had insurance to cover this!

‡See the Résumé Outline in Appendix F, developed to help students prepare intelligible, meaningful *vitas*.

ble experience with students would be in a position to cover many of the items that schools should cover. Progressive settings with adequate staffing may develop rather elaborate orientation programs in their effort to provide content that the agency considers essential to fill in gaps between what the school does not provide and what the student needs. Some schools eventually become uncomfortable with the idea that an agency is orienting its students to general social work educational concepts and begin developing more effective orientation programs of their own. This is ideal, as it relieves the agency of a task that is actually the school's responsibility and frees it to concentrate on the specialized orientation that only the agency can give. Settings with highly developed orientation programs should share content and philosophy with local schools as one method of having a direct impact on the social work educational system.

Many of the orientation items and procedures listed below would apply to new employees as well as students. Some settings group students and new staff together for selected portions of the orientation. For example, this is sometimes done at a welcoming coffee or other special event to introduce the new students and staff.

1. Nitty-gritty items. A special student orientation handbook can be developed that covers such items as parking facilities and rules; the locations of bathrooms and eating facilities (a map of the building or agency complex may be helpful); lunch and break times; dress requirements, if any; any special agency insurance coverage; policy regarding reimbursement for travel and other expenses; scheduled agency holidays when the student does not need to report to placement (these may be different from holidays observed by the school); requirements for signing in and out (if applicable); requirements and instructions for use of the telephone, including agency policy about making and receiving personal and long distance calls; any special security precautions; other items peculiar to the agency.

2. A written orientation schedule outlining when and where all planned orientation sessions will be held and who will be leading them. Each student, field instructor and agency supervisor/administrator involved with students should receive a copy, as well as key clerical staff. It is often helpful to make a master list of each student's name, school, field instructor, area of assignment, field placement hours and office location to distribute to all staff.

3. A description of what the agency/department or service delivery system does and does not do. Provide a brief history and describe funding sources and methods of program development, the types of people served, and their primary needs. Review the various types and levels of staff and their respective roles. Clearly list the kinds of activities done by social workers in the setting and give an overview of what a staff member might do during an average day. Provide an organizational chart for the unit or department in which the student is placed. If necessary, provide a second chart that shows the department or agency's position as part of a larger complex, bureaucracy, or institution.

5. Introduce students to clerical and receptionist staff right away so they know the student by name and face and can refer calls to him. It is helpful to have each student's home telephone number and address on file in case of emergency.

6. Introduction to the agency's clerical and record-keeping system. Show newcomers where records are kept, explain the intricacies of the filing system and all master cards or cross-index files. Explain necessary clerical procedures: how to get a letter typed, something xeroxed, or a tape sent to the steno pool for transcription. Explain how mail and messages are handled. It may be necessary to remind students that agency clerical staff are not there to type student homework assignments, résumés, or other personal materials and that the agency xerox machine cannot be used for copying books, articles, and the like.

7. Procedures for compiling all agency-required statistical reports. Instructions should be available in writing along with examples of related forms. This must be taught before the student has his first client contact or participates in an activity that must be recorded statistically. Most agencies require students as well as staff to report the number and type of client and collateral contacts and perhaps also the amount of time spent in various direct and indirect service activities. Most students will have many questions as they begin to keep their statistics and must have someone they can go to for answers until they become familiar with the process.

8. Specific recording requirements of the agency. Provide copies of outlines for intake, transfer, closing, social history summaries and all other required reports. Share examples of recording in actual records and present specific requirements as to frequency or style (individual field instructors will go into much more detail on this when they start reviewing their students' recording). If general techniques of recording have not been covered by the school prior to the start of placement, the agency will need to cover this as well.* If process recording or taping is to be done, general principles and format for doing these specialized recordings must be taught.

9. Written instructions on the mechanics of operating the dictaphone equipment found in the agency, plus general

---

*One way to do this would be to have students read Suanna Jean Wilson, *Recording: Guidelines for Social Workers* (New York: Free Press, 1980), which is essentially self-instructional and written especially for students. It also teaches how to do process recording and includes examples of student interviews and recording.

techniques of dictating, should be provided and should be self-instructional.

10. State clearly how the student is to identify himself in (1) written recording in agency records; (2) written reports and correspondence that go outside the agency; and (3) oral contacts with clients, families, and others. Some settings require students to identify themselves as such; others require supervisory cosignatures on correspondence, records, and other signed documents.

11. Arrange for key supervisory or administrative personnel to meet with the students. In large programs it is possible for some students to complete an entire field placement without ever having any personal contact with upper-level administrators unless formal meetings are arranged. The student needs to put a face and a personality with the title and, depending on his educational objectives, should be encouraged to have individual contact with administrators when appropriate. Even the most sophisticated student may stand in awe of the administrator and consciously or unconsciously avoid him unless interaction is encouraged so that familiarity can begin to break down unrealistic fears of "The Supreme Authority Figure."

12. Orient the student to the agency library and available audio-visual aides. If possible, distribute written instructions for library use.

13. Teach specific confidentiality requirements of the agency. Discuss the setting's consent-to-release-of-information form and its use; talk about the right of privileged communication if it applies;* discuss information that can and cannot be released without client consent; explain what to do if the student is approached by the news media or is subpoenaed, and so on. Present specific guidelines for preserving confidentiality of material taken from the field into the classroom. Regardless of the kind and extent of confidentiality training given by the school, the agency must also cover its own specific requirements. Ask the student what he has and has not had in the classroom. Make no assumptions. Many students currently enter field placement with no orientation whatsoever on confidentiality.

14. Each student should have access to the following reference materials somewhere near his work area:

A. Intra-agency and community phone directories

*Students in federal settings will also need to learn the basics of the Federal Privacy Act of 1974 (Public Law 93-579, December 31, 1974) and other pertinent legislation. Additional legislation is currently under consideration which could extend Privacy Act provisions to state and local governmental programs as well as to some private settings receiving federal funds (such as Medicare or Medicaid reimbursement for services rendered).

B. Agency or department procedure manuals
C. Information regarding community resources
D. A dictionary
E. Other special reference books peculiar to the demands of the setting, such as a medical dictionary or a synopsis of the Federal Privacy Act
F. Any other reference materials that staff must use almost daily

15. Encourage students to read the agency personnel manual. They need to get a feel for personnel regulations and terms such as sick leave, annual leave, leave without pay, and provisions for hiring, firing, promoting, and so on. As students move from one setting to another and finally into social work employment, they can become more discriminating job applicants if they already have some familiarity with various personnel practices and benefits. This also enables them to compare their benefits and responsibilities as students with those of regular paid staff.

16. Explain where the student can find a private interviewing area when needed. There is nothing more embarrassing for a student than to have a client or family waiting in the hallway while he searches frantically for an unoccupied office.

17. Describe special security precautions. Purses may need to be kept under lock and key. Perhaps the door is locked at 5:00 P.M. sharp each day and uninformed students could find themselves unable to get in or out without a key. If the agency serves a high-crime area, special precautions should be described. Many students have little experience with such neighborhoods and may have unrealistic fears or a false feeling of security that "nothing could ever happen to me." Locked wards or sexually aggressive clients may dictate special precautions. Students may need to be advised to avoid certain isolated areas of the institution or the grounds at night, and so on. Students in medical settings may have fears regarding the contagion of certain diseases, and it may be necessary to teach techniques for observing medical precautions.

18. Tell students that it is permissible to read during field placement time. Many students feel guilty if they open a book while in field. Yet a dynamic, structured approach to field instruction demands that students read about the presenting problems of their specific assignments. If a student is working with a client who seems highly suspicious of everyone, the student must feel free to read about paranoia. On the other hand, students should not use field placement time to complete classroom readings; if this is occurring, it may be an indication that the student either is having difficulty completing agency assignments or simply needs more to do. A fully challenging placement experience usually leaves little time for unrelated activities.

19. Provide a bibliography (annotated if possible) of suggested readings to orient the student to the service delivery system, the specialized field of practice (e.g. psychiatric social work), primary characteristics of the client population (e.g. the aging, schizophrenics, drug addicts), and key skills used in service delivery. List only materials that can be located readily, without an exhaustive search or a trip across town to a remote library.

20. Engage the students in a discussion of the human elements of social work practice. Social workers are human beings first and social workers second. They cannot be all things to all people all the time. They will overidentify with certain clients; everyone has unique life experiences that make him especially effective in certain kinds of situations and very uncomfortable and resistant to working with others. Talk about "third-year medical student's disease"* if the student is in a medical setting; indicate that a social work student with a psychotic parent may have difficulty working with a sixty-year-old psychotic having a similar diagnosis. Explain that situations occur where a social worker may need to transfer the case to someone else, which will not necessarily mean the student is ineffective. Acknowledge and clarify fears of physicians, common misconceptions about drug users, or unrealistic fears of "catching" cancer. Warn the students that they may experience some anxiety upon discovering that doctors, psychiatrists, social work staff, and other professionals are human and imperfect and that these anxieties are normal.

21. Hold a session on "being consumers of supervision." Even if the school has given a similar orientation, the agency may have specific concepts of its own that characterize its approach to field instruction. Students need to be informed of specialized approaches, supervisory styles, and expectations.

22. Provide students with a glossary of abbreviations, symbols, agency jargon, and technical terms peculiar to the setting. The material should be in a format that the student can carry with him as he reads records.

23. Orientation to key community resources may be provided. However, this must be approached with considerable caution. Many programs provide dull tours of their physical plant, and once a student has seen one or two such settings, he's really seen them all. Others provide irrelevant or sketchy information that doesn't really meet the student's needs. Students usually welcome agency tours—they give them a chance to travel a bit, disrupt the work routine, and are very nonthreatening. However, visits to community agencies should not take time away from completion of meaningful assignments. Students can always visit community resources at any time in their career. What they cannot do later is be in the special student role with its accompanying learning opportunities in a given agency. Thus, this must take priority. When community resources are visited, they should be primary facilities or programs with which the agency interacts almost daily. For example, students placed in a pediatric clinic might visit the state protective services unit that deals with child abuse; those placed in an outpatient mental health clinic might visit a local mental hospital; and so on. Foster homes, nursing homes, boarding homes, and similar facilities may be appropriate visitation sites. A large, complex agency or a department within an institution or larger bureaucratic structure may also need to orient students to key departments within the organizational network. Some students may even apply for services and go through the system as if they were clients in order to experience first hand what it is like to be the target of a service delivery system.

24. Peer review and other accountability activities in which agency staff participate should be discussed. Student cases might be pulled for peer review; there might be opportunities later for participation on review committees. Accountability is rapidly becoming an integral part of social work practice, and new employees will be better prepared to handle it if exposed to the process as students.

25. Finally, the agency might examine the student's classroom curriculum, looking especially at content received prior to the commencement of placement, to identify knowledge gaps that could hinder functioning in field placement. Schools cannot cover everything before field placement, and some material may be presented too late to benefit the student. Thus, the agency may want to develop special training on the diagnostic thinking process, recording, confidentiality, techniques of job hunting, psychodynamics of illness, and similar subjects.

Checklist of Written Handouts for Agencies to Distribute

1. Student orientation handbook
2. Orientation schedule
3. Instructions for completing agency statistical reports and simple forms
4. Outlines for use in recording
5. Instructions and general techniques for use of the dictating equipment
6. Library rules and regulations

---

*A phenomenon whereby medical students, as they become aware of the symptoms and diagnoses of their patients, identify similar symptoms in themselves and are fearful that they may have the same illness. The stage usually passes rather quickly as they gain more knowledge and exposure and realize that most people have one or more symptoms of physical or mental illness in varying degrees, but that a pattern of symptoms, present in a specified degree over a given period of time, is usually required before the person can be diagnosed as "ill."

7. Bibliography of suggested readings
8. List of staff members in the department/agency, giving name, title, location, area of assignment, work schedule, and phone extension
9. List of abbreviations, symbols, and technical terminology peculiar to the setting
10. Organizational charts
11. Map of agency, city, or county
12. Dress code
13. List of holidays observed by the agency
14. Examples of peer review forms, protocols, and related materials

15. A form for the student to evaluate the effectiveness of the agency's student orientation program
16. Agency procedure manual (one copy may be shared by several persons)
17. Copies of key memos covering resources and policies that update the procedure manual or existing materials
18. General job description for all levels of social work staff in the agency (if not included in the procedure manual or other readily available reference source)

6 The Educational Contract

An educational contract with an individual student provides a road map for the field instruction experience. Suppose we want to travel from New York City to "somewhere out west." We would have to decide whether we wanted to go only as far as Chicago or all the way to San Francisco. We would decide whether we wanted to take the fastest or the most scenic route. We would consult a road map to help us make this decision and would examine alternate routes and possible side trips along the way. We'd have a way of knowing when we reached Chicago or San Francisco and might even make allowances for changing the ultimate destination en route. In the absence of an itinerary and a map, we might know where we want to go but not the best route for getting there, and we could expect to get lost along the way. Furthermore, it would be difficult to control the time it would take us to reach our destination.

The field instruction experience is analogous in many respects. The student is there to learn certain things and have specific experiences. There are definite time limitations involved. Both field instructor and student need to have some idea of where they are going (objectives), how to get there (learning experiences) and how they will know when they arrive (assessment/measurement). This provides the overall structure for the placement experience, with periodic performance evaluations describing the student's progress or problems in achieving the desired objectives.

Educational contracts range in complexity from a simple oral understanding of field instruction goals to a detailed breakdown of behavioral objectives, learning experiences, and assessment mechanisms and criteria. Most contracts are developed during the first few weeks of placement and represent a joint effort of field instructor and student. Whether written or not, all contracts should be treated as highly flexible: Objectives will change throughout the placement experience as some are achieved, new ones are set, and existing ones are revised or dropped. Most educational plans need a complete reassessment and review midway through placement. While most are written to cover the entire placement experience, many mini-objectives are set along the way, and these may be time-limited. Yet, added together, they enable the student to reach the overall objectives of the total placement experience.

Most students with social work experience or a prior field placement should be able to participate actively in the development of an educational plan or a formal contract. They have some idea of what their educational needs are; they have some awareness of their professional strengths and weaknesses and areas they would like to work on; often they have some understanding of the skills needed to go along with their stated career goals. However, they should not be turned loose to write their own educational plans. The field instructor's input is needed if the process is to have real meaning.

In contrast, students entering an initial field placement with no prior social work experience usually have very limited ability to contribute to an educational plan or contract. They expect the school and field instructor to tell them what they need to learn since they have no other information to go by. They do not know the kinds of learning experiences available in a given placement setting or the tools commonly used in assessing student activity. Thus, the supervisor must develop most of the plan, soliciting student input and reactions where appropriate. The student must accept and agree with the plan and express willingness to strive for the goals it presents. When it is reviewed midway through the placement, the student will have a better understanding of social work education and his internship training and should be able to contribute more meaningfully to the discussion and revision of the contract.

A formal educational contract also outlines performance

expectations, providing an opportunity to discuss the evaluation process with the student. Once the student knows what he will be evaluated for and how, his anxiety regarding the process should decrease. If the objectives specify the degree of skill necessary to be rated unsatisfactory, satisfactory, or outstanding the student may even contract with himself regarding the level of competence he wants to strive for. Not all students have the ability or even the desire to be outstanding. Some quite consciously decide not to put forth the extra effort required and aim instead for a solid satisfactory rating. This is perfectly acceptable, unless the student is capable of performing at a significantly higher level.

A meaningful educational plan cannot be fully developed in the first week or two of placement. The field instructor must have time to get to know the student's individual needs, goals, experiences, existing skills, knowledge gaps, and so forth* in order to develop an individualized plan. If the student is actively involved in the process of attaining this awareness, the very process itself becomes a learning experience.

An educational plan must be realistic. The experiences provided to help students achieve their objectives must enable them to practice and apply the desired skills. For example, if the ability to meet deadlines is an expectation, the student must be given deadlines to meet. These should be real deadlines—that is, it must make a difference if they are met or not. The student must not be overprotected to the extent that he is never allowed to test his newly developing skills. In addition, a realistic contract will spell out exceptions and areas where a student might be permitted to fall short of stated objectives. For example, a student might be expected to follow agency policies except when the policy manual is confusing, outdated, or incomplete. Or the student might be required to establish positive relationships with clients except for ones known to be hostile toward all professional helping persons.

There are several types of educational plans or contracts. To simplify this discussion I have labeled these Levels I through IV. Many field instructors use Level I without thinking of the process as an educational plan. Very few schools or field instructors use Level IV regularly. Faculty and field instructors who are just learning to develop educational plans should start with Level I and gradually work up to more complex levels. Level III or IV is recommended for most field instructors in social work education.

Level I: Broad Objectives for All Students

The general objectives are usually stated in writing and are developed by the school rather than by individual field instructors. They are most often found in field instruction

*Some people refer to this assessment process as the "educational diagnosis." The educational plan or contract then becomes the counterpart of a "treatment plan."

manuals and other literature published by the school. These statements simply list the areas to which the student will be exposed both in the classroom and in the field. The objectives vary depending on the student's area of concentration: clinical practice, administration, research or some other. There is no attempt to define the level of competence he is expected to attain. Typical statements read as follows: "attain skill in establishing interpersonal relationships," "gain an understanding of the psychodynamics of human behavior," "develop skill in administrative planning," "develop conscious use of self in therapeutic relationships."

These objectives apply to all students. Many schools stop at Level I, leaving it up to the field instructor to develop an individualized educational plan that suits the needs of a particular student within the context of the broader objectives.

Level II: Simple Understanding Between Student and Field Instructor

This plan consists of a very simple oral agreement between field instructor and student regarding the skills and experiences it is hoped the student will gain, for example: "Okay, we'll work on helping you achieve greater depth in your interviewing; you want to become more effective working with manipulative clients; our goal is to help you become more independent in doing routine tasks." Subsequent supervisory sessions and performance evaluations may or may not pick up on these initial goals. If the goals change in midstream, there may be no awareness or discussion of the process. The change simply takes place with little or no conscious analysis of the process or reason behind the change.

Level III: The Formal Written Contract—Without the Competence-Based Component

At this level of complexity, the student and field instructor commit to writing rather simple statements regarding their (1) objectives, (2) learning experiences, and (3) assessment. It is understood that the objectives will be accomplished by the time the student finishes field placement, though this may not appear in the formal contract. The following material might go under each heading:

Objectives: what it is the student is to learn. A simple objective might be, "The student is to follow agency procedures." No attempt is made to define this phrase further or break it down into behavioral components. It is assumed that field instructor and student have at least a rough mutual understanding of the meaning of each objective. There is no attempt to define the desired level or degree of skill or competence. The objectives often appear in the general format described for Level I but are specific to the needs of an individual student.

Learning Experiences: the experiences, resources, activities, opportunities, teaching methods, tasks, assignments, and so on the student will be exposed to in field that will presumably help him learn or achieve the desired objectives. What can we have this student do that will help him learn "to follow agency procedures"? Obviously the student will require assignments and experiences that require him to apply knowledge of agency procedures. What kinds of activities should be involved? Perhaps completing the paperwork necessary to process an application for financial assistance or transfering a patient to a nursing home would provide an effective learning experience to help the student achieve this particular objective. (See the checklist of learning experiences on pp. 95–100 for additional ideas.)

Measurement (assessment): What methods will be used to examine the student's work and progress in meeting the stated objectives? What techniques will be used to determine how well the student is doing: process recordings, tape recordings, one-way mirrors, verbal feedback from the student, direct observation by the field instructor? Notice that these measurement techniques do not state the desired results of the assessment, only the type of assessment mechanism that will be used.*

This kind of educational plan or contract is becoming quite common and can be learned by most field instructors relatively quickly. It sets forth objectives and some specifics regarding the way in which they will be learned and measured.

Level IV. Formal Educational Contract with Competence-Based Component

This level adds a further dimension by specifying the degree of skill the student must achieve in order to satisfy the desired objective. Terms such as "satisfactory, adequate, effective, good, thoroughly, in-depth, be able to recognize, demonstrate," and so forth are defined clearly so that both student and supervisor know exactly what they mean. A well-developed contract at this level spells out what constitutes unsatisfactory, satisfactory, and above-average performance of the stated objectives. One column may list a broad objective (similar to Level II), with another expressing in behavioral terms the degree of skill that must be attained. Some contracts list both elements in one column. For example, "The student will apply agency policy correctly in eight out of ten intake applications." This sets a minimum standard to strive for and makes it quite easy for both field instructor and student to assess the learner's pro-

gress in achieving the objective. Most adult learners welcome clearly expressed expectations and standards against which they can measure themselves so that they are not totally dependent upon feedback from others to tell them how they are doing.

Each objective also contains a definite time frame: The student must attain the desired level of skill by the end of the field placement. However, additional dates may be used as markers along the way as the student gradually increases his skill. Perhaps he will be able to achieve part of the overall objective by November, most of it by February and all of it by May.

Another approach is to state the learning objective in rather general terms and specify the desired outcome in the assessment column. When evaluatory methods are applied, what results or outcome must be present to tell us that the student has achieved the desired degree of competence in the stated objective? For example, the student's intake applications may be reviewed to determine his ability to apply agency policy correctly, but what outcome, results or findings will indicate that he has the desired skill level? Answer: "Eight out of ten applications will be done in accordance with agency policy when reviewed by the field instructor" (or whatever standard is set by field instructor and student).

The following example of a basic educational contract regarding "confrontation" defines the desired satisfactory skill level for the student in question but does not describe unsatisfactory or outstanding performance. There are some undefined terms in the degree-of-skill column. However, the assessment/measurement column is quite specific, although it calls for some professional judgment on the part of the supervisor.

Another example is the following rather complex contract concerning "Professional Work Habits." The area in which skill or knowledge is required: "The student will display appropriate professional work habits while in field placement." The "satisfactory" level is considered minimally acceptable for a newly graduating BSW or MSW student. The first column regarding subskills breaks the broad objective down into its various components (personal appearance, attendance, punctuality, and so forth), and other columns present specific illustrations of behavioral expectations at the satisfactory, outstanding, and unsatisfactory levels. The assessment column lists methods the supervisor will use to measure the student's level of performance for each of the various subobjectives. Thus, several persons could observe a given student's performance and arrive at a basically similar rating and assessment, using the criteria presented in this contract.

Most field instructors cannot expect to do so complex a breakdown of performance expectations with every student or every aspect of a given student's learning experience. However, the Level IV concept can be implemented on a much simpler scale through oral discussions or even by assigning the task as a learning experience by having the

*See Chapters 9 and 10 for further discussion of measurement/assessment tools and techniques.

Example of an Educational Contract Regarding "Confrontation"

The following contract sets goals for an MSW student at the point of graduation (or completion of the final field placement). It was developed with input of ideas from seven field instructors representing four different settings. This example is not intended as an ideal or recommended standard, merely an example of the thinking of several field instructors.

Skill	Degree of Skill	Learning Experiences	Assessment/ Measurement
CONFRONTATION Definition: questioning or challenging facts, defenses, feelings, and client perceptions. Spot-lighting or calling attention to these things. The skill requires some conscious assertive behavior on the part of the social worker.	1. Will be able to recognize therapeutically when confrontation should and should not be used. 2. Will internalize recognition that confrontation is an effective treatment technique when used appropriately. 3. Will recognize his own reaction/feelings to using confrontation. 4. Will seek supervision for help with feelings that might interfere with effective use of confrontation. 5. Will be able to anticipate client reactions to use of confrontation. 6. Will be able to confront clients with both concrete and non-concrete (emotional/behavioral) material. 7. Will be able to explain and defend conscious, purposeful use of confrontation. 8. Will be able to distinguish between confrontation as used in personal, interprofessional, and client interactions. 9. Will be able to confront through the use of	1. Assign clients with the following characteristics: manipulative, sophisticated re the system, using resistance or denial as a defense, angry, using projection, non-verbal. 2. Role-play the use of confrontation with field instructor. 3. Role model—when field instructor or student uses confrontation in their relationship, point it out and discuss how it was used and the results. 4. Observe others using confrontation effectively in interactions with clients, other professionals, at meetings, etc. 5. See videotapes (hear audiotapes) of skillful counselors using confrontation. 6. Do reading on the use of confrontation. 7. Talk with student re his feelings about confrontation, based on his past experiences with and exposure to it.	1. Have student explain why he did or did not use confrontation in his process recordings, audio or visual tapes, self-reports on interviews, etc. 2. The following kinds of client responses as seen in process recordings, taped interviews, or observation could indicate effective use of confrontation: surprise, silence, defensiveness, anger, outpouring of emotions, agreement, joint resolution of something, relief. 3. Six out of ten interviews where confrontation should have been used will show the responses listed above. 4. In six out of ten instances where confrontation should not be used, the student will use other techniques/responses instead. 5. Direct observation of student interviews will show that when student uses confrontation, he will use constructive facial expressions and body language, will not become defensive if client becomes defensive; will not raise his voice in anger; will not retreat from his confrontative response when he shouldn't if chal-

Skill	Degree of Skill	Learning Experiences	Assessment/Measurement
	direct verbal behavior as well as nonverbal communication.		lenged by client; will not become passive-aggressive in response to client's reaction to his use of confrontation. In six out of ten observed interviews in which confrontation is used, the above negative responses will be absent.

Expectations for BSWs would be different from those for MSWs in the "Degree of Skill" area. The BSW would not be expected to internalize completely the conviction that confrontation is an effective technique—they may still have some doubts upon graduation. The BSW should be able to use confrontation to confront clients with inconsistencies regarding concrete needs and areas but would not be expected to do so with emotional areas or patterns of client behavior. The BSW should know when to confront and when not to confront and know when to put a cap on the client's response. The BSW should know when he lacks skills to deal with client's response to use of confrontation. However, he should be able to use other techniques to close any Pandora's boxes that he opens for the client emotionally through his use of confrontation.

Level IV—Formal Educational Contract Regarding Professional Work Habits

Subskills/Knowledge Necessary to Learn or Do the Identified Skill (Prerequisites)	Experiences to Help Student Learn the Objective	Level or Degree of Skill/ Knowledge Student Must Achieve to Be Considered "Satisfactory"
1. GENERAL NEATNESS	1. Student will share a work area with others; will have his own desk.	1. Student need not be an especially neat worker, but neatness creates a good impression; most of the "mess" on his desk should consist of papers and items related to work.
2. PERSONAL APPEARANCE	2. Give assignments that put student in personal contact with clients, staff, others; read or think about the effect of worker appearance on inter-relationships.	2. Student expresses his individuality through style of dress and appearance and may occasionally stretch the limits somewhat in respect to good taste or appropriateness. However, it never presents a problem in relating to colleagues or clients, and questionable matters are quickly corrected.

student develop some aspects of a contract himself. If a trainee is having rather serious problems in one or two areas of performance, a formal contract containing behavioral objectives can be a crucial part of the learning experience, and the performance evaluation process can be designed to help field instructor and student define together exactly how much improvement is necessary or what skill level must be attained before the student can be considered "satisfactory" in the areas in question. The final written evaluation will then hold no surprises for the student, even if it should indicate failure to attain the specified level of skill. Should the performance evaluation, subsequent recommendations, or assigned grade be challenged by the student, the written contract covering identified problem areas can prove very valuable in describing the supervisory approach used, the method of providing educational feedback and guidance to help the student overcome the problem, and the assessment criteria applied.

Table A (p. 297) is a self-instructional worksheet that can be used to practice developing Level IV contracts containing a statement of a learning objective; learning experiences to be provided; levels of skill for satisfactory, outstanding, and unsatisfactory ratings; and assessment methods that will be applied to determine the student's level of functioning. The form can also be used as a worksheet by student and field instructor when developing a contract together.

Instructions for Completing the Worksheet

1. Select the stage of student education you want to set a standard for (e.g. newly graduating MSW, BSW student at end of first field placement).

2. Decide whether your expectations will be based on classroom performance/knowledge only, on field placement only, or on a combination of the two.

3. Choose a knowledge/skill area to work on. The topic should be as specific as possible. For example, standard-setting for the ability to handle transference would be much easier to break down qualitatively than would the objective of being an "effective caseworker." The following examples of objectives are taken from handbooks and official publications of various schools of social work and may help

Level or Degree of Skill/Knowledge Student Must Achieve to Be Considered "Outstanding"	Level or Degree of Skill/Knowledge that Would Be Considered "Unsatisfactory"	What Methods Will Be Used to Measure or Assess Student Performance to Determine the Level at Which He Is Functioning?
1. Work area is neat, organized, and not an embarrassment to anyone.	1. Candy wrappers, soft drink bottles and cans, partly eaten snack foods, and similar items litter student's work area.	1. Direct observation; feedback from others who share student's work area; presence or absence of odors, insects, etc.
2. Always dresses appropriately to agency and clients it serves. There is never any question re student's attire or appearance.	2. Student's style of dress is not in step with other employees in the agency (or fellow students) and field instructor has received negative feedback from staff, clients, or others. Appearance may be poor because of lack of cleanliness; poor taste; sloppiness (e.g. a roll of fat hanging out between shirt and pants, thongs on dirty feet); dress inappropriate to the setting (i.e. much expensive jewelery, heavy makeup, and spike heels in rural poverty	2. Direct observation; feedback from others who come into contact with student; comparison of student's dress/appearance with that of other students and staff; look at student's ability to establish relationships—difficulties may or may not indicate that personal appearance is a factor.

(Continued)

Subskills/Knowledge Necessary to Learn or Do the Identified Skill (Prerequisites)	Experiences to Help Student Learn the Objective	Level or Degree of Skill/ Knowledge Student Must Achieve to Be Considered "Satisfactory"
3. ATTENDANCE	3. Require sign-in book; let him schedule appointments on his own so that he experiences direct feedback or consequences of missed/late appointments. Give sufficient work so that student would fall behind if absences were excessive.	3. Calls in when absent, keeps supervisor informed of late arrivals or irregularities in work schedule, without supervisor's having to ask each time. Absence or tardiness usually occurs for obviously valid reasons, and does not exceed two days per semester except in unusual circumstances (death in family, etc.)
4. ADHERENCE TO REQUIRED WORK HOURS	4. Give full experience with plenty to keep student productively busy. Offer extra experiences if student is interested (but do not require them.)	4. Puts in the required number of hours in field for the entire semester (quarter/year). Makes up missed time when required; may stay late or put in extra hours when suggested by field instructor, but rarely initiates staying late, taking work home, or doing extra work.
5. PUNCTUALITY	5. (Same as for #3)	5. Occasionally misses deadlines or fails to keep appointments on time, but this is the exception and does not interfere with overall performance.
6. PRESENTATION OF WRITTEN ASSIGNMENTS	6. Require written reports; give assignments where various things must be organized.	6. Work may vary in degree of organization, thoroughness, and legibility, but it almost always meets requirements.
7. USE OF TIME	7. Give sufficient work that if student spent too much time in inappropriate activities it would interfere with ability to get the work done.	7. May occasionally take longer than the allotted time for breaks, lunch. May make and receive personal phone calls and spend field placement time chatting, reading, or doing classroom work. However, these activities are not highly noticeable and do not interfere with student's "satisfactory" performance of field work. Student may or may not let

Level or Degree of Skill/ Knowledge Student Must Achieve to Be Considered "Outstanding"	Level or Degree of Skill/ Knowledge That Would Be Considered "Unsatisfactory"	What Methods Will Be Used to Measure or Assess Student Performance to Determine the Level at Which He Is Functioning?
	program requiring frequent home visits).	
3. Always keeps supervisor informed of irregularities in work schedule. Initiates a plan for making up missed time. Absence and tardiness are due to obviously valid reasons (but more than a minor cold). Student is almost never absent or late.	3. Student is late or absent one out of every three field placement days or is absent/ late less frequently, but consistently offers inadequate or questionable explanations. The field instructor frequently feels that the student could have attended or come on time had he/she really wanted to.	3. Student will sign in and out at the end of each day and/or keep a daily log of time spent in field. Feedback from clerical staff and others who may wonder where student is, notice irregularities in schedule, or have difficulty locating him.
4. Student often comes early, stays late, puts in extra time, takes work home, and may even come to field on nonscheduled days—all at his own initiative. Student often takes on extra work, knowing he'll have to put in extra time to get the added experiences.	4. Problems with attendance, absences and/or irregular hours make it difficult for student to put in the required total number of hours. Student is a "clockwatcher" and resists staying late or making arrangements to make up lost time, even when encouraged to do so by supervisor.	4. Direct observation; feedback from others who notice student's presence or absence during or after normal hours; student's log of hours in field; volume of work student produces (in combination with other factors).
5. Never misses a deadline except in most unusual circumstances; follows instructions very independently.	5. Consistently misses deadlines, fails to follow instructions, procrastinates on turning work in, misses or "forgets" appointments.	5. Direct experience of the field instructor; feedback from others.
6. Can be counted on always to turn in work that is well organized, neat, and thorough.	6. Consistently turns in work that is illegible, incomplete, or disorganized so that complete revision/rewriting is necessary to make it usable.	6. Direct observation; feedback from others.
7. May occasionally take longer than the allotted time for breaks, lunch. May make and receive personal phone calls and spend field placement time chatting, reading, or doing classroom work. However, these activities are not noticeable and do not interfere with student's ability to complete field assignments on time. As student's performance is actu-	7. Consistently takes longer than the allotted time for breaks, lunches. Spends field time reading newspapers or non-work-related materials; chats about nonschool activities with fellow students/ staff to the point that others wonder how he/she finds time to do his work. Makes lengthy and frequent personal phone calls during field placement time.	7. Ease with which student completes assignments satisfactorily and on time; direct observation; feedback from others.

(Continued)

Subskills/Knowledge Necessary to Learn or Do the Identified Skill (Prerequisites)	Experiences to Help Student Learn the Objective	Level or Degree of Skill/ Knowledge Student Must Achieve to Be Considered "Satisfactory"
		field instructor know when he doesn't have enough to do—is apt to use the time for classroom assignments or chatting with fellow students.
8. RESPONSIBILITY	8. Let student borrow things; give him responsibility without always checking up after him or intervening to rescue from irresponsible behavior.	8. Student occasionally (an exception) forgets to return something or needs reminders to follow through with something, but student responds to field instructor's reminders and corrects the problem so that only occasional lapses occur. Student is generally reliable and responsible.
9. RESPECT FOR CLIENTS	9. Give direct client contact or let him read confidential records and related materials.	9. Talks about his clients with obvious respect for them as persons, though there may be some joking and "letting off steam" with fellow students/ staff. While an occasional remark may seem questionable, there is never any doubt about the student's basic respect for the people he is working with (clients or large-system personnel).

Level or Degree of Skill/ Knowledge Student Must Achieve to Be Considered "Outstanding"	Level or Degree of Skill/ Knowledge That Would Be Considered "Unsatisfactory"	What Methods Will Be Used to Measure or Assess Student Performance to Determine the Level at Which He Is Functioning?
ally "outstanding" in many areas, supervisor is not concerned with occasional liberties. If student doesn't have enough to do, he'll notify field instructor rather than spend the free time in nonfield activities.	May do classroom work during field while field assignments are not being done in a timely, acceptable fashion.	
8. Student almost never loses things or forgets to do things. Student develops a reputation that "no matter what, he will be responsible about things." The student can be told to do something and the field instructor can forget about it—it will get done. He never has to check up behind the student to see if he is following through. The student's pattern of extreme reliability is broken only under unusual circumstances: getting sick on the job, extreme personal crisis, etc.	8. Student is consistently unreliable. Fails to return library books even after several reminders; forgets to turn light out or lock office door; doesn't always follow through with assignments; loses things; and so forth.	8. Feedback from others; direct experience of field instructor.
9. Student seems almost "superhuman" in that he will never joke about a client or talk disrespectfully of someone he serves. (there may be a fine line between indicating a rigid, overly controlled person who is unable to relax and use normal ways of releasing job tension, and indicating a mature individual who is unusually professional).	9. Student is overheard talking disrespectfully of clients; making fun of them and their problems; overdramatizing and clearly getting some kind of personal satisfaction out of discussing gory details about personal problems of his clients. This behavior is usually seen in conversations with students/staff, but field instructor wonders if confidentiality violations and unprofessionalism are also being carried outside the field placement.	9. Feedback from others; direct observation.

in selecting a topic. Notice that some of them are quite broad while others are more specific:

Display understanding of human behavior

Be able to manage daily work load

Be able to write an effective diagnostic statement

Get a group organized

Do social work recording in agency records

Show identity with social work as a profession

Use supervision appropriately

Develop a working knowledge of community resources

Prepare a departmental budget

Be skillful in the use of empathy in casework relationships

Be able to recognize and effectively handle transference

Display a nonjudgmental attitude

Have knowledge of basic interviewing skills

Be able to communicate complex concepts and ideas clearly and succinctly

Be able to ''start where the client is''

Be able to work independently

Have knowledge of defense mechanisms

Be able to attend a community meeting and effectively analyze the politics of the meeting

Use interpretation effectively

Make conscious and effective use of self in interpersonal relationships

4. Write the broad objective topic you have chosen at the top of the worksheet.

5. Fill in each of the columns, working from left to right. Work all five columns for each subskill entered in the first column.

The Checklist for Determining Level of Interviewing Skill that appears on pages 144–149 is a detailed listing of characteristics that distinguish beginning from more advanced students. It is one way of describing end competences behaviorally. A contract could be built around the objective that the student would achieve the skills listed in the right-hand column with a specified frequency.

See Appendix E, page 297, for Table A: Level IV

Written Contract—Worksheet for use in completing the exercise described above.

Table B describes personal characteristics that characterize unsatisfactory, satisfactory, and outstanding students in a medical setting. It was compiled by the author in consultation with department staff attending a course on field instruction. Participants mentally reviewed the evaluations they had assigned students in recent years and concluded that, in this particular field placement setting, certain qualities tended to distinguish the three levels of performance. Field instructors and supervisors employed in a different setting may or may not agree with these expectations; the list given here is not intended to present a standard that all field instructors, schools, or agencies must adopt but, rather, illustrates the thinking process that schools and student supervisors must undertake in the process of setting standards and expectations.

There are certain personal attributes and qualities that characterize the outstanding as against the satisfactory or unsatisfactory student regardless of the level of training. Of course, no student will be either outstanding or unsatisfactory in all areas. In order to warrant an ''outstanding'' or ''unsatisfactory'' rating, the attributes listed must *predominate,* form a pattern, and exist in the most important areas of functioning. That is, a student could be ''unsatisfactory'' for a brief period in one of the less important items and still warrant an overall rating of ''satisfactory'' or better. Likewise, the satisfactory student very often is outstanding in several areas and perhaps marginal in others, but with ''satisfactory'' performance predominating.

If a listing of performance expectations is shared with students at the beginning of placement, it can serve as a part of the educational contract. It can also permit the student to decide consciously which level of performance he wishes to strive for. He also knows exactly what he is being evaluated against and exactly what is required in order to earn a certain rating. If such a listing of expectations can be adopted by an entire school faculty or group of agency staff, it can lead to increased consistency in evaluations and assignment of ratings.

Individual field instructors, or an entire agency, may want to develop standardized minimum skill/performance

Table B. Characteristics of Outstanding, Satisfactory, and Unsatisfactory Student Performance

Outstanding	Satisfactory	Unsatisfactory
1. Consistently takes work home; asks to come in at off hours; volunteers to take on extra experiences, knowing that he will have to put in extra hours. (Note: some students have personal situations that do not permit working extra hours, and they should not be penalized because of this.)	May occasionally stay late to finish something, but this is the exception rather than the rule; may occasionally take work home; does what he and field instructor plan with full enthusiasm, but does not usually seek out extra experiences that would require additional time.	Puts in extra hours because he works slowly or inefficiently in completing assignments; or tries to short-cut hours by lengthening lunch breaks, coming in late, going home early, etc. Quite often resists staying late and may become defensive when asked to do so. Does not see the occasional need for remaining late as part of the basic job of of a professional social worker.
2. Aggressively seeks field instructor out—does not wait for supervisor to come to him all the time. Consistently asks questions, expresses opinions, even if in disagreement with the field instructor. Consistently brings up new things for discussion in supervisory conferences and forces the field instructor to work hard to keep up.	Seeks field instructor whenever needed, but if he is unavailable or does not respond, frequently stops trying. Welcomes the supervisor's reaching out to him to discuss things, but rarely initiates these contacts. May occasionally and temporarily react defensively to supervisory feedback.	Sometimes comes late for or misses supervisory sessions; usually comes unprepared, with nothing to present for discussion; may use the conference in a negative rather than a positive manner; consistently rather than occasionally reacts defensively to supervisory feedback.
3. Consistent, unsolicited, and very specifically positive comments come from other field instructors, interdisciplinary staff, clients, and others regarding the quality of the student's work, his personality, and so on.	Upon inquiry, field instructor will receive positive feedback regarding the student. There may be occasional unsolicited positive feedback as well. Feedback may also be absent, indicating the absence of problems or the absence of outstanding behavior.	Feedback, both solicited and unsolicited, is negative, or people are hesitant to comment regarding the student. The student's interactions with others cause problems for them, which the field instructor hears about as a result.
4. When the student leaves placement, other social workers, members of other disciplines, and others comment on how much they miss him and why and describe what he contributed while he was there. This is usually unsolicited.	When the student leaves, people notice that he is gone but do not usually specify how and why they miss him or comment specifically on his contributions. There may be an absence of comments when the student leaves.	People express relief that the student is gone. There may also be a total absence of unsolicited feedback. A flood of "I never told you about this, but while that student was here, we had these problems..." may come forth. When a new student is assigned to the same area, people may compare him favorably with the previous student: "He sure is a lot better than that last one we had—don't send us any more like that!"
5. The student does some-	The student has had a definite	The student leaves behind a

(Continued)

Table B. (*cont.*)

Outstanding	Satisfactory	Unsatisfactory
thing, brings about a change, or has an impact that continues to affect the department or the agency after he has left the scene.	impact on individuals served, but does not ordinarily make any special impact on the department or setting that remains after he has left.	negative impact that requires time and effort on the part of the staff or the field instructor to resolve or remove.
6. The student seems always to be present and never absent except for obvious illness or unusual personal crises. The student may come to field placement when obviously ill or take work home when he should be staying in bed instead. This student will initiate, without supervisory suggestion, a plan for making up lost time, not because it is required, but because he wants to be able to complete his work and continue his learning experience without disrupting service to his clients or others with whom he is working.	The student is occasionally absent, but not in excess of the maximum absences permitted by the school. When excess absences do occur, it is because of unusual circumstances and with good cause. The student makes up lost time and plans this with the field instructor. He does this willingly.	There are many absences with questionable explanations and excuses. The absences interfere with the continuity of the student's learning experience, and the field instructor feels frustrated for lack of time to teach the student what he needs to learn and because of problems that come up with his work in his absence. This student may also resist making up lost time. (On the other hand, an otherwise satisfactory student may be absent for extensive time periods due to genuine, uncontrollable emergencies or illness.)
7. The student is emotionally stable and mature in his response to stress except perhaps in highly unusual situations. This student is known for his even temper, good disposition, common sense, and ability to handle stress. He may have personal problems that temporarily affect field placement performance and may or may not get outside counseling. However, these are very temporary and do not affect adversely the clients being served or the student's overall performance.	The student is emotionally stable and mature in his response to stress except perhaps in highly unusual situations. He may have personal problems that temporarily affect field placement performance and may or may not get outside counseling. However, these are temporary and do not affect adversely the clients being served or the student's overall performance.	The student has emotional or personal problems that affect field placement performance. These may be situational or chronic, and the student may or may not get professional counseling. In any event, the problem continues to have an adverse effect on field placement performance, severely handicapping the student's functioning. The difficulties may be sufficiently severe to require intervention for the protection of clients, the student, or others.
8. The student recognizes that he cannot serve all people equally effectively and has awareness of personal limitations and biases. However, he is virtually always able to control and channel any less-than-positive feelings toward clients or others so that they do not affect adversely his working relationships or his	May occasionally fail to use the best or most effective approach with some individuals or situations. He may even feel uncomfortable with and reject or be biased toward certain clients. However, any effect on the client is extremely temporary and quickly remedied through the casework relationship or the skills of the	The student's approach to clients actually harms them emotionally as a result of prejudicial attitudes; inappropriate advice-giving; unusually cold, rejecting, or punitive approach; etc. The student may or may not agree that this behavior exists and is creating a problem. Such behavior occurs as a pattern

Table B. (*cont.*)

Outstanding	Satisfactory	Unsatisfactory
treatment activities. The student's approach consistently facilitates growth, relationships, and positive outcomes, even with difficult situations and individuals whom most social workers would find "unlikable," "incorrigible," or "untreatable."	student. These are isolated incidents in an otherwise benign or constructive relationship or otherwise effective performance.	and typifies the student's relationships and interactions with people.
9. Very <u>rarely</u> becomes defensive in response to constructive criticism from the supervisor. Will almost always directly voice differences of opinion with the field instructor rather than engage in indirect verbalizations, avoidance, or projection.	May <u>occasionally</u> become somewhat defensive or resistant to constructive criticism from the field instructor, but the response usually does not last long and is not typical of the student's normal behavior. It does not affect the working relationship with the supervisor.	Cannot accept helpful, constructive criticism. <u>Often</u> becomes defensive, dissolves into tears, leaves the room, engages in passive-aggressive behavior or other responses that make it extremely difficult for the field instructor to teach and deal directly with the issues involved.
10. <u>Always</u> follows through. The field instructor can give an assignment and literally forget about it, knowing that the student will follow through without reminder. The individual is known for always getting things in on time no matter what happens.	Occasionally procrastinates or avoids certain experiences, but consistently follows through with assignments in a timely fashion. Occasional reminders may be needed for some assignments to ensure their completion on time.	Consistently fails to complete assignments on time. Does not turn in recording or does so only after much procrastination and frequent reminders and imposition of deadlines; may avoid seeing clients. Especially resists turning in work that would enable the supervisor to evaluate his performance.
11. Forms casework relationships quickly and effectively and seems to get results that even "some of our regular staff cannot get." Successfully handles unusually difficult presenting problems, e.g. a phone call to a patient who has left the hospital against medical advice or the patient who refuses to talk to anyone. Uses some of the more difficult counseling techniques, such as confrontation, effectively and handles transference and countertransference rather than avoiding it. The supervisor sometimes says to himself, "I don't think I could have done a better job than my student with that situation."	Forms relationships effectively, and the field instructor can see client growth and movement as a result of the student's efforts. He may do well with an occasional difficult client, but this does not typify the student's experience. On the other hand, there may be a few situations where minimum client growth occurs and the field instructor feels that if he himself were serving the individual, he might have been able to bring about a different outcome.	Has great difficulty in forming relationships and working with clients in treatment. The field instructor can see very little movement or growth as a result of the student's efforts. The student may actually harm his clients through his approach. It often appears that there are no changes in the client's situation, with or without student intervention. Such behavior and outcomes typify the student's performance.

(*Continued*)

Table B.   *(cont.)*

Outstanding	Satisfactory	Unsatisfactory
12. The student seems comfortable with authority figures. He is able to see them as people as well as authority figures. He seeks out contacts with authority figures at various levels. Has respect for them but little fear. He may even disagree with top-level authority figures to their face (in a positive, constructive, professional manner).	Student is somewhat fearful of administration and may tend to avoid top-level authority figures. His discomfort is not necessarily due to negative attitudes, but simply lack of experience in interacting with these individuals and lack of internalization of the realization that they are people as well as authority figures. Student may welcome contacts with authority figures when arranged by supervisor but will experience some anxiety.	Student has negative feelings toward authority figures, which causes him to avoid interaction with them or results in negative, defensive, nonconstructive interactions. This typifies the student's response to authority figures.
13. Student conducts himself in a very businesslike manner (without being told) and is very professional at all times. Because of this, along with his personal maturity, he becomes an unofficial "leader" whom other students look up to and go to for peer consultation.	The student is usually businesslike in his behavior and approach. He may not be the neatest, most organized worker, but this does not negatively affect his performance or generate complaints. He conducts himself in a mature and businesslike manner most of the time.	Student's work habits are offensive to others. The work area may be littered with candy wrappers and soda cans, even after reminders to correct the problem. This student may have a loud voice, use offensive language, conduct himself "like a bull in a china shop," be consistently impatient and complaining, and perhaps dress inappropriately—to the point that others notice the behavior and complain. Interpersonal relationships are adversely affected by the student's lack of professionalism and businesslike behavior.
14. The student consistently writes clearly, concisely, and professionally. Even if he does not really know his subject well, written reports will be so well done that the opposite impression is given. Not only is the student's communication acceptable, but the supervisor experiences real pride when reports go outside the department and may even think to himself, "I wish our staff could communicate as well as my student!" The student may be producing an unusually high volume of work through his ability to write quickly and effectively.	Student does not use perfect English but can organize his thoughts in a logical manner, spelling most common words correctly and using grammar and sentence structure that facilitate, rather than hinder, the reader's understanding of what he is trying to say. The student takes an appropriate length of time to complete written assignments—work is turned in on time.	The student does not read, write, or communicate at a college level appropriate to the degree for which he is studying. He uses incomplete sentences, obvious misspellings, and awkward grammar that obscure the meaning of what he is trying to say. The student may use unprofessional language or laymen's terms instead of appropriate professional terminology. The field instructor shudders at the thought of this student's making entries in interdisciplinary records or sending reports to outside agencies. Many rewrites may be necessary

Table B. (*cont.*)

Outstanding	Satisfactory	Unsatisfactory
		before the student can produce an acceptable product, and he spends a disproportionate amount of time completing written assignments.
15. The student constantly asks questions, challenges concepts, and comes up with creative ideas, goals, or approaches. He wears the field instructor out. The supervisor may feel that his "brain is being picked clean" and has a difficult time keeping one step ahead of his student. The supervisor may even feel threatened on occasion by the student, who literally can do some things better than he. This student will not settle for routine or pat answers and constantly looks behind the obvious, seeking more subtle causes and explanations.	The student responds eagerly and openly to learning, although with some repetition of instructions needed. He asks questions, has an inquiring mind, and critically analyzes ideas and concepts. He may occasionally provide a real challenge to the field instructor with a questioning attitude, but this is not typical.	The student seems slow to learn. Instructions must be repeated over and over. He has difficulty with analytical kinds of thinking. He tends to be very concrete in his thinking process. The student does not appear very bright and is obviously having difficulty grasping academic and/or practice materials.
16. Student may occasionally complain or ventilate negative feelings but is very careful when, where, and to whom this is done. When this student has a gripe against someone or something, he is almost always able to share it constructively with the person involved or with an appropriate authority figure. He is consciously careful not to ventilate negative feelings in such a way that would affect others adversely. This student is very often looked up to by fellow students as a leader. They may ventilate their feelings to him and this student then provides guidance to help them deal with their feelings appropriately. This behind-the-scenes guidance often has a calming influence on other students.	The student has gripes and complaints and airs them, but does so as a ventilation device—he does not attempt to undermine the agency or the authority figure or whatever he is angry at. He does not try to convert others to his negative way of thinking. He may be consciously aware of the need to avoid negatively affecting others around him through inappropriate ventilation of feelings. On the other hand, he may keep quiet and not share his less-than-positive feelings with anyone.	This person is a troublemaker, constantly griping and aggressively trying to convert others to his negative way of thinking. He may even, openly or behind the scenes, attack the reputation, behavior, or competence of the field instructor or other staff members. This person seems to be all criticism with no constructive comments or suggestions. He will seek out indications of morale problems of other students and staff and then use this to encourage acting-out behavior and gain support for his own problems. He may review the work of other students and try to tell them that their field instructor does not know what he is doing, and so on.
17. The truly outstanding student will stand out. He may not be outstanding in every area of performance or knowl-	This student may be outstanding in some areas and marginal in a few minor areas but is not noticed for being unusually	The truly unsatisfactory student also stands out. He may be satisfactory in several areas or even outstanding in a few

(*Continued*)

Table B. (*cont.*)

Outstanding	Satisfactory	Unsatisfactory
edge, but his outstanding per- formance shows up virtually everywhere and simply cannot be overlooked.	good or for having unusual problems. He is a good, steady, solid, satisfactory. There is no need for negative feedback; on the other hand, highly out- standing performance is transitory or limited to only a few incidents or case situa- tions.	areas (such as being very bright, eager to learn, or writing well). However, the unsatisfactory part of his performance or behavior is so obvious and so all- emcompassing that it over- whelms everything else, and people usually know "that's a student who has problems."

expectations that would apply to every student in placement at a certain level. Field instructors could then concentrate on developing individualized contracts that build on these basic skills and address the specific student's educational needs and the kind of learning experiences available in the supervisor's area of assignment. This approach has several advantages. First, once the standardized material has been developed, individual field instructors need not repeat the thinking process for each contract. Copies can be given to the school, providing a picture of the kinds of expectations and experiences associated with a particular placement. With this information at hand, field instruction faculty can be highly selective in matching students with agencies. Copies can also be given to prospective students or those accepted for placement. This can facilitate the preplacement interview as well as the performance evaluation process. If all field instructors are in agreement regarding basic expectations and experiences, no individual supervisor will feel alone in imposing standards upon his student. The support of colleagues can be a very important factor if a field instructor finds his expectations challenged by a student or his school.

Level IV contracts may specify the degree of skill expected for students at various levels of training—end of first placement, at the point of graduation, BSW or MSW, and so on. It can be helpful for an individual student to see what level of skill he is expected to have acquired by the time he graduates. This sets an overall goal for him to strive toward and helps him assess his readiness for practice at the professional level upon graduation.

Field instructors commonly develop objectives in comparison with ultimate expectations. "Just how skillful must a student be in handling transference before I'd hire him to work in my mental health clinic? If he must have 'X' level of skill by the time he graduates, how far should he get by the end of his first placement?" It may take us ten days to drive from New York City to San Francisco, but how far should we be at the end of the fifth day if we expect to make it in ten days? Level IV contracts may specify interim time periods for achieving objectives. Some will take the whole quarter, semester, or year to achieve; others should be

reached midway through placement and form prerequisite stepping stones to the achievement of more complex objectives.

It is difficult for the average field instructor to develop Level IV contracts. Ideally, each school should have developed specific behavioral objectives specifying the degree of skill students in various concentrations must have before they are permitted to graduate. Field instructors would then be able to take these overall statements and convert them to individualized contracts for their students which would reflect the specific learning experiences available under their supervision. The educational objectives would be those stated by the school, with subobjectives and some specialized objectives added following discussion and negotiation with the student. Until schools actually begin functioning at Level IV, most field instructors will have great difficulty getting beyond Level III in their development of educational contracts.

Example of a Modified Level IV Contract for an Entire Field Experience (Casework)

The following educational contract was prepared by a field instructor and her graduate student.* The student is taking a special shortened MSW program and completed her first year of placement by being in field five days a week from June through August. She then took a regular second-year placement of three days a week from September through May—all under the same field instructor. The educational contract covers both placements and establishes goals that the student should attain by the end of her entire experience. She is studying casework and is placed in the medical social work department of a large hospital.

The contract is similar to the Level IV contract described earlier. However, this version omits the "assessment/measurement" column and instead breaks

---

*Special thanks to Jennifer Howells, formerly with Jackson Memorial Hospital and her Barry College student, Estrella P. Valdes, for sharing this comprehensive contract. It was developed in the summer of 1979.

down each objective into specific skills to be learned. Each objective is clearly stated, then described in some detail in the second column. A number of the specific skills to be learned are expressed behaviorally, and some incorporate the concept of degree or level of skill to be learned. Learning experiences are described, and several are quite creative, while others are obviously basic to the student's entire experience (such as reading and attending in-service training sessions). A few learning experiences appear somewhat unrelated to the objective or skills to be learned but obviously have some meaning to the student and field instructor. The "degree of skill" column is sometimes descriptive or repetitive rather than behaviorally specific in expressing the exact level of competence the student must attain. At any rate, many hours of work went into producing this contract, and it goes far beyond what the average field instructor would be expected to do. In reality most supervisors and their students might develop a Level IV contract around just one of the objectives listed in this example or might develop

a contract to deal with a particular problem area that crops up during placement.

This contract example presents a very comprehensive picture of the kinds of activities the student will be involved with and also illustrates the kind of supervision she will be receiving and the approach of her field instructor. It provides a clear road map for the student's educational experience. Some phrases may be unclear to others who read the material, but they obviously have a very specific meaning to the student and her supervisor. The contract has been shared with the school and will undoubtedly prove helpful to it in presenting a picture of the kinds of learning experiences available in this particular setting and under the direction of this particular field instructor. One can also see that the supervisor's task in evaluating the student's performance will be facilitated by the existence of this contract, against which she can measure the student's progress. It is written in such a way that the student can also monitor her own progress in achieving identified goals.

Objective	Skills to Be Learned	Experiences to Learn Skills	Degree of Skill
I. Be able to identify social worker's role and function in the medical setting.	1. Be able to identify what a social worker does in: —Medical Division— general floors —Maternal/child division —Renal dialysis area 2. Be able to explain social worker's role in the discharge planning process. 3. Be able to explain social worker's role in assisting patient in understanding his illness. 4. Be able to explain interdisciplinary approach to patient care. 5. Be able to explain the role of co-professionals and identify when it is appropriate to utilize each discipline (e.g. psychi-	1. Observation of field instructor: (a) counseling patient and family (b) advocating for the patient (c) educating patient, family, hospital staff (d) referring patient and family for services (e) manipulating the patient's environment. 2. Interview social workers in different divisions in the Social Work Department (e.g. maternal/child, medical and renal dialysis). 3. Read the JMH Social Service Procedure Manual; read articles related to the medical social worker's role and function; read our department's job description for social	1. By the end of placement, be able to verbalize and/or put in writing to the field instructor, specific statements demonstrating knowledge of the role and function of social workers in: Adult medical service, Renal dialysis and Maternal/Child division. 2. Be able to verbalize both to the field instructor and to members of other disciplines the appropriate functions and role(s) of a medical social worker in several patient situations that have been referred to the student. 3. Be able to explain to the field instructor which interdisciplinary team member(s) are, will be, or have been utilized

(Continued)

Objective	Skills to Be Learned	Experiences to Learn Skills	Degree of Skill
	atric nurse, psychiatrist, dietician, nurse, physician, discharge planning nurse, consulting physicians).	work staff. 4. Observe interdisciplinary rounds in several areas and discuss them with field instructor. 5. Process-record several interviews with members of other disciplines.	in each case situation, and the reason for involving them. 4. Be able to participate in interdisciplinary rounds. Ask appropriate questions of co-professionals representing various disciplines and take notes.
II. Be able to understand and use diagnostic skills, to design intervention plans, and to implement treatment plans.	1. Be able to establish a relationship and conduct an interview with client (and/or family) and do it in such a way that the patient feels free to reveal deep feelings should he desire to do so. 2. Be able to make descriptive statements of the patient (and/or family) and his situation. 3. Be able to follow a specific process when assigned a new case: review the medical chart, read about the kind of illness the patient has, interview patient/family, respond to the referring consult, take action, enter progress notes into the medical chart, keep members of other disciplines informed of social work activity both orally and in writing and as often as needed, write a closing summary, and close the case via the standard procedure as outlined in the department's procedure manual.	Skill #1—Establish a relationship 1. Interview and process-record interactions with a variety of patients/families (age, race, sex). 2. Discuss interactions with clients with the field instructor. 3. Solicit feedback from others (including the patient on occasion) on "how I am coming across." 4. Observe the field instructor establishing a relationship with a client. 5. Observe interviews conducted by other social workers. 6. Interview voluntary and nonvoluntary clients. 7. Do related reading. Skill #2—Gain ability to make descriptive statements 1. Observe client and	Skill #1—Establish a relationship 1. Be able to assess expressed and unexpressed needs of clients and to determine if client should be brought into a relationship. This will be done with each patient who is interviewed. 2. Be able to establish a relationship with virtually every client. Skill #2—Gain ability to make descriptive statements 1. Be able to relay

Objective	Skills to Be Learned	Experiences to Learn Skills	Degree of Skill
	4. Be able to identify major defense mechanisms used by clients to cope with stress and to recognize when the defenses are inappropriate for the situation the patient is facing.	record facts in process-recordings. 2. Relay facts and feelings of patient and significant others to the field instructor.	accurate factual information regarding a client's situation in four out of five situations. This information will be relayed orally and in process and medical record recording.
	5. Be able to identify and use eight interview techniques.	3. Interview client jointly with field instructor and describe client's situation to supervisor.	2. Be able to relay accurate factual information gained from a majority of meetings attended.
	6. Be able to identify advanced casework techniques and to provide service to clients whose primary concern centers on emotional/relationship problems.	4. Discuss "information-seeking skills" used in process-recordings and be able to indicate to the field instructor those situations where student gained information as a result of using these skills in interviews.	
	7. Generally strive for and gain lack of prejudice.		
	8. Gain confidence in ability to make diagnostic statements in retrospect and while counseling is occurring, and be able consciously to select and apply appropriate responses.	5. Observe a role-played interview with other students and describe what happened in the interview. 6. Relay facts and information from unit and staff meetings to the supervisor and others.	
	9. Be able to formulate a treatment plan.		
		Skill #3—Follow a specific process when assigned new cases	Skill #3—Follow a specific process when assigned new cases
		1. Receive several case assignments requiring the use of this process.	1. Be able to identify and use the process independent of field instructor input by the end of placement. This will occur with each new case assigned.
		2. Discuss process with field instructor on a regular basis.	
		3. Read the section pertaining to these	

(Continued)

Objective	Skills to Be Learned	Experiences to Learn Skills	Degree of Skill
		procedures in the procedure manual for the department. 4. Participate in inservice training sessions concerning this process. 5. Utilize clerical expertise to assist in following proper procedures for closing cases. Skill #4—Identify major defense mechanisms 1. Read on defense mechanisms. 2. Gain information from field instructor about defense mechanisms. 3. Label defense mechanisms in process-recording. 4. Identify with the field instructor what appear to be healthy and unhealthy defense mechanisms. 5. Observe interviews and/or group sessions in action and identify possible defense mechanisms that are exhibited. These will be identified through discussion with the field instructor. Skill #5—Identify and use eight interview techniques Note: These interview techniques will include:	Skill #4—Identify major defense mechanisms 1. Be able to identify eight of the most common defense mechanisms and to label three out of four accurately in process recordings and/or observed interviews/ group sessions. Skill #5—Identify and use eight interview techniques 1. Be able to define these skills in dis-

Objective	Skills to Be Learned	Experiences to Learn Skills	Degree of Skill
		empathy advice vs. information giving acceptance clarification interpretation confrontation reflection starting where the client is	cussions with field instructor. 2. Be able to use each skill with comfort. 3. Be able to identify each time these skills are used by labeling them in all process-recordings. 4. Be able to identify, in one process-recording, at least two situations where a particular interviewing skill should have been used instead of the one actually used.
		1. Read on these interview techniques. 2. Discuss with field instructor the use of these techniques. 3. Observe supervisor and other staff using these skills. 4. Use role-playing (video tape if available) with other students. 5. Label these techniques in process recordings.	

		Skill #6—Identify advanced casework techniques
		
		1. Obtain a social history on each patient seen.
		
		2. Read about each of the casework techniques listed below.
		
		3. Practice and discuss with the field instructor the use of each of the following casework techniques:
		
		  history-taking
		  handling transference and countertransference
		  knowing when to put the lid on
			Skill #6—Identify advanced casework techniques
			
			1. Be able to identify at least one situation where techniques listed in experience #3 were consciously and effectively used by the student.

(Continued)

Objective	Skills to Be Learned	Experiences to Learn Skills	Degree of Skill
		effective use of silence reality testing focusing the interview provision of positive experiences for patient/family limit—setting contracting summarization use of termination	
		4. Counsel at least one patient/family on a long—term basis (at least 8 months).	
		5. Observe the field instructor and other staff using these casework techniques.	
		6. Participate in in—service training sessions on these techniques.	
		Skill #7—Lack of prejudice	Skill #7—Lack of prejudice
		1. Discuss with field instructor conscious awareness of personal values and those of client.	1. Identify feelings of client and respond nonjudgmentally a majority of the time.
		2. Read about and discuss with field instructor cultural beliefs and their effect on the client (the culture of poverty as well as ethnic culture).	2. Describe the effect of cultural influences accurately in at least two patient situations.
		3. Work with a variety of patients/families and practice the principle "begin where the client is."	3. Identify the principle of "beginning where the client is" in three process recordings.
		4. Label the above principle when it occurs in process—recordings.	

Objective	Skills to Be Learned	Experiences to Learn Skills	Degree of Skill
		5. Participate in in-service training sessions related to this skill.	
		Skill #8—Confidence in ability to make diagnostic statements	Skill #8—Confidence in ability to make diagnostic statements
		1. Use of process-recording.	1. By the end of placement, will be able to identify, with the field instructor, 3 to 5 situations where assessment and immediate appropriate response was used during the interview. These situations will be reflected in process recordings or client interviews.
		2. Verbal processing of cases with field instructor.	
		3. Use of tape recording.	
		4. Participation in departmental in-service training.	
		5. Observation of field instructor and other staff social workers.	
		6. Reading on human behavior and related material concerning psychosis, neurosis, psychosomatic disorders, and personality disorders.	
		7. Read and understand defense mechanisms and discuss them with the field instructor.	
		Skill #9—Formulate a treatment plan	Skill #9—Formulate a treatment plan
		1. Interview a variety of patients with similar and dissimilar psychosocial characteristics.	1. By the end of placement, the student will be able to identify treatment plans and develop them independent of the field instructor, on a consistent basis.
		2. Discuss client situations and proposed treatment plans	

(*Continued*)

Objective	Skills to Be Learned	Experiences to Learn Skills	Degree of Skill
		with the field instructor.	
		3. Read articles on emotional reactions to various illnesses; defense mechanisms; and normal and abnormal behavior.	
		4. Obtain a list of community resources.	
		5. Write out goals for provision of both concrete and counseling services to patients/families.	
		6. Participate in diagnostic thinking and Analytical Thinking Model training and write a treatment plan as part of this training.	
III. Develop an understanding of medical conditions and medical terminology.	1. Be able to identify major illnesses common to adult medical floors (including physical limitations as a result of the illness, prognosis, and general treatment): TB alcoholism diabetes high blood pressure cancer congestive heart failure 2. Be able to use common medical terminology and abbreviations.	1. Read material in the social service library on illnesses, including the psychosocial component. 2. Read the manual of medical abbreviations. 3. Discuss illness with physicians, nurses, and members of other medical disciplines, both in interdisciplinary rounds and individually. 4. Interview the field instructor to get information about some terms that are used. 5. Review medical charts. 6. Participate in hospital in-service training sessions.	1. Be able to identify four major medical illnesses common to the adult areas and to give treatment, prognosis, and psychosocial components. 2. Be able to understand and use many medical abbreviations by the end of placement. 3. Review each patient's medical chart and, by the end of placement; be able to elicit disease and current proposed treatment from reading the chart.

Objective	Skills to Be Learned	Experiences to Learn Skills	Degree of Skill
IV. Be able to discuss delicate topics and see patients who are ill. The student will do this with occasional discomfort.	1. Be able to see/help patients and their families who experience physically/emotionally disabling illness. For example: TB patient who must be institutionalized dying patient dealing with sexual adjustments necessitated by illness tracheostomy patient patient who is in pain patient who cries 2. Be able to interview patients who present normally censured language and/or behavior: child abuse prostitution drug abuse the person who "cusses you out"	1. The student will be assigned a variety of case situations including illnesses and behaviors listed under "skills to be learned." 2. Discuss case situations with the field instructor. 3. Read about the emotional/social aspects of patients with life-threatening or disabling illnesses. 4. Discuss, with field instructor, values and interview skills used with patients who present "immoral" behavior.	1. Be able to accept each referral and establish a relationship with patients having the diagnoses/behaviors described for this objective. 2. Be able to discuss personal needs and concerns of patient/family in four out of five situations, to the maximum benefit of the patient (and not to meet the worker's needs).
V. Be able to record information required, using formal outlines provided by the agency for recording: consults social histories summaries medical chart entries statistical reports memos and letters process-recording	1. Understand and be able to verbalize the purpose of recording, per agency requirements. 2. Be able to demonstrate concise and accurate use of English language and punctuation. 3. Be able to verbalize deficits in ability to communicate and make efforts to deal with them. 4. Be able to read and interpret written data.	1. Get constructive feedback from field instructor on all written recording required by the agency. 2. Read procedure manual. 3. Read the recording of field instructor and other staff. 4. Use the dictaphone, following instructions given in procedure manual. 5. Take notes at meetings. 6. Read written re-	1. Be able to do all agency recording and verbalize the purpose with very limited input from field instructor by the end of placement. 2. Feel comfortable with use of the dictaphone. 3. Consistently meet deadlines for submission of all written material. 4. Record minutes of meetings with accuracy three out of five times.

(*Continued*)

Objective	Skills to Be Learned	Experiences to Learn Skills	Degree of Skill
	5. Be able to do process-recording and other recording (per list under "objective").	ports, correspondence, policy statements circulated among social work staff. Give feedback to field instructor on the content of this material.	
	6. Be able to take accurate notes of meetings.		
	7. Be able to understand the department procedural manual.	7. Read Recording: Guidelines for Social Workers and complete recording exercises.	
	8. Be able to prepare written material so that deadlines are met.		
	9. Be able to use the dictaphone.		
VI. Be able to identify and use community resources.	1. Identify agencies most frequently used, the type of service offered, and the type of client to refer to: Social Security AFDC County Welfare Vocational Rehab nursing homes—PSP, HRS, and Medicare boarding homes TB hospital Visiting Nurses's Association homemaker services Home Care program	1. Refer patients to each of the resources stated under "skills to be learned" and discuss the referrals with field instructor.	1. Be able to refer patients to appropriate resources (for concrete and counseling needs) with minimal input from the supervisor by the end of placement.
	2. Be able to identify gaps or lacks in community resources.	2. Identify, with field instructor and other staff/students, gaps in community resources.	2. Make referrals creatively and/or appropriately in four out of five situations by the end of placement.
	3. Be able to complete a referral (release of information form, letter, social history, exchange adequate verbal or written information, etc.).	3. Get consistent supervisory feedback on how to refer patients to particular services.	
		4. Will have access to lists of community resources currently being maintained by the field instructor and other staff.	
		5. Read the department's community resource directory.	
	4. Begin her own list of referral sources.	6. Call agencies and visit at least three.	

Objective	Skills to Be Learned	Experiences to Learn Skills	Degree of Skill
	5. Be able to involve the client in the referral process. 6. Be able to incorporate readings (concerning systems) into referral activity.	7. Assess community programs and their services through phone contacts, visits to the agency, feedback from those who have been referred, etc. 8. Participate in in-service training sessions concerning community resources.	
VII. Be able to identify the function of several groups: staff, unit, support, therapeutic groups.	1. Be able to identify the function of two specific groups. 2. Be able to identify the therapeutic intervention methods used by leader and facilitator in a therapeutic group. 3. Be able to identify characteristics of "beginning group" members.	1. Observe supervisor and psychiatric nurse leading a dermatology group. 2. Read information on "beginning group characteristics." 3. Discuss dynamics of two different patient groups and the interventive methods used by the group leaders. 4. Co-lead a rap session for dermatology patients. Possibly do the same thing for a group of laryngectomy patients.	1. Be able to identify the purpose of at least two groups, one of which shall be the group for laryngectomy patients. The student will do this orally or in writing. 2. Be able to identify three exchanges and appropriate responses between group members and the leader. 3. Be able to co-lead a group.
VIII. Be able to work independently.	1. Be able to relate to supervisory sessions with questions, issues, and material for discussion. 2. Be able to receive suggestions and critical analyses without becoming defensive. 3. Be able to work independently with minimal direction between regularly scheduled weekly supervision sessions.	1. Have regularly scheduled supervisory sessions. Supervisory and administrative staff will also be available to answer questions on an "as needed" basis but with some recognition of reality constraints that limit constant availability. 2. Have access to resource directories and procedure manual, as needed. 3. Participate in in-	1. By the end of placement, student will be able to use supervision at regularly scheduled times. 2. By the end of placement, the student will be able to identify two occasions when she initiated appropriate use of supervision. 3. By the end of placement, the student will be able to identify two ideas she initiated to keep her professional role clearly focused

(Continued)

Objective	Skills to Be Learned	Experiences to Learn Skills	Degree of Skill
	4. Be able to recognize and follow through on ideas—to maintain motivation.	service training on the functions of a supervisor and the use of a supervisor/field instructor.	and her learning motivated.
	5. Be able to explore new community resources as needed and be critical of gaps in service.		4. By the end of placement, student will be able to assess a case situation and make a referral without supervisory input in most situations.
	6. Be able to use supervisory and administrative channels appropriately.		
IX. Be able to identify what is professional and act in a professional manner.	1. Be able to demonstrate personal maturity and emotional stability, to cope effectively with the normal stresses and pressures of placement.	1. Meet with the field instructor on a regular basis to discuss issues related to the skills to be learned. Feedback on student's progress in achieving these skills will be provided.	1. Have feelings of stability in her role as learner and social worker in this medical setting.
	2. Be able to use common sense along with therapeutic skills in carrying out job responsibilities.	2. Participate in inservice training to learn more about self.	2. Identify two values of the social work profession and be able to describe how she used these values in her practice.
	3. In behavior, dress, attendance, and work habits, conduct self in a way that facilitates rather than hinders ongoing work relationships.	3. Read the procedure manual concerning administrative requirements.	3. By the end of placement, will be able to identify five feelings/values she has become aware of and has controlled effectively to facilitate the helping role and process.
	4. Be punctual in attendance, regular in work hours and call in advance when absence or late arrival is unavoidable.	4. Solicit feedback from other staff on her professionalism.	4. By the end of placement, will be able to identify three conflicts of values with the agency, her supervisor and/or departmental policy and state how she was able to perform her job to the fullest extent, in spite of these conflicts.
	5. Be able to identify the values of the social work profession and use them as a framework for practice.	5. Read about the values of the social work profession; read the NASW Code of Ethics.	
	6. Be aware of self: personal biases and values	6. Observe supervisor and other professional staff as they perform their professional roles.	

Objective	Skills to Be Learned	Experiences to Learn Skills	Degree of Skill
	personality traits that may be projected onto client and affect counseling adversely Be able to control personal feelings and values when having client contact 7. Be able to identify conflicts of personal feelings and values, not only with clients but also with the agency, the supervisor, and policies of the social work department or hospital. 8. Even when she does not agree with them, the student will be able to meet policy requirements of the department and related deadlines; she will perform administrative functions (such as statistical reports) on schedule.		
X. Be able to identify a large systems problem that affects delivery of social services to patients; plan a course of action to work on this problem.	1. Develop an understanding of the Cuban Refugee Assistance Program, and differences and similarities between it and the regular American Health and Rehabilitative Services Program (financial assistance and services). 2. Develop a plan of action should either program not be practicing its prescribed policies with regard to service delivery. This involves an advocacy role in behalf of the client.	1. Supervisory conferences regarding the problem and proposed plan of action. 2. Read about the policy of department with regard to proposed action. 3. Interview the director of social work department to discuss the proposed action. 4. Read classroom material and relate it to a course of action for social change.	1. Be able to identify one large-system problem and develop a realistic measure to deal with the problem. 2. Be able to begin to implement the proposed plan of action to deal with the identified problem.

Macro System Contract

The following contract was developed between a second year MSW student who was specializing in staff development and supervision and her field instructor. It is not entirely behavioral or quantitative in its assessment criteria, but it represents the field instructor's beginning efforts to commit to writing (with input from the student) a formal contract for the student. The student is in a concurrent placement plan for three days a week from September through May.

I STAFF DEVELOPMENT

Learning Objective

A. The student will be able to critically evaluate, both orally and in writing, observed in-service training conducted by others to assess whether the training was effective and if it met the need of the learners. This includes identifying specific instructional techniques used by the leader and identifying positives and negatives in the instructor's approach.

Learning Experiences

1. Will attend in-service training sessions for social service staff.

2. Will observe nursing orientation lectures which are given every two weeks (with eventual goal that the student will take over giving these presentations).

3. Will attend most in-service training sessions given to anyone by her field instructor so that she may observe.

4. Will act as co-facilitator of two self-awareness classes which are taught by her field instructor in her role as adjunct instructor at a local university. These classes meet once weekly for four hours. One class is held during the quarter from September to December, and the second will be from January to March. The student will do weekly self-evaluation of the class experience. There will be ongoing discussion with the field instructor regarding content, process, and teaching methods used in these classes.

5. The student will actually lead some staff development activities herself (see section C).

6. Selected readings on staff development, social work education, and adult education will be assigned.

Assessment Methods

1. The accuracy with which the student is able to assess observed teaching by others can be determined somewhat by comparing her assessments with those of the participants and/or the leader who was giving the training. For example, if student feels training was ineffective, others should agree.

2. The student's field instructor has a reputation for being generally effective at staff development. Thus, subjectively, does student's critique of observed staff development agree with the critique of the more experienced field instructor? This is admittedly a highly subjective measuring mechanism.

B. The student will acquire a working knowledge of group dynamics including awareness of similarities and differences between dynamics encountered in in-service training groups versus therapeutically oriented groups.

Learning Experiences

1. See A, numbers 1 through 4.

2. Selected readings in group therapy and practice.

3. Continuous discussion with the field instructor regarding group dynamics of groups in which the student participates either as a learner-participant or as a leader.

4. The student will serve as co-therapist with field instructor for a therapeutically oriented weight control prorgram beginning second semester. This group will consist of eight to ten members meeting once weekly for 1½ hours over a several-month period. The primary psychodynamics will be dealing with inadequate self concepts, use of food as a defense mechanism, and the necessity of helping group members achieve awareness of this pattern and develop new coping mechanisms or come to a realization that they should not attempt to change their present defense mechanism.

Measurement

1. There will be assessment of student's written and oral feedback regarding analysis of group dynamics.

2. The degree of effectiveness that the student achieves in actually leading groups will be the most important measurement of her achievement of this educational goal.

C. The student will acquire beginning skills in group facilitation in a staff development role. The student will be able, on at least one occasion, to lead groups or present material in such a manner that she is able to facilitate each of the four following types of learning:

a. Imparting facts. Presenting to the group something someone else has already drawn up or written out for her.

b. Researching her own data in order to organize them and present them to the group in lecture style (still imparting facts).

c. Lead group discussions where the primary goal is for group members to learn from one another as well as from the leader.

d. Through the use of (a) through (c), achieve the goal of bringing about attitudinal change among participants.

Learning Experiences

1. See letters A and B.

2. The student will have the opportunity to lead several social service staff meetings (1½ hours each) and take charge of giving selected training to members of other disciplines (i.e., a two-hour presentation on interviewing techniques to nurses). The field instructor will sit in on some of these and not on others.

3. The student will eventually "take over" orienting newly hired nurses to the role of the social worker. This presentation lasts 1½ hours and is given every two weeks throughout the year.

4. The student will serve as co-leader of a small group experiential exercise in a workshop put on by the social service department.

5. The student will serve as co-facilitator of a self-awareness course (see A-4). In the second semester, the student will take charge not only of selected exercises within each class period, but of entire class sessions.

Measurement

1. Unsolicited feedback from persons participating in training led by the student will be "acceptable" or "positive"—a feeling that participants learned something.

2. Formal, solicited feedback from participants. For example, the nursing department in charge of orienting newly hired nurses to the hospital uses its own evaluation form. Social service presentations are rated each month. The rating shall be "good" or "average" for those sessions led by the student. The university also uses a formal course evaluation form with a 1- to 5-point rating scale. The overall rating for the self-awareness class on the majority of items shall be at least a three.

3. Participants in training given by the student will or can be observed to be applying newly learned factual material or exhibiting the desired attitudinal change.

4. Students in the self-awareness course keep weekly "diaries" of their responses to each self-awareness class. These are reviewed by the instructor periodically. Entries will indicate whether student facilitator is functioning effectively.

D. Student will have useful skills (as a participant) and beginning skills as a leader in planning, organizing, and putting on a large-scale workshop, including selecting and securing a nationally known speaker, dealing with publicity, finances, and other matters that go along with such an undertaking.

Educational Experiences

1. Participates as a member of the social service department Workshop Committee to plan several small, one-day workshops put on by members of our own social service department. Meets once weekly with the committee in planning all aspects, including program materials. In one instance, acts as co-leader for one small group session at one workshop.

2. Observes and works with her field instructor who is chairman of the workshop committee.

3. Functions as member of a program committee to plan a large workshop (for several hundred people from throughout the state) with a nationally known speaker. As such, has opportunity to:

   a. Discuss setting up of various committees.

   b. Participate in the nitty-gritty of selecting and securing the guest speaker.

   c. Serves as member of the steering committee to oversee the activities of the various subcommittees.

   d. Helps out and attends the actual workshop.

II SUPERVISORY SKILLS

Educational Objectives

A. The student will acquire beginning skills in supervision and more specifically in supervision of a first- or second-quarter undergraduate student.

Educational Experiences

1. Participates as a learner in departmentally sponsored training program for supervisors of students. This meets for 1½ to 2 hours weekly for ten weeks. The student will complete this training program during the first semester and acquire her student the second semester. The training includes readings, "homework assignments," and handouts of illustrative materials.

2. Student will be supervising a BSW student. She will attend seminars given twice each quarter by the student's school for their current and potential field instructors.

3. The student will read and become familiar with field instruction handbooks for local social work schools to learn about social work education in field instruction.

4. It would be highly desirable for student to attend workshops given by the local MSW program for field instructors, including the new course for field instructors. However, thus far, the school has not granted permission for this.

5. Through discussion with field instructor, student will reflect on and be made consciously aware of supervisory process between herself and her field instructor.

6. Student will have total responsibility for direct supervision of an undergraduate student who is in the field for 24 hours weekly for ten weeks. This will require:

   a. Planning for student's arrival.

   b. Learning enough about how a social worker functions at the grassroots level in the social service department to be able to teach this to a student supervisee.

   c. Select and plan case assignments for the student.

   d. Develop and set with the student specific educational objectives, learning experiences, and measurement techniques.

   e. Do process-recording herself as a prelude to using this tool with her student.

   f. Monitor and give feedback to the student regarding quantity and quality of the student's work throughout the quarter.

   g. Prepare the final written performance evaluation.

   h. Communicate directly with the director of field instruction in the BSW program regarding the supervisee's performance and any problem areas.

   i. Receive very close direction from her own field instructor during this process: the field instructor will not be directly involved with the student's supervisee except in the student's absence from field.

7. Selected readings will be assigned.

Measurement

1. The BSW program requires each student evaluate his or her field placement experience. The supervisee's evaluation of the student field instructor may have some negatives, but will contain more positives than negatives and will indicate that learning and growth did occur.

2. The feedback from the director of field instruction in the BSW program will be neutral or absent (indicating absence of problem areas) or positive.

3. Solicited and unsolicited feedback from the student supervisee throughout the quarter will be evaluated.

4. The student will share with her field instructor copies of the supervisee's process recordings. These will indicate if the student field instructor is providing appropriate instructional feedback and whether or not growth is occurring in student's basic interviewing and casework skills.

5. The supervisee will complete the quarter in field placement without undue difficulties. However, it is recognized that it is possible that a student may experience difficulties of their own which have little to do with the field instructor and which may lead to premature termination from the field.

B. The student will acquire beginning skills in supervision of regular paid employees. This will be on a theoretical level only except for transfer of techniques from the experiences under objective A above.

Learning Experiences

1. It will not be possible in this setting this year for student actually to experience supervising a paid employee.

2. The social service department is actually "run" by a task force group consisting of five MSW supervisors, the assistant director, and the director, who meet once weekly for two hours to discuss problems and positives, and determine departmental policy. The student will participate during the second semester as a member of this committee. She may be excluded from selected meetings at the discretion of the supervisors.

3. Selected readings and discussion with the field instructor will occur.

Measurement

1. There is no way to measure meaningfully the student's performance in this area since the student will not actually be doing it. The degree of effectiveness in supervision of the undergraduate student is expected to give some indication of potential effectiveness with regular employees.

C. The student will have very beginning level skills in teaching techniques of supervision to others.

Learning Experiences

1. All experiences under I—STAFF DEVELOPMENT should prepare student for techniques of teaching various concepts to others. These techniques can be applied to the teaching of supervisory skills as well, and some transfer is expected.

2. As student is learning how to do supervision herself, she will not be ready this year to actually teach techniques of supervision to others. However, as she gains post–master's experience supervising, she will become prepared.

3. Observe her own field instructor leading a training program for student supervisors (ten weeks at 1½ hours weekly) and also a small group training session at the departmental workshop.

4. Selected readings will be assigned.

Measurement

1. This objective cannot be meaningfully measured as student will not actually be teaching supervision to others. However, her potential for doing so can be guessed at from assessment of student's experience in areas I and II–A.

III PROGRAM EVALUATION

Learning Objectives

A. The student will be able to analyze meaningfully and critically the functioning of the social service department in some areas of administration, staffing, and service delivery. The student will, by the end of the second semester, be able to provide some input which is actually utilized by the director and/or supervisory task force in policy or decision making.

Learning Experiences

1. Will function as a member of a peer review committee, which reviews randomly selected social service cases each month for quality of provision of social work services in selected areas.

2. Will assist her field instructor in compiling monthly reports of the peer review findings.

3. Will work with the director and assistant director in analyzing monthly statistical reports submitted by all social service staff and students regarding their direct and indirect service activity.

4. Will be given a special assignment to review critically and evaluate the functioning of the social service department in a specific area and will work closely with the director and assistant director in doing so. The student will be expected to present findings and recommendations to administration

5. Will attend, with the director, hospital–wide utilization review committee meetings.

6. Will attend other selected hopsital–level administrative meetings.

7. There will be individual discussions with the director and assistant director of social service regarding program evaluation.

8. Selected readings.

Measurement

1. Subjective evaluation by the director of the department and assistant director (her field instructor) of the relevance and usefulness of student's input in the evaluation process.

2. Feedback from the supervisory MSW staff and the degree of comfort they experience with the student being a member of their task force meetings and peer review committee will be some indication of student's effectiveness and comfort with this role.

3. Evaluation will be made by the director and hospital administration of the input and written reports done by the student either in a contributing role or through individual projects.

4. Do any of the student's findings, input, or recommendations actually result in:

   a. Recognition of the existence of a problem?

   b. Extensive supervisory-administrative level discussion regarding an area that needs attention?

   c. An actual policy or procedural change?

IV PLANNING AND PROGRAM DESIGN

Educational Objective

A. The student will, building on program evaluation skills, be able to have meaningful input into planning and program design for the social service department.

Educational Experiences

1. See all of Number III—PROGRAM EVALUATION.

2. The student will participate in weekly supervisory task force meetings (See II—B—2).

3. Will work closely with her field instructor (who is in charge of staff development for the social services department) in identifying staff development needs and then planning and implementing programs to meet these needs.

4. Will attend local and state meetings of the American Hospital Association Society for Hospital Social Work Directors as an observer.

5. May actually work with the director and/or supervisory task force in planning and developing a selected program or project of an administrative nature.

6. Selected readings will be assigned.

Measurement

1. This will be essentially the same as for III—PROGRAM EVALUATION

V OVERALL COMMENTS REGARDING TRAINING PLAN

The student will have some exposure in all the areas identified in this training plan. The primary concentration is on staff development which includes supervision. Secondary emphasis is on program design and program development. It is anticipated that student will become more deeply involved with some areas than others. Also, the amount of pressure of assignments from the classroom and student's willingness or ability to exceed 24 hours a week in field placement would affect the degree to which some of these objectives can be pursued. However, the training plan is designed around a student being in field approximately 24 hours per week. Opportunity to participate in co-facilitating a self-awareness class and the weight control therapy group may necessitate more than 24 hours weekly and therefore is optional. This particular student has chosen to pursue the option and thus is having this experience.

Difficulties in Setting Specific Degree-of-Skill Expectations

Most schools and field instructors feel quite comfortable working with educational plans at levels I, II, and even III, but the enforced structure may be anxiety-provoking to educators and supervisors who are accustomed to a more informal approach. However, no one is asked to risk anything; there are plenty of loopholes. Field instructor A may give an "outstanding" to a student and supervisor B may flunk that same student—working from the same educational contract at level I, II, or III. The contracts leave plenty of room for individual judgment and interpretation of what constitutes acceptable or unacceptable skills or attainment of objectives.

As soon as the competence-based component is added in Level IV, the instructor is committed to a set standard. If a student fails to measure up to or achieve the stated degree of skill, the supervisor must deal with it; it cannot be ignored. Hence a primary anxiety arises: "As long as standards are unspecified, I can weasel out of having to give unsatisfactory evaluations if I want to; but if a standard has been set and it's obvious my student can't meet it, I'll have to do something or else do some fast explaining to the school." When standards are set, we must be willing to recognize and accept the fact that there are effective and ineffective social workers and some people who just do not belong in or are not ready for social work practice. No longer is performance evaluation a mysterious process that occurs between the student and field instructor. It becomes more objective as student, school, and others can review the student's work and arrive at reasonably consistent assessments. Others can read the contract and evaluate the field instructor's competence in carrying out the educational plan. Others can agree or disagree with the performance evaluation based on the stated behavioral objectives and level of skill expectations. These persons can disagree with or challenge the field instructor's assessments because they know what the expectations were. His methods of evaluating the student's skill may be challenged. Furthermore, others may question the standards the field instructor has set: "That's too high. You can't expect a BSW student to achieve that level of skill." Or, "That's too low. I wouldn't hire an MSW who graduated with only that degree of skill." If expectations are vague or unexpressed, no one can challenge them.

Most schools do not provide behavioral objectives for use with contracts. Thus, when a field instructor defines a level of skill expectation for a student, he is often on his own. He may not know if the school supports his idea, because the school hasn't yet dealt with the issue or has decided not to take a stand. This places the student supervisor in a lonely position, resulting in considerable insecurity, anxiety, and perhaps hostility toward the school for not providing more definite standards. Yet, as stated earlier, field instructors are in a unique position to set meaningful standards: They know what new graduates must be able to do before they would want to hire them. They know what minimum skills a student must have to survive and function effectively as a practitioner-employee after graduation. If schools fail to provide specific standards and expectations regarding degree of skill, field instructors can certainly do so on the basis of their own experiences as social work practitioners, supervisors, and employers. Of course, this is not ideal; it should be a joint process between the school and the field. But who will make the first move?* Another problem is that we have not figured out how to convert subjective material and observations into quantitative rating scales. There are no standard criteria or assessment tools for measuring *overall* social work effectiveness. Most field instructors have never been trained in the application of these kinds of concepts. Thus, we as a profession are saying, "Set standards and assess performance," but are providing few tools for use by field instructors to accomplish this goal.

The process of standard setting in student educational contracts forces the field instructor to examine himself. Is *he* meeting the expectations and standards he is setting for his student? We dare not set standards for students that we cannot achieve ourselves. Thus, expectations are lowered and expressed in safe, vague terms.

Another area of difficulty is the weighting of skill expectations. Suppose a student fully meets standards in one area of practice and falls short in another. Must he achieve the desired minimum level of skill for all areas listed in his educational contract, or can he fall short on some and still be rated satisfactory? If so, in which areas can he fail to achieve the desired competence and still pass? Are there some areas so singularly important that if the individual fails to attain the specified degree of skill he cannot or should not

---

*A few progressive schools have developed specific standards. For example, see pp. 174–181 for an example of a field placement performance evaluation form that spells out behavioral expectations for various performance ratings.

pass field placement? There are no social work cookbooks to help field instructors grapple with this question.

Furthermore, many field instructors work exclusively with either BSW or MSW students. They have little opportunity to experience or view the continuum of skills from the beginning undergraduate student to the MSW graduate. Thus, many field instructors set standards in a vacuum—"They seem appropriate to me for a BSW student." But how does this standard fit with expectations being set at the MSW level? What is the difference, if any, between the degree of skill for various areas at the BSW level and that at the MSW level? The first and subsequent field placements? Part of the controversy in social work education today centers on this problem. No one has listed basic component skills of social work practice, developed a Level IV degree-of-skill breakdown, and expressed it on a continuum covering the BSW and MSW levels of training. As a result, some BSW's entering MSW programs experience considerable repetition in their first year; others experience gaps because the MSW program assumes they come with certain skills and knowledge from their undergraduate training when in fact these are lacking. The two levels of training programs disagree sharply over which should be preparing students for what, and both seem to overlook the expectations of field instructors and of the practitioners who employ the BSW and MSW graduates.

An educational issue that causes anxiety for field instructors is this simple question: "Should skill expectations be different for different types of students at the same level of training, or should qualitative expectations be the same for all students graduating with, say, an MSW degree? For example, should I set higher expectations for a forty-year-old student with five years of premaster's social work experience under ACSW supervision than for a twenty-one-year-old who has never had full-time work experience of any kind?" Again, the lack of definition of the minimum degree of skill a BSW or MSW student should achieve prior to receiving the degree places the field instructor in a quandary. If these standards were specified, the background of individual students would not determine the expectations.

Instead, each student would be expected to meet the minimum expectations, but with the recognition that it may take some longer than others, and that some may require more specialized and intensive learning experiences to reach the minimum standard.

The degree-of-skill issue places field instructors in another bind. Students must achieve the minimum expectations in a set time period—a quarter, six months, one semester, or whatever. What if the student needs more time before he is ready to move on to a subsequent field placement or to graduate? The tendency is to set expectations low enough so that every student is likely to reach them in the allotted time for each field placement. Perhaps social work degrees should not be granted based on specified time in a training program. Perhaps degrees should be awarded on the basis of mastery of specified types and levels of skill, regardless of whether the student can accomplish this in one year or three.

Any school contemplating adoption of a Level IV approach to educational plans and contracts must be prepared to deal with all these factors. Some faculty will be threatened by the process of specifying standards. Both students and field instructors will demand more of classroom instructors, and their effectiveness and instructional content will come under close scrutiny to determine whether they are effectively preparing students for achieving the stated objectives. Field instructor resistance and anxiety will have to be recognized and dealt with, yet the school may be in a poor position to compel its agency-based field instructors to implement a Level IV approach to student education. Thus, the biggest hurdle is preparing faculty and field instructors to accept the standard-setting process. The actual process of defining the standards and levels of skill will be an arduous, time-consuming task that is guaranteed to bring about considerable controversy among faculty, field instructors, and social work employers. Finally, field instructors will need much training and help in preparing performance evaluations based on Level IV educational contracts; student supervisors will also need to let the school know what kind of training is needed.

7 Selecting Appropriate Learning Experiences for the Student

The typical social work setting offers opportunities for observing, doing, evaluating, and perhaps teaching others. How does a field instructor go about determining which experiences should come first and which will teach the desired skill or concept most effectively? This process involves several concepts.

The Social Work Student as Adult Learner

The field instructor needs an awareness of what adult learners are like—how they learn, how they respond to educational experiences, and their special needs. Next, both field instructor and student should participate in making an educational diagnosis of the individual student—what specific skills or knowledge he has or is lacking—with consideration to how he might react to the field placement learning experience. Specific educational objectives are set with the student, and the supervisor and student examine the various kinds of learning experience available in the setting that would help the student achieve his objectives. Finally, a means of assessing the student's progress in achieving the objectives is developed and implemented.

Some Characteristics of Adult Learners

Social work students are adults. True enough, some students will have hardly reached the age of legal adulthood, whereas others may be middle-aged but still behave in some instances like adolescents. However, anyone who is learning to help people with their problems is entering an adult world of the most complex order. If a student consistently must be treated as an adolescent rather than an adult, this is a good indication that he lacks the personal maturity

necessary to be an effective social worker. Field instructors should expect their supervisees to respond as adults and structure their experiences accordingly.

Learners should start with the simple and gradually progress to more complex situations and experiences. The student who is new to a large, bureaucratic social service delivery system should be exposed initially to only one small part of the overall program. He should have contact with a limited number of people, departments, client diagnoses, presenting problems, or community groups in the beginning of field placement. The student should know his way around a given department or geographical area before branching out into other areas. Likewise, he should interview individuals before he sees clients and family members jointly.

A student's sense of mastery over a relatively small arena will give him confidence to apply his skills to broader horizons. Students who are prematurely exposed to a wide variety of people, offices, and presenting problems often report a fast-moving and interesting experience but soon feel fragmented and experience a lack of depth or a lack of mastery over any given area. If a continuous smattering of new experiences covering a broad spectrum characterizes the student's total field placement experience, he will graduate having had exposure to many areas but with few meaningful skills in any given area of practice. He may talk impressively about the many situations in which he is "experienced," but the astute prospective employer will soon detect the superficiality of the student's experience and skills.

Some learners eagerly encourage the field instructor to expose them to many varied experiences. It may take some time for the supervisor to realize that such a student is afraid to get into too much depth in any single area, where he might have to reveal his ignorance, test the limits of his skills, and take risks. Thus he distracts and impresses the supervisor with his desire to learn and be exposed superficially to a lot of fascinating experiences so that his skills won't be examined too closely. A little supportive and, if possible, humorous confrontation regarding the behavior pattern, followed by a redirection of learning experiences, usually takes care of this problem.

Many learners express a strong need for a physical space—a work area or a safety zone—that is their exclusive territory. It can be a desk in a corner somewhere, a regular office, or a library-style carrel in a crowded "student room"—just so long as it is a place the student can always come back to and where he can feel secure and at ease. Having a secure home territory enhances the learner's ability to go out into the unknown and risk himself through new experiences.

Many social work students have inadequate communication skills. Ineffective or inadequate grammar school education and insufficient challenge and instruction in communication skills at the college level can produce barely literate social work learners at both the undergraduate and graduate levels. Yet these same individuals may have excellent innate skills for interacting with people. The importance of written skills in social work practice must be explained and special experiences provided, with the school's assistance if necessary, to remedy basic deficiencies. However, the existence of the deficiencies means that the field instructor may have to use instructional methods and experiences that encourage student learning without heavy dependence on written skills. That is, the student may need to learn about basic defense mechanisms or the theoretical intricacies of undifferentiated schizophrenia through experiences involving a specific case in field rather than, or in addition to, reading assignments. Recognition of this situation may eliminate some traditional learning experiences for a given student. However, if the deficits are too severe, the field instructor and school will need to assess the realities of social work practice against the student's competence. If his communication skills are so poor that the student's functioning in his chosen area of practice would be seriously handicapped, some formal counseling or remedial action will need to be provided.

The adult learner benefits from experiencing the gap between what he thinks he knows and what will be required of him after graduation. An adult will not learn without a purpose. That purpose might be to achieve a given grade, earn a higher salary through acquisition of an advanced degree, please a field instructor, or simply improve his own skills. The educator, of course, prefers learning for learning's sake rather than for an external reward. Unfortunately, the educational system itself encourages learning to achieve a grade. However, this can be deemphasized, especially by the agency-based field instructor who is in a position to know what kinds of skills he looks for when hiring new staff and what level of competence a social worker must have

before he is capable of dealing with a suicidal patient, for example. Field instructors are training students to function effectively as social workers once they graduate, not solely to ensure that the student will have a degree to hang on his office wall. Adult learners benefit from experiencing the gap between what they think they know (or should know) and what they must be able to do as a competent social work practitioner after graduation. Usually the resultant anxiety is not overwhelming but sufficiently motivating to encourage the student to head for the nearest library, ask questions of everyone around him and try to learn as much as possible during placement.

Perhaps a few examples will illustrate the importance of this principle. In one practice setting all students received training in diagnostic thinking and treatment planning shortly after entering placement. (This was given routinely because it was found that most students, regardless of their school, background, or level of training, were weak in this area and needed certain basics at the beginning of field placement to enable them to get the most out of their experience.) Each received a case example with an actual diagnostic summary and treatment plan and was asked to state whether or not he felt it was well written. Debate teams were formed and participants were forced to defend their points of view. By the end of the two-hour session, participants had experienced the impact of ineffective diagnostic thinking and treatment planning on casework services and a specific client's life. At the conclusion of the discussion, the students had discovered experientially that social workers who cannot make meaningful diagnostic assessments can do a tremendous disservice to clients. No further motivation was needed as the students moved through additional intensive training that provided specific skills and techniques in diagnostic assessment.

Recently a gifted student gave me a paper she had written, indicating that I might find it of interest. I found that the paper plagiarized copyrighted material with no citation of the source, had no subheadings to organize content and inadequate bibliographical references, presented a complex table with no reference in the narrative regarding its purpose or interpretation, and used poor grammar and spelling throughout. It had been written for a second-year graduate course, and the grade assigned was "A—very well done." This student was two months away from an MSW degree and two months away from assuming a position as director of a social work department in a large facility. When she asked for my comments on the paper I said, "Suppose your program administrator asked you to submit a proposal outlining the goals of your social work department and your rationale for adding additional staff and you wrote it the way you did this paper—what do you think would happen?" It didn't take long for the student to admit that it would probably get laughed right off the administrator's desk and no additional staff positions would be granted. A frank discussion ensued, and she revealed a pattern of preparing sloppily written papers for the classroom because she had found she could get by with that and still receive A's. There was no reason or motivation for putting forth any additional effort. She knew the paper was poorly done when she submitted it to me for review, and this was clearly her way of letting me know she needed more challenge. When she suddenly realized that similar work on the job would cause ineffective department administration, she began working very hard to improve her writing skills. She had *experienced* the reason for this necessity and internalized it.

The reasonably motivated adult learner often needs to experience things to believe them. He usually does not accept that something is so just because the instructor says it is. This doubting attitude often remains unverbalized. A social work student can be told that alcoholics sometimes deny they have ever had d.t.'s, even as they are coming out of rather severe d.t.'s in the hospital. The student may discuss the theoretical reasons for this behavior with his field instructor and still inwardly refuse to believe that this can really happen. Similarly, the field instructor may remark that it is easy for beginning students to lose control of an interview and become the interviewee for at least brief periods. The student may respond appropriately and still be thinking, "That could never happen to *me*." Six weeks later, when he overidentifies with a client and loses control for a significant portion of an interview, real learning occurs as the student experiences the phenomenon for himself.

Most social work students who enter field placement with some skills operate largely by instinct rather than through conscious self-awareness. Most aspiring social workers have some innate ability to relate to people. They are often warm, supportive, imaginative, attentive, and perhaps even reflective and interpretive. Yet many operate by sheer instinct: "Well, nothing has blown up yet, so I must be doing something right." One of the goals of social work education is to help the student learn the labels that go with the techniques he already uses effectively. This involves knowing why certain approaches are or are not effective, and when they should be used or avoided. The student eventually becomes able consciously, differentially, and purposefully to identify, recognize, and use selected techniques. However, this learning almost always starts with intuitive responses. Conscious awareness of what is happening and why and differential application of techniques usually come later.

Totally new skills often are learned initially by rote. A new application of an existing skill may produce this pattern: "reflection—that's when you repeat back a word or phrase to the client for the purpose of . . ." The student then goes out and tries to do this, looking for every possible opportunity to be reflective in his interviews. When he goes back and evaluates his recorded sessions, he may be able to identify retroactively instances when reflection was used or should have been communicated. However, during the interview itself he must constantly say to himself, "Let's

see—I wonder if I should give a reflective response here." Internalization and instinctual or automatic use of a specific technique come only after considerable practice.

Adults learn by doing. Observation must be followed rather quickly by an opportunity to put to use what has been observed. Thus, observation should be followed by periods of application, followed by additional observation to study alternative approaches or witness competent application of skills the student is trying to learn.

Intellectual understanding comes before internalization. The student needs to try a new concept or value on for size, see what it feels like to express adherence to and understanding of it, and perhaps initially go along with it simply because he knows it is what his field instructor expects. This is a necessary part of the learning process, and sensitive field instructors are not easily fooled into believing that verbal intellectualizations mean that internalization has occurred.

Adult learners often harbor seemingly inappropriate insecurities. Even a really bright student with exceptional skills who appears self-confident and in total control to the casual observer can show anxiety-provoking insecurities regarding his skills behind the closed door of his field instructor's office. Every student has a continuing need for validation and reassurance that "I really *am* being effective. It's not my imagination."

Most learning does not occur in a straight upward direction. There are peaks, valleys, and plateaus where learning and growth seem to cease for a time. These periods are normal and can often be predicted. Following an intensive period of personal and professional growth, the learner must have some time to think about what is happening, sort out where he's been and where he's going, develop a new or revised self-concept to go along with his increasing skills, and internalize what he has learned. Since most of this activity is internal, it may appear to the field instructor that nothing much is happening. As the student stabilizes and sorts things out within himself, he prepares for the new growth spurt which inevitably follows.

External stresses having nothing to do with field placement can affect responsiveness to learning. Most adults have significant life responsibilities outside of field placement. A sick child, financial pressures, stressful relationships with family members, an auto accident, pregnancy, a son caught using drugs at school—all can detract from the student's available energy for learning in field placement. A student may hold a full- or part-time job, have a family with several young children, and attend classes at school in addition to reporting to field placement. Combined family, school, and work responsibilities may produce mental and physical exhaustion, either situational or chronic, that inhibits learning.

Most adults have some unlearning to do. Adults have a lifetime of experiences that have made them what they are. Certain values and approaches to people may exist because of specific past experiences. Perhaps the student worked in a welfare agency for three years with virtually no supervision. He may have gotten into the habit of using some rather unproductive interviewing approaches simply because no one questioned them or suggested more effective alternatives. Yet the individual may feel he was effective and not even realize that he has some unlearning to do. A forty-five-year-old housewife with years of volunteer experience may have a deeply ingrained but inaccurate concept of the role of the social worker that will need to be altered drastically or discarded if she is to identify fully with the role of the professional social worker. Thus, the field instructor must "start where the student is" and find out what he already knows or thinks he knows before a meaningful and individualized educational plan can be developed.

Most learners acquire new skills by first copying others or following instructions blindly. After he begins to feel comfortable with what is being learned, the student begins to criticize others: "Why is it done *that* way? What would happen if it were done some other way? Didn't that just make the client more upset?" And so on. Finally, he will develop his own approach, taking bits and pieces from everything he has been exposed to, rejecting what he finds unacceptable, and combining the remainder with his own personality to form his particular style. This is the end goal of social work education and signals the student's emerging identity as an individual professional with some independence. In reality, many new graduates do not discover and feel fully comfortable with their own professional identity for months or even years after graduation.

Mature adults with significant life experience are usually rather independent. Even when they do not know much, there may be a tendency to be secretly creative with the field instructor's suggested approaches. They may follow suggestions pretty much as given, but with a little individual touch that they may not reveal to the field instructor until later on, when they have proved to themselves that it works and feel secure enough to tell the supervisor that they've taken a few liberties with his instructions. This kind of behavior is normal and to be expected. Occasional innovations in the application of suggested techniques should not, of course, be confused with insubordination, which is refusal to follow a supervisory instruction regarding policy, procedure, or social work practice approaches. If a student refuses to use certain techniques suggested by his supervisor and service to clients is affected adversely as a result, the student would be engaging in very problematic insubordinate behavior.

Adults often gain as much from informal learning as from structured, planned experiences. Ventilation of feelings and ideas in a rap session with the secretary may have as great an impact as more formal experiences. Students can also participate in a specific learning experience and instead learn something quite different from, but just as important as, what had been planned. Flexibility in the field instruc-

tor's approach can allow for these situations and build on them to enhance the student's total experience.

No learner can be expected to teach others until he has first learned the content or skill himself. Consider the inexperienced student who undergoes a four-month graduate field placement and then selects staff development as his major area of practice for the second year. How can the field instructor teach him to hold in-service training sessions for supervisors when he has never been a supervisor himself? How can he help BA-level workers deal with resistive clients when his own skills for doing so are very uncertain? Likewise, a casework student cannot meaningfully explain his role at an interdisciplinary team conference if he has been in the agency only two weeks and isn't sure what his role is. The basics must be learned before the student is placed in a leadership or educational role.

The extensive life experiences of most social work students make transference and countertransference predictable occurrences during field placement. Social work students as a group often seem to have more than their share of significant life experiences, thus rendering them more susceptible to transference than persons with less exposure to problematic situations and less ability to experience and communicate intense emotions. Field instructors need to help the student watch for indicators of transference and countertransference and work with these phenomena as expected parts of field placement and social work practice.

Adults need to participate in structuring their learning experiences. Obviously a student with limited exposure to social work will have much less input than one with several years of experience who knows just what he wants out of his formal education. However, every student can and should participate in setting objectives to some degree, to enhance his involvement in the learning process.

The typical adult social work student is highly skilled at "psyching out" the field instructor and giving him exactly what he wants or what will be rewarded. Insecurities and anxieties can produce this behavior, or it may simply be the result of a lifetime pattern of striving to please authority figures. Most students spend some time in this phase and then relate more honestly with increased risk-taking as they begin to feel more comfortable in field placement. The student who stagnates in the desire-to-please stage presents a real challenge as the field instructor struggles to find out just what the student is thinking and feeling so he can adjust the learning objectives and experiences accordingly.

Most adults have little respect for a field instructor whom they can manipulate consistently. This obviously will decrease response to learning experiences.

Special Needs of Adult Learners

The foregoing description of some of the characteristics of social work students as learners suggests some special needs that field instructors must address in providing educational experiences and supervision.

First of all, *the student needs to know the qualifications and background of his field instructor.* The instructor's educational degrees and areas of practice experience or expertise, his professional biases, and his approach to student supervision should be shared and discussed.*

The student must have one primary supervisor who is responsible for regularly scheduled supervisory conferences and the writing of performance evaluations. Other staff may assist or perhaps even supervise the student for selected assignments; however, the primary supervisor must be available, involved, and continually coordinating and overseeing the student's total experience. The trainee with several supervisors may receive conflicting or inconsistent evaluative feedback along with an unrealistic and uncoordinated volume and quality of work assignments if the various supervisors do not communicate effectively with one another. The insecure or overanxious student may even play one supervisor off against the other through various manipulative techniques.

Adults may seem to prefer unstructured experiences and considerable independence. Indeed, the naive learner may even respond with enthusiasm to this approach. However, *some structure must be provided for maximum learning to occur.* Students who are turned loose to "do their own thing" undergo a directionless experience equivalent to taking a cross-country trip without a road map or even a definite destination. Structure reinforces, supports, evaluates, sets goals, extinguishes counterproductive behaviors, counsels, oversees experiences, and educates as the student moves through field placement.

Evaluative feedback must be given as soon as circumstances permit. Indeed, some methods make simultaneous feedback possible, such as a "bug in the ear" device whereby the supervisor can give a student private direction as he interviews and is observed through a one-way mirror.† A field instructor can also sit next to a student during a board meeting, workshop, audit committee or whatever and exchange impressions and reactions through unobtrusive written notes. Delays of only a few hours can frustrate the learner who needs to know his field instructor's thoughts while the experience is fresh in his mind. Once he moves on to other activities, it will be much more difficult to relive the experience and the accompanying feelings. The result is a less effective learning experience. Students may also continue nonproductive approaches and activities in subsequent situations simply because they haven't yet been informed that changes are needed or that more effective techniques exist. On the other hand, when feedback is immediate the learner's self-confidence increases markedly, giving him

*This also takes place in the preplacement interview. See Chapter 4.
†See the discussion in Alfred Kadushin, *Supervision in Social Work* (New York: Columbia University Press, 1976), pp. 427–430.

added incentive and assurance to do his best with the next and perhaps more challenging assignment.

Most responsible students are fully capable of conducting self-evaluations and welcome this opportunity to take some responsibility for their own growth. The field instructor needs to encourage this process continually so that the student becomes an involved learner rather than a passive recipient of a one-sided evaluatory process.

Likewise, *mature learners benefit from participating in structuring their own learning experiences.* Again, an involved learner feels a sense of responsibility for the success of the experience and the commitment usually maximizes his learning experience.

Students should start off the school term with assignments that bring rather immediate and specific results. Even the most bumbling, insecure, and anxious student will often receive a direct "thank you" from his client when a lost welfare check is replaced, an eviction is forestalled, or home delivery of low-cost meals is arranged. The client need not know that the student had to call the landlord four times because he got incomplete information each time or that it took him a dozen calls to find the right office to get the welfare funds replaced. The rewards for conducting an effective interview or providing a counseling service are less obvious and usually much delayed. Consumers rarely overtly thank their counselors for helping them face unpleasant realities, work through a complex transference, or gain added insight into a masochistic marital relationship. It takes a certain amount of security and self-confidence for the counselor to wait for such indirect rewards. Indeed, many beginning students don't know enough to recognize when improvement occurs and may thus be denied even this form of gratification and reinforcement of competence.

Adult learners require a highly individualized approach. The field instructor must get to know his student's skills and limitations in order for a meaningful educational plan to be developed. Existing abilities must be identified so that new concepts and challenges will build on them rather than require the student to handle an experience using totally untested skills.

Complex or long-term assignments must be broken down into small, manageable steps that build on one another and eventually achieve the overall educational goal or desired outcome (partialized learning). Have the student read about techniques of leading a community meeting, then interview selected residents to see what they hope to get out of the meeting, and so on. Repeat the presentation of in-depth concepts and instructions as often as necessary, varying the ways the information is conveyed each time (e.g., supervisory discussions, then reading on the topic, and perhaps informal discussion with a staff member) until the student grasps what is being taught.

Goals must be realistic and within the reasonable grasp of the student. He should be warned in advance that he will not fully succeed in every undertaking and thus shouldn't feel a total personal failure when he proves unable to resolve an impossible situation.

Nevertheless, the student must be challenged beyond his existing capabilities. Some enter social work training with a strong professional background and existing skills that are already at a satisfactory level. The field instructor could do almost nothing, and this learner would complete field instruction with a fully satisfactory performance rating. However, if he has not been challenged to improve his skills, very limited learning will occur in a student who is potentially capable of becoming an outstanding social worker.

The student needs support and a measured amount of timely protection from certain harsh realities; however, *he must be allowed to fail occasionally and to experience directly the repercussions of his actions.* The field instructor should not always come to the student's rescue. For example, an intern may have difficulty getting his monthly statistical reports in on time. The secretary who tabulates them and must meet certain deadlines of her own goes to the field instructor and tells him about the problem. Most field instructors, at least the first time it happens, will politely remind the student to be more prompt and explain why. When it happens a third or fourth time, the secretary may issue an ultimatum: "You'd better get your student to shape up." If the student could see at first hand how his delays create problems for the department and the secretary involved, it could have a meaningful and behavior-changing impact. Turning the secretary loose with the student directly will provide a learning experience he won't soon forget as the field instructor begins cutting the sustaining umbilical cord.

Students need reassurance that it is difficult for them to harm clients or consumer groups. There may be real fear that "I could damage somebody because I don't know what I'm doing." In reality, most students are harmless. They may bumble, take longer than necessary to get at a problem or work toward a solution, and not be much help to certain individuals, but they rarely engage in behavior that damages the client.*

Students will have definite reactions to all their experiences, which they may not want to share with their field instructor. Thus, the presence of *other students can provide an important and safe outlet for ventilation of feelings,* exchange of ideas, comparison of experiences, and validation of learning. At the same time, the student needs privacy for reading, writing, dictating, and self-reflection or internalization of newly learned skills and concepts.

Finally, *the field instructor must create a comfortable climate of acceptance and support* where the student feels free to risk himself, reveal inadequacies, and make mistakes.

---

*See Suanna J. Wilson, *Recording: Guidelines for Social Workers* (New York: Free Press, 1980), for a further discussion of this issue and examples of recording illustrating a harmless interview and one where the student actually damages his client.

How Can I Tell If My Student Is Learning?

Regardless of what is being taught, certain general behaviors and responses usually indicate that learning is occurring. It must also be remembered that a variety of experiences may all produce similar learning and that any given assignment can produce unexpected and unanticipated learning.

Two rather common indicators are often assumed to show that the student is learning, and both can be quite misleading. The student who looks the field instructor in the eye and says "I am learning a lot," "I'm getting a lot out of this," or "Yes, I understand" may be right. On the other hand, he may be giving the field instructor what he thinks she wants to hear or be trying desperately to convince himself that he is learning something when he is really uncertain about it. He may simply not want to discuss the subject further and thus may give false reassurances to the field instructor to forestall further elaboration and instruction. If the student is really assimilating and using what is being taught, this will be revealed in his attitudes and behaviors, regardless of what he says.

Another pitfall occurs when the field instructor talks a great deal in supervisory conferences, expounding at length on his values, ideas, or philosophies as he draws from his years of social work training or experience. The humble student often sits quietly, appearing to absorb every word eagerly. The field instructor may be so wound up in his own verbalizations that he does not realize that his student isn't saying anything. As a result, he doesn't have any idea how his student is responding to what is being said, yet may erroneously assume that learning is occurring. Some students catch on to this game rather quickly and may deliberately open supervisory sessions with a few key sentences, producing a monologue that takes up the conference hour and prevents the student from having to deal with anything he feels insecure about or needs to improve. This student is definitely learning—how to manipulate the field instructor and avoid any *real* learning experiences!

One indication that content is being absorbed is the student's ability to repeat it back to the field instructor. The student may not have internalized the concepts, but at least the supervisor knows that he is listening and has absorbed the words that were delivered. The next level would be to have the student actually demonstrate or put to use what has been taught. Role-playing, tape-recording interviews, and a host of other experiences may all give evidence that the student has understood what he has learned intellectually. The student should also be able to identify the techniques and concepts he has been taught as observed in others' behavior or noted in written materials and reports.

Some anxiety usually accompanies learning. The totally calm, secure student may never have been asked to extend himself beyond the comfort of his existing skills. He may never have had to risk himself to reach higher levels in his abilities. However, once the skills have been taught and the student can see the effects on his daily practice, his self-confidence should increase accordingly. As he becomes more sure of himself and more involved in his educational experience, he will become more critical and less apt to accept things at face value. He will frequently ask "why," "how," and "why not some other way instead" in response to assignments, evaluatory feedback, and instructions. If he is really involved with the learning process, he may ask for special experiences to meet his needs and interests and may even initiate meaningful activities on his own in his desire to explore something further.

Learning Experiences

Once the field instructor and student have established educational objectives, the next task is to assign experiences that will enable the student to acquire new knowledge, apply what he has learned, and then evaluate the results. Experiences do not need to be limited to things that social workers ordinarily do in the setting. For example, staff in a mental hospital may not make home visits because of time limitations and priorities, relying instead on community resources to follow patients after discharge. However, what would prevent a student from following his own patient after discharge through a series of home visits? Perhaps a case is automatically transferred to another worker if the client moves to a different geographical location or a different stage of treatment. Why not have the student continue with the case instead of transferring it? Field instructors, in short, may need to think creatively to maximize their students' experiences.

There are several broad types of learning experiences. To start with the simplest and least threatening and work up to more complex assignments, a student may *read* or *be told about something* (e.g., techniques for conducting an interview); he may *observe it;* he might be the *recipient* of the service or experience (e.g., attending an in-service training session); he could undergo an experience with someone else in a *co-leader or co-therapist* capacity; he can *do the thing on his own;* the student might *be observed by others* while performing a task; he can submit the results to others for *outside evaluation*. Finally, he could conduct his own *self-evaluation*. Learning theorists could undoubtedly add to this breakdown, but for all practical purposes, this brief list covers the great majority of experiences used in most social work settings. The specific experiences suggested in subsequent pages illustrate these levels of activity and are arranged roughly in ascending order of complexity.

The following list presents a variety of actual learning experiences reported to the author by students, field instructors, and school faculty during the past several years. It is not intended to be complete, but it can serve as an introductory menu from which individualized experiences can be selected or developed. If a specific educational objective has been defined, the supervisor may want to go through the list and consider only those items that would provide the experience necessary to achieve the desired objective. The checklist should also bring to mind additional experiences that are not listed.

A special section on establishing an agency library is included at the end of this chapter. The availability of pertinent reading materials is a crucial part of most student learning, and field instructors can take a leadership role in developing and maintaining a suitable library for students, located in the agency setting.

Checklist of Experiences for Field Instructors to Assign to Students*

1. *Read about the psychodynamics of human behavior, specific casework skills, organizational theory, presenting problems of clients served by the field placement setting, or other related subjects.* The student may be directed to find reading material on, for example, drug-addicted infants. The self-directed learner could probably ferret out something appropriate. However, the school library may not contain anything on such a specialized topic. A library on the Ob-Gyn service may contain journal articles on the subject but with a strong medical focus, containing technical terminology and treatment teachniques that are incomprehensible to the student and not entirely relevant to his social work role. Thus, he may find the readings meaningless and resist such assignments in the future.

The field instructor may need to review the existing agency library and bring in something from his personal library or direct the student to a specific source. By pre-screening available materials, the supervisor can eliminate those that are too technical, inappropriate in focus, poorly written, or uninteresting. This takes time initially, but the field instructor will eventually build a bibliography of readily available references that can be assigned to future students. Readings that can be geared toward application to a specific case situation or assignment are even more meaningful. As the student experiences the direct connection between the reading and his assigned task or the presenting problem in a given case, it reinforces his desire to do additional readings in the future and also helps him bridge the gap between classroom/textbook theory and social work practice.

---

*See also Chapter 11 for a discussion of the use of some of these experiences as part of the evaluatory process. See also Appendix F, section 3, "Self-Assessment Questionnaire for Students," for a listing of additional experiences for the student's use in selecting subsequent field placements or initial employment after graduation. Also see Wilson, *Recording,* for an extensive discussion on the use of recording as an instructional and evaluative tool and for self-instructional exercises designed to teach recording skills.

2. *Read old case records* or agency reports. If recording styles and outlines have changed, advise the student of the differences between past and current practices. Warn him that some records will be poorly prepared and should not serve as models for him to copy.

3. *Observe the field instructor or others conducting an interview.* This experience comes with several potential problems, however. The field instructor may not want anyone observing his interviews and may wish the student weren't there. He must carefully select the kind of client situation he brings the student into (if one-way mirrors are not available) so that the presence of a stranger does not adversely affect the treatment goals or relationship. The role the student will play and the manner in which he will be introduced must be planned and discussed in advance. The student should be asked to do more than just "observe the interview and get whatever you can out of it." He should be directed to watch for specific behaviors, responses, or techniques, such as "how I introduce myself," "the use of reflection," or "the client's nonverbal behaviors." A field instructor may have a highly unique or even controversial style of interviewing that he has developed to fit his own personality and value system. The student may need to be prepared for this in advance, which will incidentally help him to recognize that each person must develop his own approach to a certain extent. Even with elaborate preparation and discussion, the student may still emerge from the experience viewing his field instructor as "the perfect interviewer." He may blindly try to copy the supervisor's exact approach, forgetting that this is impossible and undesirable. He may even feel that he will be a total failure if he cannot interview in exactly the same way as his much more experienced field instructor. He may also be overwhelmed when he realizes how much he has to learn "before I can interview like *that*" and feel so inadequate and bumbling in comparison that he becomes immobilized with hopelessness.

On the other hand, the beginning student's anxiety may be relieved when he sees an actual interview for the first time as many of the mysteries about the process disappear. He may find that it is not so difficult as he had thought—"Why, it's only two people talking to each other!"—and feel motivated to get started on his own interviews.

If other staff are observed by the student, the field instructor must select only those who he feels would be appropriate role models. A beginning student needs to observe at least an "average" interviewer. The more advanced student might be exposed to a variety of styles and competences so that he can compare and evaluate each approach. However, the beginning student often lacks the knowledge necessary to distinguish between effective and ineffective skills and may blindly imitate a poor role model or become upset over the experience and have difficulty discussing it with his supervisor.

4. *Listen to a tape-recorded interview or lecture or watch an audio-visual presentation.*

5. *Attend a meeting and take notes for supervisory discussion.* For example, students might attend agency board meetings, staff meetings, public or legislative hearings, interdisciplinary meetings, or meetings of community groups and professional organizations.

6. *Come to the agency at night, on a weekend, or at other "off-hours" to see what goes on then.* This is especially pertinent in settings and programs that are active beyond normal working hours.

7. *Observe interviews with persons applying for social work positions in the agency.* Ideally, the student should observe interviews with persons seeking a position similar to the kind he will qualify for upon graduation. Obviously, the applicants must be screened carefully to make certain that they are not among the student's colleagues, classmates, or acquaintances. If the employer is under pressure to interview or hire a controversial individual, students should not be present unless they are highly mature and are studying social work administration. Only advanced students should observe interviews with applicants for supervisory or administrative positions. Clinical students might consider, as they observe, "Would I want to be supervised by this person? Do I feel he could be effective?" Administration students can identify with a role that they themselves hope to be in one day. Applicants from out of town who have obtained degrees from distant schools usually provide the best candidates for student observation.

8. *Attend interdisciplinary conferences and case presentations as an observer or participant.*

9. *Sit quietly in an intake or waiting room area* and observe the atmosphere, conversation and behaviors or persons entering the service delivery system as well as of those who serve them.

10. *Take a walk through a specific kind of neighborhood.* Students might go in a group to visit an inner-city area, the living quarters in a migrant labor camp or a public housing complex, or a working farm or factory to observe these surroundings and the people who live or work there.

11. *Visit other agencies and service delivery systems in the local community.* These could include a local welfare department, a mental hospital, a "good" and a "bad" nursing home, the local jail or detention facility, a halfway house for alcoholics, a courtroom, a street-corner rescue mission program, a school for the mentally retarded, and so on. Most students find these experiences interesting and worthwhile; however, they should not consume so much of their total field placement time that other experiences are limited.

12. *Attend a court hearing* pertaining to mental competency and guardianship, a client's criminal activity, a divorce proceeding, or a client's effort to obtain custody of minor children.

13. *Have the student go through the service delivery system as if he were a client.* The student might go through intake or the hospital admission process or apply for food stamps (some may be genuinely eligible). In order for the experience to be real, the student should not be identified as such, though agency administrators may be contacted and prior approval obtained for ''sending a student through your intake system sometime in the next month.'' A modified version of this would be to have the student accompany a client who is going through the system.

14. *Participate in a course on techniques of supervision or field instruction.* Most MSW graduates will find themselves supervising eventually, if not immediately after graduation. Yet only ''large systems,'' ''macro systems,'' or ''administration'' students have exposure to supervisory training in most graduate curriculums. Even BSWs often act as supervisors for aides, clerical staff, volunteers, and students after several years of experience, yet most receive no supervisory training while in school. Students who have taken such courses frequently report that the concepts and techniques they learned helped them to be better consumers of supervision. They acquired a better understanding of their own field instructors, the supervisory relationship, and how to get the most out of it.

15. *Attend professional workshops, seminars, and lectures in the community, using field placement time.* The presentation must have some relevance to what the student is learning in field; otherwise an unstructured, disjointed experience can result, interfering with rather than facilitating the overall learning experience.

16. *Team up with another student to service the same client jointly.* Careful thought must be given to the selection of the students involved—whether they are a good match, how their dual roles will be carried out and explained to the client, and so forth.

17. *Co-lead a group.* Another student, staff member, field instructor, or even a member of another discipline could serve as the co-leader.

18. *Conduct interviews with clients and provide direct counseling services.*

19. *Make home visits.* Every student should have the ex-perience of seeing consumers in their natural environment. Many students from sheltered backgrounds need to realize that not everyone lives in the style in which they were raised. Special techniques are needed when interviewing people in their homes, where there is much less ability to control interruptions and often the presence of other people. Thus, some prior preparation is needed. Students may need to be told to stay in the car until someone comes to the door if they are greeted by a barking dog. (Unlike the city, where most people's pets are confined, rural households often have one or more dogs running freely about the property, and they may be very protective and tend to attack well-meaning social workers.) Such nitty-gritty precautions may be obvious to the field instructor but essential to the naive student. Special instructions may be needed regarding reading maps, getting directions in rural areas where the only address is ''Route 10, Hicksville,'' and dressing appropriately for home visits, especially in adverse weather. Special safety precautions may be necessary in urban inner-city areas, and so forth. Many students benefit from accompanying a regular worker on a home visit before ''soloing.'' Two students can also team up to make initial visits together.

20. *Carry a beeper (or be on call via home telephone).* A supervisor or senior staff member would need to be available as a backup person for the student to turn to with questions as he responds to the calls. This activity requires skill in crisis intervention and screening calls that come in and gives the student a sense of independence. Obviously such an exercise should be assigned only after the student has been in field for a while.

21. *Write a diagnostic summary on a specific case, using the Analytical Thinking Model.* Written recording assignments could require adherence to any outlines or forms the agency uses. See Appendix E for the ATM and for case examples to use with this exercise.

22. *Do role-playing* with the field instructor or others to try out new skills and techniques.

23. *Carry a full-sized caseload (or its equivalent) for a limited time.* Students operate in a relatively sheltered environment during field placement. The pressures, responsibilities and size of work load are usually not the same as for a regular, full-time staff member. It is important for students nearing graduation to experience at least a sample of what it would be like to be a full-time social worker. Many students can handle twelve or more cases simultaneously through careful time management. However, being responsible for eighty cases brings up issues of quality versus quantity and priority-setting of a much different dimension. The student who is in field placement three days a week may see only three different clients on any given day. Three schizophrenics may be tolerable; but what if he finds himself faced with sixty?* How does one set priorities when fifteen people need your services today and you have time to see only seven?

Once the student becomes a postgraduate social work employee, he may find no one available to help him with these adjustments. Furthermore, he is no longer in the student role and may be hesitant to reveal his need for help with caseload management. Thus, it would seem much more desirable to expose the student while still in field placement, when it is appropriate to be a learner, to make mistakes occasionally, and when the environment permits experimentation and risk-taking and gives him permission to say "I don't know how to do that." One wonders how many new graduates don't make it through their first probationary period because they were not able to cope effectively with the numerical demands of caseloads and work assignments.

Certain kinds of students are best suited to assuming a full caseload. The individual who is only a few weeks away from completion of his final field placement is a good candidate, especially if he is seriously considering applying for a job in the agency in which he has been placed or in a similar type of setting. Such students need to determine whether that particular kind of social work or job experience is *really* what they want and are best suited for. Even the full-caseload experience cannot guarantee an accurate determination, but it certainly carries fewer risks than turning the unwary student loose in the real employment world, where the penalty for failing to adjust is loss of employment, money, status, or positive references instead of loss of ego and a change of career direction.

Students in block field placement plans can more easily assume full-size caseloads for a period of several weeks at the very end of placement, especially if the nature of the service is crisis-oriented rather than long-term. Concurrent placements pose scheduling problems. If a student is in field three days a week, he might carry 3/5 of the normal caseload of a staff member with the degree the student is about to receive. Part of an extensive Christmas break, the between semester or quarter break, or Easter recess can be used for miniblock placements, with equivalent time off given later on.

Such a plan would need to be strictly optional for the student, as most schools will not support or enforce

*One student completed an extensive block placement (forty hours weekly) just before graduation with her MSW degree. She was a very capable student whose work was generally outstanding. She came to work for the agency full time following receipt of her degree and was assigned a caseload of thirty severely handicapped individuals. After several months, the former student submitted her resignation. She herself offered the reason: "I could handle six or eight sick people at once, but seeing thirty or more every day and being constantly reminded of their demands and obvious needs was just too much. Field placement had not prepared me for this." The decision to leave was an extremely difficult and personally agonizing one for the student to make. The experience caused the agency to reexamine its approach to field instruction and find a way to build in more exposure to the realities for graduating students.

schedules that conflict with the basic school calendar. However, if a setting feels strongly about the importance of the experience, it could register with the school its willingness to accept only those students who are willing and able to participate. This would then be discussed at length in pre-placement interviews, and students who could not or did not wish to deviate from the normal schedule would eliminate themselves and seek placement elsewhere. Such a stand would have to be adopted with some caution, however. For example, if too many settings established similar expectations, highly capable students who must work while attending school or who have heavy family responsibilities might be denied effective field placements.

The informed student will be on the lookout for assignments that use him as a workhorse for an understaffed program rather than treat him as a student learner. Such students may react to the idea of the full-size caseload experience as inappropriate and offer real resistance to the plan. The field instructor must introduce the concept very carefully, with full explanation of the rationale for it. If it is explained in the beginning of field placement and implemented toward the end of the student's experience, he can often see for himself that it is a planned assignment, with a specific educational purpose. Students cannot be given full caseloads and then left on their own or with limited supervision. If anything, the field instructor must be *more* available to the student than normally and able to spend as much time as necessary to help him deal with the new stresses he will face. If this component is missing, then the student is merely an independent employee, and the full caseload assignment serves no real purpose.

24. *Participate in group or peer supervision.*

25. The student might be required to *explain his professional role to others* as part of his contacts with members of other disciplines, orienting consumers to the role of the social worker, or doing public relations for the agency. Contacts with community resources could require explanation of role. Students could visit local high schools to meet with a group of students interested in studying social work, and so forth.

26. *Participate with the field instructor in developing and writing up an educational contract* (see Chapter 6).

27. *Participate in orienting new students or staff to the agency.* Obviously this is feasible only when a student has been in field placement over an extended time period when new students are starting placement.

28. *Keep a daily log of experiences in field and reactions to them.*

29. *Keep statistical reports as required of regular agency* *staff.* Some schools and/or field instructors like to look at hours spent in field instruction (both officially and unofficially through work taken home). In certain circumstances, a time study may also be done to help the student and field instructor examine use of time.

30. *Answer the phone and act as receptionist for several days* to get a feel for the role of these staff members and the demands placed upon the agency. The experience also requires use of selected skills and some knowledge of agency programs, eligibility requirements, and resources in order to screen calls and refer them appropriately. The student-receptionist may also have to deal with the angry, impatient, overtalkative, emotionally distraught, or frightened caller.*

31. *Interview upper-level administrators and supervisors to acquire specific information about the program and their roles.* Remember that some students become quite nervous in the presence of authority figures and may need a great deal of support to complete this assignment.

32. *Interview individuals who have received services from the program to assess their responses to the experience.* The student might design his own questionnaire and method of administration or use an existing instrument.

33. *Serve as a member or observer of the system's peer review, quality control, or audit process.* The student can participate in interdisciplinary and/or in-house reviews of case records, medical charts, or program activity. His own cases might also be pulled for review and findings shared with him.

34. *Assist in writing the program's policy and procedure manual.* (But don't use the student as a workhorse on jobs no one else wants to do!)

35. *Write a report for the administrator of the program.* This might be a standard report that is periodically required or a special report recommending changes or proposing new policies or approaches to service delivery or organizational administration.

36. *Work with the program administrator to gather information for and prepare an annual budget.*

37. *Join and participate in local/national professional organizations* (e.g., NASW, NAACP, Federation of Student Social Workers). The student might attend as an observer at a meeting of an organization that does not grant membership

to students (such as the Society for Hospital Social Work Directors).

38. *Participate (or assume a leadership role) on a committee to plan a major workshop, sponsored by the student's field placement setting.*

39. *Plan and conduct an in-service training session or course.* This could be done for agency staff, though it must be recognized that students often feel quite anxious presenting material to persons whom they may view as professional superiors. The learner might prepare something just for his fellow students or for members of another discipline or a special classification of agency staff (e.g., clerical workers, social work aides, or associates). Bear in mind that in-service training involves several levels:

A. Determining the needs and desires of the target group
B. Arranging for films and guest speakers who actually do the training
C. Teaching content that someone else has prepared, using the suggested format for presentation
D. Teaching someone else's material but developing one's own method for presenting it dynamically
E. Researching and developing one's own content material and instructional methodology
F. Teaching not just to impart facts but also to bring about attitudinal change
G. Assessing the effectiveness of the training and providing follow-up training as needed

40. *Help set up a computerized data bank system* (or learn how to use an existing program).

41. *Develop a bill (in cooperation with appropriate others) for presentation to a local, state, or national lawmaking body* and perhaps even be present to lobby for its passage.

42. *Plan, lead, and conduct a fund-raising activity.* The student could recruit fellow students and staff to bring homemade goodies for a bake sale. He could plan a used-book sale or a car wash to raise funds to purchase books for the agency library, pay for a special field trip, defray costs for attending a distant conference (such as the annual meeting of the Federation of Student Social Workers), or obtain a service or costly item for a client.

43. *Prepare a grant proposal.*

44. *Set up and lead a group.* Groups could have a recreation or activity focus or be therapeutic in nature. Other groups could be primarily informational, while still others could bring together community or organizational groups to form one group to work toward common goals or resolve problems.

*This particular learning experience is often abused, however. Students should not be put into this role until they have been in the setting for some time. Furthermore, they should not be doing this activity simply because there is nothing else for them to do or because someone is hesitant to provide more challenging tasks.

45. *Be a supervisor for a period of time.* The student could assume some of the duties of an agency supervisor and participate in related activities, under very close supervision. He could also supervise another student or a volunteer. The supervisee must be a BSW student if the learner is working toward his MSW and should be hand-picked to ensure a good match between student supervisor and supervisee. The student supervisor will also require very close supervision and should have completed some special training on techniques of supervision and/or field instruction before assuming this role. The student supervisor should also meet most of the prerequisites for field instructors enumerated in Chapter 2.

46. *Act as a consultant to an individual, a group, or a program.* This must concern an area in which the student has significant experience and knowledge.

47. *Process-record* an individual interview, group session, committee meeting, supervisory conference, telephone contact with a community resource, or some other procedure. (See Chapter 9 for a discussion of this exercise and examples of recordings containing supervisory comments.)

48. *Participate in a one-way mirror observation,* either as an observer or as the "subject." It is important that the privacy rights of all participants be protected. Recent legislation and court decisions are making it imperative that all persons who are being observed give permission (preferably in writing) for the observation and be aware of when and by whom they are being observed.

49. *Tape-record an interaction or experience for later review and discussion with the field instructor.*

50. *Be observed by another student during a conference with the field instructor* (or by any other significant individual) and receive feedback designed to increase self-awareness.

51. *Write one's own performance evaluation.* This cannot serve as the student's final evaluation but can be used as a learning experience. Field instructor and student should discuss the student's ideas, which may or may not affect the official performance evaluation prepared by the supervisor.

52. *Prepare an evaluation of the field placement experience and the supervision received.* Many schools require this as part of field placement.

53. *Design and/or implement a mechanism for evaluating the effectiveness of something the student does.* For example, the student may be trying to bring several community groups together toward a common goal. He can be challenged to figure out a way to determine whether he really is accomplishing what he set out to do and how the various community group members are responding to his approach.

Establishing an Agency Library

When this author joined the staff of a large hospital social service department a few years ago, the "library" consisted of a collection of musty, malodorous volumes that hardly anyone ever used. Five years later, a full library-conference room of some size existed, with wall-to-wall shelves filled with more than a thousand current books and several hundred issues of major social work journals. The library was so heavily used by both staff and students that a formal card catalog and regular library sign-out system were instituted. All this was achieved with virtually no funds. How was it possible? Could other settings do the same?

Reading and reference materials need to be physically close at hand if students and staff are to make full use of them. If a casework problem or special challenge comes up at field placement, the learner will not want to traipse halfway across town to his school's library two days later to check out desired references. Furthermore, if it is January in Michigan, only the unusually motivated student will brave below-zero temperatures and a 20-mph wind to visit a library in another building during field placement hours. Thus, each setting that accepts students should examine the possibility of having a small library in an area where both staff and students can come on a regular basis as they go about their daily activities. The clerical work area, a convenient conference room, or even a field instructor's office could hold a few shelves to get a library started.

Most social workers have professional books filling their shelves at home, some of which are rarely used. Even one field instructor can start an agency library by bringing in books from home. Simple 3 x 5 cards can be used to record the full title, author, publisher, and date and place of publication. The cost of the book (should it need to be replaced) might also be noted along with the name of the book's owner. Draw lines across the card on which borrowers can sign and place the date. A space should be reserved for the "librarian" to mark the date the book is returned. Hundreds of these cards will fit in a standard file box less than a foot long. Someone with artistic talent can draw up a humorous "overdue notice" that can be reproduced. Its message should be complete so that the "librarian" has only to fill in the offender's name, the title of the overdue book, and the due date. If the notices are placed in unmarked envelopes (so that they look like a social card or "something special") they will attract attention when received by the borrower.

A few basic rules must be established even at this young stage of development. The author's were quite simple:

1. Help yourself to as many books as you want, but if they pass through my office door, they *must* be

signed out. No exceptions (such as "I'm just going to take it to my desk for one minute.").

2. Everything can be taken out for two weeks and renewed for two more weeks except items on the "reference only" shelf.

3. The library is in my office. You may come in and use it if I'm not there, or if I'm not in conference.

4. You must see me to sign out a book. (The unorthodox "Wilson Sign-out System" necessitated this. It seemed cumbersome initially, but brought enormous benefits. I knew the library and what was in it, and if someone walked in with a vague, "I'm looking for something on . . ." I could usually fill their arms with books before they left.)

5. If you lose something or your dog chews it up or whatever, you must replace it.

6. When a book is returned, put it in my mailbox or on my desk, never on the shelf. It might take me six months to discover you've returned the book.

7. Donations welcome.

There are many benefits to having at least a few books in one's office. When discussing a particular phenomenon or technique with a supervisee, the supervisor can merely reach over and pull out a book to refer to and suggest the student read it. If someone comes into your office and has to wait till you get off the phone, he will usually start browsing through your books to kill the boredom—and leave with several checked out that he had no intention of borrowing. Many fruitful and educational conversations can get started when someone comes to see the field instructor–librarian to check out a book, and so on.

As staff and students make increasing use of the library, the traffic jam in the field instructor's private office may get to be a little much. Some staff may also stay away for fear of disturbing you. If the office is small, you may grow tired of competing for space with the growing library. As borrowers reap the benefits of the library, they gradually begin to feel it is "theirs," and the atmosphere becomes ripe for expansion. The field instructor is no longer alone in his project.

Where will additional books come from? This was the author's first question when she inherited the historical collection described at the beginning of this section. There *had* to be more books somewhere. The department director had a few items on her office bookshelves and was soon persuaded of the benefits of letting her books repose on the official library shelves instead of in her private sanctuary. But there were no social work journals of any kind to be found anywhere, which seemed rather strange. Inquiries among staff who had been there for years produced the same response: "It seems that there must be some around here someplace." But no journals existed.

Things remained status quo until a staff member began working on her doctorate at night. She knew I was trying to

get a library going, and she stormed into my office one day giving voice to a very loud complaint: "Would you please get those *!# social work journals out of the ladies' bathroom—it's a real hassle trying to find what I want in there!" Well! It seemed that I had overlooked one location in trying to find the missing journals. The xerox machine was in the restroom, so why not the social work journals? Surely anyone could figure that out!

The ladies' shower stall contained a number of nondescript boxes, buried under trash, broken items that no one wanted to discard, and reserve toilet paper. But the journals were there: *Social Work* and *Social Casework* going back nearly twenty years. It took several days to wash off the termite wings and arrange them chronologically. Funds were found to renew the subscriptions annually to keep the collection updated. Moral: Library materials can be found in the most unlikely places, and no possible resource or location should be overlooked.

One day a graduate student finished field placement and took a job several thousand miles away. Before leaving, he donated more than fifty books to the humble library—virtually every textbook he'd used through graduate school. Other staff and students soon followed suit, and the library grew by leaps and bounds. Some did not want to give up their books but agreed to have them catalogued as being "on loan" to the library so that others could use them. These individuals always had the right to retrieve their books upon leaving the agency, but many chose instead to donate them at the time of their departure.

Retiring professionals or social workers who are going into a different career may wish to donate their professional books to a worthy cause. Libraries affiliated with schools of social work receive many of these donations, but in one instance the individual simply called his colleagues and told them to help themselves to whatever they wanted from his library, which was extensive. Such windfalls are very infrequent and require being in the right place at the right time. However, these possibilities should not be overlooked.

All donations must be screened carefully by the professional (not a secretary) acting as librarian. If a small agency or departmental library is to be effective, it must contain only the most pertinent readings on the type of social work practiced in that setting and on the needs and presenting problems of those served. A few basic psychology/psychiatry and generic texts are also needed to round out the collection. However, if the main field of practice is mental health, the library should not use its limited funds, space, and energy to acquire the world's greatest collection of readings on social work with unwed mothers or public welfare administration. If potential library customers must sort through piles of materials not related to their daily work, they will use the resource about as often as they do the public library for professional research. Well-meaning staff who are house-cleaning may be glad to get rid of a text on biology dated 1953, but that dosen't mean that the library must accept the donation. Let staff and students know what kinds of materials are needed, and keep inappropriate items off the shelves. If tact, politics, or public relations require that something questionable be accepted, store it in a box somewhere or put it in a back corner or on a special shelf marked "nonprofessional texts" or "historical items."

Do not overlook the importance of novels. Many individuals who will not read anything else will read fiction or biographical books. If these are carefully selected to represent issues of social concern, stories of people with the kinds of problems many of the agency's clients have, or stories of helping professionals, they will be devoured eagerly.

It won't be long before agency personnel will begin wanting some say about what goes into the library. One may work with a lot of drug abusers and want some reading on that; another may be heavily involved with joint marital counseling and want some references at hand. A "Library Committee" can be formed to evaluate the existing library, identify which areas need more references, review new publications, publishers' advertisements, and book reviews to get ideas, and communicate needs to prospective donors. The committee can also screen incoming donations. However, the need for money will surface eventually as staff begin wanting new publications and specialty journals that no one is likely to donate. The committee must then consider fund-raising activities.

Perhaps the most direct method is to take up a collection from staff. This is fraught with risks, however, as some may resent being asked to donate voluntarily and may avoid the library in retaliation. If there is any resistance, the idea should be dropped and an alternate activity pursued. If the atmosphere is right, collection can be highly successful. For example, in one large welfare program employing more than 150 social workers assigned to about twenty different units housed on several floors of a large building, each floor and some units designated a representative to collect twenty-five cents each pay period from willing donors in their area. The funds came rolling in, and staff members' pride increased significantly when they saw the new books being added from their own funds.

Another source of funds is through bake sales, used book sales (it's amazing how many used paperbacks some people dig up), car washes, and similar activities. One student came up with the idea of a "bake and book sale" to raise money for the agency library. She contacted staff, got commitments to bake, gathered hundreds of old non–social work books, got permission to set up display tables in a heavily traveled part of the institution, and sold out within hours, netting nearly two hundred dollars.

The agency or departmental budget should also be examined carefully. It may contain a little-used "miscellaneous" fund that could be used for the library. There may even be funds for journal subscriptions or "professional publications" that carry over from year to year because no one has ever asked for them. Such a budget item may have existed at one time and been discontinued, leaving some hope for having it reinstated.

As the library grows, shelving and space can become increasing problems. Shelving is expensive, and capital equipment budgets may or may not provide for this item. If not, large institutional settings may have a maintenance crew or workshop facilities where shelves could be made. Shelving can be improvised for very little cost by using bricks, concrete blocks, and long boards (make sure the floor will support the weight).

Once the library outgrows an individual staff member's office, it must be relocated. This can be anxiety-provoking to the social worker–librarian, who has thus far been able to maintain tight control on the borrowing of books by making certain that they are properly signed out. When no one is living in the library to monitor this process, an honor system takes effect, and the sign-out procedure may need to be modified accordingly. Written, formal library rules should be distributed to all potential users and included in orientation packages for new staff and students.

The standard sign-out system in use in most libraries requires that each book be numbered and that a packet be pasted in the book to hold the sign-out card. The borrower fills in his name and the borrowing date along with the due date and deposits the card in a designated box. He also stamps the due date on the slip that stays in the book and serves as his reminder. Returned books are dropped in a twenty-four-hour box or returned in person to the circulation desk. Obviously, such a formal system is impractical for most settings unless the library is part of a larger collection within a facility that does have librarians and regular library equipment. Large libraries also contain card catalogs listing holdings by title, author, and subject. The file drawers have special rods to prevent removal of the cards by browsers. Special hardwood or metal shelving eliminates sagging, and book ends keep books upright so the spines won't warp. And so on ad infinitum.*

The small to moderate-size agency library (up to perhaps a thousand volumes plus journals and pamphlets) can probably get by with a modified version of the more ideal system used by larger libraries. Adequate space will be required, and at least one individual must have a genuine interest in the library and assume responsibility for overseeing it on a regular basis. The system described here requires no more than an hour or two of someone's time each week to keep it in order and process returned books, once it has

---

*There are companies that specialize in the sale of library supplies and equipment, ranging from furniture to card catalog file drawers to pamphlet boxes for holding journals to sign-out cards and materials for repairing damaged books. Two large companies are Demco Library Supplies, Box 1488, Madison, Wisconsin 53701, and Gaylord Library Supplies and Equipment, Syracuse, New York 13201 (and Stockton, California 95208). They will send detailed catalogs upon request.

been established. Additional time is required whenever new books are added, however.

This author has set up two libraries during the past eight years, using these guidelines. The system has proved effective and, with some modifications, could undoubtedly be implemented effectively in a variety of settings.

Setting Up a Library: Mechanics

1. Have a stamp made up that says "property of _____ library."

2. Enter the name of the book's owner in the inside cover of all items received. Donated materials are stamped as being the property of the agency. It is a nice gesture to give recognition to the donor by entering his name as well in a conspicuous place inside the cover.

3. Make up a 3 x 5 card for every new and existing library item. This should indicate:

A. Exact title
B. Full name of author(s)
C. Publisher
D. Date and place of publication
E. Edition
F. Cost (give estimate if not known)
G. Date acquired by the library
H. Name of book's owner

A card should be made up for each magazine and journal in the collection, with the volumes, dates, and issue numbers on file in the library listed on the card. If some issues are on loan to the library, this should be noted.

These cards will be retained by the librarian to serve as master control cards for inventory and replacement of lost or damaged items. If an item is known to be out of print, this should be noted both on the card and in the book itself.

4. Use a three-ring notebook binder to set up a "library record book." Ordinary notebook pages can be used to record all library transactions. Pages labeled "Additions" should record the name of item, the date added, the cost, and how it was obtained (by donation, purchase, and so on). "Deletions" can be recorded in a similar manner. This will provide a quick reference to new material and document how funds are being used.

5. Arrange books on shelves by subject area (e.g., "Casework," "Aging," "Children," "Marriage and Family"). Label each shelf and also give each subject heading a number.

6. Put the number of the subject heading inside each book in pencil. This facilitates returning materials to the proper shelf.

7. Put up a corkboard or bulletin board to post a copy of the library rules, notices about new books, or special library activities.

8. Develop a sign-out sheet that can be posted on the bulletin board. It should contain headings asking borrowers to give the following information:

A. Today's date
B. Borrower's name
C. Complete title of book
D. Author
E. Name of book's owner (important because there may be more than one copy of the same book)
F. Date returned

Instruct borrowers that each individual journal or magazine must also be signed out, giving the title, volume, issue number, and date along with the other required information.

9. Returned books should never be returned to the shelves by the borrower. All returned items should be placed in a central collection point (which may be a staff member's "in" box or desk top). The borrower may indicate that he has returned a book by drawing a line lightly through his name on the sign-out sheet. When the librarian processes the book by returning it to the shelf, he can use a distinctive colored pen to mark it off, thus indicating that the book is back in circulation.

Borrowers can renew items by marking "renewed" and the date next to their original entry on the sign-out sheet.

10. Establish a "reference only" shelf for out-of-print items, heavily used reference books, unusually expensive books, or items the owner does not want in general circulation.

11. Check the books and journals periodically for signs of wear, worn covers that need repair, misfiled books, and other minor problems.

12. Conduct an annual inventory by going through the master cards and locating the book that goes with each one. Mark the card in some manner to indicate completion of inventory.

13. Check the sign-out sheet regularly for overdue books. Send humorous preprinted reminders. If this does not produce results, send a second reminder. If a third is needed, a simple statement addressed to the offender has proved effective: "Please return this book by Friday, July 18, or see me before that date to discuss purchasing a replacement." If this doesn't work, bring the problem to the individual's supervisor and request his help.

The library committee may or may not want to institute

a fine for overdue books. This is a source of revenue (though a limited one), but it can also cause hard feelings and delicate collection problems if the majority of library users do not genuinely support the concept. It would seem preferable to begin with no fines and consider this approach only if problems develop later.

14. Consider holding periodic ''open houses'' or parties to display new books or show off a complete reorganization of the library. Display new acquisitions on tables with a separate sign-out sheet attached so that all interested persons can put their names on a waiting list to borrow it. Various creative ideas, with staff and student input, can be used to call attention to the library and thus increase patronage.

8 Handling Case Assignments

Micro/Casework Students

Once a student has begun placement and general learning experiences have been identified, the field instructor must begin assigning actual "cases." This process can cause considerable anxiety for the new supervisor, who often has little idea of the kinds of challenges and presenting problems that should be assigned early in the field experience. Certain types of experiences are definitely not appropriate for beginning students, while others are ideal. Assignments must also be carefully selected for any student who is an "unknown." Some enter field with impressive-sounding backgrounds and/or social work experience. Others may be in a second or even third field placement. Such experiences are no guarantee that these students have appropriate skills. For example, a student with an intensive family counseling or public welfare employment history may find adjustment to an inpatient medical or psychiatric setting just as difficult as an inexperienced student would. Thus, until the field instructor has some feel for the student's skills and limitations, initial case assignments must be screened carefully. If possible, he should read the reason for referral, an intake interview, and the existing case record or transfer summary. Perhaps the presenting problem is for "financial assistance" but in reality the individual is terminally ill or psychotic with a history of child abuse. Obviously, such a case should not be given to a beginning student with no prior social work experience, yet it may seem appropriate if only the reason for the referral or the initial presenting problem is examined.

It may be necessary to get ideas for appropriate cases from other staff. This must be approached with some caution, however. If the supervisor does not communicate clear guidelines as to the kinds of situations he seeks, co-workers may eagerly give up all cases that they find difficult to work with, that do not interest them, or that have been sitting without services for so long they are feeling guilty. Thus, prescreening is essential and must be performed personally by the field instructor in cooperation with the referring staff member.

The field instructor who is carrying a caseload of his own may want to take his student with him to observe a few interviews. If a client is being seen for the first time and the student expresses genuine interest in him and his situation, the situation could then be assigned to the student, although field instructor and student have interviewed the person jointly for the initial contact. This gives the supervisor the advantage of having a feel for the client, which facilitates supervision and interpretation of the student's assessments and also eases the student into involvement with the client.

Beginning students should never be required to find people needing services in order to assign themselves cases (though this can be a very appropriate assignment for a more advanced student).

It is impossible to prescreen all cases accurately and completely. A genuinely simple presenting problem may develop into something more complicated later on. For example, I recently assigned a situation that appeared "stable" though possible child neglect was involved. Within three days of assignment to the student, several family members erupted in physical violence and one key family member died under rather suspicious circumstances. On their initial visit, the two students who had been assigned to the case as co-workers were greeted by a very hostile family member who made threats against their lives. Obviously, I would not have assigned this case had I known this was going to develop.

Occasionally the field instructor will not realize that a student has had a specific life experience that causes him to have difficulty dealing with a particular kind of problem or client. Factual information or existing record materials may be incomplete, inaccurate, or misleading. Thus, the student must be advised that there will be times when the field instructor may need to transfer his case to a more experienced or more highly trained worker. The kinds of circumstances that would necessitate such a transfer should be reviewed, along with a frank recognition that should this occur, it does not mean the student is an ineffective social worker. If this situation is presented as a natural part of the learning experience (and not as a "punishment" for lack of skills), the student can experience meaningful growth in recognizing, understanding, and accepting his own personal and professional limitations. In some instances, it may be possible for the student to continue servicing the case as a co-worker with the regular staff member.

Some supervisors deliberately assign highly complex cases that the student cannot possibly handle (even with good supervision) in order to teach him at first hand the kinds of skills he will need to acquire and the kinds of situations with which he will be expected to work after graduation. This technique may be effective in certain situations with a student who has been in field placement for some time and perhaps feels that he has little to learn or is having difficulty understanding the full professional role that accompanies the degree for which he is studying. However, such an approach carries a great deal of risk for both client and student. A severely disturbed individual being serviced by a student who obviously lacks key skills may regress, withdraw from services, engage in destructive acting-out behavior, and experience needless anxiety and discomfort. Deliberate assignment of overwhelming cases to students who do not have the necessary skills constitutes malpractice. Such assignments will prove anxiety-provoking to the student. If one is made early in field placement, when the supervisor does not know his student well, the field instructor's ability to assess and handle any problems that arise will be at a minimum. Thus, deliberate assignment of difficult cases early in the placement is not recommended.

It can be beneficial to assign two students to serve the same consumer together as a team. They can be equally responsible for all client contacts, all recording, and so forth, or they can divide responsibilities and contacts with clients and family members. Another variation would be to have one student assume a leadership role and carry primary responsibility for serving the client and the second take a more passive, observer role. Or two students can conduct an intake interview jointly, then advise the client that one of them will be following up on his situation as the second student drops out of the picture. The team approach can be effective in providing needed security for first home visits by inexperienced students. A strong student can be paired with one whose skills are not so advanced. If they relate well together, a great deal of important peer learning can take place, and the weaker student may accept criticism and

suggestions from his more advanced counterpart more freely than from the supervisor. Obviously, the stronger student must be a mature individual who will not tear down his partner or compete with him in a destructive manner. Two students can also work together on especially challenging situations where one alone might not have all the skills necessary to handle the problem. By combining two students with various areas of skills, the client can be served effectively and a meaningful learning experience provided. A man and woman might work together in group sessions or family therapy sessions; a male student might accompany a female student on a visit to an unusually hostile individual or a home visit in a dangerous neighborhood. Students of different ethnic and cultural backgrounds and with diverse life experiences will often learn as much from each other as from their client contacts if required to work together. Prejudices can be identified and dealt with, and students who have never interacted meaningfully with blacks, for example, can have this opportunity through a pairing experience.

The field instructor usually assigns very concrete, "easy" situations in the beginning until he can get to know each individual student's areas of skill and limitations. However, students also appreciate an opportunity to select their own cases. For example, each student can be assigned one or more hand-picked cases. The field instructor can have at hand four or five additional cases that he has pre-screened and determined are suitable for students in the beginning of placement, but having varying presenting problems, ethnic backgrounds, family composition, and so on. The supervisor gives a brief description of each case and the kinds of thing the social worker would need to do and presents this to his students so that they can choose one that appeals to them. Each student (if the field instructor is supervising more than one) can select a case on which he will be the primary worker but will have another student work with him as a secondary observer or aide. He can also serve as an observer for another student's primary case. This approach brings about rapid group bonding as students in a unit become familiar with each others' cases and start sharing reactions and experiences both during and after the case assignments have been made. Trainees consistently use good judgment in selecting cases; those with more advanced skills and greater self-confidence do tend to pick the more complex cases, and the remainder express relief that "I didn't get that case." Thus students begin learning their own limitations and can also examine why they gravitate toward or tend to avoid certain situations being presented for possible assignment. Notice that this approach is not quite the same as turning the student loose to find his own cases. All cases presented to the students for possible assignment need to be carefully prescreened by the field instructor and found appropriate.

A student's first few cases should be very task-oriented. The reason for the client's involvement with the agency should be clear and specific. Beginning students have a great deal of difficulty introducing themselves to someone when their role is not clear and it is uncertain why the individual needs to see a social worker or if he wants this contact. Furthermore, the presenting problem should be a tangible matter that can be resolved rather quickly. If a "chronic undifferentiated schizophrenic" is assigned to a student for "supportive contacts," his role and approach are very vague. In addition, it may not be possible for *anyone* to accomplish very much with such an individual. Thus, the student could experience considerable frustration before (if ever) he realizes any reward or sense of accomplishment in working with this client. However, if the presenting problem is concrete and can be resolved through contacts with community resources or by playing an advocacy role, the student can experience rapid and tangible success for which his client may even thank him directly. This gradually eases him into the social work role, builds his self-confidence, and eventually prepares him for more difficult challenges.*

Tell the student what he is to do if the client asks questions he cannot answer and warn him that this may well occur. Let him know that it is permissible to say, "I don't know, but I'll find out and get back to you"—and that his need to do so will decrease as he gains more experience and knowledge. Explain that even experienced, highly skillful staff have to do this on occasion.

Even though assignments ideally should be hand-picked, they should be typical of tasks performed by staff who have the degree for which the student is studying. Do not assign hopeless cases that no one can do anything with or all the drudgery tasks that others avoid doing. Resist the temptation to give clerical tasks out of fear of turning the student loose with clients: He is not attending secretarial school. If necessary, have the student do only one or two rather simple activities as part of a more complex case being served by another staff member.

Try to avoid overwhelming the student by requiring him to learn all the agency's policies, procedures, and forms before he can actually see clients. Instead, assign initial tasks that do not require knowledge of specific agency policies or that permit him to learn these step by step as needed to perform a specific task. Bear in mind that the student is not being trained to work for your agency alone but is there to learn generic social work skills that could be applied to various kinds of settings.

Think creatively. Students can have experiences beyond those performed by staff. For example, the size of regular staff caseloads and priorities may permit only brief, superficial contacts with a lonely elderly person. However, a student could take the time to provide the frequent supportive contacts such a person needs and could gain a significant learning experience in the process. Students could also take the time to make home visits and see persons in their natural environment even though regular staff might not be able to do so.

The following list of more specific do's and don'ts of early case assignment is based on the author's experiences and input provided by a large number of field instructors and students. This list is intended to guide assignments made at the beginning of field placement. Most students will and should have exposure to the more complex situations described in the right-hand column as they gain in self-confidence, experience, and skills, and those who enter field placement with special personal or professional qualifications may be able to handle these complex situations immediately.

Some agencies specialize in the kinds of cases described in the "Don't Assign" column; for example, they may serve only involuntary clients referred for counseling by court order. Such settings should of course describe this reality in detail in preplacement interviews and in their communications with the school and should accept only students who are able to deal with such client characteristics. Even in these settings, some situations will be comparatively more difficult than others; obviously, the simpler ones would be preferred for initial case assignments.

Criteria for Selecting Beginning Assignments for Casework Students

DO ASSIGN

1. Situations where the prior record is well organized and clear. It is possible, though it may take some effort, to figure out who is who and the nature of interrelationships. It is also possible to identify one or more specific problem areas or needs to work on

DO NOT ASSIGN

1. Situations where the prior record is a tangle of disorganized entries, making reference to many different people by name only, making it virtually impossible to figure out who these people are and the nature of their relationship with the client. The family constellation or

---

*The sense of panic that many students feel over their first contact with a "live client" cannot be underestimated. I can sill remember my own first contact. The assignment was to go out to the client's home, pick up a special diet form that her doctor had completed, and bring it back to the office so that it could be decided whether to increase her welfare allowance

to provide for the diet. This was probably the simplest assignment in the history of the agency, and ordinarily the client would simply have mailed the form to the agency. However, I still remember her name, her house, and my intense anxiety over the task. What a relief it was when I actually met her and discovered she was a person like me and didn't bite!

DO ASSIGN

the significant others who are involved may be numerous, presenting a confusing, overwhelming picture. The reader is left with a frustrated feeling that he doesn't know where to begin

2. Clients who have asked to see a social worker—who want the service

2. Involuntary clients and/or those who are likely to reject the social worker during the first contact

3. Situations in which only one person is interviewed at a time and where this factor can be controlled easily

3. Joint interviews or situations where others are apt to be present to participate in or interrupt the interview

4. Mentally alert individuals who can talk about their situation and their needs

4. Individuals in acute pain or who are comatose, mute, heavily drugged or nonalert and cannot or will not communicate verbally

5. Individuals who have some contact with reality

5. Psychotic persons who are totally out of touch with reality (a family member could be assigned instead)

6. Individuals whose personal appearance and/or behavior is not especially frightening

6. Acting-out psychotic individuals; persons with severe and obvious physical handicaps or disfigurements; severe retardates; an infant with bruises and cigarette burns from parental abuse; a patient hooked up to a dialysis machine, respirator, suctioning machine, or other equipment; a patient with a large open wound or severe scarring; and so on

7. Clients whose use of alcohol is moderate

7. Individuals who might be found drunk or "tripped out" on drugs at the time of the student's contact

8. Persons who can reasonably be expected to recover from or overcome their presenting problems, and whom it is possible to serve or help

8. Terminally ill patients (Students can experience severe trauma when their client dies, especially in the beginning of a first field placement.) or individuals in hopeless situations (certain long-standing psychiatric problems or other chronic difficulties for which thorough research by regular staff has discovered no resource)

9. Safe situations where no matter how incompetent or naive the student is, he will not be in any physical danger or unknowingly worsen a hazardous situation for his client

9. Home visits in tough neighborhoods where students could be mugged, harassed, raped, or taken advantage of if certain precautions are not followed; dangerous clients who are known to act out their hostilities physically; sexually seductive or aggressive individuals; child abuse cases involving violent people

DO ASSIGN

DO NOT ASSIGN

10. Clients who will be around for a while in case the student needs to see them several times to complete an assessment or a service; situations where decisions can be made at a leisurely pace

10. Institutionalized or hospitalized patients who are about to be discharged; individuals coming to a crises center where there may be only one chance to engage them in treatment; any crisis situation where decisions and actions must be taken on the spot

11. Situations where the client contact will take place in the agency with the supervisor nearby and available should the student run into any difficulties

11. Home visits, interviews in remote locations or branches of the agency; setting up the first client contact at a time when the field instructor will be absent or tied up in meetings all day

12. Situations requiring contacts with community resources and members of other disciplines who are known to be friendly and at least accepting of the social worker's role

12. Assignments where collateral contacts, other team members, or staff are known to be unreceptive toward or have a poor concept of the social worker's role. These individuals may even reject the social work student, challenge his reason for seeing the client, or display overt hostility toward him

13. A case with a specific, concrete reason for involvement

13. A situation where the reason for social work involvement is vague or dubious

14. Cases involving a long-standing psychiatric or medical problem of some severity, but where the current presenting problem is specific and concrete (e.g. a financial problem)

14. Severely ill or emotionally disturbed individuals who are in an acute phase of their illness and/or have just been diagnosed. These individuals often need to talk about the impact of the diagnosis on their lives and undergo acute anxieties and life changes which a beginning student may find overwhelming and lack skills for handling professionally

15. Individuals who are pleasant, passive, or positive in their feelings toward the service delivery system and its staff

15. Inpatients who are severe management problems owing to lack of cooperation with the treatment program; persons who are basically unhappy with the agency and/or its personnel

16. Highly verbal persons with a need to ventilate; persons with mild senility who are somewhat overtalkative. These individuals often carry the momentum of an interview with little prompting necessary from the student

16. The advanced senility patient who is a nonstop talker; the verbal individual expressing extreme feelings of anger that may be projected onto the social work student; the withdrawn, nonverbal person who will not talk no matter what approach is used

17. Situations requiring basic interviewing (fact-gathering) rather than advanced problem-solving skills (behavior change, insight production, environmental manipulation, for example)

17. Situations requiring intensive diagnostic assessment and therapeutic intervention skills that are treatment-oriented. The emphasis is on emotional, subjective, latent, intangible, covert feelings and/or behaviors rather than on facts, information, overt, or concrete needs

DO ASSIGN	DO NOT ASSIGN
18. A case not previously known to the agency or one where the previous social worker or student was doing a satisfactory job	18. A case handled by a previous worker who had poor skills or who ''botched the case''; any situation where the client might have reason to be angry with the previous worker; a case handled by a staff member who was fired or resigned under less than favorable circumstances. Cases handled by an unusually skilled staff member may also prove threatening for the student as the client recognizes the difference in skill level and may experience difficulty transferring his relationship to the new student
19. A case involving legal issues related to obtaining service for the client, e.g. referral to Legal Aid for help in preventing an eviction or obtaining a low-cost divorce	19. Cases where legal issues involve the agency or service delivery system (The individual may be threatening to sue the agency or staff or may have a history of taking legal action against service providers.); situations involving legally sensitive information necessitating special precautions in recording and handling of information; situations subject to news media publicity
20. Situations where the time lapse between referral or initial intake contact and the student's first contact is brief	20. Situations where a long time has elapsed since the initial referral or agency contact and no one has seen the client in the interim. (Such a consumer may greet the student with resistance or complaints regarding the delay in receipt of services.)
21. An individual with some denial, manipulation, and similar behaviors	21. A highly manipulative client who engages in this behavior as an overall pattern of relating to people (e.g. the alcoholic; sociopathic personalities) to the extent that confrontation regarding the manipulative pattern is necessary. (Even an experienced social worker might find this difficult and achieve minimal success.)
22. Individuals who are sufficiently stable that they will not be harmed by the beginning student's comparative lack of skill (benign ineffectiveness)	22. Clients who could decompensate, withdraw from service, resist counseling efforts by others, or have a key covert need remain unmet if the student lacks adequate skills
23. Cases where the right of self-determination is a relatively abstract concept and not a major factor in the client's life	23. Situations where the client is consciously exercising his right of self-determination and making decisions that appear obviously detrimental to his welfare (e.g. threatening to leave a hospital against medical advice; refusing lifesaving measures or treatment; insisting on living alone when he is blind and can barely walk; legal issues such as mental competence may be involved, and the social

DO ASSIGN

DO NOT ASSIGN

worker may agonize over his responsibility to society versus his client and wonder how far he can let the right of self-determination go before he can or feels he must intervene)

24. For students with prior social work experience, cases similar in nature or presenting problem to those served in the previous employment

24. Clients with diagnoses or problematic life situations known to be similar to significant or traumatic experiences in the student's personal life (e.g. assigning an alcoholic to a student who has told the field instructor that he has an alcoholic parent)

25. Persons who speak the same language as the student but perhaps have a dialect peculiar to their area or ethnic group

25. Individuals whose command of English is too limited to engage in any meaningful discussion without the services of a translator

26. Someone who does not know what a social worker is or does, so that this must be explained by the student

26. Someone with known negative attitudes toward social workers

27. A task requiring completion of paperwork, *in direct relation to a service to a consumer*

27. General clerical tasks or paperwork *not* associated with provision of a service to an individual case—paperwork for paperwork's sake rather than as a professional tool in service provision

28. (Individual field instructors can undoubtedly add more items to both lists)

28. Individuals who are the student's "peers"—e.g. another social work student who also happens to be a client; a professionally trained helping person who is a client (Such cases should not be assigned to students on any level; many such individuals would not accept counseling services from a student.)

29. Clients with *unusually* strong language, who punctuate every sentence with spicy four-letter words or engage in explicit sexual talk (Such behavior can be extremely disturbing to students from sheltered backgrounds and is more appropriately assigned later on in the student's experience.)

Assignments for Noncasework/Macro Students

Many of the same principles of case assignment apply to administrative or macro system students. Perhaps the main difference is that the field instructor must determine whether the student has the required basic skills before he is expected to supervise, teach, or organize community groups. A considerable amount of personal maturity and ease in relating to people is mandatory. The macro system student will be having an impact on a larger number of people than will the average direct services student, and the ramifications of inept performance or significant difficulties will be widespread and could reflect on the agency or system as a whole rather than on just one small segment. The following list presents a sampling of some of the guidelines that should apply and precautions to consider when selecting assignments for macro system students in the beginning of an initial field placement. Bear in mind that many of the exercises listed in the right-hand column would constitute an appropriate assignment for an advanced student; indeed, these situations will be encountered eventually at some time after graduation, and macro system students need exposure to some of the stressful realities of their potential job while still in school.

Criteria for Selecting Beginning Assignments for Macro System Students

DO ASSIGN	DO NOT ASSIGN
1. Supervision of nonpaid staff, students, or volunteers who will not be affected adversely by a change in supervisor when the student completes placement	1. Supervision of paid agency staff or others who would be affected adversely by a change in supervisor when the student completes placement
2. Supervisees having limited social work training and/or experience who will represent the least possible threat to a beginning student supervisor	2. Persons with significant training or social work experience who obviously have skills or experiences equal to or more advanced than those of the student supervisor
3. Supervision of nonproblematic individuals who respond positively to the supervisory process	3. Persons with known negative feelings toward authority figures or who have created problems for previous supervisors
4. Supervisees whose performance is known to be or can be predicted to be at least satisfactory	4. Problematic individuals whose performance is less than satisfactory; situations where the student supervisor might be required to evaluate someone as unsatisfactory, fail a student supervisee, or terminate a paid employee
5. Individuals who have never received social work supervision (volunteers, other social work students) or have had basically positive experiences with former supervisors	5. Individuals who have had bad experiences with previous supervisors (have received poor or inadequate supervision)
6. Supervisees in training for a *lesser* degree than that for which the student supervisor is studying	6. Supervisees who are studying for the same degree as the student supervisor
7. In-service training responsibilities with persons having a neutral or positive attitude toward self-development	7. Training responsibilities with staff or groups known to have negative, nonreceptive attitudes toward receipt of training (If such a response appears likely, the assignment is inappropriate.)
8. An assignment to train persons with professional social work training or experience *less than* that of the student	8. An assignment to train persons having equal or greater social work training than the student (with the exception of fellow students)
9. Having to train others on concepts and techniques in which the student has specialized or possesses significant knowledge and/or experience	9. Having to teach concepts or techniques for dealing with something with which the student has limited experience, e.g. training persons on techniques of supervision when he has never supervised anyone; teaching advanced casework skills when he has completed only a basic casework course and has beginning skills himself

DO ASSIGN

DO NOT ASSIGN

10. Being asked to evaluate a program, committee, or community group that is basically functional—with some problem areas, but no major areas of dysfunction

10. Evaluating a highly problematic program whose participants have strongly negative feelings and in which significant areas of dysfunction exist

11. Observing or participating in a job interview with someone who is applying for a position that does not require the degree for which the student is studying (an MSW student would observe an interview with a BSW applicant, for example)

11. Participating in an employment interview with someone who might be the student's peer or supervisor were he to be hired following completion of field placement

12. Participating in an employment interview with nonproblematic applicants, a "routine" interview

12. Problematic situations where political pressure requires the interview; a minority group candidate who feels discriminated against is being reinterviewed; a person suspected of being terminated from a previous job in the local community is being considered; a fellow student who is about to graduate; anyone the student knows personally or professionally; anyone who objects to the presence of a student during his employment interview

13. Being asked to develop a program, policy, or goal that is wanted by those involved or viewed neutrally

13. Developing a program, policy, or goal that will be received negatively or with resistance by those involved

14. Developing a budget or a proposal that can be implemented in some manner

14. Developing something that is purely hypothetical and does not allow for implementation of the student's ideas in any manner

15. Tackling something that will engender neutral or positive feelings toward the student because it has a positive focus and will benefit those involved in some way

15. Doing a "dirty" organizational job that no one else wants to do because it would decrease the popularity of the person involved

16. Researching, evaluating, studying something that can be readily assessed that lends itself to objective measurement techniques

16. Trying to assess something that doesn't lend itself to measurement or for which no effective evaluation instrument and assessment techniques have been developed

17. Attending and/or participating in administrative meetings, planning sessions, board meetings, and the like where the student's presence is accepted

17. Participating in administrative activities with persons who feel threatened by or uneasy over the student's presence

18. Exposing the student to "inside information" of a relatively safe and insensitive nature (that is, no great harm would be done if the student took the information outside the agency or mishandled it)

18. Participating in activities that expose the student to highly sensitive, confidential information about organizational functioning or staff

19. Allowing the student to observe some problem areas in organizational functioning

19. Permitting the student to be exposed to severe and highly problematic intra- or interorganizational problem areas

20. Exposing the student to colleagues and staff with basically satisfactory performance

20. Involving the student in activities or situations where he learns about disciplinary actions taken, unsatisfactory performance, or termination of a social work staff member; likewise, situations where the student might learn the confidential performance evaluations of student peers

21. Assignments where the student observes, assists, or participates with, rather than as a substitute for, his field instructor/administrator

21. Assignments that force the student to "compete" with the field instructor to perform an identical task, in which observers or participants may readily observe and be upset by any obvious difference in skill between the field instructor/administrator and his student (e.g. a community group that has worked with the field instructor for some time and is taken over by the student; a training course for clerical staff taken over by the student)

22. Experiences that will reinforce rather than challenge the student's belief in service delivery systems

22. Experiences that shock the student prematurely with the realities of the unpleasant side of service delivery systems; situations that could arouse strong and anxiety-provoking feelings and reactions on the part of the student

23. An assignment the student can complete based on his newly acquired knowledge of the service delivery system, agency policy, lines of communication, staff attitudes, and so forth

23. Assignments that the student cannot complete fully in a meaningful or even realistic manner for lack of specialized knowledge about the system (having a student develop a procedure manual for a department or program; set up a peer review mechanism after being in field placement for three weeks; and so on)

24. Experiences requiring exposure to and interaction with middle management and line supervisors

24. Assignments requiring interaction with the highest-level administrator (unless there is no alternative because of the nature of the placement)

25. Situations requiring skills of observation, critique, information-giving, scheduling meetings, making recommendations, and the like

25. Assignments demanding skills in organizational or attitudinal change, facilitating intergroup relationships, policy decision-making, and the like

26. Involvement in situations where "benign incompetency" will have little or no adverse effect on organizational goals or functioning; situations where adverse effects could be corrected speedily and effectively

26. Assignments where student naiveté or incompetence could create serious, complex, delicate, or difficult-to-correct legal or other problems for the delivery system

A Step-by-Step Approach to the First Client Contact

Students are often lost when assigned to their first case: What do I do first? Where do I start? Their anxiety can be decreased considerably if a structured, step-by-step approach to handling the first case is provided. If the student learns a systematic approach, he will develop basic work habits that should remain with him throughout his career.

The following outline presents one such approach that can be adapted to a variety of social work settings. The steps are very detailed and require frequent checking back with the field instructor. Much hand-holding is built into the process. It is also lengthy: A student may spend half a day or even an entire day going through the preliminary steps before he actually sees his client. It is usually necessary for students to go through every step only with the first client or two. Most of the in-between supervisory contacts can be eliminated as the student gains experience and as some things that initially are done in writing are handled orally instead, or merely thought over silently. Steps marked with a bullet (•) are those that should be retained, in one form or another, throughout the student's career. The remaining items can be eliminated as the student gains experience.

•1. *Read brief, current identifying data pertaining to the client.* The student should review the intake interview report or client application for services; a master card file notation giving identifying data; a written referral form, and so forth.

•2. *Do reading on the primary diagnosis or presenting problem.* If the client comes with a diagnosis of "diabetes," "paranoia," "educable retardate," or "amyotrophic lateral sclerosis," the student must understand what these terms mean before he can begin to think about their implications for his client.* If the presenting problem is unwed motherhood, alcoholism, poverty, or a recent divorce, reading can be done in these areas as well.† This step has proved highly effective in helping students integrate classroom theory with field work practice. Textbooks suddenly become alive and meaningful when the student starts applying them to real case situations.

3. *Think hypothetically about the needs of a person (or persons) with this problem or diagnosis.* What needs might a heart patient have? How does a psychotic break affect a person's life? What special needs might an alcoholic have because of his drinking habit and/or the physiological and psychological factors that led to his alcoholism? What might be the needs of an elderly, arthritic individual?‡

4. *Discuss step 3 with the field instructor.* The field instructor can determine what the student has learned from his reading and help him explore possible problem areas as he prepares to think about the needs of his individual client (as opposed to just anyone with the same diagnosis or presenting problem).

•5. *Read the primary case record and/or interdisciplinary chart for the client.* With this step, the student starts to consider the needs of the particular client within the context of what he has already learned. Warn the student that he probably will not understand most of what he reads in medical or psychiatric charts because of illegible handwriting or medical symbols, abbreviations, and terminology.** If an interdisciplinary chart is involved, it may be desirable for field instructor and student to go through the first record together, so that the instructor can point out where certain types of information can be found, the sections most useful to social service and those which are highly technical and not really of interest. Encourage the student to write down questions that come to mind as he reviews the record. These might pertain to the record itself or to things he wants to ask others about. If he is reading an old social service record, discuss the kinds of things that are recorded (or not recorded) and indicate if recording styles and expectations have changed since the record was written. It may be pertinent to discuss some of the pros and cons of reading records in advance as opposed to seeing a client "cold."

•6. *Hypothesize very specifically regarding the possible needs of the particular client on the basis of all that is known up to this point.* This could be done orally or in writing. (Notice that step 3 can eventually be eliminated, but this one must remain. Experienced social workers move directly into thinking about a specific client after completing pertinent readings or research.)

7. *Discuss Step 6 with the field instructor.* The student is encouraged to think analytically and fit together the knowledge he has gained thus far to come up with conclusions.

---

*I once reviewed a random sampling of service cases in a welfare program. One continually repeated a lengthy, strange-sounding medical diagnosis; it described a woman in her thirties, living in an apartment with a teenage son, having difficulty working and supporting herself on her welfare check. I happened to have a medical dictionary handy and looked up the diagnosis. It was a rare skin disease from which most patients died. In the end stages it becomes so excruciatingly painful that the individual cannot stand to wear any type of clothing. How could the welfare worker in this case possibly understand and meet his client's needs without knowing this key bit of information? Yet it was obvious that he was totally unaware of the meaning of the diagnosis.

†See Chapter 7 for suggestions on how to select readings for students as well as how to create an agency library without funds.

‡See the Analytical Thinking Model (ATM) described on pp. 280–282 for a suggested approach to teaching analytical, diagnostic thinking. The student could apply all or part of the ATM to steps 3 and 6 if desired, although it is most effectively applied following a period of actual involvement with the case situation.

**Presumably he has been provided with a glossary of the most commonly used terms.

Reassure him that these are not iron-clad and are subject to change. Some will be confirmed and others eliminated as he actually gets to know his client. This step provides an excellent opportunity for the field instructor to engage in real teaching and allows him to get a beginning sense of where his student is in terms of existing skill and knowledge. It can also lead to a discussion of possible interviewing or treatment approaches and the client's probable response to the social worker's involvement.

8. *Role-play the first contact with the client.* It is important that the beginning student have an opportunity to "practice" before he is faced with a real interview. The supervisor demonstrates approaches to introducing oneself and the purpose of the contact—an area of considerable anxiety for most beginning students. The student then takes the part of the interviewer while the field instructor role-plays probable client responses based on what is known thus far. The student should be prepared for a variety of responses; otherwise he may become immobilized if the client does not respond as anticipated.*

If a student is working in an interdisciplinary setting, it may be valuable to talk to a member of another discipline to get certain information prior to the first contact. The student may need guidance in preparing for this experience. Some professionals (e.g., physicians) have little patience for certain types of approaches on the part of a social worker. For example, they like their colleague to get right to the point. Thus, role-playing may be helpful. It may or may not be desirable to have some discussion between field instructor and student after the contact has been made and before the student goes to step 9. This mini-interview could also be process-recorded.

9. *Interview the client.*

10. *Process-record the contact with the client.*† It is important that the student's schedule allow this to be done *immediately* after the first interview if possible. First interviews are usually brief (perhaps ten to twenty minutes) but can take several hours to process-record. Some students will drop into the field instructor's office right after their interview to report that they survived, express feelings about the experience, and raise questions. Such spontaneous feedback should be encouraged but should not replace the more detailed process-recording. If the student goes into too much oral discussion about the content of the interview, his subsequent recording will be less complete, as he will tend to omit things he feels he has already shared with the field instructor. This may or may not be a problem, depending on the field instructor's objectives and the student's responses to the interview situation.

A definite time limit should be set so that all process-recordings are completed within forty-eight hours after the interview occurs. Otherwise, the student may procrastinate and/or forget important details.

11. *Give the process-recording to the field instructor for review and feedback.* The field instructor reviews the recording, makes comments in the Supervisory Comments Column (see pp. 119-144), and returns it to the student *before* the next regularly scheduled conference.

12. *Student and field instructor meet to discuss the process-recording and plan for subsequent contacts with the client.* This discussion should take place as soon as possible after the student has completed his recording. The student should be encouraged to comment on the supervisory remarks written on his recording, raise questions, and give his ideas regarding the next contact with the client. He should play an active role in the discussion—not just listen passively as the field instructor presents his wisdom about what should be done next. Student and supervisor might role-play and re-create selected interchanges from the process-recording to see what alternative responses and techniques suggest themselves. Additional readings might also be assigned. Specific plans should be made for the next contact with the client, so that a definite purpose and approach are clearly established.

Size of Caseload

How many cases should the average student be expected to carry at once? How many different cases should he have during the course of his field placement? Unfortunately, there are no easy answers to these questions, which plague even experienced field instructors.

The primary guiding force in the student's field experience should be the overall educational objectives—what must be learned and the best way to teach it. This should determine the size of the caseload, not the reverse. Obviously, a beginning student with no prior experience, who must apply all twelve steps, will take a long time to prepare to see just one person and write up his contact. If he is learning basic skills and attitudes, it may not matter if it takes several weeks before he gets a second or third case. If

---

*For example, a student and her field instructor prepared for a first interview with considerable discussion and role-playing. The individual was hospitalized and recovering from recent surgery. Therefore, the emphasis was on preparing the student to have a brief contact with a person who would probably be lying in bed, somewhat groggy, and perhaps in some pain. The student left the field instructor's office and went directly to the patient's room for the interview. Five minutes later there was a knock on the supervisor's door, and a panic-stricken student blurted out "Help! My patient is awake and sitting up and talking! What do I do now?"

†See Chapter 9 on the use of process-recording in student education. Tape-recording or direct observation by the field instructor is too threatening to use in first interviews; summary recording does not provide the supervisor with sufficient detail about the interchange that took place during the interview. Thus, process-recording is the most desirable reporting method under the circumstances. Of course, it is not placed into the formal agency record but is used only for teaching purposes.

a student has had a very sheltered life experience and needs exposure to people of diverse backgrounds, he may be assigned a larger number of cases but work with simple, concrete, brief problems. On the other hand, an advanced student who is focusing on the intricacies of transference in a long-term relationship or studying family therapy may carry very few cases but have intensive, frequent, lengthy involvement with each one. A beginning student may be having difficulty establishing relationships or developing an appropriate interviewing style for getting at basic factual information. Thus, he may have only one or two clients and may spend hours developing certain basic skills before he takes on more.

The field instructor often feels anxious if his student has completed a term of field placement and has seen only four or five clients. There is a fear that someone will think he hasn't been an effective supervisor/educator. However, there may be a very good and educationally appropriate rationale for giving a student only a few cases. The performance evaluation should refer to the educational objectives established with the student (see Chapters 6 and 11). It should comment on the learning experiences provided and how they fit in with the assessment of the student's skills and objectives. A large volume of cases does not necessarily indicate an effective field experience and may even be detrimental if it does not fit the student's educational needs. Bear in mind, however, that if a student is completing field placement with a rather small total caseload, he will experience a stressful adjustment when he finds himself employed and coping with a much larger work load. Thus, the field instructor needs to discuss at length with the student differences between what he is doing in field and the realities of a full caseload and build in some educational experiences that will equip him with beginning skills in caseload management. If a student is able to function effectively as a social worker only if he carries no more than three or four cases simultaneously while receiving three hours of supervision per week, this individual is obviously not ready for the demands of professional social work practice and should not receive a passing grade. In other words, the expectations and experiences of field placement must be sufficiently similar to what an employed social worker is expected to do for the placement experience to be a valid measure of the student's ability and readiness to function as a social work employee.

Other factors can also affect size of caseload. Perhaps the most basic is the total number of hours the student is in field. Obviously, one who is in a block placement of forty hours a week for six months will carry a much larger caseload than one who is in the field only two days a week for twelve weeks. Some students put in hours beyond the minimum required and carry a heavier work load by choice. More advanced students can usually handle a larger volume of cases, especially if they have prior social work experience. However, some advanced students studying in-depth therapeutic techniques may actually carry a smaller than average caseload. They may run groups and see families in addition to seeing clients individually. These activities require many more contacts than serving one lone individual. One complex case involving contacts with many significant others may be equivalent to four or five cases where all contacts are with the client only. Thus, the nature of the field placement setting, its clients, and the service delivery system often affect caseloads and renders comparison between settings virtually meaningless.

Size of caseload, then, is a highly individual matter depending on the setting, the student's needs and qualifications, and the expectations of the field instructor and the school. Supervisors and students should not become concerned if purely numerical comparisons appear inconsistent or their own experience differs from that of someone else.

9 Process-Recording: A New Approach to an Old Technique for Assessment and Teaching

Process-recording can be an effective way of monitoring student interviews and also a dynamic teaching tool. Unfortunately, it has been so misused that most students have never heard of it, and many field instructors have horrendous memories of having to do it in their own apprenticeship. Let's see if a more creative application of process-recording can overcome some of these problems.*

Process-recording must be used as a teaching device, not presented as "the way we record in social work practice." Process-recordings should never become part of a formal case record; once they are no longer needed by the student or field instructor, they should be destroyed. When a student process-records, he will also need to prepare an appropriate summary entry for the case record.

Process-recording requires that the student write down, as best as he can remember, everything that took place in an interview, including everything said by both the interviewer and the client. Nonverbal actions should also be described. For example:

I looked through the door and saw Mrs. W. sitting with a partly finished lunch in her lap. I knocked on the door and she motioned me in.

W (Worker): Good afternoon, Mrs. W. How are you today?

Mrs. W.: Hi, honey. Oh, about as well as can be expected at my age.

W: You're not feeling well?

Mrs. W.: Just about to starve to death on this diet the doctor gave me.

W: What can you have on the diet?

She got up and went into the other room. When she returned she showed me the diet her doctor had written out for her.

W: It sure doesn't look like much food!

Mrs. W.: It sure isn't!

---

*See Suanna J. Wilson, *Recording: Guidelines for Social Workers* (New York: Free Press, 1980), for a more detailed discussion of the use of process-recording including more than twenty examples of process-recorded interviews. Many contain supervisory comments and illustrate interviewing techniques as well as showing how to process-record. The text is written in an informal style and can be assigned to students by field instructors as a self-instructional manual to teach the basics of recording.

Some students attempt to summarize or paraphrase what each person said. This is not as effective, as the recording will not show how the student communicated his ideas or exactly what the client said in response; the recorder may be omitting things he considers insignificant. The following example is typical of this less effective style of process recording:

I went this morning to visit with Mrs. Nancy Brown and was greeted at the door by Mrs. Mary Adams, Nancy's mother. I introduced myself and asked if Mrs. Brown was home. She said, "I don't know, I'll see." She went to the back of the house and returned with Mrs. Brown. I introduced myself to Mrs. Brown and told her that I was her new worker and was going to continue where her last worker left off.

    Present in the living room were Mrs. Brown, Mrs. Adams, Billy, and I assume Mrs. Belinda Adams (the great-grandmother). I asked Mrs. Brown how she had been getting along lately. She said "Fine." I asked her if there was anything she needed and she shook her head "no." I asked her how Billy had been—if he had been sick or anything, and she said "no."

    There was a pause, and I said that I remembered that she was considering divorce and asked if she had changed her mind or made any plans toward it. She said she had written her husband a letter the day before yesterday. I asked if she had had any contact with her husband since the last worker's visit.*

This style of recording makes it much more difficult for the reader to zero in on a particular technique used by the student in order to reinforce skillful approaches or strengthen weaker ones.

Nor is a mere verbatim account of the interview sufficient. Students need to be aware of the feelings they experience as they interact with consumers. Self-awareness is basic to effective social work practice and helps students identify judgmental attitudes, countertransference, over-identification and loss of objectivity, normal human feelings, and so on. I recommend that students record their gut-level feelings parallel to the interview they are reporting.

Finally, process-recording gives the field instructor an opportunity to comment on each remark made by the student and the client. The field instructor can enter his remarks in a third column, opposite the interchange the student has recorded. Thus, a creative approach to process recording would use three columns:

It is difficult to put one's feelings into writing, and students may tend to use the "gut-level" column to analyze or comment on the client's responses instead of to record their own feelings. If this occurs, a fourth column can be added for "analysis." This will encourage the student's developing diagnostic skills by providing a place for recording his interpretations while also forcing him to separate out his own feelings from his professional assessments.

The following process-recording illustrates the three-column method. Notice in column 3 the several spots where one would think the student would have had a feeling response, yet didn't record anything. Notice also the remarks entered in the supervisor's column. Some are critical, others raise questions, and still others label and reinforce positives and effective techniques. The opening preliminaries in the interview have been omitted.

This beginning-level undergraduate student had returned from the home visit asking for permission to close the case as she felt that she had explored everything and that if there

Supervisor's Comments	Dialogue	Student's Gut-Level Feelings
In this column, the supervisor enters his comments opposite the material recorded in the "dialogue" column. He may point out techniques used by the student, comment on the meaning of a client's response, raise questions for the student to think about, suggest alternate responses or techniques, and so forth.	This is where the student records the content of what took place in the interview, using the style described on pp. 118–119. W: Hi, how are you today? Mrs. S.: Fine, how are you? and so on.	The recorder puts down any feelings he was aware of as the dialogue was taking place. For example, "I felt anxious."

*Names and identifying details in all recording examples have been altered to preserve confidentiality.

Supervisory Comments	Dialogue	Gut-Level Feelings
I'm sure your being more comfortable affected the interview positively.	Mrs. B: I got a letter from my husband on Monday and he said to go ahead and file for divorce.	I felt a little more confident than last time.
I wonder why the sudden change?	W (worker): So you are filing for divorce?	I was surprised—Mrs. B. was very willing to talk this time!
I'll believe it when I see it!	Mrs. B.: Yeah—I'm going to go ahead and do it.	
	W: Are you planning on filing soon, or are you going to wait a while?	I'm feeling more at ease.
I wonder what other feelings she has about what's happened?	Mrs. B: Pretty soon, I hope. I may as well get a divorce since he's going to be in jail for 15 years.	
What are the four kids doing while you all are talking?	Sister: I think she ought to go ahead and get one.	
	W: Where is your husband now?	
	Mrs. B.: In Puerto Rico.	
	W: What jail is he going to?	
	Mrs. B: I don't know.	
Your bias is showing (for her to get the divorce!)	W: Would transportation to Legal Aid be a problem—if so, I'll be glad to take you.	
	Sister: The car wouldn't be a problem—we've all got the family car.	
She should know if she's filed before.	Mrs. B: How much would the divorce cost me?	
	W: I'm not real sure—probably nothing or maybe just a small amount. I'll check on it for you.	
	Mrs. B.: OK. I've filed for divorce once before.	
I wonder if she filed thru Legal Aid?	W: When did you file?	I feel like I'm getting somewhere—not far, but somewhere.
	Mrs. B: Back in 1973.	
Yes, you're making a start.	W: Well, whatever happened?	

Supervisory Comments	Dialogue	Gut-Level Feelings
	Mrs. B: Nothing.	
	W: Did you not follow through with it?	
	Mrs. B: No, my husband cross-filed.	
Good! This was a natural place to bring this up.	W: I remember that your husband filed for divorce back in 1973. Whatever happened to that?	
This could be explored further.	Mrs. B: (looking puzzled) I don't know—maybe he didn't follow through.	
OK. How might this have been said interpretively?	W: (Mrs. B. was looking around). Are you uncomfortable talking with me?	Her looking uncomfortable made me feel uncomfortable too.
	Mrs. B: No, why?	
	W: I just thought that you might feel a little uneasy in here (the room was full of people).	
	Mrs. B: No, not at all.	
	Sister: It's OK—we're all family.	
	W: OK. That's fine with me. I just want us to be on a comfortable basis with each other.	
Let's talk about this some re your needs and hers.	Mrs. B: I am (smiling).	Relieved.
	W: Good.	
	W: Where's Billy today?	
	Mrs. B: My mother went out of town to visit some friends and she took him with her.	
Good—you clarify your purpose. I hope she realized you hadn't gotten a new report and were just following thru on old reports.	W: Well, you know the reason I'm here is because of a report we had that Billy had been seen in the streets and that he wasn't supervised properly.	I finally got to the purpose of my being there.
This is certainly better than the grandmother keeping him all the time.	Mrs. B: I know. But there's always somebody with him now.	

(Continued)

Supervisory Comments	Dialogue	Gut-Level Feelings
	When I go places I usually take him with me, but when I can't take him my mother keeps him.	
	W: So there is somebody with him all the time?	
	Mrs. B: Yes.	
It sounds like you're not sure what to say next.	W: Well, that's what I wanted to know.	
	W: (looking at sister): Is that your sister?	
	Mrs. B: Yes (smiling).	
Natural, honest, relaxed communication. Good for building rapport and putting everyone at ease.	W: You two look exactly alike. When I first drove up I thought it was you. The last time I saw you you had your hair in curlers and I didn't know what you looked like with your hair down.	
	Mrs. B: (laughing). And now you see me with it dyed!	
	W: Oh, it doesn't bother me (laughed).	It felt good to laugh.
	W: I'm sorry I missed seeing Billy today; tell him I said "Hi."	
	Mrs. B: OK.	
Now what did you really expect her to say here?	W: Is there anything else on your mind or that I should know?	
	Mrs. B: I can't think of anything.	
	W: Well, I guess I'll be going, but please let me know if you should check into your divorce or if I can help in any way.	
Purpose of next contact?	Mrs. B: OK, I will.	
OK. How long did your interview last this time?	W: I'll be seeing you again next week, OK?	

Supervisory Comments	Dialogue	Gut-Level Feelings
Sorry—I don't think you can close this case yet. Can you figure out why? A much better interview than the first one! You might go back and check your responses—can you find any times when you used reflection, interpretation? How many times did you ask a direct question?	Mrs. B: OK—come back! W: I will, bye.	I felt great! It wasn't half as bad as the initial visit.

were any problems she had missed, the client would have mentioned them. After the process-recording was discussed in supervisory conference, she changed her mind.

No student will remember everything that was said in an interview, nor will he record everything exactly the way it was said. However, process-recording does provide a picture of the student's interviewing style and the kinds of client responses he had to deal with and requires that he record everything he can remember, whether or not he considers it important. This avoids many of the problems discussed in connection with the use of summary reports as a monitoring method (see pp. 152–160). Surprisingly, the fact that process-recording doesn't reveal everything can be a bonus. Students don't feel quite as exposed as with taping, where they have nowhere to hide. Thus, process-recording is not viewed as a particularly threatening activity and can be used very effectively with students just starting placement who are usually too insecure to use taping effectively. Process-recording can also be done in conjunction with taping to help students compare their recall of the interview with what really was said. The significant omissions and inaccuracies can then be examined with an eye to what causes an interviewer to remember certain things and not others.

Most students respond positively to getting specific, detailed supervisory feedback written right on their recording. If the material is returned to the student prior to a supervisory conference, he can look it over, think about any questions the field instructor has raised, and come prepared to discuss the interview in depth or perhaps even to challenge the supervisor's comments. The recording can be used for role-playing during the supervisory conference (with the student in the part of the client, the recording is read almost like a script in a play). When the problematic interchange is reached, the field instructor can demonstrate the use of alternate responses, and the student responds as he feels his client might have responded. The roles can be reversed as the student practices using a reflective or interpretive response instead of a close-ended question, for example, to

see if this gets at the client's underlying feelings more effectively.

More advanced students can be asked to critique their own process-recording by pretending to be the supervisor and entering comments in the left-hand column or perhaps labeling each interviewing technique they have used. (See pp. 131–137 for an example of this kind of recording.)

The following interview was conducted by an undergraduate student in her final month of placement. She was very young, had no prior social work experience, and entered placement with virtually no knowledge of interviewing skills. Her initial interviews relied heavily on closed-ended (yes or no) questions, and her first client wouldn't talk to her beyond monosyllabic responses. Thus, she had spent the quarter learning how to use a variety of interviewing techniques and how to look beneath the surface to explore more subtle meanings and feelings. The student had been making good progress but one day came storming into the field instructor's office, very angry over this particular interview. She felt she had been manipulated by her client and was angry that she had let it happen. She had long since stopped process-recording her interviews but suggested that she process-record this one so that she and the instructor could try to figure out how she had been manipulated. The interview took place during a home visit, and the interviewees are a mother and a grandmother (Mrs. T.'s mother). Notice how the supervisor's comments don't give the student all the answers but instead challenge her to think. Some patterns of client behavior are identified, and some tidbits are tossed out to stimulate the student to want to learn more.

In this case situation, other staff from the agency had been working with the family for some time around budgeting, because Mrs. T. always ran out of money toward the end of the month and needed emergency food. She often spent her money on foolish things, seeming to have no understanding of priorities or budgeting. She asked almost everyone she saw for food or money, and the worker was expecting that this might happen to her. It is also interesting to note that after the worker talked with the child's school-teacher, it was discovered that he was being physically abused. Had the student not been helped to look at the content and approach to the client as evidenced through her process-recordings, this information might never have come to light.

Supervisory Comments	Dialogue	Gut-Level Feelings
	W: Hello, Mrs. T.?	
	Mrs. T.: Yes.	
Did you give a purpose of your visit?	W: Hi. I'm Henrietta Feldman and I'm your new worker from the ABC Agency. Can I come in and talk with you for a while?	
	Mrs. T: Yes, come on in. (The eighteen-month-old son was wandering around and also the grandmother.)	
	W: How have you been?	
	Mrs. T: Oh, pretty good, I guess. I'm so glad it's pretty outside now so the kids can go out and play. I hate the snow.	
	W: I'm glad it's warm outside too. This must be Gary (the youngster) and you're Mrs. T. also (the grandmother)?	
	Mrs. T: Yes, this is Gary and my mother-in-law. I was just getting ready to feed Gary again. He eats two eggs for breakfast and sometimes a bowl of cereal.	Big eater for a little kid!
	W: Boy, it sounds like he eats pretty good.	
Is this a proper diet for a kid his age? Does she serve the meat regular, mash it, etc.?	Mrs. T: Oh, he does, and he loves potatoes and potted meat too.	
	W: Has he been pretty healthy lately?	
	Mrs. T: Oh, yes, he hasn't been sick in a long time, and he's been eating like a pig.	
	G (grandmother): I've already fed him once this morning and he's hungry again. He drinks a lot of milk, too. He goes through about a jug a week. We get it from the milk-	

Supervisory Comments	Dialogue	Gut-Level Feelings
	man and he lets us pay him later. We've just about got him weaned. He drinks from a glass but at night we put him in bed with a bottle. We weaned him from the pacifier already.	
	W: That's great. So he does eat pretty good?	
Beans, bread and potato—100% starch—with a little protein.	Mrs. T: Oh yes. We're having beans and bread for supper tonight. But we don't have any potatoes.	
	W: Tell me, how is Bruce?	
	Mrs. T: Oh, just fine. He's in school. He hasn't missed a day in a long time. He loves school.	
	W: How's he been feeling?	
Denial?? What has client been told?	Mrs. T: Good, except he's got that problem about wetting his pants. It's a bowel problem. He does fine on his main job but will just wet all over himself. The doctors won't tell us what's wrong. I don't think they want us to know. Sara has tried to find out and they won't tell her even.	Physical or psychological— maybe request a psychological exam.
Check with Sara on this.		
Good!	W: Sara who?	
Who is Sara? Is she a social worker?	Mrs. T: Sara Williams. She comes out here some, but she hasn't been back out here since about a week and a half ago. Yes, she helps me a lot.	
	G: And Bruce has that heart problem too.	I didn't know about this.
Good reflection!	W: Heart problem?	
	G: Yes, the doctor said it was a heart murmur and he may grow out of it.	
	W: I didn't know he had a heart condition. Who is your doctor?	
Interesting. What could this mean?	Mrs. T: Oh, we just go to different ones.	

(Continued)

Supervisory Comments	Dialogue	Gut-Level Feelings
	W: Where do you go to the doctors?	
	Mrs. T: At the emergency room.	
	W: At the pediatrics clinic there?	
Boy, she just jumps from one subject to another.	Mrs. T: Yes. And what bugs me are the kids that pick on Bruce out here.	
	W: What do you mean by "pick on Bruce"?	
	Mrs. T: Oh, just like the other day. This girl was whipping him like his mammy because he was rolling a barrel down the sidewalk and she said that it was making her mother nervous. She was beating on his back.	Why doesn't she crack down? I wouldn't let anybody whip my kid.
	W: Is she a big girl?	
	Mrs. T: Yes. I told her that the only people that should whip him was his mama and daddy. She shouldn't be beating up on him.	
	W: Have you talked with her mother?	
Have you read up on enuresis or incontinence? There are definite psychological as well as physical implications.	Mrs. T: No. But I may have to. That's just not right. And the kids make fun of him too because he wets his pants. But he can't help it. I told them that too.	Poor Bruce.
Good! What technique was this?	W: Sometimes kids can be mean.	
Gads—one complaint or problem after another—what's she really trying to say? A certain interpretive comment needed somewhere in here—do you know what it is?	Mrs. T: I know it, and there's some mean ones around here too. These old boys set the trash cans on fire and put sugar in your gas tanks. They stand around and smoke that old pot and drink a lot. I'm scared of them. I always lock my doors when I'm here and when I'm not.	Rough environment.
	W: That's good that you lock your door.	
	Mrs. T: And you know, they keep upping our rent.	

Supervisory Comments	Dialogue	Gut-Level Feelings
	W: How much is it now?	
Aha! I see why you got manipulated. Let's discuss the dynamics of what she's doing in the first pages of this recording. Can you figure it out?	Mrs. T: It's $107.00 because every time my old man gets a raise they up the rent. It's hard to manage because we only get $50.00 food stamps and it's just hardly enough. All we have to eat tonight is beans and bread. We don't even have any potatoes for the boys—and they love potatoes. Do you think you can get us some money for food? Our food stamp card hasn't come yet. It probably won't be here until the end of this week.	
	W: Have you used all of your stamps?	
	Mrs. T: Yes. It's hard to feed five on $50.00 a month. It usually goes in one week.	
	W: Do you have enough food to last until the weekend?	
	Mrs. T: No. All we have is beans and bread.	
	W: Do you have any money to buy some food with?	
If he gets paid every two weeks and he doesn't get paid again for two weeks, it means he just got paid! Confrontation or exploration needed here!	Mrs. T: No, and my old man don't get paid until two weeks. He gets paid every two weeks now. He used to get paid every week and it was easier.	
	W: Well, about the food, let's wait until the mail comes today and see if your card comes. What time does it usually come?	
	Mrs. T: Between one and two o'clock.	
"Does this happen often? What have you done to get food when it has happened before?"—possible responses.	W: Why don't you call me after the mail runs and let me know if you got your card. And if it doesn't come we'll see what we can do about some food. OK?	
	Mrs. T: OK, but I really don't think we can make it until next week.	

(Continued)

Supervisory Comments	Dialogue	Gut-Level Feelings
Good question.	W: How do you and your husband budget your money?	
	Mrs. T: Oh, we don't. When we get it we just get what we want.	No wonder!!
Was this the best possible response here?	W: It's helpful to budget money because sometimes if we don't, we sort of run short at times at the end of the month.	
Many people (e.g. your supervisor) get paid once a month!	Mrs. T: I know, but it's hard since he's just getting paid every two weeks.	
	W: How would you feel about making out a monthly budget?	
	Mrs. T: It would be all right, I guess.	
A good example of advice giving.	W: A budget might be helpful to you in that you would know how much money you had to spend on different things and it might help you come out even at the end of the month.	She didn't seem real enthused.
Yes—I wonder what her change of subject means.	Mrs. T: That would be good, because it is usually hard at the end of the month. Did I tell you about Bruce?	A quick change of subject.
	W: No, what about Bruce?	
The first noncomplaint!	Mrs. T: He was in a track and running contest at that gym last Friday and we went and watched him. He won two ribbons.	Special olympics—good!!
	W: He did! That's great! Two ribbons?	
	Mrs. T: Yes, one in running and one in long jumping.	
	W: Sounds like he's pretty good.	
Good. I'm curious what teacher will say.	Mrs. T: He is. His daddy and him stand in here on the floor and see how many blocks they can jump. His teacher said he's doing real good in school too.	

Supervisory Comments	Dialogue	Gut-Level Feelings
	W: Where does Bruce go to school?	
	Mrs. T: At the elementary school over the hill. He'll be in the second grade next year.	
	W: What time does Bruce get home from school?	
	Mrs. T: About four-fifteen. He rides the bus.	
	W: I'd like to meet Bruce. Would it be OK to talk with him at school since it would be kind of hard for me to catch him here?	
I'm getting an uneasy feeling throughout this interview—she's painting a picture of a perfect family.	Mrs. T: Yes, that's fine. Teacher says he's doing real good in school.	Good.
	W: I'd like to get to know your husband too.	
	Mrs. T: Well, he works every day.	
	W: What are his hours?	
"He works such long hours you'd never be able to see him 'cause I know you work from 8 to 5 p.m." Avoidance?	Mrs. T: He goes in at seven a.m. and doesn't get home until about six. Sometimes he doesn't get home until eight. He works for the county. He just got a raise.	
	W: That's great, he must be a hard worker.	
"See, it's not my fault he wets his pants or is made to feel bad—it's their fault."	Mrs. T: Oh, he is. He works like a dog. And he loves his boys more than anything. That little Gary takes up for his brother Bruce too when those other kids pick on him. I hate that these kids do that to him. They make fun of him too and he can't help it.	
	W: You might want to talk with the kids' parents—that might help.	
	G: That's what I think she	Granny just butts right in.

Supervisory Comments	**Dialogue**	**Gut-Level Feelings**
"At least <u>we</u> don't do <u>that</u>.	ought to do. I hate to see our kids mistreated. There's some mistreated children down there. Their parents just go off anywhere and leave their kids.	
	W: They leave their kids?	
	Mrs. T: They do—by themselves. They've already taken the kids away from them four times. They'll probably do it again for good.	
Good question! Do you know why?	W: Who stays with Bruce and Gary when you're not here?	
	Mrs. T: Oh, I usually take them with me but when I don't she (pointing to grandmother) does. I never leave them by themselves. I would never do	
I was right! (see quote above)	that.	
You fell right into it with both feet! Can you figure out what I mean?	W: That's good. You know, you should never leave small children by themselves. There's no telling what they can get into.	
	Mrs. T: That's right.	
Why did you choose to end the interview here?	W: Well, I'd better be going. After your mail runs, give me a call and let me know if you got your food card or not. If you did, fine, but if it doesn't come, we'll see what we can do. And you don't have any extra money you could use for food?	
Wait! I thought she said he wouldn't get paid for two weeks?	Mrs. T: No, he don't get paid until next Friday.	
	W: Well, all right. Here's my name and phone number. What times does the mail usually run?	
	Mrs. T: About one or two.	
	W: OK, then, give me a call.	
	Mrs. T: I will—bye.	
	W: Bye.	

Process-recording takes a long time to do. For example, it took at least an hour of intense concentration for the student to produce the recording just cited. Process-recording should be done as soon as possible after the interview has been completed, preferably no more than twenty-four hours later. Ideally, beginning students' schedules should be arranged to allow one or two hours after each of their first few interviews to do detailed recording, reading, and just plain thinking about the interview. This is obviously impractical after the first couple of weeks of placement, and process-recording should then be used selectively and in combination with, if not replaced by, other methods of monitoring the student's activities and providing instructional feedback (see Chapter 10). If students are allowed sufficient time for process-recordings and they are consistently turned in late, a frank discussion should ensue to explore this problem. Perhaps the student doesn't understand how to do the recording or perhaps he feels insecure about his interviewing skills and consciously or unconsciously is resisting receipt of supervisory feedback. Feedback on summary recordings and self-assessments is much less threatening, because only the outcome or only the part that the student wants to share with the field instructor is subject to assessment. Areas of weakness are more evident in process-recording. This factor can also be anxiety-producing for the field instructor: As long as he avoids direct observation, he can avoid confronting the student with specific areas where growth is needed. When weak areas are obvious, the field instructor feels very keenly his responsibility to do something. Sometimes life seems simpler for everyone if problem areas just aren't discovered.

The following process-recording was completed by an unusually advanced undergraduate student about halfway through her field placement. She was able to use a variety of interviewing and counseling skills consciously and differentially and label the techniques used in the third column. She includes very few feelings of her own but gives some very significant analytical comments regarding her client's responses.

The client was a middle-aged woman. Her case was about to be closed by the agency because she had refused rather simple surgery and it was felt that nothing further could be done for her as she was exercising her right of self-determination. However, the student learned that she was actually dying of another illness no one knew about. The trainee had learned this through a rather routine contact with the client's physician (with her permission), and the client had hinted that she knew she was quite ill.

The student's primary goal in this interview was to help the client begin talking about her feelings about death. This was very difficult for the student, who first had to become aware of and face her own feelings about death and dying. Several intense supervisory discussions took place, and considerable role-playing was done to desensitize the student and help her feel comfortable talking with someone about how it feels to die. The student had had several interviews with Mrs. W. in which Mrs. W. provided opportunity for this discussion, but the student had always backed off because of her own discomfort and insecurity about her skills in discussing such a sensitive topic. The student approached this interview prepared to use interpretation, reflection, empathy, and confrontation along with open-ended questions to help the client express her feelings. Notice the strong positive reinforcement in the supervisory comments column; the student's summary recording is included at the end of the process-recording.

Supervisor's Comments	Interview Content	Gut-Level Feelings
Date? Client's name?	I looked through the door and saw Mrs. W. sitting with a partly finished lunch in her lap. I knocked on the door. She motioned me in.	
Open—ended question.	W. Good afternoon, Mrs. W. how are you today?	
	Mrs. W.: Hi, honey; oh, about as well as can be expected at my age.	
Good interpretation.	W: You're not feeling well?	
	Mrs. W.: Just about to starve to death on this little diet the doctor gave me, just about 1,800 calories you know.	Why does everything go so fast? I don't even have time to get acquainted with her.

(Continued)

Supervisor's Comments	Interview Content	Gut-Level Feelings
Open-ended question.	W: What can you have on the diet?	
	Mrs. W.: Not much—no salt or no sweetener. Look at this little cup of beans and half a tomato and cottage cheese and I've still gained weight.	
Reflection and closed-ended question.	W: Gained weight—is that bad?	
	Mrs. W.: Yeah, the doctor wants me to lose weight.	
??	W: What does he think that will do?	Try to get at the extent of her knowledge of the disease.
	Mrs. W.: On account of my liver disease.	
Was there a better way of asking this?	W: Does he think that will cure you?	
	Mrs. W.: No, just keep me from getting worse.	
Reflection.	W: Worse?	
	Mrs. W.: Well, dying is just a part of life.	OK. She slipped right into it.
Good. You've got another chance. Good reflection (could also be interpretive or clarifying).	W: So if you don't follow the diet you may die?	Interpretation.
	Mrs. W.: (nods yes) (no eye contact)	
	W: How do you feel about dying?	Confrontation. I feel a tightening inside of me though.
Denial?	Mrs. W.: Like I said, it's a part of life.	
Good interpretation! You're putting her underlying emotion into words for the first time.	W: Are you afraid to die?	Suggesting this to her.
	Mrs. W.: No honey, I've had a long life.	Denial.
The silence must have been really uncomfortable for you—congratulations on your effective use of silence!	W: (Silence)	
	Mrs. W.: I'll tell you, nobody ought to be afraid if they're ready to die!	Ah—is she ready to die?
	W: Ready to die?	
Hm—what's she saying here—	Mrs. W.: You know: got things	I'm remembering the last in-

Supervisor's Comments	Interview Content	Gut-Level Feelings
guilt? Something unresolved in past or present life?	right, begged God to forgive 'em, go to church and stuff.	terview where she said she recently started going to church and wants to go more.
	W: And are you ready to die?	
Good question—picking up on her contradictions.	Mrs. W.: No (pause)—not that I've done any real bad sin or anything.	Careful... remember what we talked about in supervisory conference. I don't want to shut you off.
Good confrontation!	W: But you say you're not ready to die?	Clarification and confrontation.
She admits her fear.	Mrs. W.: No, I guess not.	What does she feel will get her ready to die?
Clarification—and also what else?	W: You said if someone is ready to die they shouldn't be afraid. Does that mean you're afraid?	Clarification.
	Mrs. W.: (Avoids eye contact and no answer) I'm not afraid to be dead, it's like a sleep— no pain or nothing.	Ah—a difference here between death and the process of dying. I'm glad I did the reading.
Good—you keep pursuing!	W: No pain, is that what you're afraid of, suffering?	Interpretation.
	Mrs. W.: I guess no one likes to suffer, but you have to take the bitter with the sweet.	Yes, she's afraid.
Good reflection and interpretation throughout this section.	W: Mrs. W., you said you wouldn't be afraid to be dead. Are you afraid of the process of dying?	Interesting. Suffering and dying are related.
Right—I'm sure she is also tense.	Mrs. W.: Like I said, I guess no one wants to suffer, but sometimes you just don't have control over it.	I feel so much tension. I don't think it's all me either.
Great interpretation—feelings of increasing dependency, potential loss of ability to function, etc.	W: You feel helpless, then.

Mrs. W.: Yeah (she gets out of the chair and starts for the kitchen). I'm going to get me some more beans. Can I get you something to eat? | Client flight. I'm glad. If it hadn't been her I'm afraid it would have been me. I feel like an intruder, probing and playing games. I'm ashamed of myself. |
| Obviously this was too uncomfortable for her, so she left the scene. | W: No thank you.

W: Mrs. W., you said you had a liver disease. Do you know the name of the disease? | |
| Let's discuss your discomfort here. | Mrs. W.: Yes. See, it's a leak | I want her to tell me about the alcohol. |

(Continued)

Supervisor's Comments	Interview Content	Gut-Level Feelings
	in my liver. It's called cir-rhosis.	
Good—you're trying to find out what she knows about her illness.	W: Cirrhosis. Wonder what causes that?	
	Mrs. W.: Oh a lot of people get that....	Generalization (a defense).
She rationalizes.	W: I wonder if you know what causes it, though.	
	Mrs. W.: Oh, lots of things, I heard.	
	W: What kinds of things?	
Could you have confronted her with your observation that she didn't seem to want to talk about the cause of her cirrho-sis?	Mrs. W.: I can't remember just now—I'll think on it. What's that you got in your hand there, something for me?	Avoidance. She's not ready to talk to me about the alcohol.
	W: This is a Medicaid form. I thought we'd fill out.	
	Mrs. W.: What do they want to know, a lot of questions they have no business asking?	Felt like she wasn't just talking about the ques-tionnaire—maybe I'm overly suspicious.
No, I don't think you're overly suspicious. It may have been a stab at you—you've just been asking her a lot of anxiety-provoking questions.	W: Yeah, it looks that way (we both laughed, seemed to ease the tension).	
	We started filling out the form. Date of spouse's death.	
	W: Mrs. W. when did your hus-band die?	Let's approach death in a less threatening way.
	Mrs. W.: Last year, January 6, 1978.	
OK—kind of an empathic com-ment. You could use a few more of them—there's quite a few questions throughout the in-terview without too many em-pathic comments mixed in.	W: Just a year—that's not a long time.	Empathic.
	Mrs. W.: You're right, it seems like it was yesterday.	
	W: (Silence)	I used silence here inten-tionally.
Guilt again?	Mrs. W.: I'll tell you one thing, when they're gone you think about all the things that happened in the past, times you quarreled with them and didn't do right by them.	

Supervisor's Comments	Interview Content	Gut-Level Feelings
	W: Did you and Mr. W. fight a lot?	
	Mrs. W.: Well, not a lot, but all married people fight. We did fight right before he had his stroke though.	Yes—feelings of guilt.
Guilt!		
Good reflection.	W: His stroke?	
	Mrs. W.: The stroke he had and went into the hospital with.	
Gads! Does she feel responsible for causing his stroke and subsequent death? No wonder she has strong feelings re death.	W: Is that what he died of?	
	Mrs. W.: No, they found out he had a pancreas problem but couldn't operate because it was so close to his heart. But they kept getting him out of bed when he was so weak and then he fell. After that he had three heart attacks two hours apart and died.	
A pancreas problem.... many alcoholics get this. Did Mr. and Mrs. W. by any chance drink together?		
	W: How did you feel at that time?	Exploring.
	Mrs. W.: Confused. I don't remember too much about it after he died.	
	W: Who took care of all the arrangements after he died?	
	Mrs. W.: His daughter did, she would come at night and take care of him and I'd go home. I would be there from eight-thirty every morning to almost six each night.	
	W: That's a long time to be at the hospital each day. How long did he stay there?	Empathic.
Aha! She doesn't want to suffer like he did when she dies! This is her real fear!	Mrs. W.: Five weeks, but he suffered for a long time 'fore he went in the hospital. The doctors said in the hospital they could keep him alive on some machine but...	Guilt.
	W: Did you make that decision that he not be kept on the machine?	Let's explore.

(Continued)

Supervisor's Comments	Interview Content	Gut-Level Feelings
	Mrs. W.: No, his daughter did. She said he wouldn't want that.	
Good.	W: How did you feel about the decision?	
This seems hard to believe.	Mrs. W.: I don't remember much about it. I told his girl to do what she thought best.	
	W: How do you feel about it now?	
She's also saying she wouldn't want to be kept alive artificially.	Mrs. W.: I don't tell somebody to do what they think is best and then hold it against them, but I'm glad she didn't keep him alive; it's hard to let them go but it's better than keeping them alive to be a burden on others and in pain.	
	W: Be a burden on others?	Reflection.
	Mrs. W.: You know, expense and everything, when they just lay there and don't know you or anything and are in like a deep sleep.	
	W: A deep sleep. Like they are already dead.	
	Mrs. W.: Yeah.	
Fantastic! You don't miss a thing do you?!	W: How would you feel if it were you?	
	Mrs. W.: I'd want to just go on and die. I wouldn't want to be in pain or have anyone keep me alive. It's better to die quick than linger on in pain. Don't get me wrong, I wouldn't do anything crazy or anything.	Suicide! Glad I did the reading.
OK—now you begin to get at this.		
Reflection.	W: Anything crazy?	Reflection.
Is she thinking of suicide—or has she in the past?	Mrs. W.: You know, stop taking my medicine or take too much or something.	She's thought about it!
	W: (Silence) Have you thought about doing just that?	Confrontation.

Supervisor's Comments	Interview Content	Gut-Level Feelings
Fantastic—you aren't afraid to explore this, and it must be explored.	Mrs. W.: No, I'm not in that much pain. Besides, it's wrong (quickly).	
Great—you make her specify—you don't assume anything.	W: What's wrong?	Reflection.
	Mrs. W.: You know, taking your own life.	
I wonder if she would feel differently if she were in a great deal of pain.	W: Do you have a lot of pain now?	
Hey! What happened? You got so close, and then suddenly the interview goes off in another direction. What do you think happened?	Mrs. W.: Not now, especially since Mrs. Chapman is helping me out a lot, bind up this rupture and everything.	Avoidance.
	W: Rupture?	Reflection.
	Mrs. W.: One doctor calls it a rupture, the other calls it a hernia. Mrs. Chapman knows just where to put it when she binds it. She works at the hospital, you know.	
	W: Is she a nurse?	
	Mrs. W.: No, she's a first aid worker.	
	W: Did she use that special wrap Dr. Powell gave you?	
	Mrs. W.: Yeah, she's been real good to me (pause). Well, let's get on with this form.	Flight.
This was a really good counseling session. You handled your own feelings really well.	We finished filling out the form without further incident.	
	W: Thank you for talking to me today, Mrs. W. I'll be back to see you next week.	
Let's work some on how you might have ended this more effectively with less worker flight.	Mrs. W.: Okay, bye, honey.	

SUMMARY

In my interview with Mrs. W. we discussed her knowledge of the extent of the liver disease. She told me she was aware she had cirrhosis and is dying. She indicated she was not afraid of being dead, but doesn't feel she is ready as she hasn't made peace with God. She has started going back to church and plans to attend more. I feel she is making a step in this reconciliation. She is afraid of suffering, pain, and dying and has equated these three as being the same. She indicated that she had thought about suicide but wasn't about to cope with the fact she had even thought about this. She was very reluctant to talk about these feelings with me.

She has not revealed to me whether she did/does drink. I have not confronted her with the fact that I am aware of her past history of drinking. She seems to have some guilt feelings concerning the attack her husband had before entering the hospital which terminated in his death. She seems to have resolved this, however, and has stated the reason she feels he died was the accident he had while at the hospital. I hope to pursue these areas in further contacts. We filled out a medical insurance form, and the date Mrs. W.'s insurance takes effect is 2–3–76. She is receiving help from a neighbor with some household chores.

The following interview is typical of those conducted by first-year graduate students or undergraduate students just starting placement. Notice the heavy reliance on closed- and open-ended questions. A field instructor reading the interview might feel frustrated because of a strong desire to explore further some of the areas the student has touched on but has obviously not discussed in sufficient depth really to understand the client's needs and feelings.

Supervisor's Comments	Interview Content	Gut-Level Feelings
	W: Hello, Mr. and Mrs. Smith. I'm Sally Brown, your new worker. How are you?	
	Mr. Smith: Oh, we're pretty good, I guess. We're waiting on it to rain.	
	W: It looks like you've been doing some mowing.	
	Mrs. Smith: Yes. He works himself to death. He mows different lawns around here.	
	Mr. S.: Yes, that lady down there likes me. She just pays regular help $2.90 an hour but she gives me more. She tells me that I'm one of the poorest men she's ever seen.	
	Mrs. S: What size shoe do you wear?	
	W: An 8. Why?	
	Mrs. S.: She gave me some real pretty shoes but some of them are 7½ and they're too small.	

Supervisor's Comments	Interview Content	Gut-Level Feelings
	W: Oh. I bet they'd be too small for me too. Do you mow a lot of yards?	
	Mr. S.: Yes, it gives me a little extra money.	
	Mrs. S.: He's going to kill himself. I don't see how he does it.	
	W: The children look good. Have they been sick lately?	
	Mrs. S.: No. We've still got a lot of medicine left over from when they were sick. I don't know what to do with it.	
	W: You could save some things like cough syrup in case they should get sick again.	
	Mrs. S.: Yeah, I believe I will.	
	W: Are the children caught up on their shots?	
	Mrs. S.: Yes. We had them to the doctor about two weeks ago.	
	W: Do you have much problem with transportation?	
	Mrs. S.: Well, usually his nephew takes us, but he ain't very reliable.	Why?
	Mr. S.: I'm scared of his driving.	
	Mrs. S.: Well, I'm kind of used to it now.	
	Mr. S.: Oh, why don't you just tell her the truth?	What's going on here???
	W: The truth?	
	Mrs. S.: Well... he drinks a lot and we're sort of scared to ride with him.	
	W: He drinks a lot?	

(Continued)

Supervisor's Comments	Interview Content	Gut-Level Feelings
	Mr. S.: Yes, and he weaves and carries on and we're scared to ride with him.	
	W: Boy! I don't really blame you, when it could be endangering your lives and your children's. Do you have anyone else to take you?	Really!
	Mr. S.: Sometimes the neighbors take us if it's an emergency.	
	W: That's good that you have someone you can depend on without being scared to ride with them.	
	Mr. S.: Look, Joe is wanting to walk real bad. He can walk if he holds your fingers.	The children look good.
	W: He is trying to walk, isn't he?	
	Mrs. S.: Yes. I think he's doing real good. He ought to be flying around here in no time.	
	W: I bet he will. It will take a lot to keep up with him.	
	Mrs. S.: Me and my husband take turns watching the boys to give each other a break.	
	W: That seems to be a good idea.	
	Mr. S.: Looks like it's going to rain.	
	W: Yes, it does. It's so pretty up here. Do you enjoy living here?	They could use some better housing.
	Mr. S.: Yeah, we like it, but I wish we could find a place closer into town.	
	Mrs. S.: Yes, I just hate living so far away from everything.	

Supervisor's Comments	Interview Content	Gut-Level Feelings
	W: Have you considered moving closer in?	
	Mr. S.: Yes, but we don't know of any place to look.	
	W: Would you rather live in an apartment or house?	Don't blame them. They're so used to living off by themselves.
	Mr. S.: A house. I don't want to live in an apartment. You're too close to everybody.	
	W: You're used to living away from everybody up here.	
	Mrs. S.: Yes—if we had a yard where the kids could play. But I'd live in an apartment just as well I guess.	
	W: Maybe that's something we could check into together. How do you feel about that?	
	Mrs. S.: I think it is a good idea. Don't you?	
	Mr. S.: Yes, I reckon.	
	Mrs. S.: Look at them blades (lawnmower).	
	Mr. S.: Yeah, you can't get them any sharper than when you do it yourself.	
	W: They look pretty sharp to me. Do you do all your repairs on your mowers?	
	Mr. S.: Yes, I try to.	
	W: That's great. You must know a lot about mowers.	
	Mr. S.: (grinning) I do my own repairs.	
	W: How are you fixed on food and necessities?	
	Mr. S.: I need to go pick up my green stamps. My card came the	I guess he got mixed up!!!

(Continued)

Supervisor's Comments	Interview Content	Gut-Level Feelings
	other day and I guess we need to go on to the store, don't we honey?	
	Mrs. S.: Yeah, we are getting kind of low.	
	W: Who will take you to pick up your stamps?	
	Mrs. S.: I reckon his nephew, unless you could take us.	
	W: When would you need to go?	
	Mr. S.: Any time that's good for you.	
	W: OK, how about tomorrow at eleven-thirty?	
	Mr. S.: Oh that's fine, little lady. We'll be ready and I'll give you some money for gas, little miss.	
	W: Oh, no. I'll take you but I don't want any money for gas.	
	Mr. S.: Well miss, I've always paid my way or at least tried to.	
	W: I appreciate it but the Department pays for my gas. OK?	
	Mr. S.: Well, if you're sure.	
	W: I'm sure. Here, let me give you my name and phone number so if any emergencies arise you can let me know.	
	Mrs. S.: OK. I'll keep it with Joann's.	
	W: Joann who?	
	Mrs. S.: Joann Billingsly. You know her? She comes out about once a week. She loves these boys better than any- thing. She always talks about them.	

Supervisor's Comments	Interview Content	Gut-Level Feelings
	W: I'd like to meet her. Is she a help to you?	
	Mrs. S.: Yes, she's real good to us.	
	W: That's good. Well, listen, I'll be back tomorrow about eleven-thirty and we'll go to the food stamp office and the store. OK?	
	Mr. S.: OK, Miss, that's fine, and we're much obliged to you.	
	W: You're welcome. I'll see you tomorrow.	
	Mrs. S.: Bye. See you tomorrow.	
	W: Bye.	

Suppose you were this student's field instructor. What comments would you put in the supervisory column? In reviewing a process-recording (or a taped interview), it can be useful to consider the following kinds of questions:

How many times did the student's comments consist of questions?

Do the student's responses appear appropriate to the behaviors and statements of the client(s)?

Does the student pick up on subtle clues and communications, or do the student's responses indicate that these were ignored or passed over?

Are there some rather abrupt changes of subject when the client brings out feelings rather than discussing tangible, concrete needs?

Are there interactions that you feel certain the student must have had a gut-level response to, yet the third column is blank?

Does it appear that the student knows what techniques he is using and why? If he did something effectively, does it appear that he knows *why* it was effective? (Don't make too many assumptions!)

Does it appear that the student has some specific things in mind for the next contact, based on what happened in this interview? Are there some things you and the student will need to discuss and role-play in preparation for the next interview?

Can the student benefit from reading up on certain defense mechanisms, interviewing techniques, physical or mental diagnoses, or other phenomena to help him understand his client better?

Is there a pattern to the client's responses that the student seems to be missing?

The supervisory comments column can be used to provide comments, questions, and guidance to the student on these matters. Effective techniques must be noted and acknowledged. Strive for constructive criticism that motivates rather than stifles the student. Avoid giving him all the answers; challenge him to figure out some things for himself with a few hints and key questions from you to get him started. Supervisory feedback should be given as soon as possible after the student's recording has been received: Delays of more than two or three days lessen the impact considerably.

One problem in assessing process-recorded or taped interviews is the lack of standards against which to measure them. Directly observational assessment methods are recommended for monitoring and assessing student performance, but how do we interpret what we see, hear, or read? What do we look for that tells us the student is functioning at a beginning, intermediate, or advanced level? Would there be any consistency in assessment if, say, six different field instructors listened to the same tape or read the same recording?

The following checklist for assessing taped, recorded, or observed interviews was developed by the author with input from a group of field instructors. It represents a beginning attempt to rate interviews quantitatively and objectively. The rating scale has not yet been tested fully, but it does yield surprisingly consistent ratings (less than a .5 spread in scores in many instances) even when persons with markedly differing levels of professional training and experience use the checklist to rate the same interview.

Most of the items on the checklist can be evaluated immediately after observing, hearing, or recording a student's interview. A few items require postinterview discussion with the student to achieve full assessment. Notice that several items make reference to the three-column method of process-recording.

Instructions for Completing the Rating

Items in the left column represent characteristics typically associated with beginning-level skill in interviewing. The right-hand column describes the same characteristics as they would be demonstrated by a more highly skilled interviewer. Review the checklist before reading the interview. Then number a sheet of paper from 1 to 32. Each of the checklist items is to be rated on a scale of one to five. A score of ''1'' would indicate low-level skill; ''5'' would represent advanced skill (the right-hand column). Thus, if your student's interviewing behavior for item 3 on the checklist is as described in the left-hand column, assign a low rating; if it is more like the description in the right-hand column, assign a higher rating. Rate each of the thirty-two items in a similar manner. If an item appears not to be applicable, mark it ''NA.'' Note, however, that the mere absence of the behavior or characteristic described in the item may not necessarily mean that the item is not applica-

ble. Perhaps the skill should be present, in which case a ''1'' rating is appropriate. For example, item 3 concerns introductions to new clients on initial interviews. If an introduction should have occurred but did not, assign a ''1'' rating. However, if the student's contact is his third or fourth interview with the client, an introduction would be inappropriate and the item should be marked ''NA.''

Add up the thirty-two raw scores and divide the total by the number of items to which you assigned a numerical rating to determine the average raw score for the interview. For example, let's suppose you assigned ratings to twenty-five of the thirty-two items and that the total raw score is 100. The overall rating for this interview is 4.0, indicating a fairly advanced level of interviewing skill. Whether this level is above average or not will depend on the student's stage of training. A student with no prior social work experience in a first undergraduate field placement would be functioning at an ''outstanding'' level if he earned a ''4'' on interviews. A student finishing a second-year graduate field placement in casework, on the other hand, would be expected to perform at a 4 or 5 level for these basic interviewing skills, and anything less than that would really be unsatisfactory. Thus, the performance rating will vary depending on each student's situation.*

*See Suanna J. Wilson, *Interviewing: How to Do It* (New York: Free Press, forthcoming), for further discussion of practical interviewing skills and additional approaches to and tools for rating interviewing effectiveness.

Checklist for Determining Level of Interviewing Skill*

BEGINNING INTERVIEWER	MORE ADVANCED INTERVIEWER
1. Student usually sees client or client's family members one at a time rather than jointly. There is no group interaction, or very little.	1. Student is assigned cases requiring sessions with family members as a group (as in family therapy).
2. The purpose of the interview concerns concrete needs rather than emotional needs. The student focuses on the concrete needs.	2. Student deals with concrete needs but uses various interviewing techniques to elicit and explore feelings associated with these needs.
3. In initial interviews, the student fails to introduce himself fully to the client by giving his name, where he is from, and why he is seeing the person. He often starts asking the client questions without explaining why he is there. If an explanation is forthcoming later during the interview, it is usually in response to a direct question from the client (''Who are you?'' ''Why are you here?'' ''Who asked you to see me?'')	3. The student almost always introduces himself to a new client by giving his name, where he is from (the social service department), and why he is there before asking any questions or getting beyond the preliminary, small-talk phase of the interview.

*This checklist is a modified version of one that appears on pp. 25–32 of Wilson, *Recording*.

BEGINNING INTERVIEWER

MORE ADVANCED INTERVIEWER

4. The student uses the same basic introduction with all new clients regardless of their situation or presenting problem. He seems to have a stock approach for use in all situations.*

4. Introductions to new clients are varied. The student obviously responds differently to each person, depending on the nature of the situation and the presenting problem.

5. The reader gets the feeling that the student is not fully comfortable with his client or himself in the interview situation. There are obviously awkward moments when the reader can feel the student's desperate struggle to conduct the interview.

5. The reader gets the feeling that the student is basically comfortable with himself, his role as a social worker, and the interview. Awkward moments are brief and rare.

6. The gut-level-feelings column has comments such as "I felt like I was prying," or "This isn't any of my business," or "I felt uneasy asking these personal questions." The student appears unclear or uncomfortable with the professional role of the social worker. He appears unsure of his purpose for being there and seems unconvinced of the necessity to ask personal questions.

6. Appropriate questions are asked without apparent hesitance or discomfort.

7. The student enters the interview situation with a rather structured and clear idea of the approach he plans to use. He may or may not be able to abandon the preplanned approach if greeted with something unexpected or if client shows strong overt behaviors or feelings such as by crying or acting-out in a hostile fashion.

7. Student enters interview with an idea of the purpose and some techniques that he plans to use, but is open to change. He is almost always able to change the planned approach or to abandon it if client's presenting behavior or needs at the beginning the interview indicate a need for this action.

8. Student is generally unable to change or abandon the preplanned interview approach *in the middle of* the interview. He might be able to deviate from the planned approach for isolated responses to the client but usually reverts almost immediately to the preplanned approach.

8. Student is able to shift gears and abandon or alter his preplanned approach in the middle of the interview if client's behavior, feelings, or needs necessitate a different approach.

9. Uses direct questioning as the primary interviewing technique. The reader may receive the impression that the student has a checklist of information that he is trying to obtain.

9. Uses questioning selectively and in combination with other interviewing techniques. The questions flow naturally and with an obvious purpose. There is no feeling that the interviewer is getting answers for a checklist.

10. Relies primarily on closed rather than open-ended questions when questioning is used. Such questions require simply a yes or no response and they constitute a majority of the kinds of questions asked.

10. When questions are asked, they are *primarily* open-ended questions that cannot be answered with a yes or no. Such questions usually start with "tell me," "why," "how," "what," and the like. The *majority* of questions used are open-ended.

*It may be necessary to review more than one interview in order to rate this item. If the evaluator is familiar with the general pattern of the student's work, the item can be rated. Otherwise, it should be marked "NA."

<table>
<tr><td>BEGINNING INTERVIEWER</td><td>MORE ADVANCED INTERVIEWER</td></tr>
</table>

BEGINNING INTERVIEWER

11. The student often changes the subject by asking a direct question when the client brings up emotionally sensitive material or makes a statement that indicates strong feelings. There is a definite pattern of quickly changing the subject to safer, more concrete topics.

12. The interviewer jumps from one topic to another without exploring any one area in real depth. There appears to be no overall direction or focus to the interview. Things "happen as they happen."

13. When techniques such as interpretation, reflection, confrontation, and empathy are used, it is usually by accident and without conscious awareness of the name of the technique that was used or why.

14. May be able to label some techniques retroactively or figure out, after discussion with the supervisor, why a given technique was or was not effective but usually cannot do this *as the interview is taking place.*

15. The recording contains comments, usually in the "gut-level feelings" column, to the effect that "I felt good because the client was happy" or "client was smiling and laughing so everything is better now." The reader gets the feeling that the student believes one is an effective social worker if the interview concludes with the client feeling happy. In other words, the goal of social work is to make clients happy.

16. The student makes statements that give false reassurance ("I'm sure it wasn't that bad." "I know the XYZ Welfare department can help you with that." "Don't worry. Your check won't get lost." "Don't worry. The nurses here are really very nice." And so on).

17. The student uses advice-giving. "I think you should do this." "What you should do is." "If I were you, I would . . ." The reader finds himself wishing that other techniques had been used instead to explore further the problem or the client's feelings.

MORE ADVANCED INTERVIEWER

11. The student is usually able to pick up on and use appropriate techniques to explore client statements that indicate strong emotions. The interviewer does not change the subject or appear to avoid responding to client feelings.

12. The student keeps the interview focused. It flows in a logical pattern and seems to be moving toward some kind of objective or conclusion. The student may allow a digression or a free flow of ideas from the client, but it appears to have been permitted consciously and purposely.

13. Uses techniques of reflection, interpretation, confrontation, empathy, and so forth with obvious awareness. Is able to label the techniques used and explain why during supervisory conference.

14. Is aware of differential and purposeful use of selected techniques *at the time the techniques are being used in the interview.*

15. There may be occasional comments regarding a client's feeling happy, but the reader does not get the feeling that the student believes the primary goal of his interaction is to make his client happy. "Gut-level feelings" column comments indicate awareness that some discomfort may be necessary to bring about increased growth, change, or insight and that it is not realistic for people with problems to be happy all the time.

16. The interview is characterized by an almost total absence of falsely reassuring statements. Reflective, interpretive, and empathic techniques are used instead to explore further the client's feelings or to define a presenting problem.

17. There is an almost total absence of advice-giving comments. Instead, student helps client make his own decision and uses appropriate techniques to help him verbalize and explore alternatives. When advice-giving is done, student selects it as a treatment technique of choice *as the interview is taking*

BEGINNING INTERVIEWER   MORE ADVANCED INTERVIEWER

place and can explain later why he made this decision.

18. There may or may not be a feeling of genuine warmth in the interview. The reader may not be certain whether the warmth is genuine or whether the student is trying to seem warm to please his field instructor.

18. The person reading the student's interview can actually feel the warmth the student shows for the client, and it comes through as genuine. It is evident that this warmth was successfully and sincerely communicated to the client.

19. Rarely confronts client with anything. When a situation presents itself that calls for a confrontative response, student usually says nothing (ignores it) or asks an information-seeking question. May occasionally confront regarding very simple, concrete services planning.

19. Uses confrontation to bring to client's attention the interviewer's assessment of feelings, responses, and behaviors. This is done consciously with a purpose and usually, though not always, results in the client's discussing feelings and presenting emotional reactions or needs in more detail.

20. The interviewer rarely permits periods of silence. If the client fails to respond right away, the student jumps in rather quickly with a direct question.

20. The recording indicates that the interviewer permitted appropriate periods of silence where nothing was said by anyone.

21. May share personal life experiences with the client in an attempt to communicate: "I do understand what you are going through or feeling." Student is usually able to explain later that this was his motivation for sharing the experience but is unable to discuss, or is unaware of, the other pros and cons involved in using this technique.

21. May share personal life experiences with the client in an effort to communicate empathy. However, student usually considers the pros and cons of using this approach *while the interview is occurring* and consciously and deliberately chooses the technique after determining that the possible benefits outweigh any negatives in that particular instance. Student is able to describe this thinking process in later discussion with the supervisor.

22. The student may use laymen's terms rather than professional terminology to describe client behaviors. This can give the reader the impression that the student is being judgmental.

22. Professional rather than lay terminology is usually used. Diagnostic rather than judgmental terms are used.

23. The student's comments in the "gut-level feelings" column indicate lack of awareness when countertransference occurs. Student may describe the feelings he experiences in response to a client's statement or behavior but may question whether he was supposed to have these feelings or what he should have done with his own feelings. However, the student does not label the interaction as an instance of countertransference.

23. Student usually is aware when countertransference occurs. He is usually able to label it as such, at least retroactively, in the "gut-level feelings" column. Student may need supervisory guidance on how to handle the identified countertransference.

24. When the client mentions a concrete need or problem, the student often offers to do it *for*

24. When client presents a concrete need, the student explores the client's ability to take

the client (make a phone call, write a letter, contact the welfare department in his behalf, and so on).

care of the problem himself and encourages him to do so before offering to do it for him.

25. More often than not, the student moves toward problem resolution without completely exploring all possible ramifications of the problem. Student tends to suggest solutions to the client almost immediately after client tells interviewer he has a problem or a need.

25. Student almost always shows obvious efforts to explore both concrete and feeling aspects of a problem before suggesting possible solutions to the client.

26. The student presents a plan to the client as "this is what we can do for you" and does not give client an opportunity to express how he feels about the plan. He may ask the client directly if the plan "is okay." This usually elicits a monosyllable response with no further elaboration or discussion.

26. Student elicits client's feelings about all social service plans being developed and determines if client wants to follow through with them or not.

27. Student records and documents factually what took place in the interview but includes very little diagnostic or analytical assessment of what was recorded.

27. Student includes some diagnostic assessments of what took place in the interview, either in the "analysis" column or in a special diagnostic statement at the end of the recording.

28. Diagnostically significant statements or descriptions of client behaviors may be noted by the student in his process-recording. However, the absence of comments in the "analysis" or "gut-level feelings" columns about the recorded data indicate that student is not aware of the significance of what has been recorded.

28. Diagnostically significant statements and observed behaviors are recorded and the student makes analytical comments regarding the data in the "analysis" or "gut-level feelings" column. Student may or may not fully understand the significance of what he has recorded, but does respond with recognition of its importance and attempts analysis. The advanced interviewer does his analysis inside his head as the interview is occurring. Moderately advanced students will do their analysis immediately after the conclusion of the interview and before supervisory input occurs.

29. Student is able to make some preliminary analytical statements based on behaviors and statements recorded in the interview only with some supervisory guidance and direction. Student is very limited in his ability to do this while the interview is taking place. Thus, the student is not able to implement any ideas generated from his analytical thinking until the next interview.

29. Student analyzes client statements and behaviors *as the interview is taking place* and adjusts his behavior or approach during the interview to accommodate the results of his spontaneous analytical thinking. More indepth thinking may be accomplished retroactively with supervisory guidance and input.

30. Deals with or evaluates client statements in the present only; very rarely ties his analyses

30. Makes prognostic statements regarding future problems/consequences/benefits based

BEGINNING INTERVIEWER

MORE ADVANCED INTERVIEWER

into goal-setting or projects implications for the future. Student may be able to do some of this retroactively following discussion with supervisor but rarely does so *as the interview is occurring*.

on assessment of client's behavior—a projection into the future. Student is able to do this *while the interview is occurring*.

31. Often recognizes when something did not go well during the interview and expresses feelings of discomfort in the "gut-level feelings" column. Student usually does not know exactly what went wrong or why and only sometimes is able to suggest retroactively effective alternate ways of handling the situation. Supervisory guidance and input are usually needed to bring this about.

31. Student is usually able to recognize when something did not go as well as it could have during an interview and is usually able to figure out why retroactively and suggest ways it could have been handled more effectively. Such comments often appear in the "gut-level feelings" column before supervisory input or guidance is provided.

32. Only occasionally does the student end the interview in a structured, purposeful manner. The interview concludes when there is nothing more to talk about, an interruption makes continuation impossible or undesirable, or the client's behaviors or communications tell the worker clearly that it is time to end the discussion.

32. Worker concludes the interview when the objective or goal of the interview has been accomplished. There is usually a summation with the client of what has taken place during the interview and a review of any plans made. There may also be discussion regarding the purpose or agenda of future contacts.

10 Assessment of Student Activity

Previous chapters have discussed principles of selecting assignments for students, the educational contract, the importance of setting standards, and the use of process-recording as a teaching tool. All well and good. But how does a supervisor keep track of what his or her supervisee is doing? How do we know if the student really is learning? What is the best way to determine just what takes place when student and client, group, or organization interact?

There are essentially four methods of monitoring student activity: (1) student self-assessment; (2) summary reports of what happened (or on the final outcome); (3) directly observational methods, and (4) solicited and unsolicited feedback from others.* Unfortunately, supervisors rely most heavily on the first two methods, the fastest, easiest, most painless route to assessment of student performance—and also the least effective in most situations.

Student Self-assessment

Self-assessment can be a valuable learning experience for the student. It encourages him to analyze his own performance critically, and if specific educational objectives have been set (see Chapter 6), he can meaningfully monitor his own progress and growth. However, most students have a strong wish to please their field instructors. There is a temptation to give the field instructor what he or she wants to hear and withhold sharing of insecurities and recognized gaps in skill or knowledge in an effort to demonstrate competence. Thus, well-meaning, mature students may have real difficulty bringing problem areas to their field instructor's attention. They seem to prefer that the supervisor initiate such discussions. Other learners feel that they may

*Solicited and unsolicited feedback is not discussed in this chapter because it is mentioned throughout the text in other sections.

receive a good grade if they constantly tell their field instructor how well they feel they are doing and avoid revealing problem areas. On the other hand, some students are overcritical and possess greater knowledge and skill than they give themselves credit for. Thus, student self-assessments may be incomplete, inaccurate, or, at the very worst, attempts to manipulate the field instructor. While this assessment method has validity in specific situations, other methods of monitoring student activity generally prove more useful.

Student self-assessment can be a formal process in which the student submits written analyses of tape-recorded interviews or completes his own performance evaluation at the end of the term for comparison with the supervisor's evaluation. The most common form of student self-assessment is very informal, as illustrated by the following interchange between a supervisor and his student:

STUDENT (STICKING HIS HEAD IN THE FIELD INSTRUCTOR'S OFFICE, WHILE CONTINUING TO STAND OUT IN THE HALLWAY): Hey, Miss Adams, I met with my adolescent group today again— the meeting went really well!

FIELD INSTRUCTOR (LOOKING UP FROM A PILE OF PAPERS SHE HAD BEEN WORKING ON): I'm glad. Was Roger as hostile as we had feared?

STUDENT: No. He was very quiet—gave me no problem at all. I really tried to be more nondirective this time and I think it went really well. Lots of good stuff came out.

FIELD INSTRUCTOR: Yeah, it makes you feel good when you have a session like that.

STUDENT: Yeah, I feel like I'm really learning. The kids and I are both looking forward to our meeting next week.

FIELD INSTRUCTOR: Good. We'll talk some about the next meeting in our supervisory conference on Friday.

STUDENT: Okay. I gotta go see Mr. Williams now. See ya later.

FIELD INSTRUCTOR: Okay.

Were you able to identify with this sort of interchange? It is an extremely common form of communication between students and field instructors and often occurs several times daily. In this instance, probably both the field instructor and the student felt good about the conversation. Yet it tells the field instructor very little about the student's performance.

Look again at the communication between the student and his field instructor. Following is a list of statements or conclusions that might be based on the information the supervisor obtained from talking with the student. Put a check in front of the item if you agree that the supervisor can draw this conclusion from his conversation with the student:

1. _____ The student successfully used a more non-directive approach in his group session.
2. _____ The student feels he did a good job with this group meeting.
3. _____ Roger (the boy the student and field instructor feared might be hostile) was not hostile during the group meeting.
4. _____ Some significant material was discussed during the group session.
5. _____ The student used appropriate group-work skills in conducting the session.
6. _____ The student's group-work skills are improving, as evidenced by his success in conducting this week's meeting.
7. _____ The group members are looking forward to next week's meeting.
8. _____ The student did a good job with this group session; he was effective in leading the group.
9. _____ The student is looking forward to next week's meeting.
10. _____ This week's meeting went better than the one the student led last week.

Which items did you check?

Item 1 says the student "successfully" used a nondirective approach. But wait a minute. *Who* says he was "successful"? What criteria is the student using to measure his "success" in being nondirective? How do we know that the student didn't overcompensate in his eagerness to be nondirective and become *too* unstructured? What is the student's definition of "nondirective"? Is it the same as the field instructor's? If the supervisor had been present during the meeting, would he have felt that the student did indeed use a nondirective approach? And finally, how much group-work expertise does this student have: When he says he was "nondirective," can we accept that as an accurate conclusion, or is he still learning the techniques involved in being a nondirective group leader? Obviously, the field instructor could not conclude from this brief conversation that the student really was nondirective, because the supervisor

does not have enough information about what happened during the group session to be able to make that assessment.

We can safely say, for Item 2, that the student feels he did a good job with the group meeting. The field instructor may or may not agree with this, but obviously the student feels good about the meeting.

Item 3 is tricky. Many supervisors might sigh with relief upon learning that Roger was quiet and not hostile as expected and would not explore the matter any further. But the student has interpreted Roger's quietness as meaning "absence of hostility"; the field instructor, who has greater training and/or experience, may wonder if the quietness represents a cooperative attitude or merely a different way of expressing hostility. The client's quietness may even have constituted *increased* hostility, demonstrated by a passive-aggressive withdrawal. The inexperienced student might not recognize this behavior and its meaning. Yet a withdrawing, hostile group member can be more difficult to work with than one whose hostility is out in the open. If the field instructor fails to discuss this situation further with the student, he may never learn whether Roger remains hostile. Thus, once again, the supervisor needs to know more details about what actually happened in the group session before Item 3 can be checked with confidence.

Item 4 is also an erroneous conclusion. Again, the student feels that significant material was discussed, and indeed, perhaps this statement is accurate. But was everything discussed that needed to be brought out? Was some significant material discussed while other areas were consciously or unconsciously avoided by the student because of discomfort or insecurity on his part?

Item 5 is unknown. The interchange with the student tells the field instructor nothing about the skills the student used except that he feels he was "more nondirective." Does "more" mean that he was effective? No mention is made of other techniques used by the student. Obviously, if he was just nondirective, the group session would probably have foundered from lack of direction. So some interpretive, reflective, confrontative, or other techniques must have been used to lead the meeting. However, since the field instructor doesn't know what they were or how the group members responded, he is unable to evaluate the effectiveness of the student's group-work techniques.

Item 6 cannot be checked because the instructor is unable to assess the student's actual group-work skills from his report alone. The student feels there is improvement, and in all likelihood some growth is taking place. However, this cannot be known for certain without additional information.

Item 7 is misleading. The *student* feels the group members are looking forward to the next session, and perhaps they are. But maybe the student is trying so hard to succeed and wants to believe the members are looking forward to the next session so strongly that he is unable to see subtle indications to the contrary. A more thorough review of the actual interaction that took place between the student and the group members would enable the field instructor to help the student appraise the group's feelings about the next session.

Item 8 cannot be stated because of our inability to make previous statements, in particular Items 1, 3, 4, and 5.

Item 9 *can* be stated. The student is clearly looking forward to the next group session.

Finally, Item 10 is erroneous. More information is needed before a comparison can be made between the two group meetings and the student's display of skill in both sessions.

If student self-assessment is the *primary* method used by the field instructor to determine the quality of the student's performance, the supervisor might as well not exist. Most students have some ability to rate their own skills. Even the most inexperienced, uninformed learner knows that he does some things well and others less well. The supervisor is usually able to see more than one way that something could have been accomplished and may have much higher standards as to what constitutes "success" or "effectiveness" than does the student. A beginning tennis player often feels he's getting to be really good if he can manage to return the ball more or less consistently. A tennis champion, however, knows that the game involves much more than just returning the ball and has developed the finer points of strategy and technique. Similarly, the student may feel good because he kept the group members talking so they didn't just sit there and look at one another, whereas the field instructor will be concerned about the techniques used, the content and flow of the conversation, and the underlying and perhaps unverbalized feelings that affect the group process. Thus, the field instructor can use student self-assessment as a starting point but then must help the student examine closely the actual process or interaction that took place as measured against the supervisor's standards, knowledge, and expertise and the accepted standards of the profession before meaningful assessment of the student's skill can occur and goals can be set for improving skill and knowledge.

Written Summary Reports

Another common method of monitoring student activity is through written reports. The student summarizes what took place as he interacted with clients or community groups, or led a meeting. Unfortunately, the emphasis is often on content and outcome—what happened—rather than on the techniques or approach used by the student to achieve the outcome. Good summary recording in social work omits many of the details of how the worker conducted the interview or achieved the results. Thus, if the field instructor wants to examine the process used by the student to achieve what is reported in summary recording, he will need to do more than have the student meet the summary-recording requirements of the agency. Furthermore, to save time, student–supervisor conferences often consist largely of oral summations of student activity, similar in nature but more detailed than the interchange illustrated on p. 150. Unfortuntely, such reports do not enable the field instructor to examine the techniques used by the student. If the results were outstanding, the student needs to know *why* he was effective—what techniques were used and why they worked—so that he can consciously and purposefully use them again. If the results were "okay" but not spectacular, what might have been done to achieve really outstanding results? Or what factors made it impossible for anyone, no matter how skilled, to accomplish more than was accomplished? If the results of the interview, the group meeting, or the community activity were not satisfactory, the student needs to examine the causes and learn how to modify his approach to increase his effectiveness in the future.

Summary reports are also highly selective. Students will report only what they consider to be of significance, generally omitting subtle communications and nonverbal messages. Yet, had the more experienced field instructor been present, he might have recognized something important that the student neglected to explore or respond to in some manner. Consider the following diagnostic summary of an interview conducted by an undergraduate student only a few weeks from graduation:

This patient is seen as a victim of circumstances. It was my impression at first that he was a heavy drug user and is trying to run street game on me. But once I really listened, he was asking for help from someone. What the significance of the mother is, I was unable to determine because patient won't open up.

He is seen as a person who wants to be independent, but could be easily influenced. The doctor has expressed his concern about the patient returning to live with his mother because of some instability.

Although the patient admits drug use, something makes me feel he wants to get a lot out but has no one that will really listen to him.

Patient may desire rehabilitation, but not quite sure. I would recommend that he not return to his mother's to live. Also I would like to do followup after he leaves here because I believe he can improve his situation with some guidance.

Social work plan:

1. Referral to the local welfare department for financial assistance and boarding home placement.
2. Social service followup by me.

The field instructor had also asked the student to process-record this interview. The following excerpt illustrates an interchange the student omitted from his diagnostic summary. It was not even mentioned to the field instructor. Yet it is highly significant diagnostically. When the supervisor pointed this out to the student, he readily admitted that he had included it in the process-recording only because he had been told to write everything down, whether he considered it important or not. Since he didn't consider the interchange significant (or perhaps even blocked it out because of his own discomfort with its significance), he had omitted it from his summary:

He said he is not able to go back to his mother's where he was staying. I asked him why not.

He said his mother is the reason he is in this shape in the first place.

I said, "How is that?"

He said that she "just isn't right," that she had him and his brother fighting and that she "says things that a man's wife might say."

I said, "What kinds of things?"

To this I got no reply, only that "She isn't right and I never should have gone back there to live." He explained that before he had a job but she asked him to come live with her and his sister tried to discourage him. He said he didn't even have a regular place to sleep and slept on the floor.

(The student then changes the subject and he and the client discuss the client's past employment.)

What if the field instructor had never seen this process recording?

Consider the following summary recording of a home visit, prepared in accordance with agency recording requirements. The author is an undergraduate student about halfway through a block field placement. This is her first contact with a rather complex multiproblem family situation. The case has been referred to a protective services agency for child neglect. Previous workers had been quite negative and even judgmental in prior record entries, and the field instructor and student had talked at length about the case situation and had role-played the introduction to the client. The student wanted very much to approach this young mother with a more positive, accepting attitude than her predecessors had shown.

Diagnostic Summary

When I visited the client I felt that she was happy to see me. She was easy to talk to and did not try to avoid any subject. On the contrary, she eagerly talked about anything, especially her husband. She seems limited somewhat intellectually although she understands what you are talking about. She is very confused emotionally about her husband and states that she doesn't know what to do about him. Her thought pattern is very erratic and she talks about first one thing and then another. I didn't know what to attribute this to.

The children were very healthy and normal looking. Maria was shy and would not talk. Luis had a small scar on the upper lip from having the hairlip corrected. He was very talkative and easy to understand.

Service Plan

Help client obtain her prescription and help her find a job. I also want to explore further the situation with her husband.

On the surface, the recording appears simplistic but basically satisfactory. The student's beginning diagnostic ability is evident, and her service plan is specific and also appears realistic. The student obviously feels the interview went well and was relieved to find her client accepting of her and willing to talk. However, the student also process-recorded this interview. She knew it would be a difficult one, and she wanted detailed supervisory feedback on her techniques and approach to the client. The middle column contains the dialogue as reported by the student; the right hand column gives the student's gut-level feelings as the interview was taking place, and the left column shows the comments made by the field instructor. This is an actual interview, with the identities changed and only the opening remarks omitted. Read the summary recording once again and look for contradictions, inaccuracies, and omissions when compared with the more detailed process recording.

Supervisory Comments	Interview Content	Gut-Level Feelings
	At this time, her little girl came in. She was clean and healthy looking. She picked up a toy, looked me over, then whispered something to her mother and went back outside.	I felt like I failed her inspection.
	W: How are the children doing? Is Maria in Head Start now?	
	C: They are doing OK. Maria is registered and goes back for something on Monday. I guess she'll start then.	
	W: What about Luis?	
"Better" compared to what? What kind of emotional problems? Do they affect him in any way in addition to his speech? Exploration needed. What is the child like at home? How does he respond to her (from her viewpoint), etc.?	C: He is doing better. His teacher said that he is getting along better now. She feels like he has some emotional problems because of his father and this is why he wouldn't talk better. But she says he is beginning to do much better.	She started really talking and I felt very sorry for her.
	W: Does he still get special help with his speech problem?	
	C: Yes, from a teacher at school.	
	W: How often does she help him?	
What exactly does she do to help Luis? For how long? How often? See me re: why this is important.	C: Two or three times a week and I help him with certain words for homework.	I felt like she really wanted to help Luis.
Good. Now you can follow up and talk to his teacher.	W: Where does Luis go to school?	
	C: Down at XYZ School. I wanted to ask if I get a job will it cut my Medicaid out?	

Supervisory Comments	Interview Content	Gut-Level Feelings
	I really want to work but I can't pay the doctors if they cut it. I would have a lot of bills especially from Luis because of his hairlip and cleft palate. My little girl fell down off the front steps last week and broke her leg.	I felt she didn't want to jeopardize her financial situation.
This accident needs exploration. Do you know why this is important? How could you have explored it?		
How much money would she earn? Doing what? What is she really saying here? Interpretive response desirable. Do you see why?	W: I am not sure if it would cut your Medicaid or not—I don't think so but I'll have to ask someone because I'm pretty new at the department.	
Why did you change the subject somewhat here?	W: Does Luis have a lot of medical problems with his mouth?	
	C: He goes to a doctor for his mouth and ears.	
	W: Does he have problems with his ears?	
What kind of operation? Does his condition affect his hearing?	C: Not much—he has holes in his eardrums but the doctor said they would operate on them when he is older.	
	W: Can he hear pretty good?	
But to what extent is he affected? We need to get this from her and also his teacher, as well as from Luis himself.	C: Yes. He sits up close in school so he doesn't have many problems as far as I know. I would like to work part time if it won't cut my Medicaid out.	
Good! You explore.	W: Do you know where you could get a job?	
	C: I guess at the ABC grocery. They will need a checkout girl pretty soon.	
	W: Have you put in an application yet?	
She is saying a great deal here re her needs and anxieties. What feelings are behind her statements?	C: No. I really want to learn a trade because I only went to the 10th grade. What if my husband never comes back? What would I do? He had a girlfriend; I don't know if he mar-	Thank goodness—an answer to an unasked question!

(Continued)

Supervisory Comments	Interview Content	Gut-Level Feelings
	ried her or not. I don't think so. It wouldn't seem so bad if he would just come and see the kids. They need him. People ask me why I want him back after all he's done, but they don't understand. He's their father. He should take care of them even if he doesn't come back. I don't know what to do if he does come back because it will get me in trouble with my welfare worker, won't it? They stopped my checks for several months the last time he came.	She began crying here. I just let her go on talking partly because I wasn't sure what to say.
A very key statement. I've been around enough to suspect she's putting it this way to really say something else. Can you guess what it is?		I see her point.
A particular interpretive statement desperately needed here! Let's role-play it. Change of subject—not picking up on underlying feelings expressed above. You shifted from the emotional to the concrete.	W: If he comes back very often and stays they will stop your checks again. That's the reason you get them—because the father is away from the home. You had talked before about getting a divorce. Have you thought about that, in case he doesn't return? C: Yes. W: Have you talked to anyone about filing for a divorce? C: Yes, I've already filed.	
Right—it appears she didn't want to talk about the divorce. But there was something else she wanted to talk about. Can you figure out what it was?	W: When does it become final? C: I don't know. W: When did you file? C: It's been a while.	I don't think she wanted to talk about the divorce.
	At this time the door opened and Luis came in. He was just returning from school. He sat down on the sofa and started talking to his mother and looking at me.	She had stopped crying.
Did you introduce yourself to him?	W: How did school go today, Luis? Luis: OK.	He was very easy to understand (speech).
Luis thinking silently to himself: "Who's this stranger asking how I'm doing in school?!"	W: What grade are you in? Luis: I'm in the second.	

Supervisory Comments	Interview Content	Gut-Level Feelings
	W: Do you like school?	
Good for him! What feeling might have prompted Luis to ask this?	Luis: Yes. Are you a welfare worker?	Boy, did that shock me! I didn't know what to say. I was too flustered to make any sense.
How might you have responded differently? I wonder what a "welfare worker" means to him.	W: No, I'm from the Make-em-well Agency.	
	Luis: I'm on vacation from school till Monday. Mom, I'm going out.	
	Luis went outside.	
	C: He likes to hang around other people.	
Good exploration.	W: What do you mean?	
But underneath this statement are the same feelings expressed previously. What are these feelings?	C: He doesn't know anyone but his father.	Back to the father again—I think she's really confused about him.
A change of subject on your part—I wonder why.	W: Does he not have any friends to play with?	
What is she really saying here?	C: Oh yes, he has friends. He just likes to hang around with them and I don't like him to because I don't know if that's normal.	I got the feeling she was afraid he would become homosexual.
Good interpretive statement!	W: Maybe he likes to hang around them and their fathers since his is not here now.	
The <u>third</u>-opening to discuss the underlying feelings I mentioned earlier.	C: Maybe. It would be better if he could see his father.	
	W: I think it's pretty normal for boys his age to hang around with others. But it would be good for him to see his father some. How long were you married?	
OK. A natural lead into this question.		
	C: Over 6 years.	
A good empathic statement!	W: That's a pretty long time to live with someone and then have them leave you. Do you have any idea where he is now?	I wanted to find out about the father.
Could you have paused here before asking the question, to let her respond to your empathic statement?	C: No, he doesn't even tell his people.	

(Continued)

Supervisory Comments	Interview Content	Gut-Level Feelings
	W: Do you know his relatives pretty good?	
	C: Yes, they like me pretty good.	
Good.	W: Do some of them live around here?	
Does she see them often? Why were you having a hard time understanding her—did you share this with her?	C: Yes, his father's people and some sisters live not far from here. W: Does your own family live around here?	She told me the town and I never could understand what she said. I was having a hard time understanding her part of the time.
Aha! The fourth hint at certain underlying feelings.	C: No. I'm kind of by myself— my parents are dead. W: Did they live around here? C: No, they lived in another state. W: Is that where you met your husband? C: Yes. The client sat for a couple of minutes without talking. She had stopped crying completely by this time.	
A very significant statement!	C: Do you have many people like me?	
Very good response! Do you know why?	W: What do you mean?	
Yes, reaching for support— and also for something else.	C: That start crying. I don't do it much because of the kids, but sometimes I can't help it.	I felt like she was reaching out for some support.
I think you moved in rather quickly without adequate exploration. It gives the impression here of a little bit of false reassurance—can you see why? Let's discuss and role-play.	W: Everyone needs to let it out sometime. You can't keep it bottled up all the time. I realize it's hard to raise several children by yourself and I can see why you need to cry sometimes. We all need someone to talk to sometimes.	
OK, she probably was being truthful. But therapeuti-	C: I don't want to give you the wrong idea. I've got friends	I felt like she was telling me the truth.

Supervisory Comments	**Interview Content**	**Gut-Level Feelings**
cally, what did she need from you at this point? Please see your fellow student and have her give you the same readings she did on depression (but not the ones on suicide).	to talk to and sometimes I cry to them but they don't under—stand—if I catch myself cry—ing I stop because I'm feeling sorry for myself.	
A most unfortunate time for this interruption.	At this time Maria came back in and the client stopped talk—ing. When I saw she was fin—ished talking I decided to leave.	
Ouch! I'm not sure this was the best timing for you to decide to leave. Were you uncomfort—able with her expression of feelings? Can you figure out why your timing was not the best? Look again at her state—ment, "... and sometimes I cry to them but they don't under—stand" and your decision to leave, for a hint.	W: I will get in contact with the LMN Agency and let you know what you need to do to have them get that special medicine for you (this had been discussed earlier).	
	C: Dr. Adams said it would cost around $90. I've already got the prescription. When will you let me know?	I feel she is very anxious to get this prescription.
	W: I will be out of the office on Thursday and Friday, so I'll come by on Monday or Tuesday. I'll give you my number and you can call me if you need to talk to me before then, OK?	
	C: OK.	
Your confusion is very under—standable. You opened up a lot of good areas for further ex—ploration and discussion. In spite of all my comments, you didn't do too badly for your first interview with this com—plex situation. I think you'll have much to offer her and even if you never had another case, you'd learn a great deal from working with her. Please do the following:	W: Then I'll see you next week. Goodbye.	By the time I left, I was totally confused.
1. Read this through very carefully. Try to answer each of my questions. Use a differ—ent color ink and write on your recording if you want.		
2. Think. Don't ask the other students. Read on the needs of divorced women and their children.		

(Continued)

Supervisory Comments	Interview Content	Gut-Level Feelings

3. Go through and count the number of times you use direct questions, reflection, interpretation, confrontation, empathy and other techniques in your responses. Write the totals on the last page.

4. I'm going to want you to see this client twice a week for the rest of the field placement.

5. Please plan to continue process-recording your next 3-4 contacts with this client.

6. Please work on everything listed here and on your recording and come prepared to go over it in detail in supervisory conference in about two days. You probably won't have everything finished by then (especially the readings), but that's OK as long as you're well under way with it.

Notice the field instructor's feedback. There is concern about Luis: He may have some problem needing further exploration. The mother is exhibiting some feelings regarding her situation which are obvious to the field instructor but not to the student. On page 155 the field instructor feels a need for more exploration concerning the girl's accident. It probably was a genuine accident, but the supervisor knows that child abuse can sometimes produce broken legs, and the case has a long history of complaints from the community about the care of the children. On page 156 the field instructor suspects that the client may already be receiving financial assistance to which she is not entitled, a sticky area for the student to handle, especially since efforts are being made to be more accepting and less judgmental toward this client. Yet the student seems unsure of the possible message the client is trying to communicate as she expresses concern about her checks stopping. On page 158, the client says a great deal through her simple question, "Do you have many people like me?" The student's response seems excellent, indicating she understood what the client was really saying. However, when the field instructor read the remainder of the interview, it became obvious that the student's response was instinctual: She really didn't understand what the client was trying to say or what she needed. Finally, the field instructor makes a number of suggestions for the student to think about and assigns some specific tasks for the student to do prior to the next supervisory conference.

Thus, the summary recording again didn't give a complete picture of the client's situation and would not have enabled the field instructor to supply detailed instructional feedback about the student's understanding of the case dynamics and use of casework skills. It should be clear that summary reporting must be used in combination with other methods of monitoring student activity, especially with inexperienced learners.

Obviously process-recording is too time-consuming for both student and supervisor for everyday use. Most students just beginning field placement should have their work monitored through directly observational methods as much as possible, until the field instructor gets a good feel for the student's level of functioning and has had an opportunity to review and teach certain basics and identify areas of strength and limitations. As the student progresses in field, there can be greater reliance on self-assessment and summary reporting, with directly observational methods and process-recording used selectively in especially difficult situations or randomly as a sort of spot check or to assist the student with specialized skills.

Directly Observational Assessment

The most effective way to monitor and evaluate student activity is by examining the interaction that takes place between the student and the client or clients. There are various ways of doing this. None gives the field instructor a totally complete and accurate picture of the student's interactions. Some are highly threatening to the student (e.g. field instructor observation of an interview), while others are effective but costly or unavailable to many settings (e.g. videotaping).

Direct Observation by Field Instructor

This assessment method enables the field instructor to see and hear all verbal and nonverbal communication between his student and the student's client. Unfortunately, it introduces a third person who is not part of the ongoing relationship between student and client. The supervisor's presence is usually anxiety-provoking for the student and sometimes also for the client. The field instructor usually does not see the student at his best and may come away from the experience with a rather distorted view of the student's manner of relating to people. Further, the field instructor may feel acutely uncomfortable sitting in on an interview that is awkward because of the student's lack of skill. The supervisor may feel a strong temptation to take over the interview when he sees things aren't going well. For these reasons, direct observation through the physical presence of the field instructor is not generally recommended as a monitoring method. However, there are a few specialized situations in which this approach can be used effectively.

Direct observation should almost never be used with students just beginning field placement. It is simply too threatening to the student. However, once the student has developed a good and comfortable relationship with a field instructor over a period of time, he may request the supervisor's presence for a special situation. The field instructor may want to go along with the suggestion. However, an important question must be asked: "Why does my student want me to sit in?" Is the student feeling insecure and seeking support through the field instructor's presence? Does the student want an opportunity to show his supervisor how wrong the field instructor has been about something? Does he want to show off his skill and effectiveness? The reason for the direct observation should be discussed thoroughly with the student. Also, a plan must be worked out for introducing the field instructor's presence to the client. If the introduction of a stranger would be harmful to the student's relationship with his client or to social work goals, the supervisor should not participate.

Field instructors should sit in on interviews only with their student's full cooperation. If the supervisor forces the idea on an unwilling student, the supervisee will experience so much anxiety and anger during the interview that he is virtually doomed to failure. However, in rare situations involving problematic performance, the field instructor may have no choice but to observe the student's activities di-

rectly. The supervisor may fear that the student's approach is harmful to clients and need reassurance that his fears are unjustified (or evidence that they are real). Perhaps the only way the field instructor can help the student with a particular problem area is to experience it along with the student.

I was once working with a supervisee to try and wean him from his ever present notebook. He worked in a hospital and armed himself with a huge black three-ring binder every time he went to a patient's room for an interview. He admitted to taking copious notes during interviews but insisted it never bothered his clients. Yet there were indications that he was having difficulty establishing warm relationships with his patients, and his interviews reflected very little feeling content. He often took many notes during supervisory conferences and had developed a technique of looking me straight in the eye while simultaneously writing down virtually everything I said. This made *me* nervous, so I wondered how it affected his clients. I seemed to be getting nowhere in my weaning efforts until one day he issued a challenge: "Come watch me interview. I'll show you how I take notes and prove that it doesn't affect the client." I jumped at the opportunity.

During the interview, an old man talked about his increasing debility and loss of independence while my supervisee looked him in the eye and simultaneously wrote all his remarks down. The poor client seemed very uncomfortable as he kept glancing at the notebook and talking less and less. As we left the patient's room, my supervisee commented, "See, it didn't bother him at all!" I struggled with the best method of confronting him with reality, knowing he'd disagree strongly with my assessment of his performance and its impact on the client. Our next regularly scheduled supervisory conference was to consist of a general review of his performance thus far as well as discussion of my observed interview. As we talked, I pulled out the largest yellow pad I could find, and as my supervisee gave me his self-assessment regarding his performance and he responded to my evaluatory feedback, I looked him in the eye and wrote down his every word. He became so nervous I was about to offer a tranquilizer when I interrupted our supervisory conference to ask, "I wonder why you are so nervous today?" to which he responded, "The yellow pad—how come you're writing everything down? You've never done that before!" My point had been made, and he never took a big notebook with him again on his interviews.

Co-leading

Some situations lend themselves to a very natural co-leadership between student and supervisor. Both can lead group sessions and staff or community meetings or conduct an initial interview with a client. Roles must be defined clearly, as co-leadership is usually not a genuine fifty-fifty split; one person or the other periodically assumes a passive or more active role, depending on what is happening with the client. The field instructor must refrain from dominating the student or from embarrassing him publicly by contradicting or belittling his words and actions in front of the consumer. When there is true teamwork between a student and field instructor, both parties are usually relaxed; the student can learn from observing the field instructor as a role model (critically analyzing his performance as well), and the field instructor can get a good feel for his student's abilities. Effective co-leadership cannot occur if the student is extremely insecure (he will usually sit quietly and let the supervisor dominate the activity), if the student's performance is unsatisfactory or problematic, or if the relationship between student and field instructor is stressful. When effective co-leadership occurs, it can be the most meaningful and effective way for the field instructor to monitor a segment of his student's activities. Significant learning can occur as field instructor and student compare their joint experience, looking for differing perceptions, reactions, and use of various techniques.

One-way Mirror

A one-way mirror is a special piece of glass that looks like a mirror on one side but on the other is actually a window. The client sees only a mirror on the wall; observers on the other side see everything taking place in the interviewing room. Hidden microphones transmit the sound. Thus, the disadvantages of the physical presence of a field instructor are eliminated, while the ability to observe and hear everything is retained. Furthermore, a group of people can view the interview from behind the mirror. Both client and student must be advised that they are being observed, by whom, and for what purpose, but the interviewer and client can easily forget the observers, because there is no camera or other mechanical device present to serve as a reminder. In reality, most students do remember they are being observed, and only after a series of observed interviews are they able to relax and act natural. Some agencies insist on a written consent form to be signed by all concerned, to ensure full adherence to the privacy rights of both client and interviewer.

One-way mirrors are a highly effective device in monitoring student skills. Supervisors working in settings that have the required equipment usually use one-way mirrors a great deal in student training, both to observe students and to allow them to watch skilled staff in action. Unfortunately, most settings do not have the equipment for one-way mirror observation and must use other methods for assessing student activity.

Tape-recording

Taping produces a record of verbal interactions only. A tape can be listened to repeatedly to study techniques and client responses. Both group and individual interactions can be recorded. Most organizations own at least one tape recorder, and many individual staff members and students can gain access to one for personal use. Yet taping is often neglected as a means of assessing and training students.

Students know that tapes leave no room for hiding: Everything said will be recorded. Thus, the insecure student may resist taping because it "reveals all" to his supervisor. This anxiety can be alleviated somewhat by giving the student a specific time period in which he must record a certain number of interviews. He can choose which interviews to record and then pick one to share with the field instructor.

The student must practice operating the recorder until its mechanical functioning becomes so automatic that he can handle the equipment with no fumbling during an interview. Student and supervisor may need to role-play various techniques for introducing the presence of the tape recorder to the client and for obtaining his written permission to be taped. Most clients do not object; it is the interviewer who usually has the greatest resistance to the process. The client must be told the purpose of the taping, who will hear the recording; and whether he will have an opportunity to hear it or edit it. Two types of permission are necessary: one to make the tape and another for *each specific instance* in which the tape will be heard by anyone other than persons in the same agency (the student's supervisor; other students in the same placement, and so forth). The recorder should be placed in plain sight on a desk or table, but not glaringly between the interviewer and interviewee. The microphone will need to be close enough to pick up all remarks, even those that are spoken softly. Tapes should be long enough to run at least sixty minutes per side.

If the client shares unusually sensitive or possibly incriminating material during the interview, he should be allowed to have this portion erased from the tape. A tape is a type of formal record, and as such could be subject to subpoena by the courts, along with traditional written records. Thus, editing may be necessary on occasion; all tapes should be stored in a secure location and should be erased as soon as the student and field instructor have finished reviewing them. Taped material should never be taken to the classroom unless the client has given specific permission for this to occur, or unless all identifying details have been altered or disguised. As this is extremely difficult with tapes (the voice itself identifies the person), written permission should be obtained.

Certain situations contraindicate the use of tapes. The student should not even ask an individual known to be paranoid for permission to tape an interview. Obviously such a client will react with suspicion and possible rejection of the worker, even if he should agree to the taping. Any individual who expresses even the slightest resistance to taping should not be pressed further. All members of group sessions must agree to taping—even one reluctant member is a contraindication. If the presence of the recorder would have an adverse effect on the interview or social work process, there should be no taping. If students want to tape an administrative or staff meeting, all participants will need to know that the session is being taped; if delicate "in-house" material is discussed, the tape should be erased. Staff might even ask that the machine be turned off so that they can feel free to speak more openly. The person doing the taping must be alert to subtle indications that taping needs to be discontinued.

Certain kinds of interactions are also difficult to record. A play-therapy session with a young child may produce a few verbal comments mixed in with long periods of silence and banging, scuffling noises. If persons are moving about the room while talking, the words may be unintelligible on tape.

Many creative things can be done with a recorded interview. The student can do his own assessment of the interview and then submit the tape to his field instructor. After the supervisor has completed his review of it, both can compare their assessments. An interview might be taped and then process-recorded by the student for later comparison with the tape. The recording can be listened to during supervisory conferences and stopped at key points to discuss techniques and perhaps role-play alternate ways of responding. A student's first tape-recording can be set aside and listened to again at the end of placement to demonstrate the student's growth and increasing skill. Clients can listen back to their taped interviews and comment on their feelings as certain things were said, or they may critique the student's approach. One field instructor had psychotic patients dictate messages to themselves during periods of lucidity, to be listened to when they were not lucid.

If standards, expectations, and educational goals have been set, the student can monitor his own progress through a self-critique of taped interviews. Thus, he can become a real participant in the assessment process; he is not entirely dependent on the field instructor for feedback. Unfortunately, taping does have some limitations. If a taped interview lasted for one hour, it will take the supervisor one hour to listen to it. Thus, taping must be used in connection with other, more efficient methods of monitoring student activities.

Videotaping

Videotaping requires three basic pieces of equipment: a camera (with or without special spotlights), a recorder unit, and a modified TV set to play back the tapes. Microphones may be built into the camera or plugged into the recorder unit. A tripod is usually needed to hold the camera steady during filming. At this writing, the equipment costs well over $1,000 and is beyond the means of most field placement settings. Some schools of social work use the equipment in the classroom, usually in basic interviewing or practice courses where students role-play interviews and then watch themselves. Some equipment uses a camera that is hand-held and requires no spotlights. Nonetheless, some photographic skill is necessary as the lens usually will not take in an entire group of people or even the entire faces and bodies of two people. Thus, the camera operator must focus on just the face or just the upper part of the interviewee's body. The skilled photographer/social worker will aim the camera at the client's hands when they communicate something significant, or at his nervous, tapping foot, or will switch from the interviewer's face to that of the client to catch a fleeting but significant nonverbal response.

Obviously, the interviewer cannot also serve as photographer, thus necessitating the physical presence of a third person during the interview, group meeting, or whatever is being taped. A few settings have stationary equipment built into a special room where filming can be done by someone operating controls behind a wall and others set up the camera on a tripod to film all activity unattended, in a fixed position. The same principles suggested for audio taping must be followed when introducing videotaping to a client as regards obtaining consent for the taping and safeguarding his privacy. When used effectively, videotaping is a highly effective monitoring and teaching tool, as it captures both verbal and nonverbal communications. Students may be anxious over the process initially, but once exposed to the equipment they relax and actually enjoy being taped and studying themselves afterward. Obviously, taping must be planned in advance and is simply not practical except for selected interviews and meetings. Tapes are time-consuming for the field instructor to review, and it is difficult to skim over a taped one-hour counseling session. With the client's written permission, tapes can be used in training other students or staff. Tapes can be shared with clients as part of the therapeutic process or even used educationally to demonstrate to potential or current consumers of social work services just what happens when social worker and client interact. Thus, most settings that use videotaping find that the creative possibilities for both monitoring and teaching outweigh the drawback of the time required to work with the tapes.

11 Performance Evaluation

Once a student's performance has been examined through application of various methods of direct and indirect observation, the field instructor must periodically summarize his thinking. This may consist of a simple oral review of progress during a student–field instructor supervisory conference or an in-depth discussion around a formal written evaluation that is submitted to the school. Unfortunately, students and field instructors alike rate performance evaluation as one of the least enjoyable and most dreaded aspects of field instruction. Field instructors exhibit much resistance to the act of writing evaluations and sharing them with supervisees. Yet, without performance evaluation, the entire field instruction process would be meaningless.

Performance evaluation is an ongoing process that starts with the student's first day of field placement and culminates in a final written assessment at the conclusion of internship. The evaluation is the field instructor's assessment of the student's progress and difficulties in achieving agreed-upon objectives (see Chapter 6 on the educational contract). It also describes the student's current skill level and identifies areas where growth has occurred and where further improvement is needed. If there has been continuous sharing throughout placement, written evaluations should hold no surprises. The supervisee should know what his field instructor is going to say about him before they are written.

The primary purpose of performance evaluation should be growth. If an adult learner receives constant feedback and critiques along with suggestions for improvement, he will be aware of areas where growth is needed and, as a result, can apply suggested techniques to become stronger and more competent. If he is tossed into an experience and provided with little or no evaluative feedback, his existing behaviors and skills may be reinforced or expanded; but he is cheated out of the opportunity for meaningful, conscious growth. Likewise, sharing evaluatory comments only at the conclusion of a field placement prevents the student from strengthening his positive features and improving weak areas so that the final evaluation will reflect increased competence.

Another purpose of student performance evaluation is to identify those individuals who are suited for social work practice and those who are not. Thus, it serves as a screening mechanism for field instructors in their role as gatekeepers of the profession.

Special Problems with Performance Evaluation

Performance evaluation involves several steps:

1. Ascertaining the student's level of functioning upon entering field placement (see Chapter 7)
2. Determining what the student must learn and the best way to go about teaching it (see Chapter 7)
3. Establishing the level of skill or competence the student must achieve in the desired areas (see Chapter 6)
4. Determining how to monitor what the student is doing in field and applying appropriate methods for assessing his performance (see Chapter 10)
5. Determining the level of the student's performance in relation to standards and expectations (e.g. satisfactory, outstanding)
6. Communicating to the student the conclusions that have been reached
7. Putting the evaluation into writing and sharing it with the student
8. Dealing with the supervisee's reactions to the evaluation

Many supervisors have difficulty making evaluatory judgments regarding their supervisees because of their need to be liked and respected by students, which can cause them to withhold negative evaluatory results. They may recognize that the student is having difficulty in a certain area but hestitate to share the assessment with him for fear that he will disagree with it, challenge it, or become upset by it. Field instructors are often plagued with insecurities: ''Do I really know enough to evaluate someone else's performance?'' ''Who am I to say whether this person's performance is acceptable or not?'' To further complicate matters, most field instructors have received little or no formal training in techniques of performance evaluation and feel poorly prepared for this task. Social workers are trained to be non-judgmental, yet assessment of someone's performance involves judgment.

Some supervisors have little difficulty communicating their assessments orally but lack effective writing skills and produce written evaluations that do not fully reflect their feelings about the student's performance. A good written evaluation takes several hours to prepare—a heavy demand on a busy field instructor's schedule. Few social workers like to write performance evaluations, and some become highly skilled at procrastinating until the last minute in anticipation of the time and effort that must be expended.

If the supervisor has hesitated to share his evaluation with the student throughout the term, obviously critical comments cannot be communicated for the first time in a final written evaluation. If the field instructor hasn't had the courage to discuss certain observations and concerns with the student during the field placement, he may find himself unable to share them at all. Perhaps the most difficult part of performance evaluation for the supervisor is the fact that he must evaluate himself in the process. ''If my student isn't doing well in this area, it is because of *me?* Have I used the right supervisory techniques? Did I spend enough time with him? Would he have done better if he had had a more effective supervisor?'' And so on.

Some field instructors have had bad experiences with performance evaluations: schools that fail to support their evaluations, students who file grievances or complain about the field instructor to his superiors, and so on. These situations are rare, but every social work community has a few horror stories that circulate among field instructors and create anxiety and fears over the performance evaluation process. The day-to-day problems associated with student evaluation are much less dramatic, and specific techniques can be used to deal with them effectively.

Virtually all students, no matter how mature and competent, have some anxiety over their evaluations. Even those who are performing at an obviously outstanding level will feel some trepidation when the written evaluation is due. Whether or not there is a realistic reason for the individual to feel insecure, this anxiety must be recognized, dealt with, and discussed as a normal problem that commonly accompanies the evaluation process.

Individuals who have always received glowing responses from teachers and other authority figures may have special difficulties associated with field performance evaluation. A student may have received straight A's in the classroom, earned special praise for his effectiveness during summer employment, been highly effective in community fund-raising activities and volunteer work; then he enters field placement and encounters a field instructor trying to abide by the principles presented in this text. All social workers have room for continued improvement and growth, and these areas should be identified and dealt with as part of the student learning process. As a result, the adult learner now finds himself in a situation where he is being evaluated critically for what may be the first time. He may have become accustomed to regarding evaluation as a reward for outstanding performance and may experience keen disappointment and perhaps even anger when he encounters a supervisor who identifies areas where improvement is needed. He may not realize that the qualities that earned him the honors in other activities do not necessarily equip him for outstanding performance as a professional social worker.

Similarly, a student who has already worked as a social worker or experienced a first field placement and received glowing evaluations may have functioned in a setting where expectations were so low that almost anyone could have earned ''outstanding.'' His former supervisor may have mentioned only positives in evaluatory feedback, omitting areas of concern because of his own insecurities regarding the evaluation process or the supervisee. Perhaps the student really was outstanding in comparison to expectations. Thus he may enter field genuinely feeling, ''I am really good. I don't think I have too much to learn''—because he has no reason to believe otherwise. No one, including himself, may have looked closely at his performance. Perhaps former supervisors relied on self-assessments and superficial written reports to determine his level of skill instead of using direct observational techniques that revealed specific areas of competence and weakness. Such a student can become upset when he encounters a field instructor who applies an honest and thorough performance evaluation process for the first time in his adult experience. Invariably he will ask himself: ''Is it *me?* Have I deteriorated in my work? Am I doing something wrong that I wasn't doing before? or Is it the *field instructor?*'' The student may not realize that it isn't he who has changed. Instead, there have been changes in the method of evaluation, the expectations he must meet, and the effectiveness and honesty of the feedback being provided.

The most effective way to prevent and deal with this problem is for the field instructor to have a frank discussion with the student at the beginning of field placement in which he describes his approach to performance evaluation and warns the supervisee that expectations will be high and feedback painfully honest at times, but that the feedback is necessary to facilitate growth. The instructor should acknowledge his awareness that this may make the student anxious and note that this feeling is normal, particularly if this is the first time he has experienced fully honest, critical evaluatory feedback. He should display empathy and encourage the supervisee to feel free to share his feelings as he begins to receive evaluatory feedback. Reassure him that he will be receiving feedback on positive as well as negative areas.

Another rather common problem occurs when students receive a "satisfactory" rating rather than the "outstanding" they expected. Some social work students are overachievers—they are very conscientious, hard-working, mature learners who feel satisfied with nothing less than the highest possible ratings and may feel keen disappointment if a "lowly" satisfactory rating is received. There is a tendency to forget what a "satisfactory" rating for a field placement experience really means. A "satisfactory" evaluation states that the student is *fully satisfactory:* He has met all the basic expectations; he is fully suited for social work practice at his level of training, and he has the desired level of competence and mastery of skills. Such a rating is a tremendous accomplishment for a student who never saw a client until four months ago, who hasn't worked in twenty-four years, or who is twenty years old and has never worked. Students with prior social work experience may fail to realize that the same quality of performance that earned them outstanding ratings in their preplacement job won't necessarily earn outstanding ratings in their professional internship. The performance expectations for an MSW will be higher than those for employees having no professional social work training. Thus, the student must learn new skills and increase the depth and mastery of existing competences in order to meet the basic expectations of a graduate-level or BSW-level field placement. Social work students who receive "satisfactory" evaluations have every right to feel proud of their accomplishment. If expectations are appropriately high and intensive methods were used to assess performance, a student who earns a satisfactory rating will have worked hard and taken significant risks, both personally and professionally, to achieve the growth necessary to earn this rating.

"If all this hard work is necessary just to get a satisfactory rating, what must a student do to earn an outstanding rating?" Outstanding means just that: *unusual* ability to perform; *exceptional, far-over-the-standard* mastery of social work skills, work habits, attitudes, and knowledge.* The distribution of unsatisfactory, satisfactory, and out-

standing students can be expected to follow the familiar bell curve:

Unsatisfactory   Satisfactory   Outstanding

The vast majority of students will fall somewhere in the middle with a few functioning at the extremes. Thus, a student must be something super-special to earn an "outstanding." Such a rating should not be given to those who "fully meet expectations." Every social worker should "fully meet expectations" before he graduates. Thus, outstanding individuals must *exceed* this expectation. If a given field instructor consistently assigns outstanding ratings, something may be wrong. Perhaps his expectations are too low, so that everyone earns "outstanding." Perhaps he does not like to be critical so that everyone completes field placement with a 100 percent positive evaluation.

If an instructor never gives an outstanding rating, perhaps his expectations are too high for any student to meet. Some supervisors simply don't want to risk themselves or rock the boat by rating students as unusual in any manner. Or perhaps the school is sending a given field setting or individual field instructor a steady diet of "average" students or "the very best we have" without providing a more representative cross-section of interns.

To prevent misunderstandings regarding the meaning of satisfactory versus outstanding evaluations (and keen disappointments when "only" satisfactory is received), these terms should be clearly defined at the beginning of field placement. This may be done by the school, but it must also be done by each individual field instructor or field placement setting. "This is what it takes to earn an 'outstanding' in this setting. These are our expectations. These are typical characteristics of students who have earned unsatisfactory, satisfactory, and outstanding evaluations in this setting. These are the kinds of behaviors, attitudes, and problems that could cause you to receive an unsatisfactory or be counseled out of field placement," and so on. A frank discussion of these expectations at the beginning of field gives the adult learner an important tool. His anxiety is decreased upon learning the rules of the game. He can look the material over and decide consciously whether he wants to strive for the satisfactory or the outstanding rating. Most important, he can assess himself against the stated characteristics and expectations and continually monitor his own performance throughout the placement. This is an invaluable learning experience in and of itself. It increases self-awareness and provides the learner with a sense of dignity: He is an active, fully informed participant in the process rather than a help-

---

*See pp. 61–66 for a listing of qualities developed in one field placement to illustrate the distinctions among satisfactory, unsatisfactory, and outstanding performances. See also the detailed educational objective regarding professional work habits on pp. 55–59.

less pawn in a game placing him at the total mercy of authority figures. Student resistance to the evaluatory process lessens; instead, honest, critical feedback is welcomed. When expectations are communicated clearly, students are much less inclined to challenge and question supervisory ratings, and there is much greater opportunity to bring their concerns about performance into supervisory discussions.

The field instructor may forget that some students sincerely believe that they will receive a failing grade simply as a result of disagreeing with their supervisor. Others fear that one or two minor incidents will cause them to receive an unsatisfactory rating. Even mature, apparently confident students with solidly satisfactory or better performance can harbor unrealistic fears. The student grapevine may carry horror stories of students who were "doing okay one day and were counseled out without any warning the next" or who "received nothing but positive feedback all semester and got hit with an unsatisfactory evaluation at the end." Unfortunately, students hear only the side of the story presented by their peers; they usually have no way of knowing the field instructor's version of what happened. Thus they may not realize that the field instructor *did* communicate serious concerns all semester, but the student's denial and emotional blocking had prevented him from hearing and internalizing what was being communicated. The student's actions may have been so serious as to warrant overnight termination of field placement. And so on. Students who receive unsatisfactory ratings in field placement may suddenly disappear from school, preventing other students from learning more details about the situation, or they may present a version of what happened that will protect their ego and standing with their peers. Nevertheless, the horror stories can be very frightening and anxiety-provoking for other students who fail to realize that unsatisfactory evaluations and premature termination from field placement do not occur without very compelling reasons and usually only after many hours of conferences and discussions, efforts to help the student overcome the problem, and exhaustion of all other alternatives.*

Undoubtedly there are some situations where students are unjustifiably rated as unsatisfactory. This may occur if a field instructor becomes threatened by his student or is having extreme difficulty functioning effectively in his supervisory role. Agency administrators or field-work coordinators and school faculty usually detect when this is occurring and intervene before an inappropriate evaluation is given. If students nevertheless receive unjust evaluations, grievance mechanisms are provided for them to seek correction of the problem. In the vast majority of disputes over evaluations, the student's feeling that an injustice has occurred is not warranted. If the field instructor has handled genuine performance problems in an insecure and in-

adequate manner and has communicated his concerns to the student ineffectively, the supervisee may feel that the unsatisfactory rating is unjustified. Indeed, a student with genuinely unsatisfactory or problematic performance may even win a grievance action if the supervisor's evaluation does not sufficiently document and support the assigned rating.

Other problems occur when students exchange performance evaluations, as they frequently do. Two students may have worked side by side all term in a field placement. Each has formed an impression of how his peer is doing, and much sharing of common problems, concerns, assignments, and even analysis of field instructors has occurred. As a result, the students are intensely curious about each other's evaluation. However, some real problems can occur as a result of the exchange. Consider the following dialogue:

STUDENT A TO STUDENT B: Gosh, you got "outstanding"—I'm glad for you. (*Thinks silently to himself*): I don't believe it! I worked just as hard as he did and I only got "satisfactory." Something's wrong here!

On the other hand, both students may receive "satisfactory," but student A knows a few things regarding student B's behavior and attitudes that make him feel that B should have gotten a lower rating. If he knows that his fellow student has been "goofing off," leaving early without telling anyone, doing homework during field placement time, or reading novels and newspapers all day, student A may be very resentful that he has worked hard all year and yet received the same rating as his less dedicated peer. On the other hand, student A may receive a marginally satisfactory evaluation that results in a passing grade but essentially says "I'm not sure you're going to make it" and identifies many problem areas. Student B may console his peer with helpful comments such as, "How can they *do* that to you?! That's terrible. You didn't do anything to deserve that kind of rating. I wouldn't accept that. I think you ought to do something about it." Of course student B wouldn't accept that kind of evaluation: *His* performance was okay—he wasn't the one who received the marginal evaluation.

Thus, comparing one's evaluation with that of another student may cause a student to question or challenge his own evaluation. Of course, students who swap evaluations don't know what went on behind the scenes. They do not know the student's level of performance at the beginning of field placement as compared to the completion of the term. They may not know the specific level of skill that the student was expected to master and the amount of progress achieved. They do not know what problems the student had to work through to earn his evaluation. They often have limited knowledge of their fellow student's awareness of problem areas and willingness to work on them. Jealousy and competitiveness over outstanding evaluations may

*See pp. 198–201 for a discussion of common causes of unsatisfactory ratings.

cause peers to overlook the unusual qualities the student presented or gained during placement to earn his rating. My own view is that performance evaluations are a very private affair and Ann Landers's frequent advice—MYOB: "mind your own business"—should be applied liberally. A frank sharing with students at the beginning of placement regarding the pitfalls of exchanging evaluations may lead to appropriate caution at the end of the term.

Another problem with the performance evaluation process is that because of widely differing standards for performance, a student can receive "outstanding" in one setting, "satisfactory" in another, and maybe even "unsatisfactory" in yet another—*for the exact same performance*. There may be differences between the school and the field placement setting, from one field placement to another, and even between individual field instructors in the same agency. Students know this factor exists, and some who are more concerned with getting high grades than with acquiring skills will deliberately seek out easy placements, where almost everyone receives an outstanding evaluation. Sometimes it seems that schools are the last to know which settings fit this category; on the other hand, schools occasionally use such settings deliberately to enable marginal students to pass placement who would not succeed in settings with higher expectations and stricter supervisory approaches. As the problem of low standards has already been discussed fully elsewhere (see pp. 1–4), it will not be discussed further here. However, its existence and effect upon the evaluation process must be recognized.

Field instructors might face a difficult situation if they learn additional information about a student after the final performance evaluation has been written and the supervisee has left placement. The supervisor then has several choices. He can prepare a revised evaluation, but this can be unfair to the student if it interprets incidents that took place after he finished placement. The supervisor can write an addendum and submit it to the school, with a special covering letter explaining the circumstances necessitating the added material. However, the field instructor must find a way to share its content with the student. If the original was shared (a requirement of most schools and also good personnel practice), any addenda must also be shared. Under the Buckley Amendment* students have the right of access to their student files; should this right be exercised, the addendum will be seen.

Perhaps the most common approach is for the field instructor to put nothing in writing at the time the additional information is learned, instead storing it away for use later on should he be asked to give a reference for the student. However, the student may be anticipating a reference that conforms to his final evaluation and may be totally unaware

*Amends Public Law 93–568, effective November 19, 1974. See also Department of HEW, Office of the Secretary, "Privacy Rights of Parents and Students," Part II: "Final Rule on Education Records," *Federal Register*, June 17, 1976, pp. 24662–24675.

of the additional information and how it affects the supervisor's feelings. If it affects the quality of the reference in a positive manner, the student should certainly know about it for his own growth and satisfaction but probably would not object to the supervisor's including the data without his knowledge. However, if the additional information affects the reference adversely, the field instructor must share it with the student before including it in any reference statements. This may require that he contact the former student and have a formal discussion: "I feel you should know that if I am asked to give a reference, what I have to say now is a little different from what I said when you finished field placement, and I think you should know how I feel now and why."

The kind of information that would make it necessary for a field instructor to change a performance evaluation may be positive or negative, but it must be highly significant. A student might leave placement with a satisfactory evaluation, but subsequent review of his work and unsolicited feedback from others indicate that he completed some rather significant and unusual tasks—accomplishments requiring greater than average skill. On the other hand, subsequent review may reveal sloppy, incomplete, careless, and generally low-quality work, even though the field instructor thought the student's performance was at least satisfactory at the time he terminated. A supervisor may discover that the student has been returning to the agency using an outdated ID card to gain access to confidential files and become involved in inappropriate activities. He may be continuing to see clients without telling anyone, because of difficulty in termination, when the field instructor thought he had terminated. Some field instructors even encourage previous students to continue seeing clients after field placement has officially ended. This is a much more common practice than most administrators and schools realize. Some other students see clients over the summer months without the former field instructor's knowledge or approval. (Former employees, including those who have been dismissed, also do this.)

Such students are placing themselves and the agency in a very precarious position. Since they are no longer officially affiliated with the setting, the agency can provide no administrative or liability protection. Should problems develop, the agency will claim that the student is on his own: "He is no longer in placement here. We have no responsibility for his actions." Malpractice insurance provided through the school may not cover the student if he is acting on his own and engaging in an activity that is not an officially approved part of his social work educational experience. Since he is not an employee of the agency and is not qualified to engage in private practice, NASW malpractice insurance might not provide any coverage. The school also may claim no responsibility and may even terminate him from the social work program because of his irresponsible behavior.

Thus, the student in this situation is operating on his own, without adequate supervision and guidance, is functioning as an independent practitioner when he lacks the skills for doing so, and is virtually without protection. Furthermore, if the agency is unaware of his continuing involvement with a client, regular staff who serve the same client may develop plans and treatment approaches that are inconsistent with the student's approach, resulting in confusion for the client and added complications for everyone. Incidents of this sort can lead to client damage and other serious problems for the student, agency, and school. The field instructor who learns that his student is continuing to see clients in his own or another agency cannot overlook this information.

Another problem that can arise with performance evaluation occurs when a field instructor becomes convinced of the importance of a problem area just before the end of placement. He may feel guilty about not having shared his concern about the matter throughout the term, feel it's important to do so now, yet realize that he cannot surprise the student with it in the final written evaluation. If the field instructor has been giving positive feedback all term, what is the student going to think when he suddenly changes his tune at the last minute? On the other hand, a field instructor may have been leaning toward a marginal or even unsatisfactory evaluation and may have worked to prepare the student through appropriate discussions, but an administrator may disagree with the final evaluation or even ask the field instructor to give the student a "satisfactory," thus usurping the supervisor's authority at the most crucial moment. Or else an administrator may feel very strongly, and with good reason, that a field instructor's assessment is not accurate and must be changed in the best interests of the agency and the total student program.

The obvious way to avoid this problem is for the field instructor to keep his own superior or the appropriate administrator informed of the progress of students, especially those performing at a level that deviates markedly from satisfactory. Examples of the student's work should be shared and the rationale for supervisory impressions discussed *throughout* the field placement. This will enable the field instructor to find out early in the placement if his superior is not supporting his views and will allow time for reexamination of the student's performance if necessary, for strengthening of field instruction skills, or perhaps for convincing the administrator he is incorrect in his assessment—*before* consistent, definitive feedback is given to the student over a long period of time, making it nearly impossible to change the assessment later on.*

The field instructor can have a real problem in determining what expectations or standards he will use to measure student performance in the evaluation. Actually, this difficulty is first encountered during the contract phase (pp. 87–88), when objectives and skill levels are being defined. Should a student be rated against his own abilities—that is, receive a field placement grade and an evaluation based upon his progress in performing up to his individual potential and ability? Or should he be rated against other students, or against the expectations of the individual field instructor, the school, or generic social work practice? Should expectations be based on the requirements for functioning as an employee in a particular field placement setting, or should they be based on expectations for "any social work job"? There are no easy answers to these questions. Until schools (and the CSWE) develop more specific standards and expectations for both generic and specialized fields of social work education, field instructors will continue to set their expectations based on a mixture of these factors. However, this dilemma can be discussed openly with the student as the educational contract is being developed, and student and field instructor together can identify the factors that will be used to set their particular objectives and standards.

Another frustrating problem occurs if a first field instructor's performance evaluation does not reach the school in time for use in planning subsequent placements. Such planning often must begin weeks before the student has even finished his initial placement. When a school requires students to complete more than one placement, there must be some form of communication between the first and second field instructor, especially if the initial supervisor feels strongly that certain problem areas, strengths, goals, or recommendations need to be taken into consideration as the school seeks a subsequent placement for the student.

The mood of the field instructor at performance evaluation time can affect the rating given in the final written evaluation. Most supervisees, aware of this, are very careful not to anger or upset their supervisor in the week or two preceding this crucial time. They are also aware of the field instructor's tendency to remember their most recent accomplishments or difficulties as other experiences recede into the background.† If the supervisor himself is feeling inadequate in his own professional role for any reason (e.g. perhaps a case just "blew up"), he may resist being critical of the student or may give a hypercritical evaluation. The field instructor's own performance evaluation may have

---

*As a supervisor and consultant to field instructors, I have occasionally disagreed sharply with their final assessments of student performance. However, I have learned the hard way that if I have not been working with the instructor throughout the field placement, I cannot foist my impressions onto him at the last minute. If there is doubt or uneasiness about a field instructor's assessment of a student's performance and the adminis-

trative level person decides to review the student's work himself *at the end of placement*, he must be prepared to back down if he finds the assessment incompatible with his own and the field instructor indicates that the student is expecting an evaluation consistent with the field instructor's impressions. Sometimes it is better to remain uneasy and ignorant than to discover a field instructor's difficulties in assessing a student's performance at the very end of placement!

†This difficulty is best overcome by use of the supervisory notebook. See pp. 171–172.

been a recent topic of discussion with his superior, causing feelings of overidentification with the student. The field instructor may unconsciously take out his own frustrations through the student's evaluation. He himself may have low or marginal social work skills and thus may tend to see all "average" students as "outstanding." Usually these moods are temporary, and a competent field instructor will be aware of their existence and will try to see to it that they do not affect his evaluation of his student.* Not all field instructors are able to do this all the time. This happens very *rarely;* students who feel that an evaluation does not accurately reflect their performance and the content of supervisory discussions during the term should feel free to question the content during the final evaluation.

Preparing a Written Performance Evaluation

It is obvious that a great deal of thought must go into any written performance evaluation. A carefully thought out educational contract provides the road map for the field instruction experience. The performance evaluation then assesses the student's progress in meeting the stated objectives. Thus, the framework for the final evaluation is established and known to both student and supervisor from the beginning of placement. If performance feedback has been given on a regular basis throughout the term, the written evaluation merely formalizes what has already been communicated to the student. It is primarily an exercise in writing—not assessment—since the assessment has already occurred (see Chapters 9 and 10). However, supervisors who have no educational plan and have not shared their assessments face the difficult task of both assessing and writing at the end of placement. This undoubtedly accounts for much of the resistance and dislike for the process that is so widespread among supervisors.

In order to write meaningful student evaluations, we must consider how they are used by schools and prospective employers and how available information and tools can help or hinder us in this process.

How Performance Evaluations Are Used by Schools and Employers

Evaluations of student performance in field placement are submitted to the school, with a copy given to the student. The field instructor should retain a copy for his files for several years, as students may come back to a given

---

*For example, I have once or twice deliberately avoided doing an evaluation when I was aware of a mood that was not positive. Even though it made the evaluation a few days late, I chose to put it aside until my mood had passed and I could write it in a manner that would be objective and do justice to the student.

supervisor for references again and again as they apply for their first job, change jobs, or seek admission to another program.

The school files the evaluation in the student's record. It is almost never sent out verbatim to other schools, prospective employers, or other outsiders without specific permission from the student. The common practice is for a faculty member to summarize all the evaluatory material generated from the total educational experience of the student—classroom and all field placements—to form a master reference statement that presents the highlights of the student's experience. This is then sent out to persons who ask the school for references, and students are asked to sign a consent for release of information before it is released.

If the field instructor does not actually assign the student's grade in placement, the school relies heavily on his evaluation to determine the appropriate grade. Likewise, the decision as to whether a given student should continue in the social work program will take all field instruction evaluations into consideration, along with other material. Schools are aware that some students may do well in the classroom yet perform poorly in field, and vice versa. Thus, the field instructor's evaluation can be a key factor in the school's decision to counsel a student out of the program or to retain one whose classroom performance is marginal. Vague, general evaluations that contain unsubstantiated comments or are so abstract that they could describe almost any student are virtually useless to the school for any important planning or decision-making. Field instructors who produce such evaluations have little basis for complaint if the school fails to counsel out a problematic student or takes other action that the supervisor feels is inappropriate. Likewise, if the school is going to go out on a limb and back an outstanding student, it needs specifics to support its actions. A school's reference statement needs to indicate *why* a student is considered to be functioning at a certain level or to have certain strengths and limitations. Since much of this material comes from the student's field experience, the school's ability to deal effectively with problematic and outstanding students or to recognize solidly satisfactory students is impaired if details are not forthcoming from field instruction evaluations.

If the school calendar permits, a faculty adviser or member of the field instruction faculty may use an evaluation from an earlier field placement (along with other data) to determine the best setting for a student's subsequent placement. The school looks for a frank identification of the student's strengths and special abilities along with limitations and areas where further growth is needed. The student's reactions to field placement and to the field instructor may help in selecting the right setting and instructor for his particular needs in a second placement. If a student has shown a special ability to relate effectively with a particular client group and is very uncomfortable with others, this information can help the school avoid inappropriate placements and seek those that will maximize the student's potentials and abilities.

Information from an initial field placement evaluation is often made available to subsequent field instructors, either verbatim or in summarized form. Nothing frustrates and angers second field placement supervisors more than receiving a positive evaluation on a student that lures them into accepting the individual, only to discover later that the student has serious problems or deficits that were identified in the first placement but omitted from the written evaluation. A second field instructor should not have to start from scratch with an educational diagnosis of the student's strengths, limitations, and learning style. Accurate reporting from the first placement can enable him to build on, rather than duplicate, this information. This saves a great deal of time and enables the supervisor and student to move quickly into the more specialized experiences of the second placement.

Classroom instructors may consult a student's file if his academic performance triggers their curiosity regarding his application of skills in field. Students sometimes attach xeroxed copies of their most recent evaluations to résumés when they seek employment. School faculty responsible for training field instructors may review student evaluations to identify field instructors' skills in preparing meaningful evaluations and identifying areas where training is needed.

Thus, the field placement evaluation is one of the most important documents in a student's educational experience and has many possible applications in addition to its obvious use in the relationship between field instructor and student. It must be written carefully and thoughtfully, keeping in mind the various persons who are likely to read it and the ways in which it will be used.

The Supervisory Notebook

A very effective tool in student supervision, which also aids the field instructor in preparing the performance evaluation is a special notebook set aside for recording information regarding the field instructor's experience with the student. The existence and purpose of the notebook should be shared openly with the student, and the supervisor should feel free to refer to it during supervisory conferences if necessary. The student needs to feel comfortable with this process without wondering, "What's written in there about me?" The following kinds of information can be included:

1. Work assignments and deadlines. If a supervisory conference results in a plan to do "such-and-such," both the field instructor and the student should write it down. Seeing the field instructor make note of it as well, the supervisee knows that the supervisor will remember the assignment and the deadline for completion. There can be no room for disagreement later on. Most important, it helps the field in-

structor keep track of assignments (especially difficult if he supervises more than one person) and educational plans and goals. By flipping through his notes, he can quickly review all assignments throughout a given time period for his final evaluation as well as in preparation for a specific supervisory conference.

2. Things the supervisor needs to do. The field instructor may want to make a note of his promise to find a certain resource for the student, locate a specific type of case, plan an orientation to a community resource, or whatever.

3. Items for discussion in planned supervisory conferences. As the field instructor reviews student work throughout the week, he may give immediate feedback and direction on some things and hold others for discussion in the regular conference either because they are not urgent or because they require in-depth discussion. If something comes up during a conference that the supervisor wants to be certain to discuss or explore later on, this can be jotted down as well.

4. Observations of student performance on a day-to-day basis. Anything that is particularly significant should be noted and described briefly. Over a period of time, the collected examples of outstanding performance can be used to illustrate and justify outstanding ratings in a final performance evaluation. Likewise, if a student is having difficulty, examples and problematic situations can be noted. Most will be discussed with the student. However, if something occurs once and then not again, the field instructor may consider that it is not really a problem and choose to ignore it. On the other hand, if something happens repeatedly, he can see at a glance that a pattern exists and will have specific examples and dates on hand to share with the student when he presents his awareness of the pattern. If the problem persists, notations with dates and examples of the student's work can be reviewed to select appropriate illustrations of problematic areas discussed in a written evaluation. Such material could also prove invaluable in defending oneself in a grievance or legal action should one arise following a dispute over a written evaluation.

5. The student's response to supervision. If a student is responding openly or with eager acceptance, this will probably be remembered without any notes. However, if problems exist and the field instructor is sharing concerns and observations through supervisory conferences, notes on the date the problem was discussed, the content of the discussion, and the student's response can prove crucial. For example, if several weeks go by with no improvement in a problem, the field instructor may wonder if he has communicated his concerns clearly to the student. A review of the notebook may reveal that the problem was discussed on November 18, 21, and 30 and December 6 and that on

November 21 and 30 the student agreed to correct it within one week. Should a supervisee argue that he was never told about something, a review of the supervisory notebook can clarify the issue.

Some field instructors encourage their supervisees to keep their own notebooks for recording impressions and reactions to field placement, questions to bring up in supervisory conferences, reactions to supervisory discussions, reminders regarding assignments or special plans, and similar information. Students may also record notes on instructional content provided during supervisory sessions or other training. Some schools require their students to keep a log of hours spent in field placement; others require a breakdown of time spent in various activities. A field instructor may request a special time study to help a student look at how he uses and manages his time. Students could be asked to jot down reactions to the first three or four weeks of placement along with suggestions for improving orientation for new students. Thus, the student notebook can help the supervisee prepare his own evaluation of the placement at the end of the term.

The Educational Contract

The contract forms the basis, background, and framework for the performance evaluation. A copy can be attached to the evaluation to illustrate the expectations placed upon the student and to avoid repetition in referring to the various objectives and learning experiences (see Chapter 6).

Student Self-evaluation

A student can be asked to evaluate himself in preparation for a formal evaluation. What does he think the field instructor will say about him? How would he rate himself? This process facilitates thinking about assessment and is also a test of the field instructor's effectiveness in communicating evaluatory feedback on an ongoing basis. Are the student's self-perceptions in general agreement with those of the field instructor? Are there significant differences? Why?

This technique must be used with caution. Some supervisors abuse it, letting the student write his own evaluation and then, after the fact, telling him that it *is* the final evaluation. This places the student in a most unfair and unreasonable position and is a rather obvious ploy on the field instructor's part to avoid putting his own thoughts into writing. The supervisor may try to justify the practice by labeling it a ''learning experience.''

Some students become quite anxious at the thought of having to evaluate themselves. Supervisees who have become defensive when receiving critical feedback generally should not be asked to write their own evaluations. The field instructor can predict that such a student will give himself a higher rating than is warranted, and the written self-evaluation could become the focal point of a heated tug-of-war between field instructor and student. Students whose normal response to evaluatory feedback is passive and those who have participated actively in the evaluatory process will benefit from self-assessment. However, it should be made clear that this is a learning exercise—it will not become the final evaluation. Ideally the field instructor should prepare his own evaluation in draft before seeing the student's product. The two evaluations can then be compared, and if the field instructor wants to change his on the basis of the student's input, the change can be made during the discussion with the supervisee. It must be recognized that some students consistently overrate themselves, while others, very often outstanding individuals, usually underrate themselves.

Evaluation Forms and Outlines

A meaningful performance evaluation must give an accurate description of the individual's performance. It should also describe the kind of setting he worked in, the nature of the expectations placed upon him, the methods used to assess performance, and the type of supervision provided. Any special problems encountered should be mentioned, along with efforts to resolve them. Areas of growth or stagnation and areas still needing improvement should be identified. An overall rating must be assigned and recommendations given regarding future supervision, training, or employment.

Unfortunately, there is no standard recipe or format for the preparation of performance evaluations. Some schools provide detailed narrative outlines; others use special rating forms with or without narratives; some assessment sheets are highly structured and limit the evaluator to a series of check marks in the appropriate boxes. Many schools provide no outline at all and leave it entirely up to the field instructor to organize and present his information in the manner he feels most appropriate.

As long as the basic information is presented, it doesn't really matter what format is used for the evaluation. As long as objectives are clearly and behaviorally defined and the student's specific level of skill and mastery of expectations are described, the format is secondary. Unfortunately, many rating scales and predetermined outlines are restrictive, creating frustration for the evaluator who wants to comment on an area not addressed on the preprinted form.* Others set

*For example, the NASW reference form for ACSW candidates is highly structured. Yet it does not address ''adherence to the NASW Code of Ethics.'' Evaluators can therefore easily overlook it and forget to comment on problems or strengths. A candidate could conceivably receive the highest possible rating in all categories listed on the form and receive his ACSW, yet consistently violate the Code of Ethics!

up an arbitrary rating scale of 1 to 7 or whatever, with 1 representing the lowest skill level and 7 the highest. However, evaluations based on such forms are almost meaningless unless they are accompanied by some narrative to explain why the student was given a certain rating. Otherwise, one rater's 6 may mean something entirely different from another's.

Alfred Kadushin's *Supervision in Social Work* (New York: Columbia University Press, 1976) includes examples of many of the types of evaluation forms used currently. No attempt will be made to duplicate that information here. However, we will review several common formats, examine one progressive evaluation form, and present a comprehensive outline to serve as a guide in making certain that, regardless of the type of format being used, all pertinent areas are addressed in some manner.

Open narrative. Field instructors may be provided with virtually no guidelines except that "a performance evaluation is due on May 15." No direction may be provided regarding the content of the evaluation or the organization or style to be used in presenting the information. Many supervisors in this case produce rambling, disorganized narrative reports containing no subheadings, providing excessive information in some areas and incomplete data in others.

Detailed narrative outline. If an outline is provided, the field instructor is required to organize his thoughts under specific headings. Some comment must be made under each heading, so that the scope of the information provided will be fairly consistent from one evaluator to another. If they are prepared according to the guidelines suggested in these chapters, narrative evaluations can be ideal vehicles for giving meaningful descriptions of student performance, especially when performance is other than satisfactory. However, such evaluations require some writing skill, are time-consuming to produce, call for a great deal of subjective judgment on the part of the rater, and require more time to review and analyze than itemized checklist forms.

Numerical rating scale. This instrument lists various qualities or desired characteristics and asks the evaluator to assign a number to each one to signify the student's degree of competence. For example, a five-point rating scale might offer the following definitions: 1=unsatisfactory, 2=below satisfactory or needs improvement, 3=satisfactory, 4=above satisfactory, and 5=outstanding. One item may read: "relationships with others." The field instructor selects the number that matches his assessment of the student's abilities in that area and marks it on the form. Such evaluation forms are among the least effective in existence. If Jim Henderson gives his student a 2 on "casework skills" and Sandra Smith in another agency gives her student another 2 what does that mean? The reader needs to know the instructor's definition of 2 or "below satisfactory" before the evaluation can have any meaning.

Rating scale with behavioral definitions. In this format each rating number is accompanied by a behaviorized description of its meaning. For example, the NASW reference form uses a ten-point scale to evaluate fourteen areas of performance. The definition of a 2 rating for "ability to express himself in writing" is "vague and ambiguous in expression of ideas." The 8 rating is described as "shows organization and consistency in expression of ideas." Thus, anyone reading the form would know what an evaluator means when he assigns an 8 rating. In other words, the supervisor reads a series of descriptions of possible performance and picks the one that comes closest to his supervisee's performance. One difficulty with this format occurs when an individual has both 3 and 8 characteristics on the same item and doesn't seem to fit clearly into any one level as defined on the form. The frustrated rater may wish he could make up a definition of his own and assign it a number. Furthermore, unless a narrative is required, this format may limit a rater's ability to explain fully why a given rating was assigned. This is especially important if less than satisfactory scores are challenged by the supervisee.

The following evaluation form was recently developed by an undergraduate school of social work. A special committee comprising the director of field instruction, several faculty members, agency-based field instructors, and at least one student worked together to come up with an instrument that would reflect a competency-based approach to assessment, yield a quantitative rating, and require less time on the part of the rater than the narrative form previously in use. Note the instructions for completing the form and the total scores, which correspond to a specific grade. On the rating scale itself, each behavioral item actually has two possible ratings that can be assigned, depending on how strongly the supervisee fits the description given. Several narrative questions are added at the conclusion of the quantitative portion of the form to cover details and supporting data that cannot be addressed otherwise.

Behavioral Rating Scale for Evaluation of Field Placement Performance*

Final Evaluation of Student's Field Performance

Name of Student _____

Five behavioral expectations are listed after each factor on which the student is to be evaluated. Each skill level corresponds to the letter grade which appears at the top of that column.

Indicate the student's achievement level by circling the appropriate number in each column. Circle the first number if the student has barely achieved at that level. Circle the second number when the student has met expectations fully at that level.

Please write "not applicable" or "not measured" in any of the columns in which you are unable to rate the student. Space is provided for explanations in the narrative section of this form.

The first section of 20 evaluative factors is to be used in determining the student's overall field performance and final grade. The narrative section provides the field instructor the opportunity to support and clarify the evaluation.

The grading scale is as follows:

    A = 170 – 200
    B = 130 – 169
    C = 90 – 129
    D = 50 – 89
    F = 49 and below

If the student is rated on fewer than the 20 evaluative statements provided, the grading scale will be revised accordingly.

*Special thanks to Bob Lewis, Director of Field Instruction at East Tennessee State University for permission to use the form. It will undergo further refinements before it is considered in final form.

PROFESSIONAL/PERSONAL CHARACTERISTICS

	F		D		C		B		A	
	1	2	3	4	5	6	7	8	9	10
Professional Responsibility	Appears bored with his work and puts self-interests first. Has a pattern of tardiness and/or absenteeism.		Sometimes appears interested in work and will put client interests first. Wastes time even when he adheres to agency working hours.		Usually fulfills work responsibilities satisfactorily and is seldom tardy or absent from work.		Demonstrates responsibility in completing work assignments and makes good use of time.		Consistently responsible about all aspects of work and makes excellent use of time.	
Poise and Self Control	Generally fails to maintain a professional calm and objective manner even under nonstressful situations.		Occasionally fails to maintain poise and control even under the normal work situations.		Maintains poise and control under normal situations but sometimes behaves erratically under stress.		Generally maintains poise and control even when faced with very stressful situations.		Consistently maintains poise and control even under extreme stress and unexpected crises.	
Assertiveness	Extremely passive; occasionally assertive but only when inappropriate.		In most situations is too passive or assertive.		Appropriate under normal, routine situations with occasional exceptions.		Usually appropriate even in difficult situations.		Consistently appropriate even in dealing with very difficult situations.	
Personal Appearance as Related to Agency Standards	Appearance interferes with relationships with clients, agency personnel, and/or the community.		Appearance is occasionally consistent with agency standards.		Appearance is generally consistent with agency standards.		Appearance is consistent with agency standards with only rare exceptions.		Appearance is always consistent with agency standards.	

APPLICATION OF SOCIAL WORK PRACTICE SKILLS

	F (1, 2)	D (3, 4)	C (5, 6)	B (7, 8)	A (9, 10)
Effectiveness in Planning and Arranging Work Responsibilities	Unable to plan and organize work effectively.	Occasionally demonstrates effectiveness.	Has some difficulty in planning and organizing work.	Usually plans and organizes work effectively.	Consistently plans effectively, is well organized and considers priorities appropriately.
Ability to Assume Responsibility for Own Learning	Never suggests or performs work activities on own initiative.	Very limited in planning and performing tasks independently.	Usually plans and performs only routine tasks without first checking with supervisor.	Frequently acts on his own in usual activities and sometimes in difficult or nonroutine matters.	Consistently acts on his own in handling usual as well as new and difficult situations.
Ability to Work Within the Purpose, Structure, and Constraints of the Agency and to Make Suggestions for Change in a Responsible Manner	Defies agency standards and suggests changes or demands changes inappropriately.	Abides by some agency standards but usually with reluctance.	Usually abides by routine standards but has difficulty learning and applying some standards.	Almost always abides by agency standards, and suggestions for change are usually made in a responsible manner.	Consistently abides by agency standards and is very professional in making suggestions for change.
Ability to Identify and Use Community Resources	Almost no ability demonstrated.	Occasionally identifies and uses a community resource.	Usually identifies and uses the obvious resources.	Demonstrates resourcefulness in seeking out some resources not commonly known.	Very responsible in seeking out and attempting to develop resources on his own initiative.

	F		D		C		B		A	
	1	2	3	4	5	6	7	8	9	10
Interviewing Skills, Including the Ability to Recognize and Interpret the Meaning of Nonverbal Communication During the Interview	Does not demonstrate knowledge and use of social work interviewing skills and is not perceptive to nonverbal communication.		Is effective sometimes but interviewing skills are limited. Usually does not interpret or respond to nonverbal communication appropriately.		Interviewing skills are acceptable, and student can interpret the most obvious meaning of nonverbal communication.		Interviews skillfully in most situations and usually interprets and responds appropriately to nonverbal communication.		Consistently interviews skillfully and almost always interprets and responds to nonverbal communication appropriately.	
Written Communication Skills, Including the Ability to Record with Clarity and Promptness	Written material is vague and contains many errors; student cannot meet deadlines.		Somewhat limited in ability to express self in writing and generally does not meet deadlines.		Written work is acceptable and is usually submitted on time.		Shows good organization and consistency in written communication and meeting deadlines.		Written work is always clear and concise and is always completed on time.	
Ability to Assess Situations Both Within and Outside the Client System and Determine Priorities	Never assesses accurately and reaches wrong conclusion as a basis for service.		Has limited ability to assess accurately and plan appropriately.		Usually is able to assess routine situations and reach obvious conclusions.		Generally assesses routine situations and takes appropriate action. Occasionally is inaccurate in difficult situations.		Consistently assesses and follows through appropriately with both routine and difficult situations.	
Ability to Develop and Maintain Professional Relationships with Consumers from Various Cultural, Ethnic, and Racial Backgrounds.	Cannot relate to consumers on a professional level.		Has some difficulty in forming relationships except in familiar and uncomplicated situations.		Usually forms productive relationships but has occasional difficulty in unfamiliar situations.		Generally forms productive relationships in both familiar and unfamiliar situations.		Consistently forms productive relationships with a wide range of consumers in complex situations.	

	F (1–2)	D (3–4)	C (5–6)	B (7–8)	A (9–10)
Relationship with Co-workers (Other Students in the Agency as Well as Agency Staff)	Arouses resentment; quarrels with others and cannot use tact and diplomacy.	Occasionally antagonistic, creating needless conflict which impedes effective working relationships.	Working relationships are fairly smooth. Does not arouse antagonism or impede cooperative work but does not actively contribute to cooperative efforts in problematic situations.	Good working relationships; contributes to cooperative work in most situations and occasionally in problematic situations.	Promotes teamwork, very cooperative and handles delicate situations tactfully; is well liked by others.
Relationship with Staff of Other Agencies	Agency receives complaints about student's performance or unprofessional behavior. Student is hesitant to contact other agencies.	Sometimes has difficulty in relating to outside professionals. Supervisor has had to intervene because of conflict between the student and staff in other agencies.	Usually has satisfactory relationships with other agency staff.	Maintains effective working relationships with other professionals and is generally prompt and cooperative in handling referrals.	Consistently professional. Student is always cooperative and skillful in relating to other agency staff.
Demonstration of the Acceptance and Use of Basic Social Work Values, Ethics and Principles	No evidence that student has incorporated social work values, ethics, and principles.	Usually demonstrated with only occasional exceptions.	Demonstrated at an acceptable professional level.	Demonstrated frequently in routine situations and sometimes in controversial situations.	Consistently guided by social work values, ethics, and principles.
Effectiveness in Providing Services to Individuals and Families	Completely ineffective.	Seldom assesses situations accurately and is limited in ability to provide services.	Usually is effective in applying professional knowledge and skills in routine or uncomplicated situations.	Is effective most of the time even in situations requiring considerable patience and skill.	Consistently effective in both routine and extremely demanding situations.

	A (9–10)	B (7–8)	C (5–6)	D (3–4)	F (1–2)
Effectiveness in Providing Services to Small Groups	Consistently demonstrates knowledge/skill in forming/working with groups in demanding situations.	Demonstrates knowledge/skill in forming/working with groups most of the time in both routine and demanding situations.	Usually demonstrates knowledge/skill in forming/working with groups in routine or non-demanding situations.	Occasionally demonstrates knowledge and/or skill in forming/working with groups when there is considerable support from supervisor and/or co-leader.	No demonstrated knowledge and/or skill in forming or working with groups.
Effectiveness in Providing Services at the Community Level	Consistently demonstrates knowledge/skill in forming/working with community-based groups in both routine and demanding situations.	Demonstrates knowledge/skill most of time in forming/working with community-based groups in both routine and demanding situations.	Usually demonstrates knowledge/skill in forming/working with community-based groups in routine or nondemanding situations.	Shows sporadic, limited ability at the community level. Demonstrates occasional but limited ability in forming/working with community-based groups.	No demonstrated knowledge/skill in forming/working with community-based groups.
Use of Supervision	Consistently makes wise use of supervision. Is prepared for supervisory conferences and handles any disagreements with tact and diplomacy.	Seeks supervision responsibly and generally makes wise use of supervisor's suggestions. Is prepared for conferences most of the time.	Responds satisfactorily to supervision but usually does not take initiative in seeking such help. Seldom requests or makes suggestions for improvement.	Seldom seeks supervisory help and becomes defensive when work is criticized.	Resents supervision and will not follow instructions or guidelines.
Development of a Professional Self-awareness, Including the Need for Continued Professional Growth	Consistently seeks to extend knowledge and improve skills. Has a clear sense of professional responsibility and realistic plans for continuing professional growth.	Commitment to continuing professional development though student's future plans in this regard may be too self-limiting. Student shows initiative in self-evaluation.	Does not initiate many efforts toward increasing knowledge and skills. Interest is somewhat restricted but there is some evidence of commitment.	Seldom recognizes limitations and shows little motivation for improvement.	No apparent interest in professional development; is not self-critical and is apathetic about increasing skills and knowledge.

Narrative Section

1. Briefly summarize the student's work activities for the semester. Include the size and variety of his caseload with individuals and families and the nature of his work with groups and communities.

2. Comment on performance areas in which the student was outstanding; e.g. he may be especially effective with certain types of clients or a method of social work. Also comment on the student's potential for graduate study in social work.

3. Explain your rating of any factors which you feel need clarification. Also identify areas in which the student needs significant improvement, unless this is to be answered in question 5.

4. Explanation of evaluative items which you were unable to rate.

5. If the student's overall rating is a "C" or below, attach a narrative explanation of how his work performance warranted the rating he received.

Recommended Grade _____

Signature of Agency Field Instructor _____

Agency _____

Address _____

Date _____

My field instructor and faculty liaison have discussed this evaluation with me, and I have received a copy.

    I agree with the recommended grade _____

    I do not agree with the recommended grade _____

Student's Signature _____

Date _____

If the student disagrees with the recommended grade, he should explain in writing and submit a copy to his field instructor, faculty liaison and field director.

Final Grade _____

Assigned by _____

    Director of Field Instruction

Date _____

There are many variations of the four types of evaluation forms, but most forms will fit into one of them. One variation is in the type of overall rating assigned. Some schools assign a letter grade (A, B, C, and so on) to the field experience on the basis of the quality of performance reported in the evaluation. Most schools prefer a pass/fail or satisfactory/unsatisfactory system whereby the student either makes it through field placement or fails it. The content of the evaluation form, rather than the final rating, distinguishes among various levels of satisfactory or unsatisfactory performance.

A Comprehensive Outline

The following narrative outline covers all the points that ideally should appear, in one form or another, in written performance evaluations. It would be unrealistic to try to include all information under each heading in all evaluations. Depending on the objectives and the nature of the experience with the supervisee, some headings and content areas will be stressed more than others and some may be eliminated entirely. The comments given under each heading in this outline need not be responded to item by item in any evaluation. They are included to illustrate areas the supervisor may want to think about and address under that particular heading, if appropriate. If a standardized checklist type of rating form is required, the field instructor may want to attach a special narrative to explain or add to the standardized items. This type of outline produces a very detailed, comprehensive, and effective picture of a student's performance. It's main drawback is that a great deal of time is required to prepare the evaluation properly, and unfortunately most field instructors simply do not have the time to devote to this activity. However, the outline is presented here as a listing of subject areas to be addressed that may prove helpful in developing other instruments endeavoring to cover similar topics in a more efficient manner.

Performance Evaluation Outline

I. IDENTIFYING DATA

All evaluations should give the student's full name, the period of time covered by the evaluation, the date the evaluation was prepared, the student's level of training (first year, second quarter placement, and so on), the name of the agency or field placement setting, the name and title of the agency field instructor, and the area of assignment (if the agency or setting is a complex structure with various kinds of field placement assignments).

II. DESCRIPTION OF THE SETTING

In what kind of place did the student do his field placement? What kinds of clients does it serve? What kind of

department or staff did the student interact with? This section provides the background for the remaining evaluation items. Once developed, a standardized paragraph can be used for most evaluations in a given agency. Consider the following examples:

The XZY Program is a federally funded, state-administered agency providing financial assistance to Spanish-speaking Cuban refugees. Many clients arrived in the U.S. with no funds and no knowledge of English, and many have psychiatric and medical conditions requiring immediate attention. They come from all socioeconomic backgrounds. Some who achieved high positions in their homeland find their skills useless in the U.S. and must start all over again in middle age. The XYZ Program employs 150 BA-level "social workers" who determine initial and continued eligibility for financial assistance and provide counseling and other social services. The student (who speaks Spanish fluently) was assigned to a special unit serving clients who are receiving financial assistance because of physical or psychiatric disabilities.

The ABC Center is a residential treatment center for children, housing 85 youngsters, ages 7–16. The population is predominantly black, but with a significant number of Caucasians and a few American Indians. Most of the children are here because no one is willing or able to care for them or because their behavior is so problematic that they cannot be maintained at home. Some have been removed from parental figures by the courts and are in temporary custody of the Center. The six MSW staff provide intensive counseling to the children and their families. The Center also employs a recreational therapist, houseparents, resident teachers, and other specialists along with two psychologists and three psychiatrists.

The Heal-All Hospital is a 600-bed private facility serving a middle-/and upper-class population of patients being treated for medical and surgical problems. It is a teaching and research facility employing many different health-related disciplines. The Social Service Department consists of a Director, eight MSWs and two BSWs. The primary role of the medical social worker is to assist patients in planning for their discharge from the hospital and to provide counseling around patient and family reactions to illness, disability, and hospitalization. The student was assigned to the orthopedic unit. Most of her caseload consisted of adults and children with broken bones, many of whom were traumatically injured in accidents. Some have amputations, bone infections and other complications. Most remained hospitalized for at least two weeks and were followed by the student after discharge.

III. EXPERIENCES/ASSIGNMENTS

Describe the kinds of learning experience made available to the student. How many cases did he carry, and were they long- or short-term? What kinds of presenting problems did he deal with? Briefly describe the dynamics of some of the students's most significant cases or assignments: e.g. "one involved working with the family of a youngster admitted to the hospital as a result of child abuse; another concerned a seven-year-old child injured in an auto accident in which both parents died. A third involved an adolescent receiving kidney dialysis who was torn between his desire to be independent from his family and his symbiotically dependent relationship with his mother. At the time of referral, he was experiencing some suicidal thoughts."*

Any special orientation or learning programs the student attended should be described briefly, along with any other activities in which he participated. Did he attend staff meetings? Lead a group? Observe through a one-way mirror while the field instructor conducted an interview? Go on an orientation tour of a community agency? Attend a board meeting or a workshop?

Any special or extenuating circumstances that interrupted or affected the student's experience in placement should be described. Was there a change in field instructors or agency in the middle of placement? Was the field instructor or the student absent for long periods of time owing to illness? Did a massive departmental reorganization occur while the student was in placement, disrupting normal assignments and supervisory conferences? Did the student voluntarily put in extra hours in order to tackle special experiences or assignments?

IV. METHOD AND TYPE OF SUPERVISION PROVIDED

Did supervisory conferences take place on a regular basis? How often? How many hours a week were spent in supervisory conferences, and how does this figure compare with what you consider to be average? What techniques were used in supervisory conferences—role-playing, modeling, case discussions, and so forth? Was there anything unusual about your supervisory relationship or approach to the student?

V. THE STUDENT'S USE OF SUPERVISION

How well did the student relate to you? Did you initiate most ·conferences, or did he? Did he come prepared for regularly scheduled conferences or did he depend on you to prepare the agenda and lead the discussion? Was his learning experience enhanced or hindered by his ability to make use of your supervision? How did he respond to constructive criticism? Was he overly dependent or independent? If there were difficulties, what efforts were made by you and the student to resolve the problem, and what was the outcome?

VI. ASSESSMENT METHOD

Briefly describe the primary methods used to monitor and assess the student's activities (see Chapters 9 and 10). For example, "The student did process-recordings on all cases for the first two weeks and selectively thereafter; twelve interviews were taped; I observed six interviews through the one-way mirror; the student and I co-led a group throughout the placement. The student critiqued his own performance on taped and process-recorded interviews. I then reviewed the material, and in-depth discussion of each interview took place during supervisory conferences."

VII. PROFESSIONALISM

A variety of factors come under the heading of professionalism:†

Dress and Grooming. Did the student's appearance conform to agency standards and expectations? Did it interfere with his relationships with or acceptance by staff, clients, and others?

Attendance. Did the student exceed the minimum number of absences allowed by the school? Did he report to field placement on time? Stay late? Come in on off days because he wanted to? Was he willing to stay after hours if client- or agency-related crises developed at the end of the day?

Behavior and attitude. Is the student's attitude appropriately professional? Is he loud and offensive, quiet and businesslike, excessively aggressive or shy, sloppy, resistant, eager?

Identity with social work as a profession. Most students develop an identity with their particular field placement setting, but what about identity with social work as a larger profession? Does the student have a sense of loyalty to social work in general? Does he seem to understand what it means to be a social worker as well as a practitioner in a specific field placement?

Use of time. Is the student well organized, efficient, capable in priority-setting, a slow or fast worker, a time-waster, unusually productive?

Adherence to basic principles of social work practice. Does the student abide by the principles of the NASW Code of Ethics? Does he maintain confidentiality, show respect for his clients, use a basically nonjudgmental approach, and so on?

Going the extra mile. Is the student interested in pursuing extra or nonrequired readings and special experiences during field placement? Or is he doing just the minimum required to get by and no more? Is he a clock-watcher?

---

*Obviously these are case assignments for a very advanced casework student. If this student goes on to receive a satisfactory or outstanding rating, the reader knows he must have some real skills to have earned this rating with such complex cases. On the other hand, if the assignments required mostly concrete services with limited counseling, the reader would know that an "outstanding" meant something entirely different.

†See pp. 55–59 for a detailed statement of behaviorized objectives pertaining to this area.

Paper Work (other than recording). Most students keep some kind of statistics for the agency and/or the school, complete forms and do related paper work. How does the student do in these activities? Are his reports legible, accurate, on time, and so on?

VIII. SPECIFIC EDUCATIONAL/PERFORMANCE EXPECTATIONS

Section III describes experiences to which the student was exposed. This section must state the degree of skill the student was expected to acquire: What was he expected to know or be able to do? Refer to the educational contract or attach a copy.

IX. APPLICATION OF SOCIAL WORK SKILLS

This is the heart of the evaluation. On the basis of the educational objectives and goals, how is the student doing? Has he met the objectives? Where has he shown significant growth or lack of growth? What is his present level of functioning in all identified social work skill areas? How does the degree of skill he has achieved compare with objectives and expectations, and what is considered normal or average for a student at his level of training? Avoid such vague adjectives as "good," "average," "satisfactory," and "weak" and use specific behavioral descriptions or examples to support what is being said.

Are there areas of comparitive strength and weakness? Are there any remaining limitations in the student's application of social work skills?

X. RELATIONSHIPS WITH OTHERS

Consider all the various kinds of people the student has interacted with during placement: clients, authority figures, staff members, community agencies and their staff, members of other disciplines, the agency's clerical staff, other students, volunteers, and others. Did the student form relationships with comfort and ease? Were there any areas of difficulty? Has feedback from any of these individuals indicated unusual ability or inability to form and maintain effective relationships? What characteristics cause the student to be unusually effective or ineffective in relating to others? Are there some types of individuals to whom he relates more comfortably than to others?

XI. COMMUNICATION SKILLS

The student's written and oral communication skills should be addressed in every performance evaluation; nonverbal communication may or may not be of significance.

What are the quality and quantity of the student's social service reports, case record entries, and other materials? Does it take an unusually short or long time for him to produce an acceptable product? Are many revisions neces-

sary, even at the end of placement? Comment on the student's use of English: Can he write concisely and clearly with correct grammar, spelling, and sentence structure? If not, what seems to be the problem? Also comment on his ability to prepare reports, memos, summaries, and case record entries in accordance with agency guidelines and requirements or with accepted social work practice.

Comment on the student's participation in meetings and his ability to communicate questions, concerns, and ideas to others. How skillful is he in oral communication? Does he have a special ability to communicate nonverbally? Does he resort to nonverbal communications that speak louder than his verbalizations and cause problems for him and others?

XII. EMOTIONAL MATURITY

Does he have the basic personal qualities and maturity required to be effective in his chosen area of social work specialization (e.g. casework or administration)? If he does, one short sentence can cover this heading. If not, are there indications that his emotional needs or mental health problems are hindering his effectiveness in field or his readiness for social work practice?

XIII. SUMMARY OF STRENGTHS AND WEAKNESSES

What are the student's primary strengths as you see them? Mention areas in which he has room for improvement. Does he have any unusual strengths or potentially problematic limitations? What are they, and how did they affect his performance in field?

XIV. OVERALL PERFORMANCE RATING

Taking everything into consideration, has the student's overall performance during the term been outstanding, above average, satisfactory, below satisfactory, or unsatisfactory?

XV. RECOMMENDATIONS

From your experience with the student and assessment of his performance, what recommendations would you make regarding a subsequent field placement, his first job, the desirability of his entering a graduate or doctoral program, the kinds of clients he should or should not work with, his supervisory needs, and the kinds of settings in which you think he would function best as well as those he should avoid? If the student has been studying administration and other macro services, do you think he's fully ready to take such a position immediately after graduation, or would you recommend direct practice experience first? Are some of the student's professional goals unrealistic in view of his current strengths and limitations? It might be desirable to state also whether the student agrees with your assessment and recommendations.

XVI. SIGNATURES

The student's and field instructor's names should be typed at the end of the evaluation with a space for signatures and dates. It may be desirable to include a statement that the student has received and read a copy of the evaluation but that his signature does not necessarily mean that he agrees with its content.

The Thinking Process That Precedes the Writing of an Evaluation

It is 11 am. All is quiet in the field instructor's office. His student's performance evaluation is due in three days. The supervisor sits staring at a yellow pad. Time passes. A few sentences materialize on the page. More time goes by. The entire day passes into the annals of historical yesterdays. The yellow pad proclaims the results of the field instructor's evaluatory efforts—a total of four disjointed sentences. HELP!

Oh, how familiar this scene is to anyone who has ever supervised! We strive to be the best possible supervisors, carefully doing all the things the textbooks say we should. We have been communicating openly and honestly all term with our supervisees. We have laid the groundwork for the written evaluation. We know it will hold no surprises for the supervisee. Yet the words just won't come, and we find excuses to procrastinate for another day. How can we get past this stage?

First, review your feelings about doing the performance evaluation. Try to achieve some self-awareness. How do you feel about performance evaluations in general? How do you feel about having to commit your thoughts about this particular student to writing? Is there anything that's going to make it an especially difficult task?

Second, find a quiet place. It is not possible to write a meaningful performance evaluation with the phone ringing constantly, with people knocking on your door, or while sharing an office with someone who is on the telephone or dictating while you're trying to write. If necessary, pick up your yellow pad, your supervisory notebook and related materials and relocate. Hide out in the agency conference room, the library, a restaurant across the street, a picnic table on the agency grounds—any place where you can escape interruptions and distractions. If relocation is impossible, instruct the secretary to hold all calls, hang a sign on the outside of the office door proclaiming that you're "IN CONFERENCE" (with yourself of course) or "IN HIBERNATION: DO NOT INTERRUPT UNLESS THE BUILDING IS BURNING DOWN!" Exert some control over your environment so you can *think*. If all else fails, write the evaluation at home on your own time. Many supervisors end up using this alternative.

Next, *think* before writing. Mentally review your experience with the supervisee. Think about what it was like when you started working together. What stand out in your mind as the highlights of the quarter, semester, or year? What message do you want to convey through the performance evaluation? What do you want to say to the next person who will supervise your student? Pretend that this person is sitting beside you. Suppose it is another field instructor for a second or third field placement. What would you want to tell him about your student? What kind of approach would you hope he would use? If that individual were your student's first employer, what would you want to say? What would you want to know if *you* were the one hiring or supervising your student?

Now, begin to sort out those observations, experiences and facts that belong in the written evaluation from those that should not or need not appear. Perhaps the student made a really embarrassing "goof" early in the placement. It's a fact; it occurred and was discussed at length at the time. Does it need to be mentioned in your evaluation now? Perhaps you received some feedback regarding the student's behavior. How much of that detail belongs in black and white? Do you have some feelings about your student's performance that you haven't fully shared with him and thus cannot include, without warning, in the written evaluation?

As you consider these factors, jot down a few notes, using phrases, incomplete sentences, or whatever. Don't try to organize the ideas in any way or express them perfectly; just get them down so you won't forget them. It doesn't matter whether the ideas are recorded in any logical order or if they would make sense to anyone else.

Now divide the paper into two columns, labeling one "Strengths" and the other "Improvement needed." You may wish to add a third for "Areas of Significant Growth." *Think*. Even the most problematic student has *some* strengths. These might be personal work habits, attitudes, innate abilities (e.g. intelligence), or social work skills. Even the most outstanding student has some areas in which he is relatively weak; he is rarely outstanding in every area of performance and ability. If you cannot put several items in each column, this could be an indication that you really do not know the student, have not exposed him to sufficient challenges to determine the extent of his abilities, or have not used sufficiently revealing methods of assessment to know just what he is and is not capable of doing. It could also indicate some blocking on your part, resulting in inability to see or recognize certain performance characteristics.

What does your student do best? With what kinds of

clients is he most comfortable and effective? Is he reliable, conscientious, organized, a fast worker, especially skillful in handling transference, dealing with marital conflict, or bringing about change in community systems? Is he noticeably uncomfortable with home visits; sometimes insecure and ill at ease when using confrontation; a little too dependent, independent or sloppy? Does he sometimes procrastinate? Does he prefer working with children rather than the elderly? Did he start the placement having never interviewed anyone before, forgetting to introduce himself, holding superficial discussions with no direction, or coming across like a machine gun with overly structured concrete questions? Did he finish the term able to discuss covert client feelings and to focus an interview and bring it to a logical conclusion? Did he become able to abandon preplanned approaches when he found the client's needs, behaviors, or verbalizations different from what he expected?

Now you've got it made (almost). If an interruption comes at this point, you've got your key thoughts down on paper. You won't have to start the thinking process all over again and try to remember where you left off.

Once the thinking part of the evaluation has been completed, the next step is to pull together the random thoughts into a formal, organized written evaluation. Consult the rating forms or outlines provided by the school (see pp. 182–185 for a suggested outline if none is provided). Review the miscellaneous notes generated by the above thinking process and begin organizing them according to the various headings on the evaluation form or outline. If a checklist or numerical rating scale is required, mentally review your notes and select the appropriate rating. It may be desirable to add a brief narrative to explain or support your ratings, including some of the specific ideas generated from your thought process. If a rating form is used, it is tempting to short-cut the stages in the thinking process and merely assign numbers rapidly. It will take less time to complete the form than it will to do a written narrative following an outline, but those numbers, so hastily given, are very important. Furthermore, a checklist with no narrative explanation could do an injustice to an outstanding or marginal student who merits a little explanation for the primary ratings.

When you are doing a full narrative following a detailed outline, the way in which the content is stated is very important. You may have written that the student "is a lousy group worker" or "constantly bugs me with petty questions" on your yellow pad during the thinking part of the evaluation, and that's okay. But your thoughts obviously cannot be expressed in those terms in the formal evaluation. Try to find a polite, tasteful, unemotional, constructive way

of saying what must be said. Then pretend you don't know the student and are reading it for the first time. Does it really say what you are trying to convey? For example, one evaluation contained this comment: "Horace isn't the fastest worker in the world." Now, what on earth does *that* mean? Was the supervisor really trying to say "Horace is very slow and sometimes it seems he's never going to finish" or "Horace is so slow he could handle only half the volume of the average student"? Obviously, this is one of the most difficult parts of the evaluation-writing process, especially for supervisors who do not like to write or must struggle through endless drafts in order to produce an intelligible document.

It will take at least an hour or two to produce a meaningful written evaluation. At least half of this time should be used for thinking and jotting down random thoughts before the formal writing process begins. Beginning or inexperienced supervisors can expect to spend three to four hours preparing their first narrative performance evaluation and may have to do several drafts before they are fully satisfied with the results. It is recommended strongly that beginning supervisors have their own superiors review a rough draft of their evaluations before they are typed in final form or shared with students. Likewise, senior field instructors preparing an unusually difficult assessment may want to have someone else go over it. The objective reviewer can detect internal inconsistencies, unclear statements, excessive emotionalism on the part of the evaluator, and other factors that can creep into the evaluation and weaken its effectiveness.

Characteristics of Well-written Versus Poorly Written Evaluations

A field instructor may have fairly accurate perceptions regarding his student and may have done everything "according to the book." However, a superficial, poorly written evaluation may fail to communicate his thoughts, omit key information, stress some areas inappropriately, or give misleading impressions. Skimpy details may make a problem area appear worse than it really is or fail to describe fully the exceptional ability of an outstanding student. Vague generalities may produce an evaluation that could apply to virtually every social work student at any level of training (see pp. 275–276 for an example). Thus, regardless of the facts regarding a specific supervisee, there are certain characteristics that distinguish between a good evaluation and a poorly presented one. The following checklist may prove helpful.

WELL WRITTEN	POORLY WRITTEN
1. Uses basically correct grammar, spelling, and sentence structure that facilitate the reader's ability to understand what the author is trying to say.	1. Contains many obvious misspellings and grammatical errors that make the reader wonder if the author is qualified to evaluate his student. May contain awkward sentence

WELL WRITTEN

POORLY WRITTEN

structure that obscures meaning (e.g. ''the student, when he first started placement and also during the middle, when first assigned a client, especially the case of Mr. Jones, had some difficulty, though not a real serious problem, with the use of confrontation, but he did improve, though he didn't always follow through with suggested readings, and I think this is an area he need to work on some more.'')

2. Is concise, specific, and to the point. E.g. ''Peggy feels that agency staff are not accepting of her when in reality they give every indication of both liking and accepting her.''

2. Expresses thoughts in vague abstractions, e.g. ''The student's outer world reality failed to phase with his intraphysic phenomenon in several instances.''

3. Describes characteristics and actions that distinguish the student from all other students, e.g. ''Donald showed marked improvement in his ability to obtain social histories. He began the semester having to go back three or four times to the same client to get a complete history and relied on a checklist approach. However, he has now abandoned the checklist and is able to obtain pertinent background information while engaging the client in a natural and relaxed conversation. He rarely requires extra contacts to get information.''

3. Makes general statements that would describe most students in field placement, e.g. ''Donald applied himself diligently and greatly improved his interviewing skills this semester.'' (Questions: improved from what beginning to what level of functioning now? Is the author implying that there are serious problems remaining? Does the evaluator feel the student's present level of functioning is at a satisfactory or inadequate level?)

4. Explains descriptive comments or supports them with specifics, e.g. ''Mabel writes poorly. Common words are misspelled, handwriting is barely legible, and tenses are used incorrectly. Her writing style is more typical of a pre-high school student than a college junior.''

4. Descriptive terms are undefined. Terms such as ''well, good, exceptional, quickly, much, beginning-level, advanced, poorly, weak, inadequate'' appear throughout the evaluation and leave the reader with uncertainty regarding their meaning.

5. Both areas of strength and problems or areas needing improvement are clearly labeled and illustrated. No matter what overall rating is given to the student, *both* strengths and weaknesses are described in the evaluation and are specific to that student, e.g. ''Lois is not a morning person. She prefers to report to work at 9 A.M. and stay late in the day. This could be a problem if she sought employment in a setting where employees must come to work promptly at 8 or 8:30. However, she always remains on the job until 7 P.M. or later, putting in more than a regular eight- or nine-hour work day.''

5. The evaluation is totally positive, with no reference to areas where growth is needed. When mentioned, they are expressed in meaningless generalities: ''Felicia needs to improve her casework skills'' (Who doesn't?) or ''Margarite needs to learn more about dynamics of human behavior'' (Don't we all?). On the other hand, the evaluation may have a definite negative tone, failing to identify any strengths or positives.

WELL WRITTEN

POORLY WRITTEN

6. Gives sufficient details to present a clear picture of the student's functioning. For example, in the illustration above, the reader is advised that Lois isn't a typical late arriver or a "clock-watcher." There is a positive side to her late morning beginnings.

6. Details are skimpy, leaving the reader with incomplete or even false impressions. E.g. a statement that "Lois is not a morning person—she frequently reports to work at 9 A.M." with no further explanation would give a false impression that she is uncooperative, unable to abide by agency work hours, and careless in her attitude toward her work responsibilities.

7. Definitions of "satisfactory," "average" or "acceptable" are supported with specific examples.

7. Deviations from satisfactory are labeled, but no specifics are included to explain *why* the rater felt the individual's performance was "outstanding," "poor," or whatever.

8. All significant comments can be substantiated by examples of the student's work or descriptions of specific incidents, should the rater's assessment ever be challenged or questioned.

8. The evaluation contains gut-level assessments. The field instructor has a "feeling" that such-and-such is what's happening but cannot point to specifics to justify or support his feelings.

9. Unusual problem areas are described when relevant or significant, but potentially embarrassing or damaging details are omitted, e.g. "Henry went through a difficult period when a divorce occurred while he was in placement. For several weeks he had some difficulty concentrating on his work. However, he quickly regained his prior level of functioning." (Note: If his response to his divorce had been abnormal or problematic, it might then be necessary to go into more detail. However, the evaluator would bear in mind that he is preparing a field placement evaluation, not a psychosocial assessment of a "client.")

9. Problem areas are described with excessive detail that could prove embarrassing or even damaging to the student, e.g. "Henry's father died during the sixth week of placement. The other students observed him crying; he lost interest in his work, avoided his clients and was quite dysfunctional in field. He quickly regained his prior level of functioning, however." What is significant is that Henry's reactions were appropriate considering the loss he had experienced, and that he did regain his former level of functioning. Thus, inclusion of excessive details is unnecessary and punitive toward the student.

10. Problematic behavior is described in sufficient detail to present the problem, but diagnostic labels are omitted, e.g. "Roberta finds it difficult to trust people and sometimes resists accepting responsibility for errors or wrongdoings." This statement indicates a problem area but leaves it up to the reader to draw his own conclusions.

10. Psychiatrically diagnostic labels are applied with or without a description of the behavior that caused the supervisor to use the term, e.g., "Roberta shows definite paranoid tendencies and sometimes engages in sociopathic behavior." Roberta would react quite negatively to such a statement but probably could accept a nondiagnostic description of her behavior. Furthermore, labels are too easily picked up by others who may use them to categorize the student for years to come.

11. The supervisory process, relationship, and techniques used are described. The field instructor may express uncertainty regarding some of his statements or accept responsi-

11. The supervisory process, relationship, and techiques used may or may not be described. However, the field instructor uses the performance evaluation to examine his approach

WELL WRITTEN

bility for some less than positive outcomes, but it is obvious to the reader that he was and is basically competent in his role.

12. The evaluation reflects the supervisor's involvement in helping the student grow, but the emphasis is on the student's response to supervisory guidance and his own efforts at facilitating growth and making use of available resources, including his supervisor.

13. The evaluation is long enough to say what needs to be said and brief enough so that people will read it.

14. Statements describing the work load, the nature of assignments and the kinds of skill the student used include the rater's assessment as to whether these things are typical or atypical of expectations for a student at his level of training.

15. The content of the evaluation supports the final rating. Anyone could read all but the last page and conclude that the final rating will be "outstanding," "unsatisfactory," or whatever.

16. The evaluation is neatly typed.

POORLY WRITTEN

to the student, express insecurities regarding his supervisory ability, and relieve his guilt feelings. The evaluation seems to be more an assessment of the supervisor than of the supervisee.

12. The report is full of "with the help of the supervisor," "through sharing of the supervisor's knowledge," "with the support I provided," and similar remarks. The supervisor appears to be using the evaluation to brag about his effectiveness and implies that the student would not have achieved what he did without his marvelous wisdom and superior guidance.

13. The evaluation is 6 or 7 single-spaced typewritten pages long. Even if it is well written, who will have time to review and digest it? On the other hand, narrative evaluation of outstanding or problematic performance may be presented in half a page—obviously too short to do justice to the student.

14. Statements indicate that "Joe carried four cases this quarter" and so on, but there is no indication of how the evaluator feels this compares with the caseload of the average student or with what the student *should* have carried.

15. The content of the evaluation does not seem to support or illustrate the rating that is assigned, e.g. the final rating is "unsatisfactory" but no problematic behaviors or serious deficiencies are described in the narrative or rated items. An "outstanding" has been given, yet rather average performance is described. Or a "satisfactory" rating is assigned, yet it seems inconsistent with the behaviors and skills described throughout the evaluation. (These kinds of evaluations will generally not hold up if challenged by the student, regardless of his actual level of performance. He may really be unsatisfactory, but if the evaluation does not include data to support that rating, it could be overturned in a hearing or grievance process.)

16. The evaluation contains crossouts, corrections, obvious typing errors, and erasures. It does not give the appearance of a final document. Who made the changes, the student or

WELL WRITTEN

POORLY WRITTEN

the field instructor? Were they made before or after the evaluation was shared with the student and signed by him? The credibility of such an evaluation could be seriously questioned if challenged.

17. Regardless of the field instructor's personal feelings or attitude toward the student, the performance evaluation is obviously objective.

17. The tone of the evaluation clearly indicates that the field instructor did not like, was angered by, or rejected his student. A punitive, nonprofessional, nonobjective feeling comes through to the reader. On the other hand, an overflattering evaluation may reveal the field instructor's overidentification with or strong personal attachment to the student, preventing an objective assessment.

18. The evaluation contains only the information necessary to accomplish its purpose. The evaluator obviously considers who will be reading it and how it will be used as he writes it.

18. The evaluation contains excessive detail having little or nothing to do with the purpose for which it is being written.

19. The evaluation contains only information that has already been shared with the student in one form or another. While he may not be aware of the evaluator's exact wording, he knows essentially how the evaluator feels about various areas of his performance so that the written evaluation holds no surprises.

19. The evaluation contains information and assessments that have not been shared with the student. He sees them for the first time and learns about them only upon seeing the written evaluation.

Sharing the Written Evaluation with the Student

When the final document or a final draft has been prepared, it is time to share it with the student. He should be allowed to read it, sign it, and have a copy. The way this process is handled can affect the student's response to the evaluation; it can either bring about a frustrating result or provide a highly significant experience for both supervisor and supervisee.

The evaluation should be handed to the student personally, not left on his desk or in an ''in'' box. The field instructor must be available to answer questions and deal with the student's reactions to the evaluation. It is very frustrating and anxiety-provoking for a student when the field instructor hands him his evaluation, then disappears for several hours. The student will have a need to go somewhere with his reactions, and he may turn to other students or inappropriate outlets to relieve his anxiety in the supervisor's absence. Thus, the best approach is to share the written evaluation through a formal supervisory conference.

The location and timing of the conference are very im-

portant. Try not to use the student's office or work area, where uncontrollable interruptions may occur at any moment. There must be absolute privacy and a quiet, unhurried atmosphere where the student can feel he has his supervisor's full attention as the evaluation is discussed. Control interruptions by having the secretary hold all calls or by posting a sign on the door. Make the student feel that he has your undivided attention. No one feels free to discuss sensitive areas and share honest feelings if he is anticipating interruptions or feels rushed.

Try to avoid scheduling the evaluation conference at the end of the day, when attention spans are decreased and tension and exhaustion are at their peak. Allow a full hour and a half to two hours, and perhaps more if the evaluation is one that the student may have some difficulty accepting. If you know the evaluation will cause strong emotional reactions on the part of the student, schedule it at a time when he can take a break and think it over or compose himself before he has to see his next client or attend to some important community activity or assignment.

Have two copies of the evaluation available so that both you and the student can refer to it as you talk. After the supervisee has read it, elicit his response. Does he agree with it? Is he pleased? Upset? Does he understand it? Is there anything he feels you have omitted? Does he disagree with anything? Does he feel it contains anything he was unaware of? Does he agree with your overall rating? Was it what he anticipated? Enter into discussion around these issues, elaborating on the written evaluation where necessary to illustrate your feelings further. Have the supervisory notebook or examples of the student's work handy to refer to in case you want to use specific examples not mentioned in the evaluation to support or illustrate your viewpoint (this is especially important with less than satisfactory evaluations).

Very often a discussion of a student's performance evaluation brings about a spontaneous review of your experiences together, both accomplishments and difficulties. A student who feels comfortable with his evaluation may tell you frankly that he was "scared to death of you" for the first month, now that he's seen the written evaluation and feels secure about your positive feelings toward him. Thus, the evaluation conference can be a golden opportunity for sharing the student's future plans and passing along pertinent recommendations. Even an unsatisfactory evaluation can end on a positive note as field instructor and student discuss its implications and emphasize the positives. It doesn't mean that the student is "no good" as a person; he may have found out that he's not suited to social work—it's not the end of the world. It is easier for a student to learn this now than spend twenty or thirty miserable years trying to fit into a profession for which he is unsuited. Now he's free to find the career that matches his special strengths and abilities.

Some supervisors do so much talking during the evaluation conference that they don't give the student a chance to express his feelings. They emerge from the conference with a false feeling of security: "He took it really well. He seemed to accept everything I said." In reality, the supervisee may have disagreed on a number of points but discovered that it was useless to try to express his opinion. As a result, the supervisee sits in silence, appearing to raise no objections, yet leaves the conference with many unexpressed feelings. If the reactions are quite strong, his only way of expressing them may be through a grievance or complaint to a faculty member or the field instructor's supervisor. Even though it can be an anxiety-provoking exercise for the field instructor, it is especially important that the student's reactions to the evaluation be elicited if the rating is marginal or unsatisfactory. This can provide needed ventilation for the student and enable the field instructor to offer constructive support, guidance, interpretation, and recommendations.

The student may request some changes in the evaluation. Perhaps he is uncomfortable with a certain word, which he feels others might misinterpret. Perhaps you rated him a 3 and he wonders if you remembered how well he handled the client who had the psychotic break in February; perhaps he deserves a 4 or a 5 instead. The secure field instructor will be open to some changes. Perhaps he *did* forget some positive aspects of the performance or defined a rated item a little differently from the student. Perhaps a particular word is ambiguous or unnecessarily negative. These things can be changed on the spot through mutual agreement. On the other hand, the supervisor may not want to change his rating on major issues. The discussion provides a final opportunity to review his reasons for assigning the rating or to confront the student with his denial or difficulty in accepting reality and perhaps agree to disagree if necessary. If there is strong disagreement with a rating, the student should be advised that he can attach a written statement expressing his views if he wishes. Few will do so, but it provides an important outlet for those who wish to present their side of the story. This statement should then be attached to the supervisor's evaluation and sent to the school. It is generally inappropriate for the supervisor to respond to or rebut the student's comments: His evaluation already expresses his position.

The student and field instructor should sign and date the evaluation. Most students sign with no hesitation. If a supervisee has expressed strong disagreement with his evaluation, he should be reminded that his signature merely indicates that he has read the evaluation and received a copy; it does not mean that he agrees with it. Some evaluation forms come with a preprinted statement to this effect next to the signature line. If this is not present, the student may wish to add it before signing the report.

An occasional supervisee may refuse to sign the evaluation. A statement should be added and signed by a witness indicating that the student did see the evaluation and was offered the opportunity to sign. Refusal to sign is a rare occurrence and happens only when there is unusually strong disagreement with a rating. If the field instructor has been communicating evaluatory feedback on an ongoing basis, he should be able to predict such situations. He should always try to anticipate the student's response to seeing evaluatory comments in writing. If the performance has been problematic or marginal and the field instructor has been keeping the school appropriately apprised of the situation, the school should have no difficulty accepting or understanding the reason for presenting an evaluation that the student has not signed.

Part of the final performance evaluation discussion might be a review of the kind of reference the field instructor would give if asked. Perhaps he could recommend the student without reservation for a position involving work with children, but not with the elderly. A student receiving a marginal evaluation may need to know what he can expect if the field instructor is given as a reference. If the evaluation is highly positive, he can be reassured references will also be positive, unless he applies for a position requiring skills outside his areas of competency.

Some students will ask the supervisor to prepare a "to whom it may concern" reference statement. This should be avoided, because the field instructor may feel comfortable recommending the student for some positions but not for others. For example, he might want to write an entirely different reference statement if his administration student applies for a clinical rather than an administrative position after graduation.

Reactions to Performance Evaluations

A supervisor can never assume that a supervisee's reaction to seeing his written evaluation is totally predictable. The alert supervisor can usually identify those individuals who will disagree strongly or become upset over the written material, on the basis of their responses to daily oral feedback. However, some students seem to accept oral criticism well but have difficulty with the later written assessment. Outstanding individuals sometimes do not believe they are as good as their superior says they are until they see it in black and white. There is something about the finality of the written word that strips away all delusions, denials, false hopes, and rationalizations.

The most common student reaction to seeing a written evaluation is a calm, mature acceptance and discussion of content. Most supervisees respond with, "Yeah, that seems pretty accurate," "Gosh, that's great!" "Gee, it's better than I thought it'd be," or similar comments. One can almost see relief as the supervisee realizes it's over—he can relax and be what he wants to be without worrying about the effect on his evaluation. Part of the relief is a sense of accomplishment ("I made it through this field placement.") and recognition that an important bridge has been crossed, signifying readiness to move on to new and more challenging experiences and responsibilities.

A fairly common reaction, if the field instructor–student relationship has been good or was established only after much struggle and hard work, is difficulty in terminating. The reality of the ending of the student–tutor relationship is signaled by the receipt of the final evaluation. The student may express the wish to call on the field instructor for consultation in the future if necessary or to stop in and visit the agency periodically. The supervisor may be invited to lunch or presented with a parting gift. Such gestures are usually spontaneous, sincere, and indicative of a mutually positive and satisfying experience—as well as an important part of the termination process.

Silence is a rather common response. The supervisee may indicate that the evaluation "looks okay to me" and respond in monosyllables when encouraged to elaborate on his thoughts. The field instructor may become frustrated, feeling that there must be some kind of reaction that the student is not sharing. In fact, this supervisee may simply agree with the evaluation and have nothing further to say.

This feeling occurs most frequently with receipt of "satisfactory" evaluations. The "outstanding" student who responds with silence should be prodded; he should feel proud of his rating and should not be ashamed to say he earned it. The supervisor can reinforce this feeling and encourage the student to express pride in his accomplishment. He should not just accept the evaluation in silence. The "unsatisfactory" or marginal student who sits in silence may be very angry. He may not agree with the evaluation. Perhaps he has expressed his disagreement and denial many times in previous discussions and simply feels he has no more to say that hasn't already been said. He may be in a mild state of shock. Perhaps he could relate intellectually to rather critical feedback on an oral level, thinking consciously or subconsciously that "he'd never put that in writing." When reality strikes, he may be so stunned that he suffers a loss of words. This is usually temporary, however, and gentle prodding from the field instructor often elicits direct expression of questions and feelings.

Disbelief is a not uncommon reaction. The outstanding student may stare at his highly positive evaluation and comment, "Is that *me*?" or "Are you sure I deserve this?" or "I wasn't expecting this!" Most such supervisees know they have been doing a good job and probably would be keenly disappointed if they received a less than outstanding rating. But again, there is something about seeing it in black and white that makes it real and final: "It's not my imagination or an unrealistic hope. I really *am* outstanding—my supervisor says so in writing!" The individual who has never received written feedback that was not wholly positive may react with disbelief upon seeing a written criticism for the first time, even though the overall rating may be quite positive. The student who expected unrealistically to receive an outstanding rating may have difficulty believing he has received a lower rating. An unsatisfactory rating may also precipitate an "I can't believe this is really happening to me" kind of reaction. Again, the field instructor should explore the supervisee's reaction and discuss it during the evaluation conference.

Occasionally a student will respond to a satisfactory or better evaluation with obviously ingratiating behavior, making comments like, "What a great field instructor you are." The supervisor may then become uneasy: "He shouldn't be so thankful for getting an evaluation he earned. Maybe I missed something. Maybe he's feeling grateful because he really *didn't* earn the rating I gave him!" If the pattern persists, the student should be confronted with his behavior and the field instructor's concerns and observations shared. In most instances, overingratiating behavior is a reflection of termination difficulties or of the student's discomfort with his own achievements and abilities.

The shedding of tears is a rather common response of female supervisees who receive an evaluation that reflects problems and marginal or unsatisfactory performance. The young field instructor may be intensely embarrassed when a supervisee who is old enough to be a parent breaks into tears in his office. Yet this happens and in most instances is a normal and appropriate reaction under the circumstances. It is not pleasant to receive an unsatisfactory evaluation. Even a very mature, emotionally stable student can feel depressed, guilty, ashamed, and a total failure. Such an evaluation will have a drastic effect on his career and continuation in school, and he knows it. Tears may also reflect intense anger as the individual becomes so upset that the anger cannot be expressed directly.

A tearful reaction cannot be ignored. The field instructor can allow the student to cry, extending appropriate empathy and warmth. He must also treat his adult supervisee with respect so that he or she can emerge from the session with basic dignity intact. The fact that the individual broke down and cried in front of a supervisory authority figure can be as distressing as the incident that precipitated the tears. Thus, the supervisor must respond with some support, a handy box of tissues, and *patience*. This is not the time to suddenly remember another appointment or to rush the conference because someone else is waiting to see you. The supervisor must let the student release his feelings (unless he fears total decompensation) and then find a way to summarize the conference and help the supervisee pull himself back together again before he leaves the office. The field instructor will need to observe confidentiality and refrain from discussing the student's response to the evaluation with anyone who is not directly involved in the performance evaluation process.

Overt or covert disagreement with the evaluation can range from a calm expression of dissatisfaction with the wording of a sentence to angry accusations (an extremely rare reaction). The student who disagrees with his assessment will most commonly react with silence, defensiveness, or overt denial of the evaluation's content. These reactions are usually quite noticeable, but not extreme. Certainly it is normal for persons to react to perceived or actual unpleasantness and threatening experiences with these defenses. Unfortunately, some never move beyond this stage, feeling that the field instructor "didn't know what he was doing," "discriminated against me and that's why I got the poor rating," or was at fault in some other way. The student may refuse to take any responsibility for the rating that was given.

Angry students who disagree with an evaluation very often go to their faculty adviser or designated school representative with their feelings. The use of this very appropriate outlet should be encouraged. Such an individual can help both the student and the field instructor examine the evaluation and deal with the student's response. The student needs to feel he has someone he can go to who will be "on his side" when he is unable to express feelings directly to his supervisor. A suggestion from the field instructor that the student go to the faculty adviser in itself often reduces the student's defensiveness. If the supervisor becomes an-

gry, defensive, and threatened by the thought of the student's taking his reactions outside, this will only increase the student's anger and anxiety.

A few students may voice their concerns to the field instructor's superior in the agency or to a senior field instructor or designated staff member who coordinates and oversees the student program in the agency. This individual must then make certain that the student has first tried to communicate with the field instructor, avoid taking sides one way or the other, and listen objectively to the complaint. He will not be able to give an opinion as to whether or not the evaluation was merited if he has not directly supervised and evaluated the student's work. However, he can present reasons why the supervisor might have felt as he did, help the student to interpret the meaning of the evaluation, and, if appropriate, help him express and deal with his feelings. If feelings, questions, and reactions come out that need to be shared with the field instructor, the student can be helped with suggested approaches and techniques for expressing them.

If the angry student cannot find satisfaction by going to a faculty adviser or agency superior, he may initiate a grievance action to try to get the rating reversed, erased from his file, or to gain permission to repeat the placement. If this fails, he may resort to a lawsuit.* Grievances and lawsuits over field placement evaluations are extremely rare. Many schools with several hundred social work students process only one or two grievances a year (if that many), and a grievance over a field placement issue may occur only once every few years. As far as I have been able to determine, only a handful of field instructors in the entire United States have ever been sued over a field placement evaluation.

An angry supervisee may find ways to retaliate against the supervisor. A rather common form is mild passive-aggressive behavior, which may be conscious or unconscious. The individual shows up late for work, misses supervisory conferences, procrastinates, or does "exactly" as asked and no more, permitting him to blame the field instructor when something goes wrong if absurdly explicit instructions haven't been provided. This behavior pattern is most likely to occur following a midterm evaluation. Supervisees who engage in this kind of behavior often are silent or express mild disagreement during the actual supervisory conference, letting their underlying feelings come out through indirect behaviors. As soon as the supervisor identifies this pattern, his observation should be shared with the supervisee and efforts made to help him express his real feelings directly. Several attempts may need to be made, but once expression is given to the feelings, it often ends the problematic, indirect behavior.

An emotionally disturbed supervisee may react with extreme anger and retaliation by destroying agency property, slashing the supervisor's tires, and other violent actions.

*See Chapter 13 on legal aspects of field instruction.

Such a response is extremely rare. Verbal threats against the supervisor must not be taken lightly. Even though he may feel somewhat foolish, he should take precautions to protect himself and his belongings if such threats are made. Again, this response to evaluations is one of the most feared even though in almost all situations the fears are unrealistic and unjustified. Extreme reactions to less than positive evaluations are almost always predictable, although the supervisor may not be able to anticipate exactly how the person will respond—just that it will be an intense reaction.

If an emotionally disturbed student is receiving an unsatisfactory evaluation, or being terminated from field placement because of problematic behavior or personal problems that interfere with his performance, the field instructor may fear that the evaluatory confrontation will worsen or aggravate the student's symptoms. This is realistic. An individual who is barely functioning—to the point that he cannot complete field placement—probably will not respond in a stable, calm manner to the written assessment and recommendations. Perhaps the last thing he needs right then is to experience another failure or have another unpleasant reality brought to his attention. Yet to ignore the problem is to do an even greater disservice to the student, the agency, the consumers, and the social work profession. The most dreaded response is a psychotic break or complete emotional breakdown. The professionally trained social work supervisor is in a bind; he is trained to alleviate anxiety and dysfunctional responses, not to aggravate them. He wants to protect his supervisee from harsh realities, yet he cannot ignore the problem.

Let's suppose the receipt of the written evaluation does precipitate an emotional crisis in the student. It may very well be a positive turning point, though a painful one, if the student is propelled into getting desperately needed professional help. The field instructor will still retain some guilt feelings and may wish he could find some other way to earn a living for a while, but he took an action that had to be taken for the best interests of all concerned. He had no choice. And the outcome will probably be more positive for the student than if he had not acted. Almost never does a performance evaluation alone cause a breakdown or development of dysfunctional behavior. Something else had to be operating *before* receipt of the evaluation to cause the performance that necessitated the unsatisfactory rating. Emotionally disturbed, dysfunctional behavior is usually evident long before the evaluation is completed. Situations where students suffer a complete emotional breakdown in response to an evaluation are extremely rare.

Consider the alternatives. If a supervisor chooses not to give honest critical feedback to his emotionally distraught student for fear of heightening his symptoms, the long-term effects will be even more traumatic for the student. His feelings that he is more functional than he really is will be reinforced: After all, no one is telling him he is having serious problems. Defenses that prevent him from recognizing, accepting, and examining his own emotional needs or reactions will be reinforced, making it that much more difficult for professional help to be given when the student finally seeks it. He may graduate and take his first social work job. Employers generally have low tolerance for obviously disturbed, dysfunctional staff who display these symptoms during the probationary period. If the individual does not recognize the problem and its effect upon his functioning very rapidly, seek appropriate counseling, *and* show rather immediate improvement, he will usually be dismissed. It is much more traumatic for an individual to lose a job than to be counseled out as a student. The student may have to face considerable tension, rejection, failure, and confrontation with reality before he reaches the point where he finally seeks help or has it foisted upon him through a total breakdown when his defenses become ineffective. All this can usually be prevented if problems are identified and dealt with before they reach this stage, perhaps even on a preventive level, and while the individual is still sufficiently functional to respond favorably and quickly to outpatient treatment.

Many field instructors and supervisors complete lengthy careers and never face the most extreme reactions described here. Yet many use the fear of these responses to justify their reluctance to give honest written evaluatory feedback. Such fears are convenient but extreme and unwarranted. We must stop hiding behind them. There is some justification for the field instructor's anxiety in anticipation of some of the more common forms of response to evaluations, and these can be recognized and dealt with. However, many less than positive responses and unanticipated reactions can be prevented through an ongoing, open approach to performance evaluation. Such factors as the need to be liked, difficulty in passing judgment on others, and putting critical thoughts into writing are much more common reasons for problems in completing appropriate performance evaluations and for fearing extreme student reactions. Through proper training and experience, most supervisors can learn to accept and deal with these feelings and realities in an effective and constructive manner.

12 Evaluation of the "Unsatisfactory" Student

No one likes to deal with unsatisfactory performance. Many individuals serve as field instructors for years and never rate a student less than satisfactory because they have never encountered a truly unsatisfactory student. However, some supervisors never assign the rating and see every student as acceptable because of their own need to avoid the potential unpleasantness of a less than satisfactory written evaluation.* On the other hand, some field instroctors encounter a problematic student during their very first year of student supervision. Not all students who enter schools of social work should be social workers. Not all have the skills, aptitudes, interest, motivation, maturity, and emotional stability necessary to be a professional helping person. Classroom and field experiences must identify these individuals, help them grow wherever possible, and move them out of the social work program if necessary.

Every field instructor must accept the responsibility for dealing with an unsatisfactory student should it be required. This is undoubtedly one of the most difficult roles to fill. Even if a supervisor is effective in confronting his student informally with critical feedback and the suggestion that the student think about a profession other than social work, he may still resist putting such thoughts into writing. Various defenses may be used to avoid this task. Alas, many field instructors fail completely, producing satisfactory-sounding performance evaluations that do not mention prior discussions or the student's actual lack of skill.† Just why do these difficulties exist?

Factors that Make an Unsatisfactory Performance Evaluation Difficult‡

No matter how experienced a field instructor is or how many unsatisfactory students he has worked with in his career, self-doubt, insecurity, and/or lack of commitment to standards and expectations in social work education and practice can affect his ability to deal effectively with any given problematic situation.

A conscientious supervisor almost always examines his own behavior before he is willing to state that his student is unsatisfactory. "Did I contribute to the problem? Did I do something I shouldn't have? Should I have done something differently? Am I really a good field instructor?" And, finally: "Would the student be doing better if he had a different (more competent) supervisor?" If the student is the instructor's first supervisee, the anxious field instructor may rationalize that the student deserves a chance to be exposed to a "better" field instructor before he is confronted with any significant problem areas or assigned a failing grade. The inexperienced supervisor has little past experience to tell him whether the current problem is or is not due to something about his supervisory style.

Closely following this feeling comes a questioning of expectations: "Did I expect too much? Are my expectations out of line with the school's and those of other field instructors? If my expectations were lower, the student could have made it. Do I really believe so strongly in my performance

---

*One field instructor even told me that her student's school forbids field instructors even to recommend an unsatisfactory evaluation for a student in placement. Agency staff should refuse to take students from schools that have such a restrictive policy.

†Have you ever worked with a student or employee who had been so evaluated? How many have you passed on to someone else?

‡The normal needs and anxieties of field instructors discussed in chapter 3 certainly apply here. Also see Alfred Kadushin, *Supervision in Social Work* (New York: Columbia University Press, 1976), for a somewhat different approach to the difficulties associated with the performance evaluation process.

standards and expectations that I can defend them and alter a person's professional life because of them?'' Field instructors who have a regular opportunity to consult with peers, senior field instructors, supervisors, school officials, and others involved with student education can gain invaluable support to help them answer these questions and take firm stands when required.

The reality demands of practice are often taken into consideration as the supervisor struggles with his decision: ''Would I *hire* this student I am about to turn loose in the profession? Would he make it in our agency as an employee?''

I once agonized over a student who was only a few months from graduation at the MSW level. There were many problems with application of social work skills and little time remaining in field placement to achieve the growth that was required. The question was, should I try to help him throughout the rest of the field placement, hoping he might reach a satisfactory level of performance, or should I conclude that this can't be achieved and take definite action now? At the time I was seeing some patients on a part-time basis in private practice. One day I went from a particularly difficult late afternoon session with the student to an intake interview with a severely disturbed young woman with a lengthy psychiatric history complete with numerous serious suicidal attempts. As she sat in my office describing her history, which included a great deal of manipulative behavior and frequent changes of therapist in search of the impossible, she looked me in the eye, shared some sexual fantasies, and expressed her desire to walk out into the street in front of passing cars and end it all. I thought of my student. In a few weeks, he would have his MSW and be officially ''qualified'' to treat the kind of client I was now seeing. At that moment I knew he could not acquire the necessary skills in the time remaining in field placement and that I could not, in good conscience, say that I approved him for professional practice. As soon as the client walked out the door, I made my first serious attempt to specify the qualities I felt a student must have before he should be allowed to graduate. A few days later I shared them with the student and wrote the necessary performance evaluation, which terminated his field placement experience.

Field instructors know that they should be dealing with a problem, documenting it and making decisive recommendations. When they procrastinate, deny, evade, rationalize, and go through endless rough drafts of evaluations, they may experience considerable guilt, further complicating the completion of the evaluation.

Social workers are trained to be nonjudgmental of others. We are supposed to accept people for what they are and not impose our own values—*except* when we are field instructors or supervisors. When we evaluate a student's performance as unsatisfactory, we *are* imposing professional standards and values; we are saying that the student doesn't measure up. Yet if field instructors are to fulfill their gatekeeper role effectively, they must impose certain standards. Thus, a field instructor can experience significant internal struggle as he attempts to resolve apparent conflicts in values precipitated by the special requirements of the supervisory role.

Once the supervisor has submitted a written evaluation or recommendations affecting the student's continuation in a social work program, the student has the basic right to grieve against or appeal the evaluation. Field instructors who write wishy-washy evaluations that do not really say anything or who always have satisfactory students have little to fear. There is nothing for the student to challenge. However, an unsatisfactory performance evaluation may elicit a spoken or written rebuttal, anger, silent hostility, a grievance, or even, though very rarely, a lawsuit. The very thought of these responses is anxiety-producing for the field instructor and makes his performance evaluation task that much more difficult.

Parents, peers, relatives, and others sometimes challenge a performance evaluation in the student's behalf. A supervisee may accept his evaluation maturely until he shares it with a ''significant other'' who reacts with, ''How can they do this to you!'' The student may then be pushed into a battle he really doesn't want to fight. Such persons may exert political, financial, or even legal pressure on the agency, the individual field instructor, or the school to get the grade/recommendation reversed or obliterated. A significant person may be an alumnus, a school trustee, founder, former faculty member, or key financial contributor to the school. Parents may be committed to ensuring that their adult youngster becomes an educated, ''successful'' professional even if the rules must be bent to make this possible—and even if the student would prefer that they did not intervene. Schools, rather than individual field instructors, usually receive the brunt of such pressuring, and it takes real courage and conviction to stick to professional standards and refuse to allow politics to dictate who should practice social work. Problems of this kind sometimes offer the explanation for puzzled field instructors who cannot understand why a school reversed its action or ignored an obviously unsatisfactory student.*

To complicate matters further, the field instructor may genuinely like and respect his unsatisfactory student. It is much easier to give an unsatisfactory performance rating to someone we dislike. Some student supervisors may even repress their positive feelings toward the student to make it easier for them to justify doing what they know must be done. Unfortunately, many students assume that receipt of highly critical feedback means that their field instructor doesn't like them as persons. Thus, issues of like and dislike frequently get tangled up with the performance evaluation process.

---

*The ''negative solutions'' described on pp. 205–206 may be used to give the appearance of dealing with the problem while actually just marking time until the student moves through the program and receives his degree.

Field instructors were once social work students themselves. Perhaps they just barely made it, thanks to a charitable field instructor who overlooked a few things. As a result they bend over backward to be lenient now that they are field instructors. Others may have had a strict supervisor who didn't let them get away with anything and now take the same approach with their own students. Most have received critical performance evaluation feedback themselves at one time or another and know how it feels. There may be a maternalistic desire to shelter one's own student from such unpleasantness. These feelings of identification and over-identification can either strengthen or weaken a field instructor's stand on performance standards and evaluations.*

Field instructors may fear that their school will not support an unsatisfactory performance evaluation of a given student. A student supervisor must have the full backing of his school if his unsatisfactory evaluation is to hold up. Usually it is the field instructor who recommends the grade and the school that actually assigns it. If the faculty adviser or school–agency liaison person does not agree with the supervisor's assessment, he may negate it by transferring the student to another agency, assigning a satisfactory grade, or taking other actions. There must be constant communication between field instructor and school from the moment problems begin to appear.

On the other hand, a field instructor may have higher performance expectations and standards than the school does. The student may be satisfactory in the school's eyes, but not to the field instructor who is concerned with preparing the student for the realities of social work practice rather than for acceptance of a degree or a passing grade. Such differences may or may not be reconcilable. However, schools have been known to raise their standards to agree with agency expectations when student supervisors have provided structured, closely supervised learning experiences with constant, open communication and have taken a firm stand on their beliefs and assessments.

Along with a lack of support from the school, the field instructor may fear lack of agency backing for his evaluation. Most agencies will support the field instructor or at least leave him alone to do as he sees best. However, a few practice settings do not like to rock the boat and may discourage supervisors from giving potentially controversial performance evaluations. A field instructor may have a stressful relationship with his own superior, who in turn labels the difficulty with the student as the field instructor's rather than the student's problem, thereby withdrawing support. This causes great anxiety, anger, and a resolve on the part of the field instructor never to give an honestly critical evaluation again.†

There is also the ever present concern about what others will think. Other students may become anxious when one of their colleagues looks depressed, is seen crying, ventilates hostility toward the field instructor, withdraws, shares his performance evaluation with them, and challenges them to agree that it cannot possibly be accurate, or if he simply goes home one day and fails to return to field placement. This anxiety can result in questions that the field instructor wants very much to answer in order to explain and defend his actions; yet he cannot do so without violating his supervisee's confidentiality. He may feel very lonely: "If only I could explain my actions people would stop criticizing me and would realize I did what had to be done." All kinds of rumors and distortions may circulate among students in the agency and in the classroom.‡ Other students in the same setting may wonder if they are "next" as they realize that a field instructor who is capable of failing one student is capable of doing it again. Even outstanding students may become inappropriately anxious, though this is usually very temporary. The field instructor may develop a reputation among colleagues and students alike for being "tough." The field instructor who is aware of these dynamics may be uncomfortable about them or uncertain of how to handle them.**

The field instructor may be concerned about his ability to document or defend his evaluation, should he be challenged. If he has followed the guidelines presented throughout this text, he would not rate any student as unsatisfactory without first undergoing an intensive assessment process using directly observational methods and gathering specific examples to support all evaluatory comments. However, feelings of doubt and insecurity may persist. In some instances, he may have worrisome feelings about the student's performance that he cannot pin down or clearly document. He may wish that he could share these observations with the student but feel uncertain about the wisdom of doing so in view of his lack of supporting data.

A crucial factor in determining the appropriateness of an unsatisfactory rating is the supervisor's answer to this question: "Is the student's problem peculiar to this setting, a unique reaction to my field instruction approach or personality, to the kind of clients we serve, *or* is it something that he is likely to take with him wherever he goes?" Obviously, if the problem is the student's, he should receive an unsatisfactory evaluation if the deficits or problems are sufficiently

---

*See Appendix A, p. 228, for a helpful self-instructional exercise.

†However, it must be recognized that some field instructors have an approach that *does* create problems for their students. It could be fully appropriate for the supervisory person involved to call this to the field instructor's attention and deal with it. This may cause genuine anger on the part of the field instructor.

‡In one situation, a student sued several agency and school personnel over a performance evaluation. She called a meeting of the student government to present her views on why she had received a failing grade in field. It was most uncomplimentary to the field instruction staff involved and a considerable distortion of reality from their perspective. However, the agency was not in a position to publicize its version of the incident, and it took some time before students and some faculty began to realize that there were two sides to the story.

**A possible side benefit is that highly motivated, competent students may respect him for his stand and deliberately seek placement with him to accept the challenge: "If I can meet *his* standards, then I know I'll be a good social worker."

serious, and field instructors who reach this conclusion are often able to do what must be done with a relatively clear conscience and a sense of conviction. If the problem lies elsewhere, an unsatisfactory evaluation can sometimes be avoided and the student provided with an opportunity to prove himself in another setting before such a conclusion is reached.* Unfortunately, the insecure field instructor more often than not tends to feel that the problem is peculiar to the setting, thus avoiding necessary but uncomfortable evaluatory action.

There are always surprises in the performance evaluation process. A field instructor may become quite anxious, fearing the worst possible reactions from a student to whom he must give an unsatisfactory evaluation, only to have the student express genuine relief that someone has finally made the decision for him that he does not belong in social work, freeing him to pursue something else. Another student who is aware that he is not doing well may actually thank the field instructor for his frankness and for alleviating the agony of "waiting for the ax to fall." Other students may not thank the supervisor but may drop out of school for a time, pursue other life experiences, and return to social work school several years later and do quite well. Thus, the effects of an unsatisfactory evaluation on a student need not be totally negative, and awareness of this fact can strengthen the field instructor's commitment to expressing his recommendations in writing.

If an unsatisfactory evaluation results in an unusually difficult experience, the field instructor may be left with feelings of anger toward the student for not doing better or for causing him extra work and headaches. He might resent "the system" for not providing an alternative so that he could have legitimately avoided the entire situation. Angry at himself for having to fail someone, he might think to himself: "There must be an easier way to make a living. How did I ever get myself into this spot in the first place?" He may even vow never to take another student or decide that "it's not worth the hassle to be honest in evaluations." However, a difficult experience can also strengthen a supervisor's commitment to personal and professional values and standards and increase his effectiveness with all supervisees. Should he encounter problematic students subsequently, he will be more at ease in handling the situation than he was initially, and though he will still find the experience a difficult one, it will be comparatively less traumatic.

Finally, many field instructors have been helped to assign unsatisfactory ratings when necessary upon answering these three questions very honestly:

1. Would I *hire* this student?

---

*I shall be eternally grateful to a certain Miss Rothman, who, in my first field placement, concluded that my bumbling, self-conscious, relatively ineffective approach with children did not necessarily mean that I could not be effective with adults.

2. Would I be willing to *supervise* him as my employee?
3. Would I *want to be served by him* if I were the client?

Causes of Unsatisfactory Ratings

Unsatisfactory ratings (and termination from field placement) usually result from one of two behavior patterns: (1) The student performs an action that is so outrageous or damaging to others that his immediate removal from placement is necessary to protect the agency, the community, the student, and/or clients; or (2) he shows a recurrent series of lesser problems that he seems unable to overcome. In the latter case the unsatisfactory performance rating follows a lengthy and complex process of identifying problem areas, discussing them with the student, attempting to help him overcome the difficulties, and then finally determining that improvement is not likely and that an unsatisfactory rating must be assigned.

Some of the kinds of behavior that would justify rather abrupt assignment of an unsatisfactory rating and subsequent termination from placement are as follows:

1. Physically hitting or injuring a client, another student, an employee or anyone else on the premises of the agency
2. Extremely inappropriate behavior in field placement that is disruptive to the reputation or functioning of the agency and/or to its clients (for example, showing up for placement intoxicated or drugged; having a temper tantrum or otherwise losing emotional control; sexually seducing clients and/or staff. Such incidents require that the student be removed immediately from the scene. He might or might not receive an unsatisfactory rating. If the problems are emotional in nature, he might withdraw from school—or field placement only—while undergoing professional counseling or a period of inpatient treatment, and receive an "Incomplete" rather than a failing grade.)
3. Psychotic behavior that disturbs others or constitutes a danger to the student or others (A student may suffer a psychotic break while in field and become openly hostile, paranoid, or severely depressed or experience active hallucinations and delusions.)
4. Illegal or immoral behavior (A student might be caught stealing agency supplies or confidential papers, shooting heroin, stealing drugs or petty cash, or even selling drugs.)

These are serious incidents and they are *rare*. Many supervisors never encounter these behaviors and find it difficult to believe that such things do happen. Others are not so fortunate. Such incidents, when they occur, are often so extreme and so obvious that other supervisees and students can guess why the individual stops coming to field placement. However, severely problematic behavior can also occur in an individual whom fellow students like and feel is a competent social worker. His sudden departure could cause rumors of "unjustified termination from field placement without warning." Yet the school and field instructor cannot defend their actions without violating the student's right to confidentiality regarding the incident.

The other principal cause of an unsatisfactory rating is more common, though still relatively rare. A minor or moderately serious problem occurs and is identified. The field instructor shares his concerns with the student and suggests ways of dealing with it and improving the situation. There may or may not be improvement for a period of time, but the problem returns or continues in conjunction with other problems, which prevent the student from being effective in his role. These areas of weakness or difficulty do not occur just once or twice but form a pattern and typify the student's manner of handling certain situations. Thus, a student will not receive an unsatisfactory rating for occasional "goofs," displays of poor skill, and the like. These must be recurrent, with little or no growth, over a reasonable period of time. Following a series of discussions regarding specific incidents, the field instructor begins to point out the pattern he is observing. Together he and the student talk about the pattern, the possible reasons for it, and ways of breaking it. Every opportunity is given to the student to work the problem through. Only after many discussions, attempts to bring about growth, supervisory conferences (often involving the school as well as the field instructor and student), and special learning experiences fail to produce minimum-level performance is an unsatisfactory rating assigned.

Such students are often performing satisfactorily in a number of areas and may even be outstanding in some (refer again to the list on pp. 61–66). The individual may be a likable, conscientious person who is really trying hard to do a good job and meet his field instructor's expectations. Since he is not likely to share his recognition of problem areas with his fellow students, they may see only the positive side of his performance—his skills, conscientious attitude, likable personality, and efforts to perform well. When he receives an "unsatisfactory," his peers may be horrified ("What happened?") and conclude that the supervisor must be at fault and didn't know what he was doing.

Problems that can result in an unsatisfactory rating of this less dramatic type include the following:

1. *A hostile, resistant attitude toward learning.* No matter how much the supervisor tries, the student becomes defensive, does not listen, denies the reality of what the field instructor is trying to say, and *habitually* responds to constructive criticism with tears, anger, leaving the room, and similar behaviors. Because of the student's unwillingness to accept and recognize areas where growth is needed, it be-

comes impossible for the field instructor to teach him, and he therefore cannot achieve the minimum skills and attitudes necessary to pass field placement.

2. *Chronic absenteeism.* Field instructors cannot teach students who are not physically present in field. If too much time is missed a failing grade can result. Allowances are often made for extenuating emergency circumstances (death in the family, illness, and so on) permitting these students to withdraw from field with an "incomplete," put in extra hours to make up the lost time, or extend the length of the placement. However, some students are continually absent with obviously flimsy excuses; saunter into the agency late with no notification to anyone; repeatedly sneak out early or extend lunch breaks; and otherwise disrupt their learning experience. They display attitudes of irresponsibility and a lack of dedication to and concern with the needs of their clients and the agency. Again, such behavior must occur more than once or twice and take place without good reason and/or with no prior discussion, negotiation, or approval from the field instructor.

3. *A personality unsuited to social work.* This is one of the most difficult areas for field instructors to assess and for students to accept. Fellow students often have no idea that this is the reason for an individual's failing grade in field. However, certain personality attributes are incompatible with effective social work practice: highly punitive, rigid, or judgmental approaches to people; abrupt, curt, overly businesslike approaches; a cold, reserved, unapproachable appearance or attitude; extreme compulsiveness, perfectionistic habits that interfere with the ability to get the job done; and so on. Such behavior must characterize the student's approach to people and persist in spite of efforts on the part of the field instructor to help him develop more constructive ways of relating.

4. *Emotional immaturity or unusual naiveté.* This usually, though not always, pertains to a student very young in chronological age. He or she may never have lived away from home, may have led a very sheltered existence, and may find himself completely overwhelmed by the real world of people with problems. Because of insufficient personal maturity, he may lack basic defenses and techniques for responding to people different from himself and the kind of common sense that is crucial to successful social work practice at any level. If his parents have always bought everything for him and he has never even had his own checking account, how can he possibly help a welfare mother with six children with her budget? If he was raised in an extremely conservative environment and comes to placement equipped with biases against blacks, Jews, Italians, Hispanics, poor people, and the like, how can he learn to serve a wide range of clients with sincerity and warmth? If his own behavior is immature and adolescent, how can he possibly learn to provide marital counseling to a couple in their forties, help an elderly woman talk about death, or try to bring about change in a service delivery system in the community? Certainly no one would want him as a supervisor or would be comfortable with his assignment to administrative or program-management responsibilities. Such students are often counseled out and encouraged to get more life experience, possibly to return to social work school at a later date.

5. *Unprofessional behavior.* Students who consistently violate the NASW Code of Ethics, not out of ignorance but out of apparent disregard for their clients, their agency, and their field instructor, usually find themselves failing field placement. Blatant disregard for basic agency policies, rules, and regulations could produce similar results.

6. *Inability to communicate in English.* With the increased emphasis on admission of minority students, this is becoming a more common problem as foreign-born students enroll and enter field placement. A few simply do not have enough command of English to be able to engage in a rapid discussion with a client around emotionally laden issues or cannot compose coherent entries for social work or interdisciplinary records. Others are American-born but have serious gaps in written communication skills. If these are sufficiently serious to prevent performance of basic social work skills and remedial English courses and other special training efforts (not provided by the field instructor directly) fail to bring about the required degree of proficiency in time for completion of field placement, such students may fail field placement. Every effort is usually made to assign incomplete rather than failing grades to such students, since with time and effort many of them can gain the basic communication skills necessary for effective social work practice. A BSW or MSW degree should attest to advanced intellectual and academic accomplishments, and spoken and written communication skills must be compatible with those usually expected of college graduates. Those who cannot achieve this level may not make it through the social work program.

7. *Behavior that is emotionally damaging to clients.* Most students in their initial interactions with clients do not know enough to be very helpful, but they don't really harm the client. However, some students, often out of their own conscious needs, say and do things that obviously upset the client, reinforce his defenses, heighten his mistrust of people, hurt his feelings, and leave behind emotional wreckage that must be repaired by a more skilled social worker. The field placement's first obligation must be to its clients; students cannot be trained at their expense. Thus, students who exhibit harmful behavior toward clients are usually counseled out unless drastic and almost instantaneous improvement occurs.*

*See pp. 240–243 for an example of a process-recorded interview where the student's responses damaged the client, as opposed to an example where the student is inept but does no harm.

8. *Emotional problems and needs that interfere with the student's ability to work with clients.* Most adults have some neuroses, unmet needs, and problem areas in their own lives. These may bring about certain behaviors and responses that are dysfunctional but still do not interfere significantly with the individual's effective performance on the job or his relationships with people in his social work role. However, some students have unresolved personal problems or areas of unmet needs that carry over into and adversely affect their relationships and effectiveness in field. Such students are not psychotic or even necessarily "emotionally disturbed." However, they may be able to see clients only through the mirror of their own experiences. For example, a person may assume that because he feels a certain way, his client must feel the same and should respond accordingly. He explores his client's feelings with real eagerness, not for the primary purpose of helping him, but to satisfy his curiosity and examine his own problems in comparison with those of his client. This student may share life experiences inappropriately and have great difficulty seeing himself as a professional helping person, rather than as a client, in his social work relationships. It may take some time for the field instructor to identify such a pattern, and more time yet to help the student recognize its interference with his social work training. The individual is often encouraged to seek outside professional counseling and may or may not remain in field placement.

Some students have specific life experiences that make it difficult for them to work with certain kinds of clients or behaviors at any given time. A student whose parent has died of cancer will have difficulty working on an oncology service for some time following the death of his family member. A woman married to an alcoholic may find it difficult to work with alcoholics, and so on. Many students can be helped to work these feelings through, use them constructively and therapeutically, or recognize their own limitations. Most settings provide a sufficient variety of assignments for the few situations the student cannot handle to be avoidable. If a setting consists only of those situations the student cannot handle without overidentification, a switch to a different field placement may solve the problem. However, a few students, out of their own needs, overidentify and experience uncontrollable transference with virtually every client. These individuals would have difficulty in almost any social work setting and could end up with an unsatisfactory grade in placement if the pattern persists.

When working with a student who presents emotional difficulties, the key question is, *Do the problems interfere with the individual's performance on the job or in field placement?* If the answer is no, the supervisor has no business including his observations in a performance evaluation or requiring the individual to change his behavior. If the supervisor cares about the student as a person and senses some emotional struggle or pain, it may be appropriate for him to reach out by sharing his observations and his concern, and perhaps suggest that the student seek outside help. If the supervisee refuses or does not respond, the supervisor has no right to pursue the matter further, as long as the behavior or attitudes do not adversely affect the supervisee's performance.

When emotional needs exist but are not affecting the individual's performance, the resultant feelings and behaviors may or may not be noticeable. Temporary mood changes or short-lived changes in work habits may occur. The student may appear preoccupied, may be less outspoken and spontaneous than usual, may slip from above-average to average in his work, and so on. But at no point is there any danger that he will harm clients or disrupt ongoing relationships with colleagues and others; no one is in need of protection from him. In this case the individual seems basically able to deal with the problem in a constructive, mature manner.

When he knows his supervisee is facing an unusual crisis but is reacting to it normally under the circumstances, the supervisor can make some special allowances and overlook a few things for a while. He might withhold more difficult assignments or screen cases more carefully than usual so as not to subject the student to any extra stress. Presumably he remains basically functional and will soon recover his full ability to handle more difficult assignments.

When a student's emotional needs or problems do begin to affect performance, the supervisor not only has a right to become involved but *must* do so if he is to be effective in his educational/managerial role. However, his involvement must be *job- or performance-related:* The supervisor must not attempt to become the primary direct-treatment person for resolution of the emotional need or problem.

Indicators of Unusual Emotional Needs or Problems

When an individual's personal needs are affecting his social work performance adversely, there are usually several factors present, not just one, to indicate his situation, and their effect is felt keenly by others. Strong or acute problems are impossible to overlook; the supervisor is forced to deal with them in some manner. Subtle difficulties may show up in tape-recorded interviews and other materials seen only by the supervisor. The field instructor who uses direct observation methods of assessing performance is apt to detect problems early in their development.

Certain behaviors and emotions usually signal the onset or existence of personal problems that affect social work functioning. If a supervisor observes any of these (or has them reported to him by others), they merit special attention and further exploration. They cannot be ignored or overlooked.

Any sudden change in affect or behavior can indicate personal problems. A cheerful, outgoing, aggressive learner may become withdrawn, passive, and sullen. A quiet, ma-

ture, business like adult may become silly, giggly, and frivolous. A conscientious learner who really tries hard may become careless and lackadaisical toward his work.

Increased absenteeism with questionable explanations may indicate outside pressure, especially if it marks a change from previous attendance habits and if the absenteeism fits a pattern. The supervisor must be careful not to jump to drastic conclusions. A sudden period of arriving late for work may in fact be attributable to car troubles. On the other hand, emotional or alcoholic hangovers from a weekend could account for difficulties in getting to the agency on Monday mornings. A divorce in process may necessitate lengthy lunches for meetings with attorneys and court appearances. Thus, attendance difficulties must be evaluated carefully to determine whether they are indicative of concrete problems or unusual underlying personal stress.

A sudden fall in performance level is usually rather obvious. An outstanding student may suddenly lose motivation and drop to "satisfactory." Even though he may still be fully functional, an abrupt change from his *normal* level of functioning gives the supervisor reason for concern. If no other behavior or change accompanies the drop in performance and if the student resists attempts to explore what has happened, the supervisor may be curtailed in his exploration of the problem; after all, the supervisee's performance is still all right, even though it isn't what it once was. If the drop is from "satisfactory" or above to something less than "satisfactory," the field instructor has a ready opening for discussion: "Jim, I've been working with you now for eight weeks. The first four or five weeks you were doing really well in such-and-such areas. Now, lately, I've noticed a real change, and I'm concerned and puzzled. I wonder if you've noticed the change as well, and if we could talk about this a little?" Perhaps through discussion with the supervisor or with outside help, the individual can get his performance back up to an acceptable level. If not, the unsatisfactory level of performance will need to be dealt with in the evaluation process.

Bizarre behavior is usually quite obvious. Staff and other students may consider the individual "weird." Personal mannerisms, emotions, and behaviors may be inappropriate to the situation at hand. If colleagues notice it, the individual is probably displaying the affect with clients as well, necessitating immediate supervisory intervention.

Excessive or inappropriate crying may provide a clue to underlying problems affecting functioning. We have said that crying in response to stressful performance evaluations can be very appropriate; shedding tears when a client dies or when the student experiences a "wipeout" because of a heavy emotional experience over a client is also quite normal. Indeed, the expression of such feelings should be encouraged, not discouraged. However, the emotionally distraught supervisee may cry over situations that, to the supervisor, do not appear especially stressful. He may go around with bloodshot eyes ringed with dark circles. Others may report seeing the individual crying and may express discomfort because this happens often or without apparent reason. Obviously forces other than field placement or the job are bringing about a breakdown of the student's defenses. If this continues for any length of time, the individual can become virtually nonfunctional. To subject himself to the demands of the job and his clients in addition to his own personal problems may even aggravate his emotional state. Thus, supervisory intervention is required for the protection of the supervisee as well as to facilitate his personal or professional functioning.

The individual who suddenly or chronically has difficulty concentrating may be bored or insufficiently challenged. However, he may also be experiencing internal conflict, stress, and anxiety that are sapping his energy and preoccupying his mind.

Inappropriate responses to client and work situations may also indicate a problem. This is not a matter of skill versus lack of skill but rather a response that appears to be unrelated to the needs expressed by the other person. Exploration and discussion with the supervisee usually reveal a specific reason for the response based on a strong feeling or past experience.

Students with personal problems affecting performance may inappropriately share their personal feelings and life experiences with clients, not once or twice but as a regular pattern, so that the client seems to be the helping person and the student the client. This pattern often occurs in close connection with overidentification. A one-time occurrence deserves exploration: Perhaps the student *did* overidentify and become the client, in which case he probably needs the self-awareness that supervisory discussion can provide for growth. Overidentification or transference problems occasionally occur with even the most skilled therapists. But a pattern indicating loss of emotional control in various areas can handicap the student's functioning and affect clients adversely.

Finally, extreme resistance to self-examination through the usual field instructor–student relationship and process can indicate some underlying problems. The student may be afraid to face himself and fearful of losing control if forced to examine certain areas of his functioning. Perhaps he prefers to avoid or deny his own needs, emotions, or problems. The supervisor may not need to press further. Some supervisees are simply very private people who do not like to share much about themselves personally. They should not be forced to do so if they are functioninal and effective. Even though the supervisor may become curious, anxious, or frustrated because they won't reveal more of themselves, such disclosure may be unnecessary for the task at hand. However, if satisfactory functioning requires that certain areas be explored and discussed, resistance must be identified, confronted, explored, and dealt with in some manner.

Social workers like to believe that professional counseling works; indeed, many of us make our living providing this service to others. But do we *really* believe that a student who suffers a breakdown can return to normal functioning? Do we believe in the service we offer? How do we *really* feel about mental illness and situational emotional crises when they happen to someone who is not a "client"? Do we react to an emotionally distraught or disturbed supervisee with diagnostic labeling, rejection, and disgust? If we really believe in the effectiveness of counseling, we will not hesitate to make referrals when necessary. If we really believe that individuals with problems can often return to normal and even more effective functioning, we will talk more frequently about return to school, field placement, or social work practice rather than stigmatizing the individual and regarding him as "disturbed" forever. Would we hire someone who we know has had an emotional crisis or is in therapy? Would we knowingly take on such a person as a student supervisee? If we ourselves are prejudiced against supervisees who encounter emotional difficulties, how can we possibly provide them with unbiased, objective, and constructive guidance? Why is it okay for "clients" to have emotional needs and problems, but not for those we supervise or even for ourselves?

Of course, there are those whose problems are so overwhelming or deeply ingrained or of such a nature that they should not attempt to pursue social work as a career, either now or at any forseeable future date. Very few students with emotional problems will fit into this category, however.

Many social work supervisors are trained diagnosticians and counselors as well as supervisors or administrators. Whether we want to or not, we can see symptoms of emotional difficulties in those we supervise. However, we cannot become the student's therapist. There is a fine line between appropriate counseling within the supervisory relationship and inappropriate therapy and "caseworking." Appropriate counseling occurs when a supervisor identifies a problem area and shares the observation with the supervisee; explores it with a focus on how it is affecting job performance; and looks for solutions outside of as well as within the context of the supervisory relationship. Therapy occurs when a supervisor delves into personal problem areas for their own sake, regardless of their connection with job performance, and strives to bring about attitudinal or behavior changes in areas having no bearing on the work situation.

As the supervisor explores emotional problem areas, the student may be ready to share a great deal more than the supervisor really wants or needs to hear. The supervisee may later regret having revealed so much of himself and become uncomfortable with the supervisor, knowing that he writes the evaluation and has seen a painful and very personal area that perhaps did not need to be disclosed in such detail. He may wonder how the supervisor will use this information and whether he'll continue to treat the student with respect, dignity, and objectivity in assessing performance. A supervisor may need to know why a student is crying much of the time, for instance, to evaluate the kind of help he needs and for future planning, but perhaps he does not need to know all the details of his marital problem or whatever. Thus, he may not want to encourage or permit a total unburdening of the problem if this can be prevented or controlled. On the other hand, if the student is experiencing strong transference with a client, it may be necessary to explore the problem area in detail in order to help him gain awareness of the transference process and learn and apply skills for controlling it. If the transference results from an unresolved personal need or problem, the individual can be referred out for appropriate counseling. The supervisor would not become the therapist.

A problematic question for the supervisor can be: "Do I deal with the emotional problem in a therapeutic or an evaluatory manner?" The emotional need or problem must be dealt with in a therapeutic manner, though usually not by the supervisor himself. The effect on the individual's performance is dealt with in an evaluatory manner—if necessary. The individual's functioning or difficulties in functioning can be discussed and documented if necessary; however, the diagnostic interpretations of the reasons for the performance difficulties should be omitted from written assessments. If the effects on performance are minor or transitory in an otherwise satisfactory individual, many supervisors humanely omit any reference to the problem in their written evaluations. If improvement does not occur rather quickly, evaluation recommendations must be based on the individual's level of performance.

Perhaps the most difficult task for the supervisor is to share his observation and concerns with the emotionally unstable student. The supervisor must come across in a calm, kind, caring manner rather than in a punitive or threatening approach. It might be helpful for the field instructor and student to begin by reviewing their experiences together, including areas of growth and lack of progress, past discussions and efforts to help. Positives should be emphasized and problem areas presented in a direct, frank manner, but gently. Keep refocusing the conversation on the matters at hand if there is a tendency to stray off the subject. Be prepared to support general observations with specific examples and illustrations. Point out the benefits of obtaining outside help, recognize the difficulties, and clarify your supervisory role as necessary. Have the names, addresses, and phone numbers of specific referral sources at hand to share if appropriate.* Refer a student to agencies, mental health clinics, or private practitioners who have a sliding fee scale, if possible. The student may want to avoid settings that train social work students for fear of running into a classmate. Discuss these factors fully and openly and be supportive without being punitive, demanding, or threatening.

*Many schools have a formal counseling program for students at little or no cost, but some students may not want to use it for fear that information may leak back to their school.

The student may or may not agree to seek outside help. If he does, it can be tempting to contact his counselor and share your professional opinions. Don't do it! Except in *very* unusual circumstances involving danger to the student or others, or with express student permission, the supervisor must keep out of the relationship between the student and his therapist. Even if the two professionals know each other, there must be no informal discussion regarding the supervisee. If the student even suspects that such a process is occurring, his trust in the supervisor and in his therapist can be destroyed, severely limiting any positive impact the supervisory relationship (and the therapy!) may have had. Furthermore, the supervisee should not be pursued with, "How's it going in therapy?" or other leading questions. If the supervisor-supervisee relationship is a warm, friendly one with mutual feelings of trust, such questions might be asked casually, but they should be dropped immediately if the individual chooses not to respond or to respond vaguely. On the other hand, if the supervisor knows an individual is in therapy, there may be times when he will appropriately refer the student back to his therapist to discuss, explore, or work on something that comes up in the placement experience.

In summary, unsatisfactory grades are not given because a student "looked at his field instructor funny one day," disagreed with him during a supervisory conference, or showed up late twice because his car broke down, or because "my field instructor doesn't like me." Most students who are failing know it well in advance (though they may not admit it to their peers), have participated in intense and often lengthy discussions and experiences to help them improve, and will be failed only after repeated efforts to resolve problem areas have failed. In other words, there must be specific reasons for assignment of a failing grade, and these must be of a rather serious nature and *virtually always* are discussed with the student in advance of receipt of the written performance evaluation.

Special Techniques for Writing Unsatisfactory Performance Evaluations

Any evaluation that rates a student as "unsatisfactory" must be carefully written. It must be factual, accurate, humane yet honest and must be written in a manner that substantiates the rating being given. It must hold up if challenged by anyone.

The writing of an unsatisfactory evaluation demands a *better than average* level of communication. This is an occasion when virtually every field instructor should make use of his or her own supervisor or a senior field instructor in the same agency for consultation. Let one such person see a rough draft of the evaluation before it is typed. The objective reader can tell whether the words communicate what the writer thinks he is saying and can spot contradictions, inconsistencies, and confusing statements.* New field instructors (and even more experienced supervisors) should not feel bad if they spend several hours preparing a difficult performance evaluation and three or four drafts are produced before it becomes final.

Poorly written performance evaluations can precipitate grievances, appeals, and lawsuits.† When rulings go against the supervisor, it is often because the content of the evaluation did not merit or support the recommendations being made. An unsatisfactory assessment is a serious matter. The evaluation must indicate and illustrate serious problems; otherwise such a rating should not be given. The reader must be able to read the entire evaluation except for the final rating and reach the conclusion himself that it will be "unsatisfactory."

Problematic performance evaluations should give more than usual detail regarding the nature of assignments, learning experiences, and special training received so that the reader gets a clear picture of the experiences the student had and the expectations placed upon him. For example, if an undergraduate in the first semester of field placement is rated unsatisfactory and the evaluation states that he got the rating because he was not effective in treating psychotic outpatients, something is wrong: The expectations were obviously inappropriate for the student's level of training. On the other hand, if an evaluation describes efforts to teach the student to make welfare referrals, do simple interviews, and obtain concrete services for clients and he *still* had problems, it says something quite different.

The evaluation should attach a copy of the educational contract or any written educational objectives developed with the student. Performance expectations should be expressed behaviorally, as such objectives are more easily measured. Thus, preparation for an effective unsatisfactory evaluation must start at the *beginning* of field placement, before the field instructor even knows there are going to be problems. If he waits until the middle of the experience, it may be too late to lay the foundation for providing effective evaluative feedback.

The evaluation should address each educational objective and should assess the student in terms of his progress and existing skills in reaching the objective. If objectives are written qualitatively—spelling out level of skill as well as identifying areas of skill—there can be no doubt that such an evaluation is an objective assessment of the student's performance. The standards against which the student is being measured will be clear, and no one could argue that expectations were unclear or never communicated.

The evaluation should present a clear picture of the student's skills at the beginning of placement, the efforts made to help him grow, how he responded, and his *current level of funtioning*. Many evaluations omit the last item, instead making vague reference to "the student's growth this quarter" and "the need for continued growth."

Give more details than usual regarding the type of supervision provided and the student's response to this process. It is one thing to say that a student was told about a problem once and showed no improvement, another to describe a process of many supervisory sessions, informal discussions, and special experiences, after which the problem *still* persists. State (and illustrate if necessary) the student's pattern of response to supervisory feedback and discussion: Was he responsive, but without really following through? Did the problem area improve for a time and then reappear when supervisory surveillance was relaxed? Or was the student responsive, resulting in genuine improvement or elimination of the problem?

Indicate whether or not the student agrees with your assessment of performance in various areas. If the evaluation deals with matters that have been previously shared and discussed, it should clearly indicate that this process has occurred. It should be clear that the performance evaluation rating is not coming as a surprise to the student. (If it were, he could probably challenge it successfully.)

List sources of information that led to the evaluative conclusions and describe techniques used to assess the student's work.

A general guideline is that the evaluation should contain no comments or adjectives that cannot be substantiated through examples and other illustrative material. Use entries and observations recorded in the supervisory notebook‡ throughout the field placement to illustrate points made. It is not necessary to mention everything you know to illustrate a point, but at least one example should be given.

Use a separate paragraph (with or without a heading) to describe positive aspects of the student's performance. All students have some strengths. It is especially important that these be listed clearly for individuals who are receiving an overall unsatisfactory rating. Some students will be so concerned over the negatives that they will not even see the positives, thus they should stand out in a special section. If an evaluation contains no clear reference to positives, it will appear to the reader that it lacks objectivity, and its validity may be challenged or questioned.

Save examples of the student's work, the supervisory

---

*One new field instructor had been coming to me regularly for consultation regarding an especially challenging student. We reviewed and discussed examples of the student's work and even role-played supervisory approaches. There was much discussion of the student's obviously less than satisfactory performance in several areas, and the field instructor was able to convey her observations objectively to the student during supervisory conferences. Yet, the rough draft of the final performance evaluation was cloaked in vague generalities that would have described almost any student at any level and concluded with the statement that "the student's performance is fully satisfactory." When this was explored, the supervisor admitted her reluctance to put her honest assessment in writing. She did not doubt her assessment and was committed to it but just could not bring herself to put her thoughts into writing.

†Lawsuits are rare but sometimes can occur even in response to well-written evaluations. However, a poorly prepared evaluation can so anger a supervisee that he will take stronger retaliatory action than he might have considered otherwise, and the supervisor's chances of losing the grievance or lawsuit are greatly increased if the evaluation is not well written.

‡See pp. 171–172.

notebook, and all written evaluations for at least two or three years.*

Avoid the use of diagnostic labels if a student has emotional problems affecting field placement performance. Describe the effect on the student's daily performance if necessary, but without using psychiatric terminology. Emotional problems are often transitory, and field instructors can inflict real damage on a student by labeling him with negative diagnostic terms that may hurt him for years after the problem has been resolved. And whether we like it or not, social workers with a past history of emotional problems *are* discriminated against by other social workers, schools, and potential employers, especially if references and evaluations contain psychiatric labels.

It is not necessary to document all the gory details of a student's problem. It is usually possible to make the point without committing to writing elaborate and embarrassing descriptions of dysfunctional behavior or performance. Allow the student to retain some dignity. However, if he initiates a grievance or lawsuit, he must realize that explicit details will come out at that time. Some will be material that he wants divulged, but others might not be in his best interests, and could have remained "unspecified" had he not initiated a formal challenge to his evaluation.

By now it should be obvious that implementation of these suggestions for preparing evaluations in problematic situations requires some kind of narrative report. Most checklists and other rating-scale evaluation forms simply do not cover the special items that must be addressed. However, prescribed outlines can also be adjusted through the addition of special headings to cover what needs to be said.

Alternatives to Failing an Unsatisfactory Student

When a student's performance in field placement is genuinely problematic, the writing of an unsatisfactory performance evaluation is only one alternative for dealing with the situation. Many schools have policies that terminate a student from the social work program if he receives a failing grade in any field placement. Therefore, this outcome must occur only as a last resort. Schools and field instructors have developed some rather interesting and creative methods for avoiding this outcome. Some are real contributions in that they work to the best interests of the individual student and the profession; others are negatives in that they do not really deal with the problem, allow the student to deny reality, and foster his ability to assume blissfully that the problem was someone else's and not his.

One obvious alternative is to ignore a problematic performance and give the student a "satisfactory" in field. The reasons this is an undesirable solution have been presented throughout this text.

Another negative but often-used alternative is to lower performance expectations. If they are sufficiently decreased, even a severely retarded adult with overt psychosis could pass field placement!† Another version of this approach is to shift the student to a different field instructor or agency with lower expectations. This is often done in the middle of field placement or for a second placement if the student just barely made it through the first. Welfare settings are favorite spots for such students. Field instructors there may lack professional social work training, are heavily burdened with routine paper work, and often place more emphasis on concrete services than on more advanced professional skills. The problem is that we are not preparing students to graduate with degrees that contain a restrictive clause: "Warning: This MSW degree is valid only in welfare settings dealing primarily with concrete services." When we turn the student loose with a BSW or MSW degree, we are certifying him as qualified for practice in *any* social work setting that will hire him.

Another version of this alternative is to place the student in a setting where his work is not examined closely, where the student is left more or less on his own, with few if any direct observation methods used to assess his performance. Thus, no one needs to be bothered with observation of problematic performance, reality can be ignored, and the student receives a passing grade.

A transfer to another setting in the middle of field placement is usually a negative solution. This approach merely moves the problem from one location to another. Unless the difficulty is clearly related to the individual field instructor or setting, the student should be evaluated for his ability to make it in the setting to which he is assigned. Indeed, this challenge can be a constructive growth experience if the student is not permitted to flee the situation at the first signs of stress. Agencies that accept students who have done poorly in field placement elsewhere must be careful not to accept unsatisfactory students; to do so supports denial of the real problem and subjects consumers in the new setting to well-documented incompetence. However, a midplacement transfer could be necessary if unusual circumstances made it impossible or undesirable for the student to continue in the original placement, for example, massive reorganizational changes in the agency or the sudden illness or even death of the field instructor.

Another approach is called, "Let's wait to see if he does better in the next field placement." This negative solution has been discussed.

*In one instance a student sued her field instructor. The grievance process took place over approximately six months after the performance evaluation was written; the lawsuit extended over eighteen months subsequently, with multiple depositions and consultations. Had all materials been destroyed at the time the student terminated field placement, it would have been very difficult to recall and substantitate necessary details up to two years later.

†Indeed, the author has heard of several students who exhibited clearly psychotic behavior in class and field and yet made it through a social work program. These incidents were reported by fellow students who were annoyed and puzzled by the failure of classroom and field instructors to deal with a very obvious problem.

Another highly negative solution actually suggested by some supervisors is to make the student's experience so miserable that he will voluntarily withdraw from field placement. Little benefits and niceties are withheld, and a rigid, punitive approach is taken by the supervisor. Feedback is given on negatives only. Normal supervisory support is not provided, and the student is left to sink or swim. Standards may be set so high that he cannot possibly succeed, making it easy to document the fact that he failed. The student's every word and action may be scrutinized, or else he may be ignored completely. He may receive all the routine, dull, unpleasant, or undesirable assignments that no one else wants. The supervisor may refuse to take his word for anything, questioning everything he says and does. The pressure to perform may be increased to the breaking point, as all rules, even unrealistic ones, are enforced rigidly. Such an approach might achieve the desired objective, but if the student ever challenged the supervisor's evaluation, the field instructor would lose, for the student could easily prove discrimination (he was treated differently from others). A supervisor of paid agency staff could easily find himself demoted or dismissed if it was proved that he consciously used such tactics.

Fortunately, there are a number of potentially positive alternatives that can be used to avoid giving an unsatisfactory rating.

If a student is close to achieving satisfactory performance for a given field placement experience and basically needs more time, his placement could be extended a few extra weeks if schedules permit and if the student, field instructor, and school agree to such an arrangement. The student might work extra hours—at night, on weekends, over holiday breaks—*if* appropriate supervision is available and if it is felt that he is sincerely motivated and would benefit from the experience. He might complete an extra field placement before starting his second placement, to bring his skills up to the desired level. He might even repeat a field placement. This last choice is viewed negatively by many educators, as it often does not help a student who lacks basic qualities for being an effective social worker and is unfair to students who are capable of completing the degree program in the usual manner. It is not realistic to put a student through a given course ten times until he passes; he will not have ten chances to be effective with the same consumers of social work services after he graduates. Thus, repetition of field placement, in most instances, represents a lowering of standards.

However, there are bona fide situations where a student might be permitted to repeat a placement. The student may have had unexpected illness, a death in the family, or other situational events that interrupted his attendance in field. Unusual irregularities in the provision of supervision may have occurred, interfering with the quality of the student's experience. Thus, even though problems may exist, the school may determine that certain events beyond the student's control prevented him from getting the most out of his experience. If it is felt that the student has the potential for growth, he may be permitted to repeat placement under more favorable circumstances.

Another potentially positive approach is to assign the student an incomplete instead of a failing grade. This is done when students will be extending their field placement for a specified period of time or dropping out of school for a while with a definite intent to return. If the student's performance is unsatisfactory because of emotional problems, he might be referred for intensive counseling and encouraged to withdraw from school during its course. When the emotional crises is over and he is again fully functional, he may return and could very well be a better than average student as a result of having gone through his experience.*

When students are "counseled out" it usually occurs as the result of lengthy and intensive discussions involving the student, the field instructor, and the school faculty. Such students are usually encouraged to drop out of school voluntarily, switch to a different program of study, or find a job in a different field. If the student's performance is poor but close to satisfactory, there may be some negotiation to give him a low-satisfactory rating to facilitate his acceptance into another program.

If an unsatisfactory evaluation is rendered at the end of a field placement, school policy may prevent the student from enrolling in further social work courses. If such a policy does not exist and unacceptable approaches are used instead to deal with the problem student, the field instructor should press for stronger, more definitive action, perhaps even deciding not to take further students from a given school if his experiences with the school's failure to support unsatisfactory evaluations have been negative and problematic.

Finally, a potentially positive approach (especially for consumers of social work services) would be to terminate an unsatisfactory student from field placement before the scheduled end of the term. If behavior is highly problematic and the field instructor knows he cannot bring the student up to a satisfactory level by the end of field placement no matter how much time and energy he puts into the process, there is no point in keeping the student in the agency.

---

*This plan has worked effectively for several very competent students known to the author.

13 Legal Aspects of Field Instruction

Most field instructors give little thought to the legal aspects of their educational role, either assuming that the school will take care of everything if any problems arise or naively believing that field instruction is an activity that never involves legal issues. Both assumptions are erroneous. As has been indicated, individual field instructors can become the object of a student grievance or lawsuit. Certain precautions can be taken to prevent some of these actions or to enable the student supervisor to deal with them in the most effective manner possible.

The Agency—School Contract

It is important that a written document exist stating that the agency and its staff have assumed the responsibility of student supervision. Otherwise, should legal problems arise, there would be no evidence that student supervision is part of the job description of an individual field instructor or an overall commitment of the agency. Attorneys who normally represent the agency might feel no obligation to defend a field instructor in an issue that appears external to his duties as an agency staff member.

A formal contract should spell out areas of responsibility and benefits for both the school and the agency. Expectations, restrictions, and specific rights should be described, along with insurance and malpractice coverage requirements for all concerned. The contract should be signed by top-level administrators in both programs and be subject to annual review and renewal.

The following checklist covers items that should be basic to every contract. Other conditions may need to be added to meet the needs of specific programs. A properly written contract will appear balanced—not heavily favoring or placing more requirements or restrictions on either the school or the agency.

Contract Content

1. The names of the parties to the agreement (school and agency)
2. A statement of the purpose of the agreement (e.g. to provide a field placement experience for students in a particular setting)
3. Rights, responsibilities, and limitations regarding the assignment of students, for example, the length of advance notice required by the agency for placement of prospective students; the requirement that preplacement interviews occur (see Chapter 4); and the agency's right to refuse to accept certain students
4. Basic experiences and benefits the agency will and will not provide for all students, for example, space, supervision, free lunches, emergency medical care, access to records and agency activities, and so on
5. An understanding that the agency will provide suitable personnel to supervise the students (perhaps specifying also that someone in the agency will act as liaison, overseer, or coordinator of the field instruction program there)
6. Description of the role, responsibility, and availability of the faculty liaison person
7. Insurance coverage, possibly including malpractice coverage for students; auto insurance requirements for students who use their private cars during placement; and accident, injury, or health insurance, especially against accidents occurring during or related to the field placement experience or on agency premises (A special malpractice policy or an indemnification clause may provide for legal representation and payment of court-awarded damages if field instructors are sued by students as a result of their field placement role.)

8. The agency's right to terminate students from placement under certain conditions; the school's right to remove students from the placement if it feels the contractual requirements are not being met or that such removal would be in the best interests of the student

9. A section covering student responsibilities while in field

10. Conditions under which the contract can be broken, along with protective clauses to allow students currently in field to finish their placement should the contract be terminated or permitted to expire while students are still in placement

11. Time period covered by the contract and the process for renewal

12. Signatures and dates

Sample Contracts

Contract A, between "Learn-All University" and the "XYZ Hospital," was initiated by the hospital's administrative and legal staff. Thus, it probably reflects the agency's viewpoint to a greater degree than usual and requires related protections from the school.

Contract B was developed by a school of social work.* It is quite comprehensive and includes a number of factors not illustrated in the first contract example. Even though it was developed by school faculty and legal counsel, it is sensitive to the needs of field instructors and agencies as well and is not strongly biased in favor of the school.

*Loyola University of Chicago, School of Social Work. It is used with the school's permission.

SAMPLE CONTRACT A†

A G R E E M E N T

THIS AGREEMENT is entered into this _____ day of _____, 19____, by and between LEARN-ALL UNIVERSITY, an educational corporation of the State of New York (hereinafter referred to as the "UNIVERSITY") and the XYZ HOSPITAL, an agency and instrumentality of ABC County, New York (hereinafter referred to as the "HOSPITAL").

W I T N E S S E T H :

WHEREAS, the UNIVERSITY provides a course of study embodying theory and practice to students who have enrolled in undergraduate and/or graduate social work courses (which social work students are hereinafter referred to as "STUDENTS"); and

WHEREAS, the UNIVERSITY desires that said STUDENTS obtain clinical social work experience ("field practice") in a planned program of social services in the HOSPITAL; and

WHEREAS, the HOSPITAL is willing to provide the necessary facilities for said clinical social work experience;

NOW, THEREFORE, for and in consideration of the premises and the mutual covenants and agreements herein contained, the parties hereto agree as follows:

I. THE UNIVERSITY AGREES

1. To assume total responsibility for the educational experience and final grades of the STUDENTS.

2. To the provision that it does not and will not discriminate against any employee or applicant for employment or registration in a course of study because of race, color, creed, sex or national origin.

†This is a slightly modified version of an actual contract, reviewed and approved by attorneys representing both parties. The names of the school and field instruction setting have been changed. This contract is not intended as a model—merely an example that might or might not be applicable to other settings. It was drawn up by the agency, and all schools that use the setting for student training are required to sign it.

Clinical Social Work Experience
XYZ Hospital – Learn–All University
_____, 19____ to _____, 19____

3. To request assignment of STUDENTS approximately sixty (60) days prior to the beginning date of each period of field work placement. The request will specify the dates and length of training. The HOSPITAL reserves the right to determine the number of STUDENTS accepted each quarter/semester/year for field work placement.

4. STUDENTS must assume responsibility for their own medical care and hospitalization, with the exception of emergency treatment for injury or illness occurring during the performance of assigned duties.

5. That an administrative faculty member for the UNIVERSITY'S Office of Field Instruction will be available for consultation as needed.

6. The HOSPITAL social service staff will provide supervision and teaching for STUDENTS enrolled in the field experience program. A faculty member from the UNIVERSITY will be designated as a Coordinator and will be responsible for the coordination and implementation of the program of learning.

    The UNIVERSITY Coordinator will:

    a) Review with the HOSPITAL's Director of social service (or his designated representative) the finalized schedules prior to commencement of the clinical experience programs.

    b) Plan with appropriate HOSPITAL personnel for the use of HOSPITAL facilities including assigned patient areas and office space.

II. THE HOSPITAL AGREES

1. To the provision that it does not and will not discriminate against any employee or applicant for employment or registration in the course of study because of race, color, creed, sex or national origin.

2. The HOSPITAL reserves the right to refuse or discontinue the availability of its facilities and services to any STUDENT who does not continuously meet the professional or other requirements, qualifications, and standards of the HOSPITAL or any appropriate authority controlling and directing said HOSPITAL.

3. The HOSPITAL will provide, insofar as possible, as varied an experience as will be allowed within the specified period of field work placement. The STUDENTS will participate, under supervision, in direct services to patients and will be offered the opportunity to learn agency functions and community resources, and to attend agency staff meetings and case conferences.

4. To provide necessary orientation, administrative guides and procedures, office space (as available), and other media deemed essential to the conduct of the work experience.

Clinical Social Work Experience
XYZ Hospital – Learn–All University
_____, 19____ to _____, 19____

Page 3 of 5

5. To maintain administrative and professional supervision of STUDENTS insofar as their presence affects the operation of the HOSPITAL and/or direct or indirect services to clients.

6. The HOSPITAL will provide STUDENTS, at their own expense, the use of the cafeteria facilities in the HOSPITAL.

7. Emergency out–patient service for STUDENTS who become ill on assignment at the hospital will be provided without charge. The attending physician in the Health Office or Emergency Room will administer necessary emergency treatment and will send a referral slip with the STUDENT, either back to the UNIVERSITY or back to the assigned supervisor.

III. THE HOSPITAL AND THE UNIVERSITY AGREE

1. Orientation to the HOSPITAL will be provided for the faculty prior to commencement of the STUDENTS' field experience. Orientation shall be agreed upon by both parties to this Agreement.

2. Acceptable schedules and work assignments developed will not interfere with the primary mission of the HOSPITAL.

3. An annual review of programs and policies will be made.

4. Both parties to this Agreement reserve the right to withhold placement of STUDENTS during the planned period of field placement depending upon change within the UNIVERSITY School of Social Work or the HOSPITAL which would appear to present inadequate learning situations.

5. The HOSPITAL and UNIVERSITY shall acquaint the STUDENTS with the policies and standards and the rules and regulations of the HOSPITAL. In the event of any inappropriate actions by the STUDENTS, the HOSPITAL staff will notify the UNIVERSITY Coordinator in order that appropriate action may be taken by the UNIVERSITY.

6. There shall be a meeting of faculty and field supervisors prior to the placement of the STUDENTS in the HOSPITAL.

IV. INDEMNIFICATION AND INSURANCE*

1. The UNIVERSITY agrees to indemnify and hold harmless, the XYZ HOSPITAL and the HOSPITAL's field instructors, from any and all claims, liabilities, and causes of action arising out of the operation of this Agreement. The UNIVERSITY shall pay all claims and losses of any nature whatsoever in connection therewith and shall defend all suits, in the name of the XYZ

---

*Note: This is the clause that provides legal representation and coverage for field instructors in the event of lawsuits by student supervisees. The last sentence of the paragraph attempts to protect the university from claims against it by proclaiming field instructors to be separate entities not affiliated with the university. Note that this contradicts the usual philosophy of most universities that consider field instructors to be a part of university faculty for instructional purposes, although they are not paid by the school.

Clinical Social Work Experience
XYZ Hospital – Learn–All University
_____, 19___ to _____, 19___
Page 4 of 5

      HOSPITAL and the HOSPITAL's field instructors, when applicable, and shall pay all costs and judgments which may issue thereon. It is further provided that in no event shall the STUDENTS of the UNIVERSITY be considered to be agents, officers, servants, or employees, of the HOSPITAL. Additionally, in no event shall the HOSPITAL's field instructors be considered to be agents, officers, servants, or employees of the UNIVERSITY.

    2. The UNIVERSITY agrees to maintain during the term of this Agreement professional liability insurance with a single limit of liability of no less than One Million Dollars ($1,000,000.00). ABC County, the XYZ HOSPITAL and the HOSPITAL's field instructors shall be named as additional insureds. A certificate of insurance in evidence of compliance with this paragraph shall be forwarded to _____ at least ten (10) days prior to the commencement of this Agreement, failing which, no students shall be accepted by the HOSPITAL.

V. TERM

    The term of this Agreement shall commence on _____, 19___, and shall terminate on _____, 19___. This Agreement may be renewed by both parties to the Agreement each year for additional one year periods, subject to the approval of the HOSPITAL governing board, following a mutual written request by the UNIVERSITY and the HOSPITAL.

VI. TERMINATION

    This Agreement may be terminated by either party by notification in writing of desire to cancel, delivered to the other party by certified or registered U.S. mail not less than thirty (30) days before the anniversary date of the Agreement; provided, however, this Agreement shall not be cancelled in full until all courses of instruction scheduled have been offered to STUDENTS then enrolled. However, no other STUDENT shall be enrolled after the date upon which this Agreement is cancelled.

VII. NOTICE

    Every notice that may be required by this Agreement shall be in writing and delivered by certified or registered mail, return receipt requested, to the parties at their respective addresses as follows:

As to the HOSPITAL: (name and address)

As to the UNIVERSITY: (name and address)

VIII. SOLE AGREEMENT

    Both parties agree that this Agreement contains the entire agreement of the parties and that there are no conditions or limitations to this undertaking except those stated herein. After the execution hereof, no alteration, change or modification hereof shall be binding or effective unless executed in writing and signed by both parties hereto.

Clinical Social Work Experience
XYZ Hospital — Learn–All University
_____, 19____ to _____, 19____
Page 5 of 5

    IN WITNESS WHEREOF, the parties hereto have caused this Agreement to be executed by their officials thereunto duly authorized.

(SEAL)   LEARN–ALL UNIVERSITY

Attest:

_____   _____
(name)   (name)
(title)   (title)

(SEAL)   XYZ HOSPITAL

Attest:

_____   _____
(name)   (name)
(title)   (title)

Sample Contract B*

I. This memorandum of understanding is made this _____ day of _____ 19___, by and between the School of Social Work of Loyola University of Chicago (hereinafter called the "University"), and the _____ (hereinafter called the "Agency").

II. WHEREAS, the University is desirous of utilizing clinical facilities of the Agency for students enrolled in various social work educational programs of the University; and WHEREAS, the Agency has such clinical facilities and is desirous of cooperating with the University in making them available for educational purposes; NOW THEREFORE, in consideration of these premises and the mutual understandings hereinafter stated, it is hereby understood and agreed as follows:

A. The University and the Agency jointly agree:
1. As of _____, 19___, the Agency will allow the University to use its facilities for the teaching of social work to students enrolled in the School of Social Work at the University.
2. This agreement shall be effective for a period of _____ year(s). Either party may terminate this agreement by giving the other written notice of termination, not less than three (3) months prior to the scheduled date for the next class of students.
3. The Agency and School cooperate in the placement of students, each sharing responsibility for the final selection of students. The Agency has no obligation to work with students who are initially considered to be, or are later found to be, unsuited to the Agency program.
4. Neither party of this understanding shall be legally liable for the consequences, whether bodily injury or property damage, occasioned by act, neglect, or operation of law, chargeable to the other party. Where Workmen's Compensation, or other obligation for payments of benefits may arise, the Agreement will neither enlarge nor diminish such obligation. It shall be the intent of each party to be responsible, both factually and legally, only for its own employees and its own acts or omissions. However, it is recognized that students from the University could or might become entitled to benefits or damages from the Agency or that patients or staff members of the Agency could or might become entitled to benefits or damages from the University, and to the extent that such liabilities could or might exist, each party shall idemnify and hold harmless each other in the event, and to the extent, such contingency shall occur.
5. No party to this agreement shall, in connection with any aspect of its performance, discriminate against any person by reason of race, color, sex or national or ethnic origin.
B. Responsibilities of the School of Social Work:
1. The School provides a faculty consultant to the Agency. Educational requirements for field instructors are found in the School's Field Work Manual (dated _____). Also refer to the Manual for the responsibilities of the faculty consultant to the Agency and the student.
2. The School will confer with the Agency prior to the placement of any student in order to establish or to review the purpose, provisions and responsibilities involved in the field experience.
3. The School is responsible for monitoring the learning experiences of the student.
4. When circumstances beyond the control of the School or Agency indicate the

student must be replaced, or if the Agency is unable to meet the conditions of the agreement, the School has the responsibility to withdraw the student from the agency. This action would be taken only in consultation with the Agency field instructor and other Agency personnel involved in the placement program.

5. The School provides group meetings throughout the year for administrators, Agency liaison staff and field instructors. These programs are planned to promote understanding of curriculum of the School, encourage communication and interaction between practice and social work education and develop competence in field instruction.

6. The School offers workshops and other learning opportunities in field instruction which field instructors may attend without payment of tuition.

7. The University shall permit its social work faculty members to partitipate as resource persons at Agency activities on invitation from the Agency and with the approval of the Dean of the School of Social Work.

8. The School lists the Agency and names of the field instructors in its <u>Bulletin</u>.

9. The School provides library privileges for field instructors.

C. Responsibilities of the Agency:

1. The Agency designates one primary field instructor for the student. If there are multiple supervisors, the primary field instructor coordinates the total learning experience and is responsible for the final evaluation report. These subsidiary supervisors should be utilized only after consultation with the faculty consultant.

2. The Agency provides time for the field instructor to hold an individual conference with the student for at least one hour per week. Time is provided for group conferences with the students as needed during the school year and for teaching preparation in advance of the conferences.

3. The Agency provides time for the field instructor to attend approximately three meetings of field instructors during the school year.

4. The Agency provides office supplies, telephone facilities and office arrangements which enable the student to function effectively. There also is adequate provision for safeguarding confidential material such as case material and student records.

5. The Agency provides learning experiences, including orientation to the Agency, case assignments and a group assignment.

6. For students in the direct practice concentration, the Agency requires the student to do process recording, summary recording, psycho–social diagnosis and treatment summaries and to record for accountability consonant with Agency policy.

7. The Agency communicates immediately with the faculty consultant any concern regarding the student's learning.

8. The field instructor is responsible for prompt submission of statistical and formal evaluation reports in proper form and content which adequately describes the student's field learning.

9. The Agency will consult with the School immediately if specific circumstances arise which require the Agency to ask that the student be withdrawn from the placement during the school year.

10. The determination of the number of students to be assigned to the placement shall be negotiated between the Agency and the University. The Agency has the final decision on the number of students it can accommodate.

D. Responsibilities of the Student; the School informs the student that:

1. The student will follow Agency and School policies, procedures, programs and operating standards. Examples are rules for hours of agency operation, necessary absence, monthly statistical reports, narrative reports and

provision for continuity of services and treatment during school holidays which may be necessary and which are planned for in advance with the field instructor.

2. The student will complete all required documentation such as process recording, treatment summary recording and reports required by the School of Social Work and the field instructor.

3. The student will prepare for and participate in regular evaluation conferences.

4. The student has the responsibility to act professionally and ethically, to maintain confidentiality, and to give priority to the clients' rights and needs over his own.

5. The student is responsible for his own health and accident insurance since these will not be provided by the Agency in all instances. If the Agency has health requirements, the student is expected to meet the requirements of the Agency.

6. The student is not an employee and is not entitled to financial remuneration during placement unless otherwise arranged for with the Agency and School. The Agency reimburses the student for travel expenses incurred in fulfilling duties at the Agency. Travel to and from the field placement is paid by the student.

III. The following supplements to this agreement are attached hereto and made a part hereof: <u>None</u>

APPROVED

_____	_____
Agency	University
_____	_____
Executive	Vice President & Dean of Faculties
_____	_____
Director of Social Services	Dean, School of Social Work
Date: _____	Date: _____

Prior to beginning each field placement, students are asked to read the Memorandum of Understanding between the University and the placement Agency. The following statement must be signed by the student before the placement begins.

"I have read the Memorandum of Understanding between the placement Agency and the University and understand section D, Responsibilities of the Student."

Signed: _____   Date: _____

Grievances

Most schools have a formal grievance procedure for use by students who wish to challenge decisions, recommendations, evaluations, and policies pertaining to their educational experience. A written policy often explains the conditions under which grievances can be brought and the procedures for conducting the grievance and for appealing its outcome. Students who are members of NASW can also use the NASW grievance mechanism for complaints regarding violations of the NASW Code of Ethics, NASW's recommended personnel practices, or ethics issues. The majority of student grievances concern grades assigned by classroom faculty. Only a minute percentage pertain to field instruction issues, and of these, an even smaller number directly challenge the actions of an agency-based field instructor. However, the potential exists and will increase as student supervisors fulfill their gatekeeper role more effectively, implement and enforce adherence to high standards of practice, and provide honest evaluatory feedback.

When a student disagrees with a supervisor or classroom instructor on an action, his first step is to discuss the matter directly with the individual making the decision or taking the action. If that fails to produce the desired result, the student then goes to the field instructor's supervisor, to his faculty adviser, or to the director of field instruction, the dean, or some other administrative faculty member. If informal discussions fail to bring satisfaction, the student may initiate a grievance. Most grievance procedures require that all informal channels be tried and exhausted before the formal complaint is filed. Furthermore, the action the student is challenging must be significant; not every complaint can be aired through the grievance mechanism.

The student usually has a specified and rather brief period of time in which to request the grievance after he receives his failing grade (or other grievable action). He is usually required to describe the action in writing, state his reasons for disagreeing with it, and indicate what he feels is necessary to "make him whole"—that is, what he would like to have done about it (reversal of the action, opportunity to repeat a course, and so on). A designated group of faculty or the grievance committee itself then meets to consider the request for a grievance hearing and determine whether it meets the specified requirements for a "grievable issue." No attempt is made at this stage to consider the merits of the grievance. The only purpose is to determine if it can be heard. This decision must be reached within a specific period of time. If the grievance is to be heard, then the committee will convene to hear it. The ideal grievance committee comprises a chairman, a recording secretary, and a representative balance of students, field instructors, and faculty. It meets as often as needed to hear grievances, deliberate, and render its decisions.

The student prepares his case by gathering all appropriate materials to support his viewpoint, lining up individuals who can serve as witnesses and perhaps also a personal representative to appear with him at the grievance hearing. This may be another student, a faculty member, a personal friend or family member, or an attorney. The chairman of the grievance committee reviews the student's written statement and shares it with the committee members for their confidential review prior to the hearing. Individuals being grieved against are notified of the process and are also invited to submit statements or appear at the hearing. While witnesses (and "defendants") can be encouraged to appear, school grievance mechanisms have no power to issue subpoenas,* and witnesses cannot be forced to appear, as for a court hearing. This factor can have obvious advantages or disadvantages for either party, and the failure of key witnesses to appear could render the hearing process virtually meaningless or one-sided. No matter how ridiculous a field instructor may feel his student's grievance against him is, he should always appear to present his defense. Supervisors have lost grievances that might not have gone against them had they been present to respond to the supervisee's allegations.

The grievance hearing itself usually takes several hours and is conducted informally. Minutes are taken (the session may be taped). The individual bringing the grievance (the complainant) is usually present throughout the hearing; witnesses come in to give their testimony and then leave; the respondent should be present throughout the hearing. Once all sides have been heard, the committee meets in private to consider the information that has been presented and render its decision, which should be communicated to all parties in writing. Some school grievance mechanisms require the grievance committee to submit its recommended action to the dean or program chairperson for approval before the decision becomes final. The student then either accepts the decision or can appeal it within a specified time period. An appeal hearing follows a similar process, but witnesses may or may not be called. The composition of the appeal committee is not the same as that of the original committee, and the appeal committee may render its decision by reviewing the notes and material generated from the initial hearing without recalling the person filing the grievance or others. When a grievance decision is appealed and the appeal committee renders its decision, the action becomes final.

Some schools permit students to remain in class and/or field while their grievance is being heard. Others require that the student drop out (if this is what would be required if he lost his grievance) or accept the failing grade until a grievance decision rules otherwise. The initial grievance and appeal process can easily take three to six months, causing considerable inconvenience for the anxious student awaiting the decision. The delay can also work to his advantage by stalling the repercussions of an adverse action. Out-

*However, some hearings regarding paid employees are more formal and can use subpoenas to force witnesses to appear.

comes reached through grievance appeals usually result in the change of a failing grade to passing, permission to repeat a course and obliterate the first failing grade, or expunging the notation of problems or receipt of a failing grade from the student's record as if it never occurred. The outcome may also be that the original decision or action is upheld. Notes from grievance sessions and written material generated through the process are usually kept in a separate file and may be destroyed or summarized after a given time. Strict policies should restrict access to only those faculty with "a need to know," thus preserving confidentiality.

The manner in which a grievance is conducted is extremely important. Should a student continue to be dissatisfied with a grievance appeal ruling and engage an attorney to bring legal action against someone associated with the school or his field instructor, the grievance process will be examined closely. The student may argue that he did not receive a fair hearing in the grievance process. If so, his attorney will look closely for irregularities in the way the grievance was conducted that might invalidate or weaken the decision rendered. Such a tiny percentage of grievances turn into lawsuits that few grievance committees consider the possibility and conduct their affairs on the assumption that no one will ever examine the *process* used to render their decision. However, on a preventive level, all the participants in a grievance must be sure that the grievance is handled in an ethical, organized, confidential, responsible manner and in compliance with the school's written policies regarding grievances. The NASW guidelines for grievances can give some idea of proper techniques for conducting grievances,* but they are for use within NASW, and schools are not necessarily obligated to adopt them. School accrediting bodies may specify the need for certain types of grievance mechanisms, leaving it up to the school to work out the details for implementing a grievance process. Interested parties should obtain a copy of the school's written grievances procedure and constantly contrast and compare the stated policies with the actual manner in which their own grievance is being conducted.

Characteristics of Properly Run Grievance Hearings

The following list presents some of the characteristics of a properly run grievance mechanism and some of the irregularities that could cause difficulty in rendering a just decision or weaken the decision should it be challenged. This list is not intended as a model, nor is it complete. However, it should aid field instructors, students, and faculty in identifying when potentially unfair or damaging irregularities are occurring.

PROPER CONDUCT

1. A written procedure exists detailing the conditions and procedures for filing a grievance; the composition of the grievance committee; and the process by which the grievance is heard. The impact of decisions and the appeal mechanism should be described along with the kinds of records kept on general procedings and who has access to them.

2. Students and field instructors, as well as full-time faculty, know the grievance policies exist and how to gain access to them should they so desire. When someone asks to see them, they are shared openly and willingly, without hesitation.

3. The grievance procedure is handled in obvious compliance with the stated written procedures.

IRREGULARITIES

1. No written procedure exists because the school has never had a grievance or has never put its policies into writing. Existing descriptions of the grievance policy are sketchy, incomplete, vague, and contradictory or leave the reader with key questions unanswered. The procedures do not clearly spell out exactly how one goes about filing a grievance and the procedure that must be followed.

2. Students, field instructors, and faculty do not know that a written grievance procedure exists, nor are they routinely advised how to gain access to it. When requests for access are made, there is obvious reluctance or resistance to disclosing the information or making copies available.

3. There are obvious deviations from the written procedures: Deadlines are not met or are extended; the necessity of following some of the procedures outlined in the policy is rationalized away; and other procedures seem to be ignored or overlooked as the grievance takes place.

*A copy of the most current NASW Grievance Procedures can be obtained by writing the National Committee on Inquiry, National Association of Social Workers, 1425 H St., N.W., Suite 600, Washington, D.C. 20005.

PROPER CONDUCT

4. The committee shows absolutely no bias toward either party during the hearing process. Both complainant and respondent are treated with equal respect.

5. The grievance committee is composed of approximately equal representation from students, classroom faculty, and field instructors.

6. The chairman is a mature individual who has some experience with grievances and has leadership qualities. He is someone who will not leave the geographical area at the termination of the quarter/semester/school year should the grievance procedure need to be conducted during the summer months or between school terms.

7. The chairman of the committee is definitely in charge of the hearing. While there may be periods of open discussion between the various parties present in the hearing room, the chairman keeps the discussion focused and intervenes if things get out of hand.

8. The grievance committee consists of objective individuals who have no direct involvement with the parties to the grievance or the matter being brought before the committee.

9. Hearings involving outside persons are scheduled well in advance, and every effort is made to schedule them at a time and place when all parties and witnesses involved can attend, even if it means holding a nighttime or weekend session.

10. Notices of all meetings and decisions reached are conveyed in writing to all key parties.

11. Committee decisions are communicated to all key parties in such a manner that they will all receive the information about the same time.

12. The individual initiating the grievance as well as the party being grieved against are encouraged to bring witnesses.

13. The party initiating the grievance and the person being grieved against are both allowed to be present throughout the entire hearing (except when the committee meets to deliberate).

14. Members of the grievance committee discuss the process and the content only among themselves.

IRREGULARITIES

4. The committee appears "gentler" or more respectful toward one party than toward the other and does not appear objective in the manner in which it conducts the hearing.

5. The grievance committee is composed primarily of either students, classroom faculty, or field instructors.

6. The chairman is an individual who does not command the respect of the other committee members and has questionable or unknown leadership abilities. It may be an individual so new to his student, faculty, or field instruction role with the school that his lack of general knowledge proves to be a handicap.

7. The chairman provides limited or delayed leadership, allowing those present to get "out of order," engage in free-for-all discussion, and have several different conversations going on simultaneously.

8. One or more of the committee members appear obviously biased by virtue of personal involvement with the matter at hand or the parties to it.

9. Hearings are scheduled on short notice with little or no effort made to ensure that all key parties and witnesses can attend.

10. Notices and decisions are communicated orally in a rather informal manner.

11. Outcomes are communicated in such a manner that some key parties receive word long before others.

12. Witnesses are discouraged *or* inappropriately pressured to attend through direct or implied threats.

13. One party or the other is permitted to be present and hear the testimony of witnesses, while the other is not granted this right.

14. There is obvious "fraternizing" between members of the grievance committee and one of the two parties involved; committee members discuss

PROPER CONDUCT

the grievance process and content with noninvolved third parties or with witnesses and key parties, outside of formal grievance hearings and meetings.

15. Witnesses are present only while testifying; they are not permitted to hear the testimony of anyone else, including the complainant and respondent. Likewise, witnesses are prevented from talking with one another about the grievance or the issue at hand while waiting to be called into the hearing room.

15. The chairman fails to ask witnesses to leave when they have finished testifying and fails to advise them not to discuss the case with each other while waiting to be called.

16. The hearing is tape-recorded.

16. No notes are taken, or they are taken by one person designated as note-taker. This relies heavily on the selective recording and memory of the recorder and does not provide a full, accurate record of content as well as conclusions and process.

17. Hearings are held in a private place with no interruptions permitted and in a room where committee deliberations cannot be overheard by others.

17. There are interruptions for phone calls and nongrievance matters; the room is noisy, ''freezing cold'' or otherwise uncomfortable, and not conducive to confidential, important discussions and decision-making.

18. The committee follows a time schedule as it conducts the hearing. This ensures roughly equal time for both parties during all phases of the hearing.

18. No time schedule is followed, with the result that one side or the other consumes a disproportionate or excessive amount of time presenting its arguments.

19. Both parties and all witnesses are allowed to bring out their point of view and all pertinent factors through objective questioning and attentive listening from committee members.

19. Key parties and witnesses are ''interrogated'' in such a way that they are not able to present their complete viewpoint or facts.

20. Detailed reports regarding the general procedings and the findings are kept out of the student's individual personnel folder. If something must be entered, it is done in brief, summary form.

20. Detailed reports regarding the process and content of the grievance are filed in the student's file, regardless of the grievance outcome. Additional copies float around rather freely among committee members (after they are no longer on the committee), faculty, and others.

21. The fact that a grievance was held, the names of the key parties, the final outcome, and perhaps some of the key issues addressed may become known to other students, faculty, and field instructors *after* the entire procedure is finished.

21. Not only the bare facts, but also the details of what was said by each party and personal viewpoints judging or reacting to this material are shared by committee members in informal discussions with faculty, field instructors, and students following completion of the grievance.

22. School newspaper reporters, the public news media, and other outsiders are not permitted to be present during the grievance or to hear or see tapes and transcripts of the proceedings (unless special state or federal laws mandate access by such persons).

22. Outsiders are present during the grievance or have access to tapes and transcripts.

Lawsuits

Consumers of various kinds of services are becoming increasingly lawsuit-minded. When something does not go their way, there is a tendency to head for the nearest attorney and sue the offending party. The vast majority of disputes among students, classroom faculty, and field instructors are resolved through an informal discussion process or the school grievance mechanism. However, a few students remain unsatisfied and bring suit or threaten to take legal action against the school or its field instructors. Thus, field instructors must ask themselves, their school, and their employer a few key questions: "If I am sued, who will defend me? Who will pay my attorney's fees? Will I be given time off with pay to attend the many meetings a suit would involve? If I should lose the suit, who will pay court-awarded damages?"

Field instructors should be aware that their NASW malpractice coverage will *not* cover disputes between students and field instructors or supervisees and supervisors. If a client accuses the supervisee of malpractice and names the supervisor in the suit, the field instructor is covered. But if the student sues the supervisor for "malpractice," the NASW insurance coverage does not apply.*

A student who wants to sue someone first consults his attorney to see if he has a case. If the attorney is interested and agrees to represent him, the defendant receives a formal notice that the student has brought action against him. The plaintiff may seek a reversal or negation of the action he opposes, or he may seek "damages" as well: cash payment for alleged direct or indirect losses, inconveniences, or expenses incurred as a result of the action or decision. The trend is to ask for extremely high damages; the court may award the full amount but probably will not, even if it rules in favor of the plaintiff. The defendant then obtains his own attorney. If the suit seems absolutely absurd, the defendant's attorney can suggest to the opposing side that the case be dropped or an out-of-court settlement reached. Of the few suits brought by social work students, most never get past this stage. However, if no agreement is reached, both attorneys begin their "depositions." The plaintiff and defendant, as well as witnesses, are interviewed with a court reporter present to take verbatim notes. The transcripts are typed up, and both plaintiff and defendant receive copies. These are reviewed in depth, and each side may produce written statements answering questions or responding to issues and points raised in these documents. Depending on the nature of the suit, this process can take months, perhaps even a year or two. When key witnesses have been identified and all parties interviewed, a date is set for a formal

court hearing. This may take place rather informally in the judge's chambers, may or may not be open to the public (with prior news media publicity), and may or may not involve a jury. Once the court decision has been reached, the student either accepts the decision or challenges it through various appeal mechanisms.

The fact that a lawsuit has been filed is usually a matter of public record. Some details regarding the case will be on file in the courthouse and open to review by anyone, unless it is of a highly sensitive nature. This would rarely be the case in a suit involving social work education issues, unless accusations of mental illness, sexual harassment, or similar issues are involved. Certain information (such as the content of depositions) may be withheld in an otherwise public record. Thus, the field instructor would be technically free to talk with others about some of the details of his suit. However, this may not be in his best interests, and he should consult his attorney before discussing the case in the community. The plaintiff often talks about his point of view rather freely, which makes the defendant want to present his viewpoint to other students and his social work collegues in the community. But this could make it more difficult for the attorney to represent him effectively.

A lawsuit can drag on interminably. Mountains of papers will be generated, and a field instructor who is involved will find it a tremendous drain on his time and energy. Because it can be such a lengthy process, he should keep all notes, examples of the student's work, and related materials so that he will need to rely as little as possible on memory alone. As soon as the field instructor knows he is becoming involved in a suit, key witnesses should be located and their whereabouts shared with the attorney. Key communications with potential witnesses should be "process-recorded" immediately after they occur, to help in recalling them later on if necessary. However, do not tape-record these communications without the individual's knowledge and permission. Some state laws regard information obtained in this manner as "inadmissable": The information cannot be presented in court and is therefore useless.

In summary, if a field instructor is threatened with a lawsuit, he should not overreact. If the student wishes to sue, he'll sue regardless of what the supervisor says or does. A defensive, "you-can't-do-that-to-me" reaction only whets the plaintiff's appetite for a suit. Remain calm and try to work out the difference of opinion through all available mechanisms other than the courts. If a lawsuit actually occurs, the field instructor must consult *immediately* with his own attorney. The school and professional colleagues may all offer advice, but the defendant's own attorney must become involved at the earliest possible moment. If a supervisee threatens to sue, the attorney should be advised that a suit may occur and be fully informed of the issues so that he is prepared to become formally involved if necessary. If the school considers its agency-based field instructors to be a part of its faculty, some negotiation may be needed between

*Letter from Richard C. Imbert, President, American Professional Agency, Inc., October 11, 1979. He further states: "Disputes between employer and employees arising out of performance or hiring and firing procedures are not covered by any policy issued by any company in the country. These are obviously areas that are not insurable."

the agency and the school attorneys to determine which should represent the field instructor in the action. Is he considered an agent of the school or of the agency for purposes of the suit? Would there be any special advantage or disadvantage to the field instructor if he were considered in either category?

Preventing Grievances and Lawsuits

The key to preventing most grievances and lawsuits is communication. Supervisees who are treated with respect, as adult learners and as human beings with feelings, rarely sue when constructive criticism, even of a serious nature, is communicated in a positive manner. Students who know well in advance about their poor performance and impending failing grade generally will not sue out of retaliation. Application of the principles presented in Chapters 11 and 12 on sharing evaluatory feedback with supervisees will reduce the probability of grievances and suits.

However, a few supervisees may file grievances or bring legal action even if the best possible educational and supervisory approaches have been used. Some do so because they feel they are right and simply do not agree with the assessment or recommendation; others block out reality factors through their own emotional needs and reactions, failing to see that perhaps the assessment was accurate and the action taken justified. Supervisors who keep detailed notes throughout their experience with the supervisee and who implement the approaches suggested throughout this text will be in a much stronger position for preventing formal challenges and defending their viewpoints than supervisors who do not.*

Confidentiality Issues

Confidentiality is a quasi-legal issue. Field instructors must protect the confidentiality of information pertaining to clients and certain aspects of the internal workings of the agencies that employ them. Violations can occur if students take undisguised material from the field into the classroom. Classroom instructors may or may not provide clear guidelines for students to follow to disguise identifying data appropriately. If the student's placement is in a federal program (a veterans' hospital or the Social Security Administration, for example), it is a violation of federal law to take undisguised material from the agency.† It is possible that some version of the Privacy Act will become mandatory for local government and some private settings in the very near future.

---

*Of course, adherence to the desired principles is no guarantee that a supervisee will not challenge assessments and decisions.

†The Federal Privacy Act of 1974, Public Law 93-579, Enacted December 31, 1974, and effective September 27, 1975, *Federal Register*, Part V–VI, October 8, 1975.

Most schools of social work ask their students to bring "live" case examples from their field placement experience into the classroom at various points during their training. Casework faculty may ask for diagnostic analyses of case dynamics, a social history, or an illustration of a certain type of behavior or interviewing technique. Assignments may call for bringing process-recordings, summaries, tape recordings, or other materials into the classroom. Unfortunately, many schools provide very limited guidance on how to preserve the confidentiality of this material. In fact, unbeknownst to most students, some faculty who have had no direct client contact in years may rely on student-produced examples for live cases to work with in future classes or for use as examples in papers they are writing. Thus, the material may receive a rather wide distribution, and appropriate precautions must be taken to preserve confidentiality. The guidelines presented here should be followed along with any provided by the school. If the ideas presented here, the confidentiality requirements presented by the school, and those of the agency do not agree, select the ones that are *strictest* and follow them.

Confidentiality Guidelines for Students Who Take Case Material from the Field into the Classroom

1. All names of clients, relatives, and significant others mentioned by name in a case record or recording must be altered. Fake names or incorrect initials can be used. If names are changed rather than simply erased or obliterated, a notation should appear clearly indicating that this has been done.

2. If the interview or case material concerns a highly unusual or much-publicized situation that could be identified easily even after the client's name has been changed, the nature of the primary diagnosis or presenting problem, proper nouns, and certain identifying information may also need alteration. True, this may affect the reality of the situation and make it more difficult for the student to adequately present what really happened, but if it comes to a choice between presenting accurate recordings in the classroom and preserving the privacy and confidentiality of the consumers served, the client's needs *must* take priority.

3. Material of a highly confidential or incriminating nature should not be taken into the classroom at all. If a student is not certain whether his recording fits into this category or not, he should consult his field instructor for guidance.

4. Process-recordings are the property of the agency and should not be copied or retained by the student. They should be turned in to the student's field instructor when their usefulness has ended or at the termination of field placement and should be stored separately from the official case record.

5. All material which students wish to take into the classroom should be reviewed first by the field instructor to ensure that proper measures have been taken to preserve confidentiality.

6. Tape and video-recorded material cannot be adequately disguised to preserve confidentiality. Thus, the client's permission must be secured before a student takes it into the classroom. Furthermore, certain technical steps should be taken to conceal identity even when the client has given permission for use of the material. Students should seek specific direction from their supervisor.*

The Family Educational Rights and Privacy Act (the "Buckley Amendment")† regulates the confidentiality of academic records for individual students. The most important aspect of concern to students and field instructors is the fact that this federal law grants students the right of access to their files, and their written consent must be obtained before information from the record can be revealed to others. Many schools consider their field instructors to be part of the faculty and thus grant them access to the files without student permission. However, this access is generally limited to those students whom the person will be supervising, and students may or may not be aware that field instructors can and do review their files. In addition, when schools gather references on prospective students, the reference request may contain a statement that it will be shared with the student and should be written with this in mind. This occurs because of the law's requirement that the school not keep information regarding the student to which he does not have access. In keeping with this principle, all evaluations and references written by the field instructor, even after the

student has completed placement, should be shared with the student, and he should receive a copy for his own use.

A student's performance in field is a matter that field instructors must keep confidential. Many students graduate and become practitioners in the local community. Thus, those who supervise them must refrain from irresponsible gossip regarding their supervisee's abilities, problems, and performance. Such details should be discussed only with those persons directly involved with the field placement experience (e.g., the field instructor's supervisor, a faculty liaison person). Several field instructors in the same agency may consult one another regarding their students in a form of peer supervision, and this is acceptable as long as their discussions go no further. Field instructors must also avoid discussing one student's performance with another and make certain that appropriate precautions are observed to prevent unauthorized access to or disclosures of written performance evaluations. If a client or recipient of services is a friend, colleague, or relative of the student in placement, the field instructor may need to ensure that the student does not gain access to that individual's record out of curiosity. Students should have access only to those official agency records with whom they will be working. In addition, students must be oriented to the procedures to be followed should they receive a subpoena to appear in court or produce a case record in connection with their work, and be advised of other legal/ethical confidentiality procedures required by the setting. Students may also need to be informed of coverage under state privileged communication statutes or special state statutes regulating the confidentiality of certain record materials (e.g. medical or mental health records) and governing the type and manner of disclosures that can be made from such records.‡

---

*From Suanna J. Wilson, *Confidentiality in Social Work: Issues and Principles* (New York: Free Press, 1978), pp. 35–36.

†Amends Public Law 93-568, effective November 19, 1974. See also Department of HEW, Office of the Secretary, "Privacy Rights of Parents and Students," Part II, "Final Rule on Education Records," *Federal Register* (June 17, 1976), pp. 24662–24675.

‡See Wilson, *Confidentiality in Social Work: Issues and Principles*, for a much more detailed discussion of ethical and legal aspects of confidentiality and privileged communication.

Conclusion

Field instruction is a serious matter and one that must be conducted jointly by field instructor, school, and student. Schools have a responsibility to select and train field instructors for maximum effectiveness in their role, and field instructors must view themselves as part of the educational team and seek ways to share information and have an impact on their local social work programs as well as on their individual student supervisees. Informed students are best equipped to make mature use of their field experience and should be consulted for reactions and suggestions to improve their experiences. All involved with field instruction must be assertive in expressing their needs, ideas, and recommendations for change in a constructive manner. It is hoped that the ideas presented in this text have provided food for thought, factual information, and a sense of support for all those concerned with improving the field instruction process so that they may work together toward developing and maintaining effective programs and approaches that will produce BSW and MSW graduates with the skills necessary for effective social work practice in today's complex society.

Appendixes

APPENDIX A

Increasing Self-awareness as a Field Instructor

There is much emphasis on the need for students to achieve "self-awareness" as part of their social work training. However, it is equally important for those who supervise students to achieve their own form of self-awareness as field instructors. What are we like as supervisors? What characterizes our supervisory style? What would it be like to work under our supervision? There may be significant differences between the way in which students perceive us in our role and how we perceive ourselves.

The following exercises are designed to stimulate the field instructor to think about himself and some of the subjective factors that influence his manner of interacting with supervisees. Honest and perhaps painful soul-searching must occur in order to complete these exercises effectively. Private inadequacies and insecurities may surface and be stated in writing. Thus, trainers who ask field instructors or supervisors to do these exercises *must not require that the answers be shared with anyone, including themselves*. The mere process of thinking about the exercises will produce the desired learning experience, and privacy must be assured to bring about maximum learning. Of course, trainers can make themselves available to discuss the results with instructors who wish consultation or feedback.

1. Assessing the impact of your own field placement experience

If you are a field instructor who is qualified for this role in accordance with the standards presented in this text, it is very likely that you yourself underwent a student internship or field placement while studying for your social work degree. This experience and your reaction to it will affect your approach to the students you now supervise. The following exercise is designed to increase your awareness of its impact on your own supervisory approaches and values.

A. Turn a large sheet of paper lengthwise and divide it into columns like this:

POSITIVES		NEGATIVES	
Experiences	Feelings	Experiences	Feelings

In the first column, list each experience you had as a student in field placement that you consider "good." For example, "My field instructor was warm and supportive," "I was allowed to be creative," "He never let me give up," "Staff took us out to lunch at the end of field placement," "We used a written educational contract," "Explanations were clear," and so on. In the second column, put an adjective that describes how you *felt* as a result of each good experience you have listed: "secure," "wanted," and so forth. In the third column, list experiences, attitudes, approaches, and other factors that you consider to be "bad" things about your field placement experience, and in the last column the feelings you had as a result.

Now, analyze your results. Is the first column much longer than the third? Did you have difficulty remembering how you felt in response to either positive or negative experiences? Did you relive some of your feelings and reactions as you completed the form?

B. Now take another piece of paper and create three columns labeled "experience," "impact," and "action." In the "experience" column, list each experience, positive and negative, that you have given in the first and third columns in Part A.

In the "impact" column, for each experience listed, describe how you feel it might affect your approach to field instruction now that you are (or are about to become) a student supervisor. Be totally honest. Some of your experiences may have a favorable impact; they may cause you to be more effective than if you had not had the experience. On the other hand, some may cause you to overreact, overidentify, overcompensate, be excessively lenient or rigid, or view field instruction through rose-colored glasses. Some elements of your experience will hinder rather than facilitate your effectiveness as a field instructor. Achieving self-awareness in these areas will help you channel your experiences and feelings constructively rather than destructively in your supervisory role.

Finally, use the "action" column to describe anything you feel you should do or avoid doing to ensure that your experiences and resulting feelings do not interfere with your effectiveness as a supervisor.

2. Examining your positive and negative qualities and your own supervisor's response to them

It is important that you be aware of your own professional strengths and limitations. An awareness of your own supervisor's knowledge and handling of these areas will also enable you to be more sensitive to issues and techniques in handling evaluatory feedback with your supervisees.

Think about those aspects of your personality, attitudes, abilities, work habits, skills, and personal attributes that are *positives*. What characteristics do you feel especially proud of? Be *personal*—avoid listing professional accomplishments such as "I have my MSW degree" or "I published an article in a social work journal." Instead, describe *personal qualities* such as "I'm always on time," "I work extra hours when required, and I'm not a clockwatcher," "I take criticism without becoming defensive," "I always follow through," "I'm very patient," or "I'm always neat and well organized." List as many things as you can think of in a column labeled "positives."

Now, in a second column list all *negatives* (deficits or limitations). Again, be personal and frank. Don't say, "I need more training," "I've never supervised anyone before," or "I need to do more reading." Instead, "I lose my temper easily," "I have trouble being critical of others," "I tend to procrastinate," "I hate paperwork and sometimes make sloppy errors," "I am sometimes rigid" or "I react defensively when criticized" are much more meaningful responses.

When you have finished both lists, think about your relationship with the person who evaluates your performance now. Do you think he or she is aware of all of the positives and negatives that you have listed about yourself? Go back over both lists, and put a check mark by those items that your supervisor is aware of *and* has discussed with you or put into a written performance evaluation. Put an "X" by items you feel certain he or she is aware of but has *not* discussed with you or put into an evaluation. The remaining items will be those that you feel he or she has no knowledge of.

Study the results. Do you feel your superior is sharing reactions with you in a frank, honest manner? Are you getting sufficient recognition for your positives? Are you "waiting for the ax to fall" when he or she discovers some of your negative qualities? Do you think the two of you are in agreement as to what constitute your positive and negative qualities, or are you thinking that he or she really doesn't know you at all? Did you have difficulty listing either positives or negatives? Why? If your supervisor were aware of your less than positive qualities and they were affecting your job performance, how would you hope that he or she would handle evaluatory feedback with you?

Now consider your current or potential supervisee. What do you think he will want and need from you in your evaluation of his strengths and limitations? How do you think he would want you to give him evaluatory feedback regarding positives and negatives? How do you think he might feel as a result of this process?

3. Working under your supervision

What would you be like to work for? What would it be like to be a student under your supervision? Pretend that you are the student and have been assigned to yourself for supervision. Write a short description.

4. Expectations of supervisees

Everyone has certain unique expectations of supervisees, different from those of other supervisors. What basic kinds of attitudes, behaviors, or work habits do you expect of anyone you would supervise, regardless of their level of training?

On the other hand, what kinds of attitudes or behaviors on the part of supervisees would irritate you the most? What kinds of things do you feel you have the least tolerance for?

5. Your own supervisory needs

What kinds of things would you like or need from your own supervisor when you start supervising students? Be very specific. Do you need this person to relate to you differently from the way he or she did before you assumed your supervisory role?

6. Areas of difficulty

What kinds of things do you think will give you the most difficulty as a new field instructor? Are there situations that you feel especially insecure about handling? On the other hand, are there any aspects of your role as a field instructor that you feel especially confident about, things that you feel you could handle effectively?

7. Reactions to specific problem situations

The following are characteristics or problems that you might encounter with student supervisees. Use the following code to rate *each* item:

C : I have worked with this kind of thing before and feel comfortable with it.

U : I have worked with this kind of thing before and know from experience that I am not comfortable with it.

NC : I have never worked with this kind of situation or student, but I feel I could do so effectively and with comfort.

? : I have never worked with this kind of situation or student and am not certain whether I'd be comfortable with it or not.

A. ____ The supervisee who comes to you repeatedly throughout the day with simple questions

B. ____ The individual who rarely comes with questions—who seems to function almost too independently

C. ____ The student who seems to know everything already

D. ____ The student who is older than you are

E. ____ The student who is a good deal younger than you are

F. ____ The supervisee who has more knowledge or expertise than you do in some areas

G. ____ The intellectually gifted student

H. ____ The student who seems not to learn very quickly

I. ____ The student who questions or challenges your knowledge and/or authority (a defensive learner)

J. ____ The student who needs to be given the same instructions over and over

K. ____ The supervisee who can't seem to be kept busy, who works so quickly you can't keep up with him

L. ____ The student who insists on putting in extra hours and sometimes keeps you late because of his involvement in so many things

M. ____ The student with significant deficits in grammar, spelling, sentence structure, or some other aspect of written communication

N. _____ The student you have to keep after all the time because he doesn't follow through with things

O. _____ The student with a lot of past experience and some unlearning to do

P. _____ The student with emotional problems affecting performance in field

Q. _____ The student who keeps bringing you articles to read and discuss with him

R. _____ The student who sticks close to you and obviously wants to join you almost daily for coffee breaks and lunch

S. _____ The student who sits silently when you give feedback regarding his performance, although you sense that he doesn't agree with everything or is having some other reaction that he is not sharing with you

T. _____ The student who is a member of an ethnic minority group

U. _____ A physically handicapped student (blind, an amputee, wheelchair bound, deaf, etc.)

V. _____ The student who is a middle-aged woman with years of volunteer experience

W. _____ The individual whose attendance is irregular

X. _____ The student who idealizes all professionals

Y. _____ The student with a recent or current personal experience with illness, disability, divorce, death in the family, or other major crisis

Z. _____ The student who analyzes you as a field instructor in his discussions with fellow students

AA. _____ The supervisee who is naive and easily shocked and requires much hand-holding in the beginning of placement

BB. _____ The supervisee who seems to show little or no emotion

CC. _____ The student who doesn't seem especially interested in his field placement experience

8. "What would you do if..."

Following are some situations that a field instructor typically encounters in working with students. Various responses are suggested. None is absolutely "right" or "wrong," although one or two may be more effective than the others. All possible choices have been used by field instructors at one time or another. Circle the response that most nearly matches how you would handle the situation. Be honest with yourself in responding; avoid giving answers that you think you ought to give. If you don't like any of the suggested answers, write in your own, but avoid doing this excessively. There may also be times when you will want to do more than one thing in response to the situation presented. If so, rank the choices in the order in which you would take the actions.

Experienced field instructors or trainers will recognize patterns in trainee responses to these items. For example, certain responses would indicate that the person tends to give the student a great deal of responsibility rather than sheltering him; other patterns might indicate a very protective attitude, and so on. The interpretation of these patterns is not provided here so that this can remain a self-instructional exercise. Those who use this exercise for training can undoubtedly provide their own interpretations for individual learners or for feedback to the group.

A. It is the first day of field placement. Your student was told to meet you at 10 A.M. He arrives instead at 8:30 A.M., eager to meet with you and get started. You aren't ready to see him then and are very busy. What would you do?

  I. You send him out for coffee and a self-guided tour of the agency and have him meet you at 10 A.M. in your office.

  II. You call your supervisor or someone in charge of in-service training and ask that person to give the student some reading to do until 10 A.M.

  III. You take the student with you to whatever you had planned to do at 8:30.

  IV. You personally select several library books for the student to read until 10 A.M., even though this makes you a few minutes late for your 8:30 appointment.

B. You refer your student to the procedure manual to look up a procedure. Even though he says he's read it and it made sense to him, he keeps asking you the same questions over and over about the procedure, and you know the answers are in the manual. How would you respond?

  I. Confront the student with his behavior pattern.

  II. Simply tell him to stop asking you these questions.

  III. Do nothing.

  IV. Double-check what's in the manual.

  V. Make yourself less available to the student as a means of curtailing his inappropriate questions and forcing him to rely more on the manual.

  VI. Refer him to another staff member to get his questions answered.

C. Your student attends interdisciplinary medical rounds with you. One of the doctors is obviously having a bad day and makes some very inappropriate, judgmental, and rather crude remarks regarding a patient during the rounds. It's a bad scene.

Your student sits there quietly and doesn't say anything. When rounds end, the *first* thing you do is:

   I. Nothing. The student has got to learn that this is part of reality in a medical setting.

   II. Assume the student was upset and comfort him afterward in private.

   III. Explain your point of view and give the student an explanation for the doctor's behavior.

   IV. Ask the student what he thought about the whole thing.

   V. Share with the student honestly and openly your feelings toward the doctor for acting as he did.

D. Your student shows up for field placement one day wearing thong sandals. This, in combination with a mod hairdo and a casual manner of dress, gives the student a definite "hippie" look. The student is doing all right in field placement and actually relates rather well to his clients.

   I. Say nothing. If he relates well with this clients, his manner of dress must not be causing any problem. Thus you feel there's no need to deal with it.

   II. Say nothing. How the student dresses is his or her own business.

   III. Thongs are unprofessional in this setting. You confront the student with this and require that he wear more appropriate shoes in the future.

   IV. More power to him! He's able to be an individual and is not afraid to express it.

   V. Send him home for an instant change of shoes.

   VI. Say nothing, but keep him away from clients and in the office so the fewest possible people will see his attire.

E. Your student has done some process-recording. You have read it, made written supervisory comments, and returned it to him. Several days later, at your regularly scheduled conference, the student takes issue with your interpretation of some of his behavior in the interview situation and becomes quite defensive.

   I. Confront him with his defensiveness.

   II. Explain your point of view until he understands it.

   III. Stop discussing it—you're not accomplishing anything—he's just not listening to what you have to say.

   IV. Agree to disagree.

   V. Ask him why he's projecting so much anger onto you.

F. You work closely with a psychologist in your setting. One day he complains to you about your student. "What's with Henry Smith? He seems so slow about everything and doesn't seem to know what he's doing. He keeps asking me all these stupid questions." Obviously he is annoyed with your student's simplistic, beginning-level questions and bumbling approach (typical of many new students).

   I. Tell the student what the psychologist said and discuss it with him.

   II. Say nothing about the incident to the student.

   III. Say nothing now, but plan definitely to do so at a later date.

G. You have been working with your student for about six weeks and he has had exposure to a variety of case situations. He seems quite uncomfortable with middle-aged adults. His contacts with these individuals are more superficial and less effective than with other kinds of clients.

   I. Tell him you realize that there must be some kind of transference taking place or something from his personal life that is making it difficult for him to work with middle-aged adults. Explain that this is quite evident in his interviews. Would he like to talk about it?

   II. Confront him with your observation and see how he responds.

   III. Say nothing. Maybe it will pass with time and more exposure to this kind of client.

   IV. Make a note to yourself to mention this in his performance evaluation and recommend there that it would be best that he not work with middle-aged adults.

H. A fellow field instructor tells you he saw your student doing something highly inappropriate that he knows you'd disapprove of. However, he asks you not to mention to anyone that he told you about it.

   I. Thank him for the information and do nothing further.

   II. Confront the student: "Someone told me . . ."

   III. Tell the fellow field instructor that you *must* tell your student and cannot keep it quiet.

   IV. Ask around to see if anyone else observed the incident.

   V. Do nothing now, but make a note of it so you'll remember to mention it in the student's performance evaluation when it comes due.

I. Your student has been in field placement for four months. For the third time, he has failed to turn in his statistics when due. The clerical supervisor tells you angrily that you'd better do something about this chronic problem because it's making it difficult for her to meet her own deadlines.

   I. Support the student—after all, you sometimes get your own statistical report in late too—but give him a gentle reminder that he needs to be more prompt.

   II. Tell the student what the clerical supervisor said and let him have it (constructively, of course).

III. Do nothing and wait for the clerical supervisor to let the student have it.

IV. Don't tell the student what the clerical supervisor said but issue a sort of ultimatum: You expect the statistics to be in on time from now on!

J. Your supervisor has an informal contact with your student when you aren't around. You discover later that she gave the student some advice that goes directly against what you have been telling him. How would you handle this?

I. Tell your supervisor you found out about the incident and you resent her interference with your student.

II. Ignore it for now and wait to see if it happens again before doing anything about it.

III. Tell the student he is to seek guidance from you and not your supervisor. Clarify the chain of command for him.

IV. Ventilate about the incident to a fellow field instructor or nonsupervisory staff member.

K. You learn that your student has spoken to your supervisor in confidence. You are afraid she has complained about you or made negative comments about you as a field instructor.

I. Tell your student she must share with you what she discussed with your supervisor.

II. Tell your supervisor he's to let you know in the future when students come to him—this should be automatic.

III. Figure that when your supervisor gets ready to share with you what happened with the student, he will. You can't or shouldn't interfere. He'll let you know about it when he thinks it best to do so.

IV. Tell your supervisor you feel uneasy about the situation and ask him how he handled it with the student and why.

L. Your student wants to know why Jack Doe's student doesn't have to do some of the things you've been asking her to do.

I. Check with Jack Doe. Perhaps you *have* been asking your student to do too much.

II. Tell your student it doesn't matter what Jack Doe's student is doing. You, not Jack Doe, are her field instructor.

III. Explain why you feel the things you've been asking her to do are important and emphasize that you expect her to continue.

IV. Ask her how she feels about the situation.

V. Ask her why she told you about Jack Doe's student.

M. You give your student things to do and he doesn't follow through or is very slow. Which of the following would you do?

I. Explain your perception of the problem to the student and point out that he needs to change his behavior.

II. Ask him what's going on.

III. You're too busy to keep after him all the time, so you let it ride and let the student suffer the consequences.

N. Your student tells you that you haven't been spending enough time with him. You have been spending about an hour and a half a week in supervisory conferences with the student. You *have* been very busy with a lot of crises in your caseload. However, your agency is also somewhat understaffed, and everyone carries a heavy work load at all times.

I. Apologize and promise to spend more time with him.

II. Explain why you haven't been able to spend more time with him and promise to try to do better.

III. Explain why you haven't been able to spend more time, and let him know that this situation may not change and he'll have to learn to adjust to it.

IV. Tell the student you're giving him the amount of time recommended by the school and it is unrealistic of him to ask for more.

V. Talk to your supervisor or another field instructor about helping out with some of the training of your student because you're so busy, or maybe even explore the possibility of having him transferred to another field instructor who has more time to give.

O. You've done your final written performance evaluation on your student and have shared it with him. It is a rather low satisfactory: He just barely made it. He doesn't agree with it, however, and refuses to sign it.

I. Tell him it's okay if he doesn't want to sign.

II. Tell him he's got to sign. It is required by the school.

III. Get two witnesses to sign, stating that the student refused to sign.

IV. Tell him he has the right to add a written statement if he doesn't agree with your evaluation.

V. Explain to him in detail why it's important that he sign the evaluation.

P. You have told your student that his process-recordings are due within two days after each interview, but he meets this deadline only rarely and offers various reasons for his persistent delays. This problem has been discussed repeatedly in your supervisory conferences, yet it persists.

I. Tell him his process-recordings must be in on time from now on "or else."

II. Tell him you'll have to put a comment in his performance evaluation regarding this problem if he doesn't cooperate better.

III. Forget about it. It's obvious his behavioral pattern isn't going to change. Perhaps you should be more flexible in your requirements regarding due dates for recordings.

IV. Stop giving him process-recording to do. Obviously he is resisting it for some reason, and it would be better to select some other instructional method.

V. Ask the student what he thinks you should do about this problem.

VI. Ask him what the problem is.

Q. You want your casework student to take a training course for new field instructors given by your agency. You feel it's important for graduate students to take this training, since most of them will be supervising someone soon after graduation. However, the school feels that only administration students should take the course, because it's not part of the overall educational objectives for casework students and takes too much time away from casework activities.

    I. Explain to the student why she will be unable to take the course. You do not share your disappointment at the school's viewpoint or the fact that you do not agree with it.

    II. Explain why she will be unable to take the course. You do share with the student your disappointment in the school's viewpoint and the fact that you do not agree with it.

    III. Try to get the school to change its mind. If unsuccessful, you would then do (I).

    IV. Try to get the school to change its mind. If unsuccessful, you would then do (II).

    V. Try to get the school to change its mind. If unsuccessful, you let the student take the course, but do not tell the school until the end of the field placement.

    VI. Complain to your supervisor or administrator about the problem and let him see what he can do about it. You will accept whatever he and the school decide, even if it means that the student will be unable to take the course.

    VII. Same as (VI), but let the student take the course even if the school still doesn't go along with the idea, without telling the school.

R. You are a new field instructor and have just written your first performance evaluation at the end of your student's field placement Your own supervisor has asked to review it. You have rated the student as outstanding. However, your supervisor reacts strongly, claiming that "this is not an outstanding student—he's only satisfactory" and asks you to change your rating. You've been giving positive feedback to the student all semester, and this puts you in a very awkward position.

    I. Swallow hard and do as your supervisor asks.

    II. Look him in the eye, tell him it's your student, not his, and refuse to change the evaluation.

    III. Explain the problems you feel this action would create for you and the student at this point and ask your supervisor to let it pass the way you've written it. If he doesn't agree, you go along with his decision.

    IV. Same as (III), but if he doesn't agree, you fight him tooth and nail, refusing to change your evaluation.

    V. Take the matter up with your supervisor's supervisor.

Would you tell the student about this incident and/or your feelings about it? _____ yes _____ no.

S. You and your student have been planning for some time for her to do a major case presentation at a meeting involving twelve interdisciplinary staff on Wednesday at 9:30 A.M. Your student's presentation is the main agenda. At 9:15 the student calls in sick.

    I. Cancel or postpone the meeting and plan to talk with the student about the possible meaning of her untimely illness.

    II. Cancel or postpone the meeting and hope your student feels better tomorrow.

    III. Pinch-hit for the student and plan to talk with her about the possible meaning of her untimely illness.

    IV. Pinch-hit for the student and hope she feels better tomorrow.

    V. Cancel or postpone the meeting and plan to let the student have it for leaving you in an awkward situation on such short notice.

    V. Review the student's past absences and see if this same kind of thing has happened before.

    VII. Make a note to mention this incident in the student's written performance evaluation.

APPENDIX B

Typical Problem Situations for Field Instructors

The following situations are all based on actual incidents reported by field instructors, students and faculty. They are typical of the problems that supervisors face as they work with students, especially in providing casework or administrative guidance.

These situations are designed for use in group training sessions with field instructors; they can be assigned as homework or used for group discussion as well as individual reflection. Some include portions of student interviews.* If

training is being provided in a group situation, the trainer might have two members act out the interview by reading the parts of the student and the interviewee rather than distribute written copies to the group. Most of the problem situations can be role-played in various ways so as to demonstrate the field instructor's chosen approach. Most experienced student supervisors will identify readily with many of the issues reflected in these exercises.

Problems involving students

1. A Student Is Very Ineffective in Leading a Staff Meeting

Your administration student is halfway through his field placement and has been learning, among other things, how to lead staff meetings. He has prepared an agenda and presented it to staff. You attended the meeting but played no active role. It was a terrible experience. The student was disorganized and obviously nervous, and gave inaccurate and conflicting information during his presentation. Staff showed obvious boredom and impatience with the student's bumbling efforts. At the close of the session the student distributed a form seeking evaluative feedback from the audience. You glance at the forms as you help collect them. The staff are merciless and several make downright unkind remarks about the student. You and your student had

planned to meet immediately after the session to critique it together. Questions for consideration:

- A. What kind of evaluative feedback would you give the student when he asks how *you* think the meeting went?
- B. Would you let him see the staff evaluation forms you collected?
- C. Would you apologize for staff's inattentive behavior during the meeting and/or their unkind remarks on the evaluation forms?
- D. Would you permit the student to lead another staff meeting? If so, how would you deal with staff resistance to meeting with him again?

2. A Student Makes a Bad Blunder That Could Result in a Lawsuit Against the Agency

Your first-year graduate student is in the beginning weeks of field placement in a mental hospital. He has been working with John H., a twenty-four-year-old schizophrenic with acute adult onset. You have been too busy to

*See Suanna J. Wilson, *Recording: Guidelines for Social Workers* (New York: Free Press, 1980), for many additional examples of process-recordings and student interviews using the three- and four-column method of recording interview dialogue, the student's feelings as the dialogue was occurring, his analysis of the client's responses, and supervisory comments. It also contains an extensive discussion on the use of process-recordings in student teaching.

meet formally with your student for about a week, but you know he is working on several process-recordings and has taped one interview with John's parents. The student submits the tape three days before your scheduled conference and you listen to it alone in your office after reviewing the written recordings. These report that John was hospitalized two months ago following a psychotic episode but a couple days ago became nearly comatose and suffered extensive kidney damage. As a result, he was transferred from the psychiatric to the special medical care section of the hospital, where he has been placed on dialysis.* As you listen to the tape, you hear very hysterical parents ventilating a great deal of anger and anxiety over what has happened (their son nearly died). As you listen, the following exchange occurs:

FATHER: I can't understand it. John has always been healthy—I mean, until his emotional upset. He's never had anything physically wrong.
STUDENT: It must be a frightening experience for you.
FATHER: You bet. I'm going to get to the bottom of this. Things like this just don't happen without a reason.
STUDENT: What do you mean?
FATHER: Something must have happened, I just know it. I don't trust those doctors—never have and never will. Martha, I told you we never should have brought him here.
STUDENT: You think they did something to John?
FATHER: Well, that's certainly a possibility, isn't it? You tell me—you work here—what do you think?
STUDENT: Gosh, I'm not sure.
MOTHER: Whad'ya mean "not sure"? You work here, don't you? You don't even know what happens in your own hospital? What kind of a social worker are you anyway?
(silence)
FATHER: Well, what's your supervisor's name? I gotta get some answers around here, and you obviously don't know what you're doing—just like everybody else around this place.
STUDENT: I did read his record last night and there was a report about a possible mix-up in medication. Could that have been it?
FATHER: (sound of chair scraping). What? Give me that again . . .
STUDENT: Now, don't get upset, Mr. H. These kinds of things do happen sometimes, you know. Doctors are human just like everybody else. They try to do their best.
FATHER: Yeah, but he just about murdered my son. Am I supposed to overlook that?
STUDENT: Well, it could have been worse. One of the nurses told me about a man that died in a medical mix-up in a hospital out in California. You should be thankful your son is still alive!
FATHER: C'mon Martha, it's not doing us any good to sit here talking to this guy. Let's get out of here.
(sound of people getting up and leaving and door slamming). End of interview.

Good grief! You would give anything to erase this interview from your mind—to retract its existence. Yet you sit here

*A technique of using a machine to take over the functioning of the kidneys. Most dialysis patients are connected to the machines for four to six hours a day several times a week and would die without this treatment.

listening to it. Obviously your student got in way over his head. He tried as best he could to deal with an unpredictable situation, but he left things in quite a mess!

A. What are the legal ramifications for (1) the patient and his family; (2) the hospital; (3) the school of social work; (4) your student; and (5) yourself?
B. What action, if any, would you take to try to patch up or remedy the situation (in addition to dealing directly with your student)?
C. What would you say to and do with your student? (Role-play your supervisory conference or write it up as if it were a process-recording or taped interview.)
D. Would you tell the school anything about this incident? Why or why not?

3. A Client Living in Filthy Conditions Offers Your Student Some Homemade Food

Your student is about to make his first home visit. The previous worker wrote in the record that the client's house was "the filthiest mess I ever saw; the floor was covered with newspapers and soiled clothing (including diapers), and two infants crawled around through the mess, covered with flies; there was a strong odor of urine and what smelled like rotting garbage; roaches were in abundance." Midway through the interview the former worker reports he was offered a glass of tea and some homemade cookies. How would you advise your student to handle this situation should the same thing happen to him?

4. Preparing a Student for His First Exposure to a Back Ward for Adult Mental Retardates

You and your student are in a facility serving the mentally retarded. For his first few weeks of field placement, the student has been seeing outpatients and their families. He has seen a few mildly retarded children and some retarded adults who have learned a simple skill but are not self-supporting and require some supervision in the community. It is time for the student to experience the other half: institutionalized adults with gross mental deficiency (IQs of 20 to 30 or lower). You can visualize what he'll see when he walks into the ward for the first time: old-looking, adult-size babies in oversized cribs; foul odors from incontinence that no amount of quality nursing care can remove; drooling, crosseyed, poorly coordinated fully grown individuals who sit on the floor picking at their hair and sexual organs indiscriminately or twirl in continuous circles and sometimes clutch at anyone who approaches.

How would you prepare your student for his first exposure to this scene?

5. A Naive Student Makes Her First Home Visit in a High-Crime Neighborhood

Your twenty-one-year-old student is in a first field placement. She has spent her whole life before graduate school in a rural area. Your agency is located in a high-crime neighborhood and serves a hard-core inner-city population. The nature of the field placement requires that the student go out into the community and occasionally make home visits, alone or with another professional. The student was informed of the nature of the setting during the pre-placement interview and wanted to come anyway. You accepted her because she seemed mature and level-headed, though young and inexperienced.

What guidelines would you give her regarding dress, behavior, safety precautions, and so on to help her cope with the neighborhood and move about with minimum risk to herself?

6. You Compliment Your Student for a Job Well Done and Learn Later That He Actually Performed Poorly

Your administration student has been learning to do some public relations. You send him out alone to talk to a local agency regarding the nature of your program and some of the unique characteristics of your client population. You and the student rehearsed his presentation carefully and he seemed well prepared for the assignment. The day afterward he reported that all went well; he felt that he was well received and that staff in the other agency were receptive and responsive. The student reports on some of the audience response to his presentation, and it does appear that he did an effective job. You help him look at some of the reasons why it went over so well and compliment him on his developing skills.

Two weeks later you attend a meeting of a professional group. Several members of the other agency descend on you with complaints regarding your student. Apparently he made a few remarks they didn't exactly appreciate; instead of enhancing public relations, his presentation has caused some ill will between the two agencies. But you had complimented your student on his presentation, which seemed to have gone well!

What do you do now? Do you tell the student about your contact with the staff from the other agency? How would you tell him he really didn't do such a good job after all?

7. A Student Tries to Convert Others to Her Religious Beliefs

Your student is an undergraduate in her first field placement. A deeply religious person, she makes no secret of the fact that she has been "born again" and believes others should have the same experience. One day she comes to field placement wearing a T-shirt with "Repent your sins today!" emblazoned across the back. Your administrator takes one look and exclaims in horror, "*What* is that! Is that one of *our* students?"

A. Suppose you do not share your student's basic beliefs. How would you handle the situation with the student, your administrator, and the school?

B. Suppose you yourself are a "born again" Christian and personally share your student's beliefs (though not her manner of "witnessing"). How would you handle the situation with your student? With the administrator? Would you involve or inform the school in any way? Why?

8. Your Student Seeks Out Another Staff Member for Supervision Without Your Knowledge

You have been working with your student for three months. The placement is about half over. The student has a lot to learn; many behavior and attitude changes are needed to mold her into an effective social worker. Some of your supervisory sessions have been rather "heavy." However, you feel she has real potential. One day a fellow staff member tells you that he had a discussion with your student regarding a case situation "when you weren't around." In exploring this matter further, you discover that the student has been going to your colleague for more than a month, apparently to question and check out your supervisory approach and guidance. The other staff member "just assumed you knew about this" and didn't tell you. As it turns out, some of the advice he has been giving the student directly contradicts some of your suggested approaches, permitting the student to manipulate the two of you and avoid dealing with some important problem areas. You are so angry at the other staff member you could choke him on the spot. However, society frowns upon such action, so you must find another way of handling your anger.

A. What *do* you do with your anger?

B. What do you say to the offending staff member?

C. How do you handle the situation with the student?

D. Do you say anything to your supervisor or administrator or the other staff member's supervisor? Why or why not?

9. When Should a Field Instructor Become a Counselor?

You and Mary have been working together for several weeks now. She has several months left in her final undergraduate field placement. Mary has been having some attendance problems. She frequently comes in late or has to leave suddenly in the middle of the day for a problem at home with her children. Her reasons for being absent always appear valid, but still the problem is annoying. You decide to discuss this with her more fully in your next scheduled supervisory conference.

As you begin sharing your concern about this pattern, Mary offers rather standard explanations: She has an old car that breaks down frequently; one child is sickly; she sometimes has babysitter problems. You move in on each of these areas, offering suggestions for working out the problem. She sits in silence. Suddenly she bursts into uncontrollable sobs. After a few minutes she tells you that she is going through a divorce; her husband has been beating her and the children when he gets drunk, and she has moved out of the house. She feels lonely, helpless, depressed, and unable to cope with the demands of her four young children. And she's got to make it through this field placement so that she can graduate on schedule in six months and begin supporting herself. She needs the income desperately.

A. What is your immediate response when she starts to cry. What do you say or do?

B. What is your approach when she starts to tell you about her family and personal problems? How much do you encourage her to tell you?

C. Do you make any effort to deal with the personal problems she reveals? What do you say or do? How involved should you get?

D. Are you willing to promise her that she needn't worry—that you'll make sure she finishes field placement? She is obviously letting you know that you'll be complicating her already upset life if you cause any problems for her in completing her field placement. How should you handle this?

10. A Student Uses an Unorthodox Interviewing Approach

Your undergraduate student (one month away from graduation) turns in the process-recording below.* She's fairly honest about recording things the way they actually happened. She attaches a note telling you she's proud of the outcome of this interview.

A. What do you think of the student's rather unorthodox language and approach to this man whom she had never met?

B. Does the outcome justify the approach used?

C. Would you compliment or criticize the student?

This client had been hospitalized in preparation for surgery. At the last minute, he left the hospital against medical advice, refusing the surgery. The doctor requested social service help with this problem, as the surgery was really needed. An undergraduate student in her second quarter of field placement had called the patient's home and left a message for him to return her call. He did, and the following interview took place by phone.

Supervisory Comments	Dialogue	Gut-Level Feelings
	Wkr: "Mr. D., what happened?"	
	Pt: "Well, I was going to call you. They came to get me and I decided that I should come home and prepare myself for the operation."	
	Wkr: "Prepare yourself? How?"	
	Pt: "Well, you know, straighten out my affairs and build myself up a little bit."	
	Wkr: "You feel you aren't ready for surgery yet?"	Good, he's undecided—do a good job—maybe he'll come back.

*This is an actual recording presented exactly as recorded by the student, except for changes in identifying data to preserve confidentiality. It first appeared in Suanna J. Wilson, *Recording: Guidelines for Social Workers* (New York: Free Press, 1980), p. 69.

Supervisory Comments	Dialogue	Gut-Level Feelings
	Pt: "Well, I don't know!"	
	Wkr: "Let's talk about it."	
	Pt: "Well, my doctor told me it was OK to check out for awhile. I have a funeral I wanted to go to and I felt I had to be there. And I need to straighten out my affairs too."	I talked with his doctor and he didn't tell him it was OK. Can I level with him? I'll try it.
	Wkr: "Mr. D., you know the reason I called you is because I care what happens to you?"	
	Pt: "Yes, I know that."	
	Wkr: "Then cut the crap and level with me. I've talked with your doctor and it's hard to believe he would let you go."	
	(pause)	
	Pt: "Well, I don't know what they will find."	Good!
	Wkr: "You're afraid of what they will find?"	
	Pt: "Yes, I don't know if I'll ever be able to go back to work and I don't want to be a burden on anyone."	
	Wkr: "So you're afraid of something really bad happening?"	(get back on the track—don't lose that!)
	Pt: "I just wish I knew."	
	Wkr: "What did your doctor say about that?"	
	Pt: "Well he said I should have the surgery."	
	Wkr: "And you don't know what to do?"	
	Pt: "That's right, I have an appointment with the clinic on Friday, so I'll be in the clinic."	

Supervisory Comments	Dialogue	Gut-Level Feelings
	Wkr: "You mentioned you didn't want to be a burden, could you explain that to me?"	Didn't want to lose track of that statement.
	Pt: "You know—a burden on anyone."	
	Wkr: "You mean you don't want to have to depend on anyone?"	
	Pt: "Right."	
	Wkr: "Have you given any thought to what might happen if you don't have the surgery?"	
	Pt: "Well, not really."	
	Wkr: "Do you think it would be a good idea to look at both sides of the situation?"	
	Pt: "What way?"	
	Wkr: "Well, you're still a young man. If you don't have the surgery, what do you think could possibly happen?"	
	Pt: "That's true."	
	Wkr: "What's true?"	
	Pt: "It could be worse. But when I left I had felt OK."	
	Wkr: "How do you feel now?"	
	Pt: "Still OK."	
	Wkr: "Well, I hope you continue to feel OK."	
	Pt: "I'm coming into the clinic on Friday."	He's trying to tell me something—he's reaching out.
	Wkr: "What for?"	
	Pt: "For a checkup."	
	Wkr: "I'd really like to see you when you come in."	
	Pt: "OK."	

(Continued)

Supervisory Comments	Dialogue	Gut-Level Feelings
	Wkr: "Maybe we could even meet with the doctor and he could explain things in more detail to you."	
	Pt: "That would be fine."	
	(pause)	
	Wkr: "If you need to talk to me before, you can call me here."	
	Pt: "OK."	
	(we hung up)	

11. A Student Damages Her Client

Your graduate student produced the following process recording* during the seventh week of a twelve-week block field placement (forty hours weekly). Study it carefully and respond to the questions at the end.

SETTING

The student is placed in a unit conducting eligibility studies for persons applying for AFDC (Aid to Families with Dependent Children). The applicant is a recently divorced forty-three-year-old woman with seven children. The portion of the interview that follows takes place during a home visit. Only the dialogue content is given in this interview. The preliminaries of the interview have been omitted.

Supervisory Comments	Dialogue
	W.: How long have you been divorced?
	C.: Uh, one year.
	W.: Can you tell me what happened?
	C.: I'd rather not talk about it.
	W.: How come you left him?
	C.: Who said I left him?
	W.: That's what I read in your case record at the office.
	C.: I said I don't wanna talk about it. Do I have to answer any more questions?
	W.: Well, I do need to learn about your divorce. It's important we have a complete social history. Did you fight a lot?

*This is not an actual recording. However, it illustrates problematic communication and an interviewing approach that is sometimes (rarely) seen in actual student recordings. This interview is taken from Wilson, *Recording; Guidelines for Social Workers*, p. 87.

Supervisory Comments	**Dialogue**
	C.: Yeah, we fought. Why don't you ask me about finances or something? It's money I need, and I don't see what my marriage has to do with that.
	W.: I can't give assistance without the complete social history. You must give me some more information. Look, if it helps... my parents just got divorced. I know what it's like. My father beat my mother when he got angry and she had to get out of the house for her own protection. Men who do that to their wives ought to be outlawed.
	C.: (Silence)
	W.: So, getting divorced isn't so bad. I mean you probably did the right thing under the circumstances. So, it's OK to tell me about it. I'll understand.
	C.: What if the husband leaves you instead?
	W.: Well, oh—is that what happened with you?
	C.: Yeah. Left me for another woman, the miserable *!#*.
	W.: I'm working with another case where that happened. The woman was so upset she had a total breakdown. So, I can understand that that's a pretty rotten thing you've had done to you. How'd it make you feel?
	C.: Look, I thought I said I didn't want to discuss this.
	W.: Were you having any sexual problems? I mean, a lot of times when there are marital problems, there are sexual problems.
	C.: It's none of your business (rising and moving toward the door).
	W.: That kind of thing can be hard to talk about. A lot of times sexual problems are really the symptom of other problems that are much more serious.
	C.: I've decided I don't want none of your AFDC. I'll beg or steal if I have to. Just get out of my house (showing worker to the door) and don't you come back, you hear?
	W.: But I...
	C.: Get out of here!

What do you think of this interview?

A. Notice the blank column for entering supervisory remarks on the process-recording. Enter your remarks as if you were the supervisor.
B. What would you say to this student when you meet to discuss the recording?
C. What impact, if any, would this recording have on the student's overall performance evaluation in field and your recommendations for the future? What issues are involved here?

12. An Inexperienced Student Gets Nowhere in His Very First Interview

You are supervising a young undergraduate in his first field placement. He has no work experience (except during the summers while in high school and college) and has had only a few courses in social work. After much discussion and preliminary planning, he has his first interview with a real live "client" and submits the following process-recording.*

Supervisory Comments	Dialogue—Interview Content	Gut-Level Feelings
(What comments would you make if this were your student?)	Good afternoon. Are you V.M.?	
	Client: Yes. Who are you?	
	My name is Albert Smith and I work for social service here. I received your...	Client interrupts me at this point. Anger comes to me because of his interruption.
	C: Oh yeah! Well, I was talking to some others about my financial situation, but young man, I think you won't be able to help after I tell you what I have to say.	
	What may that be, Mr. M.?	
	C: Well, you see I have always been a self-supporting man, and I never needed charity or have been on public relief. So to make the long story short, my financial problems as far as food and shelter, they have been accounted for.	At this point he pats on my knee and gives me a wink.
	Well, how do you do that, if you do not mind my asking?	
	C: Simple. I have many friends. Now, the real financial problems I have are my car payments, my rent, and my insurance payments. I think you won't be able to help me with that.	
	It seems like so.	
	C: Well, anyway, thanks for trying, but anyway I'm leaving today.	Client shakes my hand as if he was trying to get rid of me as soon and as politely as possible.
	OK, Mr. M. I hope everything turns out well. Goodbye.	
	C: Oh, it will son. Goodbye now.	

*Taken from Wilson, *Recording: Guidelines for Social Workers*, p. 73.

It appears that the student was rejected by his client. He just didn't know how to get into any meaningful exploration of the client's needs and feelings. You don't want to make him feel like a total failure; he is insecure enough as it is. Thus, you need to give him some supportive feedback, but also some constructive criticism and discussion that will help him do better next time.

A. Enter your remarks in the column for supervisory comments.
B. What would you say to the student in your supervisory conference when this recording is discussed? What techniques would you use to teach him the things you feel he needs to learn as a result of his experience with this interview?

13. A Student Produces a Poor Interview in Comparison to Her Usual Outstanding Performance

The undergraduate student who wrote the following recording was only two weeks away from graduation. She had performed at a very advanced level throughout field placement. The student felt that this particular interview was the opposite of everything she had demonstrated in previous interviews. It was a difficult first interview. The record indicated that Mr. B. had been hostile to previous social workers, and considerable supervisory discussion and some role-playing preceded the first interview. The student felt she had used a machine-gun questioning approach and lacked warmth. She said she had been very anxious during the interview, felt she came on too fast, and didn't handle confrontation very effectively. It appears that her anxiety may have hindered the effectiveness of her contact, and the student knew this.

What comments would you put in the "Supervisory Comments" column if you were this student's supervisor? What kind of discussion would you have with the student in your next supervisory conference? What rating would you assign the interview, using the checklist on pp. 144–149?

Supervisory Comments	Dialogue—Interview Content	Gut-Level Feelings
	As I drove up, Mr. B. was sitting on the porch with three children. Sitting on the rail looked like a beer can; as I drove up Mr. B. went inside, taking the can with him. When I got out of the car and went to the porch, Mr. B. was standing in the door with a coffee cup in his hand.	Oh no, he's home! Help me, Father.
	W: Mr. B.?	
	C: Yes.	
	W: Mr. B., my name is Nina Schroeder. I'm your new worker from the Human Resources Agency and I would like to speak to you and your wife.	
	C: Where did you say you were from?	Oh.
	W: Human Resources.	
	C: Sure, come on in.	Surprise. He actually seems friendly.
	I entered the house and was swamped by three children. Two were holding on to my legs. The oldest (about four) stood back	

(Continued)

Supervisory Comments	Dialogue—Interview Content	Gut-Level Feelings
	and observed me, not saying a word. Sally was sitting on the couch when I entered. She glanced up but went back to feeding the baby on the couch without speaking.	
	W: Hello, Mrs. B. How are you?	
	Mrs. B.: Oh, okay.	
	W: (to the three children) And who are you all?	I thought they only had three kids.
	Mr. B.: This is Allen (four years old) and Frank (two years old). And this is one of the neighbor's little boys. We keep him for her while she works.	Oh, a neighbor boy.
	W: They sure are cute (and turning attention to Sally and the baby). And this must be Jimmy. How old is this big boy now?	
	Mrs. B. (smiles): about seven months now.	
	W: Is he growing pretty good?	
	Mr. B.: Yes, sir. He's really putting on weight now. Doctor said give him as much milk as he'll take. He's taking about five bottles a day.	He's talking for Sally. I wonder if this is a typical interaction pattern.
	W: No wonder he's really growing.	
	pause—a deafening sound...	Well, here we go!
	W: Mr. and Mrs. B., are you aware of the reason I'm here?	
	Mr. B.: Frankly, no.	He's not going to make this easy for me.
	W: Several months ago there was a referral that the children were being neglected. You've seen several workers since then and I'm here to pick up where they left off.	

Supervisory Comments	Dialogue—Interview Content	Gut-Level Feelings
	Mr. B.: It was none of their business and it's none of yours. I'd like to know just who made this referral anyway. I bet it was her *!# mother.	Shock. But an unreal calm.
	W: (Silence)	
	Mr. B.: Well, who was it?	He's trying to intimidate me.
	W: Mr. B., I'm not authorized to release that information.	
	Mr. B.: That's what that other worker said.	He's tried it before.
	W: Mr. B., you seem extremely angry, which is understandable (pause). Would you like to talk about it?	Thanks for the training (referring to field instructor)! Empathize—it's all right to feel angry.
	Mr. B.: I just don't understand why someone would call in and tell you all something like that. I was without a job for a while, but we managed.	
	W: Why do you think someone would call in?	
	Mr. B.: Well, her mother hates me and doesn't think I take care of Sally and the other kids.	
	W: What gives her that idea?	
	Mr. B.: I used to drink but I've quit that and now we're back in church. I don't have a job right now but I've got several good possibilities; one Tuesday and two Thursday.	Not drinking—was that a beer can I saw? Everything a good father should be!!
	W: You said before that you were without a job for a while. Does that mean you've had a job since then and now?	Clarify.... why did he lose job?
	Mr. B.: Yeah, but I had a promised job at Phil's gas station, so I quit, but it didn't come through.	Why didn't it come through? Past job record, drinking??
	W: You said you have several possibilities next week.	

Supervisory Comments	Dialogue—Interview Content	Gut-Level Feelings
	Mr. B.: Yes, one definite and two maybes.	
	W: Then you have a definite job offer.	
	Mr. B.: Yeah, but I'd rather not work at night, and if those others come in then I've told 'em I'm going to take it.	BUT...
	W: Why wouldn't you want to work at night?	
	Mr. B.: I'd just rather be at home at night; I'd rather get more money anyway. Besides, I have bad legs. I don't know why but lately after I stand for about 2–3 hours, then pains like needles run through my legs.	Wonder when and why his legs start hurting. Gap: why would he have less leg pain in the day than at night, or he'd get more money?
	W: What do you think caused the pain?	Could the reason he wants to be at home at night be that he doesn't beat his wife then?
	Mr. B.: Just standing on a hard floor for hours at a time pumping gas.	
	W: How long have you been pumping gas?	
	Mr. B.: About four years, I guess.	
	W: When was the first time you remember having the pain?	
	Mr. B.: I don't remember.	Let's explore.
	W: Do you enjoy pumping gas?	Could it be the job?
	Mr. B.: Yeah, I guess. It's what I do best.	Don't feel he really enjoys it.
	W: Have you thought of some-thing you would like to do better?	
	Mr. B.: Shoot pool.	Shoot pool. No real responsi-bility.
	W: You like to shoot pool.	

Supervisory Comments	Dialogue	Gut-Level Feelings
	Mr. B.: Yeah, I'll take spells when I do and then sometimes I don't—depends on how I do at it. Last week me and my brother shot pool together and made a few bucks.	
	W: Your brother?	
	Mr. B.: Yeah, he's a pretty good guy. But I don't get a chance to go much because of working.	Working keeps him from doing a lot of things. Traps.
	W: When you work it pretty well restricts you, huh?	
	Mr. B.: Yeah, cuts out everything but sleepin', eatin', and work.	
	W: How do you feel then?	
	Mr. B.: Trapped—just like the fish down in that pond by the road.	Right on.
	W: How do you react when you feel trapped?	
	Mr. B.: Mad. I just want out.	Wants out.
	W: What happens in the family when you start feeling trapped?	Hindsight: I seem judgmental—imposing my values. "What's the matter with you—you've got a family to think about!"
	Mr. B.: I don't hit them or anything, if that's what you mean.	Defensive.
	W: I wonder why you would think that's what I mean?	
	Mr. B.: Well, everybody gets mad.	
	W: How do you work off being mad, Mr. B.?	I feel defensive because he's defensive.
	Mr. B.: Mostly I just leave and go shoot pool.	
	W: Is there any other way?	
	Mr. B.: No.	Mr. B. ends flat—no argument.

(Continued)

Supervisory Comments	**Dialogue**	**Gut-Level Feelings**
	W: (Pause)	
	Mrs. B.: He stays here some-times and lets me visit a neighbor.	I handled this lousy. Mrs. B. is defensive of Mr. B. and is running interference. I'd like to know more about their relationship.
	W: Do you ever have a chance to go out together?	
	Mrs. B.: Not with these kids.	
	W: I guess with these children it is hard to get away.	Empathize.
	Mrs. B.: I don't ever have any time for myself, hardly even to think.	
	W: It's pretty rough on you. How do you feel about this?	
	Mrs. B.: I'm not complaining. I manage.	
	She stops and looks at Mr. B. (nonverbal behavior; children misbehaving). Mr. B. walks to door and calls two of the boys. He walks back.	
	Mr. B.: The doctor says we're going to have to take Jimmy to have an operation.	Now Mr. B. is running inter-ference.
	W: What kind of operation?	
	Mr. B.: He has a hernia. The doctor says that's not uncom-mon in a lot of babies.	How will they pay for this?
	W: Does Jimmy have a lot of pain or discomfort?	
	Mrs. B.: Yes, he's real ir-ritable and cries a lot.	
	W: What does the doctor say?	
	Mr. B.: It's not uncommon for a baby to have one.	
	Mrs. B.: He gave me some oint-ment for him and said when he was 18 months old (student didn't finish the sentence)	

Supervisory Comments	Dialogue	Gut-Level Feelings
	Mrs. B. looked at Mr. B. again, and he yelled at the children in the yard. The oldest boy was standing next to me. I reached out to touch him. He didn't withdraw but didn't make any facial expression either.	
	W: Tom, how are you? Have you been a good boy?	
	Tom doesn't look at me but looks up at his dad. Still no expression change—then he looks back at me.	Is this normal reaction for a four-year-old? Fear?
	Mr. B.: Tom's been getting a lot of spankings lately.	I was startled. Would like to get child's feelings.
	W: Oh. (pause). Tom, have you been acting bad?	
	Mr. B.: Yeah, he's been very bad, won't mind or anything. I can't stand a child who won't mind.	
	Tom just looks at me; no facial expression, a dullness in his eyes. No verbal response.	
	Mrs. B.: Well, it's getting late. I guess I better get sup- per started.	Client ends interview.
	W: It is about 4:00. I guess I'd better be going. I will be back next week.	
	Mr. B.: Stay.	
	W: I guess I'd better be going. I hope your job comes through. I will be back to see you next week.	
	Mr. and Mrs. B.: Goodbye.	On leaving I don't feel I've accomplished very much. I'm disappointed in my reactions to Mr. B. I hope I haven't dam- aged it too badly. I really feel Sally needed someone to talk to. I hope I can establish a relationship with her. Mr. B. has some problems.

14. A City-Bred Student Must Adapt to the Special Requirements of a Poor Rural Area

You and your student are in a setting that serves a very rural, mostly indigent population. Many clients live in substandard wooden frame housing located on rutted dirt roads in the middle of nowhere. Your student, a first field placement graduate student born and bred in a large city, is about to make her very first home visit. She shows up for work on the appointed date dressed as usual: open sandals with three-inch heels; short skirt and tight-fitting silk blouse; heavy makeup; four or five pieces of obviously expensive jewelry; and a bouffant hairdo.

    A. Pretend you are a male supervisor (if you are not). Would you say anything to the student? If so, what and how?

    B. Suppose you are a female field instructor (if you are not). Would you say anything? If so, what and how?

    C. How would you help prepare this student for survival and effectiveness in a rural as opposed to an urban environment?

15. The Right of Self-determination Issue Becomes a Reality That Can Mean Life or Death for the Student's Client

You and your second-year graduate student are in a general medical hospital in a Northern farming state. The student has been working closely with Mr. Smith, a fifty-five-year-old man who suffered a stroke eight weeks ago. Prior to admission to the hospital, he was living alone in his own home, a farmhouse located on 20 acres. The property is his free and clear and has been in his family for several generations. Mr. Smith supported himself by farming the land and doing some light carpentry on the side. His only income now is $122 month Social Security. He is now partially paralyzed on one side and walks slowly and unsteadily with a special four-pronged cane. He has expressive aphasia; that is, he can understand fully what is being said to him but cannot express himself orally. All that comes out are unintelligible sounds. However, it is obvious that he is mentally alert and aware of everything going on around him. He is able to respond to questions with nonverbal gestures.

You and your student attend a special planning conference on Mr. Smith. He is about ready for discharge, and the medical staff are recommending nursing home placement. They do not see him as able to care for himself in his present condition. However, Mr. Smith has made it quite clear that he will not go to a nursing home. He has expressed his feeling that he can manage at home, even though he would be living alone and has no family in the area. He indicates that a neighbor does live nearby. Since he is not senile, disoriented, psychotic, or out of touch with reality, he can-

not be declared incompetent. Yet the medical team predicts deterioration and possibly death if he returns home alone. It is decided that you and your student will make a home visit before the patient's discharge to see if he really could return home.

Your home visit only complicates matters. Mr. Smith lives in a rundown, wooden frame house that appears well over one hundred years old. Clothing, papers, and miscellaneous items are piled from floor to ceiling in several rooms, including the "bedroom," a tiny room crammed with junk and barely enough space for a cot. Light comes from a lone bare bulb hanging from exposed wiring. The kitchen contains no modern appliances. The only source of heat is a wood stove with dangerous-appearing pipe and chimney connections (It goes to 30 below zero in the winter!). There is no running water. Four rickety, steep steps must be climbed to get in and out of the house and to get to the outdoor toilet. Water comes from a hand pump connected to a well located several hundred feet from the house. The nearest neighbor appears to be about ¾ mile away.

    A. What would you want your student to recommend to the discharge planning team at the hospital?

    B. Are any legal issues involved here for you and your student, the patient, and/or the hospital?

    C. How would you handle the right of self-determination issues involved here with your student?

    D. What problems, complications, and benefits do you see in this situation for your relationship with the student and his learning experience?

16. A Student's Personality Appears Unsuited to Social Work

Jim, at forty-three, has a strong business background and entered social work school late in life, when he decided he wanted to contribute more to helping mankind. He worked for two years as an aide in the local public welfare department before going to school to get his BSW. He has continued to work at the welfare office part time while attending school and coming to field placement.

Jim has done well in the classroom, with a high B average. He has applied himself seriously to his studies. His first field placement was in a psychiatric setting, and now he's in your agency. He is scheduled to graduate in three months.

Jim approached field placement eagerly but with a number of complaints regarding his previous placement. His attendance has been perfect; his dress is always appropriate; and he is very businesslike in his behavior. In fact, he is too businesslike, and you have found that he is quite rigid and sometimes gets himself and his clients into a bureaucratic straitjacket with excessively rigid application of your department's policies and procedures. He seems to be rather judgmental and has had difficulty emphathizing with clients from backgrounds different from his own. Other staff have commented that he seems ''cold'' and ''like a computer,'' and it is evident that he has some difficulty in communicating feelings of warmth and empathy. Yet, when this is discussed with him, he denies that there is any problem. His basic philosophy and approach to people seem to be deeply rooted in his years of experience in a rather competitive business setting, compounded by his public welfare experience.

As Jim described his first field placement to you, it was apparent that he recieved very little supervision there. He did little professional recording, and because of his efficiency he was actually used like a regular worker, but primarily handling paper work. His current paid aide position with the welfare department appears also to be heavily paper work–oriented. You're concerned that with his rigid attitude he probably is communicating the old-fashioned ''investigator'' image of social work to his clients, the very thing we are trying so hard to avoid in our profession today. Therefore, you question how well he is doing even in that type of setting, let alone your agency.

Jim's end-of-quarter evaluation is due. You have shared your concerns with the school and the student. Jim is actively planning on graudation and plans to seek social work employment in a psychiatric setting. Because so many of his problems this quarter seem to be an integral part of his basic personality and the results of years of life experience, you don't see much hope for change. Therefore, you very much dislike the idea of turning him loose into the field of social work, as his approach goes against several of the profession's most basic ideals. He is only three months away from graduation.

    A. Pretend that you have written all of the end-of-quarter evaluation except the material under the heading ''limitations.'' Using the information given above, say what needs to be said in a manner that would be appropriate for inclusion in a written performance evaluation.

    B. What recommendations would you make at the end of the evaluation, based on your assessment and the description of his limitations? Should this student graduate?

    C. How will you handle the conference with Jim when the performance evaluation is shared? How do you think he will respond to what you have to say, and how will you deal with his response?

17. A Student's Performance Declines Markedly

Peggy Jones is thirty-four years old, has lived in this city all her life, and has three children, aged eleven, eight, and four. She married in her early twenties, dropped out of college, and for several years helped her husband in his business, a small retail store. After the birth of her third child, she began attending night classes at a local junior college and then entered the undergraduate social work program at the university. She did very well in her classes—all passing grades with a number of honors credits. The school felt she would do well in her first field placement.

Mrs. Jones has been active with PTA, Boy Scouts, and other volunteer groups in the community and is sincerely interested in working with people in a helping capacity. Comments from the director of field instruction indicate that she is bright though somewhat insecure, warm, sensitive, highly responsible, and highly motivated.

It is now early November, and Mrs. Jones is under your supervision for her first field placement. She has been in field three days a week since September 21 and will terminate on December 11. She has been very regular in her attendance, follows through with supervisory guidance, and participates actively in supervisory conferences. Her skills are at an acceptable beginning level. She has expressed some anxiety about returning to school at an older stage in life, but this has not created any significant problems for you or her.

During the past few weeks you've been noticing some things that concern you. Mrs. Jones has called in several times at the last minute to say she'd be absent, giving rather flimsy excuses. She has come in late several days without calling. The quality of her work is slipping: She's not turning in her reports on time; she's not getting as involved with her clients; she's showing up late for supervisory appointments—quite a change from her previous work habits. Yesterday a fellow supervisor told you she saw Peggy crying and encouraged her to come to you, but she refused. You've shared with Peggy your observations regarding her performance and she has denied that she has any problems and offered reasonable-sounding excuses. You've been afraid to push her too hard for fear she'll become angry and even more defensive.

Now you have scheduled a special supervisory conference to attempt again to share with Peggy your observations of her performance and your concerns. How would you handle this conference (role-play it if possible)?

18. A Student Takes Sides in a Family Dispute

You have assigned the case of Mrs. G. to your beginning graduate student. The patient is eighty-six years old and was admitted to your hospital on August 1 following a stroke. As a result, she is paralyzed on the right side and is aphasic. She appears able to understand some spoken language but is unable to speak intelligibly. She was referred to social service by a physician on August 14 for ''nursing home placement.''

Prior to admission, Mrs. G. was living alone in a small, rather rundown house in a rural area of the country. The house is on 2 acres of land. She has been receiving monthly Social Security payments of $150. She has a son and daughter living in the local area. Both are in their fifties with grown children of their own. Two other daughters live in distant parts of the United States.

Your student has had the case for approximately a week. He is somewhat behind in his recording, but in answer to your questions he indicates that everything is going fine. Bill has consulted with you several times during the past week to plan for a visiting nurse, as it was decided that Mrs. G. would live with her son after discharge rather than go to a nursing home. The student's planning seems appropriate.

At 3 P.M. on Friday, February 23, the student tells you rather casually that he will not be in the office for a couple of hours on Monday morning even though that is his regular field placement day, because he has to appear in court. This is the first you've heard about it. Upon questioning him further, you piece together the following story:

The patient owns a rather valuable piece of property. Her local son and daughter are apparently engaged in a family battle, as each is hoping to inherit it from Mrs. G. Both opposed nursing home placement and have insisted on taking the patient into their homes. The son had quite a few discussions with the student regarding his opinion that his sister would be physically unable to care for the patient, even though she wants to do so, and told the student repeatedly that "all my sister wants is my mother's property." The student evidently believed the son and thus has been working closely with him to plan for the patient's discharge to his home. The son is in the process of applying for legal guardianship for his mother and asked the student, as the social worker on the case, to appear in court in his behalf. The attorney has talked several times with your student by phone. The hearing is scheduled for Monday morning, and your student has promised the son that he would be there.

A. Would you permit the student to appear at the hearing?

B. If so, what guidance would you give him?
C. If not, why not? Since you would be asking your student to break a promise, how would you help him handle this? What would you advise him to tell Mrs. G.'s son?
D. Do you see any legal ramifications associated with your student's involvement with the son?
E. Would you let your student continue to carry this case, or would you transfer it to someone else? Why or why not?

19. A Family Accuses your Student of Causing the Father's Heart Attack

It is 1979. You and your first-year graduate student, Carmen, are in a special program providing financial assistance and social work services to Cuban refugees. They left their homeland by the thousands in the 1960s, 1970s, and early 1980s seeking political asylum and a better way of life in the United States. Most lost or left behind everything they had in Cuba and arrived penniless, unable to speak English. Many found their former professional training and skills useless or meaningless in this country and had to start all over again. At the time your student is in placement, an agency policy requires that all recipients of financial assistance between the ages of eighteen and sixty-four be evaluated to determine if (1) they could be rehabilitated through special programs and vocational planning to get them off financial assistance, or (2) they were permanently and totally disabled and thus eligible for a more permanent form of financial assistance offering greater benefits.

Carmen has been assigned to evaluate the Perez family for possible rehabilitation or disability benefits. Previous social workers have been active with the family in granting special Cuban refugee financial assistance. The following background information is already in the record:

Mr. Perez is fifty-six; his wife is fifty. A son and daughter-in-law and their nine-month-old baby also live in the home.

In Cuba, Mr. Perez began working while still a teenager as a sweeper in a factory and, through hard work, moved up to the level of foreman and had a total of thirty-five years' experience in one factory. He has a sixth-grade Cuban education. He suffered his first heart attack in 1968, which caused him to retire from his job. He lived on a retirement pension until he came to the United States in 1976. Mrs. Perez has never worked outside the home, as is typical for a Cuban family. This couple started receiving financial assistance upon their arrival in the United States in 1976. Six months ago, Mr. Perez was referred to a special medical clinic for evaluation of rehabilitation potential, and at that time physicians discovered that he was on the verge of a heart attack. He was immediately referred to a local hospital for treatment. The incident was not serious, and he soon returned home.

Two months later your student interviewed Mr. Perez regarding rehabilitation potential in conformity with the policies of the agency. This process required completing a form which asked questions regarding his background, education, physical condition, and so on. Carmen explained carefully to Mr. Perez why she was having the contact with him (hundreds of other recipients were also being evaluated in a similar manner). It was discovered that Mr. Perez had applied a year earlier for the special assistance based on disability and had been rejected because he hadn't been considered sufficiently or permanently disabled. During Carmen's interview, Mr. Perez appeared motivated toward rehabilitation, was quiet, appeared intelligent, seemed to understand and accept his cardiac condition, and was fully cooperative and eager to get off financial assistance. It was not until later that the student discovered he had been extremely upset by the interview.

Carmen recently made a home visit to check out a rather routine matter and found the family very hostile toward her. Mr. Perez was in bed complaining of an upset stomach. While Carmen was interviewing him, he began suffering acute chest pains and appeared to be in the process of having another heart attack. The ambulance was called, and he was taken to the hospital, where he was placed in the coronary intensive care unit. The family blamed Carmen openly for upsetting Mr. Perez by discussing rehabilitation planning with him when he was obviously sick, causing the heart attack.

Carmen was quite distressed by this development. You and she discussed the matter at length and agreed that in time, the family would probably get over their anger and see things more realistically. Yesterday, two weeks after the home visit incident, you and Carmen learn that Mr. Perez has died. The family is actively blaming your student for his death.

Carmen is now extremely upset, threatening to drop out of field placement and leave social work entirely. She repeats one theme over and over again: This man lived in Cuba under Communism for fourteen years after having had his first heart attack and yet did not have another one; he then went through the trauma of coming to the United States as a Cuban refugee and even then did not have a second heart attack. His second (and fatal) attack occurred only after his interview with her, and it is Carmen's feeling that the family may be right for holding her responsible.

Carmen is feeling guilty and questions whether or not she should have followed the required agency policy with Mr. Perez by even conducting the interview in the first place. Was there any way she could have detected that this was going to happen before she had the interview? Perhaps if she had been more knowledgeable or perceptive during her interview she would have recognized that Mr. Perez was really upset by it instead of perceiving him as responsive and cooperative. Agency policy dictates that someone con-

tinue to be involved with Mrs. Perez because she is still eligible for financial assistance, and Carmen wonders whether she should continue or whether another worker should be assigned to the case. Furthermore, she wonders if you knew what you were doing when you assigned her this case: Shouldn't you have taken a more active role to protect her?

A. How would you deal with your student's feelings (not her skill or lack thereof, but her *feelings* about what has happened)?

B. Would you want Carmen to continue as Mrs. Perez's social worker?

C. Is Carmen reacting normally or abnormally to this situation?

D. Is there any way this situation could have been avoided or handled differently? Should Carmen have deliberately disobeyed the agency policy?

E. Assuming you speak Spanish fluently, would you yourself establish direct contact with the Perez family?

F. Would you mention this incident in the student's evaluation at the end of the semester? If so, what would you say?

20. Your Supervisee Is Treated Rudely by a Community Agency

Your brand-new supervisee contacts a local community resource to get a service for his client. He comes storming into your office a few minutes later and, with much emotion, acts out the following interchange:

(Phone receiver is picked up. Nothing is said.)
STUDENT: Hello? Anybody there?
AGENCY: Yeah. Whaddya want?
STUDENT: I was told this is the supervisor's office—Miss Jewel.
AGENCY: Yes, what do you want? Oh, Harry, put that over there. I'll be with you in just a second as soon as I get this caller off the phone.
STUDENT: Listen, I'm Henry Williams, a social worker at the Brandon Clinic. I was referred to Miss Jewel because I'm trying . . .
AGENCY (interrupting): Hurry up, will you? I gotta go.
STUDENT: May I speak to your supervisor, please?
AGENCY: He's not here. He's in a meeting.
STUDENT: What's his name? I'll . . .
AGENCY: Sorry, I gotta go. Call back later (hangs up).

How would you react? What advice would you give your student? How would you deal with his feelings about the incident?

21. Responding to a Process-Recording

Your student turns in the following process recording. She is an undergraduate less than a month from graduation.

She is in a protective services setting, and the prior record indicates that this particular client doesn't welcome social workers with open arms. It is obvious that the client did not want to talk to the worker. Enter your comments in the "Supervisory Comments" column.

Also, how would you help the student get this client to open up and talk? Describe the supervisory techniques you would use in your next supervisory conference with the student to help her learn from this interview and prepare for her next contact with this client. Don't merely describe what you think the student needs to do; describe the *supervisory techniques* you would use to convey this information to the student and help her learn what you want to teach her.

Supervisory Comments	Dialogue	Gut-Level Feelings
	W: Hi, are you Judy Newton? (she met me on the dirt road outside her house)	
	J (Judy): Yeah.	
	W: Well, I'm Rebecca Brown—I called you—from the PQR Agency.	
	J: Yeah—come on this way.	I knew she didn't want me there.
	A (one of the children): This is my Daddy's dog.	
	W: It is?	
	A: Yeah.	
	J: Suzy, get out of that water.	
	(She took me into the house and we sat down. The couch was very dusty)	
	W: I'm your new worker from the PQR Agency. See, when you moved into this county your case was transferred to us and I am required by law to come out and see you and see how things are.	She said something before this like "What did you want to talk about?"
	(She sat there and stared at me. Also, her 17-year-old sister came in and began "cleaning" the table)	Began to panic because she was not responding—my first one!
	W: Who is living here with you?	Felt resentment toward the sister and from the sister.
	J: My mother and father and my two sisters—besides my kids.	
	W: Does your father or mother work?	
	J: No, my father is disabled and my mother can't work.	Can't work? Didn't ask—should have.

Supervisory Comments	Dialogue	Gut-Level Feelings
	W: Do you work?	
	J: Yes, I work at the JD Restaurant at night. You woke me up when you called.	Should have asked who keeps the kids!!!! I'm sure Mother does or sister.
	W: I'm sorry, I didn't know you worked at night.	
	(long pause)	
	W: Can you tell me about the fire you had where you were living before?	
	J: It happened about 4:00 in the morning. My sister woke me up when she smelled smoke and we got the kids out.	
	W: I know that must have scared you to death.	
	J: Yeah.	
	W: So you all moved to this county.	I _hated_ questioning her, but it seemed the only way to get anything out of her. Felt I had a bad start.
	J: Yeah.	
	W: What about your husband, Judy?	
	J: We are separated.	
	W: Not divorced?	
	J: No.	
	W: Are you planning on getting a divorce?	
	J: Yeah, I have an appointment with the legal agency on the 15th. He's down here from Wisconsin visiting the kids now.	
	W: Visiting the kids?	Didn't work—should have pursued.
	J: Yeah.	
	(about this time I noticed the hickies on her neck)	_Some_ man's been here for sure
	W: Judy, can you tell me about the referral from the other county?	

Supervisory Comments	Dialogue	Gut-Level Feelings
	J: Yeah, the neighbors called it in. They had been having a fight with my parents. I know that's why they did it. My mother went down and straightened it out, though. (the kids had come in by now, and were climbing on us)	
	E (one of the children): Are those holes in your ears?	
	W: Yeah, see, my earrings go in them.	
	E: Yeah, Mom has holes in her ears. Did it hurt?	
	W: No, did it hurt you, Judy?	
	J: No, my sister did it with ice.	
	(polite conversation about infection—first common ground)	
	W: Judy, are you getting any financial aid through the Department?	
	J: No, my parents want to apply for food stamps. (Maybe she said they are going to.)	
	W: Where are they now?	
	J: They're out for the morning (in town?).	
	W: Well, Judy, I want you to know that I want to help you. I'll be coming out to see you some.	
	J: OK, but remember, I work at night, so I won't be here in the late afternoons.	Felt she was becoming more receptive—because I was leaving?
	W: OK.	
	I said goodbye to the kids and the sister (who didn't speak when I said hello) and Judy walked me out to the dirt road.	I felt this interview was horrible, but that she will be more receptive next time. I will also be a little less nervous!
	Kathy told me the children were healthy and rarely sick.	

22. Students Who Don't Got Good English

You are supervising a very young student in her junior year of an undergraduate program. She has just started her first field placement. Following is her first effort at social work recording. Read it carefully and respond to the following questions.

A. What feedback would you give the student regarding her writing skills?
B. Would you allow her to write in social service records? Interdisciplinary records?
C. Suppose she relates well with people. Would you overlook her writing deficits?
D. What level of ability to communicate in writing must a student have:
   I. Before you would give her a passing grade in a first field placement
   II. before you would grant a passing grade in a final undergraduate field placement
   III. before you would hire her to work as a BSW in your agency under your supervision?

September 18

The mother was seen in the office today by me again. It was as a result of my calling her up yesterday that she showed up. Her dress was very simple, not what I espected at all. She seem ambivalent about coming to see me—didn't know what I was going to do I guess. Most of the time we talked about Charlie. He keeps running away from home. She can't understand this behavior. Last time the police aprehended him he was on the cornar of 20th and Bylor stret, about 8 miles from the center. Hitchhiking was how he had to have got there the way Mrs. Milton figured it. I'm not so sure because with his low IQ (78) I gues he would have gotten a bus and just kept riding till he decide he want to get off. Then maybe from here somebody gave him a ride. With Mr. Milton working now things are much better at home for Mrs. M. Her other kids are having lots of problems. Charlie went to the Dr. yesterday and the dr. told him he was coranary insuficency and she's real worried about him expecially seeing that he eats so poorly and just doesn't do like she asks him too and runs off and is gone for hours at a time so she just doesn't now where he's at or what he's doing or if he's alright or even when he'll come back home if at all. Anyway, she's real worried. About Charlie being in the high security area of our home was explained and Mrs. M. appreciate why the action was necessary. She's glad we have him controled now so she don't have to worry about him anymore. The fact she could visit him in one week when he's back in the regular building was all explained and she thought she'd come see him next tuesday. She's going to the welfare office then to see about her application and expects that'll relief her financial worries some. In the meanwhile, she's looking for a new place to live where it won't be so costley. Upon parting, we agreed she would come in to see me again next week so we could discuss her problems and situation some more, expecially since Charlie will be out of detention and she'll be able to visit him again.*

23. What Level Student Wrote This Process Recording?

The following recording is a real one; it appears exactly as the student wrote it. Only identifying details have been changed to preserve the confidentiality of both client and interviewer. This is the first real contact with this particular client. The student had had a brief contact the day before when she made a home visit and found the client about to leave for a doctor's appointment. She told Mrs. N. she'd return the next day. Mrs. N. had been resisting having surgery, and the agency is considering closing her case because they feel they are not getting anywhere. She is in her sixties and lives alone. The student has been encouraged to use the "Gut-Level Feelings" column both to record her feelings and to label techniques used in the interview. She also includes some analytical comments regarding Mrs. N.

A. Read the recording. What level of student do you think wrote it? Check the item below that comes closest to your assessment:

_____ Undergraduate BSW student in very first field placement
_____ Undergraduate BSW student at very end of first field placement or in beginning of a second field placement
_____ Undergraduate BSW student at point of graduation
_____ Graduate (MSW) student in very first field placement

*Some social workers and students actually do write like this! This material also appears as a slightly different exercise in Wilson, *Recording: Guidelines for Social Workers*, p. 203.

_____ Graduate (MSW) student at very end of first field placement or in beginning of a second field placement
_____ One-year MSW student *or* large systems (non-casework) MSW student at point of graduation
_____ Two-year MSW student at point of graduation

If you are doing this exercise as part of a group, compare your results. Did you all agree? Why or why not?

B. Now go back to the ''supervisory comments'' column and enter your remarks as the student's field instructor. Be specific, constructive, and critical when indicated. If something was well done, identify it and state why it was effective; label interviewing techniques; offer alternative approaches if something could have been done more effectively. You might also want to comment on some of the dynamics, needs, emotions, and areas for further exploration and discussion that are hinted at throughout the interview.

C. What approach and techniques would you use in your supervisory conference with the student to help prepare her for her next contact with this client?

Supervisory Comments	Dialogue	Gut-Level Feelings
	I arrived at Mrs. N.'s house at 1:30 for a previously arranged appointment. I knocked at the door and I heard the television on.	
	Mrs. N.: Come on in.	
	W: Mrs. N., my name is Pam Crowell. I am your new worker from the Family Counseling Agency. I spoke to you yesterday. Do you mind if we talk some?	
	Mrs. N.: Law, no. Come on in.	
	W: Thank you. Mrs. N., I just came by to introduce myself and see if there is anything you needed and to pick up where your last worker left off.	Sounds repetitious but I don't think she caught my name and who I was.
	Mrs. N.: Well, I don't reckon there's anything I need; I've gotten along this far with no help, I guess I can get along well enough.	Sounds like some bitterness. Also someone with past history of a lot of help from neighbors; doesn't sound right.
	W: Well, how are you feeling? You said something yesterday when I was here about going to the doctor.	
	Mrs. N.: Well, I feel okay I guess. I got swelling in my feet and legs, but it's better than it used to be as I used to weigh 217 pounds. The swelling in my stomach has gotten worse, though.	

Supervisory Comments	Dialogue	Gut-Level Feelings
	W: What did the doctor say about the swelling in your stomach?	
	Mrs. N.: Oh, well, this doctor I went to yesterday is not my doctor. He's a surgeon. I just went to him to see what he would say. My doctor is Dr. Williams. He's nice and good looking also.	Avoiding the question. Let's try it again.
	W: What was the doctor's name you saw yesterday?	
	Mrs. N.: Dr. Hunt. He's a surgeon.	
	W: Mrs. N., what did Dr. Hunt say about the swelling?	
	Mrs. N.: Well, not much.	
	W: Did Dr. Hunt recommend surgery?	Oh, my, confrontation.
	Mrs. N.: No, he said he wouldn't touch it unless he had to—if it burst or something.	Contrary evidence to neighbor's information.
	W: Did he see that as a possibility?	
	Mrs. N.: Uh huh.	Avoidance.
	W: Mrs. N., how do you feel about the possibility of surgery?	
	Mrs. N.: Well, it scares me, but I reckon what will be will be.	Oh, she admitted she's scared. And shows fatalism typical of this geographical area.
	W: Scares you?	
	Mrs. N.: I don't like anyone cutting on me, but I try to trust my doctor just like the preachers. If you don't trust them there's not much use to go to them.	Reflection.
	W: And you trust your doctor, Dr. Williams.	Good relationship with doctor.

(Continued)

Supervisory Comments	Dialogue	Gut-Level Feelings
	Mrs. N.: Yes, he's a good doctor.	
	W: And what does he say about the swelling in your stomach?	I wonder if she understood what he was saying?
	Mrs. N.: Well, they pretty much both said the same thing.	She never told me exactly what Dr. Williams said.
	W: The same thing?	Reflection.
	Mrs. N.: Yes, the swelling is caused by water because of a hole in my liver.	I don't understand—must investigate.
	W: There's a hole in your liver. Did he say what caused the hole?	
	Mrs. N.: Something like a hernia or something.	
	W: Mrs. N., did your doctor sit down and explain what was wrong?	
	Mrs. N.: Oh, yes. Dr. Williams is a very nice man. He even drew a diagram, but you know how doctor talk is.	The dr. attempted communication.
	W: He explained it to you but you didn't quite understand?	Interpretation.
	Mrs. N.: Yes, I guess; but it doesn't matter. What will be will be.	She knows more than she's telling. She's avoiding the issue.
	W: Did the doctor give you any specific instructions like a diet or special medication?	
	Mrs. N.: Well, I have to take my medication to get rid of the water every two hours and a pill to replace some of the water. He also put me on a diet—salt-free, 1,800 calories.	
	W: Do you have any problems staying on your diet or fixing the food—salt-free?	What are her needs?
	Mrs. N.: Well, no, but I love home-canned food but I have to	

Supervisory Comments	Dialogue	Gut-Level Feelings
	soak them in water to get rid of the salt. They don't have much taste after that. I love fresh vegetables but they're hard to get now that I can't work in the garden. I use to have the best garden and the prettiest flowers. This side of the hill was covered in dahlias—big ones—and there's a rose bush over there that he planted the year he died. I wouldn't give anything for it.	First mention of her husband.
	W: "He"? Do you mean your husband?	
	Mrs. N.: Yes. He died two years ago.	
	W: What did your husband die of?	I visibly saw her withdraw.
	As I spoke I reached out to touch her hand as she had folded her hands in her lap and was looking down.	
	Mrs. N.: He had an enlarged spleen like mine but his liver burst but he was getting better until they dropped him in the bathroom.	Shock. I wonder if she has internalized this fear?
	W: Dropped him?	
	Mrs. N.: They got him up before he could walk and left him in the bathroom by himself and when he fell they just let him fall without trying to catch him. It was after that, he got real bad and died.	
	W: Do you feel that fall caused your husband to die?	She feels this was the reason her husband died.
	Mrs. N.: I wouldn't say that.	Why wouldn't she say that if she feels that way? Fear, or realizes unconsciously it's not the real reason.
	W: But you feel that way.	
	Mrs. N.: I'd say it didn't help.	
	W: Would you be afraid something like that would happen if you had to go into the hospital?	Confrontation.

Supervisory Comments	Dialogue	Gut-Level Feelings
	Mrs. N.: I'd tell my doctor that I didn't think I was able to stand up yet if I wasn't strong enough. I trust Dr. Williams.	
	W: What if you weren't able to tell Dr. Williams?	I wonder how much she has thought about this possibility.
	Mrs. N.: Well, honey, I don't know.	
	At this Mrs. N. started poking in the fire (wood stove). She had started to cry.	
	Mrs. N.: I feel cold—how about you?	She doesn't want to continue. Let's try another direction.
	W: I'm fine, Mrs. N. Mrs. N., do you feel lonely a lot?	
	Mrs. N.: Yes, I guess after you've lived with someone you don't ever get used to them being gone.	
	W: Do you have a lot of people that come by?	What is her relationship with neighbors?
	Mrs. N.: Well, I don't have any family in the area. I have a brother. He may be down this spring to help me clean this place up. My husband has a son— an engineer—in _____. He would do anything for me.	
	W: Are there people in the area that come and see you?	
	Mrs. N.: Yes, the people from the church come over to help me. The preacher's wife is real good to me. She took me to the doctor yesterday.	
	W: Do you attend the church next door?	
	Mrs. N.: Well, I go but I'm not a Christian. They stop by all the time anyway.	She goes but is not a Christian. I wonder why she goes?
	W: Mrs. N., do you feel depressed or discouraged any?	

Supervisory Comments	**Dialogue**	**Gut-Level Feelings**

Mrs. N.: Well, yes.

W: Do you have anyone you can talk to when you feel discouraged?

Mrs. N.: Yes, there is this girl—well, she's an older woman, but she has a young figure and wears real young clothes, but we talk a lot. She just lost her sister and a son not long ago. She comes by to help me out some.

W: Do you have problems managing getting along with household chores?

Mrs. N.: Well, I get around about the best I can, but I do have problems.

W: Problems—would you care to tell me what kinds of problems?

Mrs. N.: Well, I stumble all over the place.

W: Why do you think that is?

Mrs. N.: Well, I thought about the medication, but the doctor says not.

W: Do you think it may be your eyes?

Mrs. N.: That's what I think. Honey, I can't even see the screen on that television.

W: Do you have glasses?

Mrs. N.: I went to the doctor and he gave me some glasses but I couldn't see out of them so I went back and he said glasses couldn't make me see better, that if I wanted to see I was going to have to have surgery.

W: And how did you feel about that?

Mrs. N.: I'd like to go to that eye hospital downtown.

Obviously the reason this lady doesn't want surgery is more than just the surgery itself. Besides, if something is terribly wrong this is secondary, but I've got a one-track mind.

(Continued)

Supervisory Comments	Dialogue	Gut-Level Feelings
	W: The Adam–Smith Hospital.	
	Mrs. N.: Yes, that's the one. I think they can make me glasses that I can see out of.	She doesn't trust that doctor.
	W: You don't trust the doctor you went to about the glasses the first time.	
	Mrs. N.: I'd just like to get a second opinion.	
	W: Do you know someone down at the eye hospital?	
	Mrs. N.: No, not really. I heard they were good, though.	
	W: If I got you an appointment at the eye hospital, would you go?	
	Mrs. N.: If I was able, honey...	An excuse.
	W: If you are able?	Reflection.
	Mrs. N.: My stomach, honey. It's so swollen and my feet and ankles. I try to stay off them as much as possible.	I'd pursue this, but feel this is really secondary until I get more information.
	W: Do you have problems with transportation, like getting to and from the store?	
	Mrs. N.: I just go once a month and this other woman and I go together.	
	W: How about the wood for the stove? Does that pose any problems—to get it in the house?	
	Mrs. N.: I ask a boy in the neighborhood to bring it in and I paid him. You can't ask anyone to do anything any more without paying them. I'd like to keep the yard clean, but there's no way I can.	She wants to be independent but feels bad about having to be dependent.
	W: Do you think someone from the church would do it?	

Supervisory Comments	Dialogue	Gut-Level Feelings
	Mrs. N.: I'm going to talk to my sister. Maybe she can. We're talking about fixing up this house to sell it.	Talking about selling— doesn't sound right for a woman in her sixties and disabled. Either she knows she's not going to be around long or... what?
	W: Sell the house? Would you want to move?	
	Mrs. N.: Oh no!! But when you get where you can't manage you have to do a lot of things you don't like to do.	Gap in what she's saying. Maybe she knows she's not going to be able to manage for long.
	W: But you said you manage now. Are you expecting a time when you can't manage?	
	Mrs. N.: As I'm getting older, I'd say the time will come.	Is it the vision or is it the problem causing the swelling in her stomach?
	W: And how do you feel about this?	
	Mrs. N.: Well, it's just part of life—what will be will be.	I really felt this woman was being sarcastic with me. She can see right thru me.
	W: Mrs. N., is there any other problems that maybe I can help with?	At this (her statment "what will be will be") I'm at a loss for words—it's time to go.
	Mrs. N.: No, I don't think so.	
	W: I would like to contact your doctor to try and understand your physical problems better and see if there is any service that we at the Agency can provide. May I have your permission?	
	Mrs. N.: Sure, honey.	
	W: Well, thank you for talking to me. If I can help you in any way, here is my number. Please call me.	
	Mrs. N.: Hurry back now. I'm never busy.	
	W: I'll see you next week. Goodbye.	

24. A Student Gets Stuck in a Ditch on Her First Home Visit

Your undergraduate student has gone out on her very first home visit and has been gone from the office for about two hours. Your secretary tells you that you have an urgent call from the student. As you get on the phone, she tells you, virtually in tears, that she is stuck in the ditch by her client's driveway. The road is steep, and she somehow went off the edge. She has no cash with her and desperately asks you what to do. What would you tell her? What would you do, if anything?

25. A Client Asks the Student to Hold Her Newborn Infant

While on a home visit, the client shows off her three-month-old baby. She is preparing something to eat while talking with the student, and casually asks the student to hold the baby "for just a minute" while she tends to something. The baby has obviously wet and smelly diapers; her nose is runny and it looks as though she has some kind of skin sores. What should this student do? How can this situation be handled tactfully?

Problems in the relationship of field instructor and school

1. The Field Liaison Person Doesn't Visit the Agency Very Often

Your student is in a nine-month concurrent field placement that started in September. It is now February and you haven't seen a faculty adviser or school representative all year. Your student is doing well and is beginning to complain that faculty liaison people never visit the field instruction site unless there are problems. You share your student's feelings, appreciating his need for positive feedback and recognition from the school for good performance. How would you relate your concerns to the school?

Suppose you tell the school about your student's concerns and your faculty liaison person responds with, "I most certainly agree. Unfortunately I have thirty students out in the field, and between them and my classroom teaching load, there's just no way I can visit field placements routinely. I have to use the time I do have for problem situations." What would you do now?

2. Your Student Gets an "A" in Class on a Paper That You Feel Barely Deserves a Passing Grade

Your graduate student is nearing the end of her first field placement. You have some rather specialized knowledge of the role of the social worker in the criminal justice system, since that is your area of practice, and you've also done extensive reading on the subject. Your student chooses that topic for a paper for one of her class assignments. She shows it to you when she gets it back from the instructor. You review it eagerly. You've never seen such sloppy work in your life. The paper is poorly written, poorly researched, and downright inaccurate in spots. Footnotes are incomplete; there is no bibliography—but there *is* an "A" grade assigned. You are horrified. You'd never have gotten an "A" for such poor-quality work when *you* were in school. The student has asked for your feedback regarding her paper and seems quite proud to have gotten the "A" grade.

A. What would you say to her?
B. Would you do anything else? If so, what? If not, why not?

3. Students Don't Seem to be Getting Certain Basic Concepts in the Classroom

You are working with a student who is in the beginning of a second field placement. You have been discussing some case dynamics together, involving basic psychiatric diagnoses. You're getting the feeling that the student doesn't really understand what you're talking about when you discuss paranoia, major defense mechanisms, and the like, but assume he must have been exposed to this material in the classroom by now. You try to give the student the benefit of the doubt as you ask gently, "I'm not sure I'm getting through to you. Have you been exposed to these terms in the classroom yet?" The student responds with a definite no. He's had basic casework techniques, social work history, beginning group work, human growth and development, and some other courses, but he hasn't had anything on abnormal behavior yet. How can this be? How can a student get halfway through a professional education in social work and not be exposed to abnormal psych? "What's the matter with that school anyway?"

A. What do you say to the student?
B. Is it possible that he really hasn't received this training in the classroom?
C. Would you say anything to the school? If so, what? If not, why not?

4. Your Students Voice Some Criticisms About Their School—and You Agree with Them

You supervise two graduate students in a second field placement. You sometimes meet for joint as well as individual supervisory conferences. They are both intelligent, motivated, hard-working students, though with very different personalities and areas of strength. However, they are united in their criticism of their graduate program. They have been talking all year about the "incompetence" of two of their classroom instructors. If the experiences they relate are true, it is rather obvious that the school's written policy and program description and the way they are being implemented are entirely different things. The students have brought back juicy tidbits about other students who are having real problems in the field, which the school seems to be ignoring, and tell you it is well known that the school is using a number of field placements that are highly questionable. You tend to agree with the students. You know from observation and input from other sources that there are problems, and you've had some experiences of your own that substantiate some of their concerns.

   A. How do you react when your students share their concerns? Do you let them know how you feel? Do you express your agreement with the students frankly? Do you try to present the positive side of the school's program and thus defend it, or do you try to straddle the fence?

   B. At what point, if any, would you say anything to the school? Why or why not? What would you say?

5. You Learn That an MSW Who Was Fired from Your Agency for Incompetence Is Now Employed in Another Setting and Being Used by the School as a Field Instructor

You are a supervisor working in a large social service agency where there has been constant staff turnover for various reasons. Six months ago you dismissed an MSW who had almost no grasp of basic casework skills, became very defensive when criticized, and generally had difficulty relating to people. You find it hard to believe that she actually had an MSW degree, even though you've seen her diploma. Now you hear that she's supervising graduate students. Your students have volunteered the fact that a friend of theirs is under her supervision and is miserable. They don't know that this indivdiual used to work under your supervision or the circumstances surrounding her change of jobs. You are quite concerned. Part of you rationalizes, "It's the school's job to select field instructors, and if they are dumb enough or blind enough to make that person a field instructor, that's *their* problem. There's nothing I can do." However, the professional, superego side is arguing, "But I know the students are getting a terrible experience; maybe the school doesn't know what it got itself into. If I know about it and do nothing, then in a way I'm responsible."

   A. What would you do and why?

   B. What would you say to your students when they

share concerns about their friend's bad experience with your former supervisee?

   C. What are the ethical issues involved here?

6. Your Student Complains to You About a Classroom Instructor's Inappropriate Behavior in the Classroom While "Stoned" on Drugs

Your student is in her final year of school. This is your first year as a field instructor for this particular school, though you have worked with several other schools. About halfway through field placement you and several other students from your agency are having an informal coffee break together, and they start discussing their classroom faculty. There seems to be a mixture of positive and negative comments. Suddenly a student comments on Mr. X's "problem": His drug use is rather obvious to the students and sometimes leaves him staring into space in the classroom. When he is not "stoned," he is described as brilliant and a reasonably good teacher. The student group seems to feel that this professor's behavior is known and tolerated by the school. However, you are shocked to learn about it.

   A. What do you say, if anything, to the students? They are obviously watching for your verbal and nonverbal response.

   B. Do you do anything else?

7. The School Disagrees with Your Assessment of a Problem Student's Performance, Hinting That the Problem Is You, Not the Student

You have been supervising Joan, a first-year graduate student whose performance is described on pp. 227-228. You are very concerned about this student, as her performance is obviously unsatisfactory. You have shared your concerns with the faculty liaison person and have recommended immediate termination from placement. The student has talked with the faculty person, and one conference was held involving all three of you. However, the school seems ambivalent about your evaluation. It is rather obvious that they feel that the student's problem may have been aggravated or even caused by something in the relationship between the two of you or by characteristics of your placement setting or its clients. The school's plan is to transfer Joan to a different field placement. You are familiar with the setting the school has in mind, and it is one known for lenient supervision with low, very concrete expectations. Just about anybody could make it there. You feel very strongly that the school is doing the wrong thing, and you are angry and frustrated over the lack of support for your very careful evaluation and recommendation.

   What would you do? How would you handle your feelings with the school? With the student? Would this experience affect your future relationship with the school or your attitude toward subsequent students? How and why?

8. You Wish the School Would Provide More Training for Field Instructors, but So Far Your Requests Have Yielded Minimal Response

You attended a recent NASW meeting and got to talking with a group of people who also supervise students. You all seem to have one common concern: the school's once-a-year field placement orientation day for student supervisors is just not enough. You need some kind of ongoing seminar on techniques of supervision and related matters. Past efforts to communicate this need to the school have gotten a rather standard response: "we agree completely and we're working on it, but it may be a while yet before we're ready to offer anything specific." What do you do now?

APPENDIX C

Problem Situations for Consultants, Supervisors, and Trainers of Field Instructors

The following exercises present complex problems that might confront administrators, supervisors, consultants, and trainers of persons who supervise students. They involve advanced concepts requiring considerable exposure to supervisory theory and/or practice. The exercises are included in the hope that agencies and schools will recognize and respond to the need for specialized training for those agency-based individuals (and school faculty) who must face such issues. Persons in training to become field instructors might benefit from exposure to these exercises to increase their awareness of the responsibility and role of their own superiors. The exercises are designed for use in group discussions but can also be given as "homework" assignments for individual reflection.

1. A student complains to you about her field instructor

You supervise three paid staff. One is a field instructor. You met his student when she started field placement and have seen her in staff meetings and informal contacts around the office but have not interacted with her on a personal or meaningful level since you participated in the preplacement interview process. At that time, the student seemed like a bright, enthusiastic learner, though she didn't have much work experience. Lately you've noticed that she seems unhappy. It's nothing drastic, but she seems to be tolerating rather than enjoying her field placement as she once did. You've mentioned this to Fred, her field instructor and your supervisee, but Fred is quick to reassure you that everything is fine—perhaps she's just overwhelmed by the total field placement experience at this point. You accept his explanation and file it away in the back of your mind.

One day, about midway through field placement, the student knocks on your door and asks if she can see you for a few minutes. You invite her in, and a two-hour session follows as the student reveals many problems with her field instructor, shedding a few tears as she expresses her sense of frustration. She is afraid to tell Fred how she feels for fear he'll become defensive and take it out on her in his performance evaluation. She is obviously very unhappy. Even though you encourage her to talk with Fred about her con-

cerns (which seem valid), she refuses, and perhaps with some justification.

What would you do? Respond to each of the following questions.

A. What plan would you make with the student before she leaves your office? What feedback, if any, would you give her regarding your analysis or observations about the situation?

B. Would you tend to side with the student or with Fred? Would you let the student know which side you are on?

C. Would you say anything to Fred about the incident? If so, how would you handle the discussion? What would you say?

D. What goal or outcome would you strive for to improve this situation? (Be specific. Say more than just "resolution of the problem.")

E. Would you tell the school (faculty liaison person or whomever) about the situation? If not, why not? If yes, what would you say, and would you tell the student and the field instructor that you are involving the school in the situation?

2. You disagree with a field instructor's evaluation of his student

You supervise Frank Adams, a paid staff member and field instructor. He has supervised several students, and you feel quite comfortable with his effectiveness and approach to students. His current student is in the second of three short graduate field placements. Her performance evaluation is due in two weeks, as her field placement will be ending then (the third placement will be done in a different agency). Frank has been telling you that she seems to be a good student—not outstanding, but perhaps somewhat above average. You haven't interacted with her directly except in staff meetings and informal contacts and have relied upon Frank's reports for an indication of the quality of her performance. You've accepted Frank's assessments ever since you started supervising him two years ago. You've never had any reason to question his effectiveness with his students or to get involved directly with his supervisees.

A few days ago Frank was out for some minor surgery. It was arranged that his student would come to you if she had any problems or questions. Frank felt there wouldn't be anything, since she is finishing her field placement, can function quite independently now, and has sufficient work to keep her busy. However, she gets involved in a sticky interview situation in the morning and asks you to go over the tape recording with her as she wants feedback before a scheduled contact with the family the next morning. She has also completed several special summaries on the case that provide background and diagnostic information and submits them to you so you can get a better understanding of the context of her taped interview.

You play the tape while doing some paper work, sort of half listening while working on other things. However, your full attention is engaged when you begin hearing a surprisingly ineffective approach on the part of the student. Some of her comments are quite judgmental and obviously hinder rather than facilitate the client's expression of feelings and needs. Obvious opportunities for the use of basic casework approaches (reflection, interpretation) are missed, and the interview sounds like that of a beginning-level student, not

one completing a second graduate field placement. Your review of the student's special summaries also reveals superficial, poorly written reports that are not indicative of an advanced-level student. You ask the student to supply you with some other examples of her recordings and tapes, and she complies willingly. You spend most of the day reviewing the material and emerge quite concerned. How can Frank possibly give this student a satisfactory evaluation? "There's no way I'd assign a satisfactory grade if she were *my* student!"

Frank returns to work four days later. What do you do? Address each of the following issues in your response.

A. It appears that either your expectations for student performance are greater than Frank's, or Frank just doesn't know what his student is doing. Do you have a right to intervene in his assessment of his student? Is it possible that Frank isn't as good a field instructor as you had thought, or that he has blinders on regarding this particular student for some reason? What is your opinion?

B. When Frank reports back to work, he gives you a rough draft of the student's final performance evaluation, which he completed while at home. It describes fully satisfactory performance and assigns an "above average" rating. This seems highly incongruent with the quality of the student's work that you have reviewed. Do you share your feelings with Frank? If so, how do you handle the discussion?

C. Frank argues that she's his student and he's the one who has been working with her directly, not you. He wants to submit his performance evaluation to the school as he has written it. What do you do?

D. Would you inform the school of the incident? Why or why not?

E. Frank wants another student next term. You will continue to be his supervisor. How do you handle this?

3. A student asks you to switch him to a different field instructor

You supervise Sally Brown, field instructor and paid agency staff member. Her student, Bob, is a rather nervous-appearing middle-aged man who is quite outspoken in staff meetings and other group sessions. He can be quite critical of others and of the agency. He has been in placement for two months and will be in field a total of six months. One day he comes to you and asks to be assigned to a different field instructor in your agency. He feels that he and Sally aren't getting along well and that he'd be much more comfortable relating to a male supervisor. He tells you

he has talked with Jim, a new field instructor also under your supervision, and reports that Jim has agreed to take him on as his student if you will approve the transfer.

What would you do? Comment on each of the following items.

A. Would you approve the request for transfer? Why or why not?
B. Describe the thinking process you would go through as you try to make your decision. What things would

you take into consideration before deciding what to do?

C. What is your reaction to Jim's offer to take on this student?

D. If you decide to permit the transfer, how would you explain it to Sally and to the school?

E. If you decide to forbid the transfer, how would you handle this with Sally, Jim, Bob, and the school?

4. A field instructor's performance declines to "unsatisfactory" and your middle-management supervisor is having difficulty handling the situation

You are an agency administrator in a large outpatient, interdisciplinary mental health setting. The organizational structure that pertains to your department is depicted on the accompanying chart.

You review and approve performance evaluations for all social work staff. You usually do not see student evaluations unless there is a problem or the field instructor comes to you for consultation regarding the preparation of the evaluation. All of your students are in block placement from a local social work school and are in the clinic for six months. They are all graduate students.

Everything seems to be going well until the second month of placement. Frances Maypole's performance has

declined rather markedly in the past six weeks. Her supervisor, Mr. Fleishman, reports that there are an increasing number of careless errors in her work; she misses appointments, doesn't follow through on things, does incomplete planning with her clients, and seems rather disorganized. Absenteeism has increased, though not to a problematic level; there has been resistance to complying with certain clinic policies; several clients have complained of poor service.

Mr. Fleishman is a fairly new supervisor, but he has significant post-MSW experience. This is the first time he has had to deal with unsatisfactory or problematic performance. It took him a while to bring Frances's problems to

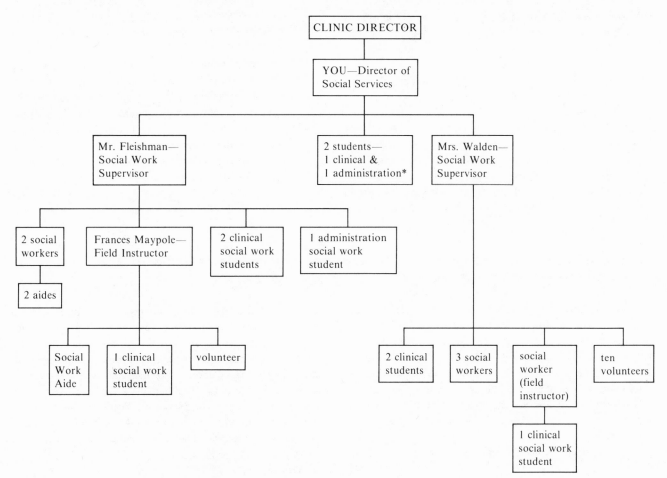

*The terms "clinical" and "administration" refer to social work students studying casework and administration. All are graduate students.

your attention, and you facilitated the process by sharing with Mr. Fleishman several client complaints you had heard about. Mr. Fleishman is eager to "do the right thing"—he is conscientious and dedicated. You both hope that Frances's decline in performance is due to situational factors, something that will correct itself shortly and permit her performance to return to its normal satisfactory level. However, another month passes, and in spite of intensive counseling and evaluatory feedback to Frances, there is little indication of change. Both you and Mr. Fleishman begin to worry about Frances's student.

The student appears okay to you and Mr. Fleishman. If he is affected by the decline in his field instructor's job performance, it doesn't show. But you both wonder how Frances can be providing a good role model under the circumstances. What is the student really learning? You both realize that if Frances's performance continues much longer at its present level, you are going to have to let her go (she has been with the clinic for only eighteen months, and this is her first student). What would happen to the student if this occurred while he was still in field placement?

Mr. Fleishman wants to wait and give Frances the benefit of the doubt; maybe things will get better. But you've been an administrator for fifteen years and know that new supervisors would prefer to avoid dealing with problems of this nature when they feel uncertain and insecure and wish to avoid unpleasantness. Furthermore, the student's field experience is nearly half over.

What would you do? Address each of the following questions.

A. Would you transfer the student to a different field instructor or a different agency altogether, or would you leave him with his current field instructor? Explain why you made the decision.*

B. If you decided to leave the student with his current field instructor:

I. What would you do to determine/evaluate the quality of this student's experience to protect him from negatives or gaps in training because of the problems with his field instructor's performance and her own obvious limitations at this point?

II. How would you use or work through Mr. Fleishman in this process?

III. What would you do if it became necessary to fire Frances while the student is still in field placement? How would you handle this situation? Who would supervise the student and how would you explain the sudden departure of the field instructor to the student and the school?

IV. What, if anything, would you tell the school about this situation (assuming that there is no change in field instructor)?

C. If you decided to transfer the student to a different field instructor or a different agency:

I. Would you handle this yourself or let Mr. Fleishman handle it?

II. How would you (or Mr. Fleishman) go about telling Frances that her student is being assigned to someone else? How do you think she would react, and how would you deal with her reaction?

III. What explanation would be given to the student regarding the reason for the change in field instructors? How do you think he would react?

IV. What, if anything, would you tell the school?

D. What impact do you feel this entire situation will have on the other students in placement and their field instructors, regardless of the action taken by you and Mr. Fleishman?

5. The school wants to assign a student to someone you don't feel would be an effective field instructor

You oversee the student program in your agency, being the senior field instructor among staff. Wilma Smith has three years of post-MSW experience and meets the school's requirements for supervision of graduate students. She has attended some school meetings, and the faculty have been impressed with her and would like to use her as a field instructor this year. Wilma wants a student and feels she's ready for this responsibility. You, however, have some doubts.

Her job performance is "low satisfactory." She hasn't

taken any real interest in the other students who have been in placement during the three years she's been with your agency and in fact has resisted getting involved with them. She has a rather strange personality. It doesn't interfere with her job performance enough to render her "unsatisfactory," but other staff tend to avoid her. On a gut level, you really hate to see her supervising students. You're afraid there will be problems, though you can't point to anything concrete to back up your feelings. The school is pressing you for permission to send her a student.

What should you do?

A. Do you let her take a student? Why or why not?

*One approach to this exercise would be to apply the Analytical Thinking Model for large systems. See p. 282.

B. If you let her take a student, would you have any ongoing involvement once the decision has been made?

C. If you don't give her a student, how would you handle this with Wilma? How do you think she'd react to your decision? What would you tell her is your reason for not letting her take a student? Do you really have a right to tell staff they can't take students?

D. If Wilma takes a student, would you share anything with the school regarding your concerns over her ability to be an effective field instructor? If she is not permitted to have a student, how would you explain this to the school?

6. A trainee in your seminar for field instructors reveals an obviously inappropriate approach to student supervision

You are leading a seminar for field instructors, both new and experienced. There is much opportunity for discussion in the small group and much sharing of "this is how we do it in our setting." One person has considerable experience with students, yet makes remarks that describe a rather unorthodox approach to field instruction that goes against some of the values and philosophy you are presenting. You don't see how students can be getting a good experience in his setting. The other field instructors in the group have given him several looks that say, "I don't believe what I'm hearing. I'd never do that to a student!" Yet the individual seems self-confident and obviously feels he's developed an ideal approach to student supervision.

A. How would you respond to the errant field instructor's remarks *during the group discussion?* How would you respond to the other field instructors' obvious dislike and lack of respect for what they are hearing from their colleague?

B. Would you do anything with this person on an individual basis?

C. What else would you do?

APPENDIX D

Performance Evaluation Exercises

These exercises require supervisors to grapple with issues involved in writing evaluations of student performance in field placement. Each situation should be responded to with an appropriate *written* product.

1. Evaluating a performance evaluation

The following performance evaluation concerns an undergraduate student who has completed an initial twelve-week undergraduate placement of twenty hours weekly. You are a field instructor for the school, which would like you to take this student for his second field placement and has given you the first field instructor's evaluation to help you reach a decision. Read it carefully and consider: Would you take this student? What does this evaluation tell you about Harry? Is there anything you wish it included that appears to be omitted? Is it a well-done performance evaluation? Why or why not?

Harry Smith began placement on September 22nd. He was sick alot during the first month, but then attended more regularly during the last two months. He met once a week for supervision and my administrator also provided some supervision when I wasn't available. Harry was assigned to the intake unit of a welfare department and had opportunity for contact with a wide variety of clients seeking financial assistance. He interviewed 8-10 different people each week and carried several long-term cases, and made home visits on three cases. He dealt with housing problems, families with disabled and retarded children, divorce, a suicidal woman, several alcoholics and drug abusers and two cases of suspected child abuse. In spite of a lack of social work experience, Harry moved in quickly and wasn't hesitant to interact with any of these individuals. His efforts provided a considerable relief for other staff as one intake worker was out on maternity leave. Harry completed all appropriate forms and reports accurately and completely. He became quite skilled at interviewing applicants and effectively gathered the necessary information to process their applications. Harry read the procedure manuals and seemed able to apply them effectively. He is not an especially fast learner, but when he learns something, he retains it accurately. He can perform his work quite independently and came to me only occasionally with questions (I suspect the staff working with him in Intake answered many of his daily questions). He did some readings from the Public Welfare journal and has a sincere desire to better the living conditions of the people he worked with.

Harry dresses informally, but that presented no problem since he is in an informal setting. He was well liked by our staff and the clients seemed to react well to him—none resisted giving him information at intake. We have enjoyed working with Harry. He is bright, dedicated and eager to get involved. We would seriously consider hiring him if we had a vacancy when he graduates.

Harry's evaluation for the semester is "outstanding."

2. Providing consultation to the author of a meaningless evaluation

The following example of a performance evaluation written by a field instructor illustrates a style of writing and level of assessment that characterize all too many evaluations. The student is completing his first semester of field placement. Notice how nicely the supervisor avoids individualization of Mr. T.; this evaluation could apply to almost any student in a variety of situations. Furthermore, the reader would not be able to determine whether the student in question was an undergraduate or a graduate. Notice also that the report emphasizes the kinds of experience the student was exposed to without describing the *level* of skill he has attained. Even though the field instructor makes repeated reference to the student's "growth" and "improvement," the terms are virtually meaningless, because he tells nothing about the student's level of functioning upon entering placement as against his skill at the completion of the semester. The reader does not know how much improvement took place or whether the student is performing at the level he should be for an end-of-first-semester concurrent field placement. When the evaluator rates the student as "satisfactory," we do not know what this means. What did this student have to be able to do to earn this instructor's "satisfactory" rating? What standards was the student being measured against?

The most positive aspect of this evaluation is that it lists the techniques employed to assess the student's performance. However, even this list fails to provide any glimpse of how the student did when the supervisor reviewed the results of these evalatory mechanisms.

Your task: In the left-hand column, indicate the questions you would raise were you providing consultation to the author of this evaluation.

Application of Social Work Skills

Mr. T. started out this semester at a rather low level. He has applied himself diligently and has grown considerably. Interviewing is still not his strongest area; however we look for continued improvement next semester. We worked on techniques such as reflection, interpretation and confrontation. While Mr. T. has made some progress, he needs to become more skillful in these areas.

At first, Mr. T. showed some lack of motivation when given assignments. This was discussed at length, and he has now improved.

Mr. T. was asked to do process recordings, summary recordings, and two tape recordings during the semester. These, plus supervisory discussions, were used to evaluate his performance.

The student had some difficulty working with the resistant client. He had two individuals who really did not see the need for social work services. Various techniques and approaches were discussed to help Mr. T. He did become more skillful, but has room for continued growth.

Summary of Strengths and Weaknesses

Mr. T. is bright, responsible, punctual, and professional in his dress and behavior. He seems especially at ease with the elderly. He uses supervision well, recognizes the areas where he needs to grow and is what I would call a nondefensive learner. He has grown considerably in a number of areas this semester.

Mr. T. is not a very fast worker, and takes longer than average to complete assignments. He has a tendency to get overinvolved with some client situations, and needs to continue working on this. Mr. T. is familiar with many of the basic interviewing skills, but will need to study them further next semester.

Performance Rating

Mr. T.'s performance is rated as satisfactory.

3. Writing a performance evaluation

You are a field instructor. You have been supervising an MSW student in his final (or only) field placement. It has been a block permanent, forty hours a week for four months. The student will return to campus for one term and then graduate. He will be under your supervision for one more week, and you must now write his final performance evaluation. As you prepare for this process, you go back through your notes regarding his assignments, supervisory sessions, and performance observations throughout the past four months. You also review again some of the key examples of his work. A lot of ideas and observations are running around in your head.

What follows is a random list of adjectives, notes, and thoughts. They are numbered but not in any significant order. Your task is to organize the list into a coherent, well-written performance evaluation. Use (1) the performance evaluation outline or form actually used by the school from which you take students; (2) the outline on pp. 182–185 of this text; *or* (3) an outline or form provided by your instructor if you are doing this exercise as part of a course on field instruction or supervision. You must conclude by labeling the student's overall performance as ''unsatisfactory,'' ''below satisfactory,'' ''satisfactory,'' ''above satisfactory,'' or ''outstanding.''*

1. Car has broken down several times
2. Established relationships with a patient who frequently ordered nurses and doctors out of his room
3. Is constantly reading
4. Came in some nights and twice on weekends
5. Had a dispute with a staff member who labeled student "overly aggressive"
6. Constantly asking me questions
7. Appears to be at least 50 lbs. overweight and dresses kind of sloppily
8. Does reports on time
9. Succeeded in getting a patient who left the hospital against medical advice to come back in for surgery
10. Knows and uses knowledge of all basic defense mechanisms
11. Is very quiet in staff meetings
12. Co-led two groups with staff therapists
13. Patients have come in asking specifically to be seen by Joe
14. Had trouble terminating with one patient
15. A young medical student called me up to complain about Joe when he tried to tell him he couldn't discharge the patient into the street with no place to go (the doctor needed the bed for another patient)
16. My supervisor has been turned off by student's personal appearance, which isn't the greatest
17. Doesn't seem to mingle much with the other students

*As an alternate exercise, several supervisors might complete this exercise and compare their results. Do they all give this student the same rating? Do they agree in their interpretation of the ''facts'' listed, or do some evaluators see some items as positives while others express concern over the same factors? What considerations affected the interpretation of observed performance?

18. Quiet, reflective
19. Has conflicted with staff on several occasions with intellectual disagreements
20. Doesn't become defensive when criticized
21. Took my undergraduate student under his wing (unofficially) when he was starting placement and was scared to death of the whole process
22. Sometimes questions the standard way of doing things
23. Hates statistics and never really did them right
24. Clerical staff like to work with Joe—he's warm and friendly and not too demanding of them
25. Seems businesslike in interactions with clients and staff
26. Caseload averaged 10 patients per month (not all the same each month)
27. Learned the hard way that he doesn't relate well to the elderly (transference involving a despised grandfather figure)
28. Doesn't get manipulated easily by alcoholics and sociopaths
29. Work area sometimes littered with candy and snack wrappers and soft drink cans
30. Writes much better than he communicates verbally
31. A little uneasy around authority figures, but nothing serious
32. Initiated a research study to learn more about characteristics of diabetics
33. Doesn't find it very easy to talk about his own feelings
34. Has a very Freudian orientation to casework
35. Gets detailed social histories
36. Not too comfortable making home visits—would rather work in his office
37. Dependable and reliable
38. Made a suggestion for improving the referral system—it was implemented
39. Got a middle-aged alcoholic into a rehab program—he's been dry now for 3 months
40. Comes in late fairly often, but always calls in, and automatically stays late to make it up

4. Writing an evaluation on a problematic supervisee

You have been supervising Joan for four months of a nine-month concurrent field placement, two and a half days a week. She is a first-year graduate student with some public welfare experience. You are very concerned about her performance. There have been a number of fairly serious problems. Her midterm evaluation is now due. You decide you have no choice but to write a less than satisfactory performance evaluation.

A. Use the following list of experiences with Joan to form the content of a performance evaluation. Use your imagination to elaborate or fill out the items if necessary.

B. The evaluation must conclude with an overall rating of "unsatisfactory." Be sure to write it in such a way that it would hold up if challenged by the student or school.

C. Make specific recommendations for the second half of field placement based on your unsatisfactory rating for the first half.

D. Write a paragraph explaining how you plan to share the evaluation with your student. What approach or techniques would you use? What response do you expect from Joan, and how would you deal with it?

Facts/Observations/Experiences

-Has rigid, insensitive approach to clients
-Hasn't completed any assignments on time in spite of repeated coaxing
-Statistics, written reports—full of careless errors
-Can write very well when she applies herself
-Has better than average intellectual understanding of casework theory and human behavior
-Three staff have complained regarding inappropriate behavior:
  -seductive dressing on occasion

- was overheard calling one of her clients "a stupid, fat clod who lives like a king off the rest of us" (student doesn't know I know about this)
  - told a clerical staff member to "go to _____" when told she had to follow a procedure she didn't like (student doesn't know I know about this as clerical person doesn't want Joan to know she complained)
- Always trying to get me to have lunch with her
- Spends most of supervisory conferences talking about herself and her life experiences
- Is very punctual for meetings, reporting to work, etc.
- Wants to be a supervisor when she graduates
- Wants very much to be a good social worker
- Two clients have complained that they "can't stand that weird social worker." They complain she asks about their marital problems when all they want is public housing and she tells them how rotten the welfare system is. They would like to tell her where to go, but they have to have their welfare checks to survive.
- Asks a lot of questions
- Learns fast
- Knows how to do things, but can't seem to carry them off effectively
- Does not feel that her temper is a problem and says she can control it when she really wants to
- Puts in extra hours in field
- Likes me and feels she's getting a good learning experience
- Has gone to my supervisor three times without telling me first when she disagreed with me over something
- Faculty advisor from the school called to meet with me. Joan had called to tell them I was rigid, unrealistic and punitive in my supervisory approach. Following the meeting, I'm not really sure who the school believes.
- I strongly suspect her of going through my desk in my absence, but can't prove it
- Gets complete details regarding financial situation regardless of the presenting problem
- Has great difficulty demonstrating empathy in role playing with supervisory input
- Seems to misunderstand sometimes why her clients feel and act as they do
- Tends to get one interpretation in mind and doesn't want to consider other possibilities
- Seems compulsive in some work habits and disorganized in others
- Is working 20 hours a week while going to school and is on a scholarship based on financial need and academic grades
- Meticulous personal appearance
- Sometimes really tries hard
- Either becomes angry and defensive, withdrawn and silent or tearful when confronted with less than satisfactory behavior or problems
- She's interested in research—perhaps she'd do well in an area like that if she didn't have to work much with people?

5. Preplacement interview—would you take this student?

Background

You are a field instructor for a social service agency. Your setting takes both BSW and MSW students and often has more than one student in placement at the same time. A preplacement interview is done with all students. Following the interview, student and field instructor decide whether or not they will work together. The school sometimes participates in this decision-making process also. Your agency, you as an individual field instructor, and the student have the right to say no and request that the school place the student elsewhere if for any reason placement in your setting does not seem appropriate or desirable.

The field instruction office at the school has asked you to interview an MSW student who wants to do his second field placement in your setting. He has completed two terms of classroom training. They tell you some basic background information, including the fact that the student received all A's and B's during his first term. Halfway through his first field placement, he was evaluated and considered "average" in ability to get along with others, use of community resources, and written communication skills. The previous field instructor felt that he was better than average in handling his caseload, response to supervision, verbal communication skills, motivation for learning, responsibility, and flexibility. There was some initial difficulty in written communication skills, but this has improved. A number of positive personal qualities are mentioned. The final field evaluation for the first term and the most recent classroom grades are not yet available.

The Situation

You have just finished a preplacement interview with François ("Frank"). The school has a modified block field placement plan: Students are in seminars one day a week and in field four days a week from September through January. During the interview, you learn the following information:

Frank is twenty-six, married, and from France. He has been living in the United States for the past five years but was educated here during his teenage years. He speaks with a rather heavy accent. While able to communicate his ideas, he often used incomplete sentences and rather awkward grammar. You sometimes asked for illustrations of what he was saying to be certain that you were understanding him correctly.

Frank has a BS degree in business and sociology (a double major). He worked for two years after college as a lower-level supervisor in a large department store chain. He is interested in industrial counseling. Therefore, he decided to enter social work school to pursue this specialized field.

He initially described his first field placement experience in a very positive manner. After some discussion, however, Frank expressed the feeling that he did not get some things that he considered important. During the first half of his placement, he met weekly with his field instructor for supervision, and the instructor was also available as needed. Many of Frank's interviews were observed through a one-way mirror. He did no process-recording and very little formal recording of any kind in any case records. During the second half of the first placement, he reported, the field instructor "was busy and didn't have as much time for us, so I only got to see him once every two weeks or so, and I usually had to initiate the contacts." He led an adolescent group for eight weeks, until "members stopped coming because it conflicted with after-school activities that they wanted to attend instead." Also, "Another student started a group, and some of the kids chose to be in that one instead of mine." Frank had a total of twelve cases during the year. He stated he did marital counseling that was "supportive" in nature and saw each case only a few times before transferring it out to another agency for long-term casework followup.

Frank identified his strengths as being in diagnostic assessment and treatment planning, stating that he had gained in self-confidence during the year. His educational goals for second-year placement were to learn "greater depth in treatment." Repeated questions regarding the specific treatment techniques he wanted to study produced general responses such as "I want to learn greater depth" or "I want to improve my treatment skills." When asked to list some of the common techniques used in interviewing, counseling, or casework therapy, he could not name any, stating that he had never studied them. When asked to name some common defense mechanisms, Frank named denial and defined it very superficially. "Projection" was named after a few moments' thought and defined as "when the client thinks something is going to happen and can tell it." He then added, "It's sorta like prediction." Transference was named as a defense mechanism and defined as "feelings between me and the person I'm counseling." Frank could not name any other defense mechanisms, said that he had never studied abnormal psychology or human growth and development, and admitted needing to learn more about these matters.

Frank came across as warm and eager to learn. He repeatedly indicated that he would be fully willing to do extra work at home or over the summer if he was accepted in field placement at your agency.

Your Task

1. You must decide whether or not you will take this student in field placement. Check either the "yes" or the "no" response; do not hedge or fence-sit. Write nothing else in response to this question. Do *not* say "but" or "if."

_____YES!   _____NO!

2. As you finish talking with the student, he suddenly looks you in the eye and asks, "Will you take me as a student next year?" Answer as if you were responding directly to Frank.

3. You check with the school for more information and share your response to the preplacement interview. The field placement office reminds you that the evaluation from the first-year field instructor was above satisfactory and that Frank's classroom grades are good. The school encourages you to take the student, pointing out his motivation to learn and the feeling that you can provide the kind of experience Frank needs for his second placement. Write a paragraph defending your point of view as if you were talking to the school. Explain why you will or will not take this student in field placement. Comment on any areas of uncertainty you might have. If this situation raises any special issues in your mind, mention them briefly. Keep your answer concise and to the point. Be firm about your convictions!

APPENDIX E

Group Training Exercises Based on the Analytical Thinking Model

Application of the analytical thinking model to casework

The Analytical Thinking Model (ATM)* is a structured, step-by-step approach to analytical and diagnostic thinking. It can be assigned to students as a self-instructional exercise or taught in a group situation (see pp. 282–285). Review the problem situations presented on pages 286–294 and 294–296 for some examples that could be used for individual study or for group discussion.

A professional helping person must learn how to think analytically before effective diagnostic statements can be produced. Analytical thinking refers to the ability to take a situation apart so that its dynamics can be studied meaningfully and the appropriate "solution" selected. Achieving this ability does not mean that the practitioner will also be able to diagnose. Even after the worker has learned to analyze a situation, he may not be able to select the appropriate diagnostic label to apply to what he is recording or observing. His ability to do this will depend upon his knowledge of the dynamics of human behavior. However, the analytical thinking process will lay the groundwork for application of this knowledge.

The following method is suggested for analyzing case situations. The professional or student should put himself through this process in preparation for writing the diagnostic summary and treatment plan that will be placed in the formal case record. As the worker goes through the process, his "answers" should be put in writing on a work sheet and then summarized to make up the formal diagnostic summary and treatment plan. This process could easily take several hours, obviously impractical for daily social work practice.

The goal is that the worker learn the thinking process and eventually be able to do it automatically, in his head, as he works with clients and prepares written diagnostic statements.

1. *Review mentally everything that is known about the client's situation* up to the point that you are preparing to do a diagnostic summary.

2. *List, in outline form, ten to fifteen key facts known about the situation.* Do not give impressions or analyses. Try to select only the major facts that are known about the client and/or his situation. This requires sorting out what is relevant from what is not. If some significant information about the case is unknown, this could be a key fact that should be listed.

3. Review the list of facts you have written down. *Think: What feelings might the client be experiencing, knowing what I know about him?* Focus on the client *only*. Do not describe feelings of family members or others, though the client's attitudes toward these people might be included here. List individually each feeling you think the the client might have, and *for each feeling:*

    A. *State who or what the feeling might be directed at.* This will not be appropriate for all feelings (such as guilt, depression, and so on), but would apply to feelings such as anger, resentment, and love.

    B. *State why you think he might have the feeling.*

    C. *State how the feeling might be manifested behaviorally.* In other words, how might the client express his feelings? What kinds of behavior or actions would tell you that the feeling is present? It might

*Material on pp. 280–282 is taken from Suanna J. Wilson, *Recording: Guidelines for Social Workers* (New York: Free Press, 1980). It also contains additional discussion regarding the writing of diagnostic statements, including examples of summaries produced by students and practitioners.

be helpful to review mentally the common ways that most people might deal with, express, or not express the feeling, and then consider how your particular client might express the feeling.

You will get your ideas about the kinds of feelings your client may be experiencing and the ways in which he might express them from several sources:

A. Your own personal life experience. A review of how you have handled certain feelings may help you identify feelings and potential behaviors on the part of your client.
B. Your professional work experience. This has put you in touch with many people, experiencing and expressing many diverse feelings. If you have several months' experience, you are probably able to identify patterns that tend to produce certain feelings or cause people to express them in certain ways.
C. Your knowledge of the client's specific situation. This could include what others have told you about him, past case records, statements he has made, or nonverbal communication you have observed.
D. Your knowledge of human behavior in general. Classes taken, preparation for a professional degree, attendance at workshops or training sessions given by an agency, and readings could inform you how most people in the client's situation would probably feel or behave. Bear in mind that you are thinking theoretically at this point. You are not wholly certain your client has the feelings you have identified but are simply listing all possible feelings he *might* have. As you get to know him better, some of your ideas will be either substantiated or eliminated.

It is important in this step to list *all* possible feelings you think your client might have. This means you may need to read some literature about the environmental, physiological, or emotional factors that are known to be affecting your client in order to determine what feelings and reactions a person in your client's situation might be expected to have.

4. *Consider who are the "significant others" in the client's life.* Select one or two persons with whom he relates most closely and go through step 3 with them. In view of the key facts known about the client and his situation, the possible feelings he might be experiencing as a result, and the associated behaviors, what are the feelings these significant others might be having? Look at and describe the actual or possible interactional patterns between the client and these other persons. Bear in mind that the professional helping person can also be a significant other with feelings.

5. Develop a treatment plan.

A. *List all possible case outcomes or treatment goals, regardless of whether they appear realistic or unrealistic.* (For example, "get Mr. S. to go to a nursing home;" "remove six-year-old Sarah from the home;" "help Mrs. J. prepare for her death due to her illness.") These should be broad, basic objectives or outcomes. Do not list subgoals or steps for achieving the outcomes listed.
B. *Label each plan or outcome suggested in (A) as either realistic or unrealistic.* Also determine which outcomes or goals are unrealistic to plan for consciously but may happen anyway through circumstances beyond the client's or the worker's control. For example, Mrs. S. has been an alcoholic for fifty years and is now seventy. It is not realistic to expect her to stop drinking at this point. But, as her health deteriorates, she may be forced into an inpatient medical facility where she is unable to obtain alcohol, thus bringing about an involuntary withdrawal from alcohol.
C. *For each realistic goal, (1) state the goal; (2) break it down into subgoals that must be achieved before the overall goal can be accomplished, and (3) state exactly what specific treatment techniques will be used to accomplish the goal or subgoals.* For example, a realistic goal might be for Mrs. C. to gain better control over her children and use more effective parenting techniques. However, a subgoal might be to help her alleviate her depression and feel better about herself as a step toward helping her relate more effectively to her children. If a treatment technique such as "empathy" is listed, state exactly *how* you would communicate empathy to this particular client in this particular situation. What would you say or do? Or, exactly how would you get your client to "ventilate unexpressed feelings of anger," if you have put that down as one of your goals or treatment plan objectives.
D. *Rank the treatment goals in order of priority.* Which ones will you work on first? Watch for some goals that, if accomplished, would automatically bring about accomplishment or progress toward achieving other goals.
E. *For each treatment goal, give an estimate of the length of time you feel it will take to accomplish the goal.*

6. *Finally, write a diagnostic statement that summarizes your main thoughts in steps 3 and 4. Also, under the heading "treatment plan," summarize what you came up with in step 5.* Only the written material you produce in this final step should be placed in the official case record. The work sheets from steps 1 through 5 should not become part of the permanent case file. They should be kept in a secure location in a separate folder until no longer needed by the worker, at which time they should be destroyed.

Application of the Analytical Thinking Model to a supervisory-administrative problem

Supervisory and administrative staff are often faced with difficult decisions affecting employees, consumers, and others. Human elements can make such decisions particularly difficult for the individual who is especially attuned to human needs and who is trained professionally to be a "helping person." What is needed is an objective, *structured* method of attacking the problem.

The Analytical Thinking Model can be used in several ways for administrative decision-making. A field instructor who is facing a difficult decision regarding a student supervisee may want to put himself through the ATM privately. Someone leading a seminar, workshop, or training course for field instructors could have the group apply the ATM to one of the problem situations presented on pages 271 and 278. Finally, an individual field instructor, a supervisor, or someone teaching supervision and administration might have students apply the ATM as a direct learning experience.

The following steps should be completed in writing:

1. *Review mentally everything that is known about the situation or problem.*
2. *List ten to fifteen key facts known about the situation or problem.* Use outline form. Do not give impressions or analyses. Sort out the relevant from the irrelevant facts in the situation.
3. *What feelings might the key person in the situation be experiencing? List each feeling individually, and for each one:*
   A. *State who or what the feeling might be directed at.* For example, if you have listed "anger" as a feeling that your supervisee might have, state whom he might be angry at, and so on.
   B. *State why you think the feeling might be present.*
   C. *State how the feeling might be manifested behaviorally.* How might the supervisee express his feelings? What kinds of behaviors or actions would tell you that the feeling is present? What are some of the ways that supervisees deal with

and express feelings of anger, for example, toward a supervisor?
4. *What feelings might the person who will have to make the decision or take the necessary action have in this situation?* (In a supervisory problem this would be the supervisor; in an administrative situation it could be the administrator or perhaps the department or agency collectively.)
5. *What feelings might significant others be experiencing in this situation?* Select *only* significant others whose feelings are *relevant* to the problem at hand. A number of significant persons may have feelings (e.g., the family of the employee in a supervisory problem), but these feelings might not necessarily affect the handling of the problem. Consider: *Should family feelings about a supervisee's dismissal determine what action the supervisor should take?* Typical significant others whose feelings might be relevant could include co-workers, the administration, clients, other agencies, the community, the taxpayers (in a government agency), or funding and accrediting bodies.
6. *List all possible solutions or actions that might be taken to resolve the problem.* List all possible alternatives, even those that may seem undesirable or impossible. Do not permit the reality constraints of the system to limit your creative thinking in this step.
7. *For each possible action listed in step 6, list all possible repercussions, both positive and negative, that might occur if the action were to be taken.* Be sure to consider the reactions of persons identified in steps 3, 4, and 5 as you work on this step. At the completion of this step, label each possible action as realistic or unrealistic, desirable or undesirable.
8. *Select the option or solution or possible action that comes closest to resolving the problem and has the fewest potentially negative factors that would make it impossible or undesirable to accomplish or implement.*

Teaching the Analytical Thinking Model in a group situation*

This section is included for those trainers, field instructors, or classroom faculty who want to teach the Analytical Thinking Model to learners through group analysis of a case situation. The group goes through the Analytical Thinking Model step by step to arrive at the assessment and treatment

plan. The most important concept to teach is the ATM itself. It is easy for learners to get so involved with the case situation that they lose sight of the thinking process that they are learning. The instructor must keep the discussion focused on the thinking process rather than try to achieve a complete understanding of the case example.

The following steps should be followed in giving this instruction. Those marked with a bullet (•) are optional, depending on time. The exercise, minus the optional items,

---

*This is designed for use with the casework Analytical Thinking Model but could easily be adapted for use with the supervisory/administrative ATM. The outline for teaching the ATM first appeared in Wilson, *Recording: Guidelines for Social Workers,* pp. 147–150.

will take three to four hours to complete. If the optional items are included, time must naturally be added for each.

1. Explain to the group that they will be learning a structured, step-by-step method for taking a case apart analytically and developing a diagnostic assessment and treatment plan. Comment that this technique is lacking in social work practice and, as a result, many social workers cannot perform meaningful diagnostic thinking and treatment planning.

2. Explain that time will probably not permit going through each of the steps of the Analytical Thinking Model. However, enough will be done so that participants can become familiar with the thinking process and apply it to other cases they are working with.

3. Explain that this thinking model is not necessarily the sole approach to diagnostic thinking. It is only one approach that a number of people have found helpful.

4. Explain that the Analytical Thinking Model exercise that they will be doing can easily take two to four hours. Therefore, it is not a practical method for working with every case in a caseload. However, once the thinking process has been mastered and two or three cases have been put through the model in its entirety, the process will become more or less automatic and much less time consuming.

5. Distribute the case example to be studied. Allow sufficient time for everyone to read it. This should take no more than five minutes, since the case example is usually a one- or two-page summary.*

•6. (Optional) Have group members write a diagnostic summary and treatment plan based on the case summary they have just read. Ask them to be very specific in their treatment plan as to what techniques they will use and what goals they hope to accomplish. Fifteen to thirty minutes will need to be allowed for this exercise. Ask people to put their names on their products, and collect them. Explain that they will be returned later in the training.†

7. Distribute the Analytical Thinking Model outline. Allow as much time as necessary for everyone to read through it quickly.

•8. (Optional) While the group is reading the Analytical Thinking Model handout, look through the initial diagnostic

*See pp. 285–296 for case examples that can be used in this exercise. Trainers might also want to make up examples of their own.

†If teaching the supervisory/administrative ATM, have the group write, briefly and specifically, what they would do with the problem in question. Then, in step 7, share the results with the group and compare them with suggested solutions arrived at when the exercise has been completed.

summary efforts that were collected in step 6. Take a quick survey of the treatment plans given. Write down the primary goals suggested by the members of the audience. For example, one goal might be to ''get him to go to a nursing home'' or ''get him to accept surgery.'' Each time a different major goal is suggested, write it down on a large piece of paper and then note how many people suggest that as a goal. The result will usually show conflicting goals. Some people will state ''get Mr. A to go to a nursing home'' while others will say ''Mr. A should not be pushed to go to a nursing home.'' The contradictions will be quite interesting.

•9. (Optional) When the group has finished reading the Analytical Thinking Model handout, share with them the results of your brief survey. Do not comment on the quality of the product offered by the group, but simply list how many people suggested the various goals. Make a comment such as, ''Isn't it interesting that there are so many different ideas as to what should be done with this client?'' The group will usually respond with equal interest. (Your goal as instructor is to point out how professionals possess various degrees of skill and view a client's situation in various ways. You realize that after they have gone through the analytical thinking training and produce a second diagnostic summary at its conclusion, there will be much greater consistency in their goals and plans for the client. However, you do not share this knowledge with the group until the very end.)

10. Have someone from the group read step 1 from the outline (''Review everything that is known about the case''). Explain that this has been accomplished by their reading the summary that was distributed.

11. Have someone read step 2 (''List key facts known about the case''). Ask people to take a minute to review the case summary and think about the *key* facts that should be listed. Solicit ideas from the group and write them on the blackboard. Have someone take notes of what is being written so that it can be erased and referred to later if necessary. Guide the discussion so that group members do not just list everything they can think of about the case—force them to be selective and list key facts only. If you know of several important facts that the group has failed to include, give them hints and use other techniques to encourage them to supply the missing items. If they cannot, list them yourself. There should be a total of about ten to fifteen items when this exercise is completed. Move quickly so that it takes no more than five or ten minutes.

12. Have someone read step 3 from the outline (''Feelings the client might be experiencing based on what is known about him''). Explain that knowledge of these feelings can come from several sources: e.g. knowledge of the client specifically and knowledge of the general psychodynamics of human behavior, normal and abnormal psychology, and coping and defense mechanisms. Explain that the more knowledge and training one has in these areas, the greater the depth possible in this step of the Analytical Thinking Model.

Comment also that much of this will be hypothetical—we are trying to list every possible feeling that the client might have. We will not know until we get to know him better whether he actually has these feelings. They will be confirmed or discounted as we work further with him. However, it is important to have these thoughts in mind so that we can be alert to possible feelings as we work with the individual.

Ask the group to list all the various feelings they think this client might have, using only one or two words for each. This will take only a minute or so. Most groups will list such feelings as anger, fear, anxiety, and depression. Write them on the blackboard. When five or six feelings have been listed, including the major ones that you have in mind, stop the discussion. Explain that there will be time to go into depth in only two or three of these feeling areas. You make the decision as to which areas will be discussed. The first feeling to be discussed should be one that is manifested behaviorally in rather obvious ways. Anger and denial are good ones to start with. Try also to start with feelings that will build on one another to result in yet another feeling being suggested. For example, when anger and guilt are discussed in depth, the group may be able to recognize that the client could also be experiencing some depression. Then take depression and work through it. This helps the group see how feelings can build on one another, enabling them to come up with additional feelings. This portion of the discussion will probably take half an hour to forty-five minutes. Use a directive approach and do not allow the group to get sidetracked or so wound up in the case that they forget the thinking process they are learning.

When one feeling has been completely worked through on the blackboard, go back and ask the group to think about how the feeling might be manifested behaviorally. "How would we know that this individual has this feeling—what in his behavior or actions will tell us that this feeling is present?" Proceed to list these ideas on the board. Time will probably permit going through only one or two of the feelings that have been worked through.

13. Ask the group to read the next step in the process (feelings of significant others). Explain that time will not permit going through this step in detail but that the thinking process is very similar to what has just been done regarding the client's feelings. Ask the group simply to list who the significant others are in the individual's life, and write these on the blackboard. If there is strong interest in pursuing one of these key figures, this can be done if time permits. Some groups will choose to explore the feelings of the professional helping person as a significant other. If the group suggests this, it should be pursued if time permits.

14. As this discussion is taking place, be alert for ideas that directly suggest a treatment plan, and comment on this. This is important to help the group see the connection between their analyses and the treatment plan they will subsequently be developing. Trainees need to see that these two processes are not isolated from one another but are actually interwoven.

•(Optional break) A natural time for a break is just prior to discussion of the treatment plan. If the training must be broken up into two sessions on separate days, this is the place to do it. The instructor should have the notes from steps 11–13 typed up so they can be distributed at the second session, since the learners will need this material to refer to as they develop the treatment plan.

15. Explain that the group will now develop a treatment plan. Ask the members to review the notes that have been developed in the previous discussion. Explain that one of the most difficult things about a treatment plan is determining the main objective. Ask the group to list all of the idealistic goals (e.g. get the man to stop drinking, get him to accept nursing home placement, get him to enter a vocational rehabilitation program, help the couple reunite). What do we really want to accomplish as professional helping people in working with this individual? List the idealistic suggestions on the blackboard. Keep them brief and use phrases only. Comment on why they are idealistic and that the client's motivation, the feelings that have already been identified by the group, and other external factors will determine whether the client is able to follow through, or whether the goal is even desirable or workable.

Engage the group in a discussion to select two or three realistic goals. Explain that it is important to think consciously of idealistic versus realistic goals so that we do not automatically select goals that turn out to be unworkable. List each realistic goal suggested by the group.

16. Take each realistic goal separately. Write the first goal on the blackboard. Comment that a goal is admirable, but we need to talk about how we are going to accomplish it. Force the group to be very specific during this part of the exercise. Do not allow them to get away with textbook generalities that cover up lack of knowledge of specific social work treatment skills. For example, if the group suggests that one goal is to "help client ventilate his feelings," ask how we will accomplish that miracle. Someone may suggest "by being empathetic." Write that down and explain that empathy is kind of a subgoal. How does one go about communicating empathy to a client? Elicit specific ideas such as "sitting close to the client" or making comments such as, "I can see why you're angry." Use outline form to list these things on the blackboard. Go through as many of the realistic goals suggested by the group as time permits.

17. Summarize for the group the experience they have been through during the past two to three hours. Comment on how they have moved from a complex presenting situation where there were multiple problems and confusion about which to approach first, to developing a rather specific assessment and treatment plan. Review again how important is one's knowledge of the psychodynamics of human behavior in social work assessment and treatment. Comment again on the fact that, while learning the process, learners should write out the exercise on long yellow sheets of paper, and that it may take several hours. Explain again that this is not realistic in day-to-day social work practice but that, once the thinking process has been mastered, it will take no more time than whatever nonstructured process they are using now, which probably results in less effective assessment and treatment planning. If the group argues, "We don't have time for this," the response is simple: "If we don't have time to relate to our clientele in this way, than what are we here for?"

•18. (Optional) If time and group interest permit, ask group members once again to write a diagnostic summary and treatment plan now that they have gone through the Analytical Thinking Method. Ask them to write the diagnostic summary in summary style as it might appear in a case record. Explain that they are to take into consideration the ideas that have arisen from today's discussion. Do not make any reference to their first effort at the beginning of the exercise (if this was done). Allow at least forty-five minutes for completion of this portion of the exercise.

•19. (Optional) When everyone has finished writing his diagnostic summary and treatment plan, return the original efforts from the beginning of the training session. Ask them to compare the two. There should be considerable verbal and nonverbal feedback from the group indicating their recognition and awareness of the improvement they have achieved. Comment on how the treatment plans and goals that the group identified in the beginning are quite different from the ideas developed by the group following the analytical thinking process (many diagnostic summary efforts at the beginning of the training come up with unrealistic goals, as opposed to more realistic goals presented at the conclusion of the training). If time permits, read a few of the final products to the group.

•20. (Optional) Offer to give individual feedback on the second diagnostic summary effort. Collect both the first and second diagnostic summary efforts of those who are interested in your critiques. Be honest in your comments, pointing out factual statements as opposed to analytical remarks, unrealistic goals and planning, as well as giving specific positive feedback regarding something that is appropriate, very analytical, or well expressed. If you should wish to retain some of the examples for use in training, secure permission from the author.

•21. Distribute copies of a bibliography of pertinent readings on diagnostic-analytical thinking. Devise the bibliography yourself, making certain that the readings included are readily available in your agency or local library. The group should be ready to receive this and eager to pursue additional research now that they realize the importance of increased knowledge of human behavior in achieving proper assessment and treatment planning. Comment that the bibliography is only a sampling of the kinds of material that are available.

Case examples for use with the casework Analytical Thinking Model

The following examples are included here for those who wish to use them in group training or for individual assignments. However, field instructors and trainers are encouraged to develop additional case situations of their own, using these guidelines:

1. Case examples should be based on real-life situations, with modifications to preserve confidentiality. Some alterations of the actual situation may also be necessary to include factors that are especially important to the learning experience.

2. The case situation should be highly complex, with no obvious, easy solution. The reader should react by thinking, "Wow! Where do I begin?"

3. All examples should typify the kind of situations that could be encountered and the skills that must be used by persons functioning at the degree-level for which the student is studying.

4. It is desirable to have an actual, known case outcome for some of the examples. There will be meaningful learning if the trainer can have students work through the ATM using a given case example and then say, "Would you like to know what *really* happened to Mr. P.?" The contrast or similarity between the learner's projected outcome and the actual outcome often produces considerable discussion.

5. Some case examples can be presented in stages. A problem situation is described in step 1. A second handout then states that "the following events have now occurred" and challenges the learner to deal with the added complications (e.g. see the case of Mr. H. on pp. 290–293).

6. All cases should provide:

A. Factual background information. The trainer may want to include deliberate inconsistencies or errors or to omit certain items of information to challenge the learner's assessment skills.
B. Some background information describing the events leading up to the present situation or presenting problem
C. It may be desirable to include an example of an actual diagnostic summary or portion of an actual recording as part of the case description
D. A brief statement of the current problem
E. A footnote explaining that identifying details have been altered to preserve condentiality.

7. The written example may contain technical medical or psychiatric terms. It may be preferable to leave them undefined as an additional challenge for the learner. If he glosses over the terms and never really examines their meaning, the trainer can use this to point out the hazards of diagnostic thinking and treatment planning when key diagnoses are not understood. On the other hand, unexplained abbreviations and specialized terms may frustrate the learner and hinder his application of the ATM.

8. Supervisory/administrative problems involving unsatisfactory performance usually bring up many issues and provide opportunities for discussing many techniques and aspects of supervision or administration.

9. Cases concerning problem employees or students *should not represent an actual person or situation*. Details must be carefully checked so that *no one* could possibly associate the situation with any given individual. This is usually accomplished by taking bits and pieces from several situations and combining them to make up one representative situation.

10. It is suggested that persons who develop case examples for use in formal training exercises include their name, agency or school, date, and restrictions on reproduction of the material. Our profession's eagerness for dynamic case examples can cause widespread borrowing of ideas and materials that could result in distribution and use that go much beyond or even against the author's original intentions.

A. Mrs. T: An Elderly, Independent Woman Wants to Die at Home*

BACKGROUND

Mrs. T., sixty-eight, has been receiving financial assistance continuously since her husband's death more than

*See Suanna J. Wilson, *Recording: Guidelines for Social Workers* (N.Y.: Free Press, 1980), pp. 221–229, for nine additional case examples for general use in student training or for studying the ATM.

fifteen years ago. Thus, the agency knows her quite well.

Mrs. T. is illiterate and signs all papers with an X. She has not worked under Social Security, and thus her financial assistance (SSI) has been her only source of income. She lives in an older house that is large enough so that she could rent out a room to someone if she wished. However, Mrs. T. has consistently refused to consider this, preferring instead to live alone.

Mrs. T.'s biggest problem has been her severe diabetes. She had her right leg amputated "years ago" and she has been confined to a wheelchair since then. Five years ago her left leg was amputated because of complications from her diabetes. Mrs. T. is on a strict diabetic diet and takes daily insulin injections. Because of her decreasing vision, a neighbor has been coming in to fix her meals and give her her shots. Various social workers have noted that Mrs. T. appears "shaky and nervous."

In spite of her serious physical limitations, Mrs. T. has actually been managing very well. She is well known in the neighborhood and has many friends who look after her. Her home has been modified to accommodate her wheelchair, and she gets along surprisingly well by herself. She is consistently cheerful, outgoing, and friendly and is well liked by everyone, including her social workers.

CURRENT PROBLEM

Some changes began taking place about a month ago. Mrs. T. became disagreeable and difficult to get along with. The neighbor who had been giving her insulin shots and cooking her meals so faithfully for so many years quit when Mrs. T. accused her of stealing food and personal belongings. The agency helped her hire two new housekeepers, who both subsequently quit for similar reasons. All resources are now exhausted; no one wants to work for Mrs. T., yet she cannot continue to live at home alone without help. When the worker suggests nursing home placement as the only other alternative, Mrs. T. states that she'd rather die in her own home then go to a nursing home.

YOUR TASK

Apply the ATM to determine the best course of action in this long-term situation, which is now in a state of crisis. This client could die from a diabetic reaction if she does not receive daily insulin shots, and the local public health department will continue this service on a daily basis for only four more days; then they can come only twice weekly. You have four days to arrive at an appropriate plan.

B. Mr. and Mrs. Z.: A Father Files a Formal Complaint Contesting His Rejection for AFDC

FAMILY COMPOSITION

Mr. Z., forty-four years old
Mrs. Z., forty-one

son, fourteen
son, eleven
daughter, nine
son, eight

BACKGROUND

You are an intake eligibility worker for AFDC (Aid to Families with Dependent Children). In order to qualify for this type of financial assistance, the children must be deprived of the parental support and care of one or both parents. This deprivation can occur through death, disability, divorce, separation, or desertion by one or both parents. The family also must have income that is below the poverty level according to the specific standards set by the state and used by the AFDC program.

Mr. Z. applied for AFDC for his family thirty-five days ago. He has been employed regularly but is temporarily out of work because of a recent illness. However, he expects to return to work in about ten days.

According to Mr. Z., Mrs. Z. has a long history of mental illness and has been in and out of the state mental hospital for several years. She is able to do the housework and provide basic concrete care for the children but cannot leave the house alone. Therefore, Mr. Z. felt that the family was eligible for AFDC because of his wife's emotional disability and his reduced income.

A further review of their situation over the next two weeks finds Mrs. Z. rated as able to do simple work, and thus not considered sufficiently disabled to qualify for AFDC. Furthermore, Mr. Z. returned to work parttime, giving the family just enough income to make them ineligible. Therefore, their application was rejected.

CURRENT PROBLEM

Your supervisor has just informed you that Mr. Z. has requested an appointment with him to contest his rejection. He has also filed an appeal to the rejection decision and, in addition, has written a letter to Congressman Smith and the regional director. He says he plans to see you after he meets with your supervisor, and you know he's really going to let you have it.

YOUR TASK

Use the ATM approach to help you plan for your meeting with Mr. Z.

C. Helen Smith: An Obese Woman Won't Follow Her Special Diet

BACKGROUND

Mrs. Smith is a fifty-four-year-old white female with a long medical history. She has received outpatient care for a number of years and has had several hospitalizations within the past two years. Certain physical problems appear more or less chronic: hypertension, persistent fluid retention in the lower extremeties in spite of low sodium, low calorie diet prescriptions; various dermatological problems, which clear up but then return; anemia; and varicose veins. There are some irregularities in pulmonary function, and Mrs. Smith's obesity is potentially life-threatening.

Mrs. Smith reports that she has been overweight most of her life. She is 5′4″ and on last hospital admission four months ago weighed 268 pounds. She has been on many diets, ranging from sensible low-calorie plans prescribed by her physician to the diet pill regime through local "obesity clinics." Mrs. Smith has been advised over and over of her need to lose weight by just about every nurse and physician who has had contact with her. She's been fully informed of the life-threatening implications and says she sincerely does try to follow her low-calorie diet. Yet, she continues to present physical symptoms that clearly indicate she is not doing this successfully.

Socially, Mrs. Smith is somewhat alone. She has been divorced for many years. Her children are grown and living in other parts of the country, and she has little contact with them. She lives alone in a small apartment and receives financial assistance due to her inability to work combined with her lack of skills. She has been rejected by Vocational Rehabilitation as not being a suitable candidate for vocational rehabilitation in view of her age and physical condition. Mrs. Smith spends most of her time visiting with her neighbors and doing some knitting, and maintains that she really eats very little because she simply cannot afford it.

THE PROBLEM

You have been following Mrs. Smith for some time. You are becoming quite concerned about her apparent denial of the seriousness of her weight problem and her continuing refusal to comply fully with medical recommendations. What kind of counseling approach should you take?

D. "Hubert": A Psychotic Man Frightens the Neighbors

You work for a local family services agency and have been working with Mrs. Schreiber for several months. One day she tells you about "Hubert." This middle-aged man has lived in the rural community where Mrs. Schreiber lives for several years. He is well known to the local residents as the "local crazy man." His behavior is usually ignored or tolerated benevolently by the neighbors. However, Mrs. Schreiber says that she and many others are now frightened of him. He walks the roads talking to himself and has walked up to people working out in their fields and "started cussing them out for no reason at all." Hubert was in military service and talks about a "disability," and it's known that he draws a pension and has spent time in a mental hospital. Mrs. Schreiber says someone called the sheriff, but he told them he could do nothing unless Hubert actually threatened someone and was caught in the act of being dangerous to himself or others. Several community leaders are very protective of Hubert and view the mental hospital and the mental health system as a ''place where bad things happen, and we wouldn't want to do anything to hurt Hubert—such as have him sent back to one of those awful places.''

Mrs. Schreiber lives alone, is elderly, and is obviously frightened, yet she clearly finds it difficult to bring the matter to your attention. What should be done?

E. Mr. Y.: A Diabetic Refuses Lifesaving Surgery

MEDICAL SITUATION

Mr. Y. is a forty-six-year-old black male who was admitted to the hospital with a diagnosis of diabetes mellitus—uncontrolled, with diabetic neuropathy. Prior to admission, the patient had been giving himself insulin injections; on the day of admission, he experienced unusual pain in his lower extremities, to the point that he had difficulty in walking. Medical history indicates that Mr. Y. has been hospitalized four times during the past three years for various problems connected with his diabetic condition. Onset of diabetes occurred at age forty-one. During his hospitalization, it was discovered that Mr. Y. had gangrene involving three of his left toes, necessitating amputation of the affected toes. The patient remained hospitalized several weeks, and discharge home was planned. However, a few days before discharge, it became obvious that Mr. Y.'s vascular insufficiency was quite advanced; as a result, the gangrenous condition was spreading throughout his entire foot. Amputation of the foot was scheduled. However, Mr. Y. told his physician he would not permit this surgery and is threatening to leave the hospital against medical advice. It is at this point that a referral is made to social service by the medical staff.

BACKGROUND INFORMATION

Before the social worker has a chance to see Mr. Y., the nursing staff receive a very anxious phone call from the patient's wife, and they refer her to the social worker. She is concerned over her husband's refusal to permit the surgery, because the doctor has told her that he could die if this is not done. As she talks, the social worker learns the following information:

Mr. and Mrs. Y. have been married for seventeen years. They have five children. Four are grown and out of the home; the fifth, a son aged sixteen, is still living at home. He was recently diagnosed as having a mild case of diabetes, which is adequately controlled with diet alone. Mr. Y., the son of migrant farm workers, received a sporadic education. He left school at twelve to work with his family in the fields. He was drafted at eighteen and served three years in the U.S. Army, where he obtained his high school equivalency and was taught to be a mechanic. He has worked most of his life as an auto mechanic for various small service stations. After being laid off from his last job, he worked for a brief time as a security guard but quit when he had to be hospitalized about a year ago and has been unemployed ever since. Mrs. Y. has done mostly day work, earning approximately $50–$60 weekly. Their son has had a paper route for several years. Their savings are exhausted, and they have been trying to live on Mrs. Y.'s earnings. They are one month behind on their house payments and their late-model car is about to be repossessed. Mr. and Mrs. Y. have never been seen by social service before.

CURRENT PROBLEM

With this information, the social worker prepares for the first interview with Mr. Y. Upon arriving on the floor, the worker finds several nursing staff standing around outside Mr. Y.'s room, listening as Mr. Y. orders the head nurse out of his room as she tries to persuade him to remain in the hospital. He is obviously quite upset and angry.

YOUR TASK

1. Write a diagnostic summary and treatment plan based on the information given on this case thus far.
2. Describe *exactly* what techniques you will use for your first interview with Mr. Y. (see ''Current Problem'' for the setting of this interview). Also tell what you think will happen during your interview with Mr. Y. or what you think the outcome will be.

F. Mrs. P.: A Chronic, Multiproblem Protective Services Situation

The P. family has been known to Protective Services for more than ten years. Their situation is typical of long-term multiproblem families. The following information has been summarized from a very thick case record. Apply the ATM to break down the overwhelmingly complicated situation into manageable bits and pieces and develop a realistic service plan, with appropriate priorities.

FAMILY COMPOSITION

Mrs. P., in her forties, widowed four years
Son, eighteen
Son, sixteen and a half
Son, fourteen

Daughter, twelve
Daughter, eleven
Daughter, eight
Four additional adult children, in and out of the home

BACKGROUND

The family has been receiving AFDC and protective services for more than ten years. During that time, four children have grown up and left home. On one occasion a daughter returned to live at home. So many men kept coming in and out of the home that a neighbor called the police. When the social service department intervened, the daughter moved back out of the home for good.

Mr. P. died in a motorcycle accident that caused injury to his head and face. Prior to his death, Mrs. P. talked repeatedly of her intense dislike for him. Yet she paid several thousand dollars to have plastic surgery performed on his face after death so he would look presentable for an open-casket funeral. The funeral took place on a very hot summer day, and she paid extra to have the casket specially aid conditioned to keep the plastic from melting.

The children and the house are rarely clean. Dirty clothes are piled all over, several days' accumulation of unwashed dishes are evident, and bugs abound. One or more rooms are cleaned when Mrs. P. is notified in advance of the worker's visit. However, the record contains repeated warnings to avoid the red rug in the middle of the living room floor: The hole in the floor underneath it serves as the family's garbage disposal.

The younger children have had repeated illnesses, and Mrs. P. has a history of providing poor care. At one point the two youngest girls had tonsillitis, and Mrs. P. waited so long before she sought medical attention that they nearly went deaf. The school has complained of poor attendance for all the children. The Health Department has visited the home on several occasions to check out complaints of sickness when the children have been kept out of school for supposed illnesses. All of the children are doing poorly in school. All four of the older children (who are no longer in the home) dropped out of school at age sixteen. Mrs. P. talks constantly to her workers about herself, her ideals as a mother, her desire to raise the children properly, the importance of their education, and so on. She expounds at length about why it is important to keep the children clean and expresses some basically good ideas on how to raise children. But there is no evidence that she is implementing her ideals.

The sixteen-year-old has just dropped out of school, because he says, he didn't like it. He is a juvenile diabetic, poorly controlled. He cannot do heavy work and has occasional blackouts. He says he's interested in being a mechanic but has no desire to take any special training in this field or to return to school. He is currently looking for work and feels he'll have no difficulty finding it. The youngest child is mentally retarded and attends special classes at school. She has been described as having a pleasant, outgoing personality. However, her teachers feel that Mrs. P.'s lack of interest in helping her hinders her progress and that environmental factors may be affecting her intellectual performance.

Complaints from neighbors and others come in every one or two years on this family. Most concern poor housekeeping standards, noise, or the men seen frequently in the home when the oldest daughter was there for her visits. The most recent complaint, received nine months ago, charged that the children were not clean and were not attending school regularly. The neighbor who complained added that Mrs. P.'s older children were in fact in the home even though she had been telling everyone they were not living there.

Mrs. P. sometimes reacts defensively to the worker's visits but always agrees that she could probably do a better job with her family and promises to try harder. Her situation usually improves somewhat for a time. Service plans repeatedly mention the goal of "continuing to encourage Mrs. P. to take better care of her family."

What should the worker do now?

G. Mr. and Mrs. S.: A Protective Services Case Appears Significantly Improved

CLIENTS

Mr. S., twenty-four years old
Mrs. S., eighteen
Daughter, two

BACKGROUND

This family became known to the agency eighteen months ago, when someone, desiring to remain anonymous, reported seeing the mother with the baby slung over her back in a carrier while shopping in a grocery store. The baby was observed wearing only diapers, was not clean, and "squalled his head off up and down the aisles." The caller reported that the mother seemed oblivious to the baby's discomfort. Subsequent contacts found the family living in a humble but clean and orderly apartment. Mrs. S. explained that the baby had a type of colic for which she had been to the doctor and that she had been feeling poorly for several days and crying a great deal as a result. Mrs. S. had to go shopping, had no one to sit with the baby, and thus took the child with her, knowing that she would probably cry. As it was a hot summer day she saw no need to dress her more warmly, especially knowing that she would be in the store for only a few minutes.

The agency continued to visit the family regularly on a preventive basis and helped Mrs. S. with obtaining eyeglasses, getting a new mattress, referral to GED training (since she failed to finish high school), and miscellaneous other services including some guidance on basic childcare techniques. Mrs. S.'s goal is to get a job and become self-supporting. Things went along well until about a year ago when a complaint was received from a neighbor that "Mr. and Mrs. S. had a big fight" and she feared for the baby's safety. Mrs. S. explained that they were under severe financial stress at the time as Mr. S. had lost his job and they were fighting over money. The worker helped them obtain emergency food stamps. In a few weeks Mr. S. found another job and the situation was eased.

Recently, the worker has reported that "Mrs. S. seems to be becoming dependent on the worker." For example, she called the worker and asked her to come out to the house to help her complete a rather routine form that the food stamp worker had sent her. The social worker helped her with it by phone and planned a home visit in two or three weeks. At the time of that visit, the baby seemed well cared for, and Mr. S. continued to be employed, though Mrs. S. reported that things were a little tight financially. In subsequent contacts, Mrs. S. seemed to have things pretty well in hand, was preparing to take her high school equivalency exams, and expressed confidence that she and her husband and baby could make it, though, they knew it wasn't going to be easy. There have been no additional complaints filed regarding the family.

PRESENT SITUATION AND WORKER'S TASK

A reassessment is due on this case now. The worker is considering closing the case. What would you do if you were the worker?

H. Joe Brown: A Mentally Alert Man Refuses Nursing Home Placement

Mr. Brown, aged fifty-seven, has been hospitalized for one month following a stroke. Prior to admission he was living alone in his farmhouse located in a rather rural area of the country. Now his right arm is paralyzed and his right leg is partially paralyzed. As a result, he is very unsteady on his feet, shuffling very slowly and tiring a great deal after walking only short distances (such as across the room). He is also aphasic. He can understand what is said to him, but his speech is garbled. Thus he answers questions through gestures and nods, as he is illiterate.

PROBLEM

It is now time for Mr. Brown to be discharged from the hospital. Medical staff, including the social worker, feel he should enter a nursing home, because he is believed to be incapable of caring for himself. Everyone agrees this would be the best plan since he lives alone, has no close relatives or family nearby, and is so unsteady on this feet. However, Mr. Brown refuses to go to a nursing home and insists that he wants to return home. The medical team considered having him declared mentally incompetent so a guardian could be appointed to order him to go to a nursing home. However, psychological tests revealed that he is fully alert mentally in spite of his speech disorder. Finally a decision was made to send a social worker and public health nurse out on a home visit to see what his living arrangement is like and determine if it is feasible for Mr. Brown to return home. They find his situation even worse than imagined.

Mr. Brown lives in a very old, rundown farmhouse. The nearest neighbor is half a mile away. The house is about to fall down. It sits on 80 acres that have been in Mr. Brown's family for several generations. The house has no running water. The well (with a hand pump) is located several hundred feet from the house and is the only source of water on the property. The only source of heat (in a part of the country where it goes to 25° below zero in the winter) is an old wood-burning stove with an unsafe-appearing chimney connection. Cooking is done over a one-burner camp-type stove. All the rooms in the house are piled virtually to the ceiling with old clothing and assorted miscellany. An old mattress without sheets obviously serves as Mr. Brown's bed. Eight rickety steps must be climbed to get into the house and to get outside to the outhouse. There is no phone. Mr. Brown's only income is $122 Social Security.

When the report of the home visit is made to the medical team, they feel even more strongly that Mr. Brown simply cannot return home: He must go to a nursing home. Yet Mr. Brown makes it very clear that he's lived in that farmhouse for more than forty years and, regardless of what anyone says, intends to return there. The medical staff, including the social worker, feel almost certain Mr. Brown will die or suffer severe and life-threatening medical complications if he is allowed to return home.

What should be done? What is the role of the social worker in this situation?

I. Mr. H.: A Multiproblem AFDC Family

The following information has been summarized from a social service case record with details disguised to preserve confidentiality. It is necessary to understand the background information and facts regarding the case in order to respond properly to the diagnostic summary that follows.

FACTUAL DATA AND CASE SUMMARY

Ages: Mr. H. is forty-one; Mrs. H., twenty-eight; daughter, six; daughter, nine; son, twelve.

Household composition: Mr. and Mrs. H. and their children live in a three-bedroom apartment with Mr.

H.'s sixty-year-old mother. She is totally blind from glaucoma and receives financial assistance based on her blindness and inability to work.

Ethnic factor: This is a black family.

Contact with agency: Mrs. H. came to the AFDC office to apply for financial assistance in October 1979, when her husband had to stop working because of physical problems. The application was subsequently approved, and the family was assigned to a service worker.

BACKGROUND

Mrs. H. appeared in the AFDC intake office in October 1979. Since then, there have been two home visits and another contact in the office with Mrs. H. A complete social history was done at the time of the home visits, and what follows is a summary of information in the record based on these three contacts with the family thus far:

Mrs. H. had her first child at age twelve (it was placed for adoption). She has a sixth-grade education and has never worked outside the home except for occasional domestic work. Her health is fair.

Mr. H.'s mother used to live with a common-law husband. He died of a heart attack ten years ago, and since then she has lived with the H.'s. Her vision became progressively worse, and she became totally blind approximately five years ago. She just recently began receiving financial assistance based on her blindness.

Mr. H. dropped out of high school at an early age to help support his ten siblings. Mr. and Mrs. H. were married in 1969. He has been a construction worker for the past ten years, doing heavy labor. He was laid off from his job several weeks ago because he was absent so much from work. The H.'s have exhausted their savings, and this has made them apply for financial assistance. Mr. H. has had diabetes since age fifteen and has been hospitalized several times since then with various physical problems. There have been no recent incidents that required inpatient care. He has been complaining of some numbness in his legs. Medical reports indicated that he would be unable to work for quite a while, and the AFDC application was subsequently approved.

DIAGNOSTIC SUMMARY

In February 1980 the worker wrote the following diagnostic summary. It appears here exactly as written by the worker:

Mr. and Mrs. H have been the subject of several home visits. It was Mrs. H who provided most of the details regarding this family's situation and needs. Satisfactory progress in school is reported for all the children. However, the oldest boy does tend to oversleep in the morning and frequently arrives tardy to school. According to Mrs. H, her husband engages in some behaviors that are quite problematic for her. One illustration is his approach to foods. He is highly selective in his choice of foods and this is a source of conflict for Mrs. H who resists cooking special meals for him. Mrs. H sees her husband as being a fiercely independent person who has difficulty expressing underlying feelings openly. It is important that he be masculine at all times in her eyes. She has attempted to communicate to him her feeling that such a manner is not necessary for her to love him, but his behavior remains unchanged. Mrs. H suspects that her husband has not been feeling well for some time and told this worker that "his refusal to discuss these things with me is worse than outright rejection." Her perceptions of how Mr. H became unemployed is that he "got laid off." However, she confided in the worker her feeling that he was actually fired for some reason unknown to her. Mrs. H reports that her husband has been leaving the house every morning and she assumed he was reporting to work. Mr. H told the worker he had been going to work daily and could not understand why he lost his job. He does complain of a "bum leg" that bothers him from time to time; but he is quick to follow up with a statement that he takes good care of his "sugar" and insists that this had nothing to do with his being laid off.

Mr. H gives the appearance of a healthy man—he is big, muscular, and well developed. Hopefully he will be able to return to work shortly. This client obviously does not relate well to social workers. It was necessary for Mrs. H to cajole him into signing the AFDC application form and he has attempted to avoid me. For example, he was present for the first home visit, but was absent the second time. Mr. H spends much of his time keeping in touch with friends at his former place of employment and talks repeatedly of getting odd jobs on the side so he will not have to work for anyone else. His eating habits were discussed, and Mr. H explained that since he does not have to be on any special diet, he has been eating whatever he desires without restriction. He describes his wife as having a strong dislike for cooking, stating that she prefers fast-fix foods which comprise the bulk of their menu. Mr. H described several contacts with his physician and explained his physician's feeling that he would be able to start looking for work again soon. The worker was very supportive of this aspiration, as it is certainly important for Mr. H to have a hopeful goal to work toward. He is a relatively young man and does have an intact family.

Since Mr. H has been out of work for some time, he views his main problem right now as financial. He considers that his health problems are primarily behind him and looks forward to returning to work soon. When this hope was supported by the worker, he seemed to respond more positively to interactions with me. Some of the behavioral modification implications of Mrs. H's dietary demands were reviewed with Mrs. H. She was advised not to reinforce his eating habits by catering to his demands for special food. She found this idea reasonable and will be implementing it. Mr. H appears quite difficult to reach and it is suspected that he will not respond to suggestions this worker might offer. Thus, we will be working with him indirectly through Mrs. H—striving to use her as a vehicle for reaching him.

<u>Treatment</u> <u>Plan</u>: This case is being referred to Vocational Rehabilitation. A copy of this diagnostic summary was shared with the DVR representative. He concurred that Mr. H would be a good candidate for rehabilitation and has decided to accept the case, pending receipt of additional medical information.

This worker plans to see Mrs. H in the office in two weeks to discuss the home situation further. As she has worked as a domestic outside the home and since all of her children are in school, there is a possibility that she might obtain some part-time domestic work to help out financially until her husband can return to work. Their apartment rent is $250 monthly, which is obviously excessive for their AFDC budget. Thus, they have been placed on the application list for public housing, though it may be several years before a vacancy occurs. Finally, this worker plans to talk to Mr. H's former employer to determine his perception of Mr. H's situation and the circumstances that led to his loss of employment.

<u>Recommendation</u>: This case will remain active for services until the above goals have been accomplished.

FOLLOW-UP REPORT AND CASE OUTCOME

Three months after the diagnostic summary was written, the following events occurred:

Mr. H. did do odd jobs for various people for several weeks, though he never made enough to get off AFDC. One day Mr. H. was found by the police lying on the street in a coma. He was taken to an alcoholic rehabilitation program as he had a strong odor of alcohol on his breath. It was several hours before anyone realized he was actually in a diabetic coma. He was then rushed to the local county hospital. It was found there that Mr. H. suffered from juvenile diabetes and that it had been out of control for some time. He had not been observing any dietary precautions and had been careless in urinary testing and insulin administration. He had ignored symptoms of diabetic neuropathy. Gangrene developed in his "bum leg," and Mr. H. subsequently underwent an above-the-knee amputation. There is some loss of sensation in his other leg, and it is questionable whether it can be saved. An eye exam revealed diabetic retinopathy and a prognosis that blindness will result in a few years. It is doubtful that Mr. H. will ever be able to work again. After six weeks, he continues hospitalized.

Mr. H.'s case never became active with Vocational Rehabilitation. When the DVR counselor obtained the medical reports, they showed the true seriousness of Mr. H.'s condition. DVR predicted that he was undoubtedly heading for some complications shortly and therefore felt that it would not be appropriate to start rehabilitation planning at this time.

Mrs. H. became hysterical upon Mr. H.'s admission and at first refused to leave his bedside. She "ordered the nurses around" and seemed to want to take charge of everything on the floor. She became highly anxious if the nurses did not respond immediately to her calls and resented their spending time with other patients. After several weeks, Mrs. H. suddenly stopped visiting and now calls infrequently to inquire about her husband's condition. She has not responded to the worker's calls.

Mr. H. refuses to see his family, does not want to see his friends from work, is not motivated to participate in physical therapy and other hospital treatment programs, and refuses to talk to the AFDC social worker. He has been losing weight and spends much of his time sleeping. Whereas he once was ambitious, self-confident, and somewhat explosive in temperament, he is now passive, apathetic, quiet, but somewhat concerned about his wife and puzzled by her behavior. Mr. H. has commented several times that his life is ruined and he has nothing to look forward to now.

The family continues to receive AFDC. Their housing

problem has not been resolved. The new AFDC service worker plans to provide intensive counseling services.

LEARNER'S TASK

1. The original AFDC worker left her job. Since you have some experience and advanced training, this multiproblem case has been assigned to you for intensive casework services. As the new AFDC service worker, you have a copy of the summary of the case, the diagnostic summary, and the follow-up report. Do the following:

   A. Study the diagnostic summary carefully. Is it a well-written diagnostic summary? Why or why not? Look again at the case outcome. Did it appear that the first worker picked up on everything that was really happening in this case? Do you agree with the service plan made by the prior worker? Do you see any connection between the activity/plans made by the prior worker and the case outcome?

   B. Write a diagnostic summary as you feel it should be written. Be certain it includes your analysis of what you think is really happening in this case situation. Focus on the things described in the case outcome. Use the Analytical Thinking Model on pp. 280–282 to help you prepare your summary.

   C. State why you think Mr. H. is responding the way he is to his hospitalization.

   D. State why you think Mrs. H. has stopped visiting her husband and why she gave the nursing staff on the floor such a hard time when she was visiting regularly.

2. Write a treatment plan. Be sure to include the following:

   A. Your short-term plans. Be very specific. State what you would do when you walk into the room to see Mr. H. for the first time.

   B. Your long-term plans. Again, be very specific.

   C. State what you think will eventually happen to Mr. and Mrs. H. If you could look into the future, what do you think will be this family's situation, say, five years from now? Be very brief; confine your comments to one or two sentences.

ALTERNATE EXERCISE (LESS DIFFICULT)*

Read all the material on the case of Mr. H. Analyze the diagnostic summary written by the AFDC worker.

1. Read up on diagnostic summaries and how they should be written. State whether you think the diagnostic summary written in February 1980 is a well-written or poorly written

*Instructors may want to set this up as a debate-team exercise if this training is being given in a group situation.

diagnostic summary and treatment plan. There may be both good and bad things about it. However, it has to be either "more bad than good" or "more well-written than poorly written." Don't hedge. Take one side or the other.

2. List all the reasons you feel it was a well-written or poorly written diagnostic summary. Use everything possible to substantiate your point of view.

J. Mrs. X.: An Elderly Woman Who Is Going Blind Refuses Cataract Surgery†

BACKGROUND

Mrs. X. is sixty-five years old and lives alone in a small shack. Even though it is in the country, neighbors are close by. The case became known to the agency one year ago when a neighbor called, concerned because Mrs. X. was gradually going blind and had no family to help her. Subsequent home visits found Mrs. X. to be a pleasant, talkative person who did indeed complain of decreased vision but felt she could continue taking care of her basic needs without difficulty. She expressed no other needs and appeared obviously alert and able to get around, though quite overweight.

After six months, Mrs. X. began telling the worker she occasionally tripped over chairs and tables. With the agency's encouragement, Mrs. X. made an appointment with an ophthalmologist and reported that he advised her that cataracts were advancing on her eyes and surgery was needed. The worker's follow-up contact with the opthalmologist verified that this was indeed the case, and he predicted decreasing vision unless she had the surgery.

PRESENTING PROBLEM

Mrs. X. adamantly refused to undergo surgery, explaining that her husband died two years ago in a hospital and was treated poorly by hospital staff. She denies that her decreasing vision is a serious problem, reassuring the worker that friends and neighbors and especially her church help her with groceries and other needs (this was subsequently verified by the worker). She maintains that she really has no other needs at this time and either changes the subject or flatly refuses to consider surgery when advised to do so by the worker.

What would you do now if you were the worker? Be very specific.

†This exercise includes a case outcome (see next page). Trainers or supervisors might wish to have students work with the first part and share the outcome only after all ideas for dealing with the situation have been exhausted. The Analytical Thinking Model could also be applied to the situation after students learn the case outcome. See also pp. 131–137 for a process-recording of an interview with Mrs. X, in which the student worker talks with her about her forthcoming death (the client is referred to as "Mrs. W" instead of "Mrs. X").

MRS. X.: CASE OUTCOME

A new worker was assigned to the case. No contact had occurred in more than one month since the prior worker left the agency. The case record was reviewed from start to finish to determine just what was known about Mrs. X. The worker made a home visit, planning to focus on feelings, find out what her daily life is like, and try to get to know her as a person, deemphasizing advice-giving to undergo surgery.

Upon arrival at Mrs. X.'s home, the worker found her standing on the front porch, waiting for a friend to take her to her doctor. She complained of some pain and readily showed the worker a large sore on her abdomen. The worker observed that while she appeared overweight, most of the weight was around her stomach, which appeared quite distended. A home visit was planned for her immediate return from the doctor. During this contact, Mrs. X. told the worker the doctor recommended hospitalization and surgery to take care of her open sore and the excess fluids caused by "the hole in my liver." However, she refused hospitalization and instead returned home. The worker subsequently talked directly with Mrs. X.'s doctor and learned that he had been treating her for some time for cirrhosis. The liver is now severely damaged, and there is little more that can be done for Mrs. X. except some medication and dietary precautions to reduce fluid accumulation. Mrs. X. is not expected to live very long; no surgery has been recommended, as her condition is too far advanced.

Case examples for use with the administrative Analytical Thinking Model

A. A Student's Dilemma

Your name is David and you are doing your field placement at the local program for substance abuse. Harold Williams is your faculty liaison person from the school. You feel comfortable with this arrangement, as you've had him for several classes. You have been assigned to the branch of the program that works with DWI cases—persons arrested on charges of driving while intoxicated. Offenders are required to attend a special driving safety course, to attend lectures on the effects of drugs and alcohol, and also to meet individually and in groups with counselors to discuss personal or family problems that might be involved with the offender's use of drugs and to evaluate the extent and impact of substance abuse on the offender's life situation. You have been in field placement for several months now and have reached the point where you review the list of new referrals on a routine basis and pick up on certain ones to add to your caseload.

Today as you review the roster, a man's name grabs your attention: Harold Williams! As you check the identifying data, you realize that it is indeed your faculty liaison person. The police report states that he and a female passenger (not his wife, whom you have met) were stopped at 12:30 A.M. because the car was weaving wildly back and forth across the road. During the arrest, the vehicle struck another car, resulting in minor injuries for the other driver and for Mr. Williams. A search of the car turned up several ounces of marijuana, four six-packs of beer, and two bottles of whisky.

Help! Do you let anyone know what you've learned? Should you even tell your field instructor?

B. A Group Leader Faces a Difficult Decision

Sally, fourteen years old, recently enrolled in an activity group for teenagers, sponsored by the local YWCA. This particular YWCA is large and well equipped and employs several professionally trained social workers. Robert Hazelton, twenty-seven, is Sally's group leader. Sally was referred to the group by another social worker who recognized her isolation from her peers and her desperate need for acceptance and a sense of belonging to something. At first Sally responded eagerly to the group and seemed to make several friends. However, after four meetings she has become a serious problem. She often comes in late, makes rude remarks to everyone around her, and ridicules other members who attempt to express feelings of any kind. Last week the problem became so intense that several youngsters actually ran from the room in tears under Sally's scathing attack. The group leader's efforts to intervene were useless, and the impact on the two youngsters involved will be very negative as they are shy and hesitant to express themselves, and they were just beginning to gain self-confidence and come out of their shells. Sally's behavior will probably undo several months of progress.

Sally's behavior seems to become worse with each meeting rather than better. The group leader sees in Sally a desperate need for acceptance and a definite cry for help. She needs to continue in the group if at all possible. Yet the emotional needs of the other youngsters must also be considered. What should be done?

C. Public Housing Versus Bayview Heights Community

The local public housing authority has been picketed for several days by residents of the community who live near the newly opened public housing development. Extensive public relations meetings were held prior to completion of the project in an effort to minimize these problems and to increase acceptance of the project by the more well-to-do neighborhood known as Bayview Heights. The picketers complain of increased vandalism in their neighborhood and related problems since the project opened. They are demanding that the Housing Authority pay for extra police protection and place certain restrictions on the project residents, prohibiting them from entering Bayview Heights after 9 P.M. and so forth. On the other hand, project residents complain of a hostile attitude on the part of Bayview residents, rejection and isolation by their peers in the local public school, and an unfriendly attitude on the part of local shopowners. Bayview is a middle- to upper-middle-class community; the residents of the project are 70 percent black, 20 percent Puerto Rican, and 10 percent white and mostly of lower socioeconomic status.

Social work staff in the Housing Authority are concerned about the tensions in the community and the impact on all concerned, including the Housing Authority. What can be done?

D. A Seductive Field Instructor*

Your name is Angela and you are doing your field placement at one of the local institutions, which employs several hundred staff. Your field instructor is Mr. Jones. He is new to the school but seems to be very friendly and helpful. The nature of your field placement requires that you work irregular hours, as the institution is active eighteen hours a day and off-hours emergencies sometimes arise. One evening as you and Mr. Jones are working late, he pulls two cans of beer out of his desk drawer and offers you one along with a sandwich for dinner while you work—a simple-appearing, friendly gesture. However, after several more cans of beer, Mr. Jones loosens up considerably and, to your horror, changes from a dignified professional into an "amorous slob." Before you know what's happening, he becomes just a little too friendly and propositions you. The janitor accidentally interrupts just as you're desperately trying to get away from Mr. Jones, and you take advantage of the opportunity to flee.

What should you say and do now? No real physical harm was done, and you actually feel a little sorry for the man after you've had a chance to calm down. However, Mr. Jones will be your field instructor for six more months. What could happen if you did or did not do something about this incident?

E. Steve Hunt: A Problem Employee Forces the Supervisor to Make a Difficult Decision

There is no real "Steve Hunt." Bits and pieces have been taken from various situations to arrive at this fictitious case. It is not intended to represent any past or present employee or supervisee in any setting. Even though it is not

*Such incidents are extremely rare but have been reported by students on occasion. The fact that such incidents occur between employers and employees has been well documented in private industry.

based on an actual employee situation, it does illustrate a typical problem that can arise when there is a decline in a supervisee's performance.

INSTRUCTIONS

1. Read the case example.
2. Write a *brief* paragraph telling what you would do if you were this person's supervisor. Be *very* specific. Do not respond with "I would consult with *my* supervisor."
3. Now go back and apply the Analytical Thinking Model for large systems. Go through all the steps described on p. 282. Do this in writing.
4. Write a brief statement telling what you would do with this problem situation. Be very specific.
5. Compare your statement in step 4 with your initial decision in step 2, before you applied the ATM.

BACKGROUND PRIOR TO PRESENT EMPLOYMENT

Mr. Hunt is seventy-one years old. After he finished high school, he spent several years in the service, then worked for several more years before going on to college under the GI Bill. He received his BA degree in English at the age of thirty, then taught in public schools for ten years and spent several more years in an unsuccessful small business. During this time Mr. Hunt realized that he had a strong need and desire to work with people in a helping relationship and thus sought employment in the local public welfare department. After several years there, he obtained a stipend from his agency to attend graduate school and subsequently obtained his MSW at the age of forty-eight. He continued working in the public welfare department as a supervisor for four years until he completed his commitment to them. He spent the next five years in a family service agency and then a brief period in a public health department, where he was rather unhappy, as he found the work was not what he thought it would be. Eighteen years ago he began working for another branch of the setting where he is now employed. Twelve years ago he transferred, with retirement and seniority benefits intact, to his present setting. It is a large, multidisciplinary environment. Mr. Hunt is employed as a mental health caseworker.

HIS PRESENT EMPLOYMENT SITUATION

Mr. Hunt has been in social service here for twelve years. There are no mandatory retirement requirements. He has been a loyal, steady worker—not highly creative, not especially eager to move upward administratively—just reliable and consistently acceptable (average) in his performance. A few years ago some supervisory responsibilities were assigned to him when a vacancy occurred in the department, but Mr. Hunt soon chose to return to direct services, where he has since remained. He has supervised several undergraduate and graduate students and currently has a graduate student under his supervision.

Mr. Hunt's relationships with co-workers and his supervisors have been generally satisfactory. He is usually pleasant. However, as he is considerably older than the majority of social service staff (including his supervisor), he sometimes seems to feel out of step and out of touch with the eager new crop of recent graduates who have joined the department in the past two to three years.

PRESENTING PROBLEM

Mr. Hunt will complete his twenty years' employment eighteen months from now. He has verbalized rather strongly his intention to retire at that time and collect full benefits. He does not want to retire earlier, as these benefits would be substantially reduced.

Mr. Hunt has been married for many years. His wife is not well, and medical expenses have been high. They have two grown children. One is married and living in a distant state. The second suffers from a birth defect resulting in limited ambulation, poor coordination, moderate mental retardation, and a visual handicap. This forty-year-old son lives at home with the Hunts and has required considerable care over the years. Mrs. Hunt has never worked outside the home. Mr. and Mrs. Hunt are buying their home; their mortgage will be paid off during the same year Mr. Hunt plans to retire. He figures if he can keep working until then, he'll be able to make it on his retirement income.

During the past year, there has been a marked change in Mr. Hunt's performance. He has always used an "average" amount of sick leave, but during the past year he was absent for more than thirty days with various physical problems. His work has slowed down considerably, to the point where he is not able to handle an average work load. He is slow to adapt to changes, and the supervisor has had to repeat instructions to him numerous times. Sometimes he seems to

be staring off into space, and it appears that his concentration span is lessening. His rate of careless errors on reports, forms, and dictation has reached an unacceptable level in recent weeks. Mr. Hunt has been wearing a hearing aid for several months now, but it apparently does not or cannot completely correct his increasing hearing deficit, which sometimes causes problems in communication. He is also developing a noticeable tremor of his hands. The supervisor concluded some time ago that Mr. Hunt is suffering from some of the typical problems of advancing age, which are affecting his functioning both mentally and physically. His graduate student, who has been with him for four months and has three more to go in placement, is not handling the situation very maturely; she is loudly and sometimes unprofessionally critical and disrespectful of her supervisor.

Mr. Hunt's supervisor has been meeting regularly with him during the past year to discuss his changed performance. Mr. Hunt always promises to do better and makes a sincere effort. His performance does improve for a time but then slips back into the problematic pattern. He is not usually defensive, but when the supervisor suggests that perhaps he should take advantage of his eighteen years of faithful service to the agency and retire now, he becomes quite upset and emphasizes his plan to continue working until he can retire with full benefits, in a year and a half. In fact, the last time the supervisor made this suggestion, Mr. Hunt became quite angry and indicated that his brother is a practicing attorney in the area and that he has a close friend who is a congressman, and "you aren't going to force *me* to retire!"

The supervisor is aware of Mr. Hunt's home situation and fully emphasizes with his need to continue working, but at the same time the department is suffering from his declining performance, and there is little indication that he will be able to get back up to his previous level. His Annual Performance Evaluation is due in four months.

What should this supervisor do?

Standard-setting and educational contract exercises

A. Think about the student you are supervising or are about to supervise. Name three skills (educational objectives) you would expect the student to acquire.

Now list five learning experiences that you could give the student to help him learn each of the three skills. What kinds of things must he be exposed to or have an opportunity to do or have contact with in order to acquire the skills?

Finally, what would tell you whether the student had acquired each skill? How would you know he had learned it?

B. All social workers need to be able to "establish relationships effectively." What does that phrase mean to you?

Describe the specific behaviors or outcomes that would tell you your student is "effective" at establishing relationships.

Now take a piece of paper and make three columns, labeled "Unsatisfactory," "Average—acceptable" and "Above average." Describe the behaviors or outcome that would tell you what your student's ability to establish relationships was at each of these three levels.

C. Your beginning graduate student has asked you, "How will I know when I become a good caseworker?" Answer as if you were addressing the student.

D. Develop a Level II educational contract with a hypothetical student around transference and countertransference. (See Chapter 6, p. 51, for ideas.)

E. Develop a Level III educational contract with a hypothetical student around skills in leading committee meetings. (See pp. 51-60.)

F. Read the instructions on pp. 55 and 60 for completing the "Qualitative Performance Expectations Sheet" and complete the exercise. See Table A for the worksheet. Pick a skill area that is not illustrated elsewhere in this text.

G. We all know that an essential skill for a counselor or interviewer is the ability to "start where the client is." However, some students are more effective in applying this skill than others. What is the difference between a student who has only minimal skill in this area and one who is highly skilled at "starting where the client is"?

Let us assume that this ability can be expressed on a rating scale from zero to ten, with zero representing no skill and 10 highly superior skill. Indicate the number on the scale that symbolically represents your thinking as to the degree of skill a newly graduating BSW *or* MSW must have.

Table A.   Level IV Written Contract—Worksheet

_____ End of first field placement for BSW student

_____ Newly graduating BSW

* * *

_____ Expectations based on classroom performance/ knowledge only

OR

_____ Small systems (casework) MSW student one-half way through graduate school

_____ Newly graduating MSW casework student

* * *

_____ Expectations based on field placement performance/knowledge only

OR

_____ Large system (Admin., C.O., etc.) MSW student one-half way through graduate school

_____ Newly graduating MSW administration student

* * *

_____ Expectations based on combined field placement and classroom performance

Subskills/Knowledge Necessary to Learn or Do the Identified Skill (Prerequisites)	Experiences to Help Student Learn the Objective	Level or Degree of Skill/ Knowledge Student Must Achieve to Be Considered "Satisfactory"	Level or Degree of Skill/ Knowledge Student Must Achieve to Be Considered "Outstanding"	Level or Degree of Skill/ Knowledge That Would Be Considered "Unsatisfactory"	What Methods Will Be Used to Measure or Assess Student Performance to Determine the Level at Which He Is Functioning?

Now describe, very specifically and *behaviorally,* the degree of skill in "starting where the client is" that you would require/expect of a newly graduating BSW *and also* of an MSW before you would grant the degree. Don't say, "Okay, but it depends on what he is doing in other areas." Either we expect students to achieve a minimal level of skill in "staring where the client is" and educate them accordingly, or we have no expectation or standard in this regard. So what is the minimum acceptable level? Answer on the basis of *your* professional expectation, not on what you think your school or agency expects or should expect.

If you are doing this exercise in a group situation, compare your responses and analyze and discuss them together. Look for similarities and differences and discuss the impact of these on social work education and field instruction.

H. Write an educational statement regarding "use of supervisory conference time." Develop a Level III contract containing three components: objectives, experiences, and measurement (see pp. 51–60).

I. Define the degree of skill you expect of newly graduating BSW *or* MSW students around the skill "recording" (substitute "written correspondence and reports" for administration students). Divide your paper into three columns: "Unsatisfactory," "Average—acceptable," and "Above average." List specific characteristics for each column. Consider the various purposes and uses of social work recording in your setting as you respond.

J. Have your student develop a statement of expectations regarding supervision. Ask him to divide a piece of paper in half vertically and label one side "expectations" and the other "how I will know I'm getting it." Have him list what he expects of you as a field instructor in the first column. In the second, have him list what will tell him the expectation is being met.

Now do the same thing for yourself, referring instead to your student. What do you expect from him in your supervisory relationship, and how will you know you are getting what you expect?

Compare and discuss your results with those of the student.

K. Develop a Level IV educational contract on a simple, concrete educational objective of your choice. Refer to pp. 52–86 for guidance. Try to select a specific objective that is limited in scope—one that is not discussed elsewhere in this text. Avoid broad objectives such as "will be an effective interviewer" or "will be a good supervisor." Instead, select one of the many skill components that go into making an individual an effective interviewer, supervisor, or whatever.

L. Review your school's field instruction manual or other written material that describes educational objectives. The material may be discussed very generally with vague, unspecified objectives, such as "will use community resources effectively," or may describe exposure to experiences rather than skill levels ("will study the interface between environmental systems and intrapsychic adjustment"). You may find the objectives quite behaviorally specific. In any event, select *two* and break them down into the four-column approach described for a Level IV contract on pp. 52–54.

Miscellaneous group exercise

Have three or more field instructors observe a brief role-played interview (no more than ten minutes). Tape-record the interview. Teach the field instructors how to do the three-column method of process-recording described on pages 118–123. Have them observe the interview without taking any notes. Then have the group process record it, striving to remember accurately everything they can from the observed interchange. Ask them to use the "gut-level feelings" column to describe their own reactions as they were observing the interview.

Now compare the various recordings. If possible, have them typed up on a long sheet of paper side by side for easier comparison. How were they different, and why? What accounts for differences in recall, perceptions, and feelings? Discuss the implications for use of process-recording and other observational/assessment techniques in student training.

Play back the tape recording and let each person study his own process-recording as the tape is played. Discuss and analyze the meaning of the results and the trainees' reactions to the exercises.

APPENDIX F

Documents for Use in Field Instruction

1. Field instruction learning experience inventory

This document was prepared at the request of a local school of social work, which wanted to compile a resource file of learning experiences available in all field placements to be used by school faculty and also to be made available to students who wished to learn more about prospective settings before deciding if they wanted to pursue a placement there. This description provides considerably more detail than is requested by the school, as it covers a variety of placement experiences within a single complex department. Each individual field instructor had also completed a form provided by the school, giving more specific information about learning experiences available in his particular area of assignment. Thus, the following description was intended to give an overview of the hospital itself and of the functioning of the social work department within that framework as well as the experiences available with individual staff field instructors. This example is provided to help other settings develop similar reports for submission to their schools (see pp. 31-32). Some minor modifications have been made to render it useful to a nationwide audience.

LEARNING EXPERIENCE INVENTORY

AGENCY: ABC Hospital
UNIT OR DIVISION: Medical Social Service Department
ADDRESS: _____
DATE: _____

Description of what field placement is like in the Medical Social Service Department

The Medical Social Service Department consists of thirty-seven social workers, most of whom have an MSW. We serve a 1,200-bed general medical hospital (psychiatric patients are seen by a different social work department). The patient population is very diverse, representing a full cross-section of social, economic, sex, ethnic, age and other variables. The role of a medical social worker is to help patients and their families with adjustment to illness and hospitalization. There may be strong emotional reactions. Concrete needs may exist concerning financial problems, unemployment, and housing. Many patients require a change in living arrangements after discharge, such as going to a boarding or nursing home. Other return home with the help of community supports such as homemaker services, the securing of prosthetic devices or special care by family members. Marital or family counseling may be needed. Some patients are followed on an outpatient basis after discharge; the majority are referred to community resources if continued services are needed. Our staff sometimes help medical staff deal with their reactions to the patient who dies or with whom they find it difficult to work. Staff in the department serve specialized areas according to patient diagnosis or other characteristics, i.e., dialysis, general surgery, burn unit, pediatrics, spinal cord injured, and so on. The nature of a student's experience can be quite different depending on the specific unit or area to which he is assigned.

We take both administration and casework students; graduate and undergraduate students. Students may be in placement here from three different schools of social work.

All ABC Hospital medical social service placements are coordinated through the staff member identified as the liaison person between agency and school. Students should not contact any individual field instructor until after their interview with this individual. One reason for this is the fact that staff may change their area of assignment or changes in their area may affect their ability to take a student. Thus, all students are referred to the agency liaison person through the school field instruction office, and she then matches them up with a prospective field instructor.

The various areas where placements could exist are described briefly below. There may or may not be opportunities for students to be placed in all of these areas during any given school year.

1. The Medical Unit. This covers quite a few floors in the hospital and services patients hospitalized for various medical problems, such as diabetes, alcoholism, tuberculosis, heart conditions, etc. Patients with dermatology problems are also seen in this unit and a well-developed patient group exists to help them deal with the impact of skin disease upon their body image. There is a rapid turnover of cases but some opportunity exists for long-term involvement. Almost all patients are age 18 or older.

2. The Surgical Unit. This serves adults hospitalized for various kinds of surgery. Some are terminally ill or have had multilative surgery. The majority come for a short time and are discharged with various degrees of recovery. Some longer-term casework is presently offered to the laryngectomy patient through outpatient clinic follow-up.

3. The Orthopedics-Neurology Unit. This unit includes patients hospitalized with orthopedic, neurological and neurosurgical problems. Patients with fractured hips or amputations and diseases of the bones, spine and joints are found in this area. Neurology patients cover those having diseases affecting the brain and nervous system such as strokes, multiple sclerosis, epilepsy and cancer of the brain. Neurosurgery deals with surgery of the nerve tissue including the brain and spinal cord. Common problems are removal of tumors or blood clots from the brain. Most of the patients in the orthopedic-neurology unit stay for a short period of time and require crisis-intervention casework and discharge planning. A number of neurology and neurosurgical patients are left quite seriously handicapped (i.e., paralyzed), and intensive casework services are needed. These patients may be transferred to the Rehabilitation Center and therefore stay hospitalized for a longer time, up to 6 months. While most are adults, a few are teenagers.

4. The Rehabilitation Center. The average length of stay for patients here is three to six months. There is opportunity for intense, long-term therapeutic follow-up with patients both during hospitalization and after discharge. Most are quite severally handicapped, including the spinal-cord injured (paraplegics and quadraplegics), amputees, and stroke patients with paralysis and speech disorders. Many are adolescents or young adults. A high number are drug-involved or sociopathic and/or have multiple social problems. Most have been injured suddenly and traumatically. This is generally not a suitable setting for a student who has never had exposure to a medical setting before or who has not had considerable experience as a social worker or counselor.

5. Ambulatory Care. Social workers are on duty in the Emergency Room from 7:00 A.M. to 11:30 P.M., Monday through Friday, and on weekends and holidays from noon until 8:30 P.M. There is much short-term crisis intervention with patients and families. The majority of patients are not admitted to the hospital but return to the community following receipt of emergency medical or surgical treatment. Several social workers in the Outpatient clinic see patients who come to the hospital for strictly outpatient services. They frequently present many psychosocial needs and economic difficulties. These patients are of all ages.

6. Oncology. These patients are physically housed in a building adjacent to the main hospital grounds and are there because of a diagnosis of cancer. Some are terminally ill and require counseling regarding death and dying. Others have had radical or multilative surgery and need assistance with all of the adjustments required. Still others are in various stages of recovery, receiving chemotherapy, radiotherapy and other treatments that can have side effects or cause complications in their lives. This setting is for experienced students with previous exposure to medical settings.

7. Dialysis. Both children and adults receive dialysis because of kidney failure. Others have received transplants or are awaiting kidney transplants. These are long-term patients. Most are outpatients who live at home and come to the hospital several times weekly for their dialysis treatments. They present multiple social-emotional-financial-family problems. This is a setting for mature students with some previous medical exposure or experience.

8. Maternal/Child-OB/GYN Unit. This unit serves new mothers, teenage mothers, unwed mothers, women with gynecological problems including cancer, women who have recently had abortions, and children and infants with various physical problems including the effects of child abuse. Many cases are highly complex requiring involvement with community resources and protective intervention. Most are short-term and require assertive crisis intervention with patients, families, staff and community agencies.

9. Burn Unit. These are patients who have been severely burned. They range in age from infants to the elderly. The stay is usually fairly long, with follow-up post-discharge provided through the outpatient clinic. The treatment for burns is often painful, and not all social workers can tolerate the physical appearance of the burned patient and the treatment procedures that are given. Much intensive counseling work occurs with patients and families. This setting is appropriate only for students with significant prior exposure to medical settings and some social work experience.

10. Staff Development, Supervision and Administration. Students placed in this speciality can have exposure to in-service training of social service staff and students and members of other disciplines. They may attend the training course for field instructors given by the department; supervise an undergraduate student; participate in planning major workshops; become involved with peer review and accountability, and perform various other administrative activities within the department and interdepartmentally. These students must have considerable personal maturity and must have mastered the basics of casework. Only students with significant previous social work experience or unusual life experiences are accepted for this specialized placement.

Approach to Field Instruction

We have a definite style of student supervision. It is not necessarily suited to all students and their needs. Students placed here can expect the following:

1. All students seeking placement in the department are interviewed first by the department's liaison person who oversees the student program. If she and the

student feel that the setting would meet joint needs and expectations, the student then interviews with the individual staff member for the specialty area in which he wishes to be placed. The student is encouraged to think about his needs as a learner and his educational and career goals before coming to the preplacement interview. Not all students who are interviewed are accepted.

2. Highly structured supervision with regular weekly conference times and field instructor availability as needed.

3. There is a highly structured and very formal orientation provided to all students as a group. Training covers the diagnostic thinking process, confidentiality, how to be a consumer of supervision as a social work student, as well as orientation to the department, the hospital and the community.

4. Students are required to do reading in connection with their field placement and time is allotted during field placement hours for this activity.

5. All students will be required to do some process-recording and/or taping and participate in other methods that enable the field instructor to directly assess the student's skills and provide feedback.

6. Each student will make at least one home visit while in field placement, regardless of the area of assignment.

7. Performance evaluation feedback is continuous and honest. Students will receive feedback on areas where they are doing well and also constructive feedback and guidance on areas where they have room for growth. Students who do not wish to become heavily involved with their field placement experience or who do not want their work examined closely should avoid this setting.

8. Students are expected to work hard in terms of both quantity and quality. Expectations are high but we feel, and our students agree, that we give a lot.

9. All field instructors in the department are required to go through a special training course on techniques of field instruction provided by the Social Service Department as well as to attend training offered by the local schools.

10. All students are encouraged to be creative and reasonably independent in field placement. However, responsibility is placed upon the student to communicate his needs and to participate in the educational experience as an adult learner.

2. Outline for résumé

1. <u>Personal Data</u>

    a. Your name
    b. Address and phone number(s) where you can be reached
    *c. Date and place of birth
    *d. Marital status
    *e. Dependents
    *f. Sex (especially if first name doesn't reveal this)

2. <u>Educational Background</u>

    a. Start with high school and work up to the most recent degree. For each school you attended, give:

        1. Name and address of school attended
        2. Dates attended
        3. Degree received (if any)

*These items are considered sensitive, and concerns about discrimination prevent many employers from asking about them. You may or may not want to include them on your résumé. Some employment applications also ask for height, weight, and related physical characteristics. This information is not pertinent to most social work positions and should not appear on résumés.

b. Mention any special honors received while in school

c. Describe specifically the nature of any field placement experience you had while in school

3. Employment Experience

Start with the most recent and work backward. For each position held, give:

a. Name, exact address, and phone number of place of employment
b. Starting and ending dates of employment
c. Your exact title while employed there
d. Your beginning and ending salary (optional)
e. The nature of your responsibilities
f. Your reason for leaving each place of employment (optional)
g. Name of immediate supervisor who can be contacted for reference (optional for older employments; should be given for most recent and current positions)

(Note: Field placement experiences should be described under "educational background." They should not be treated as employment.)

4. Volunteer Experience

If you have had any volunteer experience even remotely related to social work, this should be listed. Give the same information as for employment, but omit information regarding salary and reason for leaving.

5. Professional Licenses, Membership in Professional Organizations, and other Professional Activities

For each license held that is related to the helping professions give:

a. The exact title of the license
b. The number of the license
c. The expiration date of the license

For each membership in a professional organization that is related to the helping professions, give:
a. The exact title of the organization

6. Publications

List any social work or related materials you have published or presented orally at workshops or professional conferences. Give complete references, including co-authors.

7. Hobbies and Special Interests (optional)

Briefly list any hobbies or special interests which might be relevant to an employment situation and/or which might help the prospective employer understand better what type of person you are.

8. Career Goals—Short and Long Range (optional)

Describe the type of position you are seeking immediately and what your long-range professional, educational, and/or career goals are.

9. <u>Minimum</u> <u>Salary</u> <u>Required</u> <u>(optional)</u>

   Highly optional. Unless you have considerable background and social work
   experience, you could be closing doors by including this item.

10. <u>References</u>*

    These should be persons in addition to names given as immediate supervisors in the
    employment section. Avoid using personal friends unless they are professionals in
    the social work field. For each reference, give:

    a. The full name
    b. Official title (if any) or degree
    c. Business address if available; otherwise home address
    d. Phone number(s) where person can be reached

    NOTE: Permission should be secured from each person listed before you give that
           person as a reference.

3. A tool to help students choose field placements or employment: Self-assessment Questionnaire

The following questionnaire was developed to help students choose a second field placement or an initial employment post-graduation. The questions force the student to think about his educational, personal, and supervisory needs in a very formal and structured manner. They should also increase self-awareness in a number of important educational areas.

The questionnaire is written in a manner that addresses the student directly. Field instructors, faculty, and others can assign it as a self-instructional exercise if desired. It is helpful for field instructors to be aware of the items included as they conduct preplacement interviews and develop educational plans with their students. Schools can ask students to complete the form as a prerequisite for their preplacement interview with a prospective field instructor.

Self-Assessment Questionnaire for Students

INSTRUCTIONS FOR COMPLETION

Students must undergo meaningful self-assessment before they can select appropriate field placements or seek employment successfully. This form provides a structured method for you to conduct this self-assessment. When students encounter difficulties in field placement or employment, it is frequently because of poor matching between their expectations, needs, and educational goals and those of the setting or employer.

This form should be considered highly confidential and completed in total privacy, in a quiet setting where you have time to think through each answer. Responses should be completely honest and as "gut-level" as possible.

The form should be completed with *either* field placement *or* employment in mind. Do *not* try to deal with both things on the same form, as needs and answers will not be the same for both experiences.

Some questions are relevant to field placement only; some pertain to employment only; and others cover both situations. Write "NA" for all nonapplicable items.

Be sure to respond to *each* item. Don't be afraid to say "I don't know" if that is the answer. Actually, if you have had an effective field placement experience and/or are now about to graduate, you should know yourself well enough to answer most of the questions here, though some may require real thought. Lack of such knowledge could indicate blocking on your part or insufficient meaningful feedback from those who should have provided it during field placement and/or classroom experiences.

If you have not had a field placement, base your answers on previous social work experience or an employment situation where you had to relate to a supervisor. This questionnaire is recommended for use by students who are choosing a second rather than a first field placement. Most persons without significant social work or employment experience simply do not have enough professional self-awareness to be able to answer these questions. However, the form may still prove useful by presenting a picture of the kinds of self-awareness such students should achieve during the first year.

You should not be pressured to share the content of this questionnaire with anyone. Field instructors should not feel

---

*If a current employer does not know you are job-hunting, do not give his name on the resume as a reference, or do so with a note "do not contact." Most prospective employers will want to contact this person, but you can discuss this in your interview and you should plan to tell him of your job-hunting efforts before someone else breaks the news to him.

threatened if you choose not to share this form with them. How much and what is shared should be left entirely up to you.

Save the form, when it is completed, so that you can review it for comparative purposes as you gain additional experience and professional maturity. It should be completed at the beginning and at the end of each field placement; at the point of graduation; and perhaps again after one or two years of paid social work experience.

1. List below ten things that you liked about your present (or most recent) field placement, such as the types of learning experiences you had, the kind of supervision you received, and so on. Be very specific. For each of the ten responses, state why you liked that aspect of your experience.

2. List below all the things about your current (or most recent) field placement that you did not like, did not get an opportunity to do, and/or wish could have been different. For each item, state why.

3. List the main characteristics of your personality (e.g. passive, aggressive, easily intimidated, eager, anxious, creative).

4. Describe the kind of emotional or supervisory environment in which you function best. What kind of climate is necessary in a field placement or work setting in order for you to learn, or to be really productive, and so forth.

5. What do you want from a supervisor?

6. What do you need from a supervisor?

7. Following is a list of some of the kinds of things that can happen in a relationship between a supervisee and supervisor (or student and field instructor). Some are things that should occur; others are problems some supervisees experience. A few instructional techniques are also listed. Use the following code to mark each item:

       OK = I have experienced this <u>and</u> it was okay – I had no major problem or discomfort with it.
        X = I have experienced this <u>and</u> it made me very uncomfortable <u>but</u> I never really told my supervisor how I felt.
        S = I have experienced this <u>and</u> it made me uncomfortable <u>and</u> I was able to voice my discomfort to my supervisor and/or the school <u>and</u> I tried to change it.
     N–OK = I have never experienced this, but I think I could handle it okay.
      N–U = I have never experienced this, and I am not sure how well I could handle it.
        W = I wish I could do (or could have done) this.

1. _____ Do process-recording.
2. _____ Supervisor observes me interviewing.
3. _____ I observe supervisor interviewing.
4. _____ Tape-record interviews.
5. _____ Videotape interviews.
6. _____ Supervisor not present or on the job the same hours I am in field placement.
7. _____ Not meeting with my field instructor often enough (minimum should be once a week for one to two hours.)
8. _____ Get written comments from my field instructor on my recordings, summaries, etc.
9. _____ Not having enough to do.
10. _____ Being "caseworked" (field instructor digging into my personal life).
11. _____ Field instructor seems too busy for me.
12. _____ A long delay (weeks) before getting my first case after starting field placement.
13. _____ Not knowing how the field instructor thinks I'm doing.
14. _____ Unexpected absence of field instructor due to illness, etc.
15. _____ Unexpected change of field instructor in the middle of field placement.
16. _____ Being left more or less on my own.
17. _____ Receiving highly structured, close supervision.
18. _____ Receiving 100 percent positive feedback regarding my performance in field.
19. _____ Receiving critical feedback.
20. _____ Receiving a "satisfactory" in field instead of above satisfactory or "outstanding."
21. _____ Having the field instructor share examples of my work with the school (i.e., faculty liaison person).
22. _____ Being supervised by someone whose knowledge/skill I do not respect.
23. _____ Disagreeing with my field instructor on assessment of my work.
24. _____ A personality clash with a field instructor.
25. _____ Doing a formal educational contract with the field instructor that spells out learning objectives for the quarter/semester/year.
26. _____ Getting critical feedback in public.
27. _____ Being angry at the field instructor about something.
28. _____ Telling the field instructor directly what she/he needs to do differently to meet my needs better.
29. _____ The field instructor advises/involves my faculty liaison person regarding how I am doing, especially if there is a problem.
30. _____ When I do something well, I am told <u>why</u> it worked.
31. _____ When I do something that is "not so good," I am told why and instructed on alternate ways of handling it that might be more effective.
32. _____ Having too much to do: too many cases, or excessive expectations regarding work load.

33. ____ Pinch–hitting for a regular staff member who is absent, or helping out in a staff shortage; being treated more like an employee than a student/learner.

34. ____ Being supervised by someone other than the person the school thinks is supervising me.

35. ____ Having a field instructor who has no professional training in social work (psychologist, administrator, etc.)

36. ____ Being supervised by someone younger than I am.

8. List at least _five_ things about you that you consider to be your assets—your strongest points. Be very specific and personal; don't just say, "I have a BSW degree" or "I think my casework skills are good." Be personal: "I learn quickly," or "I can handle a lot of pressure" are much more meaningful gut–level responses.

9. List at least _five_ things about you that you consider to be your weak points, things you need to work on improving. Don't cop out by saying, "I need more training." Be _personal_: "I tend to get defensive when criticized" or "I don't work well under pressure" are much more meaningful responses.

10. The following list describes client groups that might be found in some settings. Put an "X" by the ones you would feel most comfortable or most skilled in working with, and put an "O" by the ones you would feel less comfortable working with or would rather not work with at all. (Be honest; all social workers have some client groups they would rather not work with or just plain don't like.)

____ Infants
____ Children
____ Adolescents
____ Adults
____ The aged
____ Physically handicapped
____ Mentally retarded
____ Emotionally/mentally disturbed
____ The voluntary client (he asks for your services)
____ The involuntary client
____ Dependent personalities
____ Aggressive/acting out persons
____ Psychotics
____ Law offenders
____ Highly religious people
____ Institutionalized persons
____ Family units
____ Persons with marital problems
____ Character disorders (sociopath)
____ Unwed mothers
____ Homosexuals/lesbians
____ The disfigured
____ Senile persons (OBS)
____ Grossly obese persons

____ Lower–income groups
____ Middle–income groups
____ Upper–income groups
____ Urban clients
____ Rural clients
____ Well–educated clients
____ People who lack education
____ Blacks
____ Whites
____ Latins
____ Indians
____ Other minority groups
____ Alcoholics
____ Drug abusers
____ Persons with sexual adjustment problems
____ Males
____ Females
____ Dying patients
____ Hospitalized persons
____ A client who is also a professional helping person
____ The intellectually gifted
____ Women having abortions
____ Atheists
____ child abusers

Use the remaining space on this page to list any other types of client groups that you would feel comfortable or uncomfortable working with.

11. Following are some common defense mechanisms and behaviors that may present themselves during client—social work relationships. Mark each item, using the following code:

X = I know what this is, have dealt with it, and feel confident about my skills for doing so.
C = I have dealt with this but don't yet feel confident of my ability for doing so.
0 = I have never dealt with this.
? = I don't really know what this is.
U = For some reason, I just don't feel comfortable working with this.

____ Transference and countertransference
____ Denial
____ Projection
____ Client rejects social worker
____ Client cancels/fails to keep appointments
____ Overt hostility
____ Client cries
____ Resistance
____ Passive-aggressive behavior
____ Overidentification on my part
____ Anger
____ Free-floating anxiety
____ The manipulative client
____ Repression
____ Regression
____ Sublimation
____ Ingratiating behavior
____ Client who accuses me of violating his confidentiality
____ Success in treatment/outcome
____ Failure in treatment/outcome
____ The nonverbal person
____ The overtalkative person
____ The client who swears a lot
____ Client who terminates treatment prematurely
____ Having to transfer client to another social worker or counselor
____ The client (or family) who accuses me of making him worse instead of better

____ A psychotic person (out of touch with reality) who is not hospitalized
____ Mentally alert persons who can't communicate normally (deaf, mute, speech disorders)
____ Compliments from clients
____ Questioning my credentials and skills
____ Personal questions from clients
____ Knowing when a goal has been achieved
____ Suspiciousness (paranoia)
____ Dependency
____ Expressions of guilt feelings
____ The lying client
____ Seductive behavior toward therapist
____ Verbalized suicidal thoughts
____ Client threatens to harm therapist
____ A psychotic client who is hospitalized
____ Client who doesn't speak English
____ Acceptance
____ A mistake on my part that adversely affects treatment or relationship
____ Client who gives me gifts
____ The very demanding client
____ Family members who constantly fight among themselves
____ The client who chain-smokes during interviews
____ The person who smells terrible and/or has obviously not bathed in some time
____ Withdrawal

Use the space provided below to list any other kinds of client behavior or defense mechanism that you have experienced and/or are concerned about one day having to deal with. Be sure to mark each item you list according to the above-given code.

12. Following are some concepts or techniques used in social work intervention. Mark each one, using the following key:

  X = I have used this modality or technique and I feel confident of my skill in using it.
  I = I have used this technique, but I don't feel very confident of my ability to do so effectively.
  N = I have never used this technique/approach.
  ? = I don't know what this is and need to learn more about it.
  B = I am familiar with the modality, but I don't really believe in it, so I prefer not to use it.
  C = I am familiar with the modality and believe it can be effective, but I don't feel comfortable using it; it's just not my style.

____ Confrontation
____ Reality therapy
____ Behavior modification
____ Interpretation
____ Reflection
____ Empathy
____ Establishing contracts with clients
____ Termination
____ Crisis intervention
____ Diagnostic assessment
____ Treatment planning
____ Obtaining social histories
____ Artificial stimulation
____ Environmental manipulation
____ Joint counseling (family therapy)
____ Writing social histories
____ Systems theory
____ Advocate
____ Broker
____ Casework
____ Group work
____ Role-playing
____ Psychodrama
____ Taping an interview

____ Videotaping an interview
____ My interview being observed through special mirror
____ Acceptance
____ Questioning
____ "Starting where the client is"
____ Transactional analysis
____ The functional approach
____ Modeling
____ Knowing "when to put the lid on"
____ Advice giving, knowing its pitfalls; when it should and should not be used
____ Purposeful silence
____ The nondirective approach
____ Supportive therapy
____ Psychoanalytical approach
____ Insight-production
____ Clarification
____ Note-taking during interviews
____ Play therapy
____ Understanding/using nonverbal communication
____ Community organization

Use the space provided below to list any other treatment approaches or modalities you have used. Rate each one according to the above-given key.

13. The following phrases describe working conditions and characteristics of some social work settings. Put an "X" by the ones that you could accept—that would be agreeable to you and you could deal with effectively. Put a "U" by those that you do not feel you could live with or would not want to have to deal with or would find unacceptable. Think about some of your answers to the previous questions as you answer this one.

____ Lots of paperwork and detail
____ Constant pressure to meet deadlines
____ Large, diverse caseloads with fast turnover
____ Small, intense caseloads with long-term cases
____ Settings where I might see shocking things

―――Lots of structure and supervisory guidance

―――Limited supervision and lots of independence

―――Crisis-oriented problems to solve

―――A setting where appointments are scheduled in advance and few crises occur to interrupt routine

―――A place where when I leave at 5:00 P.M., I know the work is done, and will rarely have to stay late

―――A place where the work seems never to be done and where I may have to put in extra hours on short notice

―――A place where I have opportunity to advance into better paying positions within the same agency

―――Opportunities for advancement to supervisory positions

―――Lack of promotional opportunities

―――Supervision from an MSW

―――Supervision from an ACSW

―――Supervision by a non-social worker or person with less formal training than I have

―――A place with a formal in-service training program

―――A place with no in-service training program

―――Working primarily with other social workers

―――An interdisciplinary setting

―――A setting with a lot of bureaucratic structure (i.e., governmental)

―――Lack of bureaucratic structure, as is found in many small, private agencies

―――A chance to be with other single people, as I depend on my field placement or job to help meet my social needs

―――A place where most staff are the same sex as I, or in a different age bracket

―――Providing <u>primarily</u> concrete services

―――Doing <u>primarily</u> intensive counseling

―――Normal working hours (8–5 P.M.)

―――Odd hours (evenings and/or weekneds, being "on call")

―――Located in a high crime or inner-city neighborhood

―――Freedom, with time off and/or pay to attend workshops and seminars on agency time

―――Having to use my own car in connection with my job

―――Having to pay for parking every day

―――Making home visits in an urban ghetto/poverty neighborhood

―――Making home visits in a poor rural area

―――A setting where the social worker's role is clearly defined and is accepted readily by clients

―――A setting where the social worker's role is <u>not</u> clearly defined and the worker must constantly explain and demonstrate his role to clients, other disciplines, and so on

―――A place where I have to do much of my own typing because of lack of clerical support

―――A place with air conditioning

―――An office without windows (a basement-level or modern building with no windows)

―――Having to walk two or three blocks or more from the parking lot to my office

―――Sharing my office with a smoker

―――A place where most of the work is with the client himself (limited opportunity for working with families or significant others)

―――A setting where work with families is a daily part of serving the primary client

―――An agency where the nature of politics plays an important role in determining who gets what, eligibility criteria, and other policies (the Veteran's Administration; welfare programs)

―――A position funded by grant monies with some sense of insecurity; if the grant runs out of money or is not renewed, my employment could come to an abrupt end (a reality in many social work jobs)

Now go back and put an asterisk (*) by each item that you absolutely will not compromise on. In other words, you would not take a job or accept a field placement in a setting that did not provide these things or in which these conditions prevail. Add any significant items that you feel were omitted from the above list and rate each one.

14. Write in the figure that answers the following items.

_____a. The largest number of cases you've ever worked with at the same time (caseload)

_____b. The longest you've ever worked with the same client or family

_____c. The largest number of people you've had in the same interview

_____d. The number of group meetings/sessions you have co-led

_____e. The number of group meetings/seesions you have led alone

_____f. The total number (estimate) of interviews and/or group sessions you have observed someone else leading (exclude co-led sessions)

_____g. The average number of times you met with or had a significant contact with you field instructor (or supervisor) per week

_____h. The total number of client interviews (estimate) you had in your last field placement

_____i. The total number of administrative/committee/staff meetings you attended in your last field placement (estimate)

Are you satisfied with the totals? _____ Do you want/need more or less of some things? _____
Comment below:

15. List anything significant from your own past life or experiences that would make you especially dedicated to working with a particular client group or social work modality. Name the client group and/or the modality, and state why you feel a special affinity to it.

16. List anything significant from your past life or experiences that would make it especially difficult or emotionally stressful for you to work with certain client groups or social work modalities. Name the client group and/or the modality, and state why it would be difficult for you to work with.

17. What are your short-range career goals? What do you see yourself doing two to three years from now?

18. What are your long-range career goals? What do you see yourself doing five to ten years from now in social work? (Include plans for furthering your professional education, as well as what you envision yourself doing in your work.)

19. The following questions pertain to possible personnel benefits. Comment briefly on each one:

a. Minimum salary you must have to <u>survive</u> (pay bills with nothing left over): _____

b. Minimum salary you would <u>like</u> to have: the ideal (based on what you think you're worth): _____

c. You have the following special needs with regard to health insurance: _____ _____ _____

d. Is it important whether or not Social Security is deducted from your pay? (Federal employers do not deduct Social Security—they have their own retirement plan.): _____

e. Do you need access to educational leave so you can stop working and go to school full time, yet be guaranteed return to your old job or a better position when you finish? _____

f. Do you require flexible working hours so you can go to classes while working full time? _____

g. Do you have any special feelings about working in a setting where social workers are unionized? _____

h. Are you willing to start work immediately after you graduate, with no break in between? _____

i. How much time, <u>ideally</u>, would you like to take off between finishing school and starting your first job? _____

j. If a job were available but you had to start immediately and couldn't take any time off after finishing school, would you be willing to lose the job opportunity in order to get your time off? _____

k. Do you have any special requirements in terms of the amount of sick leave or annual leave you require annually? _____

20. How far are you willing to commute to work or field placement? _____

21. Are you willing to take anything you can get because you need the money? _____

22. Answering the questionnaire should make you keenly aware of some of the things you consider important in a job or field placement situation. Do you think you would actually be able, in a job or preplacement interview, to ask questions so you can find out if the experience will give you the things you consider important? _____

23. Is there anything that might affect your permanency on the job (pregnancy; plans to start a family; chance of husband being transferred out of town; going through a divorce that might affect where you want to live; plans to return to school)?

24. Considering your responses to the previous questions and your current situation and desires, what kind of setting would you want for field placement or work? List several types of agencies, or specific agencies or settings, that you believe meet your conditions and expectations. If you don't know of any, state that and write down how you might go about finding out which ones would and would not meet your needs.

25. In question 24 you indicated the kind of setting you want. Is this the same as what you <u>need</u> for your professional development? If so, state this. If not, answer the question again, substituting the word <u>need</u> for the word <u>want</u>.

26. Review, in your mind, your answers to all the previous questions. Is there anything you expect from a field placement or work experience that has not been covered? If so, list the items below and comment on each one.

27. Following are some tasks and skills that very realistically could be expected of a macro-systems graduate student shortly after he enters his first work situation as an administrator, supervisor, staff development person, or community organizer. Persons functioning in these capacities usually receive rather limited supervision, and often from non-social workers. Thus, to be effective, the individual must be able to perform these skills or tasks rather independently. Use the following key to rate <u>each</u> of the tasks that follow (some items might get more than one rating):

X = I have done this before and feel confident of my ability to do so effectively
0 = I have done this before, but I do <u>not</u> feel confident of my ability to do so effectively
S = I have never done this, though I have studied how to in the classroom. I think I could handle it.
N = I have never done this and have never studied how to do it in the classroom.
U = I just don't enjoy doing this or don't feel comfortable doing it and wouldn't want to have to do it on the job.

____ Interview social work applicants for a job vacancy and make decisions as to who should be hired
____ Do therapeutic group work with clients
____ Do group work (leadership, educational, administrative) with staff
____ Supervise regular social work staff with less education than I have
____ Supervise staff with as much or more education than I have in social work
____ Supervise persons younger than I am
____ Supervise persons older than I am
____ Supervise social work supervisors

———Dismiss an employee whose performance I had determined was unsatisfactory

———Write performance evaluations

———Work with and/or relate to, an agency governing board

———Be an administrator in charge of an entire social work program

———Develop and implement a statistical reporting system for my agency or department

———Lead a committee that plans and puts on a workshop for 100 people or more from various parts of the country

———Present a paper or give a formal presentation to a group of thirty or more professionals

———Set up a consumer advisory committee

———Teach how to do social work: concrete services

———Teach how to do social work: casework, interviewing skills

———Teach how to do group work

———Teach techniques of supervision to persons who have never supervised before

———Teach techniques of supervision to experienced supervisors

———Teach staff how to be field instructors for the first time

———Take an undergraduate student in field placement (me personally)

———Take a graduate student in field placement

———Write, and present for approval, a budget for my agency or department

———Write a grant application and try to get it approved

———Work with community groups

———Take a leadership role in professional groups, e.g. NASW.

———Prepare a report for a "superior" explaining why I feel I need more staff

———Write a procedure manual for my agency

———Make use of an outside consultant for a special problem I am facing

———Act as a consultant myself to other agencies/programs

———Settle a dispute between two employees who both want their vacations at the same time, and only one can have it at that time

———An employee (supervisee) brings a grievance against me because of some action I have taken

———Give a news release to the press regarding something happening in my agency

———Develop a contract with schools of social work for taking students for field placement

———Explain and/or teach the proper role of social workers to other disciplines within my setting

———Help an employee whose communication has broken down with his supervisor (I am not his immediate supervisor)

———Check out a complaint lodged against one of my employees by a client or someone else within my system

———Try to get two community groups to work effectively together (they have a history of not working well together)

———Set up a client advocacy program

———Set up a flow chart

———Set up, and get my staff to carry out effectively, a time study. Then, analyze the results and present a report to upper administrators

———Conduct, or have charge of, a fund-raising campaign

———Write, and actually get published, an article for a professional journal in, or related to, social work

———Develop, as well as actually teach, a curriculum for an entire course in a school of social work

———Develop and implement a peer review or accountability mechanism in a social work program

———Write a detailed report, pulling together many facts, that adequately and properly supports what I have to say and present the material in a well-organized, readable fashion

———Write a paper or a report using proper footnoting style, including a bibliography

____Write a lengthy report using correct spelling, grammar, and sentence structure: no incomplete sentences, confusing phrases, or other grammatical errors that obscure the meaning of what I am trying to communicate

If many of your responses are O, U, or N, you should seriously question whether you are ready for administrative or community-focused employment. You should aim for a direct service job first, until you gain additional experience.

28. Pretend you are applying for a position of your choice (or having a preplacement interview for field placement). Write a brief paragraph selling yourself: Why should <u>you</u> be hired and not someone else?

29. Now is the time to determine how honest you have been with yourself in answering this questionnaire. Go back to question 12. One of the items listed is called "artificial stimulation." Look at how you marked this item. Was it with a "?"? It should have been: There is no such thing as "artificial stimulation." It was made up by the author of this questionnaire! Thus, if you marked the item with anything other than a "?" you are not being honest with yourself and are trying to pretend you have knowledge where you do not. Go back and review your answers to <u>all</u> the items on this questionnaire to be certain you have not guessed at them or avoided recognizing lack of knowledge.

4. A form for students to evaluate their field placement experience

Many schools provide a mechanism for students to evaluate their field placement experience and the perceived effectiveness of their field instructor. A checklist rating form or an outline may be provided. All student evaluations of placement should include the identifying data listed on p. 317.

The school may or may not want to guarantee anonymity to the student. If field instructors are required to share their evaluations with students, it would appear to be good professional practice for the student to share his as well. However, many students fear possible reprisal through the performance evaluation or references after field placement has ended. Therefore student evaluations of field placement should be shared with the field instructor, if at all, only *after* the student has received his final written evaluation for the entire placement. This still may not relieve the student's anxiety regarding its impact on subsequent references, causing some students to produce innocuous, superficial assessments that give the field instructor what they think he wants to hear but are essentially meaningless. Guaranteed anonymity, on the other hand, generally results in honest and useful feedback that helps the school to identify problematic or highly effective placements and make decisions regarding future students for that setting. It can, of course,

lead to irresponsible criticism that is emotionally laden and without support. If the school faculty liaison person is in touch with his students and their placements, student evaluations of settings should come as no surprise to the school and in any case should not form the sole basis for decisions to use or avoid certain placements.

Forms for evaluating field placement experiences run the gamut from simple checklists and rating scales to detailed narrative outlines and questionnaires requiring narrative responses. An effective form will provide space for students to enter spontaneous comments in addition to or instead of restricted checklists or boxes. A questionnaire-style form is preferred, as illustrated here. However, an example of a detailed outline is also provided for those wishing a more comprehensive instrument.

The following form is narrative in format, encouraging students to elaborate on their responses. (The actual form provides space for responses to each question.) A group of students in a field placement unit and their faculty-member field instructor developed the form. The students preferred the narrative rather than the checklist format. The evaluation form is completed at the very end of placement and is not shared with the field instructor or school until the final grade has been assigned.

STUDENT EVALUATION OF FIELD EXPERIENCE

Your name_____
Agency_____
Date_____
Field Instructor_____

Did you request the placement agency to which you were assigned? ____yes   ____no

1. Briefly summarize your work activities during field placement.
2. Did you have the kinds of experiences that you wanted to have? Explain.
3. What do you consider to be the most important things you learned during field placement?
4. What did you like most about your field placement experience?
5. What did you not like about your placement experience?
6. Comment on the quality of supervision you received. What about the frequency and length of supervisory conferences? Explain how your field instructor's approach to supervising you did or did not meet your needs.
7. Describe how your field instructor assessed the nature of your involvement with individuals, groups, communities, and agency staff.
8. How did your field instructor help you to integrate classroom knowledge with field learning?
9. Did your field placement provide opportunities for:

   ____work with individuals and families?
   ____leading a group (or getting one started)?
   ____work with organizations and community resources?
   ____work with community groups?

   Comment on your answer by describing what you did.
10. Comment on the physical facilities in this setting. How did they affect your field learning in either a positive or a negative way?
11. What suggestions do you have for improving the overall quality and effectiveness of this field placement?
12. Do you feel that the social work curriculum prepared you adequately for field experience? Please explain the reasons for your answer.
13. Comment on the field integration seminars. Were these sessions helpful? Not helpful? Why or why not? Was information covered that you considered not pertinent? Is there anything you would like to see covered in these sessions that was not covered?
14. Comment on the nature and effectiveness of your contacts with your field liaison faculty person. How could this person have been more helpful to you during field placement?
15. Please make any suggestions you might have for improving the field experience program, from the time you made application for field placement through the planning meetings and agency placement process, to the final evaluation of your performance.

5. An outline for student evaluation of field placement

The following outline is very long and detailed and would constitute a significant assignment for the student if completed properly. Most schools find it more practical to use a briefer form. However, the following example can serve as a kind of menu of areas on which individual field instructors or schools may want to solicit student feedback.

Face Sheet
  1. Name of Student_____
  2. Student ID Number_____
  3. Date_____
  4. Agency_____
  5. Address of Field Agency_____
  6. Phone_____
  7. Field Instructor_____
  8. Field Instructor's Title_____
  9. Period Covered: From_____ to_____
 10. Quarter (semester/year)_____
 11. Placement Number ____one; ____two; ____three

I. Description of Field Placement Setting

   A. What are the purposes, functions, goals and kinds of services provided by the agency or service delivery system?
   B. Describe the clientele of the agency.
   C. What are the primary problems presented by clients requesting services?
   D. How is the agency/institution/service delivery system funded? Does it get its support from public or private sources?
   E. Is it your impression that clients understand the scope of services available to them through the setting? Explain.
   F. Was it made clear what social workers do in this setting?

II. Relationship to the Setting

   A. Did you receive support and cooperation from administration and staff? Explain.
   B. Did you feel accepted as a student by regular staff? What were the positives and/or negatives, if any, in this area?
   C. Do you believe the structure of the setting encouraged or discouraged creativity on the part of students? Why?
   D. What did you like most and what did you like least about this setting?
   E. What do you see as having been your role in the setting?
   F. How would you rate the overall experiences you had in this setting? Describe.

III. Experiences Provided by the Field Placement Setting

   A. Was an educational contract developed that outlined educational objectives, learning experiences, and the degree of skill you were expected to achieve? Did it also describe assessment mechanisms that would be used to determine how well you were doing?
   B. Describe the types of learning experiences provided fo you by this field placement.
   C. Describe some of the assignments you were given. Did you feel adequately prepared for each assignment by previous course content or life experiences?
   D. Do you believe that you received sufficient advance information about your assignments from the field instructor to know what was expected of you? Explain.
   E. You probably had some idea about what you wanted to learn in this field placement experience. Did you have the kinds of experience that you wanted or needed to help you learn what you wanted to learn? Explain.

IV. The Field Instructor

   A. Did you receive individual or group supervision?
   B. Did you have a fixed time to meet with your field instructor? How frequent were your meetings, and for how long did you meet each time (on the average)?

C. Was the field instructor (or other responsible person) available to you at times other than the fixed meeting time? When and how? Was he/she present at the agency during the hours you were in placement?

D. How much time did you spend with your field instructor each week, counting both formal and informal discussions (on the average)? Do you feel this was enough or too much time?

E. Do you believe that the access you had to your supervisor was adequate? Describe.

F. Did you receive a planned orientation to your placement setting? How?

G. Did your field instructor assist you in integrating classroom material with the field experience? How?

H. Did your field instructor assist you in learning and developing social work skills and techniques? Explain.

I. What techniques did your field instructor use to assess your performance and to familiarize himself with your work? (Did you tape-record interviews, do process-recordings, do interviews while the field instructor observed?)

J. What did you like most and what did you like least about your experience with your field instructor?

K. Were the expectations of your performance by the setting and/or the field instructor adequately explained to you, and were you provided with sufficient time and opportunities to learn the skills needed to meet those expectations? Explain.

V. Actual Learning

A. List in rank order the social work methods you received help with learning in this field experience. Also name any specific skills you worked intensively on.

B. Briefly list the main things you feel you have learned during this placement. Include areas in which you feel you have grown professionally or personally as a result of this field placement experience.

C. What do you feel are your greatest strengths, both personal and professional? What do you consider to be the areas in which you need further growth?

VI. The Future

How has this field placement experience affected, if at all, your future goals or plans, both while still in school and after you graduate?

_____

Student's Signature

_____

Field Instructor's Signature

_____

Date

_____

Date

APPENDIX G

Ingredients of a Comprehensive Field Instruction Program

The Council on Social Work Education sets forth some standards for schools to follow in developing and implementing their field instruction programs (see pp. 323–325). However, schools vary tremendously in the extent and manner in which they adapt and implement these broad guidelines. Thus, a field instructor cannot assume that a school will provide, permit, or encourage certain benefits, activities, and materials merely because a field placement program exists. Most schools do provide several of the features described below; very few provide them all. Agency-based practitioners often have no mechanism for seeing beyond what their local school(s) offer and may not realize that certain essential elements exist elsewhere or that their own school is actually quite progressive compared with what many others are doing.

1. *A director of field instruction.* A single faculty member should have the primary responsibility of overseeing the entire field instruction program. If he also teaches in the classroom, this is usually restricted to one course or seminar plus training for field instructors. Large schools with several hundred students may have a full-time director, plus one or more additional faculty assigned part time to specific field instruction responsibilities to act as assistants. In small or less progressive schools, a faculty member whose primary responsibility is classroom teaching is also asked to take charge of field instruction.

2. *A field instruction manual.* CSWE encourages accredited schools to prepare a special manual that describes the field instruction program. However, many schools lack such manuals. In others, a manual exists but is given very limited distribution. A single comprehensive manual is generally prepared for use by faculty, field instructors, and students. Special handouts may emphasize requirements of

students, but they are usually referred to the field instruction manual for more details regarding their field experience. Some schools make a point of telling students where copies can be obtained; others do not tell the students that such a thing exists or do not make copies readily available to them. Most schools give each field instructor a copy; some are not as generous.

Field instruction manuals vary greatly in content. Some are skimpy and obviously done simply to meet an external requirement; they provide no real guidelines for field instructors or students. Others are much more comprehensive; there may even be separate manuals for the undergraduate and graduate programs of a given school.

A fully comprehensive field instruction manual includes the following kinds of material:

A. Description of the field instruction program, including scheduling, prerequisites for entering placement, hours, recommended dress, and other nitty-gritty details

B. The school calendar

C. The entire curriculum schedule for the degree involved, listing all courses (including electives) and the sequence in which they are normally taken (This enables field instructors to know what their students have or have not been exposed to in the classroom as well as what they are getting concurrently with field placement. Detailed course syllabi or bibliographies may be included in the manual as an appendix or distributed separately.)

D. Requirements for being a field instructor and description of the method by which agencies and individual field supervisors are selected

E. Requirements and responsibilities of students, field instructors, faculty advisers, and other key school personnel in the placement process

F. Specific performance/knowledge expectations for each level of field placement for which the field instructor is required to do a performance evaluation, with detailed instructions and related forms used for completing student performance evaluations and a detailed outline and/or form for the student to complete in evaluating his field placement experience, plus a description of how student and field instructor evaluations are used by the school

G. A description of the school's grading system, including options for dealing with special situations (e.g. the use of incomplete rather than unsatisfactory grades in field placement)* If the school has any special policies regarding students who receive unsatisfactory evaluations in field, these will be stated.

H. Discussion and examples of special forms or materials used by the student in field (e.g. a special log sheet to record time and activity, a form for noting mileage)

I. A list of aspects of field that must apply to all students, regardless of where they are placed (e.g. frequency and duration of supervisory conferences, types of recording used, and the nature of assignments)

J. Description of special seminars that may or must be taken by students in conjunction with field (A course outline with suggested readings for students may be included.)

K. Description of seminars and training programs available to or required of field instructors, with their prerequisites (A bibliography of related readings for field instructors may also be provided.)

L. A list of special benefits available to field instructors, such as tuition-free credit hours, use of the library or other campus facilities, special title, or faculty discount at the bookstore

M. Description of any special insurance coverage required or provided by the school for students and/or field instructors

N. Legal contracts and/or agreements that must be signed by the school, the student, and/or the agency in connection with placement

O. A list by name of all field instructors and their respective agencies

3. *A description of each field placement setting used by the school,* including the nature of the program, the kind of clientele served, the training and background of the staff who work there, and the kinds of learning experiences available to students. It should include any special restrictions regarding the kinds or levels of students that will be accepted. This resource file is used most heavily by the

*See Chapter 12, pp. 205–206.

school in arranging placements for individual students but can also be made available to students to assist them in selecting placement preferences.

4. *Various kinds of seminars for students.* Some schools hold an informal seminar (or perhaps a student government association meeting) where students can orally present data regarding agencies where they have had field placement and can make themselves available for questions from students who are seeking placements. Other programs hold formal seminars to orient students to field placement and/or help them select subsequent field placements and ongoing seminars throughout field placement to help students make maximum use of supervision and provide a structured opportunity for comparing and sharing experiences. A special seminar for seniors may acquaint advanced students with techniques of résumé preparation and job-hunting.

5. *An annual orientation day* (or seminar or several day workshop) for field instructors, to acquaint them with the current direction of the social work and field instruction program, issues in social work education, objectives, and goals. Newly revised field manuals are often distributed at these meetings.

6. *Special seminars or courses for field instructors,* including (1) practitioners who have never supervised students before; (2) experienced field instructors who have never had students from that particular school; (3) senior or experienced field supervisors; (4) macro as opposed to micro field instructors and special instructional approaches unique to each. An increasing number of schools are providing ongoing rather than sporadic training sessions for all field instructors and require their participation in certain types of orientation and training activities as opposed to permitting optional attendance. As a special compensation, some schools bring in well-known guest speakers on various social work topics and invite field instructors at no charge as a special continuing education experience.

7. *Encouraging field instructors to observe or give lectures in the classroom and/or having faculty spend time in the field.* The purpose for the faculty member would be not to act as adviser for the student or meet with the field instructor, but to observe the role and activities of the practitioner and the agency.

8. *A mechanism for field instructors periodically and formally to evaluate their experience with the school.* They could also evaluate the key individual with whom they relate (a faculty liaison person) in the field instruction process.

9. *A formal mechanism for students to evaluate the field instructor and field placement experience.* The results may

or may not be shared with individual field instructors but are used by the school in evaluating placements and the effectiveness of individual field instructors.

10. *A formal mechanism for the school to evaluate field instructors.* Results will be shared with them so they can improve their effectiveness and receive compliments when warranted.

11. *Field instructor access to student files.* The Family Educational Rights and Privacy Act of 1974* requires that students have access to their own files. However, schools may or may not permit or encourage field instructor access. Students may not be aware that their field supervisors have this privilege.

12. *Preplacement interviews.*† Some schools structure the mechanics of field placement so that students have virtually no choice where they go, and agencies must take whomever the school sends if they want any students at all. Other schools tolerate the process if agencies insist on a preplacement interview in their consideration of a student. Some encourage the practice, while still others require it. Students may or may not receive instruction from the school on the purposes of this interview and techniques for participation.

13. *Insurance coverage for students and field instructors.* Several types exist:

A. General health insurance that students must, or have the option of acquiring

B. Liability insurance that covers students who injure themselves while in school or in field placement or who are injured by a client

C. Malpractice insurance for students providing coverage if a client should sue over the quality of services rendered‡

D. Malpractice insurance or indemnification clauses to cover field instructors in the event a student should sue them over a grade or other action associated with fieldwork supervision** (These suits can and do happen. In one instance, a student was terminated from field placement. The school faculty supported the field instructor's recommendation. The student

exhausted the school's grievance mechanism, then brought suit against her field instructor, two other agency administrators, her faculty adviser, and the dean of the school, seeking $250,000 damages from *each* person.†† Following this experience, the agency refused to take any more students unless the schools provided some form of malpractice coverage. Two schools subsequently complied; one did not and lost use of the placement; and one obtained coverage for all its field instructors. It should be noted that some agencies will not defend or pay court-awarded damages for their field instruction staff when student suits occur. See Chapter 13 for further discussion regarding legal aspects of field instruction.)

E. Indemnification clauses that are a form of malpractice insurance for field instructors (No insurance policy may exist per se, but schools agree in writing to "hold harmless" the field instructor and provide legal representation and/or payment of any damages that might be awarded from a suit against a field instructor in the performance of his duties for the school.)

14. *A legal contract between school and agency that spells out conditions and responsibilities of both parties in connection with the setting's use as a field placement.* See Chapter 13 for further discussion and two sample contracts. Not all schools actively encourage or require such contracts. They are time-consuming, add to the paper work, and are potentially costly if either party should fail to abide by the contract's provisions. Yet a contract can provide essential protection for all parties, including students.

15. *A course sequence that enables students to receive training on basic interviewing skills before they enter field placement and are faced with their first live client.* Many schools offer general concepts during the student's first quarter/semester and gradually move into more specific practice skills. As a result, the student may be in field placement for weeks or even months before he receives "how-to" classroom training, and the full burden of providing this instruction then falls on each individual field instructor. In contrast, some schools provide meaty practice courses with role-playing, use of videotapes, and other creative instructional techniques that enable students to learn about specific skills and practice using them in the classroom before the beginning of field placement.

16. *Field placement in the last quarter or semester prior to the student's graduation.* This very common approach is

---

*Also known as the Buckley Amendment. This amends Public Law 93-568, effective November 19, 1974. See also Department of HEW, Office of the Secretary, "Privacy Rights of Parents and Students," Part II, "Final Rule on Education Records," *Federal Register,* June 17, 1976, pp. 24662–24675.

†See Chapter 4.

‡Field instructors are likely to be named in such suits, since they are the student's supervisors. However, many malpractice insurance policies, including NASW's, would cover them because the suit revolves around a specific client, even though the supervisor is named as an indirect party. A few schools are requiring all students to obtain NASW malpractice insurance to provide coverage in the event of litigation.

**NASW malpractice insurance does *not* cover these situations, as the suit does not center on services to a client. Disputes between supervisors and supervisees/students are specifically excluded from coverage.

††*Jane Ganz vs. Barry College et al.,* Case No. 75-27028, 11th Judicial Circuit Court, Dade County, Florida, August 20, 1975. The case was dropped by the plaintiff (Ganz) just prior to a court hearing scheduled nearly two years after the suit was filed.

problematic, as it places a very heavy burden on the field instructor. If the student experiences difficulties in field, everyone is aware that he is very close to graduation, and there is a powerful informal norm against failing him at this point. The field instructor will be viewed as the ultimate "bad guy" if he prevents a student from graduating only weeks short of commencement. Thus an objective assessment becomes virtually impossible because of time pressures.

17. *A requirement that a student who receives a failing grade in field cannot continue in the social work program.* Some schools permit students who fail field to repeat placement or to continue taking classroom courses. Others do not give failing grades and deal with "problem students" by transferring them to settings with lower expectations and more superficial supervision, thus avoiding the need for a policy regarding students who do not make it through field placement. In contrast, some students who fail field are dropped from the school program entirely and immediately. However, all schools must provide a grievance mechanism. Some permit students who initiate grievances over failing grades to continue attending class until the grievance has been resolved; others are not so permissive.

18. *Frequent visits from a faculty liaison person to the field instruction site,* to talk with the field instructor and student, possibly review examples of student work, and generally review progress and problems. The frequency and effectiveness of these visits vary considerably from school to school and from faculty member to faculty member within the same school. Some schools have a written policy that a faculty adviser will visit field settings a specified number of times each school term and spell out clearly what is to take place during the visit. Others leave this to the discretion of the individual faculty adviser. Some programs seek field instructor input in determining how many visits are necessary and when they should occur during the school year to be of maximum benefit; others set policies (or have no policies)

without consulting field instructors and may or may not inform them of the plan.

19. *Field instructor participation on school committees.* Social work programs consist of many committees. A certain group of faculty may be responsible for seeing that sufficient minority content is woven into classroom material and field experiences; another may handle admissions, and others may oversee or recommend policy regarding various curriculum concentrations, the grievance process, field instruction, or faculty self-development. Recommended policies may be presented to the entire faculty and/or the dean for official approval. Regular faculty, students, and/or field instructors may participate on these committees. Progressive programs actively encourage input from field instructors either through committee membership or through an active steering committee or other official mechanism.

20. *A field instructor association of some kind.* There is nothing to prevent a group of field instructors in a certain geographical area from getting together on a regular basis to discuss their common needs and concerns. School staff and paid field instruction faculty may or may not be invited to attend. Schools may discourage, encourage, actively support, or even participate fully in such an association. When joint participation exists, it can provide a powerful communication vehicle that selects field instruction representatives on school committees, shares information, and gives recommendations when needed. Continuous communication and sharing of information between school and a field instruction association can go a long ways toward resolving common problems and is much more effective than just a few individual field instructors airing their concerns among themselves or, worse yet, to their students.

21. *Funding to send selected field instructors to conferences pertaining to field instruction.* The annual program meeting of the CSWE would be an example.

APPENDIX H

CSWE Standards for BSW and MSW Field Programs

Some of the CSWE standards for BSW and MSW programs are undergoing revision. However, the basic philosophy and approach to field instruction recommended by the Council can be seen from a review of the standards that appear in the April 1971 edition of *The Manual of Accrediting Standards for Graduate Professional Schools of Social Work* (New York: CSWE) and the accompanying pamphlet for BSW programs, dated July 1, 1974. It is unknown at this time exactly what changes, if any, will be made in this material as some of the broader criteria for accreditation undergo revision.

This material is reprinted with the permission of the Council on Social Work Education. Also, I wish to extend my appreciation to Sidney Berengarten for his review of this appendix; it is recognized that neither CSWE nor Mr. Berengarten necessarily agrees with or endorses my comments regarding the material that has been quoted.

MSW Programs

In 1969 the Board of Directors approved a "Curriculum Policy for the Master's Degree Program in Graduate Schools of Social Work," which appears as Appendix I, pages 55–60, in the *Manual*. Upon approval of this Policy Statement, the Board of Directors of CSWE asked the Commission on Accreditation to develop the actual accreditation standards for MSW programs. Thus, it is important to first examine the Curriculum Policy Statement before looking at the more specific standards themselves.

The first two paragraphs of the Policy Statement describe its purpose as follows:

> This document sets forth the official curriculum policy for schools of social work that are accredited by the Commission on Accreditation of the Council on Social Work Education.

The Statement governs graduate programs leading to the master's degree and is the basis for formulation of accreditation standards. It does not state curriculum policy for post-master's education in social work or for undergraduate education relevant to social welfare and social work.

The Curriculum Policy Statement deals with the kind of substantive knowledge to be included in the master's program but does not present an organizing theme, suggest sequences, or in any other way direct how that knowledge is to be organized and conveyed. Each school carries full responsibility for the specific organization and arrangement of courses and other learning experiences. Each school is also expected to establish procedures for self-study and continuing evaluation of the effectiveness of its educational program. (p. 55)

The Statement addresses a number of areas in graduate education, concluding with the following section pertaining to field instruction (practicum) on page 60:

Learning Experiences

Curriculum objectives define what the student is expected to learn. Learning experiences, such as those provided through classroom courses, the practicum, laboratory experience, tutorial conferences, and research projects offer the student the means to achieve the goals of social work education. Responsibility to select and order specific learning experiences rests with the individual school of social work.

The social work practicum is an essential component of professional education for social work. Its patterns may vary but an essential element of the practicum *must include learning experiences that provide for students' direct engagement in service activities*. Advances in educational methods may encourage use of a variety of practicum designs, even within the same school.

The practicum is intended to enhance student learning within all areas of the curriculum. There are several major objectives of the practicum. It should provide all students with opportunities for development, integration, and reinforcement of competence through performance in actual service situations. It should permit students to acquire and test skills relevant to emerging conditions of social work practice. The practicum should also foster for all students the integration and reinforcement of knowledge, value, and skill learning acquired in the field and through particular courses and concentrations. In the practicum the student should have an opportunity to delineate and comprehend questions for research which arise in the course of practice.

These objectives may be appropriately attained through diverse practicum designs and through various instructional formats. All arrangements should, however, be derived from clearly stated educational purposes, they should be articulated with other components of the curriculum, and they should be commensurate with the resources available to the school. Subject to these general principles, each school shall have freedom to determine the particular nature of its practicum, including the degree of variation for groups of students and the timing, level, and character of instructional experience to be provided through the practicum. [Emphasis added]

The accrediting manual describes a number of standards that must be met. They are as follows (note that the word ''practicum'' is used for the term field instruction):

Cooperation Between School and Field Instruction Agencies

Planned cooperation and coordination of activity between a school and agencies selected are essential to a high level of field instruction.

A school shall assume responsibility for the development and administration of field instruction. Fulfillment of this responsibility calls for a continuing investment of time and a clear faculty assignment. Administrative responsibility includes (1) regular planned communication between school and agency regarding students, the school's educational objectives and program, and developments within the agency affecting student learning; and (2) the systematic provision for participation of field instructors in curriculum development especially as it pertains to field instruction.

A school and agency shall agree upon the fundamental goals and methods requisite to a common approach to, and internal consistency in, the educational experience offered in field instruction.

Agencies selected shall meet criteria established by the school as necessary to provide an educational program of integrity. Criteria shall be related to (1) commitment of board, administration, and staff to field instruction as an agency function and responsibility; (2) compatibility of the philosophy of agency service with the educational objectives of social work; (3) clarity in the agency about the focus of its program for service; (4) participation in local and regional activities in its field of service; (5) size and flow of program; (6) resources sufficient to provide an educational experience having diversity, breadth, and depth; (7) availability (either within the agency or from the school) of a qualified field instructor(s).

A field instructor is considered available when his assignments are adjusted to permit adequate time for field instruction *and appropriate participation in curriculum development*. Assessment of his qualifications takes into account his professional education, commitment to the

profession, competence in practice, and his interest and competence in teaching (See Appendix II, ''Criteria for Learning Experiences Provided through the Practicum.'')*

The school and agency engage *jointly* in selection of field instructors and planning the field instruction program and in assessing student progress, but the school shall assume responsibility for final decisions on educational matters.

Regular *joint* school–agency evaluation of the field instruction program shall be regarded as a part of curriculum evaluation.†

Appendix II, ''Criteria for Learning Experiences Provided Through the Practicum,'' gives more detail regarding standards for field instruction:

Each school of social work establishes its own criteria for learning experiences to be provided through the practicum in accordance with the standards set forth in the Curriculum Policy Statement Section on learning experiences. The following statement has been developed as an elaboration of these standards:

1. The learning experience should entail a programmatic commitment to service compatible with the values and ethics of the social work profession.
2. There should be clarity and specificity about the educational objectives to be achieved through the practicum, the program of the setting in which it occurs, and the methods to be pursued in implementing the objectives.‡
3. The volume and flow of the school's program should be such as to offer students a fairly wide range of learning opportunities commensurate with the school's objectives for the practicum.
4. The availability of qualified field instruction is essential. Field teachers may be chosen from the staff of the setting or may be employed by the school.

   A field teacher is considered available when his assignments are adjusted to permit adequate time for curriculum development and implementation. Assessment of his qualifications takes into account his professional education, commitment to the values of the social work profession, competence in practice, and interest and competence in teaching.

   When the field teacher is not a social worker, the school has the obligation to insure that basic planning and evaluation of the practicum experience and the organization of the teaching contribution of non–social workers are carried out by a social work

---

*Emphasis added. This clearly indicates that schools must provide some mechanism for eliciting field instructor input into planning of curriculum. Presumably this refers not just to field instruction, but to classroom curriculum that prepares students for the field experience.

†Sections 3630, pp. 16–17 of the *Manual*. Emphasis added.

‡This requires that the school and field instructor both understand what these objectives are for all field students in general as well as for each individual student. Chapter 6 concerning the educational contract presents one way of clearly meeting this requirement.

teacher through (additional) specific staff or faculty arrangements.*

5. When learning experiences are associated with an agency in a field of service in which there are standard-setting bodies, the agency should qualify for membership.

   When the practicum is located in organizations in other fields, sufficient structure must be demonstrated to provide for the necessary learning experience, acceptable field instruction, and proper assumption of responsibility by administration, staff, sponsor, or constituency.

6. The policy-setting body, administration, and staff should have respect for professional education and an acceptance of the objectives and the educational focus of the practicum program. They should be willing to undertake, individually and collectively, the responsibilities of a teaching agency, including the provision of appropriate supports to enable field instructors to maintain an educational focus in field learning and teaching.†

7. *The organization of the practicum setting must be such that its basic program can be maintained and developed without reliance on students.* However, an exception may be made when it is necessary to create a setting in which students, on a planned and time-limited basis, provide basic services not currently offered by an established social agency. [Emphasis added]

8. The setting should accept the guiding principle that any agency or setting selected for field instruction should be explored to provide educationally sound practicum placements for first and/or second year students.

9. The agency or setting should be prepared to accept the guiding principle that placement of not less than two social work students is highly desirable from the educational point of view.

10. The agency or setting should make available suitable desk space, telephones, dictating facilities, supplies, transportation costs, clerical service, and interviewing facilities. This provision may be waived under exceptional circumstances if the educational benefits resulting from a practicum experience in a particular agency or setting could not be realized otherwise.‡

*Schools meet this criterion in various ways. A faculty liaison person may visit the agency much more frequently than would be normal were the field instructor a social worker; the faculty person may meet directly with the students once per week for direct supervision; the faculty person may review much of the student's work, in cooperation with the field instructor, to assist in assessing the quality of the student's performance and determining an appropriate grade.

†This clearly implies that agencies must recognize the special skills required in being a field instructor, the time involved, and also permit field instructors to attend training sessions and meetings held by the school to help prepare field instructors for their educational role. Thus, schools may refuse placement settings that do not allow staff to attend meetings for field instructors.

‡Notice the "transportation costs" item. This clearly indicates that agencies can be required to pay students mileage for travel. If this, and the other items listed, are not provided, this must be shared with the student so he can determine if he wants a placement under these conditions. Appendix II is found in the *Manual,* pp. 61–62.

Notice that these ten items primarily indicate standards that must be met by the agencies used as placement settings. They say very little about the school's obligation to the placement setting; they do not even require that the school provide training for its field instructors to assist them in fulfilling their role, although it could be inferred that such training would be most helpful in enabling the school fully to meet stated objectives. Some of these ten items find their way into school/agency contracts (see pp. 207–215) as one way of ensuring that the criteria are met.

BSW programs

The standards for BSW programs, which are found in a four-page supplement to the *Manual* entitled "Standards for the Accreditation of Baccalaureate Degree Programs in Social Work" (effective July 1, 1974), are very similar to those for MSW programs; the primary exception is the specific clock-hours requirement for field work.

An educational program that prepares for beginning professional practice shall demonstrate that it:

1. builds on, and is integrated with, a liberal arts base that includes knowledge in the humanities, social, behavioral, and biological sciences;
2. provides content in the areas of (a) social work practice, (b) social welfare policy and services, (c) human behavior and social environment, and (d) social research;
3. requires educationally directed field experiences with engagement in service activities for at least 300 clock hours, for which academic credit commensurate with the time invested is given.

Effective preparation for beginning professional social work practice requires that the educational aspects of field experience be under the administrative direction of faculty with a graduate degree from an accredited school of social work.** The program shall demonstrate that it selects and orders specific field experiences aimed at helping the student to apply and integrate academic content and to develop skills that meet the requirements of beginning professional social work practice. Field learning shall support the total social work curriculum and should provide a breadth of learning opportunities designed to familiarize the student with a variety of interventive modes.††

Educational direction also requires ongoing liaison between faculty and appropriate staff in field instruction settings.

**This implies that all faculty who act as faculty liaison persons to field instructors and students should meet this requirement, not just the director of field instruction or the faculty member having overall responsibility for the field instruction program.

††Obviously, field instructors must know what students are learning in the classroom in order to fulfill this requirement. Furthermore, many settings require considerable assistance from the school in order to offer a "variety of interventive modes" (e.g. casework, group work, work with communities and organizations). The field instructor himself may not have skills in working with groups or communities. Training for field instructors and an effective faculty liaison role are essential if this requirement is to be met fully.

Meaningful liaison goes beyond evaluation of field instruction settings and of students and should include elements such as: identification and discussion of problems that affect the educational process; mutual involvement in experimental ventures based on new approaches to social work intervention; a demonstrated awareness of field activity by classroom faculty to serve the ultimate aim of integrating learning experiences; and an organized approach in the assignment and orientation of students to field instruction settings. Establishment of criteria for the selection of field instruction settings and field instructors is basic to the provision of educationally sound field instruction.* For field instruction settings, criteria should include evidence of acceptance by personnel of the need for professional education for professional practice, instruction of the student in adherence to the ethical values of the profession, and acceptance of the objectives of field instruction.† For field instructors, criteria should address practice and teaching competence and adequacy of time available and allocated for field instruction.‡

It is recognized that field instruction settings other than social service agencies can provide rich learning experiences for social work students. When field instruction is provided in such settings and the field teacher is not a social worker, the social work faculty has to assume additional responsibility for planning and evaluation of field instruction to assure a social work focus.**

Page 4 of the supplement for BSW programs also contains this very pertinent and interesting paragraph:

> "Selecting out" of students whose performance and aptitude have been judged unsatisfactory should be, insofar as possible,

---

*See Chapters 2 and 5 for a structured approach to assignment and orientation of students to field and a listing and discussion of criteria for selection of agencies and field instructors. Similar standards and criteria are often spelled out in field instruction manuals.

†Many field instructors are not even members of NASW and may not be familiar with the "ethical values of the profession."

‡In reality, most agencies do not reduce the work loads of staff who serve as field instructors: additional time, energy, and competence required to function as a field instructor is often not even recognized in employee performance evaluations and in considerations for merit raises and special awards.

**Supplement to the *Manual*, pp. 2–3.

the result of mutual evaluation. It should occur early to avoid unnecessary delay in the students' schedules for completion of their studies and, whenever possible, precede assignment to field instruction.

Thus, CSWE places a strong burden on the school to develop appropriate mechanisms for screening out those students who will not make it in the social work program *before they enter field*. This can be accomplished through an advisement system, where the student is assigned to a faculty member who serves as his academic adviser throughout his enrollment in the social work program. This person would meet periodically with the student, review his grade-point average and his general progress in the program, and make certain that he fully qualifies to proceed into field placement. Individual faculty who notice possible problems through their contact with students in the classroom should have a central point or committee to which they can bring their concerns for a general and objective review of the student's readiness for social work practice. Obviously, if a student exhibits inappropriate behavior in the classroom or is unusually uneasy in interacting with people on a daily basis, problems can be predicted in the field experience. Some schools incorporate "mini-field" experiences into practice or methods courses, requiring students to spend several hours each week, throughout the term, actually interacting with individuals, families, groups, organizations, or communities. Thus, students can sample social work practice before entering field placement.

Effective implementation of an early selecting-out process can exempt the field instructor from having to perform his gatekeeper function when the student is practically on his way out the door with degree in hand. However, it must also be recognized that no matter how effective a screening process is, some students will demonstrate problems in field that simply could not be detected in the classroom, or at least were not sufficiently problematic to warrant the student's discontinuance in the social work education program.

Bibliography

Field Instruction—General Concepts

AKABAS, SHEILA H. "Fieldwork in Industrial Settings: Opportunities, Rewards and Dilemmas." *Journal of Education for Social Work*, 14, No. 3 (Fall 1978): 13-19.

AMACHER, KLOH-ANN. "Explorations Into the Dynamics of Learning in Field Work." *Smith College Studies in Social Work*, 46 (1976): 163-216.

BARBARO, FRED. "The Field Instruction Component in the Administration Concentration: Some Problems and Suggested Remedies." *Journal of Education for Social Work*, 15, No. 1 (Winter 1979): 5-11.

BENEVIDES, EUSTOLIO, III; MARY MARTIN LYNCH; and JOAN SWANSON VELASQUEZ. "Toward a Culturally Relevant Fieldwork Model: The Community Learning Center Project." *Journal of Education for Social Work*, 16, No. 2 (Spring 1980): 55-62.

BRACHT, NEIL F., and INGE ANDERSON. "Community Fieldwork Collaboration Between Medical and Social Work Students." *Social Work in Health Care*, 1, No. 1 (Fall 1975): 7-18.

CAMPFENS, HUBERT, and FRED LOACH. "Political Placements in Social Work Education: The United States and Canada." *Journal of Education for Social Work*, 13, No. 2 (Spring 1977): 11-17.

COHEN, RUTH. "Student Training in a Geriatric Center." In *Issues in Human Services*, ed. Florence W. Kaslow and associates. San Francisco, Jossey-Bass, 1972, pp. 168-184.

Council on Social Work Education. "Agency Board, Executive, and Supervisory Support Conducive to Productive Field Instruction." *Workshop Report*, Annual Program Meeting of the Council on Social Work Education. New York CSWE, 1962.

———. *The Dynamics of Field Instruction: Learning Through Doing*. New York: CSWE, 1975.

———. *Field Instruction: Selected Issues*. New York: CSWE, 1959.

COX, ENID O., and ROBERT I. PAULSON. "Field Placement Alter-natives in Social Welfare Administration/Management." *Administration in Social Work*, 4, No. 2 (Summer 1980): 75-86.

CRAMER, M. "Fieldwork Preparation for Entrance into Mental Retardation Practice." *Journal of Education for Social Work*, 13 (Winter 1977): 37-43.

DANA, B. S., AND SIKKEMA, M. "Field Instruction—Fact and Fantasy." In *Proceedings, Twelfth Annual Program Meeting, Council on Social Work Education*. New York: CSWE, 1964, pp. 90-101.

DEJONG, CORNELL R. "Field Instruction for Undergraduate Social Work Education in Rural Areas," in *The Dynamics of Field Instruction: Learning Through Doing*. New York: CSWE, 1975, p. 20.

DOVER, FRANCES T. *Field Instruction in Casework: A Five-year Agency-School Demonstration Project*. New York: Jewish Guild for the Blind, 1962.

DUNCAN, MINA G. "An Experiment in Applying New Methods in Field Work." *Social Casework*, 44 (April 1963): 179-184.

DWYER, MARGARET, and MARTHA URBANOWSKI. "Field Practice Criteria: A Valuable Teaching/Learning Tool in Under-graduate Social Work Education," *Journal of Education for Social Work*, 17, No. 1 (Winter 1981): 5-11.

FINESTONE, SAMUEL. "Selected Features of Professional Field Instruction." *Journal of Education for Social Work*, 3 (Fall 1967): 14-26.

FOECKLER, MERLE M., and GERALD BOYNTON. "Creative Adult Learning-Teaching: Who's The Engineer of This Train?" *Journal of Education for Social Work*, 12, No. 3 (Fall 1976): 37-43.

FOECKLER, M. "Orientation to Field Instruction in Light of Current Needs of Social Work Education." *Social Work Education Reporter*, 16 (September 1968): 34-46.

GITTERMAN, ALEX. "The Faculty Field Instructor in Social Work Education." In *Dynamics of Field Instruction: Learning Through Doing*. New York: CSWE, 1975, p. 31.

GITTERMAN, ALEX, and NAOMI PINES GITTERMAN. "Social Work

Student Education: Format and Method.'' *Journal of Education for Social Work,* 15, No. 3 (Fall 1979): 103–108.

GOLDEN, KENNETH M. ''Client Transfer and Student Social Workers.'' *Social Work,* 21, No. 1 (1976): 65–66.

GREENBERG, I., and SARAH S. MARNEL. ''Field Supervision—A Basic Tool in Administration.'' *Social Casework,* 29 (February 1948): 70–74.

GRIMM, JAMES W. and JAMES D. ORTEN. ''Student Attitudes Toward the Poor.'' *Social Work,* 18, No. 1 (January 1973): 94.

HANNON, ELEANOR M. ''Shared Experience: Student and Client Learn About Each Other.'' *Social Casework,* 49, No. 3 (March 1968): 156.

HAWKINS, MABLE T. ''Interdisciplinary Team Training: Social Work Students in Public School Field Placement Settings.'' In *The Dynamics of Field Instruction: Learning Through Doing.* New York: CSWE, 1975, p. 40.

KENDALL, K. ''Selected Issues in Field Instruction in Education for Social Work.'' *Social Service Review,* 33 (March 1959): 1–9.

KETTNER, PETER M. ''A Conceptual Framework for Developing Learning Modules for Field Education.'' *Journal of Education for Social Work,* 15, No. 1 (Winter 1979): 51–58.

KOEGLER, RONALD R.; ENERY REYES WILLIAMSON; and CORAZON GROSSMAN. ''Individualized Educational Approach to Fieldwork in a Community Mental Health Center.'' *Journal of Education for Social Work,* 12, No. 2 (Spring 1976): 28–35.

KRAMER, SIDNEY. ''Developing a Field Placement Program.'' *Social Casework,* 42, No. 9 (November 1961): p. 456.

KURREN, OSCAR, and PAUL LISTER. ''Social Work Internship in Public Housing: An Interdisciplinary Experience.'' *Journal of Education for Social Work,* 12, No. 3 (Fall 1976): 72–79.

LAMMERT, MARILYN H. and JAN HAGEN. ''A Model for Community-oriented Field Experience.'' In *The Dynamics of Field Instruction: Learning Through Doing.* New York: CSWE, 1975, p. 60.

LIPSCOMB, NEIL. ''The Teaching-Learning Setting in a First-Year Field Instruction Program.'' In *The Dynamics of Field Instruction: Learning Through Doing.* New York: CSWE, 1975, p. 68.

LLEWELLYN, GRACE M. ''Orientation: A Conceptual Approach to Field Work,'' *Social Casework,* 45, No. 7 (July 1964): 404.

LURIE, ABRAHAM, and SIDNEY PINSKY. ''Queens Field Instruction Center: A Field Instruction Center for Multi-Level Education in Social Work,'' *Journal of Education for Social Work,* 9 (Fall 1973): 39–44.

MANIS, FRANCIS. *Field Practice in Social Work Education: Perspectives from an International Base.* Fullerton, California: Sultana Press, 1972.

MAYER, John E., and AARON ROSENBLATT. ''Sources of Stress Among Student Practitioners in Social Work: A Sociological View,'' *Journal of Education for Social Work,* 10, No. 3 (Fall 1974): 56–66.

MCNEIL, JOHN, and JOHN J. LITRIO. ''Community Service Clinics: A Fieldwork Model at the University of Texas at Arlington.'' *Journal of Education for Social Work,* 17, No. 1 (Winter 1981): 111–118.

MCQUIRE, RITA AUDREY. ''The Group Work Field Instructor-in-Action: A Study of Field Instruction Using the Critical Incident Technique.'' Unpublished dissertation, Columbia University, 1963 (available from University Microfilms Inc., Ann Arbor, Michigan).

MERRIFIELD, ELEANOR. ''Changing Patterns and Programs: Field Instruction,'' *Social Service Review,* 37 (September 1963): 274–282.

MOORE, DOROTHY E. ''Help Line: An Integrated Field-Research Learning Experience.'' In *The Dynamics of Field Instruction: Learning Through Doing.* New York: CSWE, 1975, p. 76.

PALMERA, PAUL L. ''One Foot in Academia, One in Practice.'' *Social Work,* 20, No. 4 (July 1975): 320–321.

PAWLAK, EDWARD J.; STEPHEN WEBSTER; and GIDEON FRYER. ''Field Instruction in Social Work Administration and Planning: Roles, Tasks and Practices.'' *Administration in Social Work,* 4, No. 2 (Summer 1980), 87–96.

POOR, J. ''Field Work Training of a Visually Handicapped Student.'' *The Family,* 26 (February 1946): 368–371.

ROTHMAN, J. ''Development of a Profession—Field Instruction Correlates.'' *Social Service Review* 51 (June 1977): 289–310.

ROTHMAN, JACK, and WYATT C. JONES. *A New Look at Field Instruction: Education for Application of Practice Skills in Community Organization and Social Planning.* New York: Association Press, 1971.

RUBIN, GERALD K. ''Termination of Casework: The Student, Client and Field Instructor.'' *Journal of Education for Social Work,* 4 (Spring 1968): 65–69.

SANTORE, ANTHONY F., et al. ''Field Placement for Administration Students: An Agency's View.'' *Administration in Social Work,* 4, No. 2 (Summer 1980): 97–104.

SCHUBERT, M. *Field Instruction in Social Casework: A Report of an Experiment.* Social Service Monographs, Second Series. Chicago: University of Chicago Press, 1963.

SCHUBERT, MARGARET. ''Field Work Performance: Repetition of a Study.'' *Social Service Review,* 34 (1960): 286–299.

SHAEFOR, BRADFORD W., and LOWELL E. JENKINS. ''Issues that Affect the Development of a Field Instruction Curriculum.'' *Journal of Education for Social Work,* 17, No. 1 (Winter, 1981): 12–20.

SHANNON, R. ''Developing a Framework for Field Work Instruction in a Public Assistance Agency.'' *Social Casework,* 43 (July 1962): 355–360.

SIMON, B. K. ''Design of Learning Experiences in Field Instruction.'' *Social Service Review,* 40 (December 1966): 397–409.

SNYDER, GEORGIA W.; ROSALIE A. KANE; and GLENN C. CONOVER. ''Block Placements in Rural Veteran's Administration Hospitals: A Consortium Approach.'' *Social Work in Health Care,* 3, No. 3 (Spring 1978): 331–341.

SOMERS, M., and P. GITLIN. ''Innovations in Field Instruction in Social Group Work.'' *Journal of Education for Social Work,* 2 (Spring 1966): 52–58.

SARROW, JANE. *Diary of A Student Social Worker.* London: Routledge & Kegan Paul, 1978.

ST. GEORGE, HENRY C. ''An Examination of Field Work Models at Adelphi University School of Social Work.'' *Journal of Education for Social Work,* 11 (Fall 1975): 62–68.

STRUBEL, PETER, and MARY HUTTON. "Creative Social Work Education: A Student-designed Practicum." In *The Dynamics of Field Instruction: Learning Through Doing.* New York: CSWE, 1975, p. 86.

SUMNER, D. "An Experiment with Field Work in Generic Social Work." *Social Casework,* 37 (June 1956): 288–294.

TANNAR, V. "Student Problems in Field Work in a Public Assistance Agency." *The Family,* 25 (January 1945): 345–350.

TORRE, ELIZABETH. "Student Performance in Solving Social Work Problems and Work Experience Prior to Entering the MSW Program." *Journal of Education for Social Work,* 10 (1974): 114–117.

WADDINGTON, M. "The Student Unit—Some Problems and Psychological Implications." *Social Casework,* March 1949, pp. 113–117.

WENZEL, K. *Curriculum Guides for Undergraduate Field Instruction.* New York: CSWE, 1972.

———. *Undergraduate Field Instruction Programs: Current Issues and Predictions.* New York: CSWE, 1972.

URDANG, ESTHER. "An Educational Project for First-Year Students in a Field Placement." *Social Casework,* 45, No. 1 (January 1964): 10.

Field Instruction Supervision

BARNAT, M. "Student Reactions to the First Supervisory Year—Relationship and Resolutions." *Journal of Education for Social Work,* 9 (Fall 1973): 3–8.

BAUM, O. E., and C. HERRING. "The Pregnant Psychotherapist in Training—Some Preliminary Findings and Impressions." *American Journal of Psychiatry,* 132 (April 1975): 419–422.

BERL, FRED. "The Content and Method of Supervisory Teaching." *Social Casework,* 44, No. 9 (November 1963): 516.

BERNSTEIN, SAUL. "Group Supervision of Social Work Students." *Council on Social Work Education,* New York, 1961.

BOGGS, B. "Advance Preparation of Caseworkers for the Supervision of Graduate Students." *Journal of Social Work Process,* 12 (1961): 57–72.

BROWN, CLEMENT S., and E. E. GLOYNE. *The Field Training of Social Workers.* London: Allen & Unwin, 1966.

BROWNE, MARJORIE M. "The Field Work Supervisor as Educator." *Journal of Psychiatric Social Work,* 22, No. 3 (April 1953): 141–143.

CARROLL, DONALD, and PATRICK MCCUAN. "A Specialized Role Function Approach to Field Instruction in Social Administration." In *The Dynamics of Field Instruction: Learning Through Doing.* New York: CSWE, 1975, p. 1.

CHICHESTER, E. "Group Meetings as an Aid to Student Supervision." *Social Casework,* 36 (June 1955): 264–269.

Council on Social Work Education. *The Dynamics of Field Instruction: Learning Through Doing.* New York: CSWE, 1975.

COWAN, B., et al. "Group Supervision as a Teaching-Learning Modality in Social Work." *Social Worker Travaileur,* 40 (1972): 256–261.

CRAIG, M. "Field Supervision—An Adaptation of Social Work Skills." *Social Casework,* 30 (May 1949): 200–203.

DAWSON, BETTY GUTHRIE. "Supervising the Undergraduate in a Psychiatric Setting." In *The Dynamics of Field Instruction: Learning Through Doing.* New York: CSWE, 1975, p. 10.

FELDMAN, YONATA. "The Supervisory Process: An Experience in Teaching and Learning." *Smith College Studies in Social Work,* 47, No. 2 (March 1977): 154–160.

GOLDEN, KENNETH M. "Client Transfer and Student Social Workers." *Social Work,* 21, No. 1 (January 1976): 65.

HOLTZMAN, REVA FINE. "Major Teaching Methods in Field Instruction in Casework." DSW dissertation, Columbia University School of Social Work, 1966.

KENT, BESSIE. *Social Work Supervision in Practice.* New York: Pergamon Press, 1969.

KOLEVZON, MICHAEL S. "Evaluating the Supervisory Relationship in Field Placements." *Social Work,* 24, No. 3 (May 1979): 241–244.

LANGE, DOROTHY. "Four Processes of Field Instruction in Casework: The Field Instructor's Contribution to Instructor-Student Interaction in Second Year Field Work." *Social Service Review,* 37 (September 1963): 263–273.

MACGUFFIE, ROBERT; FREDERICK V. JANZEN; and WILLIAM M. MCPHEE. "The Expression and Perception of Feelings Between Students and Supervisors in a Practicuum Setting." *Counselor Education and Supervision,* 10 (1970): 263–271.

MATORIN, SUSAN. "Dimensions of Student Supervision: A Point of View." *Social Casework,* 60 No. 3 (March 1979): 150–156.

MAYER, JOHN E., and AARON ROSENBLATT. "Strains Between Social Work Students and Their Supervisors: A Preliminary Report." Paper presented at the National Conference on Social Welfare, Atlantic City, N.J., May 1973.

MAYERS, F. "Differential Use of Group Teaching in First Year Field Work." *Social Service Review,* 44 (March 1970): 63–75.

MORTON, THOMAS D., and DAVID P. KURTZ. "Educational Supervision: A Learning Theory Approach." *Social Casework,* 61, No. 4 (April 1980): 240–246.

MURDAUGH, JESSICA. "Student Supervision Unbound." *Social Work,* 19, No. 2 (March 1974): 131.

NELSEN, J. C. "Relationship Communication in Early Fieldwork Conferences." *Social Casework,* 55 (April 1974): 237–243.

———. "Teaching Content of Early Fieldwork Conferences." *Social Casework,* 55 (March 1974): 147–153.

———. "Early Communication Between Field Instructors and Casework Students." DSW dissertation, Columbia University School of Social Work, 1973.

NEUSTAEDTER, E. "The Field Supervisor as Educator." *Social Casework,* 29 (December 1948): 375–382.

ROSE, SHELDON. "A Behavioral Model for Field Instruction and Supervision." Mimeographed. Madison: School of Social Work, University of Wisconsin, 1970.

———. "Students View Their Supervision: A Scale Analysis." *Social Work,* 10, No. 2 (April 1965): 90.

ROSE, SHELDON D.; JANE LOWENSTEIN; and PHILIP FELLIN. "Measuring Student Perception of Field Instruction." In *Current Patterns in Field Instruction in Graduate Social Work Education*, ed. Betty L. Jones. New York: CSWE, 1969, pp. 125–34.

ROSENBLATT, AARON, and JOHN MAYER. "Objectionable Supervisory Styles: Students' Views." *Social Work*, 20 (May 1975): 184–188.

SALES, ESTHER, and ELIZABETH NAVARRE. *Individual and Group Supervision in Field Instruction: A Research Report*. Ann Arbor: School of Social Work, University of Michigan, 1970.

SARNAT, R. G. "Supervision of the Experienced Student." *Social Casework*, 23 (1952): 147–152.

SCHLENOFF, MARJORIE LITWIN, and SANDRA HRICKO BUSA. "Student and Field Instructor as Group Cotherapists: Equalizing an Unequal Relationship." *Journal of Education for Social Work*, 17, No. 1 (Winter 1981): 29–35.

ST. JOHN, DAVID. "Goal-directed Supervision of Social Work Students in Field Placement." *Journal of Education for Social Work*, 11, No. 3 (Fall 1975): 89–94.

WIJNBERG, M. H., and M. C. SCHWARTZ. "Models of Student Supervision—The Apprentice, Growth and Role Systems Models." *Journal of Education for Social Work*, 13 (Fall 1977): 107–113.

Group and Peer Supervision

ALLEN, J. D. "Peer Group Supervision in Family Therapy." *Child Welfare*, 55 (March 1976): 183–189.

APAKA, TSUNEKO K.; SIDNEY HIRSCH; and SILVIA KLEIDMAN. "Establishing Group Supervision in a Hospital Social Work Department." *Social Work*, 12, No. 4 (October 1967): 54–60.

FIZDALE, R. "Peer Group Supervision." *Social Casework*, 39 (October 1958): 443–450.

GETZEL, GEORGE S.; JACK R. GOLDBERG; and ROBERT SALMON. "Supervising in Groups as a Model for Today," *Social Casework*, No. 3 (March 1971): 154–163.

HARE, RACHEL T., and SUSAN T. FRANKENA. "Peer Group Supervision," *American Journal of Orthopsychiatry*, 42 (1972): 527–529.

KASLOW, FLORENCE W. "Group Supervision." In *Issues in Human Services*, ed. Florence W. Kaslow and associates. San Francisco: Jossey-Bass, 1972, pp. 115–141.

MOORE, STEWART. "Group Supervision: Forerunner or Trend Reflector: Part I—Trends and Duties in Group Supervision." *Social Worker*, 38 (1970): 16–20.

———. "Group Supervision: Forerunner or Trend Reflector: Part II—Advantages and Disadvantages." *Social Worker*, 39 (1971): 3–7.

ROWLEY, CARL M., and EUGENE FAUX. "The Team Approach to Supervision." *Mental Hygiene*, 50 (1966): 60–65.

SMITH, DONALD M. "Group Supervision: An Experience." *Social Work Today*, 3 (London, 1972): 13–15.

WAX, JOHN. "The Pros and Cons of Group Supervision." *Social Casework*, 40, No. 6 (June 1959): 307–313.

WEINBERG, GLADYS. "Dynamics and Content of Group Supervision." *Child Welfare*, 39 (1960): 1–6.

Historical Material

COVNER, B. S. "Studies in the Phonographic Recorders of Verbal Material: III. The Completeness and Accuracy of Counselor Interview Reports." *Journal of General Psychology* 30 (1943): 181–203.

Family Welfare Association of America. *Worker and Supervisor*. New York: FWAA, 1936.

GLENDENNING, JOHN M. "Supervision Through Conferences on Specific Cases." *Family* 4 (1923): 7–10.

HILL, R. "A Field Work By-Product." *The Family*, 1 (February 1921): 22–23.

HOBART, A. "What the Visitor Expects from Supervision." *The Family*, 12 (March 1931): 17–19.

JOHNSON, V., and M. WINDAU. "The Supervisor-Worker Relationship as an Element in Training." *The Family*, 15 (October 1934): 184–187.

KOGAN, LEONARD S. "The Electrical Recording of Social Casework Inverviews." *Social Casework*, 31 (1950): 371–378.

MACKAY, E. "Organization and Supervision of Field Work from the Viewpoint of the Social Agency." *The Family*, 5 (February 1925): 253–256.

MARCUS, GRACE. "How Casework Training May Be Adapted to Meet Workers' Personal Problems." In *Proceedings of the National Conference of Social Work, 1927*. Chicago: University of Chicago Press, 1927.

WARD, C. H. "An Electronic Aide for Teaching Interviewing Techniques." *Archives of General Psychiatry*, 3 (1960): 357–358.

YEARND, J. "Credo of a Supervisor." *The Family*, February 1937, pp. 342–344.

Miscellaneous

ELLIS, JACK A. N., and VERNON E. BRYANT. "Competency-based Certification for School Social Workers." *Social Work*, 21, No. 5 (September 1976): 381–385.

FARLEY, WILLIAM O., *et al.* "Social Work—Professional Mediocrity or Maturation." *Social Casework*, 58, No. 4 (April 1977): 236–242.

GINGERICH, WALLACE J.; RONALD FELDMAN; and JOHN S. WODARSKI. "Accuracy in Assessment: Does Training Help?" *Social Work*, 21, No. 1 (January 1976): 40–48.

GOTTESFELD, MARY L., and FLORENCE LIEBERMAN. "The Pathological Therapist." *Social Casework*, 60 No. 7 (July 1979): 387–393.

INGALLS, JOHN D. *A Trainer's Guide to Androgony*. Washington: U.S. Department of HEW, revised May 1973.

LINDVALL, MAURITZ, E., ed. *Defining Educational Objectives*. Pittsburgh: Pittsburgh Press, 1964.

MAGER, ROBERT F. *Preparing Instructional Objectives*. Belmont, Calif.: Fearon Publishers, 1962.

NACMAN, MARTIN. "A Systems Approach to the Provision of Social Work Services in Health Settings: Part I." *Social Work in Health Care*, 1, No. 1 (Fall 1975): 47–54.

———. "The Provision of Social Work Services in Health Settings: Part II." *Social Work in Health Care*, 1, No. 2 (Winter 1975–76): 133–144.

REYNOLDS, BERTHA CAPEN. *Learning and Teaching in the Practice of Social Work*. New York: Russell & Russell, 1965.

SHULMAN, LAWRENCE. "A Study of Practice Skills." *Social Work*, 23, No. 4 (July 1978): 274–281.

Performance Evaluation

BLOOM, MARTIN, and STEPHEN R. BLOCK. "Evaluating One's Own Effectiveness and Efficiency." *Social Work*, 22, No. 2 (March 1977): 130–136.

CHICHESTER, E., *et al*. "Field Work Criteria for Second Year Casework Students." *Social Casework*, 31 (June 1950): 229–237.

DAILEY, WILDA J., and KENNETH IVES. "Exploring Client Reactions to Agency Service." *Social Casework*, 59, No. 4 (April 1978): 233–246.

DORNBUSCH, S. M., and W. R. SCOTT. *Evaluation and the Exercise of Authority*. San Francisco: Jossey-Bass, 1975.

FREIDSON, ELIOT, and BUFORD RHEA. "Knowledge and Judgment in Professional Evaluations." *Administrative Science Quarterly*, 10 (1965): 107–124.

FRIESEN, DELOSS D., and G. B. DUNNING. "Peer Evaluation and Practicuum Supervision." *Counselor Education and Supervision*, 13 (1973): 229–235.

FROEHLICH, CLIFFORD P. "The Completeness and Accuracy of Counseling Interview Reports." *Journal of General Psychology*, 58 (1958): 81–96.

GOULD, M. I. "Counseling the Problem Employee." *Supervisory Management*, 15, No. 11 (November 1970): 27–30.

GREEN, SOLOMON H. "Educational Assessments of Student Learning Through Practice in Field Instruction," *Social Work Education Reporter*, 20 (1972): 48–54.

HENRY, CHARLOTTE S. "Criteria for Determining Readiness of Staff to Function Without Supervision." In *Administration, Supervision, and Consultation*. New York: Family Service Association of America, 1955, pp. 34–45.

JANSSON, BRUCE S., and SAMUEL H. TAYLOR. "The Planning Contradiction in Social Agencies: Great Expectations Versus Satisfaction with Limited Performance." *Administration in Social Work*, 2, No. 2 (Summer 1978): 171–182.

KAGAN, MORRIS. "The Field Instructor's Evaluation of Student Performance: Between Fact and Fiction." *Social Worker*, 3 (1963): 15–26.

KAGLE, JILL DONER. "Evaluating Social Work Practice." *Social Work*, 24, No. 4 (July 1969): 292–296.

KANDLER, H., *et al*. "Prediction of Performance of Psychiatric Residents—A Three-Year Follow-Up Study." *American Journal of Psychiatry*, 132 (December 1975): 1286–1290.

LECHNYR, RONALD J. "Clinical Evaluation of Student Effectiveness." *Social Work*, 20 (March 1975): 148–150.

LEVY, CHARLES S. "Personal Motivation as a Criterion in Evaluating Social Work Practice." *Social Casework*, 61, No. 9 (November 1980): 541–547.

LUTZ, WERNER A. *Student Evaluation: Workshop Report*. 1956 Annual Program Meeting of the CSWE, Buffalo, N.Y. New York: CSWE, 1956.

MAGER, R. F., and P. PIPE. *Analyzing Performance Problems or "You Really Oughta Wanna."* Belmont, Calif.: Fearon Publishers, 1970.

McCAFFERY, M. "Criteria for Student Progress in Field Work." *Social Casework*, 28 (January 1947): 9–17.

MERRIFIELD, ALEXANDER; JAY LINFIELD; and EDYTHE JASTRAM. *A Standard for Measuring the Minimum Acceptable Level of Performance in First-Year Fieldwork in Social Casework*. Chicago: University of Chicago Press, 1964.

MILLER, A., *et al*. "Teaching and Evaluation of Diagnostic Skills." *Archives of General Psychiatry*, 24 (1971): 255–259.

MINER, G. "Techniques of Mutual Evaluation." *Social Casework*, December 1948, pp. 400–403.

MUSLIN, HYMAN L.; ALVIN G. BURSTEIN; JOHN E. GEDO; and LEO SADOW. "Research on the Supervisory Process: I. Supervisor's Appraisal of the Interview Data." *Archives of General Psychiatry*, 16 (1967): 427–431.

ROSE, SHELDON D.; JAY J. CAYNER; and JEFFREY L. EDLESON. "Measuring Interpersonal Competence." *Social Work*, 22, No. 2 (March 1977): 125–129.

SCHINKE, STEVEN PAUL. "Evaluating Social Work Practice: A Conceptual Model and Example." *Social Casework*, 60, No. 4 (April 1979): 195–200.

SCHMIDT, FRANCES, and MARTHA PERRY. "Values and Limitations of the Evaluation Process. I: As Seen by the Supervisor. II: As Seen by the Worker." In *Proceedings of the National Conference of Social Work*. New York: Columbia University Press, 1940, pp. 629–647.

URBANOWSKI, MARTHA L. "Recording to Measure Effectiveness." *Social Casework*, 55, No. 9 (November 1974): 546–553.

WALSH, MARGARET. "Supervisory Appraisal of the Second-Year Student in Field Work." *Social Casework*, 41 (December 1960): 530–532.

WEISS, S. S., and J. FLEMING. "Evaluation of Progress in Supervision." *Psychoanalytic Quarterly*, 44 (1975): 191–205.

WOOD, KATHERINE M. "Casework Effectiveness: A New Look at the Research Evidence." *Social Work*, 23, No. 6 (November 1978): 437–459.

Social Work Education—Standards, Values, and Issues

ARKAVA, MORTON L., and CLIFFORD E. BRENNEN. *Competency-based Education for Social Work: Evaluation and Curriculum Issues*. New York: CSWE, 1976.

BAER, BETTY L., and RONALD FEDERICO. *Educating the Baccalaureate Social Worker: Report of the Undergraduate Social*

Work Curriculum Development Project. Cambridge, Mass.: Ballinger, 1978.

BARKER, ROBERT L.; THOMAS L. BRIGGS; and DOROTHY BIRD DALY. *Educating the Undergraduate for Professional Social Work Roles*. Manpower Monograph No. 3. Syracuse, N.Y.: Syracuse University Press, 1971.

BIGGERSTAFF, MARILYN A. "Preparation of Administrators in Social Welfare: A Followup Study of Administration Concentration Graduates." *Administration in Social Work*, 2, No. 3 (Fall 1978): 359-368.

BRIAR, SCOTT, and NEIL F. BRACHT. "Collaboration Between Schools of Social Work and University Medical Centers." *Health and Social Work*, 4, No. 2 (May 1979): 72-91.

CAROFF, PHYLLIS. "A Study of School-Agency Collaboration in Social Work in Health Curriculum Building." *Social Work in Health Care*, 2, No. 3 (Spring 1977): 329-340.

COHEN, JEROME. "Selected Constraints in the Relationship Between Social Work Education and Practice." *Journal of Education for Social Work*, 13, No. 1 (Winter 1977): 3-7.

Council on Social Work Education. *Education for Social Work: Proceedings—Eleventh Anniversary Annual Program Meeting, 1963*. New York: CSWE, 1963.

———. *Field Instruction in Graduate Social Work Education: Old Problems and New Proposals*. New York: CSWE, 1966.

———. *Field Learning and Teaching: Explorations in Graduate Social Work Education*. New York: CSWE, 1968.

———. *Manual of Accrediting Standards for Graduate Professional Schools of Social Work* (with supplement for Undergraduate Programs). New York: CSWE, April 1971.

———. *Potentials and Problems in the Changing School Agency Relationships in Social Work Education*. New York: CSWE, 1967.

DOWNING, R. A. "Bridging the Gap Between Education and Practice." *Social Casework*, 55 (June 1974): 352-359.

EADES, JOE C. "Starting Where the Student Is: An Experiment in Accelerated Graduate Social Work Education." *Journal of Education for Social Work*, 12, No. 3 (Fall 1976): 22-28.

EUSTER, GERALD L. "Trends in Education for Social Work Practice With Groups." *Journal of Education for Social Work*, 15, No. 2 (Spring 1979): 94-99.

FRUMKIN, MICHAEL L. "Social Work Education and the Professional Commitment Fallacy: A Practical Guide to Field-School Relations." *Journal of Social Work Education*, 16, No. 2 (Spring 1980): 91-99.

HALE, M. "The Parameters of Agency-School Social Work Education Planning." *Journal of Education for Social Work*, 2 (Spring 1968): 32-40.

JONES, BETTY LACEY. *Current Patterns in Field Instruction in Graduate Social Work Education*. New York: CSWE, 1969.

KNOTT, B. H. "Symbolic Interaction and Social Work Education." *Journal of Education for Social Work*, 9 (Fall 1973): 24-30.

LARSEN, JO ANN. "Competency-based and Task-centered Practicum Instruction." *Journal of Education for Social Work*, 16, No. 1 (Winter 1980): 87-94.

LARSEN, JO ANN, and DEAN H. HEPWORTH. "Skill Development Through Competency-based Education." *Journal of Education for Social Work*, 14, No. 1 (Winter 1978): 73-81.

LOENBERG, FRANK. *Time and Quality in Graduate Social Work Education: Report of the Special Committee to Study the Length of Graduate Social Work Education*. New York: CSWE, 1972.

MANIS, FRANCIS. *Field Practice in Social Work Education: Perspectives from an International Base*. Fullerton, Calif.: Sultana Press, 1972.

MATSON, MARGARET B. *Field Experience in Undergraduate Programs in Social Welfare*. New York: CSWE, 1967.

MEYER, CAROL H. "Integrating Practice Demands in Social Work Education." *Social Casework*, 49 (October 1968): 481-486.

MEYERSON, E. "Educational Linkages Between Undergraduate Education in Social Welfare and Professional Social Work Education." *Journal of Education for Social Work*, 5 (Fall 1969): 31-37.

NEUGEBOREN, BERNARD. "Field Education for Social Welfare Administration: Integration of Social Policy and Administration." *Administration in Social Work*, 4, No. 2 (Summer 1980): 63-74.

PERLMAN, HELEN HARRIS. ". . . And Gladly Teach." *Journal of Education for Social Work*, Spring 1967.

———. "Believing and Doing: Values in Social Work Education." *Social Casework*, 57, No. 6 (June 1976): 381-390.

PERRETZ, EDGAR A. "Social Work Education for the Field of Health: A Report of Findings from a Survey of Curricula." *Social Work in Health Care*, 1, No. 3 (Spring 1976): 357-366.

POHEK, M. V. "Report on Developments in Teaching and Teaching Methodology." *Social Work Education Reporter*, 16 (June 1968): 20-21.

RIPPLE, LILIAN (ed.). "Innovations in Teaching." In *Social Work Practice*. New York: CSWE, 1970.

ROSENBLATT, AARON; MARRIANNE WELTER; and SOPHIE WOJCIECHOWSKI. *The Adelphi Experiment: Accelerating Social Work Education*. New York: CSWE, 1976.

SALMON, ROBERT, and JOEL WALKER. "The One-Year Residency Program: An Alternative Pattern to the Master's Degree in Social Work." *Journal of Education for Social Work*, 17, No. 1 (Winter 1981): 21-28.

SANTA CRUZ, LUCIANO A.; SUZANNE E. HEPLER; and MARK HEPLER. "Educationally Disadvantaged Students and Social Work Education." *Social Work*, 24, No. 4 (July 1969): 297-305.

SCHNEIDER, ROBERT L. "Behavioral Outcomes for Administration Majors." *Journal of Education for Social Work*, 14, No. 1 (Winter 1978): 102-109.

SHERWOOD, DAVID A. "The MSW Curriculum: Advanced Standing or Advanced Work?" *Journal of Education for Social Work*, 16, No. 1 (Winter 1980): 33-40.

SKIDMORE, REX A. "Administration Content for All Social Work Graduate Students." *Administration in Social Work*, 2, No. 1 (Spring 1978): 59-74.

SOUTHWICK, PHYLLIS C. (ed.). *Professional Education and Social Work Practice: A Partnership*. Salt Lake City: Graduate School of Social Work, University of Utah, June 1976.

STICKNEY, PATRICIA J. (ed.). *Student Participation in Decision Making in Graduate Schools of Social Work and Higher Education*. New York: CSWE, 1972.

SWACK, LOIS G. "Education and Practice: Their Responsibility to Complement Each Other." *Health and Social Work*, 5, No. 1 (February 1980): 64–70.

————. "The Unique Aspects of Short-term Teaching: How to Teach the How To's to the Doers." *Education for Social Work*, Winter 1974, pp. 90–95.

TENDLER, DIANA, and KAREN METZGER. "Training in Prevention: An Educational Model for Social Work Students." *Social Work in Health Care*, 4, No. 2 (Winter 1978): 221–232.

TOWLE, CHARLOTTE. *The Learner in Education for the Professions as Seen in Education for Social Work*. Chicago: University of Chicago Press, 1954.

TROPMAN, ELMER J. "Agency Constraints Affecting Links Between Practice and Education." *Journal of Education for Social Work*, 13, No. 1 (Winter 1977): 8–14.

TUFTS, J. *Education and Training for Social Work*. New York: Russell Sage Foundation, 1923.

Tulane University School of Social Work. *Field Learning and Teaching: Explorations in Graduate Social Work Education*. New Orleans: Tulane University School of Social Work, 1968.

WALKER, SYDNOR H. *Social Work and the Training of Social Workers*. Chapel Hill: University of North Carolina Press, 1928.

WENZEL, KRISTEN. *Curriculum Guides for Undergraduate Field Instruction Programs*. New York: CSWE, 1972.

————. (ed.). *Undergraduate Field Instruction Programs: Current Issues and Predictions*. New York: CSWE, 1972.

WITTMAN, MILTON. "Application of Knowledge About Prevention in Social Work Education and Practice." *Social Work in Health Care*, 3, No. 1 (Fall 1977): 37–48.

WODARSKI, JOHN S. "Critical Issues in Social Work Education." *Journal of Education for Social Work*, 15, No. 1 (Spring 1979): 5–13.

Student Learning

AMACHER, KLOH-ANN. "Explorations into the Dynamics of Learning in Field Work." DSW dissertation, Smith College School of Social Work, 1971.

BERENGARTEN, SIDNEY. "Identifying Learning Patterns of Individual Students: An Exploratory Study." *Social Service Review*, 31 (December 1957): 407–417.

BRUCK, MAX. "The Relationships Between Student Anxiety, Self-Awareness, and Self-Concept and Student Competence in Casework." *Social Casework*, 44 (March 1963): 125–131.

EPSTEIN, DORIS W.; SOPHIE F. LOEWENSTEIN; and MARY M. DUGGAN, "Issues in Training New Professionals." *Social Casework*, 55, No. 1 (January 1974): 36–42.

GELSO, CHARLES H. "Inhibition Due to Recording and Clients Evaluation of Counseling." *Psychological Reports*, 31 (1972): 75–77.

GOULD, ROBERT PAUL. "Students' Experience with the Termination Phase of Individual Treatment." *Smith College Studies in Social Work*, 48, No. 3 (June 1978): 235–260.

MAGER, ROBERT F. *Preparing Instructional Objectives*, Belmont, Calif.: Fearon Publishers, 1975.

REEVE, M. "An Illustration of the Learning Process in Supervision." *The Family*, 18 (June 1937): 131–133.

SCHMIDT, TERESA M. "The Development of Self Awareness in First-year Social Work Students." *Smith College Studies in Social Work*, 46, No. 3 (June 1976): 218–235.

Student Training and Supervision in Related Disciplines

BAUMAN, WILLIAM F. "Games Counselor Trainees Play: Dealing with Trainee Resistance." *Counselor Education and Supervision*, 12 (1972): 251–257.

BRUGGER, T.; G. CEASOR; A GRANK; and S. MARTZ. "Peer Supervision as a Method of Learning Psychotherapy." *Comprehensive Psychiatry*, 3 (1962): 47–53.

BURGOYNE, R. W., *et al.* "Who Gets Supervised: An Extension of Patient Selection Inequity." *American Journal of Psychiatry*, 133 (November 1976): 1313–1315.

COHEN, R. J., and B. DEBETZ. "Responsive Supervision of the Psychiatric Resident and Clinical Psychology Intern." *American Journal of Psychoanalysis*, 37 (Spring 1977): 51–64.

EBAUGH, F. "Graduate Teaching of Psychiatry Through Individual Supervision." *American Journal of Psychiatry*, 107 (1950): 274–278.

EKSTEIN, RUDOLF, and ROBERT S. WALLERSTEIN. *The Teaching and Learning of Psychotherapy*. Second ed. New York: International Universities Press, 1972.

FLEMING, J., and T. BENEDEX. *Psychoanalytic Supervision—A Method of Clinical Teaching*. New York: Grune & Stratton, 1966.

GALE M. S. "Resident Perception of Psychotherapy Supervision." *Comprehensive Psychiatry*, 17 (January–February 1976): 191–194.

GARETZ, F. K., *et al.* "The Disturbed and the Disturbing Psychiatric Resident." *Archives of General Psychiatry*, 33 (April 1976): 446–450.

GUTHEIL, T. G., and H. U. GRUNEBAUM. "The Teaching of Clinical Administration: Opportunities and Problems of Role Ambiguity." *Psychiatric Quarterly*, 49 (Winter 1977): 259–272.

HAMILTON, J. "Some Aspects of Learning Supervision and Identity Formation in the Psychiatric Residency." *Psychiatric Quarterly*, 45 (1971): 410–422.

HESTER, L., *et al.* "The Supervisor-Supervisee Relationship in Psychotherapy Training from the Perspective of Interpersonal Attraction." *Comprehensive Psychiatry*, 17 (September–October 1976): 671–681.

HEWER, VIVIAN. "An Aid to Supervision in Practicuum." *Journal of Counseling Psychology*, 21 (1974): 66–70.

HOFFMAN, F. (ed.). *The Teaching of Psychotherapy*. Boston: Little, Brown & Co., 1964.

KARLSRUHER, A. E. "The Influence of Supervision and Facilitative Conditions on the Psychotherapeutic Effectiveness of Nonprofessional and Professional Therapists." *American Journal of Community Psychology,* 4 (June 1976): 145–154.

KOGAN, W., *et al.* "Personality Changes in Psychiatric Residents During Training." *Journal of Psychology,* 62 (1966): 229–240.

LAZAR, N. D. "Some Problems in Faculty Selection of Patients for Supervised Psychoanalysis." *Psychoanalytic Quarterly,* 45 (July 1976): 416–429.

LOEBER, R., and R. G. WEISMAN. "Contingencies of Therapist and Trainer Performance—A Review." *Psychology Bulletin,* 82 (September 1975): 660–668.

MARTIN, R. M., and H. PROSEN. "Psychotherapy Supervision and Life Tasks—The Young Therapist and the Middle-aged Patient." *Bulletin of the Menninger Clinic,* 40 (March 1976): 125–133.

MATARAZZO, RUTH G. "Research on the Teaching and Learning of Psychotherapeutic Skills." In *Handbook of Psychotherapy and Behavior Change,* ed. Allen E. Bergin and Sol Y. Garfield. New York: Wiley, 1971, pp. 895–924.

MILLER, C. DEAN, and E. R. OETTING. "Students React to Supervision." *Counselor Education and Supervision,* 6 (1966): 73–74.

MUSLIN, H. L., *et al.* (eds.). *Evaluative Methods in Psychiatric Education.* Washington, D.C.: American Psychiatric Association, 1974.

NADELSON, C., and M. NOTMAN. "Psychotherapy Supervision: The Problem of Conflicting Values." *American Journal of Psychotherapy,* 31 (April 1977): 275–283.

ORNSTEIN, P. "Sorcerer's Apprentice: The Initial Phase of Training and Education in Psychiatry." *Comprehensive Psychiatry,* 9 (1968): 293–315.

RIOCH, M. J. "Changing Concepts in the Training of Therapists." *Journal of Consulting Psychology,* 30 (1966): 290–292.

ROSENBAUM, M. "Problems in Supervision of Psychiatric Residents in Psychotherapy." *Archives of Neurology and Psychiatry,* 69 (1953): 43–48.

ROSKIN, G., and C. J. RABINER. "Psychotherapists Passivity: A Major Training Problem." *International Journal of Psychoanalytic Psychotherapy,* 5 (1976): 319–331.

SCHER, M., and J. NEHREN. "A Student Experience that Taught Faculty and Hospital Staff." *Nursing Outlook,* 14 (1966): 26–29.

SCHLESSINGER, N. "Supervision of Psychotherapy: A Critical Review of the Literature." *Archives of General Psychiatry,* 15 (1966): 129–134.

SCHUSTER, DANIEL B.; JOHN J. SANDT; and OTTO P. THALER. *Clinical Supervision of the Psychiatric Resident.* New York: Brunner/Mazel, 1972.

SPIEGEL, D., and H. GRUNEBAUM. "Training Versus Treating the Psychiatric Resident." *American Journal of Psychotherapy,* 31 (October 1977): 618–625.

VAUGHAN, M., and J. N. MARKS. "Teaching Interviewing Skills to Medical Students—a Comparison of Two Methods." *Medical Education,* 10 (May 1976): 170–175.

WOLKON, G. H., *et al.* "Personality Changes and Compatibility in the Psychiatric Resident–Supervisor Relationship." *Journal of Medical Education,* 53 (January 1978): 59–63.

WOLPE, JOSEPH. "Supervision Transcripts: I. Fear of Success." *Journal of Behavior Therapy and Experimental Psychiatry,* 3 (1972): 107–110.

———. "Supervision Transcripts: II. Problems of a Novice." *Journal of Behavior Therapy and Experimental Psychiatry,* 3 (1972): 199–203.

———. "Supervision Transcripts: III. Some Problems in a Claustrophobic Case." *Journal of Behavior Therapy and Experimental Psychiatry,* 3 (1972): 301–305.

———. "Supervision Transcripts: IV. Planning Therapeutic Tactics." *Journal of Behavior Therapy and Experimental Psychiatry,* 4 (1973): 41–46.

———. "Supervision Transcripts: VII. Neglecting the Case History and Other Elementary Errors." *Journal of Behavior Therapy and Experimental Psychiatry,* 4 (1973b): 365–370.

Supervision (General Techniques of Supervision)

ABRAMCZYK, LOIS W. "The New MSW Supervisor: Problems of Role Transition." *Social Casework*, 61, No. 2 (February 1980): 83–89.

ABRAMOWITZ, S. I., and C. V. ABRAMOWITZ. "Sex Role Psychodynamics in Psychotherapy Supervision." *American Journal of Psychotherapy,* 30 (October 1976): 583–592.

American Public Welfare Association. *The Supervisor of Caseworkers in the Public Welfare Agency.* Second ed. Chicago: APWA, June 27, 1958.

ANCHOR, K. N., *et al.* "Supervisors' Perceptions of the Relationship Between Therapist Self-Disclosure and Clinical Effectiveness." *Journal of Clinical Psychology,* 32 (January 1976): 158.

APTEKAR, HERBERT H. "Significance of Dependence and Independence in Supervision." *Social Casework,* 35 (June 1954): 238–245.

———. "Supervision and the Development of Professional Responsibility: An Application of Systems Thought." *Jewish Social Work Forum,* 3, Fall 1965.

AUSTIN, LUCILLE. "An Evaluation of Supervision." *Social Casework,* 37 (October 1956): 375–382.

———. "Basic Principles of Supervision." *Social Casework,* 33 (December 1952): 411–419.

———. "Supervision of the Experienced Caseworker." *The Family,* 22 (1942): 314–320.

———. "The Changing Role of the Supervisor." *Smith College Studies in Social Work,* 31 (June 1961): 179–195.

BALSAM, A., and N. GARBER. "Characteristics of Psychotherapy Supervision." *Journal of Medical Education,* 45 (1970): 789–797.

BASCH, DON. "Portrait of a Supervisor." *Supervisory Management*, 15, No. 12 (December 1970): 2–4.

BELL, J. I. *Staff Development and Practice Supervision*. Social and Rehabilitation Service, Department of Health, Education and Welfare. Washington, D.C.: Government Printing Office, 1968.

BERKOWITZ, SIDNEY J. "The Administrative Process in Casework Supervision." *Social Casework*, 33, No. 11 (December 1952): 417–423.

BITTEL, LESTER. *What Every Supervisor Should Know*. Second Ed. New York: McGraw-Hill, 1968.

BLITZSTEN, N. L., and J. FLEMING. "What Is a Supervisory Analysis?" *Bulletin of the Menninger Clinic*, July 1953.

BLOCH, S., *et al.* "The Use of a Written Summary in Group Psychotherapy Supervision." *American Journal of Psychiatry*, 132 (October 1975): 1055–1057.

BLOOM L., and C. HERMAN. "A Problem of Relationship in Supervision." *Social Casework*, 39 (July 1958): 402–406.

BLOOM, ALLAN A. "Pitfalls of a Managerial Approach to Supervision in a Public Welfare Agency." *Administration in Social Work*, 2, No. 4 (Winter 1978): 482–488.

BRAGER, G. "A First Conference with an Inexperienced Group Leader." In Trecher, H. B. (ed.), *Group Work—Foundations and Frontiers*. New York: Association Press, 1955.

BURNS, M. "Supervision in Social Work." In Lurie, H. (ed.), *Encyclopedia of Social Work*. New York: National Association of Social Workers, 1965, pp. 785–790.

CHERNISS, CARY, and EDWARD EGNATOS. "Clinical Supervision in Community Mental Health." *Social Work*, 23, No. 3 (May 1978): 219–225.

———. "Styles of Clinical Supervision in Community Mental Health." *Journal of Consulting Clinical Psychology*, 45 (December 1977): 1195–1196.

COHEN, NEIL A., and GARY B. RHODES. "Social Work Supervision: A View Toward Leadership Style and Job Orientation in Education and Practice." *Administration in Social Work*, 1, No. 3 (Fall 1977): 281–292.

CRAWFORD, B. "Use of Color Charts in Supervision." *Social Casework*, 52, No. 4 (1971): 220–221.

CRUSER, ROBERT W. "Opinions on Supervision: A Chapter Study." *Social Work*, 3 (1958): 18–25.

DALY, D. "Supervision of the Newly Employed Experienced Worker." *The Family*, 27 (June 1946): 146–150.

DAY, R. C., and R. L. HAMBLIN. "Some Effects of Close and Punitive Styles of Supervision." In Bell, G. D. (ed.), *Organizations and Human Behavior—A Book of Readings*. Englewood Cliffs, N.J.: Prentice-Hall, 1967, pp. 172–182.

DEBELL, D. "A Critical Digest of the Literature on Psychoanalytic Supervision." *Journal of the American Psychoanalytic Association*, 11 (1963): 546–575.

DE LA TORRE, J. "Use and Misuse of Cliches in Clinical Supervision." *Archives of General Psychiatry*, 31 (September 1974): 302–306.

DEVIS, DONALD A. "Teaching and Administrative Functions in Supervision." *Social Work*, 10, No. 2 (April 1965): 83–89.

DIMOCK, H., and TRECKER, H. *The Supervision of Group Work and Recreation*. New York: Association Press, 1949.

DOEHRMAN, MARGERY J. "Parallel Processes in Supervision and Psychotherapy." Ph.D. dissertation, University of Michigan, 1962.

DOWLING, WILLIAM F., and LEONARD R. SAYLES. *How Managers Motivate: The Imperatives of Supervision*. New York: McGraw-Hill, 1971.

DRUCKER, P. F. *Management—Tasks, Responsibilities, Practices*. New York: Harper & Row, 1973.

D'ZURMA, T. L. "The Functions of Individual Supervision." In Hoffman, F. H. (ed.), *The Teaching of Psychotherapy*. Boston: Little, Brown & Co., 1964.

EDINBURG, GOLDA M.; NORMAN E. ZINBERG; and WENDY KELMAN. "Getting the Most Out of Supervision." Chapter 10 in *Clinical Interviewing and Counseling: Principles and Techniques*. New York: Appleton-Century-Crofts, 1975, pp. 113–121.

EISENBERG, SIDNEY. *Supervision in the Changing Field of Social Work*. Philadelphia: Jewish Family Service of Philadelphia, 1956.

ENGLE, PHILIP R. *Supervision of the Baccalaureate Social Worker*. Manpower Monograph No. 11. Syracuse, N.Y.: Syracuse University School of Social Work, 1977.

FELDMAN, YONATA. "Some Particular Emphasis in Supervision." *Social Work*, 1, No. 1 (January 1956): 62.

———. "The Teaching Aspect of Casework Supervision." *Social Casework*, 31 (April 1950): 156–161.

FELDMAN, YONATA; HYMAN SPONITZ; and LEO NAGELBERG. "One Aspect of Casework Training through Supervision." *Social Casework*, 34 (1953): 150–156.

FINCH, WILBUR A., JR. "Social Workers Versus Bureaucracy." *Social Work*, 21 (September 1976): 370–375.

FLEMING, JOAN, and THERESE BENEDEK. *Psychoanalytic Supervision*. New York: Grune, 1966.

FOECKLER, M. and P. DEULSCHBERGER. "Growth-oriented Supervision." *Public Welfare*, 28 (1970): 297–299.

FOX, RAYMOND. "Supervision by Contract." *Social Casework*, 55 (1974): 247–251.

GITTERMAN, ALEX. "Comparison of Educational Models and Their Influence on Supervision." In *Issues in Human Services*, ed. Florence W. Kaslow and associates. San Francisco, Jossey-Bass, 1972, pp. 18–38.

GIZYNSKI, MARTHA. "Self Awareness of the Supervisor in Supervision." *Clinical Social Work Journal*, 6, No. 3 (Fall 1978): 202–210.

GOIN, M. K., and F. KLINE. "Countertransference—A Neglected Subject in Clinical Supervision." *American Journal of Psychiatry*, 133 (January 1976): 41–44.

GOIN, MARCIA K., and FRANK M. KLINE. "Supervision Observed," *Journal of Nervous and Mental Disease*, 158 (1974): 208–213.

GOLDSTEIN, ARNOLD P., and MELVIN SORCHER. *Changing Supervisor Behavior*. New York: Pergamon Press, 1974.

GRANVOLD, DONALD K. "Supervision by Objectives." *Administration in Social Work*, 2, No. 2 (Summer 1978): 199–210.

———. "Supervisory Style and Educational Preparation of Public Welfare Supervisors." *Administration in Social Work*, 1, No. 1 (Spring 1977): 79–88.

GROSS, M. J. "Parallel Process in Supervision and Psychotherapy." *Bulletin of the Menninger Clinic,* 40 (January 1976): 1–104.

GROTJAHN, M. "Problems and Techniques of Supervision." *Psychiatry,* 18 (February 1955): 9–15.

GUTHEIL, T. G. "Ideology as Resistance: A Supervisory Challenge." *Psychiatric Quarterly,* 49 (Summer 1977): 88–96.

H. C. D. "Through Supervision with Gun and Camera: The Personal Account of a Beginning Supervisor." *Social Work Journal,* 30 (1959): 161–163.

HALLOWITZ, DAVID. "The Supervisor as Practitioner," *Social Casework,* 43 (1962): 287–292.

HAMACHEK, JOAN M. "Effects of Individual Supervision on Selected Affective and Cognitive Characteristics of Counselors-in-Training: A Pilot Study." Ph.D. dissertation, Michigan State University, 1971.

HAWTHORNE, LILLIAN. "Games Supervisors Play." *Social Work,* 20, No. 3 (May 1975): 179–183.

KADUSHIN, ALFRED. "Games People Play in Supervision." *Social Work,* 13, No. 3 (1968): 23–32.

_____. "Supervisor-Supervisee: A Survey." *Social Work,* 19 (May 1974): 288–297.

_____. *Supervision in Social Work.* New York: Columbia University Press, 1976.

KASLOW, FLORENCE, *et al. Supervision, Consultation and Staff Training in the Helping Professions.* San Francisco: Jossey-Bass, 1979.

KENDREW, MARY HYLAND. "How Perceptive Are You as a Case Supervisor?" *Social Work,* Vol. 1, No. 4 (October 1956).

KENNEDY, M., and L. KEITNER. "What Is Supervision: The Need for a Redefinition." *Social Worker,* 38 (February 1970): 50–52.

KNEZNEK, EVE. *Supervision.* New York: APWA, 1966.

KOONTZ, HAROLD, and CYRIL O'DONNELL. *Essentials of Management.* New York: McGraw-Hill, 1974.

KURPIUS, DEWAYNE; RONALD BAKER; and IRENE THOMAS. *Supervision of Applied Training: A Comparative Review.* Westport, Conn.: Greenwood Press, 1977.

LEVY, CHARLES S. "The Ethics of Supervision." *Social Work,* March 1973, pp. 14–21.

LEYENDECKER, GERTRUDE. "A Critique of Current Trends in Supervision." In *Casework Papers: National Conference on Social Welfare.* New York: Family Service Association of America, 1959.

LIDE, ·P. "A Supervisory Record." *Social Casework,* 29 (January 1948): 27–33.

LINDENBERG, R. "Changing Traditional Patterns of Supervision." *Social Work,* 2 (April 1957): 42–46.

LINDENBERG, S. *Supervision in Social Group Work.* New York: Association Press, 1939.

LINDERBERG, R. "Changing Traditional Patterns of Supervision," *Social Work,* 2 (1957): 42–46.

MANDELL, BETTY. "The 'Equality' Revolution and Supervision." In *Social Work Supervision: Classic Statements and Critical Issues.* Carlton E. Munson, ed. New York: Free Press, 1979, 311–326.

MARCUS, PHILIP M. "Supervision and Group Process," *Human Organization,* 20 (1961): 15–19.

MAROHN, RICHARD C. "The Similarity of Therapy and Supervisory Themes," *International Journal of Group Psychotherapy,* 19 (1969): 176–184.

MATTINSON, JANET. *The Reflection Process in Casework Supervision.* Washington, D.C.: NASW, 1975.

MILLER, IRVING. "Distinctive Characteristics of Supervision in Group Work," *Social Work,* 5, No. 1 (1960): 69–76.

_____. "Supervision in Social Work." *Encyclopedia of Social Work.* New York: National Association of Social Workers, 1977, pp. 1544–1550.

MUELLER, WILLIAM S., and BILL L. KELL. *Coping with Conflict: Supervisory Counselors and Psychotherapists.* New York: Appleton, 1972.

MUNSON, CARLTON E. "Evaluation of Male and Female Supervisors." *Social Work,* 24, No. 2 (March 1979): 104–111.

_____. "Professional Autonomy and Social Work Supervision." *Journal of Education for Social Work,* 12 (Fall 1976): 95–102.

_____ (ed.). *Social Work Supervision: Classic Statements and Critical Issues.* New York: Free Press, 1979.

_____. "Style and Structure in Supervision." *Journal of Education for Social Work,* 17, No. 1 (Winter 1981): 65–72.

_____. "Supervising the Family Therapist." *Social Casework,* 61, No. 3 (March 1980): 131–137.

National Association of Social Workers. *NASW Standards for Social Work Personnel Practices.* New York: NASW, 1968.

National Association of Social Workers, Western New York Chapter. "Opinions of Supervision: A Chapter Study." *Social Work,* 3, No. 1 (January 1958): p. 18.

ORCHARD, BERNICE. "The Use of Authority in Supervision," *Public Welfare,* 23 (1965): 32–40.

PASQUALINI, FRANÇOIS. "Advice for the New Supervisor." *Supervisory Management,* 15, No. 7 (July 1970): 16–18.

PAYNE, PAUL A.; DONNA E. WINTER; and GLENN E. BELL. "Effects of Supervisor Style on the Learning of Empathy in a Supervision Analogue." *Counselor Education and Supervision,* 11 (1972): 262–269.

PETERS, MARY OVERHOLT. "Supervising the Experienced Worker." *Social Casework,* 30, No. 5 (May 1949).

PETTES, D. *Supervision in Social Work—A Method of Student Training and Staff Development.* London: George Allen & Unwin Ltd., 1967.

PUVIS, LURLINE C. "Self-Awareness: A Proposal for Supervision." *Journal of Contemporary Psychotherapy,* 4 (1972): 107–112.

RAPOPORT, LYDIA. "The Use of Supervision as a Tool in Professional Development," *British Journal of Psychiatric Social Work,* 2 (1954): 66–74.

RABKIN, L. Y. "Survivor Themes in the Supervision of Psychotherapy." *American Journal of Psychotherapy,* 30 (October 1976): 593–600.

RICKERT, VERNON C., and JOHN E. TURNER. "Through the Looking Glass: Supervision in Family Therapy." *Social Casework,* 59 (March 1978): 131–137.

ROBINSON, VIRGINIA. *Supervision in Social Casework.* Chapel Hill: University of North Carolina Press, 1936.

SCHERZ, FRANCES. "A Concept of Supervision Based on Definitions of Job Responsibility." *Social Casework,* 39 (October 1958): 435–443.

SCHOUR, ESTHER. "Helping Social Workers Handle Work Stresses." *Social Casework,* 34, No. 10 (December 1953): 423–428.

SEARLES, HAROLD F. "The Informational Value of the Supervisor's Emotional Experiences." *Psychiatry,* 18 (1955): 135–146.

SHARLIN, SHLOMO, and HARRIS CHAIKLIN. "Social Work Supervision on Wheels." In *Social Work Supervision: Classic Statements and Critical Issues.* Carlton E. Munson (ed.). New York: Free Press, 1979, pp. 166–177.

SHOWALTER, J. E., and K. PRUETT. "The Supervision Process for Individual Child Psychotherapy." *Journal of the American Academy of Child Psychiatry,* 14 (Autumn 1975): 708–718.

SIPORIN, MAX. "Dual Supervision of Psychiatric Social Workers." *Social Work,* 1, No. 2 (April 1956): 32.

SPANO, ROBERT M., and SANDER H. LUND. "Management by Objectives in a Hospital Social Service Unit." *Social Work in Health Care,* 1, No. 3 (Spring 1976): 267–276.

SPERGEL, IRVING. "Role Behavior and Supervision of the Untrained Group Worker." *Social Work,* 7, No. 3 (July 1962): p. 69.

State of California Department of Social Welfare. *Training Aid No. 39A: A Training Course on The Supervision of Case Aides.* Sacramento: State of California Department of Social Welfare, August 1970.

————. *The Supervision and Training of Case Aides: A Reading Reference for Supervisors and Staff Trainers.* Sacramento: State of California Department of Social Services, August 1970.

TAUBER, L. F. "Choice Point Analysis-Formulation, Strategy, Intervention, and Result in Group Process Therapy and Supervision." *International Journal of Group Psychotherapy,* 28 (April 1978): 163–184.

TOWLE, CHARLOTTE. "The Place of Help in Supervision." *The Social Service Review,* 37, No. 4 (December 1963): 403–417.

United States Civil Service Commission. *Recognizing and Supervising Troubled Employees.* Personnel Management Series Number 18. Washington, D.C.: U.S. Civil Service Commission, July 1967.

VAN ATTA, RALPH E. "Co-Therapy as a Supervisory Process." *Psychotherapy: Theory, Research and Practice,* 6 (1969): 137–139.

WATSON, KENNETH. "Differential Supervision." *Social Work,* 18, No. 6 (November 1973): 80–88.

WAX, JOHN. "Time-Limited Supervision." *Social Work,* 8, No. 3 (1963): 37–43.

WIDEM, PAUL. "Organizational Structure for Casework Supervision." *Social Work,* 7, No. 4 (October 1962): 78.

WILLIAMSON, MARGARET. *Supervision: New Patterns and Processes.* New York, Association Press, 1961.

WOODCOCK, G. D. C., "A Study of Beginning Supervision," *British Journal of Psychiatric Social Work,* 9 (1967): 66–74.

YOUNG, RUTH. "Supervision: Challenges for the Future." In *So-cial Work Supervision: Classic Statements and Critical Issues.* Carlton E. Munson (ed.). New York: Free Press, 1979, pp. 327–335.

Teaching Approaches, Including Video and Audio Taping, Recording, and Direct Observation

ARMSTRONG, MARGARET; MARGARET HUFFMAN; and MARIANNE SPAIN. "The Use of Process and Tape Recordings as Tools in Learning Casework." MA Thesis, State University of Iowa, 1959.

BENSCHOTER, R. A.; M. T. EATON; and D. SMITH. "Use of Videotape to Provide Individual Instruction in Techniques of Psychotherapy." *Journal of Medical Education,* 40 (1965): 1159–1161.

BOYLSTON, WILLIAM H., and JUNE M. TUMA. 1972. "Training of Mental Health Professionals Through the Use of the 'Bug in the Ear.'" *American Journal of Psychiatry,* 129 (1972): 92–95.

CHODOFF, PAUL. "Supervision of Psychotherapy with Videotape: Pros and Cons." *American Journal of Psychiatry,* 128 (1972): 819–823.

CONNOLLY, J., and J. BIRD. "Video-Tape in Teaching and Examining Clinical Skills: A Short Case Format." *Medical Education,* 11 (July 1977): 271–275.

CRAWFORD, BLAINE. "Use of Color Charts in Supervision." *Social Casework,* 52, No. 4 (April 1971): 220.

DWYER, MARGARET, and MARTHA URBANOWSKI. "Student Process Recording: A Plea for Structure." *Social Casework,* 46, No. 5 (May 1965): 283.

ENGLISH, R. WILLIAM, and SERGE JELENEVSKY. "Counselor Behavior as Judged Under Audio, Visual, and Audiovisual Communication Conditions." *Journal of Counseling Psychology,* 18 (1971): 509–513.

FLEISCHMANN, O. "A Method of Teaching Psychotherapy: One-Way-Vision Room Technique." *Bulletin of the Menninger Clinic,* 19 (1955): 169–172.

FREY, LOUISE A.; EUNICE SHATZ; and EDNA-ANN KATZ. "Continuing Education: Teaching Staff to Teach." *Social Casework,* 55, No. 6 (June 1974): 360–368.

GOIN, M. K., et al. "Teaching Dynamic Psychotherapy by Observation." *American Journal of Psychotherapy,* 30 (January 1976): 112–120.

GRUENBERG, PETER B.; EDWARD H. LISTON, JR.; and GEORGE J. WAYNE. "Intensive Supervision of Psychotherapy with Videotape Recording." *American Journal of Psychotherapy,* 23 (1969): 95–105.

HARPER, ROBERT A., and JOHN W. HUDSON. "The Use of Recordings in Marriage Counseling: A Preliminary Empirical Investigation." *Marriage and Family Living,* 14 (1952): 332–334.

HIRSH, HERMAN, and HERBERT FREED. "Pattern Sensitization in Psychotherapy Supervision by Means of Video Tape Recording." In *Videotape Technique in Psychiatric Training and*

Treatment, ed. Milton M. Berger. New York, Bruner-Mazel, 1970.

ITZIN, FRANK. "The Use of Tape Recording in Field Work." *Social Casework,* 41 (1960): 197–202.

JARVIS, PAUL E., and JONATHAN F. ESTY. "The Alternative-Therapist-Observer Technique in Group Therapy Training." *International Journal of Group Psychotherapy,* 18 (1968): 95–99.

KADUSHIN, ALFRED. "Interview Observation as a Teaching Device." *Social Casework,* 37 (1956): 334–341.

———. "The Effect on the Client of Interview Observation at Intake." *Social Service Review,* 31 (1957): 22–38.

———. "The Effects of Interview Observation on the Interviewer." *Journal of Counseling Psychology,* 3 (1956). 130–135.

KAGAN, NORMAN; DAVID R. KRATHWOHL; and RALPH MILLER. "Stimulated Recall in Therapy Using Video-Tape: A Case Study." *Journal of Counseling Psychology,* 10 (1963): 237–243.

KEPECS, J. G. "Teaching Psychotherapy by Use of Brief Transcripts." *American Journal of Psychotherapy,* 31 (July 1977): 383–393.

KOHN, R. "Differential Use of the Observed Interview in Student Training." *Social Work Education Reporter,* 3 (1971): 45.

KORNER, IJA N., and WILLIAM H. BROWN. "The Mechanical Third Ear." *Journal of Consulting Psychology,* 16 (1952): 81–84.

KORNFIELD, D. S., and L. C. KOLB. "The Use of Closed Circuit Television in the Teaching of Psychiatry." *Journal of Nervous and Mental Diseases* 138 (1964): 452–459.

LAMB, RICHARD, and GEORGE MAHL. "Manifest Reactions of Patients and Interviewers to the Use of Sound Recording in the Psychiatric Interview." *American Journal of Psychiatry,* 112 (1956): 733–735.

LEADER, ARTHUR L. "Supervision and Consultations Through Observed Interviewing." *Social Casework,* 49 (May 1968): 288–293.

MELTZER, RAE. "School and Agency Cooperation in Using Videotape in Social Work Education." *Journal of Education for Social Work,* 13, No. 1 (Winter 1977): 90–95.

MEYERSON, A. T., *et al.* "Evaluation of a Psychiatric Clerkship by Videotape." *American Journal of Psychiatry,* 134 (August 1977): 883–886.

MORGAN, ROBERT. "Videotaped Telegraphic Personalized Instructional Packages for Students in Health Care Settings." *Journal of Education for Social Work,* 16, No. 2 (Spring 1980): 78–84.

NILAND, THOMAS M.; JOHN DULING; JADA ALLEN; and EDWARD PANTHER. "Student Counselors' Perception of Videotaping." *Counselor Education and Supervision,* 11 (1971): 97–101.

PERLMAN, HELEN H. "Teaching Casework by the Discussion Method." *Social Service Review,* 24 (1950): 334–346.

PITTENGER, ROBERT E.; CHARLES F. HOCKETT; and JOHN J. DANEHY. *The First Five Minutes: A Sample of Microscopic Interview Analyses.* Ithaca, N.Y.: Martineau, 1960.

POLING, E. G. "Video Tape Recordings in Counseling Practicuum. I. Environmental Considerations." *Counselor Education and Supervision,* 8 (1968): 348–356.

RHIM, BONNIE C. "The Use of Videotapes in Social Work Agencies." *Social Casework,* 57, No. 10 (December 1976): 644–650.

ROBERTS, RALPH R., and G. A. RENZAGLIA. "The Influence of Tape Recording on Counseling." *Journal of Counseling Psychology,* 12 (1965): 10–15.

RYAN, C. "Video Aids in Practicuum Supervision." *Counselor Education and Supervision,* 8 (1969): 125–129.

RYAN, FRANCIS. "Joint Interviewing by Field Instructor and Student." *Social Casework,* 45 (1964): 471–474.

SCHUR, EDITH L. "The Use of the Coworker Approach as a Teaching Model in Graduate Student Field Education." *Journal of Education for Social Work,* 15, No. 1 (Winter 1979): 72–79.

STAR, BARBARA. "Exploring the Boundaries of Videotape Self-Confrontation." *Journal of Education for Social Work,* 15, No. 1 (Winter 1979): 87–94.

SUESS, JAMES F. "Self-confrontation of Videotaped Psychotherapy as a Teaching Device for Psychiatric Students." *Journal of Medical Education,* 45 (1970): 271–282.

THOMAS, EDWIN J.; DONNA L. MCLEOD; and LYDIA F. HYLTON. "The Experimental Interview: A Technique for Studying Casework Performance." *Social Work,* 5, No. 3 (July 1960): 52.

URDANG, ESTHER. "In Defense of Process Recording." *Smith College Studies in Social Work,* 50, No. 1 (November 1979): 1–15.

VAN ATTA, R. E. "Excitory and Inhibitory Effect of Various Modes of Observation in Counseling." *Journal of Counseling Psychology,* 16 (1969): 433–439.

WALZ, G. R., and J. A. JOHNSTON. "Counselors Look at Themselves on Video Tape." *Journal of Counseling Psychology,* 10 (1963): 232–236.

WARD, C. H. "Electronic Preceptoring in Teaching Beginning Psychotherapy." *Journal of Medical Education,* 37 (1962): 1128–1129.

WIKLER, LYNN. "Consumer Involvement in the Training of Social Work Students." *Social Casework,* 60, No. 3 (March 1979): 145–149.

WILKIE, CHARLOTTE H. "A Study of Distortions in Recording Interviews." *Social Work,* 8 (1963): 31–36.

WILSON, SUANNA. *Recording: Guidelines for Social Workers.* New York: Free Press, 1980.

ZIMNY, GEORGE H.; JOSEPH E. BROWN; JOANNA J. ELLIS; and JAMES C. SORENSON. "Use of Television in the Clinical Internship Programs." *Professional Psychology,* 3 (1972): 271–276.

Teaching Specific Skills/Knowledge

ANDERSON, GARY D. "Enhancing Listening Skills for Work with Abusing Parents." *Social Casework,* 60, No. 10 (December 1979): 602–608.

BRYANT, CARL. "Introducing Students to the Treatment of Inner-City Families." *Social Casework*, 61, No. 10 (December 1980): 629–638.

CASSIDY, HELEN. "Helping the Social Work Student Deal with Death and Dying." In *Social Work with the Dying Patient and the Family,* ed. Elizabeth R. Prichard *et al.* New York: Columbia University Press, 1977, pp. 313–322.

CRAMER, MARGERY FAY. "Fieldwork Preparation for Entrance into Mental Retardation Practice." *Journal of Education for Social Work,* 13, No. 1 (Winter 1977): 37–43.

ELLIS, JACK A. "Skill Training for Social Welfare Management: Developing a Laboratory Model for Field Instruction." *Administration in Social Work,* 2, No. 2 (Summer 1978): 211–222.

FIRESTEIN, STEPHEN K. "Teaching Dynamic Psychiatry to Social Work Students." *Social Casework,* 57, No. 4 (April 1976): 265–271.

GRANVOLD, DONALD K. "Training Social Work Supervisors to Meet Organizational and Worker Objectives." *Journal of Education for Social Work*, 14, No. 2 (Spring 1978): 38–45.

GROSSMAN, BART. "Teaching Research in the Field Practicum." *Social Work,* 25, No. 1 (January 1980): 36–39.

KNAPPE, MILDRED E. "The Training Center Concept: Educating Social Workers For a Changing World." In *The Dynamics of Field Instruction: Learning Through Doing.* New York: CSWE, 1975, p. 50.

PINDERHUGHES, ELAINE B. "Teaching Empathy in Cross-Cultural Social Work." *Social Work,* 24, No. 4 (July 1969): 312–316.

PURVINE, MARGARET. *Educating MSW Students to Work with Other Social Welfare Personnel.* New York: CSWE, 1973.

SCHULMAN, GERDA L. "Teaching Family Therapy to Social Work Students." *Social Casework*, 57, No. 7 (July 1976): 448–457.

SYTZ, F. "Teaching Recording." *Social Casework,* 30 (December 1949): 399–405.

WELLS, RICHARD A. "Training in Facilitative Skills." *Social Work,* 20, No. 3 (May 1975): 242–244.

Index